Government and Polit

'This book is impeccably written – extremely clear prose and full of lucid details that even a non-specialist and non-statistician like me can understand. The amount of careful work involved in amassing all the data is extraordinary and the transparency and fluidity of the prose is impressive. It's a pleasure to read something so well-written – something I would rarely say about most academic texts.'

Professor Adam Lifshey, *Georgetown University, USA*

Written by an experienced teacher and scholar, this new and revised second edition of *Government and Politics in Taiwan* introduces students to the big questions concerning change and continuity in Taiwanese politics and governance. Taking a critical approach, Dafydd Fell provides students with the essential background to the history and development of the political system, as well as an explanation of the key structures, processes and institutions that have shaped Taiwan over the last few decades.

Using key features such as suggestions for further reading and end-of-chapter study questions, this textbook covers:

- the transition to democracy and party politics;
- cross-Strait relations and foreign policy;
- electoral politics and voting;
- social movements;
- national identity;
- gender politics.

Having been fully updated to take stock of the 2012 and 2016 General Elections, the Sunflower Movement and new developments in cross-Strait relations, this is an essential text for any course on Taiwanese politics, Chinese politics and East Asian politics.

Dafydd Fell is the Reader in Comparative Politics at the Department of Politics and International Studies and Director of the Centre of Taiwan Studies, the School of Oriental and African Studies (SOAS), University of London, UK.

Routledge Research on Taiwan
Series Editor: Dafydd Fell, SOAS, UK

The Routledge Research on Taiwan Series seeks to publish quality research on all aspects of Taiwan studies. Taking an interdisciplinary approach, the books will cover topics such as politics, economic development, culture, society, anthropology and history.

This new book series will include the best possible scholarship from the social sciences and the humanities, and welcomes submissions from established authors in the field as well as from younger authors. In addition to research monographs and edited volumes, general works or textbooks with a broader appeal will be considered.

The series is advised by an international Editorial Board and edited by Dafydd Fell of the Centre of Taiwan Studies at the School of Oriental and African Studies.

For a full list of titles in the series, please visit: www.routledge.com/asianstudies/series/ RRTAIWAN

Government and Politics in Taiwan

Second Edition

Dafydd Fell

Routledge
Taylor & Francis Group

LONDON AND NEW YORK

Second edition published 2018
by Routledge
2 Park Square, Milton Park, Abingdon, Oxon, OX14 4RN

and by Routledge
711 Third Avenue, New York, NY 10017

Routledge is an imprint of the Taylor & Francis Group, an informa business

First edition published by Routledge 2012

British Library Cataloguing-in-Publication Data
A catalogue record for this book is available from the British Library

Library of Congress Cataloging-in-Publication Data
Names: Fell, Dafydd, 1970– author.
Title: Government and politics in Taiwan / Dafydd Fell.
Description: Second Edition. | New York : Routledge, 2018. |
Series: Routledge Research on Taiwan ; 23 | "First edition published by
Routledge 2012"—T.p. verso. | Includes bibliographical references and index.
Identifiers: LCCN 2017037160| ISBN 9781138187382 (Hardback) |
ISBN 9781138187399 (Paperback) | ISBN 9781315643120 (eBook)
Subjects: LCSH: Taiwan—Politics and government.
Classification: LCC JQ1530 .F45 2018 | DDC 320.95124/9—dc23
LC record available at https://lccn.loc.gov/2017037160

ISBN: 978–1–138–18738–2 (hbk)
ISBN: 978–1–138–18739–9 (pbk)
ISBN: 978–1–315–64312–0 (ebk)

Typeset in Bembo
by Florence Production Ltd, Stoodleigh, Devon, UK

Contents

Figures

Tables

Foreword

Judged only by its population and size, Taiwan, officially known as the Republic of China, would not command much attention in the global community. With 23 million people inhabiting approximately 36,000 square kilometers – about half the size of Ireland and about one quarter that of the state of New York – Taiwan easily could be overshadowed by its neighbours. Yet it remains in the international eye, due to its geo-strategic location, its complicated relationship with the People's Republic of China, and unique political and security ties with the United States. Moreover, Taiwan has successfully developed from an agrarian base with a per capita income of US$50 in 1950 to a flourishing information technology giant today; during that time, it transformed from an authoritarian one-party state to a democracy, with minimal social costs. To some scholars, Taiwan's experience demonstrates that a non-Western culture imbued with the essentials of Confucianism can transition successfully to democracy.

In 1895, imperial China's decaying Manchu dynasty ceded Taiwan to Japan. Immediately after the Second World War ended Japanese rule, the Republic of China took control of the island; four years later, in 1949, the Nationalist Government moved to Taiwan following its defeat in China's civil war. In subsequent decades, the ruling Nationalist party – also known as the Kuomintang (KMT) – governed Taiwan and fashioned it into a de facto political entity segregated from the communist mainland China. Until 1986, the Nationalist regime practised authoritarian one-party rule and imposed martial law, severely restricting citizens' freedom and political participation. Under martial law, organized political contests were forbidden, the mass media were state controlled, and coercive force was deployed to repress political dissidents. In international affairs, Taiwan was an American ally against communism during the Cold War and an important strategic post for the United States in East Asia. Despite the suffocating political climate, however, Taiwan's people were free to engage in entrepreneurial ventures, and eventually a flourishing market sector led to spectacular economic growth.

Economic success brought about changes, even as Taiwan's international profile diminished with the increasing recognition of mainland China in multilateral organizations. Urbanization accelerated during the 1970s. As the literacy rate rose and per capita incomes soared, increasing exposure to mass media gradually led to the accommodation of dissenting voices. Group activities became pluralized, and demands for social liberalization and political participation became more vociferous. By 1986, when the first genuine opposition party came into existence, sufficient social and economic preconditions existed to support the political transition to democracy. Changing society and persistent democratic movements certainly helped lay the foundation for Taiwan's ultimate political transformation. In addition, many observers credit the ardent democrats and former president Chiang Ching-kuo, who decided at a critical moment in Taiwan's political development not to quash the birth of Democratic Progressive Party (DPP). Martial law was lifted about a year before his death on 3 January 1988.

From the time he assumed office in 1988 until 2000, former president Lee Teng-hui took additional important steps to direct Taiwan towards semi-presidential democracy. Along these lines, Lee dismantled the entrenched martial law apparatus, mobilized popular support for constitutional reforms, while battling intra-party rivals. Externally, he pressed for international activism and initiated contacts with Chinese leaders, implementing more fully the policy of gradual opening to cross-Strait relations that Chiang Ching-kuo adopted just before his departure from office. Throughout the 1990s, Taiwan's domestic politics were littered with intricate political struggles, but the road towards democracy, while bumpy, never ran over the cliff. In 1996, in the face of China's belligerent threats, the first presidential election took place on Taiwan. After the election ended – peacefully – Taiwan could boast to the international community of the successful emergence of open and competitive party politics. The transition from the nascent democracy's 'founding' parliamentary election in 1989 to a fully fledged presidential election took nine years.

The first rotation of executive power occurred in 2000 as Chen Shui-bian, candidate of the opposition DPP, won the presidential race in a three-way contest, by a plurality vote against two sets of rival candidates representing the KMT and its splinter party, the People First Party. During Chen's eight-year presidency, an independent national identity slowly evolved, accelerating the process of indigenization that began during Lee Teng-hui's administration. Although cross-Strait trade and investments were growing rapidly, efforts to delink ties with mainland China concerning education, culture and foreign affairs absorbed the DPP government's policy attention. Distrust between Beijing and Taipei steadily worsened, complicating further the already tensile cross-Strait political relationship.

The KMT regained power in 2008 when Ma Ying-jeou won the presidential contest by a substantial margin. Ma immediately undertook a course reversal concerning Taiwan's relations with the mainland and foreign affairs. Reconciliation became the centrepiece of his policy initiatives. He resumed dialogue with Beijing, implemented a long-awaited policy of direct air links and shipping across the Strait, opened up two-way tourism, and, in June 2010, signed a historic Economic Cooperation Framework Agreement (ECFA). The ECFA aims to institutionalize the already close economic ties across the Taiwan Strait.

Initial reactions towards Ma's policy directives from the United States, which maintains a pivotal role in Taiwan's foreign policy, were positive; the Obama administration, eager to maintain a peaceful environment in East Asia, has voiced its open support for Ma. However, as Taiwan and mainland China move rapidly towards social and economic integration, Washington may be compelled to reassess the political and security implications for future US Asian policy, especially concerning its own security interests in the area. And, as closer cross-Strait social and economic interactions develop, they invariably lay the foundation for changes to Taiwan's political identity. Will Taiwan gradually fall under China's sphere of influence? What would be the consequences for the United States' long-held security arrangements in the Western Pacific? Will Japan and South Korea's shipping lanes fall under the spectre of China's increasingly powerful navy if Beijing succeeds in extending its political and security influences to Taiwan? The events that transpire in Taiwan's domestic politics, and the evolving cross-Strait relations, have broader implications on the regional and international security environment.

Taiwan has experienced two consecutive rotations of power between rival political parties – a textbook example of progress in democratic consolidation. In 22 years it has moved from a nascent democracy with a newly formed opposition party to the consolidation phase of democratic development, without the drama of military coups or serious political breakdown. Meanwhile, its role in both the East Asia region and the world as a whole has become more complex, as the domestic changes accompanying democratic consolidation have, perhaps paradoxically, pushed Taiwan closer to mainland China. Given this context, the Taiwan story should fascinate students of comparative politics and Asian affairs, particularly regarding the rise of China.

And so it is with delight that I welcome the publication of Dafydd Fell's book on *Government and Politics in Taiwan*. His comprehensive studies of Taiwan politics bring updated analyses and supply a rich reservoir of information that complements my earlier book, *The Great Transition: Political and Social Change in the Republic of China* (Stanford: Hoover Institution Press, 1989). The author has devoted much of his intellectual life to the study of Taiwan politics and society, and his life in Taiwan has given him unparalleled opportunities as an on-site observer as well as interviewer. He has enjoyed access to a wealth of well-documented information, sourced from both the local academic community and the flourishing mass media. It is a mark of Taiwan's political and social evolution that these were not available when I embarked upon research for my book in the 1980s, while martial law still prevailed.

In short, this book provides a Western scholar's comprehensive perspective on Taiwan. It is a work of serious scholarship by an academic intimately familiar with the local scene, and constitutes a valuable addition to the study of Taiwan.

Hung-mao Tien
President and Chairman of the Board
Institute for National Policy Research
Taipei, Taiwan

Acknowledgements for the first and second editions

There are so many people that I want to thank for their invaluable help on this book project. However, the first must be my remarkable former student, Daniel Mojahedi. Daniel patiently worked with me on revising and editing the manuscript for the first edition. Without his support I really doubt that I could have completed the manuscript during a teaching year.

I also doubt that I could have completed the book without the support of my wife, Jewel Lo (羅寶珠). She has always been encouraging when I have suffered writer's block, resolved many IT crises and been understanding of the pressures of academic life. I do recommend any readers to try David Lodge's academic novels to get a taste of the pleasures and pain of the academic world.

I am also extremely grateful to friends and colleagues who have offered constructive suggestions in individual chapters. These include Jean-Pierre Cabestan, Ho Ming-sho, Jin Xuan, Lin Wan-I (林萬億), Chou Wan-yao (周婉窈), Charles Chen (陳以信), Hardina Ohlendorf, Isabelle Cheng (程念慈), Jonathan Sullivan and Barak Kushner. Others, such as Nathan Batto and Lin Chiung-chu (林瓊珠), have been very helpful when I was stuck on certain issues for the second edition.

For the second edition, the most useful feedback came from my students. I have now taught Taiwan politics courses at SOAS since 2002, and also shorter versions when visiting at Heidelberg University, Masaryk University and the University of California at Santa Barbara. When revising, I was able to bring in my experiences of what students found interesting over the last few years of teaching. Since the second edition was written during the 2016–17 academic year, I should especially thank my Taiwan Politics and Cross-Strait Relations, Taiwan's Politics and International Relations, as well as North East Asian Politics classes.

I am also grateful to three Taiwanese universities for hosting me while I was trying to complete the first and second editions. Particular thanks should go to Chiu Kuei-fen (邱貴芬) and Eva Jen at the Research Center for Humanities and Social Sciences, National Chung-hsing University and to Liao Da-chi (廖達琪) and Chen Chi-ching at the Graduate Institute of Political Science, National Sun Yat Sen University. For the second edition I benefited from a productive stay at the National Chung Cheng University in December 2016 and would like to thank Lin Ping (林平) and Chan Sheng-ju (詹盛如) for inviting me back.

Thanks are also due to my colleagues at Routledge, especially my editors Stephanie Rogers, Leanne Hinves, Ed Needle and Georgina Bishop. I appreciate your encouragement, suggestions on the book cover and patience when I missed my delivery deadlines too many times.

I was extremely touched that Dr Tien Hung-mao (田弘茂) agreed to write the Foreword to this book. Dr Tien's book *The Great Transition: Political and Social Change in the Republic of China* helped inspire me to study Taiwanese politics in the first place back in my undergraduate years. This book is an attempt to offer readers an updated, but similarly broad, introduction to the fascinating world of Taiwan's politics.

I would like to thank the anonymous reviewers who came back with many valuable suggestions on how to improve the structure and content of the project.

I also could not have completed this project and remained sane without the friendship and support of Robert Ash, Julia Strauss, Chang Bi-yu (張必瑜) and Laurence Fell (羅洋).

Lastly, I wish to thank countless Taiwanese people for taking the time to talk to me about their political views and experiences. It is Taiwanese people that make the field of politics on the islands such an addictive subject for me. This book is dedicated to you.

Dafydd Fell (羅達菲)

Note on Romanization

The system of Romanization for Taiwan is a troublesome and controversial issue. Whatever system we employ will lead to the writer being accused of supporting one side or the other. Until the DPP era, the accepted practice was to use the Wade Giles system for place names and names of Taiwanese people, while *Hanyu Pinyin* was used for names and places in the People's Republic of China (PRC). This all changed as the issue became politicized in the DPP era, with the KMT promoting the use of *Hanyu Pinyin* and the DPP government backing a new system called *Tongyong Pinyin*. In addition, many names use Romanization that does not tally with any recognized system. Since the KMT returned to power, *Hanyu Pinyin* has also become more widely used. Nevertheless, the Romanization situation in Taiwan remains chaotic and confusing. What I have chosen to do is to take the Romanization adopted by the *Taipei Times* for well-known Taiwanese figures, followed by Chinese characters the first time it appears in the text. I also adopt the standard Romanized form for important place names, again followed by Chinese characters the first time they are mentioned. In other cases, *Hanyu Pinyin* is used for names and place names. Where Chinese language phrases are transliterated, I use *Hanyu Pinyin*.

Abbreviations

2–28	The 1947 February 28 Incident
ARATS	Association for Relations Across the Taiwan Strait
BNHI	Bureau of National Health Insurance
CBM	Confidence Building Measures
CCP	Chinese Communist Party
CEC	Central Election Commission
CPI	Corruption Perception Index
CSDP	Chinese Social Democratic Party
CUPP	Chinese Unification Promotion Party
DOH	Department of Health
DPP	Democratic Progressive Party
ECFA	Economic Cooperation Framework Agreement
ESC	Election Survey Center (At National Chengchi University)
GIO	Government Information Office
GPT	Green Party Taiwan
GVM	Gloabl View Monthly Polling Center
IGO	International Governments Organization
KMT	Kuomintang
LGBT	Lesbian, Gay, Bisexual and Transgender
LSE	London School of Economics and Political Science
MAC	Mainland Affairs Council
MRT	Mass Rapid Transit System
NCCU	National Chengchi University
NGO	Non Government Organization
NP	New Party
NPP	New Power Party
NT$	New Taiwan Dollar
NTU	National Taiwan University
NUG	National Unification Guidelines
OCRI	One China Respective Interpretations
PCT	Presbyterian Church of Taiwan
PFP	People First Party
PLA	People's Liberation Army
PRC	People's Republic of China
ROC	Republic of China
ROT	Republic of Taiwan

SEF	Straits Exchange Foundation
SMD	Single Member (electoral) District
SOAS	School of Oriental and African Studies
SVMM	Single, Non Transferable Voting in Multi-member Districts
TAPCPR	Taiwan Alliance to Promote Civil Partnership Rights
TCTU	Taiwan Confederation of Trade Unions
TEPU	Taiwan Environmental Protection Union
TIC	Taiwan Independence Clause
TIM	Taiwan Independence Movement
TIP	Taiwan Independence Party
TISR	Taiwan Indicator Survey Research
TSU	Taiwan Solidarity Union
UN	United Nations
UNHI	Universal National Health Insurance
US	United States

1 Introduction to government and politics in Taiwan

Introduction

Taiwanese politics are never boring. I often tell my students this in their introductory Taiwan politics class. Is this a fair statement or just a marketing slogan to persuade students to take my course rather than another from the bewildering range of possible courses at my university?

In the evening of 18 March 2014, a group of mainly students broke into Taiwan's parliamentary debating chamber, occupying it until 10 April. This occupation, together with protests surrounding the parliament, became known as the Sunflower Movement. Rather than being violently evicted from parliament, this movement was able to push the government to put its proposed controversial trade deal with China on hold. For students in the UK used to harsh police treatment of protestors and governments completely ignoring protests, the Taiwan Sunflower Movement is an inspiring story. This then set off a chain of events leading the ruling Kuomintang (KMT) party to suffer historic electoral defeats at the local (2014) and then national level (2016). While I had started off the first edition of this book describing the KMT's landslide victories in 2008, the most recent national elections in January 2016 saw the Democratic Progressive Party (DPP) not only win the presidency but also for the first time to win a parliamentary majority. This was Taiwan's sixth direct presidential election and third change of ruling party through elections. The fact that these election-driven party turnovers have been so smooth and peaceful stands in stark contrast to the post-election violence seen in many other new democracies. As such, over the last three decades, Taiwan has gained a reputation as one of Asia's model liberal democracies.

Such political developments would have seemed unimaginable when I had my first taste of Taiwanese electoral politics in 1989. At the time, I was a spotty teenager, in Taipei for a year as a Chinese language student. I arrived knowing next to nothing about Taiwan, as it had barely received a mention in my year one Modern Chinese Studies courses. Spending a year in Taiwan was entirely accidental. The violent crackdown on student protestors in Beijing, known as the *Tiananmen* incident, had temporarily made the People's Republic of China (PRC) off-limits for UK students. That year, I witnessed not only Taiwan's first multi-party parliamentary election but also its own version of the student democracy movement.[1] My experiences during that transitional year sowed the seeds of my own inexhaustible fascination with the Taiwan's politics.

In 1989, it was still not clear whether Taiwan would remain a Singapore-style semi-democracy, where a change of ruling party was in effect impossible, or if it would move in the direction of a competitive multi-party liberal democracy. It is worth noting that in 1989 Taiwan was still ranked by Freedom House as only 'Partly Free'.[2] The Republic of China's (ROC) last dictator, Chiang Ching-kuo (蔣經國), had only passed away the previous year and, although martial law had been formally lifted two years earlier, many aspects of the authoritarian era remained firmly in place. National level elections were still only supplementary, with the vast majority of both the Legislative Yuan and National Assembly seats held by parliamentarians that had been elected in China in the late 1940s and frozen in office. This meant that no matter what the election results were, the ruling KMT had a guaranteed majority. Civil liberties had improved, but there was not yet freedom of speech, as activists could still be arrested for advocating Taiwan independence. I still recall clearly the uncomfortable atmosphere when I touched upon such taboo subjects with university students.

After returning to the UK to complete my undergraduate education, I decided to write my dissertation on the KMT's nation building project. Despite being at one of the largest East Asian Studies departments in Europe, I was struck by the paucity of English language material on contemporary Taiwan. At the time, the book that was particularly valuable and inspiring was Tien Hung-mao's (田弘茂) *The Great Transition: Political and Social Change in the Republic of China*. Even today, Tien's book remains one of the best guides to political life in the dying days of the martial law era. Although a rich literature on Taiwan politics has developed in the last two decades, no one to date has written a comprehensive post-transition version of *The Great Transition*. Therefore one of the motivations of this volume is to introduce modern Taiwanese politics from a comparative political science perspective and hopefully inspire readers to delve deeper into the subject.

I returned to Taiwan in 1992 and worked there as a *buxiban* (private language school) teacher through to 1999. This allowed me to witness that critical period of democratic transition and the subsequent early operation of democratic politics. Since 1999, I have often returned to Taiwan for fieldwork, first as a Ph.D. research student and then as an academic. On these visits I have observed the high hopes and fears of political change at the time of changes of the ruling parties. Looking back over the three decades since I first set foot in Taiwan, it seems hard to imagine how much and how rapidly the country has changed politically.

Why has this subject so captivated me? I am sure it must partly be the contrast between the glacial pace of political change and dull electoral campaigns that I have grown up with in Europe and Taiwan's passionate and sometimes festival-like campaigns, along with the sense that democratic politics can make a real difference there. Thus, in this book I will try to tell the colourful story of Taiwan's political change and continuity over the last three decades.

The emergence and growth of the study of Taiwan politics

In the mid-1980s, Taiwan politics was still a marginal topic in the field of Chinese studies and largely ignored by mainstream Western political science. In Taiwan itself, the lack of academic freedom and KMT party ideology meant that research and publication on Taiwan's domestic politics was also severely underdeveloped. Initially, it was Taiwan's economic achievements that caught the attention of social scientists around the globe. Three publications were to be critically important in introducing Taiwan's political affairs to a wider readership. In addition to Tien's *The Great Transition,* these were Thomas Gold's *State and Society in the Taiwan Miracle* and Cheng Tun-jen's (鄭敦仁) *World Politics* article 'Democratizing the quasi-Leninist regime in Taiwan'. Gold's volume on the political economy of the Taiwan miracle brought Taiwan to a wider audience by applying theories that had previously been used in Latin America, such as dependency, world systems and dependent development. One of the most influential scholars of Taiwan politics, Shelley Rigger, talks of Gold's volume as having 'awakened the field'.[3] Cheng's article was ground-breaking in being the work that made Taiwan's politics visible to the broader comparative politics community by applying the transition framework to the Taiwan case. Its importance was reinforced to me when I surveyed a sample of Taiwan political experts on what was the most influential English language piece on Taiwan politics over the last two decades. The most popular response was Cheng's work.

Since the publication of these landmark works, the field of Taiwan studies has expanded rapidly in terms of university courses, academic events and publications. Within the umbrella of Taiwan studies, Taiwan politics has been by far the most developed disciplinary field with its university courses being the most popular and common both on the island and abroad and, since the late 1990s, at least ten English language books have been published per year on the topic.[4,5] From my own experience as the editor for the Routledge Research on Taiwan series, politics book proposals outnumbered the combined total of all other disciplines. In the leading peer-reviewed Asian and Chinese studies journals, papers on political studies are by far the most commonly published articles focusing on Taiwan.[6] Political science presentations have also been predominant in Taiwan studies seminars and conferences in Europe and North America. For example, in the annual European Association of Taiwan Studies conferences, the number of political research papers has often exceeded other disciplines. At the world's leading politics conference, the American Political Science Association Conference, there are often more Taiwan panels than those on the PRC. Shelley Rigger's comments reflect the current vibrancy of the field, 'Given Taiwan's small size and marginal position within Chinese studies, one cannot but marvel at the breadth and depth of social scientific research engaging the island's history, economics, politics and society.'[7]

Why study Taiwan politics?

Clearly, Taiwan politics has become a popular subject of research over the last three decades. But why should you opt to study the subject instead of another regional politics course? As someone of Welsh descent, I do like to question why the politics of a country about the same size as Wales should receive such disproportionate scholarly attention. Shelley Rigger's explanations for the vibrancy of the field are a useful way to approach the question.[8]

First, she suggests that Taiwan's rapid political, social and economic change have made it a useful case for testing social science theories. The timing of Taiwan's democratic transition coincided with what Samuel Huntington calls the 'Third Wave of Democracy'.[9] This has encouraged scholars to apply various democratization theories to explain Taiwan's democratic change and compare its developments with other new democracies. In addition, there is still some scope for comparing Taiwan with China, particularly when examining their political histories. For example, exciting work is being done on comparative land reform and political persecution from the 1950s. However, the gulf between the two political systems today makes comparative research with other new democracies instead much more fruitful. Particularly prevalent have been studies comparing Taiwan with South Korea and Mexico. There is much scope for further research comparing

Taiwan with countries with similar political systems in Latin America, Europe and Asia. In this volume I will discuss studies that place Taiwan in a comparative context and examine topics as diverse as welfare state development, political communication and party systems.

Second, Rigger stresses the ease of gathering political data in Taiwan. Compared to many of the countries we focus on at my university, the School of Oriental and African Studies (SOAS), Taiwan is an extremely safe place to conduct fieldwork. Its modern public transport network, particularly the islandwide high-speed railway and Taipei and Kaohsiung metro systems, enhance one's ability to perform such research. To a certain level, Taiwan's politics can be studied without learning Chinese. In fact, because of the availability of political data in English, it is possible to take an MA in Taiwan Studies without using any Chinese language sources.[10] Increasingly, the best scholars from Taiwan, regardless of whether they are based in Taiwan, Europe or America, are now publishing in English. Perhaps because so many Taiwanese politicians and officials have Ph.D.s and spent part of their career as academics, they are much more willing to be interviewed and have far more patience with academics than their counterparts in most Western countries. Taiwan's online databases are also extremely user friendly. Getting access to Taiwanese political data is so straightforward that it is sometimes possible for a Ph.D. student to write their dissertation on Taiwan in Europe without ever visiting the island during their degree.[11] An academic studying Taiwan politics rarely fails to produce quality research due to a lack of data. Instead, a greater problem tends to be how to manage an excess of material.

A final reason Rigger suggests for the strength of the field is that the 'scholarly community in Taiwan is extremely well developed and welcoming to foreign researchers'.[12] This hospitality applies not only to established scholars, but extends as well to MA and Ph.D. candidates, with my own students, when going there for research, noting Taiwanese academics' hospitality and willingness to provide invaluable data and research guidance. Taiwan's political liberalization has also enhanced the island's research environment. The political taboos that I attempted to tackle in 1989 have long since been swept aside, so that even what were previously the most controversial issues, such as Taiwan independence or public attitudes towards national leaders, are now run-of-the-mill research topics.

Although Taiwan is still a marginal issue in Chinese studies, it remains highly relevant for those who want to understand contemporary Chinese politics. Many of the formal ROC political institutions in Taiwan originate from the time before the government fled to Taiwan. For the Chinese Communist Party (CCP), the continued existence of a regime called the ROC signifies that their civil war is still not over. Moreover, at a time when Beijing is still arguing that multi-party democracy is not suitable for China, Taiwan's status as the first and only Chinese democracy represents a rival political system.[13] During the Asian Values debates in the 1990s, Taiwan's leaders stood firmly on the side of liberal democracy. Despite its democratic flaws, Taiwan is evidence that Western democracy can work in Chinese or other Confucian societies. Taiwan is also critical to understanding contemporary Chinese nationalism. Studies suggest that, along with anti-American and Japanese sentiment, opposition to Taiwan's formal (or *de jure*) independence is a key ingredient of Chinese nationalist ideology. The fluctuations between cooperation and conflict in cross-Strait political relations, like those between North and South Korea, have attracted huge scholarly interest. The increasing economic and political ties between Taiwan and China, and the two-way human migration, all serve to make Taiwan more relevant than ever for Chinese studies.

Taiwan is also a critical case for students of international relations. The triangular relationship between Taipei, Beijing and Washington and the possibility of conflict have generated a rich literature. Apart from coverage of fighting in Taiwan's parliament, the Taiwanese political topic most likely to attract Western media attention is speculation about the outbreak of cross-Strait conflict. Analysts constantly debate whether the United States (US) would intervene in such a conflict and the role Taiwan plays in US–China relations. Taiwan has a unique and controversial international status. It has most of the standard ingredients of a state: (1) a permanent population, (2) defined territory, (3) government and (4) the capacity to enter into relations with other countries. However, it is only recognized by twenty United Nations (UN) member states and is itself completely excluded from the UN and its affiliates. An alien from outer space would surely be as confused as the Taiwanese are frustrated that failed states such as Somalia have UN membership and diplomatic recognition, but Taiwan is isolated. The squeezing of Taiwan's international space explains why its citizens refer to their country as having become the 'Orphan of Asia'.

A final explanation for the popularity of studying Taiwan politics has been the intensive debates over the island's national identity. Measuring and explaining political and cultural identities on the island has generated a huge literature. The leading French Taiwan studies scholar Stéphane Corcuff has thus described Taiwan as representing a 'Laboratory of Identities'.[14] These contending identities form the central political cleavages dividing Taiwan domestically and are also at the root of cross-Strait conflict.

This book is organized as follows.

Chapter 2: Authoritarian rule: the politics of martial law in Taiwan

This chapter will introduce how Taiwan was governed during its four-decade-long martial law period. First, I will briefly discuss the political legacy of the 50-year Japanese colonial period. This will be followed by an examination of why Taiwan's return to the ROC after 1945 went wrong so quickly and the legacy of those first few years of Chinese rule. Next, the chapter will concentrate on how the KMT was able to recover and deliver over three decades of political stability. There will be sections on the ROC's political system at the national and local levels, in addition to detailing their nation–building projects, levels of democracy, economic policy and external relations. Afterwards, the gradual shift from hard to soft authoritarianism will be introduced. Last, the chapter will consider how Taiwan's past authoritarianism compares with similar cases around the world and assess the legacies of the authoritarian era for contemporary Taiwan.

Chapter 3: Transition to democracy and democratic consolidation

After briefly reviewing the chronological process of Taiwan's democratization, this chapter will then appraise the competing explanations for Taiwan's transition and where Taiwan fits in the comparative democratization literature. Next, the chapter will look at whether Taiwan can be viewed as a consolidated democracy and how we can assess the quality of the island's democracy. How does Taiwan's democracy compare with other Third Wave democracies? Lastly, I will consider the debate over whether Taiwan's democracy is regressing.

Chapter 4: Taiwan's government and constitutional structure

This chapter will introduce Taiwan's government structure in its democratic era. It will show how the consensual nature of constitutional reform created a political system that incorporated elements of change, but also retained much of its martial law era institutional structure. The chapter will consider how we should best classify Taiwan's political system. The major rounds of these constitutional reforms will be examined along with some of the consequences of these reforms for how the political system operates. Lastly, we will look at current debates over whether Taiwan requires continued reform to the 1947 ROC constitution or whether they should discard it altogether for a more Taiwanese one.

Chapter 5: Electoral politics: milestones, electoral systems and political communication

This chapter will look at the captivating subject of Taiwan's electoral politics. I will first outline the key events in Taiwan's recent electoral history. Next, the chapter introduces the island's electoral systems, how they have been reformed and their political consequences. Then there will be a focus on how election campaigning has developed since the late 1980s, with emphasis on changes in the kinds of techniques, issues and appeals that parties and candidates employ. The analysis will be tied in with the political communications debates over whether campaigns matter and if we are seeing an Americanization or modernization of campaigning in new democracies.

Chapter 6: Party politics in Taiwan

This chapter will first introduce the main political parties that have dominated Taiwan politics since the 1980s and how they compare with parties in other democracies. Taiwan's main parties have joined international party organizations such as Liberal International. But do they really fit into such party typologies? There will be sections on their organizational structure, ideologies, party image, leadership, candidate selection methods and inner party balances of power. The success and failure of Taiwan's smaller challenger parties will also be discussed. Next, I will examine how scholars have explained change within the main parties. The remainder of the chapter will focus on Taiwan's changing party system. This will cover changes to the main dimensions of the party system, such as party system fragmentation, ideological distance, interparty relations and the openness of the party system to new entrants. In the concluding section, I will gauge the increasing popular dissatisfaction with Taiwanese parties and the challenges hindering the development of a well-functioning party system.

Chapter 7: Local and factional politics

This chapter considers the changing patterns of politics at the local level. Although Taiwan's national level elections were only fully introduced in the early 1990s, local elections had been conducted since the late 1940s. The chapter thus focuses on the KMT local factional relationships after martial law was lifted. Although the KMT tried periodically to reduce its dependency on local factions, they became increasingly influential at the national level. Electoral patterns at the local level stand in stark contrast to those at the national level, with the KMT remaining the dominant force in grassroots politics. The last section will assess the impact of changes of the ruling parties, and of electoral and administrative reform on local politics.

Chapter 8: Competing national identities

This chapter will focus on the competing nation-building projects that have been promoted by Taiwan's political elites before and after democratization. The key changing trends on national identity will be introduced along with the competing methods of measuring identity. The debate over whether elites follow the public on national identity questions or, instead, can still impose their nation-building projects on voters is discussed. I will also examine the impacts of democracy and the rise of China on national identity at the mass and elite levels, as well as the validity of claims that there was an effective anti-Chinese desinification campaign under the DPP after 2000 or deTaiwanization effort between 2008 and 2016.[15] The concluding section addresses the future prospects for Taiwan's competing nation-building projects.

Chapter 9: Taiwan's external relations: balancing international space and cross-Strait relations

In this chapter, after first reviewing Taiwan's external ties under martial law, the focus will be on developments after political liberalization. The first section will examine Taiwan's changing status in the Cold War international system. Next, I will consider how Taiwan's government attempted to enjoy the best of both worlds after democratization. In other words, it attempted to enjoy both international recognition and close relations with China. However, after the mid-1990s, cross-Strait relations deteriorated, followed by a period of political divergence and economic convergence. Next, I will assess the question of whether developments after the 2008 presidential elections represent a revolution in Taiwan's external relations. After the DPP returned to power in 2016, are we seeing a new era in Taiwan's external relations? For each period I will consider how we can best explain Taiwan's changing international status and cross-Strait policies. Are societal, leadership, institutional or international system variables most decisive in this arena? Lastly, the chapter will conclude by considering the long-term prospects for Taiwan's external relations. Is the issue likely to be resolved by peaceful or military means? Is unification, independence or a continuation of the current status quo more likely in the next two decades?

Chapter 10: From Leninist corporatist state to vibrant civil society: the emergence and role of social movements

This chapter considers the impact and strategies of Taiwan's main social movements. After reviewing some of the definitions of central concepts for the study of civil society and social movements, I will then discuss how the KMT tried to control associational life under martial law. The lifting of martial law created a new political environment for social movements, resulting in a remarkable blossoming of civil society. The remainder of the chapter will focus on the case studies of four key social movements: (1) women's rights movement, (2) labour movement, (3) environmental protection movement, and (4) the student movement. The chapter will compare their different strategies, their relative success and failure, their relationship with Taiwan's democracy and the main challenges for the future of Taiwanese civil society.

Chapter 11: Is democracy working in Taiwan? Social welfare, political corruption and LGBT rights

This chapter considers the question of whether democracy is working in Taiwan by looking at three key policy areas: social welfare systems, political corruption and Lesbian, Gay, Bisexual and Transgender (LGBT) rights. The first two areas were seriously neglected under authoritarian rule, with a highly unbalanced welfare system and the KMT record of exploiting its government position to amass a vast business empire. The chapter will focus on the impact of democracy on these salient political issues. Has democracy created a fair and adequate social security net for Taiwan's citizens and how does Taiwan's welfare system fit into global welfare typologies? The second case study asks whether democracy has actually helped reduce political corruption or exacerbated the problem. In both these policy areas, the advent of electoral politics and a free media has transformed the policy-making process. LGBT rights only became politically controversial recently in Taiwan, but this represents an important test for how democracy can deal with newly salient issues.

Chapter 12: Taiwan under divided government, 2000–8: the Chen Shui-bian era

This chapter focuses on four closely related questions on the Chen Shui-bian period: (1) How can we best explain the results of three presidential elections (2000, 2004 and 2008)? (2) How can we assess the impact of the change of ruling parties in 2000? Thus I consider the patterns of change or continuity in government policy after the first power transfer. (3) Was 2000 a genuine turning point in Taiwan's political history or what political scientists call a 'critical election?' (4) To what extent did the losing sides in these elections learn the lessons of defeat from these setbacks? In other words, did these learning experiences contribute to improved electoral performances in subsequent elections?

Chapter 13: Taiwan under Ma Ying-jeou and Tsai Ing-wen

In this chapter I will discuss how we best evaluate the political consequences of the changes of the ruling parties in 2008 and 2016. To what extent have we seen continuity or change? Will historians view these as successful or failed administrations? I will also look at a number of election campaigns from the post-2008 period and how we can explain the outcome of these contests.

Chapter 14: A multitude of political miracles and future challenges

This final chapter first summarizes some of the remarkable political miracles Taiwan has achieved over the last few decades. I will then consider the key challenges that face Taiwan's democracy. Are we more likely to see a move towards a Singapore-style one-party dominant system? Or will Taiwan be able to regain its reputation as a model liberal democracy? I make some suggestions for how Taiwan can deal with these new and old challenges to its democracy. By the end of the book I hope I have done enough to convince you that Taiwan politics are worth studying.

Discussion questions

1 Why has Taiwan politics become the most studied topic in Taiwan studies?
2 Why should students of comparative politics, international relations or modern Chinese studies be interested in Taiwan politics?
3 How should Taiwan's main political eras be divided?
4 How useful is Taiwan for testing political science theories and as a comparative case with other new democracies?
5 What have been the main themes that have attracted the interest of scholars of Taiwan's political scene?

Further reading

Fell, Dafydd (ed.). 2008. *The Politics of Modern Taiwan: Critical Issues in Modern Politics*. London: Routledge. Collection of 63 of the best and most influential English language articles and chapters on Taiwan's politics.

Gold, Thomas. 1996. 'Taiwan society at the fin de siècle'. *China Quarterly*, 148: 1091–114. Also Chapter 3 in *Politics of Modern Taiwan*. Colourful introduction to social change in Taiwan after the lifting of martial law.

Rigger, Shelley. 1999. *Politics in Taiwan: Voting for Democracy*. London: Routledge. The best single-authored introduction to Taiwan's domestic politics, it analyses Taiwan's electoral politics and democratization up to the mid-1990s.

Rubinstein, Murray (ed.). 2007. *Taiwan: A New History*. Armonk, NY: M.E. Sharpe. Best history of Taiwan available, with detailed chapters written by leading scholars of Taiwan. Covers Ming Dynasty through to the post-2000 period.

Schubert, Gunter (ed.). 2016. *Routledge Handbook of Contemporary Taiwan*. Abingdon and New York: Routledge. The most comprehensive collection of essays on contemporary Taiwan from a wide range of academic disciplines.

Useful web links

www.airiti.com/teps – Taiwan Electronic Periodical Services: this database includes all the leading social science periodicals published in Taiwan.

www.eats-taiwan.eu – The European Association of Taiwan Studies, their annual conference is the largest Taiwan studies event in Europe.

www.ercct.uni-tuebingen.de – European Research Center on Contemporary Taiwan promotes European social science research on Taiwan.

www.na-tsa-org – North American Association of Taiwan Studies: Founded in the mid-1990s, their annual conference is held at a different US campus each June. It is the oldest and largest annual Taiwan studies conference in the world.

www.soas.ac.uk/taiwanstudies – The Centre of Taiwan Studies, School of Oriental and African Studies is the world's leading centre for Taiwan studies teaching, academic events and publication.

Notes

1 It is debatable whether we take 1986 or 1989 as the first multi-party election. The DPP did contest the election in 1986, but it was still an illegal organization under martial law. By 1989 the DPP was a legally registered party, so I take that as the first multi-party contest.
2 Freedom House, 'Freedom in the World 2010', available online at: www.freedomhouse.org/template.cfm?page=505
3 Rigger (2002), 'Political Science and Taiwan's Domestic Politics: The State of the Field Politics', 50.

4 Another popular field in Taiwan studies has been Taiwan film, spurred on by the remarkable success of Taiwanese films at winning international festival prizes since the late 1980s.
5 Rigger, 53.
6 Scholars from the arts and humanities have complained how much harder it is to get their research on Taiwan published, compared with that of social scientists.
7 Rigger, 53.
8 Ibid., 53–4.
9 Huntington, *The Third Wave: Democratization in the late Twentieth Century.*
10 For example, the SOAS MA Taiwan Studies, available online at: www.soas.ac.uk/taiwanstudies/mataiwanstudies/
11 I have examined a number of Ph.D.s that fall into this category over the last few years.
12 Rigger, 54.
13 I do note that some Taiwanese disagree with my description of Taiwan as the first and only Chinese democracy. However, since Taiwan's official title remains the ROC and most Taiwanese see themselves as being culturally, but not politically Chinese, I have stuck to this usage. Although city states such as Hong Kong do have competitive multi-party elections, direct elections cannot change the ruling party or select their top executive positions. Thus, I regard them as being semi-democracies.
14 Corcuff (2002), 'Introduction: Taiwan, a Laboratory of Identities', xi.
15 Desinification refers to a process of removing Chinese cultural influences.

2   Authoritarian rule

The politics of martial law in Taiwan

The lifting of martial law in July 1987 was a key moment in Taiwan's modern political history. It marked the end of almost four decades of martial law (1949–87). If we include its Japanese colonial period (1895–1945), then Taiwan's twentieth century can be viewed as predominantly a history of authoritarianism. Today, images of military police arresting political prisoners and forcibly cutting the hair of young men whose hairstyles were deemed too long seem like ancient history. However, as this chapter will show, Taiwan's experiences and institutions under the authoritarian era have left indelible marks on contemporary Taiwanese politics.

What is authoritarianism and why should we study it?

Rod Hague and Martin Harrop suggest two definitions of authoritarianism. One more inclusive definition is 'Any form of non democratic rule'.[1] A second, narrower definition is 'nondemocratic regimes which, unlike totalitarian states, do not seek to transform society and the people in it'.[2] In contrast, they define totalitarianism as 'any regime that seeks total control of society with the theoretical aim of transforming it'.[3]

When we apply these definitions to the martial law era in Taiwan, it becomes clear that the island's former status falls in between their second definition of authoritarian rule and a totalitarian regime. Although the KMT did try to transform Taiwanese society while successfully dominating the island's political scene, it never came close to the levels of total control over society seen in Maoist China or Stalin's Soviet Union. Edwin Winkler suggests that for much of the martial law period, the KMT employed hard authoritarianism to rule Taiwan.[4] His central characteristics of hard authoritarianism were: (1) Mainlander technocratic rule,[5] (2) a one-man dictatorship, (3) elections as a control device to co-opt local elites, (4) frequent resort to repression by security forces and (5) more direct and often unconstitutional repression.[6] Winkler contends that by the early 1980s Taiwan was undergoing a transition from hard to soft authoritarianism. I will return to the concept of soft authoritarianism later in the chapter.

Although martial law was lifted well over three decades ago, understanding Taiwan's authoritarian era is important for the student of comparative politics and present-day Taiwan. After the optimism seen during the third wave of democratization of the early 1990s, it is now clear that many of the remaining authoritarian states are showing no signs of moving towards democratic reform. For much of Taiwan's martial law period there was no obvious movement towards political liberalization and even periods of democratic reversals. Therefore, Taiwan holds lessons about how authoritarian regimes today maintain or gradually reduce their political domination. There is also much scope for comparing authoritarian era Taiwan with other similar regimes, such as military regimes in South Korea or the single-party rule in contemporary China. For example, does Taiwan's experience of very gradual democratic change, started at the local level, offer a model for political change in China? Moreover, after Taiwan's former authoritarian party, the KMT, returned to office in 2008, it was often accused of reverting back to authoritarian practice – for instance, in its use of police against protestors.[7]

Nevertheless, the most important reason for studying Taiwan's authoritarian era is that it is impossible to understand current Taiwan politics without reference to it. Taiwan's political institutions, party system, core salient issue cleavages and international status, to name a few, all have their roots in political developments that transpired prior to 1987. Taiwan's authoritarian legacies have left a similar imprint to those of Communist regimes on new democracies in Eastern Europe or military rule in South Korea.

Political legacy of the 50-year Japanese colonial period

Before looking at the martial law period, I will briefly discuss the preceding authoritarian era, the Japanese colonial period and its legacy. Following the Ching Empire's defeat in the Sino-Japanese War, the Treaty of Shimonoseki ceded the Chinese province of Taiwan to Japan. Taiwan became Japan's first colony and remained under Japanese rule for the next 50 years, until the end of the Second World War.

Two contemporary political scandals reveal how controversial the issue of the Japanese colonial era remains. First, in June 1997 Chinese nationalists in Taiwan initiated a series of angry protests against proposed new high-school textbooks titled *Getting to Know Taiwan*.[8] These new textbooks included Society, Geography and History volumes and were designed to make up for the long-term neglect of Taiwan in the school curriculum. One of the features that particularly enraged these protestors was what they perceived as its positive treatment of the Japanese occupation of Taiwan.[9] The second incident followed the 2001 publication of the Chinese translation of *On Taiwan*, a cartoon history of the island by Japanese author Kobayashi Yoshinori.[10] In addition to the book's partisan analysis of recent Taiwanese history, what really raised a storm was its depiction of Taiwanese young women cheerfully volunteering to serve as 'comfort women' (military prostitutes) for the Japanese army during the Second World War.[11] The book's publication was greeted by book burnings and book-buying campaigns by rival nationalist political groupings. The root of both these scandals lies in the contrasting historical memories and interpretations of pre-1945 Taiwan held by different political and ethnic groups.

Five decades of Japanese rule had a transformative effect on Taiwan. To a large extent, the island witnessed a completely different era between 1895 and 1945 than China experienced. After an initially brutal Japanese takeover, Taiwan benefited from decades of rapid economic growth and political stability. By the time Taiwan was returned to Chinese rule, it was economically more advanced than the mainland, and its residents had a higher standard of living than those of any other Chinese province. Taiwan was largely insulated from the upheavals on the Chinese mainland, such as the Boxer Rebellion, 1911 Revolution, Warlord Period, Northern Expedition, anti-Communist suppression campaigns and the Second Sino-Japanese War. Taiwan also missed out on the battle of ideas in China surrounding the May Fourth Movement, in addition to the ideological struggles for and against Communism.

Although the Japanese colonists dominated Taiwan's political realm, a number of political processes that the Taiwanese were allowed to join had long-term legacies. In the relatively liberal 1920s, independent Taiwanese political organizations began to emerge. The Taiwan Culture Association claimed its principle objective to be promoting the island's culture, focusing on organizing public lectures, cultural performances and publishing the *Taiwan People's Journal*.[12] However, one writer described it as being 'the one organization most responsible for the development of Formosan nationalism'.[13] The importance of the Taiwan Culture Association can be seen by how presidential candidates in 2008 vied to commemorate its leading figure Chiang Wei-shui (蔣渭水) and how Taiwan's newest motorway was named after him.[14] Chiang's struggles against colonial authorities featured in Yeh Tien-lun's (葉天倫) 2014 historical comedy *Twa Tiu Tiann* (大稻埕). Another important political movement was the League for the Establishment of a Taiwan Parliament, which petitioned for home rule within the Japanese Empire. Such organizations served as forerunners of the *Tangwai* opposition of the martial law era. Taiwan's first elections also occurred during this period, with local elections under a restricted franchise starting in 1935, giving wealthier Taiwanese their first taste of voting. The electoral system employed was that used in Japan, known as the Single, Non-transferable Voting in Multi-member Districts (SVMM). Since 1945, this electoral system has been widely used for most Taiwanese elections – even to this day.[15]

During the last decade of colonial rule, efforts to assimilate the Taiwanese into Japanese citizens did accelerate. The Kominka programme involved banning Chinese publications and broadcasts, promoting Japanese religion and adopting Japanese names. A key tool in Japanese nation building was the education system. During this period Japanese was the sole language of instruction, with classical Chinese taken out of the curriculum. Japanese authorities even tried to ban Taiwanese cultural practices, such as opera and puppet shows, and encourage Japanese-style weddings and funerals. In certain sections of society some kind of Japanese nationalism did develop, visible in the numbers of Taiwanese who volunteered to join the Japanese war effort. However, Taiwanese remained second-class citizens throughout, discriminated against in the education sector, economically and politically. The fact that the ROC government was welcomed to Taiwan in 1945, followed by a quick revival of Taiwanese cultural practices, suggests the shallowness of Japan's nation-building. However, if the Japanese had begun the Kominka project earlier, or ruled for a few more decades, the picture could have been quite different.

The last two decades have seen a huge body of research on Taiwan's colonial era, creating a rich empirical literature and more balanced perspective. Historian Chou Wan-yao has talked of a shift from being a 'political taboo to a hot field of studies'.[16] These studies have debunked the idealized depictions of both Japanese rightists, such as Kobayashi, who eulogize the virtues of Japanese rule, and of Chinese nationalists who focus on Japanese brutality and the anti-Japanese movements of the time. Japanese aggression against China in the first half of the twentieth century, particularly the atrocities during the Anti-Japanese War, made anti-Japanese sentiments a core ingredient of modern Chinese nationalism. In contrast, although most Taiwanese were glad to see the back of their Japanese colonial rulers, they tend to have very different historical memories and interpretations of this period. This is why we do not see such intense anti-Japanese sentiments in Taiwan, and why the island is able to host so many Japanese tourists every year.

Taiwan's disastrous return to Chinese rule after 1945

For most of the Japanese colonial period, recovering Taiwan was not a priority for Chinese nationalists in the KMT or CCP, Republican China's two main political forces. In 1936

Mao Zedong (毛澤東) famously informed the American journalist Edgar Snow that he supported the struggle for Taiwan's independence from the Japanese.[17] However, Taiwan was listed in the Cairo Conference press communiqué as being among the stolen Chinese territories that would be returned by Japan after the Second World War.[18] In April 1944, Chiang Kai-shek's (蔣介石) government in China set up a Taiwan Investigation Committee to begin preparations for the island's return to Chinese rule. The Chairman of this committee, Chen Yi (陳儀), was to become the first Administrator of the ROC's new province of Taiwan after the Japanese surrender in August 1945. As had been the case five decades earlier, the Taiwanese population had no say in this transfer of power.

A huge body of research has been produced on the early years of ROC rule on Taiwan, and you can now learn more at the National 228 Memorial and Taipei 228 Memorial Museums when visiting Taipei.[19] However, with the aid of a double espresso, one of the best places to start in understanding Taiwan during this period is Hou Hsiao-hsien's (侯孝賢) award-winning film *City of Sadness*. The film, which opens with the Japanese Emperor's surrender broadcast, tells the tragic story of how a Taiwanese family struggles to cope in the unstable years from the end of Japanese rule, through to the 1947 February 28 Incident and its aftermath.

Although there was a degree of apprehension in Taiwan about the new regime, the ROC troops and administration were initially welcomed. However, the KMT regime's misrule ensured that this goodwill was quickly lost. One writer talks of the Taiwanese going from hope (*xiwang*), to lost hope (*shiwang*), to hopelessness (*juewang*).[20] Relations rapidly deteriorated between the Taiwanese and their new rulers. Tensions culminated in the outbreak of the 1947 February 28 Incident, commonly referred to as the 2–28 Incident. The catalyst for this episode was a relatively minor incident on the evening of 27 February. Government monopoly agents accidentally shot a bystander during a failed attempt to confiscate illegally sold cigarettes, sparking off riots and soon open rebellion. In a matter of days, Taiwanese had taken over the running of most towns and cities on the island, with numerous incidents of Mainlanders being killed or injured. One of the most memorable moments in *City of Sadness* is when the main character, who is deaf, is confronted on a train by Taiwanese rebels looking for Mainlanders. When they ask him where he is from, he struggles to reply in Taiwanese so they mistake him as a Mainlander. Fortunately, he is just saved in time by a fellow traveller.[21]

Chen Yi began negotiations with the Taiwanese Settlement Committee, which had a number of proposals for resolving the crisis and instigating political reforms, leading to greater autonomy within the ROC. However, Chen had already secretly telegrammed Nanjing for troop reinforcements. When the KMT troops arrived in March they launched a wave of revenge killings, particularly targeting both the Taiwanese elite who had been critical of the KMT and those who had been trying to negotiate and maintain order. We get horrifying eyewitness accounts of the killings and subsequent round-ups of dissidents in the countryside from books such as George Kerr's *Formosa Betrayed* along with a fictionalized portrayal in *City of Sadness*. There are conflicting figures for the numbers killed, but something in the region of 10,000 appears likely.

A combination of economic, political and cultural factors contributed to the 2–28 Incident. First, Chen Yi's economic policies and mismanagement helped to make Taiwan ripe for rebellion. His policy of government domination of the economy through monopolies and state-run firms was a disaster. The monopolies were dominated by Mainlanders, limiting business opportunities for Taiwanese entrepreneurs. Many KMT officials took advantage of their position to profit from selling Taiwanese economic assets to the mainland. There were cases of whole factories and vital railway equipment being transplanted to China, with inevitable disastrous economic consequences on the island. The lack of economic recovery meant that Taiwan was hit by unemployment while embroiled in inflation. For the first time in living memory, Taiwan suffered shortages of essential commodities such as grain and salt.

Corruption and inefficiency were key characteristics of the KMT regime. In contrast to the Japanese era, public order deteriorated seriously. This was exacerbated by an inefficient and corrupt police service, and an influx of mainland gangsters. Again, these are features portrayed in *City of Sadness*. Public health was equally dismal, with outbreaks of cholera and bubonic plague reported for the first time in decades. A key reason for these problems was that Taiwan was not a priority for the KMT, as it faced a greater challenge where the CCP was strongest in northern China. Therefore, many of the initial troops and officials sent to Taiwan were of low quality. We get a picture of this in Peng Mingmin's (彭明敏) account of how his father recalled the first arrival of Chinese troops in 1945 at Kaohsiung harbour:

> The ship docked, the gangways were lowered, and off came the troops of China, the victors. The first man to appear was a bedraggled fellow who looked and behaved more like a coolie than a soldier, walking off with a carrying pole across his shoulder, from which was suspended his umbrella, sleeping mat, cooking pot, and cup. Others like him followed, some with shoes, some without. Few had guns. With no attempts to maintain order or discipline, they pushed off the ship, glad to be on firm land, but hesitant to face the Japanese lined up and saluting smartly on both sides. My father wondered what the Japanese could possibly think. He had never felt so ashamed in his life.[22]

Politically, Taiwanese hopes of self-government were completely dashed. Instead of sharing in the administration, Taiwanese were largely excluded from the provincial government. The same was true in the civil service, where thousands of Taiwanese were laid off and replaced by mainland officials. The replacement of Japanese with Mandarin as the official language put educated Taiwanese at a severe disadvantage in the state-sector job market. Thus, there was a large pool of unemployed Taiwanese intellectuals by early 1947. Moreover, the KMT officials often treated the Taiwanese as culturally inferior, arguing that after being enslaved by the Japanese they needed to be re-educated before they could be true Chinese again.

Who should ultimately be blamed for the 2–28 Incident is still debated today. Initially, the KMT had tried to pin the blame on Communist agitation and the legacy of Japanese rule, although this was not very convincing as the Japanese had been quite successful at suppressing the tiny Taiwan Communist Party. Later in the 1990s, the KMT tried to shift the blame on to Chen Yi. In fact, back in 1950 the KMT had delighted many Taiwanese by having Chen executed in Taipei, although his crime had been negotiating with the CCP on China. Others point the finger primarily at Chiang Kai-shek. One of Chen Yi's body guards claimed that Chen had received a telegram from Chiang telling him to 'Kill them all, keep it secret'.[23]

By the spring of 1947, dissatisfaction with the Chen Yi regime was so high that any spark could have set off rebellion. For most Taiwanese, it was clear that one cruel but efficient colonial regime had been replaced by a cruel, corrupt and inefficient one.

Legacy of 2–28

In Taiwan, 2–28 became a taboo subject for decades. As such, when *City of Sadness* was released it was the first time that many university students had even heard of the Incident. Despite the public invisibility of 2–28, it was, and remains, one of the most controversial topics in Taiwan's history and politics.

The comments of historian Robert Edmondson reveal the significance that the 2–28 Incident holds in modern Taiwanese history: 'This event is perhaps the most important single event in Taiwanese history because it made Taiwanese history thinkable. The betrayal and violence of the Chinese nationalist government made the boundaries of a distinct historical subject, "the Taiwanese people", clear and compelling.'[24]

Although a sense of Taiwanese identity did begin to develop in the face of Japanese discriminatory colonial policies, the birth of Taiwanese nationalism can be dated from the 2–28 Incident in 1947. Following the Incident, we see the emergence of a Taiwan independence movement in exile, first in Japan and later in the US. Unlike earlier pre-1947 opposition movements, which sought greater autonomy, this new nationalist movement made full Taiwanese independence its ultimate objective. The 2–28 Incident served as a unifying and mobilizing symbol for the opposition to attack the KMT's legitimacy. After martial law was lifted, the KMT tried to ignore the issue but were gradually forced to make concessions, apologizing and paying compensation to the victims and their families. A sign of the degree of change is that now February 28 is treated as one of the most important national holidays of the year.

The Incident had a huge impact on ethnic relations on the island, creating tension between Mainlanders and local Taiwanese.[25] Writing three decades after 2–28, Hill Gates noted that, 'The existence of two major ethnic blocs in Taiwan is a fact obvious to everyone from the greenest tourist to my elderly Taipei landlady, who spends many cheerful hours slandering "those hillbilly Chinese" for cutting out the Taiwanese-language soap operas.'[26] Although the divisions are no longer so apparent today, as most first- generation Mainlanders have now died, politically this ethnic divide has remained influential after democratization. For the KMT, the Incident was seen as proof that Taiwanese could not be trusted, thus giving them reason to exclude islanders from top party, government and military positions for the next three decades. For many Taiwanese, the Incident created a hatred of Mainlanders, a sentiment that some politicians tried exploiting during election campaigns until only quite recently. The KMT has also employed ethnic mobilization by nurturing the sense of crisis within the Mainlander community that Mainlanders will be persecuted if the KMT loses power.

The targeted killings associated with 2–28 meant that the Incident had a particular impact on Taiwan's educated elite. Those not killed or imprisoned had a choice of self-imposed exile abroad or silence. The incident caused many to lose interest in national politics and concentrate on business interests or local politics. The severity of the KMT crackdown and subsequent decades of political persecution, known as the White Terror, showed the futility of open opposition to the KMT and meant that the party was largely free from open political challenge for decades.

How did the KMT survive its disastrous start?

After its disastrous start in Taiwan leading up to 1947, the KMT regime's plight did not immediately improve. It progressively lost control of its remaining territory on mainland China, culminating in the formal establishment of the People's Republic of China (PRC) in Beijing in October 1949. What was left of the ROC army and government fled to Taiwan after repeated defeats on the mainland. Somewhere between one and two million Mainlander refugees came to Taiwan between 1948 and 1950.[27] Considering that Taiwan's population was only six million at the end of Japan's colonial rule, this transformed Taiwan's ethnic structure, with Mainlanders making up approximately a fifth of the population. Taiwan struggled to cope with this huge population increase at a time of high unemployment and inflation. The KMT troops were deeply demoralized by late 1949 and, after numerous defections on the mainland, Chiang Kai-shek had doubts over the loyalty of many of his generals. By this time, the KMT had also lost the military and financial support of the US. This ROC government in exile was hosted by a hostile Taiwanese population, whose memories of 2–28 were still fresh. After the PRC's People's Liberation Army (PLA) captured Hainan in April 1950, it looked likely that an attack on Taiwan was just months away, as troops and landing craft were being prepared in Fujian. At the time, someone predicting a future Taiwan economic or democratic miracle would have been viewed as out of their minds by the pessimistic Taipei resident in mid-1950.

A combination of external relations and economic and political variables enabled the KMT to survive and take the first steps towards political stability on the island. Initially, what saved the KMT was the outbreak of the Korean War on 25 June 1950. As Thomas Gold notes: 'in one of the greatest twists in history, none other than Kim Il Sung, the leader of North Korea, ended up saving Chiang Kai-shek'.[28] In response, the US decided to deploy their Seventh Fleet into the Taiwan Strait to prevent a PRC invasion. This US security guarantee was formalized in the 1954 US–ROC Mutual Defence Treaty.[29] The treaty was severely tested in the 1954 and 1958 Strait Crises when the PRC launched attacks against the last two major ROC-held islands off the Chinese mainland, Kinmen and Mazu.

Publicly, Chiang Kai-shek talked of militarily retaking the mainland throughout the martial law era. However, the Mutual Defence Treaty was a defensive pact, as Chiang had privately pledged he would not attack the mainland without US consent. The security umbrella gave Chiang the breathing space to modernize and reform ROC forces. Their performance in the 1958 Second Cross-Strait Crisis suggested that these reforms had had some impact. Increasingly, though, the KMT came to accept that 'recovery of the mainland would require 70 per cent political work and 30 per cent military efforts'.[30] In the latter half of the martial law era the main slogan became 'Three People's Principles Unify China', with official reminders fading but visible on walls in the 1990s. By the end of the martial law era, the slogan had become a laughing stock. In the Blacklist Studio group's 1989 rap song *Minzhu acao* (*Democracy Bumpkin*), a boy from the country visiting Taipei happens to come across an opposition party rally and, seeing the ranks of military police in riot gear, asks a policeman, 'are you getting ready for the war to retake the mainland?'[31]

The KMT's party organizational reforms were to be as important as those in the military. The loss of the mainland led to much soul searching within the KMT. In early 1950 the KMT was a demoralized and disorganized party. Party reform was a critical step in its revival. First, Chiang set up a reform committee led by middle-aged loyalists. There was a process to re-register all members. Many seen as disloyal, corrupt or incompetent were purged from the party. In addition, thousands of party cadres went through training at the Sun Yat Sen (孫中山) Institute on Policy Research and Development. By October 1952, the party was much stronger. After three years of reform efforts, it had strong leadership and morale, and membership had expanded rapidly. In fact, almost 60 per cent of its members were Taiwanese by the early 1950s, although they were concentrated in the lower ranks until the 1980s.[32]

For most of the martial law era, cross-Strait relations amounted to little more than occasional shelling or spy missions against the other side. Taiwan was cut off from China to a greater extent than any time in the previous 400 years. There was no bilateral trade or negotiations, and visits were forbidden. This meant that the 1.5 million Mainlanders, for whom coming to Taiwan had been just a temporary move, were cut off from their Chinese homes and families. Once again, Taiwanese film can help us to understand this story. We can get a sense of the tragedy of separation in the 1989 Wang Tong (王童) film *Banana Paradise*, which focuses on the lives of lower class Mainlanders under martial law.[33]

The US alliance also provided Taiwan with critical diplomatic support. After the foundation of the PRC, most non-Communist states still recognized the ROC as the legitimate government of China. The island regime even retained its seat on the UN Security Council, while the PRC remained excluded from the world body. As more former Western colonies gained independence in the 1950s and 1960s, the ROC and PRC fought for their diplomatic recognition. Both Chinas claimed to be the sole legitimate government of all China, each maintaining their own version of the 'one China policy'. This meant that as soon as a country recognized the PRC, the ROC would cut diplomatic ties.

Economic recovery and miracle

Taiwan's economic success was a key factor in the KMT's ability to gain domestic legitimacy. Under martial law, Taiwan had a remarkable economic record. Between 1951 and 1987, the average annual economic growth rate was 8.9 per cent. In 1987, Taiwan was the eleventh largest exporter in the world, and in 1986 the country had the second largest foreign reserves in the world. The foundations of Taiwan's developmental state and this economic miracle were first laid in the 1950s.

A number of factors were critical in this economic success. First, although it had suffered from US bombings during the Second World War and early KMT economic misman-agement shortly thereafter, the previous Japanese regime had left a strong economic infrastructure that was to be crucial to the island's economic take-off. Second, in addition to US security and military aid, Taiwan benefited from American economic advice and non-military aid that amounted to approximately US$100 million per year until 1964. This aid was important in stabilizing Taiwan's economy in the early 1950s.

Another important pillar of Taiwan's economic success was land reform. The KMT had failed to carry out land reform in China and saw this as being a factor in its defeat to the CCP. The first stages of land reform involved rent reduction and, later, land redistribution of former Japanese-owned land. The next stage was more ambitious. From 1953 landlords were compelled to sell to the government any land in excess of 2.9 hectares, which the government then resold to tenant farmers. In return, the landlords received government bonds and shares in government companies. The number of owner–farmer families in the farming population rose from 38 per cent to 60 per cent between 1949 and 1957. The land reform led to increased agricultural productivity and more equitable distribution of income, and freed agricultural workers for industrial jobs. Land reform also had political repercussions. It greatly diminished the status of Taiwanese landlords, a group of potential opposition to the KMT, leaving the rural areas under their continued sway for the next few decades.

Taiwan also benefited from intelligent economic planning. Kuo and Myers's book *Taiwan's Economic Transformation* examines how the KMT government's property rights reform and institutional change laid the foundations for the country's economic success.[34] Its economic planners were able to operate relatively free of pressure from either their political superiors or big business. The key economic policies were import substitution, followed by export-orientated growth, with the latter starting in the late 1950s. In the early 1950s, the government promoted its policy of import substitution, using high tariffs to protect domestic industry. The emphasis during this phase was on labour-intensive light industry, such as textiles. By 1956, however, the domestic market was saturated and a new policy of export-led growth was launched. The New Taiwan Dollar was devalued against the US dollar, import duties were cut and the government initiated programmes to encourage foreign direct investment. For instance, in 1966 the first Export Processing Zone was set up in Kaohsiung, with special incentives for exporting firms doing business there. Since US and European markets were booming, these economic policies paid off so well that the end of US aid in 1965 did not dent economic growth.

In 1973, Taiwan entered its third phase, with a growing emphasis on high technology and capital-intensive industrial development, as by then the global economy was slowing, and both Taiwan's labour costs and global energy prices were rising. To further boost the economy and improve Taiwan's infrastructure, the government launched ten major construction projects, including expanding the island's railway network, railway electrification, developing motorways and opening Taiwan's first nuclear power plant, an integrated steel plant, Taoyuan International Airport and petrochemical complexes. The government also began promoting the development of its high-tech industry, exemplified by the opening of the Hsinchu Science Park in 1978, which has developed into one of Asia's leading Information Technology production and research and design centres.

In spite of its rapid growth figures, Taiwan achieved one of the most equitable distributions of wealth in the non-communist world. For example, the Gini coefficient, which compares the income share of the richest 20 per cent against the poorest 20 per cent, fell from 0.558 in 1953 to 0.321 in 1970. The average annual income rose, in spite of continued population growth, from US$48 in 1952 to US$4,991 in 1987. Taiwan also experienced huge social change, with large-scale rural to urban migration and the emergence of a large and well-educated middle class. In short, Taiwan's economic policies contributed to the island's significant and equitable record of growth, which bolstered the ROC regime's political legitimacy.

Despite these impressive economic statistics, it was not until the mid to late 1980s that Taiwan gained an image of a successful state. In 1964, historian Mark Mancall opened his edited volume *Formosa Today* with an essay titled 'Taiwan, Island of Resignation and Despair'.[35]

Taiwan's political system under martial law

I will now discuss the formal and informal political structure of the ROC, which will help to both clarify how the KMT was able to maintain its power and describe the nature of authoritarianism under the martial law period.

The formal political structure of the ROC during the height of martial law is shown in Table 2.1. This structure was essentially that inherited from when the regime nominally governed all of China and is based on the 1947 ROC constitution. Basically, the ROC political structure was maintained due to publicly stated desires to retake the mainland but, as such an event never took place, it could only be applied to Taiwan. It can be divided into four layers: (1) national, (2) provincial, (3) county/city and (4) grassroots (including township and village/neighbourhood).

At the top of the national power pyramid is the president. Alongside the president was the National Assembly, although it was abolished in 2005. The President is the ROC's head of state and had the power to appoint the premier and most government positions down to the provincial level. The president could serve a maximum of two six-year terms. The National Assembly was directly elected for the first time in 1947 throughout China. Its main functions were to elect the president and to revise the constitution. Below the president were the five yuans: The Executive Yuan, Legislative Yuan, Judicial Yuan, Examination Yuan and Control Yuan. For this study, the most relevant are the first two. The Executive Yuan was headed by the premier, who was appointed by the president.

Table 2.1 Republic of China political system under martial law

National level				
Representative Body: National Assembly (elected 1947 in China)				
President (elected by National Assembly)				
Five Yuan				
Premier (appointed by President) Executive Yuan	Judicial Yuan	Legislative Yuan (elected 1948 in China)	Examination Yuan	Control Yuan
Provincial level				
Provincial Governor (appointed by President)				
Provincial Government				
Representative body: Provincial Assembly (directly elected)				

	Level			
	County			*City*
Executive Representative	County (County magistrate) County Council			City (City mayor) City Council
	Rural Township (xiang)	*Urban Township (zhen)*	*City (shi)*	*District (Qu)*
Elected Executive	Township chief (*xiangzhang*)	Township chief (*zhenzhang*)	City mayor (*shizhang*)	District head (*Quzhang*) Appointed by city mayor
Representative	Township councillor (*xiangmindai*)	Township councillor (*zhenmindai*)	City councillor (*shimindai*)	None
	Village (cun)	*Neighbourhood (li)*	*Neighbourhood (li)*	*Neighbourhood (li)*
Elected representative:	Village chief (*cunzhang*)	Neighbourhood chief (*lizhang*)	Neighbourhood chief (*lizhang*)	Neighbourhood chief (*lizhang*)

The Executive Yuan included all the major government ministries and operated like a cabinet, although ministers could not concurrently serve in the parliament. The Legislative Yuan was the law-making parliament, which reviewed government budgets and laws proposed by the Executive Yuan. Members of the Legislative Yuan were elected from the various Chinese provinces in 1948. This government structure was meant to reinforce the idea that the ROC remained the government of all China, not just Taiwan. The problem arose once the legislators, National Assemblymen and president reached their term limits. As new elections on the mainland were no longer possible, these parliamentarians were frozen in office until new elections could be held, while the president's term limit was removed. To hold new elections for the national parliaments just in Taiwan would have undermined the ROC's claim to be the government of all China.

At the next level came the Provincial Governor and government, which were responsible for running the affairs of Taiwan Province. The Provincial Governor was not elected but appointed by the President. The problem was that, apart from the offshore islands of Kinmen and Mazu (counted as Fujian Province), the total territory governed by the national and provincial governments was completely overlapping.[36] The Provincial Assembly, which became directly elected in 1951, was the highest elected office in Taiwan. At the next level came the city mayors and county magistrates. These positions, once the most powerful elected executive posts on the island, covered 23 districts.[37] Their city and county governments were supervised by the elected city and county assemblies. Below the county/city level came Taiwan's grassroots local levels, with elected posts of township and county level city mayors, who were supervised by elected township representatives. The lowest elected posts were for village and neighbourhood chiefs. Since the early 1950s, Taiwan has thus been electing a huge range of positions, bolstering its claim to be Free China or Democratic China.

Table 2.1 thus shows that there were two quite distinct systems, or One Country, Two Systems. From the President down to the Provincial Governor was completely insulated from public opinion, manned by politicians frozen in office indefinitely. While at the local level almost all posts were elected. There was also a parallel ethnic division, with national level politics dominated by Mainlanders, while at the local level ethnic voting meant that elected posts were dominated by local Taiwanese.

How free and democratic was martial law in Taiwan?

Although the ROC's democratic credentials look quite impressive on paper, upon closer examination it becomes clear why it remained a hybrid of authoritarianism and totalitarianism for decades. To a large extent, Taiwan's early democracy was a façade, something to please the KMT's American allies and channel local Taiwanese political interests without really delegating any significant political power.

Taiwan's first democratic defect was that it was a one-party state. The KMT had a very unconvincing argument that the China Youth Party and Democratic Socialist Party made the ROC a multi-party system. In reality, these were KMT ally parties from China, which became known as 'flower vase parties' that did not play any oppositional role. Their role was thus quite similar to the satellite parties that can legally operate in the PRC today. Under martial law and the Temporary Provisions, the constitutional right to form new political parties was suspended. It was possible for non-KMT politicians to contest elections, but only as individuals. This meant that, as the only organized party, the KMT was able to dominate local elections. This can be seen in the election rate of

KMT nominees, which was 83.56 per cent for local executives (city mayors and county magistrates) and 85.86 per cent for provincial assemblymen from 1954 to 1989.[38] It was only after the arrival of the first genuine opposition party that this election success rate fell.

The first attempt to form a new political party revealed that the KMT would not accept an organized challenge to its one-party state. The bid to create a China Democratic Party was led in the late 1950s by the Mainlander editor of the liberal *Free China Fortnightly*, Lei Chen (雷震). This was an attempt to form an alliance between Taiwanese elected politicians and liberal Mainlander intellectuals. Initially, the KMT had tolerated the magazine, but the move to formally create a genuine opposition party crossed over the KMT's red line. In 1960, Lei was arrested on a trumped-up charge and sentenced to ten years, and the *Free China Fortnightly* was closed down. This alliance between Taiwanese elected politicians and liberal Mainland intellectuals was too much of a potential threat for the KMT. Nevertheless, it was also a wasted opportunity to create a multi-ethnic opposition as, since the island's democratization, all the relevant challenger parties have been dominated by single ethnic groups.

A second democratic defect was that elections were limited only to the local level. The most powerful bodies, such as the presidency, National Assembly, Executive Yuan and Legislative Yuan, were all unelected after the 1940s. The powers of local elected politicians were not sufficient to actually seriously threaten KMT domination. That said, some non-KMT politicians did occasionally win important elected positions such as Kao Yu-shu (高玉樹) winning Taipei's mayoral seat twice. However, as the election statistics cited above show, the KMT did dominate local politics.

As the KMT did not have a strong network in rural Taiwan, it dominated local politics by cooperating with the local factions, who were nearly all KMT affiliated. Chen Ming-tong (陳明通) defined local factions as 'a set of interpersonal networks that function, for political purposes, in the local as opposed to the national arena'.[39] For much of the martial law era, Taiwan's elections were very competitive, but the competition was among KMT factions rather than parties. The KMT was not able to attract these groups using ideological appeals but developed a patron–client relationship with them. The KMT rewarded these factions with economic privileges in return for political support. The key carrots included regional economic activities (running local credit cooperatives or transport companies), provincial level lending, provincial and county level procurement and contracting, local level interest exchanges, such as favourable land zoning, and protection of illegal businesses. The KMT also tried to control the factions by limiting their scope to the county level and encouraging competing factions. At the grassroots level the factions' foot soldiers were the vote brokers, or *tiau-a-ka*, who employed a mixture of persuasion and material incentives to ensure their patron's desired electoral outcome.[40] With no real opposition party, material rewards were more persuasive than policy promises. A senior KMT politician admitted to me how, when he first joined elections for Taipei city council in the early 1970s, only two or three candidates could get elected without vote buying.[41]

The KMT was not just an ordinary party under this political system, but was itself the state. Even today, the Republic of China's national anthem started out as a KMT party song. Just as with the CCP in China, it was the Chiangs and KMT that set government policy. To succeed in the state sector it was essential to be a KMT party member. This fact applied to the civil service, military, state-owned enterprises and education sector. Again, this practice was to have a long-term legacy, as these remain some of the most pro-KMT sections of Taiwanese society to this day. The KMT was aware of the role student movements had played in its fall. Therefore, party cells were set up in all schools, colleges and universities. Party ideology was also spread by the China Youth Corps, which served to recruit promising talent. The fact that by the end of martial law there were almost two and a half million KMT party members – over 20 per cent of the total population – gives some idea of the degree that the KMT penetrated Taiwanese society.[42]

Financially, the KMT was more than a political party; it was also a business empire. Because of the often fuzzy divide between party and state finances, the KMT was able to build up a huge business and property empire. Working in a KMT party-owned enterprise had similar status and benefits to the civil service or a state-owned enterprise. These enterprises became known as the KMT party assets. Such companies naturally also benefited from government patronage in procurement and construction contracts. These assets meant, of course, that the KMT had a huge electoral campaign fund to support its election candidates, particularly where they were threatened by popular non-party candidates. Again, this has had long-term implications, as after democratization the KMT's financial superiority meant that there was not a level election playing-field, as the KMT could always outspend its rivals in election campaigns. It was only after the third change of ruling parties in 2016 that legislation was passed to deal with the KMT's party assets.

On the surface, martial law era Taiwan had a rich number of associations to cater to its societal needs, one of the central characteristics of a civil society in a democracy. By 1987, there were 11,306 registered associations with 8.3 million members.[43] However, as is the case in the PRC, the KMT controlled the registration of these groups and penetrated almost all organizations. In order to increase the party's influence in society, it encouraged citizens to join the KMT-sponsored groups, such as the Farmers' Association, professional associations, chambers of commerce and government-run trades unions. These groups were almost all led by KMT members and were a key tool in election mobilization for the party. The largest such organization was the Farmers' Association and, due to its influence, its leadership elections were hotly contested. In 1974 a US academic found that rather than being 'run by and for the farmers . . . they were controlled by the government and used to organize the farmers and prevent spontaneous peasant organization'.[44]

Another democratic defect was the lack of a free media. The case of the *Free China Fortnightly* revealed how the KMT dealt with what it saw as threatening public discourse. The KMT controlled the media through ownership and censorship. Out of the 31 newspapers in 1987, 20 were in private hands, with the other 11 owned by the government, KMT and military, thus making them, in effect, KMT papers.[45] However, since 70 per cent of the daily newspapers sold belonged to the *China Times* and *United Daily* groups, whose directors were KMT Central Standing Committee members, they were also de facto KMT papers. New newspapers could not emerge to challenge the KMT as there was a ban on establishing new daily papers until 1988. The KMT's control of the electronic media was even tighter. The KMT-run *Broadcasting Corporation of China* dominated the radio networks. The principal owners of the three television stations were the KMT, Ministry of Defence, and Education and the Provincial Government. This, once again, guaranteed KMT control. The implications of such a KMT-dominated media were that the party dominated political communication, with the media serving as a tool for KMT propaganda. Only in the realm of magazines and journals was there some variation. It was here that writers such as Li Ao (李敖) and Po Yang (柏楊) satirized the KMT government. The price they paid was, like Lei Chen, to receive lengthy prison sentences on trumped-up charges.[46] In the film and music industries artists needed to deal with Government Information Office (GIO) censorship. The film director Wan Jen (萬仁)

has spoken of his frustrating experiences with the GIO censors in gaining approval for his early films in the 1980s.[47]

Lastly, Taiwanese political and civil rights were severely curtailed under martial law. The 1947 constitution had quite liberal provisions for human rights, such as freedom of speech and association. However, these were effectively suspended under the four decades of martial law. This meant that the KMT could basically rule without any of the checks and balances envisaged in the constitution. The widely unpopular Taiwan Garrison Command was the key body in charge of enforcing martial law. It was responsible for censorship, arresting dissidents and surveillance. There is no accurate figure for the numbers of political prisoners incarcerated under martial law, but Tien estimates that there were 10,000 military trials for civilians between 1950 and 1986.[48] The KMT was exceedingly paranoid about plots to undermine its rule, leading to the large numbers of political prisoners. The two causes that it was particularly wary of were Taiwan independence and communism. This meant that political prisoners tended to come from both major ethnic groups, the Taiwanese and Mainlanders. Where corporatism, brainwashing, material improvement and clientelism failed to work, the KMT employed severe political repression. Political prisoners who were known abroad received slightly more lenient sentences, but those less well known, such as the Taiwanese politician Su Tung-chi (蘇東啟), were treated much more harshly.[49] Su received a death sentence in 1961 for allegedly plotting rebellion, with his wife receiving a life sentence. This gave the era the name of the White Terror. Readers can get a vivid sense of the brutality of political persecution and the difficulties victims of terror faced in adjusting to post-martial law life in Wan Jen's award-winning film, *Super Citizen Ko* (超級大國民). In the long term, though, the KMT would pay a price for its repression, as the White Terror and its victims would eventually provide the opposition an election appeal to attack the party.

KMT nation–building project

As mentioned at the outset of the chapter, a key goal of the KMT's martial law authoritarianism was its attempt to transform Taiwanese society. One of the most dominant methods it used to this effect was its nation-building project. In other words, the KMT was trying to impose on the Taiwanese a new form of nationalism – what I call ROC or KMT Chinese nationalism. There were a number of key components of this kind of message. First, the KMT argued that the ROC was the sole legitimate government of all China and the protector of traditional Chinese culture. The ROC's sacred mission was to unify China by retaking the mainland. Another key message was that the Taiwanese are Chinese, and that Chinese identities should override any other local or foreign national identities. Thus, competing types of identities, such as PRC Chinese nationalism, Japanese nationalism and Taiwanese local or national identities, had to be suppressed. The KMT's position in the ROC state meant that promoting its form of Chinese nationalism was designed to support its legitimacy to rule unchallenged.

The KMT attempted to impose its nationalism through a range of avenues. One such method was in its cultural policies. Edwin Winkler compares these efforts with the economic miracle, stating 'The extraordinary success of Nationalist cultural policy in shaping Taiwan's post-war cultural development is another sort of "miracle"'.[50] A key component of this project was the Cultural Renaissance Movement that began in the 1960s. This movement was initiated to counter the PRC's attack on traditional Chinese culture during its infamous Cultural Revolution. The Cultural Renaissance Movement included a range of programmes to promote traditional Chinese cultural expressions, such as traditional painting, Peking Opera (national opera), classical Chinese literature and Confucian philosophy.[51] In contrast, local cultural practices, such as Taiwanese opera, folk arts and local religions, did not receive state funding and were viewed as being of lower status.

One of the most visible methods of nation building was the changing of street names. The vast majority of the island's roads had their names changed to promote aspects of Chinese culture, KMT political ideology and Chinese identification. Every city now had a China Street, along with streets named after Chinese cities and provinces and iconic figures such as Sun Yat Sen and Chiang Kai-shek. Others were named after Sun's Three People's Principles, the Self Strengthening Movement and the 1911 Revolution. Moreover, these tended to be the most important streets in each city. Few road names seemed to have any local Taiwanese or even international reference. Despite democratization, these symbols of ROC Chinese nationalism remain largely intact today. There was a similar pattern in the naming of schools and universities. When I lived in Kaohsiung, I was woken early every morning by the ROC national anthem playing at Wufu Junior High School, which was named after the Five Blessings from the Confucian classic *The Book of History*.

Language policies were another key tool for this nation-building project. After banning Japanese soon after 1945, the government progressively expanded its Mandarinization project. Mandarin became the sole language in the education sector and within official settings. From 1956, school children were fined for speaking local languages.[52] An important piece of language policy was the 1976 Broadcasting and Television Law, which limited non-Mandarin broadcasting. This led to a sharp drop in Taiwanese TV shows, going from 50 per cent of shows in the early 1970s to less than 10 per cent by the end of the decade. According to the linguist Henning Klöter, 'The extension of ROC language policies to Taiwan was thus not driven by linguistic considerations, but by the ideological notion that Taiwan was a province of China and that Mandarin represented the national language of China.'[53]

Along with the media, the education sector and military also played key roles in promoting ROC Chinese nationalism. With its control of the education system, the KMT developed a highly political curriculum for all levels of education. Students had to take courses in Sun Yat Sen's thought and the ROC constitution, and there was a China-centric orientation to most courses, particularly history and geography.[54] Within the schools, students were surrounded by ROC nationalist symbols, such as statues and portraits of Chiang Kai-shek and Sun Yat Sen, and the national ROC maps on the classroom wall showed Taiwan as just one tiny province within the vast country of China. Such KMT ideological indoctrination of ROC nationalism continued well into adult life. This held particularly true for all males, who had endure two to three years' compulsory military service, in what was essentially a KMT institution.

Because the KMT's ROC nationalism was so central to its claim to legitimacy, the party was especially sensitive to any attempt to undermine this ideology. Thus, when National Taiwan University (NTU) professor Peng Ming-min attempted to issue his *Declaration of Formosan Self Salvation,* he and his student helpers received lengthy prison sentences. The key crimes for which he was accused were that he attacked Chiang, arguing that retaking the mainland was impossible, and stated that Taiwan and China are different countries with Taiwan being independent since 1949 and thus having the right to become a democracy.[55] Today, these seem like mainstream opinions, but at the time they were political dynamite. If Peng had not been an internationally known scholar, he probably would have suffered a far worse fate.

Despite Winkler's description of a miracle in cultural policy, we are faced with a problem of empirically proving this. Media reports, published literature and film were so tightly censored that they cannot really answer this question. There were also no reliable public opinion surveys, as answering politically sensitive questions honestly would have been too dangerous. One realm in which this policy did have an impact was in the use of Mandarin, which had shown a huge expansion, especially among the educated and younger sections of the population. However, as Hill Gates's landlady quote revealed, the attempt to eliminate local languages was bitterly resented and would become an important symbol of opposition in the future. Nevertheless, by 1987, no language could possibly replace Mandarin as the national language.

The gradual shift from hard to soft authoritarianism?

As mentioned at the outset, Winkler argued that by the early 1980s Taiwan was making a transition away from hard to soft authoritarianism. This included the following characteristics: (1) joint Mainlander–Taiwanese technocratic rule, (2) collective party leadership, (3) elections that offered space for new social forces, (4) less frequent use of repression and (5) more legalistic and less direct repression. In the conclusion of Winkler's article he tries to put Taiwan's changed authoritarianism in a comparative light:

> Remember that Taiwan is not, for example, a part of Latin America, where military regimes have waged open warfare on their societies; or South Korea, where military officers shoot their way to power; or the Philippines, where a ruling family drains the economy. On the contrary, Taiwan is almost Mexico, where a no-longer revolutionary party remains predominant; and it may be Spain, where the question was not so much whether The Leader would enact democracy as whether the successors he appointed would succeed in doing so. Taiwan could even become Japan, whose economic and electoral system it almost resembles. In any case, it is certainly not the People's Republic of China.[56]

Gold makes a useful observation on Taiwan in this period: 'It was possible to avoid politics, beyond studying the Three Principles of the People and compulsory military service for males.'[57] Such an avoidance of politics was not an option in Maoist China at the same time.

To what extent had Taiwan softened its authoritarianism?

Let us now briefly examine some of the features of what is described as a softening of authoritarianism to see if there really was a change in the nature of the political system. I will focus on developments up to the early 1980s when Winkler published his piece, but will talk more about the remainder of that decade in the next chapter on democratization.

First, Winkler talks of a shift to collective leadership rather than the one-man dictatorship witnessed under Chiang Kai-shek. There was a shift away from the centre of power as Chiang Kai-shek reached the end of his life and his son Chiang Ching-kuo became increasingly influential in his role as Premier. However, even before becoming president, Chiang Ching-kuo was another dictator, completely dominating the political scene. Just as had been the case with Chiang Kai-shek, when Chiang Ching-kuo felt threatened by internal domestic rivals he would have them removed. It was Chiang Ching-kuo's political strength that enabled him to begin a Taiwanization of party and state. Under the junior Chiang younger and well-educated Taiwanese and Mainlander technocrats were rapidly promoted to higher positions in both the party and government for the first time. The most obvious example of this was the rise from obscurity of Lee Teng-hui (李登輝) to become Taipei mayor in 1978 and Vice President in 1984. Other figures promoted rapidly under Chiang's watch that will feature heavily in subsequent chapters are James Soong (宋楚瑜) and Ma Ying-jeou (馬英九).

From the early 1970s, there does appear to have been more scope for a political opposition to develop. We can see this in the emergence of the *Intellectual* (*Daxue*) magazine and the Protect the Diaoyutai Islands Movement it instigated in the early 1970s, along with the emergence of an organized *Tang Wai* movement later that same decade. In the first case, protests broke out against the weak ROC response to Japan's claim of sovereignty over the Diaoyutai islands, which Taipei also claimed.[58] One of the centres of criticism was *Intellectual* magazine. However, once its criticism went beyond the Diaoyutai case and on to the KMT government, then it was closed. This was essentially an elite movement of intellectuals and university students. Thus, stern warnings and the firing of a few professors resolved the issue.

The second movement was the *Tangwai,* meaning 'outside of the party' (KMT). The term already existed to refer to non-KMT candidates in the 1950s and 1960s. However, the *Tangwai* that emerged in the local elections of 1977 was stronger and more organized than before. The characteristics of this were quite different from earlier elite movements in that it was made up of local elected politicians standing for election with a unified list of candidates and a policy platform. It was like a party in all but name. Its key demands were democratization, human rights and ethnic justice. Unlike Lei Chen's aborted party, this one was overwhelmingly ethnically Taiwanese. The *Tangwai* did extremely well in their first election in 1977, winning four local executive and 21 Provincial Assembly seats.

On the edges there were also some signs of media liberalization. For the first time an opposition media appeared in the form of political magazines. The most groundbreaking initially was the short-lived *Meilidao,* which operated as the voice of the *Tangwai*, and whose offices also served as the semi-party's headquarters. Often these publications would cross KMT red lines and get closed down, only to reappear under a different name. Thus, unlike in 1960, the opposition media could not be so easily suppressed.[59]

One important factor in the rise of the new opposition was that a new form of elections created new opportunities. These were the so-called supplementary elections that began in 1969. These elections opened up a gradually increasing number of National Assembly and Legislative Yuan seats to direct election. Although these elections could not change the balance of power, they allowed Taiwanese voices to be heard in the national parliaments for the first time.

The opposition grew increasingly bold, instigating what would be known as the Chungli Incident in 1977. A crowd protesting suspected KMT vote fraud burned down the Chungli police station, inciting the first open political violence against the regime since 1947. There were also, for the first time, demonstrations and marches. By late 1979 the *Tangwai* was moving close to forming a formal political party. However, this time the KMT cracked down on the movement and its followers following what is known as the Kaohsiung Incident. The *Tangwai* had been planning a rally for International Human Rights Day in Kaohsiung on 10 December, but clashes broke out between demonstrators and the police. In response, almost all the main opposition leaders were rounded up and put on military trial, with many receiving lengthy sentences. The KMT thus revealed that it would still not accept an organized opposition. Nevertheless, the *Tangwai* was different from the China Democratic Party in that, despite the arrest of all its core leaders, the movement quickly recovered. The party's candidates were instead the defendants' wives and defence lawyers. In other words, the support foundation of the new opposition was far stronger than the intellectual basis of earlier movements.

Although levels of KMT toleration of opposition were probably slightly higher from the mid-1970s, compared to that of the 1950s or 1960s, this should not be exaggerated. According to Freedom House, Taiwan moved from 'Not Free' to 'Partly Free' in 1977. However, its ratings for civil and political rights were actually quite consistent at five and five respectively for the next ten years until the lifting of martial law.[60] Moreover, we should also not forget that many of the worst atrocities against the opposition came during the latter days of martial law, some of which remain unsolved to this day. For instance, no one has ever been tried for the murder of Kaohsiung Incident defendant Lin I-hsiung's (林義雄) mother and daughters, despite the fact that the house was under police surveillance. The same applies to the suspected murder of the US-based Taiwanese professor Chen Wen-cheng (陳文成), who was found dead at NTU a day after being taken in for questioning by the secret police. A fictionalized portrayal of this story has now been made in the 2009 film *Formosa Betrayed*.[61]

By the late 1970s, the ROC's international status was undermining its legitimacy within Taiwan itself. The ROC suffered a series of diplomatic setbacks in the 1970s, losing its UN seat, along with US and Japanese diplomatic recognition and had to deal with the termination of the US–ROC Mutual Defence Treaty. By the end of the decade, it was just left with a handful of formal diplomatic allies. This severely undermined the KMT's claim that it was the government of all China, something that had been used by the party to justify delaying full national elections. The external setbacks worked both ways. They undermined KMT legitimacy but also, at times, made the regime take a tougher line on domestic opposition. For instance, after the US switched its formal recognition to Beijing, the island's government postponed the 1978 elections in addition to its severe handling of the Kaohsiung Incident later that same year. Despite no longer officially recognizing the island's government, Washington did pressure Taiwan to liberalize politically. However, this pressure did not rise to significant levels until the mid-1980s.

Conclusions

Despite the limits to KMT tolerance of political opposition, by the early 1980s Taiwan was making a transition away from hard authoritarianism. The re-emergence of the *Tangwai* after the 1979 Kaohsiung Incident crackdown showed it was no longer possible for the KMT to wipe out the opposition the way it had in 1947 and 1960. However, it was not yet clear what kind of regime was likely to emerge.

Taiwan's authoritarianism had evolved at a glacial pace. There was not a linear movement towards political liberalization. Instead, there were a number of democratic reversals at certain points, such as 1960 or 1979. Just as with communist China or the Soviet Union, the KMT was trying to transform society. It permeated extensively the island's social order, controlled the media and education sectors, showed itself willing to use brutal political repression and maintained strong connections between the state and party. However, the KMT was prepared to leave increasing space for the private sector in the economy. Thus, we do see the emergence of an independent business class. Also, unlike the above-mentioned totalitarian states, it allowed genuinely competitive elections to take place. Although they were single-party elections, non-party candidates could and did win elections. Similar to communist states, Taiwan under martial law was able to make society more equal, with its record of growth with equity, but managed this with a system allowing for private property and enterprise. Despite the appalling human rights record that Taiwan did have, under the ROC authoritarian rule the island did witness an impressive record of increased incomes, a better educated populace and economic modernization. In other words, like its counterparts in South Korea and Singapore, it was an efficient authoritarian developmental state and thus stood in stark contrast to authoritarian regimes in Latin America or Africa or even South East Asia.

Martial law left a deep imprint on post-transition Taiwanese politics. This will be a constant theme as we delve deeper in the subsequent chapters focusing on Taiwan in the 1990s and twenty-first century. Just as Taiwan remains in China's shadow, the authoritarian era still casts a shadow over the island's civil society and institutions. With some revisions, Taiwan's 1947 constitution and government structure remains in place. Taiwan's ethnic divide, though narrowing, is still structured along the same lines that prompted the 2–28 Incident. The two-party system that emerged in embryonic form in 1977, later to settle into a rivalry between the KMT and DPP, remains in place today. By the end of this book it will be clear that the list of authoritarian era legacies is a long one in democratic Taiwan.

Discussion questions

1   What were Taiwan's inherited political legacies from Republican China and Japanese rule?
2   Why did Taiwan's return to Chinese rule after 1945 go wrong so quickly?
3   What have been the long-term political legacies of the period between 1945 and 1949 and the White Terror era?
4   How was the KMT able to recover enough to deliver over three decades of political stability?
5   How did the KMT attempt to mould its version of Chinese nationalism on the island and how successful was this project?
6   What is meant by soft authoritarianism and what brought about Taiwan's move away from hard authoritarianism?
7   To what extent has Taiwan dealt with the issue of transitional justice from the authoritarian era?

Further reading

Chu, Yun-han and Lin Jih-wen. 2001. 'Political Development in 20th Century Taiwan: State building, regime transformation and the Construction of National Identity'. *China Quarterly*, 165: 102–29. Wide-ranging analysis of state and nation building projects in the twentieth century, cutting across Japanese, martial law and democratic eras.

Dickson, Bruce. 1993. 'Lessons of Defeat: The Reorganization of the Kuomintang on Taiwan, 1950–52'. *China Quarterly*, 133: 56–84; Dickson, Bruce. 1996. 'The Kuomintang before Democratization: Organizational Change and the Role of Elections.' In Tien HUng-mao (ed.). *Taiwan's Electoral Politics and Democratic Transition: Riding the Third Wave*. Armonk, NY:

M.E. Sharpe, pp. 42–78. These two articles by Dickson discuss how the KMT reorganized after defeat and then operated under martial law.

Hague, Rod and Martin Harrop. 2001. *Comparative Government and Politics: An Introduction.* Basingstoke: Palgrave. Chapter on authoritarian rule offers a useful comparative introduction to the theme of non-democratic regimes.

Kerr, George. 2005. *Formosa Betrayed.* Taipei: Taiwan Publishing Co. Eyewitness account by US Vice Consul of the critical 1945–49 period. Now available to download at: www.pinyin. info/books/formosabetrayed/index.html

Rigger, Shelley. 1999. *Politics in Taiwan: Voting for Democracy.* London: Routledge. Especially useful for this chapter are Chapter 3 on the party-state and Chapter 4 on electoral mobilization under hard authoritarianism.

Rubinstein, Murray (ed.). 1999. *Taiwan: A New History.* Armonk, NY: M.E. Sharpe. This has very useful and detailed chapters on the colonial period and martial law era. Especially relevant are Chapter 8: Harry Lamley, 'Taiwan under Japanese Rule', pp. 201–60; Chapter 10: Steven Phillips, 'Between Assimilation and Independence', pp. 275–319; Chapter 11: Peter Wang, 'A Bastion Created, A Regime Reformed, An Economy Reengineered, 1949–1970', pp. 320–38.

Schubert, Gunter (ed). 2016. *Routledge Handbook of Contemporary Taiwan.* London: Routledge. Chapters by Chou Wan-yao (on the Japanese colonial era) and Thomas Gold (on authoritarian rule) are outstanding reviews of these two eras.

Tien, Hung-mao. 1989. *The Great Transition: Politics and Social Change in the Republic of China.* Taipei: SMC Publishing. Most comprehensive introduction to politics in Taiwan in the dying days of martial law, with detailed chapters on foreign relations, interest groups, the media and political parties.

Notes

1 Hague and Harrop, *Comparative Government and Politics: An Introduction*, 34.
2 Ibid.
3 Ibid.
4 Winkler, 'Institutionalization and Participation on Taiwan', 481–99.
5 The term 'Mainlander' (*Waishengren*) refers to Chinese from mainland China and their descendants who emigrated to the island during the communist takeover of mainland China. During the martial law era I refer to the distinction of Mainlanders and Taiwanese, with the latter referring to those that already lived in Taiwan under Japanese colonial rule. However, when discussing Taiwan after the mid-1980s I use the term Taiwanese to refer to all ROC citizens, including Mainlanders, Hokklo, Hakka and Aboriginals.
6 Winkler, 481–82.
7 After 2008, a number of concerned scholars issued a series of open letters to members of the KMT government on judicial bias, human rights abuses and democratic reversals. For example, see 'An Open Letter to Taiwan's President', *Taipei Times,* 13 November 2009, 8.
8 This incident is discussed in Corcuff, 'History Textbooks, Identity Politics and Ethnic Introspection in Taiwan', 133–69 (note this is Chapter 36 in *Politics of Modern Taiwan*); Wang Fu-chang, 'National Imagination, Ethnic Consciousness, and History', 145–208.
9 The other infuriating aspects for the Chinese nationalists were the treatment of the historical relationship between China and Taiwan and positive depiction of the then president Lee Teng-hui.
10 Kushner, 'Nationality and Nostalgia', 793–820.
11 Lin, 'Women's Groups campaign Against "On Taiwan" Comic', *Taipei Times,* 23 February 2001, 2. This time there was a rather strange coalition of activists from the women's movement and extremist Chinese nationalists, both condemning Kobayashi.
12 Lamley, 'Taiwan under Japanese Rule', 231–2.
13 Chen, 'Formosan Political Movements under Japanese Colonial Rule, 1914–1937', 489.
14 The Chiang Wei-shui Memorial Freeway links Taipei with Yilan County.
15 The electoral system will be discussed in detail in Chapters 4 and 5.

16 Chou, 'Taiwan under Japanese Rule' (1895–1945), 23.
17 Snow, *Red Star Over China*, 110.
18 There is much debate within Taiwan on the significance of the Cairo Conference. It should be noted that this was not a treaty, but was a press communiqué that was not signed by the participants Roosevelt, Churchill and Chiang Kai-shek.
19 The Taipei 228 Memorial Museum is located in the 228 Peace Park, close to National Taiwan University Hospital. The National 228 Memorial Museum was opened more recently in 2011.
20 Phillips, 'Between Assimilation and Independence', 284.
21 One complaint by some Taiwanese nationalists has been the downplaying of violence in *City of Sadness* and that, in one of the few times violence is shown, it is Mainlanders that are the victims.
22 Peng, *A Taste of Freedom*, 51.
23 Edmondson, 'The February 28 Incident and National Identity', 43.
24 Ibid., 25.
25 During this transition period of 1945 to the early 1950s I use the term 'Taiwanese' to refer to those who were already resident in Taiwan during the colonial period.
26 Gates, 'Ethnicity and Social Class', 241.
27 In correspondence with the author, the historian Chou Wan-yao (周婉窈) commented: 'it was a decades-long sensitive secret kept by the KMT as to how many Mainlanders came to Taiwan. Two million may be larger than the real number, but no one knows at this moment. Some of my colleagues guess it may be around 1 to 1.5 million. But it is just guessing.'
28 Gold, 'Retrocession and Authoritarian KMT Rule', 43.
29 For details on the US–ROC relationship in the 1950s, see Tsang, 'Chiang Kai-shek and the Kuomintang's Policy to Reconquer the Chinese Mainland, 1949–1958', 48–72.
30 Ibid., 68.
31 For analysis of this song, see Schweig, 'Hoklo Hip-Hop', 52–3.
32 For details on KMT reforms, see Dickson, 'Lessons of Defeat', 56–84.
33 For a discussion of two films that focus on the long martial law era, see Chen Kuan-hsing, 'A Borrowed Life in *Banana Paradise*: De-Cold War/Decolonization, or Modernity and Its Tears', 39–54; Haddon, 'Hou Hsiao-hsien's *City of Sadness*', 55–66.
34 Kuo and Myers, *Taiwan's Economic Transformation*.
35 Mancall, 'Taiwan, Island of Resignation and Despair'.
36 Taipei and then Kaohsiung were later upgraded to special municipality status during martial law. This put them on the same level as province but also meant their city mayors became appointed rather than democratically elected.
37 The number of cities and counties at this level did change over time as a result of administrative district changes. The number 23 applies between 1993 and 2009.
38 Chen Ming-tong, 'Local Factions and Taiwan's Democratization', 178–9.
39 Ibid., 176.
40 See Rigger, *Politics in Taiwan,* Chapter 2.
41 Wu Den-yih (吳敦義) interview by author, Nantou, 8 October 2001.
42 Huang Teh-fu, 'Elections and the Evolution of the Kuomintang', 115.
43 For a discussion of interest groups in martial law era Taiwan, see Tien, *The Great Transition,* Chapter 3.
44 Stavis, *Rural Local Governance and Agricultural Development*, 104. Cited in Rigger, *Politics in Taiwan,* 77.
45 For a discussion of the media under martial law, see Tien, Chapter 8.
46 Wang, 'A Bastion Created, A Regime Reformed, An Economy Reengineered, 1949–1970', 335.
47 See the Question and Answer session in his visit to SOAS in 2014. Available online at: www.soas.ac.uk/taiwanstudies/events/28jul2014-film-screening-super-citizen-ko-and-qa-with-director-wan-jen-.html
48 Tien, 111.
49 Roy, *Taiwan: A Political History*, 88.
50 Winkler, 'Cultural Policy in Post-War Taiwan', 22–46.
51 Peking Opera held the title of national opera until the Lee Teng-hui era. For details of this engrossing topic, see Guy, *Peking Opera and Politics in Taiwan*.

52 Klöter, 'Mandarin Remains more Equal', 209–11.
53 Ibid., 209.
54 For details on how the KMT attempted to make Taiwanese Chinese in geography courses, see Chang, *Place, Identity and National Imagination in Postwar Taiwan*, 155–206.
55 For details of Peng's arrest, see Peng, 121–36.
56 Winkler, 'Institutionalization and Participation on Taiwan', 499.
57 Gold, 'Retrocession and Authoritarian KMT Rule', 48.
58 In Japan, these islands are called the Senkaku Islands.
59 For a discussion of these opposition media outlets, see Tien, 202–4.
60 Available online at: www.freedomhouse.org/template.cfm?page=439
61 Available online at: www.formosathemovie.com

3 Transition to democracy and democratic consolidation

Democracy is one of the core shared values in Taiwanese society. It is also something that has been extensively employed as part of Taiwan's international public diplomacy since the mid 1990s. The importance of democracy was highlighted by the 2014 Sunflower Movement's core slogan, 'Defend democracy, Reject the Cross-Strait Services Trade Agreement.' But how did Taiwan make a transition from fighting to achieve democracy to fighting to defend its democracy?

In the last chapter we saw how, despite its claim to be 'Free China' and democratic, the Republic of China (ROC) was a one-party authoritarian state for most of the martial law era. When including Japan's colonial rule of the island, Taiwan's government and policy-making had thus been insulated from public opinion for the first nine decades of the twentieth century. The democratization process that began to gain pace in the 1980s, however, transformed Taiwan. The advent of multi-party politics brought genuine policy debate into election campaigns. Political parties and government could no longer impose policy but had to learn to persuade the public and sometimes even follow public opinion. Although there have been inevitable complaints about the inefficiency of democratic policy-making, electoral debate has had tangible results in certain policy areas and given government policy much greater domestic legitimacy. Democracy has also transformed the way external policy is made, as such issues have featured prominently in campaigns. Even the mere existence of democracy has had serious ramifications on Taiwan's most important external relation, China, as it has widened the political gulf across the Taiwan Strait despite the increasing economic integration between the two. Political liberalization has meant that Taiwan is no longer the research surrogate for China that it had been in the authoritarian era.[1] Nevertheless, the process has created huge potential for comparing aspects of Taiwanese politics with both new and mature democracies.

In this chapter, after reviewing competing standards and definitions of democracy and democratic consolidation, I will briefly sketch the chronological process of Taiwan's democratization. Next, the chapter will appraise the leading explanations for Taiwan's transition and assess where Taiwan fits in the comparative democratization literature. This will be followed by sections analysing whether Taiwan can be viewed as a consolidated democracy and detailing how we can assess the quality of the island's democracy. How does Taiwan's democracy compare with other Third Wave democracies? Lastly, the debate over whether Taiwan's democracy is regressing will be considered, along with some of the remaining challenges facing the island's democracy.

Definitions and standards

Before moving on to the actual story of Taiwan's democratic transition, we need to consider what we mean by the key concepts dealt with in this chapter. Democratization or democratic transition can be defined as the transformation from a non-democratic government to a representative and accountable one. However, this definition still leaves open the question of what factors we should assess when deciding whether a country is democratic or not.

Standards for what counts as a democracy range from minimalist to very broad requirements. At the most limited end of the spectrum, Joseph Schumpeter talks of democracy being merely a set of procedures for electing leaders. For him, 'Democracy means only that the people have the opportunity of accepting or refusing the men who are to rule them.'[2] Samuel Huntington proposes a slightly broader procedural definition of democracy as where, 'the most powerful collective decision makers are selected through fair, honest and periodic elections in which candidates freely compete for votes and in which virtually all the adult population is eligible to vote.'[3]

Coming mid-way in this spectrum is the concept proposed by Robert Dahl of poly-archy. For Dahl, the key institutional requirements include (1) the election of government officials, (2) free and fair elections, (3) inclusive suffrage, (4) the right to stand for election, (5) freedom of expression, (6) free access to alternative sources of information and (7) associational freedom.[4] Today, these requirements are more closely associated with the concept of a liberal democracy. Dahl's criteria are intimately linked with the most widely cited system for measuring levels of democracy devised by the non-governmental organization, Freedom House,[5] which examines data to locate countries on scales of political and civil rights. These surveys have been carried out on an annual basis from as far back as 1972 and are used to categorize countries into the three categories listed below:

- Not Free (5.5–7): basic political rights are absent, and basic civil liberties are widely and systematically denied.
- Partly Free (3–5): limited respect for political rights and civil liberties; frequently suffer from corruption, weak rule of law and ethnic and religious strife; often a single political party dominates despite a façade of limited pluralism.
- Free (2.5–1): maintains a broad scope for open political competition, climate of respect for civil liberties, significant independent civic life and an independent media.[6]

The Freedom House statistics allow us to plot Taiwan's democratic change over time, but also to compare Taiwan's democracy with other country cases.

The liberal democracy or empirical democratic theory utilized by groups such as Freedom House has come under scrutiny for being culturally blind and overemphasizing the role of elections. A more demanding approach is suggested by Jean Grugel, who defines democracies as 'political systems that translate citizens' preferences into policy, have effective states that act to protect and deepen democratic rights and count on a strong participatory and critical civil society'.[7] On a similar vein to Grugel's first require-ment, Ian Budge and Judith Bara argue that 'Democracy is a system which brings government action into line with popular preferences through party competition and voting choice in elections.'[8] Achieving this is not straightforward, even in the most mature democracies, as it requires parties to make clear their policies to voters and have distinct platforms on salient issues, voters to base their voting choice on policy preferences and parties to do what they promised once they win an election.

After a democratic breakthrough, it is not inevitable that democracy will survive or deepen enough to become consolidated. We also find a range of minimal to demanding definitions for the second major concept in this chapter – democratic consolidation. Huntington offers the often cited and best measured criteria for consolidation, named the two turnover test. According to this definition, a democracy can be considered consolidated if it can survive two changes in ruling parties through post-transition elections.[9] In contrast, Adam Przeworski's definition stresses the maturity of democratic institutions and democratic values among elites and the mass public. He states that 'Democracy is consolidated when under given political and economic conditions a particular system of institutions becomes the only game in town and when no-one can imagine acting outside the democratic institutions.'[10] Such standards require intensive surveys of both the operation of political institutions and levels of democratic values among political elites and the general public. Grugel offers a similar but broader perspective by viewing consolidation as the routinization and widespread acceptance of his definition of the democratic political system cited above. As with democracy, democratic consolidation has generated a variety of interpretations. The prevalence of conceptual confusion led Andreas Schedler to talk of 'the current Babylonian chorus of voices singing songs of democratic consolidation'.[11] Instead, he prefers to simplify the concept into the idea of democratic survival or the avoidance of democratic erosion. Thus, he argues that a consolidated democracy would be one that 'relevant observers expect to last well into the future – and nothing else'.[12]

Chronological review of Taiwan's democratization

With these competing conceptual definitions of democracy and consolidation, we can now review the chronology of Taiwan's democratization. Determining the exact date of the transition and whether Taiwan can be considered a consolidated democracy depends on which definitions we adopt. In this section we can also see how most of the democratic deficiencies of the martial law era detailed in the previous chapter were removed but how some authoritarian features remain intact.

The 1960s

The 1960s was a period of rapid economic growth contrasted with political repression, known as the White Terror. Holding local elections became routine, but even at this level the KMT was prepared to withdraw democratic political rights. For instance, the upgrading of Taipei city to a special municipality meant that the mayoral post became appointed rather than directly elected from 1968.[13] However, the most important political reform of the decade came in 1969 with the introduction of supplementary elections for the National Assembly and Legislative Yuan. Although these new parliamentarians represented only a drop in the ocean against those elected in the late 1940s, they meant that for the first time elected representatives of contemporary Taiwanese public opinion had a voice in the national parliaments.

The 1970s

In the previous chapter I showed how the KMT government fluctuated between toleration and repression of the opposition movements, culminating in crackdowns such as the Kaohsiung Incident in 1979. However, there was more political space for a political opposition by the end of the decade. In the 1970s, supplementary national elections were continued and the number of directly elected parliamentary seats gradually expanded, although not enough to affect the balance of power. The arrest of most of the leading opposition figures after the Kaohsiung Incident and the postponement of the 1978 National Assembly supplementary election suggested that Taiwan had made limited democratic progress in the decade. Thus, even if we just take Schumpeter's minimalist standards, Taiwan still fell well short of being a democracy.

Table 3.1 shows the Freedom House ratings for Taiwan from 1972 through to the lifting of martial law in 1987. This seems to support the limited liberalization suggested by Winkler in his description of a move from hard to soft authoritarianism, as Taiwan moved from a Freedom House categorization of Not Free to Partly Free in 1977.

The 1980s

After the setback of the Kaohsiung Incident's mass arrests, the *Tangwai* movement recovered quickly and mounted repeated electoral challenges to the KMT at local executive, provincial assembly and supplementary national level elections during this decade. The *Tangwai's* organization thus moved closer to becoming a de facto political party. Political persecution and arrests did continue into the 1980s but were not as severe as those of the previous decade. This was seen when the *Tangwai* formally established the Democratic Progressive Party (DPP) in September 1986 in time to contest the year-end supplementary elections. Instead of the mass arrests that many dissidents expected, the KMT chose tacit toleration. Although technically illegal, the DPP ran its first election campaign in December 1986, winning 12 legislative and 11 National Assembly seats. Thus, this could arguably be counted as Taiwan's first multi-party election.

Post-martial law and the Lee Teng-hui era, 1988–2000

Following the lifting of martial law in 1987 and the death of President Chiang Ching-kuo a year later, the pace of democratization accelerated rapidly. Many of the former democratic deficiencies were lifted as Taiwan moved closer to Dahl's standards for a polyarchy, or liberal democracy. The speed of political liberalization during this period is reflected in the Freedom House scores in Table 3.2. By 1996, Taiwan was categorized as at point 2 for civil and political rights, and thus ranked Free for the first time. This gave Taiwan a similar Freedom rating to the new East European democracies such as the Czech Republic and Hungary, and better than new Latin American cases such as Brazil and Argentina.

Shelley Rigger views 1989 as a watershed year in the democratization process.[14] In January 1989, the Law on the Organization of Civil Groups was passed, allowing the legal formation of opposition political parties for the first time. Rigger notes that by the end of the year more than 50 parties had registered.[15] A wide range of political parties thus contested the last supplementary election in December of that year, although the KMT and DPP were the only relevant parties in respect to seats won. The campaign was also the freest to date, with the first political advertising in newspapers, the lifting of the ban on new newspapers and the development of the island's vibrant political rallies. However, those elected still only accounted for about a third of parliamentarians, as the politicians elected in the late 1940s stubbornly remained in office. The senior parliamentarians also dominated the last indirect presidential election in the spring of 1990 at the National Assembly. Thus, as in Hong Kong today, elections could not yet change the balance of power.

Table 3.1 Taiwan's Freedom House ratings in the late martial law period

	1973	1974	1975	1976	1977	1978	1979	1980	1981	1982	1983–84	1984–85	1985–86	1986–87	1987–88
Political Rights	6	6	6	6	5	5	5	5	5	5	5	5	5	5	5
Civil Liberties	5	5	5	5	5	4	4	5	6	5	5	5	5	5	4
Freedom House Status	NF	NF	NF	NF	PF	PF	PF	PF	PF	PF	PF	PF	PF	PF	PF

Source: Freedom House.

Note: NF = Not Free, PF = Partly Free, and F = Free

There were also other limitations on Taiwan's democracy at this point. There was not yet absolute freedom of speech, as advocating communism or Taiwanese independence remained seditious. Moreover, despite the media liberalization, the KMT and its allies remained dominant in the print and electronic media sectors. The limitations are reflected in the poor Freedom House ranking for 1991–2 of 5 for both civil and political rights. This may partly be due to Premier Hau Pei-tsun's (郝柏村) threat to dissolve the DPP for supporting Taiwan independence and his popular but authoritarian anti-crime campaigns.

The 1990s

At the outset of the 1990s it was still not clear whether Taiwan would make the transition and become a genuine liberal democracy or remain a semi-democracy. There had been a marked improvement in political and civil rights, but elections could still not yet change the ruling party. A key moment in the transition process came with the pro-democracy student demonstrations against the National Assembly in March 1990. These demonstrations were held at the Chiang Kai-shek Memorial Hall and were the largest since the 1940s. This movement features in Yang Ya-che's (楊雅喆) 2013 film *Girlfriend, Boyfriend* (女朋友男朋友). The scenes were reminiscent of the 1989 student movement in China, but the way the KMT handled it was markedly different from government responses at both *Tiananmen* and earlier Taiwanese protests. Taiwan president Lee Teng-hui chose to engage in real dialogue with the students and pledged to hold a National Affairs Conference to deal with their concerns for political reform.

The conference was held in the summer of 1990 and included a wide variety of participants, ranging from senior KMT conservatives and reformers to academics, businessmen and DPP politicians (including former Kaohsiung Incident political prisoners). Although there were some areas where consensus was not reached, a remarkable degree of agreement was found on the overall direction of political reform. The democratization blueprint included (1) the retirement of senior parliamentarians, (2) full re-election of the Legislative Yuan and National Assembly, (3) election for Kaohsiung and Taipei mayors and the Provincial Governor and (4) election of the president (although there was disagreement over whether this should be by direct popular election or indirectly by the newly elected National Assembly).[16]

Below, I have listed the subsequent key dates in Taiwan's democratization through to the present day.

- 1991–2: Retirement of senior parliamentarians.
- 1991: First full re-election of the National Assembly.
- 1991: Television election advertising permitted.
- 1992: Article 100 of the criminal code revised, strengthening freedom of speech.[17]
- 1992: First full re-election of the Legislative Yuan.
- 1994: Direct elections for Provincial Governor and Taipei and Kaohsiung mayors.
- 1996: First direct presidential election.
- 2000: First change of ruling parties through elections.
- 2008: Second change of ruling parties, as the KMT returns to power.
- 2016: First complete change of ruling parties through elections as DPP wins both the presidency and parliament.

Table 3.2 Taiwan's Freedom House ratings in the Lee Teng-hui era, 1988–2000

	1988– 89	1989– 90	1990– 91	1991– 92	1992– 93	1993– 94	1994– 95	1995– 96	1996– 97	1997– 98	1998– 99	1999– 2000	2000– 01
Political Rights	5	4	3	5	3	4	3	4	2	2	2	2	1
Civil Liberties	3	3	3	5	3	4	3	4	2	2	2	2	2
Freedom House Status	PF	PF	PF	PF	PF	PF	PF	PF	F	F	F	F	F

Source: Freedom House.

Note: NF = Not Free, PF = Partly Free, F = Free

When did Taiwan become a democracy?

So when can we say that Taiwan became a democracy? Every year I find that students make a range of cases for different years. Here, it is useful to take note of Bruce Jacobs's point on the need to make a distinction between liberalization and democratization. Jacobs notes that in the former there may be 'some increase in freedom of speech and the press. They may allow opposition politicians to win office in elections, though they do not relinquish ultimate control.'[18]

The exact time that Taiwan became a democracy depends on whose definition we choose to adopt. The first direct presidential election in 1996 is often taken as the decisive moment. For instance, that was the year where Freedom House first gave Taiwan a Free rating. For others, the first change in ruling parties following the 2000 presidential election is given prominence. In my own research, I have taken the 1991 National Assembly elections as the first democratic election, as this was the first contest that had at least the potential to change the ruling party. However, at that point Taiwan had not yet fulfilled all Dahl's conditions. In contrast, by the late 1990s Taiwan deserved the status of a liberal democracy by most credible definitions.

Testing whether Taiwan has achieved the more demanding democratic tests suggested by Grugel or Budge and Bara is more challenging. We will return to this question again later in this chapter and in Chapters 6 (party politics) and 10 (social movements). However, at this stage we can say that the improved human rights record, intense electoral policy debate and vibrant civil society witnessed at the end of the 1990s ticked a number of the boxes in their definitions.

The question of Taiwan's democratic consolidation is also open to debate. If we take Huntington's two turnover test as our standard, then Taiwan became a consolidated democracy when the KMT returned to power in 2008. One challenge to that view is that the change of ruling parties in 2000 was only partial, as although the DPP won the presidency, it did not win a majority in parliament between 2000 and 2008. If we use Przeworski or Schedler's definitions, then consolidation could be dated earlier, as from the mid to late 1990s democracy had become the only game in town and no serious observer was predicting a return to authoritarian rule. Once again, we need more data before addressing Grugel's standards.

Theories of democratization

Before examining how Taiwan scholars have tried to explain the island's democratic transition, I will briefly introduce some of the main comparative politics approaches to democratization.

Studies on democratization can be divided into four broad types: (1) modernization theory, (2) historical sociology, (3) transition studies and (4) hybrid theories.

Modernization theory is most commonly associated with Seymour Martin Lipset's article 'Some Social Requisites of Democracy'.[19] For Lipset, democracy was a product of modern capitalism. Modernization creates a wealthier and better educated population, largely middle class, and produces cultural changes favourable to democracy, such as secularism and the erosion of traditional hierarchal values. Thus, once countries achieve certain preconditions of economic wealth, then democratization should be expected to take place. In contrast, structural or historical sociological approaches examine the historical transformation of the state through class conflict to explain the emergence, or continued absence, of democracy. An influential example of this method was Barrington

Moore's *Social Origins of Democracy and Dictatorship* which looks at state trajectories in eight countries.[20] The key classes in this process are the landowning upper class, bourgeoisie and peasantry. He argues that democracy emerged in the UK, France and the US as a result of successful bourgeois revolutions. In contrast, revolution from above led to fascism in Germany and Japan, and revolution from below to communism in Russia and China.

Modernization theory was later criticized by writers such as Dankwart Rustow for its economic preconditions for democracy and for confusing the correlation of economic wealth and democracy with any causal relationship. For Rustow, the one precondition was that of national unity whereby, 'the vast majority of citizens in a democracy-to-be must have no doubt or mental reservation as to which political community they belong'.[21] Rustow's writings represent the forerunner of what became known as transition studies or transitology. Transition studies tend to focus on elite level interactions, pacts and bargaining. The paradigm assumes that democracy will proceed through three stages: (1) opening, (2) breakthrough and (3) consolidation. According to Grugel, transitology argues, 'democracy is created by conscious committed actors, providing that they possess a degree of luck and willingness to compromise'.[22] It became popular as it offers greater hope for spreading democracy even where the structural conditions do not look favourable. So long as elites learn the right way to proceed with political reforms, democracy can be created anywhere. More recently, transition studies have also come under attack. Carothers has criticized a number of the core assumptions in this paradigm, such as the idea that transition goes through a three-stage process, its disregard for underlying conditions and its overemphasis on the importance of elections.[23]

A hybrid approach is found in Samuel Huntington's *Third Wave: Democratization in the late Twentieth Century*. This approach incorporates elements of modernization theory and the role of elites, but also stresses the importance of external international factors in democratic change. One such variable is the changing global environment (particularly changing policies of the European Union, Soviet Union and US).[24]

A final hybrid approach is suggested by Grugel, for whom the key dimensions to observe are the impact of collective action (especially social movements), whether there is a favourable global order and the building of a democratic state.[25]

Explaining Taiwan's democratization

The volume of political science studies on Taiwan's democracy and democratization can only be matched in numbers with those on national identity and cross-Strait relations. In this section, I will discuss how useful these democratization theories are for the Taiwan case and the diverse approaches that Taiwan scholars have taken to explain the process.

Of the general theories of democratization, neither historical sociology nor modernization theory has gained popularity among Taiwan specialists. As Rigger points out, by the time that democratization took place, modernization theory had already been replaced by alternative frameworks.[26] Moreover, Taiwan, like South Korea, had long been a case that seemed to disprove modernization theory, as Taiwan's transition took place long after it reached the expected prerequisite level of economic wealth with a large, well-educated middle class. In the late martial law period, Taiwan, like Singapore or the Gulf states today, seemed like one of the exceptions to the rule.

Variants of transition theory and a focus on elite politics have proved far more widely adopted for the Taiwan case. The pioneering work that positioned Taiwan in this transition studies literature was Cheng's article 'Democratizing the Quasi-Leninist Regime in Taiwan'.[27] Written at a time when it was still not certain what kind of democracy would emerge from post-martial law Taiwan, Cheng called on his readers to focus on the relationship between the political opposition and the ruling KMT rather than on economic wealth indicators. We can get a rich detailed historical account of the interplay between the KMT and opposition in the late 1980s and early 1990s in Chao and Myers's *First Chinese Democracy*. Another example of how the transition paradigm has been applied to Taiwan is Huang et al.'s 'Elite Settlements in Taiwan'.[28] In this article, they apply the concept of elite settlements to examine the consensus-building constitutional conventions of 1990 and 1996. They argue that this kind of pacted transition contributed to the island's democratic consolidation.

A useful way of considering the transition approach is the comparative cases of the student protests movements in China in 1989 and Taiwan in 1990. In the Chinese case, the Chinese Communist Party hardliners came out dominant in the power struggle, marginalizing party moderates. Unlike in states that conducted successful transitions, such as Czechoslovakia and Poland, there was no real organized opposition negotiation partner with acceptable demands for the ruling party moderates to ally with. From this perspective, the tragic *Tiananmen* outcome was quite similar to that of the *Tangwai* in 1979. At the time, the liberals in the KMT were not yet strong enough and the opposition not yet accepted as a genuine negotiating partner. In contrast, we can consider Taiwan of the 1990s as having elements of a pacted transition. This time, KMT moderates were able to negotiate and ally with opposition party moderates and the student protestors. These three blocs were able to agree on a common position on most central issues of democratic reform. In the process, both KMT and opposition hardliners were marginalized. Thus, this pacted approach contributed towards Taiwan's relatively gradual and smooth transition.

The transition approach does also have its problems in Taiwan's case. It underplays the role of grassroots actors and civil society in democratic change. Also, the elite bargaining allowed authoritarian actors to preserve aspects of the authoritarian system. For instance, unlike in many former communist states, the KMT's party assets were not returned to the state. Similarly, the style of pacted transition has also been a factor in the limited implementation of transitional justice since the island's democratic breakthrough.[29] Since these elite pacts were often made with short-term party political goals in mind, they were later to have some negative consequences, as we will see in the next chapter on constitutional reform.

Much of the academic and popular analyses have discussed the role of Taiwan's presidents in democratization. Chao and Myers state that 'Taiwan could not have experienced a peaceful democratic breakthrough without great leadership'.[30] Not only do they give credit to Chiang Ching-kuo and Lee Teng-hui, but also to Chiang Kai-shek for laying the foundations of later democratic change. In the popular press, Lee Teng-hui seems to have gained the title 'Mr. Democracy', earning more credit for reform than Chiang Ching-kuo. This was an image that Lee's spin doctors tried to cultivate in the 1990s and he received recognition in Western publications such as *Newsweek*.[31]

Academic writers are divided on Chiang and Lee's relative roles. A useful examination of Chiang's late conversion to democracy is Leng Shao-chuan's (冷紹佺) edited volume,[32] while for a balanced appraisal of Lee's contribution to Taiwanese democracy, see Lu Ya-li's (呂亞力) work.[33] Writers stressing Chiang's role emphasize the critical function of navigating the lifting of martial law, while his detractors focus on his authoritarian past

and last-minute conversion. Jacobs is critical of those writers giving credit for democratization to Chiang Ching-kuo; instead, he dates the starting point as 1988 when Lee
assumes the presidency.[34] It cannot be denied that full democratization, the transition to
liberal democracy, took place under Lee's presidency. However, Lee is also criticized for
allowing the expansion of political corruption, worsening ethnic relations and deteriorating
cross-Strait relations. This remains an open debate in Taiwan, and over the years my
own students have made convincing cases on both sides of the argument.

Other elite-centred studies have focused on the ruling KMT party. For instance, Paul
Hao stresses the role of the KMT's ideological change in the transition away from authoritarianism.[35] Bruce Dickson, in one of the best available comparative political studies
of China and Taiwan, shows how, although both the CCP and KMT adapted to their
changed political environments in the 1970s and 1980s, the distinct content of their
organizational adaption resulted in quite different political systems.[36] Dickson shows how
the limited Taiwanese martial law elections contributed to making the KMT far more
responsive to society than the CCP, which lacked such feedback mechanisms. He argues
that the different sectors of society from which the parties recruited in this period also
had an impact on political change. In other words, the KMT's focus on recruiting younger
intellectuals from the 1970s contributed to making the party more receptive to democratic change. In contrast, the CCP was much more cautious about recruiting from
intellectuals or the newly emerging economic elites (wealthy peasants and entrepreneurs).
Where the CCP did bring in intellectuals, they tended to be from older generations and
in the natural sciences. Attention should also be given to the role of the DPP, as in its
early years it was far more a movement for democracy than the vehicle for Taiwanese
nationalism it later became. In fact, for many former *Tangwai* politicians, Lee and the
KMT's hijacking of democracy is quite infuriating.

It is also important to give consideration to Huntington's stress on the impact of international variables on Taiwan's democratic reform. US pressure for political liberalization
did increase in the 1980s after the cutting of formal diplomatic relations. We should also
consider the impact of what Huntington terms 'the demonstration effect'. Clearly,
Chiang and Lee must have been affected by contemporary international developments.
Imagine how Chiang must have viewed the images of Philippine dictator Ferdinand
Marcos being helicoptered away by Americans at the height of the People Power
movement in 1986. For Chiang's successors, images of *Tiananmen* and the sudden downfall of communism in Eastern Europe served as a warning that political inertia was no
longer an option. By the mid-1990s there seemed to be an elite consensus that Taiwan
was part of a global wave of democracy. Dickson actually argues that the most important
external variable was not US pressure but a new perception among the KMT of the
reduced military threat from China. He notes that 'KMT officials interviewed emphasized
that the moderation of the Chinese threat was a necessary pre-condition to the wide-
ranging political reforms of 1986–7'.[37]

Democracy promoters often stress the importance of a strong and independent civil
society in promoting political liberalization. Although the KMT did try to avoid any
such civil society emerging under martial law by controlling all civic groups, some social
movements did emerge and contribute to democratization. Particularly important were
the Presbyterian Church, the environmental movement and, as mentioned earlier, the
student pro-democracy movement.[38] I will return to these cases in Chapter 10.

A final rewarding approach to explain Taiwan's transition has been to consider it as a
case of election-driven democratization. Using quite different theoretical frameworks and

data, Chao and Myers come to quite similar conclusions to Shelley Rigger on the democratizing role of pre-transition elections.[39] This approach is developed most thoroughly in Rigger's *Politics in Taiwan*.[40] She argues that instead of seeing elections as a consequence of democracy, in Taiwan the semi-democratic martial law elections acted as an independent variable for democratization. Adopting the framework of Bolivar Lamounier's work on democratization in Brazil, she shows how the KMT increasingly used the limited elections to gain legitimacy.[41] Since the system was designed so that it could not lose power, the KMT felt confident enough to gradually expand the scope of elections. However, elections were often treated as plebiscites, so KMT politicians nevertheless felt pressure to support reforms. Moreover, elections represented a tool for political socialization and an educational opportunity for opposition elites and the general public. For the opposition, elections were a relatively safe stage from which to attack the KMT government and get their message across. Elections, and the promise of wider ranging ones to come, encouraged the *Tangwai* to forsake radical methods or direct action. Rigger also suggests that elections served to divide the KMT into reformists and hardliners and allowed the former to quickly gain strength over the latter. Over time, as the *Tangwai* /DPP seat share in the relatively powerless parliaments rose, there was increased pressure for political reform. When we consider the large number of semi-democracies that have failed to consolidate, such as Malaysia or Hong Kong, it will be interesting to examine whether we will see a similar pattern of election-driven democratization.

Since the late 1990s, scholars have become less interested in transition and shifted more to the actual performance of democracy in Taiwan. However, recently Slater and Wong have returned to the topic in an article that looks at transition in Taiwan, South Korea and Indonesia. They have coined the term 'conceding to thrive' to show how ruling authoritarian parties can be incentivized to democratize at times of exceptional strength. They argue that this scenario is most likely when they '(1) possess substantial antecedent political strengths and resource advantages, (2) suffer ominous setbacks signaling that they have passed their apex of domination, and (3) pursue new legitimation strategies to arrest their incipient decline'.[42] They show how these former ruling parties, particularly the KMT, actually fared extremely well under democracy.

In short, Taiwan offers a very rich and diverse literature on democratic transition. It is worth repeating here Rigger's conclusion that 'As the many studies of Taiwan's democratization illustrate, the democratic transition was a complex process, one that resists a theoretically tidy explanation. Ultimately Taiwan's transition must be viewed as multi-causal, multi-dimensional, and path-dependent.'[43]

Is Taiwan's democracy dead?

In the spring of 2000, the above question would have appeared nonsensical. At the time, Taiwan was widely viewed as a model Asian democracy, having peacefully negotiated transition, consolidation and the first change of ruling parties through election. However, political developments in the post-2000 period have led to domestic and international doubts about the quality of Taiwan's democratic system.

Back in 1999, Rigger ended *Politics in Taiwan* on a cautiously optimistic note.[44] She did, however, outline a number of continuing challenges facing Taiwan's democratic future. These included (1) transforming political attitudes and behaviour, (2) balancing presidential and legislative power, (3) streamlining the administration, (4) reducing clientelism and corruption, (5) strengthening parties and (6) the challenge of cross-Strait relations. Whether these have been resolved or are still the principal challenges today is a question that we should be able to answer by the end of this book.

What is clear is that both in the popular press and academic world there are deep divisions over whether democracy is still working in Taiwan. We can see the changed perception of Taiwan's democracy in the 1990s and post-2000 period by comparing Rigger's writings on Taiwan in the two eras. In her 2005 chapter 'The Unfinished Business of Taiwan's Democratization',[45] Rigger uses a framework for testing democratic consolidation proposed by Larry Diamond. This examines the degree of democratic deepening, political institutionalization and regime performance in Taiwan after transition. Her conclusion is that although Taiwan has made progress on democratic deepening, it is performing poorly on the latter two dimensions. There appears to be a similar tone of pessimism in many of the post-2000 writings on Taiwan's democracy. With the recent comparative democratization studies, now it is clear that the euphoria of the peak of the Third Wave is over. Not only have new transitions dried up, but there have been cases of reversion to authoritarianism in addition to numerous instances where democratic consolidation has simply not taken place.[46]

Other academic writers have taken alternative approaches but also reached highly critical conclusions about Taiwan's democracy. At the height of global praise of Taiwan's democracy, Kuo Cheng-tian (郭承天) argued that Taiwan had a distorted democracy rather than economic and political miracles.[47] What he calls an 'iron rectangle' of the state, the ruling party, local factions and conglomerates has gradually come to dominate Taiwan's political economy at the expense of distributional equality and economic efficiency. Kuo suggests that this pattern of distorted democracy also applies to Japan and South Korea. Another writer highly critical of Taiwan's democracy and the way it is understood has been NTU professor Shih Chih-yu (石之瑜). Shih is damning of the view that Taiwan represents a success story of liberal democracy. For instance, Shih has discussed the human rights violations against Chinese workers by Taiwanese employers.[48] He argues instead that the rosy view of Taiwan as a model democracy is a construct of the international media.[49]

Although we will return to the problems of Taiwan's democracy in later chapters, it is worth acknowledging here that popular sentiment has been more critical of how democracy is working since 2000. This became apparent when I returned to Taiwan in late 2000 for a year's fieldwork. In March to April 2000 there had still been great optimism at Taiwan's political future, but just six months later the mood was quite different, particularly in Taipei. I noticed this at academic conferences, in the popular media and in conversations with ordinary people. The common emotion that I noticed was pessimism. Key factors in this changed perception of the post-2000 period include declining economic performance, party conflict and polarization, tense cross-Strait relations, political corruption scandals, rising levels of political violence, accusations of a biased judiciary and dissatisfaction with election results. In 2004, KMT demonstrators held up banners claiming 'democracy is dead' in Taiwan.[50] Similarly, after 2008, DPP supporters talked of a return to KMT authoritarian-style politics. Asian Barometer Surveys in 2001 and 2006 found that 40.4 and 47.5 per cent of Taiwanese respondents preferred democracy to other forms of non-democratic government, respectively.[51] This support of democracy was weaker than most of Taiwan's Asian neighbours in the survey, such as Japan and South Korea. The title of the article where this data is cited, 'Authoritarian Nostalgia in Asia', shows how Taiwan is increasingly viewed not as a democratic model for Asia, but as another Asian democracy on the rocks.

More recently, the Sunflower Movement set off a new set of debates on the state of Taiwan's democracy. Lack of democratic oversight on cross-Strait agreements, alienation from mainstream political parties and a fear that the China factor was threatening Taiwan's democracy were all factors driving protestors. Many saw the Sunflower Movement as a means to defend and revitalize Taiwan's democracy. In contrast, the KMT's perspective argued that the movement was profoundly undemocratic, as elections had given the KMT a mandate to govern and that occupying the parliament was actually undermining democracy and Taiwan's international reputation for being a model democracy.

The Freedom House rankings for the post-2000 Taiwan (Table 3.3) show some fluctuations in their evaluation of Taiwan's democracy. In 2006 Taiwan actually recorded its best ever Freedom House scores with 1 on both civil liberties and political rights. However, the Freedom House surveys have noted negative trends since 2008, such as state media interference and the handling of protests. This is reflected in the downgrading of Taiwan's ranking on civil liberties in 2010.

Nevertheless, in the post-2000 period, some authors have come to much more positive conclusions on the state of Taiwan's democracy. For instance, both Joseph Wong and I independently employed medical terminology to describe the health of Taiwan's democracy. Wong's comparative study examines the relationship between democracy and a vastly improved health system in Taiwan and Korea.[52] In my book *Party Politics in Taiwan*[53], I argue that Taiwan's electoral debate had positive impacts on policy outputs, resulting in an improved welfare system, anti-corruption measures and tacit agreement on questions related to national identity and external relations. I show how electoral forces pushed parties to move from polarized to more moderate positions, but that the parties still remained distinct enough to offer real policy choice for constituents. I called this a pattern of moderate differentiation. In short, my conclusion was that democracy was working in Taiwan. Joseph Wong also had a similar upbeat finding in his examination of democratic deepening in Taiwan.[54] He found that Taiwan performs well in human and civil rights, economic redistribution and public participation in policy making. Thus, Wong and I offer evidence that Taiwan had, in the early post-2000 period, met some of the more demanding democratic conditions suggested by Grugel and Budge. *Party Politics in Taiwan* was based on data from 1991 to late 2001. However, political developments immediately after the book was published did lead to some criticism of my moderate differentiation thesis.[55] I should admit that between 2006 and 2009 even I took a more balanced and at times critical view of Taiwan's democracy.[56] However, I remain optimistic about Taiwan's democratic system. I have often been impressed at the way Taiwan's

Table 3.3 Taiwan's Freedom House ratings in the post-2000 period

	2001–02	2003	2004	2005	2006	2007	2008	2009	2010	2011	2016
Political rights	1	2	2	2	1	2	2	2	1	1	1
Civil liberties	2	2	2	1	1	1	1	1	2	2	2
Freedom House status	F	F	F	F	F	F	F	F	F	F	F

Source: Freedom House.

Note: NF = Not Free, PF = Partly Free, F = Free

electorate has repeatedly punished parties for perceived poor government performance and extremism.

One of the repeated themes for us to consider in this book is whether democracy is working in Taiwan and if it can make a difference, or would we be better off with a benevolent dictator. This is a question that I will return to in most subsequent chapters.

Conclusions

Taiwan's democratization has had a profound impact on the way that the island is governed and on the lives of its residents. This chapter has outlined the key moments in the process and some approaches for explaining the democratic transition. In recent years, the focus of research has shifted to examining the quality of Taiwan's democracy, asking questions such as how it performs and whether it is a consolidated democracy. Here, the answers are still being heatedly debated, especially in the light of domestic concerns about democratic reversals. We have just begun our discussions here on these topics. However, by the end of the book, we should have enough material to make a balanced judgement on the health of Taiwan's democracy. Our next step is to examine the institutional continuity and change in Taiwan's constitutional and government structure in the post-transition period.

Discussion questions

1   How should we classify Taiwan's democracy? Is it a liberal democracy?
2   Can we view it as a consolidated democracy?
3   What defects/challenges does its democracy still have?
4   Which theories/explanations best explain Taiwan's transition?
5   How does Taiwan's democracy perform compared to other democracies?
6   Does Taiwan's democracy offer a model to other countries?
7   Why did confidence in Taiwanese democracy decline during the Chen and Ma presidencies?

Further reading

Chao, Linda and Ramon Myers. 1998. *The First Chinese Democracy: Political Life in the Republic of China on Taiwan*. Baltimore, MD: The Johns Hopkins University Press. This is especially useful for its rich detail on the late martial law and democratic breakthrough periods.

Cheng, Tun-jen. 1989. 'Democratizing the Quasi-Leninist Regime in Taiwan'. *World Politics*, 41(4): 471–99. Although parts may seem dated now, like Tien's *Great Transition,* it is still a rich source for understanding the complex political scene in the 1980s.

Grugel, Jean. 2002. *Democratization: A Critical Introduction*. London: Sage. Comprehensive overview of democratization studies.

Lin, Chia-long (林嘉隆). 1998. 'Paths to Democracy: Taiwan in Comparative Perspective'. Ph.D. dissertation, Yale University. It may seem odd to list a Ph.D. dissertation in further readings, but Lin's study represents an extremely rich theoretical and empirical reference book for Taiwan's democracy. I do hope that one day he will find the time to get it formally published.

Rigger, Shelley. 1999. *Politics in Taiwan Voting for Democracy*. London: Routledge. The best single authored volume on Taiwan's transition and early years of democratic politics.

Slater, Dan and Joseph Wong. 2013. 'The Strength to Concede: Ruling Parties and Democratization in Developmental Asia'. *Perspectives on Politics*, 11(3): 717–33. Slater and Wong return to the topic of democratic transition. They suggest that Taiwan's experience may hold lessons for authoritarian parties today, particularly the Chinese Communist Party.

Notes

1 For much of the Maoist era fieldwork in China was next to impossible. This meant that researchers often treated Taiwan as their research surrogate for China.
2 Schumpeter, *Capitalism, Socialism and Democracy*, 268–70.
3 Huntington, *The Third Wave*, 7.
4 Dahl, *Democracy and its Critics*, 221.
5 For details of Freedom House's *Freedom in the World* surveys, see www.freedomhouse.org/template.cfm?page=15 (accessed 20 June 2010).
6 Puddington, 'Freedom in the World 2010: Erosion of Freedom Intensifies' (Overview Essay for Freedom in the World 2010), available online at: www.freedomhouse.org/uploads/fiw10/FIW_2010_Overview_Essay.pdf (accessed 20 June 2010).
7 Grugel, *Democratization: A Critical Introduction*, 36.
8 Budge and Bara, 'Introduction: Content Analysis and Political Texts', 8.
9 Huntington, 267.
10 Przeworski, *Democracy and the Market: Political and Economic Reforms in Eastern Europe and Latin America*, 26.
11 Schedler, 'What is Democratic Consolidation?', 101.
12 Ibid., 102.
13 This also happened in Kaohsiung in 1979.
14 Rigger, *Politics in Taiwan*, 131–47. Rigger devotes a chapter to this critical year.
15 Ibid., 132.
16 For details see Chao and Myers, *First Chinese Democracy*, 196–215.
17 This article had been used by the KMT to arrest political prisoners for openly advocating Taiwan independence. For details on the struggle to remove this, see Chao and Myers, *The First Chinese Democracy*, 224–9.
18 Jacobs, 'Taiwan During and After the Democratic Transition,' 51.
19 Lipset, 'Some Social Requisites of Democracy: Economic Development and Political Legitimacy', 1.
20 Moore, *Social Origins of Democracy and Dictatorship*.
21 Rustow, 'Transition to Democracy: Toward a Dynamic Model', 350.
22 Grugel, *Democratization*, 56.
23 Carothers, 'The End of the Transition Paradigm', 5–21.
24 Huntington, 45–6.
25 Grugel, 65–7.
26 Rigger, 'Political Science and Taiwan's Domestic Politics: The State of the Field', 67.
27 Cheng, 'Democratizing the Quasi-Leninist Regime in Taiwan', 471–99.
28 Higley, Huang and Lin, 'Elite Settlements in Taiwan', 148–63.
29 On the issue of democratization and transitional justice see Wu, 'Transition without Justice, or Justice without History: Transitional Justice in Taiwan', 77–102.
30 Chao and Myers, *The First Chinese Democracy*, 300.
31 *Newsweek*, 26 March 1996.
32 Leng (ed.), *Chiang Ching-kuo's Leadership in the Development of the Republic of China on Taiwan*.
33 Lu, 'Lee Teng-hui's Role in Taiwan's Democratization', 53–72.
34 Jacobs, 51–2.
35 Hao, 'The Transformation of the KMT's Ideology', 1–31.
36 Dickson, *Democratization in China and Taiwan: The Adaptability of Leninist Parties*; Dickson, 'The Kuomintang Before Democratization', 42–78.
37 Ibid., 64.
38 On the Presbyterian Church, see Rubinstein, 'The Presbyterian Church in the Formation of Taiwan's Democratic Society', 109–35.
39 Chao and Myers, 'How Elections Promoted Democracy in Taiwan under Martial Law', 387–409; Rigger, *Politics in Taiwan*.
40 Ibid.
41 Lamounier, 'Authoritarian Brazil Revisited: The Impact of Elections on Abertura', 43–79.
42 Slater and Wong, 717.
43 Rigger, 'Political Science and Taiwan's Domestic Politics', 71.
44 Rigger, *Politics in Taiwan*, 178–94.

45 Rigger, 'The Unfinished Business of Taiwan's Democratization', 213–18.
46 For examples of this new sense of pessimism see recent Freedom House reports, but also Carothers, 'The End of the Transition Paradigm', 5–21; Diamond and Plattner (eds), *Global Divergence of Democracies*.
47 Kuo, 'Taiwan's Distorted Democracy in Comparative Perspective', 85–111.
48 Shih, 'The Global Constitution of 'Taiwan Democracy', 28.
49 Ibid., 16–38.
50 Huang Tai-lin and Joy Su, 'Chen Replies to Pan-Blue Rally Request', *Taipei Times,* 28 March 2004, 1.
51 Chang, Chu and Park, 'Authoritarian Nostalgia in Asia', 70.
52 Wong, *Healthy Democracies.*
53 Fell, *Party Politics in Taiwan*, 143–145.
54 Wong, 'Deepening Democracy in Taiwan', 57–90.
55 Chu, 'Book Review of Party Politics in Taiwan', 185, 189–90. For a more positive review, see Rubinstein, *Pacific Affairs.*
56 Fell, 'Democracy on the Rocks: Taiwan's Troubled Political System Since 2000', 21–5; Fell, 'Partisan Issue Competition in Contemporary Taiwan: Is Democracy Dead in Taiwan?', 23–39.

4 Taiwan's government and constitutional structure

On 1 January 1947, the Constitution of the Republic of China (ROC) was promulgated in Nanjing, the then capital of China. Although this document is long forgotten in its birthplace and has been revised repeatedly over the last two decades, it remains the constitution of Taiwan today. By studying the ROC constitution we can better understand the rules and structure of the political game and how these changed in different political eras.

The question of whether to essentially preserve the 1947 constitution, revise the constitution to adapt to contemporary Taiwanese circumstances or create a brand new Taiwan constitution has been bitterly debated since the outset of multi-party politics. The reason for this two-plus decade dispute on the issue is the intimate relationship between possible solutions to the constitutional question and competing nationalisms in Taiwan. It is a question that has yet to be resolved.

Wu Yu-shan (吳玉山) suggests three approaches to studying political institutions: (1) upstream studies (origin of institutions), (2) midstream studies (legal provisions and operation) and (3) downstream studies (institutional impact).[1] To put this in layman's terms, we can think of this as the how, why and so what of constitutional reforms in the democratic era. Regarding Wu's first approach, we will see how the political structure, set out in Table 2.1 in Chapter 2, was revised in the democratization process. The consensual nature of constitutional reform created a political system that incorporated elements of change, but also maintained relatively intact much of the martial law era institutional structure. Rather than opting for a completely new charter, Taiwan has revised the 1947 constitution through a number of stages. The 'why' dimension considers how we can best explain the pattern of change and the nature of Taiwan's constitutional reform. Why did Taiwan emerge as a semi-presidential rather than a parliamentary or pure presidential system? With this in mind, the major domestic debates over constitutional issues will be discussed. Lastly, we will consider the impact of these reforms – namely, the 'so what' of the reforms. Have Taiwan's constitutional reforms laid the foundations for effective democratic governance or political instability?

The 1947 constitution

Under the 1947 constitution, the Republic of China's political system incorporated elements of Imperial Chinese origin and both Western parliamentary and presidential democracy.[2] To a large extent, it was modelled on that of the Weimar Republic in Germany. The system included two leading figures, the President and Premier. The President was the head of state and chief of the armed forces and could nominate the

Premier. Thus, in Taiwan, it has often been referred to as a dual leadership system (*shuang shouzhang zhi*).[3] The President was to be indirectly elected by the National Assembly and could serve no more than two six-year terms. However, the Premier headed the Executive Yuan, the highest executive body in the state, which ran the various government ministries. It was the Premier, not the President, who chaired the cabinet of ministers, and all new laws required the Premier's countersignature. Moreover, the Premier's appointment needed the approval of the Legislative Yuan. There was a degree of ambiguity in the constitution about how powers should be divided between the Premier and President. At least on paper, the Premier appeared to be a more powerful position. This may explain why initially Chiang Kai-shek was tempted to be Premier rather than President.[4]

Although the constitution claimed to be non-partisan, it had a clear KMT imprint. The teachings of its party founder, Sun Yat-sen (孫中山), are stated as being the basis of the document, and the national flag incorporates the KMT flag. The constitution included quite an impressive list of civil rights, such as freedom of speech, assembly, publication, association and religion. It also stipulated equality before the law, regardless of gender, race, party affiliation, religion and class. Lastly, if we consider the minimalist definitions of democracy discussed in the previous chapter, then the stipulation for popular elections at all levels of government means that democracy was an integral ingredient of the 1947 constitution.

How best to classify the 1947 constitutional system has been widely debated in Taiwan. The hybrid nature of the system meant that it incorporated elements of both a presidential and parliamentary system. One of the original drafters described it as a 'revised parliamentary system'.[5] John Hsieh (謝復生) argues that 'the ROC Constitution provides essentially for a parliamentary form of government'.[6] But he goes on to note that 'Taiwan's political system operates rather like (a) presidential system in practice'.[7] Within Taiwan itself, many scholars and politicians have argued in favour of Hsieh's interpretation and believe that Taiwan should return to the parliamentary spirit of the 1947 constitution. For instance, the constitutional scholar Hu Fu (胡佛) stated, 'Our System is a responsible cabinet system.'[8] In contrast, others have promoted reforms in the direction of a pure presidential system. More often than not, the motivations for constitutional reform proposals have been based on personal and partisan interests rather than the advice of constitutional experts.

The constitution under martial law

The outbreak of the Chinese Civil War in 1947 and four decades of martial law meant that the 1947 constitution was never given a chance to be fully implemented in a unified China as its drafters had intended. According to Wu Yu-shan, Taiwan can only be classified as having enjoyed a parliamentary constitutional regime in 1948, to be followed by 43 years of presidential dictatorship (1948–91).[9] Chen Don-yun (陳敦源) attempts to apply Shugart and Carey's presidential versus parliamentary political system typology on Taiwan.[10] He concludes that for most of the martial law period, Taiwan was closer to the premier–presidential rather than parliamentary-with-president system.[11]

The imposition of martial law and the Temporary Provisions Effective During the Period of Communist Rebellion (Temporary Provisions) effectively suspended the 1947 constitution and concentrated power on the office of President.[12] Since Chiang Kai-shek was also the chairman of the KMT, he held undisputed political power until the early

1970s. In contrast to the provisions of the constitution, under martial law 'the Premier and Executive Yuan became the President's policy implementation bureau'.[13] The Temporary Provisions also lifted the President's two-term limit, making Chiang Kai-shek and, later, his son dictators for life.

So how could Chiang basically govern in a manner at complete odds with the system stipulated in the constitution? The official justification was that the extraordinary times of the communist rebellion required extraordinary powers and suspension of certain constitutional provisions. The ambiguity of the relationship between various government branches also left scope for different interpretations over how power should be distributed. In reality, Chiang Kai-shek was just so politically dominant that he had the power to tailor the system to suit his own needs. Moreover, Chiang's style of presidential rule has left what Chen Don-yun calls 'a strongman legacy' on Taiwan.[14] Even though the constitution may be parliamentary in spirit, Taiwanese voters expect their presidents to govern rather than be figureheads.

We first see some variation in the early 1970s when Chiang Kai-shek's health began to deteriorate and power gradually shifted towards his son, the Premier Chiang Ching-kuo. The strongman legacy was most apparent after Chiang Kai-shek's death in 1975. He was succeeded by his Vice President, Yen Chia-kan (嚴家淦), but real power was concentrated in Premier Chiang Ching-kuo's hands. Thus, this was the first and perhaps only time when the Premier has held greater actual power than the President. As soon as Yen's term ended in 1977, he stepped down and Chiang became President. Power became as concentrated in the presidency as it had been under Chiang Kai-shek. As Wu Yu-shan noted, 'That aberration from presidential dictatorship proved transitory.'[15]

The end of the presidential dictatorship, 1987–91

As the democratization process got off the ground, there was intense debate about Taiwan's constitutional future. Was the solution to basically return to the 1947 Constitution after lifting martial law and the Temporary Provisions? Or did the Constitution require revisions to make it a better fit for the political reality of the Republic of China on Taiwan? A third approach was that the 1947 Constitution, one designed for all China, was beyond saving. Instead, an entirely new Taiwan Constitution was required. The dynamics of reform were also more complicated than in the past, when the Chiangs could in effect dictate political reforms. Now the debate involved liberals and hardliners from the KMT, as well as academics and the new opposition party, the DPP. At least initially, Lee Teng-hui did not have the kind of political strength within the KMT to dominate the process. Nevertheless, in the four years from the lifting of martial law to the first full parliamentary elections in 1991, the foundations of what Wu Yu-shan calls a presidential dictatorship were gradually dismantled.

The debate over Taiwan's constitutional future was probably at its height during the early 1990s. One major stage for this debate was the June 1990 National Affairs Conference. The conference gathered an impressive diversity of opinions, especially considering the KMT's long tradition of trying to insulate policy-making from outside opinions. Chao and Myers describe the extraordinary scenes at the National Affairs Conference whereby television news

> showed political opponents, who for years had insulted and attacked each other, shaking hands and smiling at a banquet: President Lee smiled and chatted with Hsu

Hsin-liang (許信良); Premier Hau Pei-tsun conferred with the overseas dissident and delegate Wang Gui-rong (王桂榮); KMT Secretary-General Soong (宋楚瑜) talked with DPP member Yao Chia-wen (姚嘉文).[16]

Key areas of agreement, discussed in the previous chapter, largely amounted to a return to the operation of the 1947 Constitution. However, the parties disagreed on how to elect the President and on whether or not in the future to revise the 1947 Constitution or draft a new constitution. The KMT's official position was for a return to the Constitution's stipulation for the President to be indirectly elected by the newly elected National Assembly. In contrast, the DPP proposed a direct presidential election. Similarly, while the DPP had its own new draft constitution for a Republic of Taiwan, the KMT just wanted, at most, limited revisions to the 1947 Constitution. Two quotes give a taste of this debate. First, a group of DPP figures argued that 'The request for a new constitution matches with the requirement of our new democratic movement. If we do not restructure the constitution, our political and economic system will be adversely affected.'[17] In contrast, the KMT's Ma Ying-jeou stated:

> Any new form of a constitution would be opposed by me and many others. If that is done, it will be very difficult to reach any consensus to have a new constitutional draft, and even a new draft might not be as good as what we have now.[18]

All things considered, it was quite remarkable how the conference managed to reach such a number of important areas of agreement.

The difference between the parties was again on show during the 1991 National Assembly elections, as the parties remained poles apart. In the campaign, almost all DPP candidates carried the title *Constitution Drafting National Assembly Candidate* on their publicity material.[19] In contrast, the KMT argued that only minor revisions were required for the existing constitution and in its advertising even claimed that a new constitution would lead to recession and PRC invasion.[20] The KMT's overwhelming victory in this election suggested that voters were not yet ready for the DPP's more radical solutions.

Between 1991 and 2000, Taiwan went through six stages of constitutional reform.[21] Although the KMT rejected the DPP demand for a new Taiwan constitution, and its majority in the National Assembly meant that it was able to dictate the terms of the first three stages of constitutional reforms, the actual contents of revision often mirrored DPP demands.

The first stage occurred in the spring of 1991 and thus was carried out by a National Assembly still dominated by the senior parliamentarians, guaranteeing a KMT majority. The presence of what the DPP called the 'old thieves' meant that the first step was conflictual compared to the negotiations held at the National Affairs Conference, with DPP parliamentary violence and heavy police involvement in keeping order.[22] Nevertheless, this National Assembly session abolished the Temporary Provisions and approved ten new articles to the constitution. These included stipulations for the full re-election of the new Legislative Yuan and National Assembly and gave the President authorization to issue emergency orders.

The making of semi-presidentialism, 1992–7

The year 1992 marked the start of the next era in the constitutional order, as from this point the National Assembly was wholly Taiwan elected and reforms aimed at expanding presidential power began this year. Therefore, Wu Yu-shan views this period from 1991 to 1997 as one of an emerging semi-presidentialism.[23]

The second round of constitutional reforms came in May 1992. The scale of the KMT's National Assembly victory in 1991 meant that it could still dominate the ratification procedure as much as it did a year earlier. Once again, the process was highly antagonistic and involved violent DPP protests in the Assembly. Eventually, the DPP chose to withdraw and adopted street demonstrations to promote its demands, in particular its desire for direct presidential election. However, on this occasion KMT divisions also came to the surface. The key areas of contention were how the President should be elected, directly or indirectly, for while in 1991 the KMT and DPP stood on opposite ends of this spectrum, by 1992 the KMT itself was bitterly divided on this question.

The second stage included the following provisions:

1   The National Assembly could hold a state-of-the-nation report from the President.
2   The President would be elected in the free area (Taiwan) of the Republic of China for four-year terms.
3   The Provincial Governor and Taipei and Kaohsiung mayors would be directly elected.
4   National Assembly terms would become four years.
5   The President was given nomination powers for members of the Control Yuan, Examination Yuan, Grand Justices and President and Vice President of the Judicial Yuan, though consent was required of the National Assembly.
6   The government would be committed to promoting culture, environmental protection, modernizing the economy, protecting the rights of women, the handicapped and aboriginals.

In short, the 1992 reforms were much more substantial than those passed in 1991 and were significant in beginning the process of expanding presidential power. This process was continued in the next two stages of reform in 1994 and 1997. The key change in 1994 was provisions for a direct popular election of the President, as by now there was a majority within the KMT supporting this measure. Thus, by 1994 the KMT had adopted the DPP position. Similarly, the DPP was also moving towards the centre, as it quietly dropped its insistence on a new constitution and agreed to promote its reform agenda through constitutional revisions.

Full semi-presidentialism, 1997–2000

Partisan convergence on constitutional reform was even greater in the second half of the 1990s, as the process witnessed a more balanced and negotiated approach. The 1996 National Development Conference played a similar role to the 1990 consensus-seeking National Affairs Conference in effectively setting the rough blueprint for the next stage of reforms. In this conference it was a clear case of equal political bargaining between the KMT and DPP, while it was the New Party (NP) that felt isolated enough to walk out. In 1997 and 2000, the KMT and DPP cooperated as partners in radical constitutional reform measures. Particularly controversial was the effective elimination of the provincial level of government in 1997, thus ending elections for the Provincial Governor and Assembly. The other important measures in 1997 were stipulations that the President's appointment of the Premier no longer required legislative approval, expanding the number of legislators from 164 to 225, giving the President the power to dissolve the legislature (only when the Legislative Yuan passed a vote of no confidence on the Premier) and transferring the power to impeach the President from the Control Yuan to the Legislative Yuan. There was also cross-party support when, in 2000, the National Assembly was transformed into a 'non-standing body only responsible for endorsing future constitutional amendments'.[24] Almost all the National Assembly's powers, such as reviewing key presidential nominations and recalling the President, were transferred to the Legislative Yuan. In short, these reforms explain why Wu views the period of 1997–2000 as the birth of full semi-presidentialism on the island.[25]

By the end of the 1990s, Taiwan had reached the end of an era of constitutional change, as it had democratized much of its political system. The degree of change can be seen by comparing the martial law era political system in Table 2.1 with the radically different picture at the time of writing in 2016, shown in Table 4.1. In addition to opening up many offices to direct election, the most critical changes we see were the effective abolition

Table 4.1 Taiwan's political system after 2010

National level				
President (directly elected)				
Five Yuan				
Premier (appointed by President) Executive Yuan	Judicial Yuan	Legislative Yuan (directly elected)	Examination Yuan	Control Yuan
Special municipalities (equivalent level with province)				
City mayors of Taipei, New Taipei, Kaohsiung, Tainan, Taichung (directly elected) City governments				
Representative body		City councils (directly elected)		
Level	*County*			*City*
Executive representative	County (county magistrate) County council			City (City mayor) City council
Level	*Rural township (xiang)*	*Urban township (zhen)*	*City (shi)*	*District (Qu)*
Elected executive	Township chief (xiangzhang)	Township chief (zhenzhang)	City mayor (shizhang)	District head (Quzhang) Appointed by city mayor
Representative	Township councillor (xiangmindai)	Township councillor (zhenmindai)	City councillor (shimindai)	None
Level	*Village (cun)*	*Neighbourhood (li)*	*Neighbourhood (li)*	*Neighbourhood (li)*
Elected representative	Village chief (cunzhang)	Neighbourhood chief (lizhang)	Neighbourhood chief (lizhang)	Neighbourhood chief (lizhang)

of the National Assembly and provincial level of government and, of course, the increase in presidential power.[26] Thus, writers such as Cabestan and Wu view Taiwan as having become a semi-presidential system by the end of the 1990s. For Duverger, semi-presidentialism had three main conditions: (1) a president elected by universal suffrage, (2) a president holding considerable powers and (3) a prime minister opposite the president that holds executive and government power and can stay in office only if parliament does not show its opposition to them. Clearly, Taiwan's constitutional reforms of the 1990s moved it closer to this norm. Similarly, Wu argues that Taiwan was a president–parliamentary system using Shugart and Carey's typology, noting that this is often the most dangerous for a new emerging democracy.[27] In contrast, Chen Don-yun views Taiwan as being a premier–parliamentary system on the Shugart and Carey typology only after 1997.[28]

Comparing Taiwan's constitutional transition

A number of studies have tried to set Taiwan's constitutional reforms in a comparative context. Wu Yu-shan has compared Taiwan's approach to those of the new democracies of Eastern Europe.[29] In these cases, almost all chose to create completely new constitutions following the collapse of communism and the democratic breakthrough. In contrast, the only case of a similar model to Taiwan's incorporation of gradual revisions to the original pre-transition constitution was Hungary. Unlike the vast majority of these European former communist states, after transition the former authoritarian regime had far greater domestic legitimacy in Taiwan. This enabled the KMT to engineer a much more gradual process of constitutional reform that retained much of the old political system intact and allowed the KMT to remain the dominant political force in a way none of its East European counterparts were able to do. As Slater and Wong argue, the KMT was conceding to thrive.[30]

We can find closer similarities in the pattern of constitutional change in Taiwan with that during Spain's immediate post-Franco period under Adolfo Suarez. As Lin Chia-long explains:

> Both (Suarez and Lee) had to first conduct democratic reform within the existing institutions, and then, after reform had gained some momentum, tried to break away from the existing institutions so as to make a complete transition from authoritarian rule.[31]

In both cases we see a process of pacted reforms, with coalitions between regime liberals and opposition moderates.

Perhaps since France is the most well-known example of a semi-presidential system, a number of writers have compared it to Taiwan.[32] One major difference is that, unlike in France, the Taiwanese President does not need to seek legislative approval for his choice of Premier. In addition, while the French President can dissolve the parliament, in Taiwan this is such a complicated matter that it has not yet taken place. Taiwan's President can only dissolve parliament after the Premier has been subjected to a no-confidence vote in parliament. Since elections are so expensive in Taiwan, legislators have been unwilling to take the risk of parliament being dissolved and being forced into a snap election. Thus, they have avoided such a no-confidence vote. Also, unlike in France, Taiwan's President cannot chair cabinet meetings. Even before the change of ruling parties, there was already discussion about whether Taiwan would see a French-style cohabitation if the President's party did not hold a legislative majority. Overall, the Taiwanese President does not seem as powerful as some of their global counterparts. For instance, unlike in Russia, the Taiwan President cannot determine the basic guidelines of state policies. Despite the constitutional revisions, the dividing line in policy responsibilities of the Premier and President remains ambiguous. Thus, Taiwan also differs from the Finnish case, where there is an explicit division of labour between domestic and external policy realms.

Operation of semi-presidentialism in the Lee Teng-hui era

Following Lee's re-election and the 1997 constitutional reforms, Taiwan's semi-presidentialism appeared to be functioning relatively smoothly. In 1996–7, Lee had faced protracted Legislative Yuan opposition to his Premier Lien Chan (連戰), only receiving a narrow win in his confirmation vote.[33] However, the 1997 reforms meant that Lee no longer had to worry about his Premier getting legislative approval. Thus, after finally sacrificing Lien, Lee was able to impose Vincent Siew (蕭萬長) as Premier in 1997 without challenge. Moreover, the congruence between the KMT Legislative Yuan majority and presidency limited the scope for conflict between him and the legislative branch. This position was further strengthened when the KMT won an expanded legislative majority in 1998. Lee was also completely dominant within his own party by the late 1990s, as his internal challengers had left the party, chosen silence or been marginalized. It was no wonder that one writer talked about Taiwan now having an 'Imperial Presidency',[34] while Lin Chia-long notes how 'the revised constitutional system in Taiwan, now semi-presidential in character, has functioned more like a presidential system'.[35]

Wu Yu-shan observed one more notable feature of semi-presidentialism under Lee, in that the President has power without responsibility. Wu notes that

> the President can make final decisions without being held responsible. He can actually severely criticize the government for incompetence and wrongdoing and build his image at the expense of the government, though the President may be the ultimate decision-maker.[36]

Explaining Taiwan's constitutional reforms

Now we come to the crucial question of how can we best explain Taiwan's patterns of constitutional change in the 1990s? We need to give consideration to the following variables: (1) party and national ideology, (2) partisan, factional and personal power interests and (3) the balance of power between and within major parties.

In contrast to the above variables, Taiwan's political elites did not pay particular heed to the loud advice of constitutional experts in this reform process. Scholars were essentially marginalized during the constitutional conventions of the decade. The constitutional expert Hu Fu chose to withdraw from the 1990 National Affairs Conference days before it commenced stating, 'Its results might have nothing to do with constitutional reform and only reflect political struggle.'[37] Similarly, Yang Kuo-shu (楊國樞) complained that those scholars that attended 'were like a small vase of flowers with no opportunity to be seen and heard'.[38] There was a common view that the decisions were being made by parties and they could have no genuine input. As Yang explained: 'You either belong to one side or the other, and there is no chance to be independent.'[39] When it came to the debate in 1992 over the form of presidential elections, again most constitutional experts were on the losing side of the argument. For instance, Chou Yang-shan (周陽山) and Yang Tai-hsun (楊泰順) argued that the constitution was a cabinet rather than presidential system. And Hu Fu warned of the potential dangers of political stability that direct presidential election could bring.[40]

Party and nationalist ideology was to play an important role for both major parties in the constitutional reform process over this period. For some in the DPP, democratization and its objective of formal Taiwan independence were synonymous. Thus, full re-election of the parliaments and direct presidential elections can be viewed as steps towards this objective. The same applied to its long-standing demand for a new Taiwan constitution, as the party had long felt uncomfortable about adhering to the 1947 ROC constitution that had little legitimacy for them. By 1992, when it appeared impossible that Taiwan would get a new constitution, the DPP was forced to work within the system and revise the 1947 constitution. Thus, it aimed to remove elements that particularly signified ROC Chinese nationalism, such as the National Assembly and the provincial government structure. The latter had particular symbolic importance for the DPP, as it suggested that Taiwan was a province of China rather than a country. Removing the provincial level of government seems quite a rational move that would make government more efficient by removing essentially overlapping government structures. However, for the DPP, the prime motivation in this demand was not efficiency but removing this hated symbol of Chinese nationalism from Taiwan's political system.

For many within the KMT, the 1947 constitution is also a key symbol of ROC nationalism and thus there was a strong degree of attachment to the document. We got a sense of this from the Ma Ying-jeou's comments cited earlier from 1992 during the debate over a new constitution. The ideological attachment to the 1947 constitution was especially strong among politicians associated with the non-Mainstream faction within the KMT. This contributed to their resistance to Lee's attempts at moving away from what they saw as the parliamentary nature of the constitution. We can see a similar affection among some of the scholars supportive of the 1947 constitution. For instance, at the time of the 1990 National Affairs Conference, Hu Fu warned that 'The Republic of China might even be discarded as a by-product of crass political bargaining.'[41]

The second key variable is political interests. Many of the constitutional reforms were closely linked to the interests of Lee Teng-hui. As the island's most popular political figure in the early 1990s, direct presidential election was the best means for Lee to strengthen his own position. We thus saw how Lee attempted to progressively expand his own personal power through the reforms. Prior to constitutional reforms, Lee had been constrained by Premiers and the Legislative Yuan, and faced resistance from within the KMT. For example, Premier Hau Pei-tsun had been able to stand up to Lee in the early 1990s, but later Premiers were in effect Lee's subservient executives. In fact, the presidential election was a perfect stage for Lee to defeat two of his main inner party rivals, KMT Vice Chairmen Lin Yang-kang (林洋港) and Hau Pei-tsun, who formed a rebel presidential ticket to challenge Lee in 1996. Although the KMT still held parliamentary majorities after the democratic breakthrough, the pure parliamentary system was less appealing to Lee and his Mainstream KMT faction. They had grown frustrated by the parliamentary resistance from the ever stronger opposition parties and disunity among KMT legislators, and they expected that these trends would continue.

The DPP itself was divided between supporters of a presidential and parliamentary system until 1991. After disappointing parliamentary elections results in the early 1990s, however, it united around the appeal of direct presidential elections. It found that this was a highly effective electoral strategy for the party to gain new support against the rather vague KMT position of indirect elections. The DPP had correctly calculated that its chances of winning a presidential election, particularly against a divided KMT, were far greater than winning power through parliamentary elections. Such electoral considerations also affected the KMT's decision to support direct presidential election. Lee explained his position change as being the result of grassroots discussions during the 1991 campaign, stating, 'I came to the conclusion that many people wanted direct election.'[42]

Partisan interests also explain why the DPP opposed the idea of a second round run-off election if the winning presidential candidate failed to gain over 50 per cent of the vote. The DPP's support base of 30–40 per cent gave it a chance against a divided KMT, but meant that it would struggle in a second round run-off. In 1996, Lee was confident of winning in a first round, but wanted to avoid the risk of a second-round run-off. Lin Chia-long points out how in the late 1990s the KMT was more supportive of a run-off as a result of the dangers of a significant KMT rebel candidate, but by this time the DPP was strong enough to resist a move that would probably have stopped it from winning in 2000.[43]

The following quote from DPP leader Chang Chun-hong (張俊宏) gives us a taste of the instrumental way the DPP approached constitutional reform:

> In jail we never stopped talking of how to make the KMT collapse. We reached the conclusion that at first we should not talk of direct presidential elections, but for Provincial Governor. Of course our objective was direct presidential elections. This was the only way to end KMT rule, using localized force. But talking of direct presidential elections would not have succeeded. The way to make the KMT voluntarily introduce direct presidential elections was to have a Provincial Governor election first . . . By having the Provincial Governor election first, they would have no choice but to have direct presidential elections. Lee Teng-hui opposed direct presidential elections. However, Provincial Governor elections were easy to promote and implement. It was essential the DPP didn't win, but let the KMT win first. Then we could go home to sleep and wait for them to break up.[44]

Opposition to the shift towards a presidential system was also related to internal party factional interests. The KMT's non-Mainstream faction had traditionally been strongest in the non-elected side of the governance system. Although it held legislative seats, these tended to be concentrated in the major cities and it lacked the kind of island-wide grassroots backing of Lee and his Mainstream faction. Thus, its support of a parliamentary rather than presidential system was as related to its power position as to its Chinese nationalist ideology.

The last critical variable for explaining reform was the balance of power. Lee and his Mainstream faction had been initially constrained in achieving their constitutional reform goals by the strength of the non-Mainstream faction in the KMT and government. However, after 1993 Lee's internal rivals were marginalized, so that he could push revisions for direct presidential elections in 1994. In 1997, although Lee was dominant in the

KMT, the party no longer had the overwhelming National Assembly majority of the previous term. Thus, it had to compromise to a greater extent with the DPP in the constitutional reform's content.

Constitutional issues under the DPP

During the 1990s, the main parties moved from polarized positions to convergence on almost all key issues of constitutional reform by the end of the decade. In contrast, the subsequent ten years saw a return to divergence. The DPP's victory in 2000 was to put the semi-presidential system Lee had created to the test in a series of constitutional crises.

Operation of the constitution under divided government

Lee Teng-hui's creation of a semi-presidential system had operated relatively smoothly up to 2000, but the advent of Taiwan's first experience of divided government was to put great strain on the system. The DPP held the presidency but less than a third of Legislative Yuan seats. Under the French system we would expect either a period of cohabitation, in which the President would appoint a prime minister from the Legislative Yuan majority party until the next election, or dissolve the parliament hoping the voters would give a new majority to the President's party. However, the Taiwan President does not have the power to unilaterally dissolve the Legislative Yuan, and the new DPP President was not willing to let the KMT control the Executive Yuan. Instead, Chen Shui-bian (陳水扁) chose to nominate a KMT member to head the cabinet, but did so without negotiating with the KMT. This Premier lasted less than six months, and for the remainder of the DPP era Chen chose DPP members to be Premiers.

Under divided government, semi-presidentialism featured the kind of political instability that authors such as Wu Yu-shan had warned of. The DPP era saw highly antagonistic executive-legislative relations, often creating gridlock. During the fourth Legislative Yuan (1998–2001), we can see the impact of divided government in the success rate of cabinet bills being passed in the legislature. Prior to the 2000 change of ruling parties, the KMT government had a 72.7 per cent success rate, but after the DPP came to power it was only 38.5 per cent.[45] The 1997 constitutional reforms meant that the President could appoint a Premier without Legislative Yuan support, but this produced frequent clashes between the two branches of government and more often than not frustration for the President's reform agenda. The KMT opposition was able to block critical government bills such as on arms procurement and its attempt to adhere to an anti-nuclear power policy. For perhaps the first time in Taiwan's post-1945 history, the balance of power swung from the presidency to the legislature.

Constitutional reform under the DPP

In the early years of the Chen Shui-bian era, there was a lull in the constitutional reform process. It was not until September 2003 that Chen pledged to construct a new Taiwan constitution by 2006, proposing that such a constitution would be ratified by a national referendum.[46] A month later, Chen even suggested that the three-quarters Legislative Yuan majority required for constitutional reform made establishing a new constitution almost impossible. Instead, he proposed bypassing the Legislative Yuan and ratifying the new constitution by a referendum.[47] The pledge was at the time primarily a bid to gain support in the run-up to the 2004 presidential contest. However, it meant that the DPP was returning to its more radical stance of a brand new constitution rather than further tinkering with the old one. The KMT position also appeared to have shifted back to the one it had held in the early 1990s. In response, KMT Party Spokesman Tsai Cheng-yuan (蔡正元) equated Chen's proposal to 'a timetable for independence' and argued that constitutional reform was no longer a primary concern.[48]

Chen began his second term (2004–8) on a more moderate note, talking of constitutional re-engineering rather than a new constitution. A cross-party Constitutional Reform Committee was proposed to draw up the reform proposals, and Chen explained that 'Consensus has yet to be reached on issues related to national sovereignty, territory and the subject of unification/independence: therefore, let me explicitly propose that these particular issues be excluded from the present constitutional reengineering project.'[49] However, the high levels of interparty hostility following the contested 2004 presidential election meant that the KMT ignored Chen's call for a consensus-seeking conference along the lines of the 1996 National Development Conference. Chen continued to reach out for a consensus on further constitutional reform, again calling for a cross-party conference in December 2004 and agreeing to pursue constitutional revision rather than a new constitution in his ten-point agreement with People's First Party (PFP) leader Soong Chu-yu in February 2005.[50]

Considering the interparty tensions, it is quite remarkable that the next phase of constitutional reform received the support of all five relevant parties in the summer of 2004 to pass the Legislative Yuan, and in 2005 the KMT and DPP cooperated to see these reforms through the final National Assembly. This set of reforms was focused on the electoral system, replacing the multiple member district system with a single member district two vote system, halving the number of legislators and extending their term from three to four years, so that it would correspond with the President's terms.[51] This revision abolished the National Assembly, with its final function of constitutional reform passed to the Legislative Yuan. Lin Jih-wen (林繼文) has attempted to explain this round of constitutional reform by comparing the way that Japan and Taiwan reformed their electoral systems.[52] Lin argued that three conditions made reform possible in these two cases. These were that reformers must see benefits to change, when no party has an overall majority in parliament, and that the majority of legislators must have some incentives for change. I will return to discuss the impact of this set of reforms in a number of subsequent chapters.

After the above reforms were achieved, the parties degenerated back into polarized positions on the constitution issue. The subsequent DPP constitutional proposals were all roundly condemned or ignored by the KMT. Chen proposed what he called a second round of constitutional reforms, in which he hoped that civic groups would take the lead in drafting and promoting the creation of a new constitution. In April 2007, the Constitutional Reform Alliance claimed that it had received sufficient signatures of legislators for its draft constitution to proceed to the Legislative Yuan's Procedure Committee.[53] However, by attempting to avoid dialogue or bypass the KMT-dominated Legislative Yuan, such projects had no chance of success. The extremely high threshold of a three-quarters legislative majority for constitutional changes makes broad cross-party consensus a prerequisite for future reforms. Moreover, after Ma Ying-jeou became KMT chairman in 2005, the party took a position opposed to any further constitutional changes, with even technical revisions ruled out.[54]

Return of constitutional reform?

Recently, one of my students asked me whether I remain as pessimistic on the prospects of future constitutional reform as when I wrote the first edition of this book. I am glad to say that I am more optimistic than six years ago. After the KMT returned to power in 2008, constitutional reform almost completely disappeared from the political agenda. Thus far, the key actors in constitutional reform had been political parties, ensuring that it was a largely top-down process. In contrast in Ma's second term, it was bottom-up societal pressure that revived political interest in reform. A number of reform issues rose in salience in the build up to, during and in the aftermath of the 2014 Sunflower Movement. Key reforms that civil society has been pushing for include revising the highly restrictive Referendum Law, reducing the voting age to 18 and reforms to the electoral system that could allow greater space for smaller and alternative parties to enter parliament. In fact, one of the four core demands of the Sunflower Movement was convening a citizen's constitutional conference.[55] At this point, the KMT dismissed the idea of more constitutional change and instead proposed a National Affairs Conference on economics and trade.[56] However, in the build-up to the 2016 elections, there was a renewed interest among all the parties. After Ma Ying-jeou resigned, the KMT's new chairman Eric Chu (朱立倫) proposed moving to a parliamentary system in late 2014.[57] In June 2015, there appeared to be cross-party support to initiate constitutional reform to lower the voting age and threshold for parties to win party list seats. However, the KMT's attempt to link these reforms to two of its proposals to empower the legislature to confirm the Premier and allow absentee voting led to a breakdown in the process.[58] Once again, the way that parties dealt with the issue was closely related to their political interests.

Conclusions

Constitutional reform has transformed Taiwan from an authoritarian state into a democratic political system and from what on paper was a parliamentary system to a semi-presidential system. These reforms have been explained by partisan power interests, the balance of power and political ideologies. While in the 1990s there was a degree of political convergence on constitutional reform, in the post-2000 period the parties reverted to a similar level of polarization, as we saw at the outset of democratization.

During the post-2000 era, the parties were also guided by their ideologies and partisan interests in their treatment of constitutional issues. The parliamentary balance between the major parties meant that constitutional reform required genuine bargaining as in 1996. However, the antagonistic relationship between the main parties and the DPP's attempt to promote a more radical goal of a new constitution doomed the project to failure. The new factor that further complicated the issue is that China is now much more vocal in objecting to Taiwan's constitutional reforms. Although the KMT had a sufficient majority to carry out reforms to the constitution, under Ma's leadership new reform measures were ruled out. For the KMT it was more important to respect and implement the 1947 constitution.

In the first edition of this book I was critical of the KMT's lack of interest in constitutional reform, viewing it as a wasted opportunity. Taiwan's experience of the last decade has shown some of the serious defects of the current constitutional system. The lack of a presidential run-off allowed a president to win with only 39 per cent, contributing to his limited legitimacy. This could easily happen again. The removal of legislative approval for the Premier contributed to eight years of legislative–executive stalemate. If Taiwan reverts to divided government this could happen again. Lastly, the new electoral system resulted in a highly disproportional vote to seat share ratio, creating a sense of disenfranchisement among the losers. These are all areas that are crying out for new constitutional reforms. At least at the time of writing, the post-2016 Tsai government had yet to show signs that constitutional change would be a priority.

Discussion questions

1   How can we best explain Taiwan's pattern of constitutional reform?
2   How useful is the categorization of semi-presidentialism and how does the Taiwan case compare with that of other semi-presidential systems?
3   What have been the political consequences of Taiwan's new semi-presidentialism?
4   What kind of constitutional reforms would Taiwan benefit from?
5   How can we explain patterns of convergence and divergence on constitutional reform?

Further reading

Cabestan, Jean-Pierre. 2008. 'A New Constitutional Balance and the Prospect for Constitutional Change in Taiwan'. In Steven Goldstein and Julian Chang (eds). *Presidential Politics in Taiwan: The Administration of Chen Shui-bian*. Norwalk, CT: Eastridge, pp. 29–48. This offers a detailed discussion of constitutional issues in the post-2000 period.

Chao, Linda and Ramon Myers. 1998. *The First Chinese Democracy: Political Life in the Republic of China on Taiwan*. Baltimore, MD: The Johns Hopkins University Press. Chapters 9–11 are especially illuminating on the debates over constitutional reform and the actual reform process.

Chen, Don-yun. 1999. 'A Popularly-Elected Presidency as a Focus of Constitutional Choice: Explaining the Taiwanese Case, 1986–96'. *Issues and Studies*, 35(5): 1–42. Wide-ranging essay that tries to explain why Taiwan chose to adopt direct presidential elections.

Lin, Jih-wen. 2003. 'Transition Through Transaction: Taiwan's Constitutional Reform in the Lee Teng-hui Era'. In Lee Wei-chin and T.Y. Wang (eds). *Sayonara to the Lee Teng-hui Era: Politics in Taiwan, 1988–2000*. Lanham, MD: University Press of America, pp. 63–90. This piece is useful in delineating the content of constitutional reform in the 1990s and also offers a convincing framework for explaining the process.

Tien, Hung-mao. 1989. *The Great Transition: Politics and Social Change in the Republic of China*. Taipei: SMC Publishing. This has a good introduction to the constitutional order at the end of martial law and also the texts of the constitution and Temporary Provisions.

Wu, Yu-shan. 2000. 'The ROC's Semi-Presidentialism at Work: Unstable Compromise, Not Cohabitation'. *Issues and Studies*, 36(5): 1–40. Useful examination of Taiwan's semi-presidential system prior to 2000 and in the immediate post-2000 period.

Notes

1   Wu, 'The ROC's Semi-Presidentialism at Work', 3–4.
2   For the text, see Constitution of the Republic of China, available online at: www.gio.gov.tw/info/news/constitution.htm (accessed 4 July 2010).
3   Wu, 'Semi-presidentialism–easy to choose, difficult to operate', 201–18.
4   Cabestan, 'A New Constitutional Balance and the Prospect for Constitutional Change in Taiwan', 31.
5   Chang Chun-mai, cited in Chen, 'A Popularly-Elected Presidency as a Focus of Constitutional Choice', 8.

 6 Hsieh, 'The 2000 Presidential Election and Its Implications for Taiwan's Domestic Politics', 19.
 7 Ibid.
 8 Hu, 'Our System is a Responsible Cabinet System', 34–40.
 9 Wu, 'Semi-presidentialism–easy to choose, difficult to operate', 203.
10 Chen, 'A Popularly-Elected Presidency as a Focus of Constitutional Choice', 1–42; Shugart and Carey, *Presidents and Assemblies*. The five types suggested by Carey and Shugart are: (1) Pure Presidential, (2) Premier-presidential, (3) President-parliamentary, (4) Parliamentary with president, (5) Pure Parliamentary.
11 Chen, 12.
12 For the full text of the Temporary Provisions, see Tien, *The Great Transition*, 273–5.
13 Chen, 14.
14 Ibid., 8.
15 Wu, 'Semi-presidentialism–easy to choose, difficult to operate', 203.
16 Chao and Myers, *The First Chinese Democracy,* 206–7. Note that Yao and Hsu had been key *Tangwai* figures even before the Kaohsiung Incident.
17 Ibid., 211–12.
18 Ibid., 212.
19 See *Liberty Times,* 20 November 1991, 1.
20 These arguments were made in the KMT's 1991 TV advertisement titled 'Constitutional Revision Ad'.
21 For a comprehensive review of these six phases of reform, see Lin, 'Transition Through Transaction', 63–90.
22 'Old thieves' was a common derogatory term used to satirize the senior parliamentarians elected in China.
23 Wu, 'Semi-presidentialism–easy to choose, difficult to operate', 203.
24 Cabestan, 'A New Constitutional Balance and the Prospect for Constitutional Change in Taiwan', 38.
25 Wu, 'The ROC's Semi-Presidentialism at Work', 20.
26 I will discuss the important administrative upgrading and mergers of 2010 in Chapter 13.
27 Wu, 'Semi-presidentialism – easy to choose, difficult to operate', 215.
28 Chen, 'A Popularly-Elected Presidency as a Focus of Constitutional Choice', 40.
29 Wu, 'Legitimacy of Political Power and the Format of Constitutional Reforms', 29–62.
30 Slater and Wong, 717.
31 Lin, 'Paths to Democracy', 341–2.
32 For instance, see Cabestan, 'Constitutional Reform: Is Taiwan Moving Towards a French style Semi-Presidential System?' 40–4; Liao (廖達琪) and Chien (簡赫琳), 'Why no co-habitation in Taiwan?' 55–9.
33 Lien won by a margin of 85 to 77 votes.
34 Lu Ya-li (呂亞力), quoted in Wu, 'The ROC's Semi-Presidentialism at Work,' 20.
35 Lin, 494.
36 Wu, 21.
37 Chao and Myers, 200.
38 Ibid.
39 Ibid.
40 Ibid., 263.
41 Ibid., 211.
42 Ibid., 250.
43 Lin, 488–9. Note that Lin has quite impressive predictive analysis considering it was written two years before the 2000 election.
44 Interview with the author, Taipei, 26 September 2001.
45 Wu, 'Semi-presidentialism–easy to choose, difficult to operate', 213.
46 Chang Yun-peng and Huang Tai-lin, 'Chen Makes DPP Birthday Pledge', *Taipei Times*, 30 September 2003, 1.
47 Liao, 'An examination of the leadership elite's role in Taiwan's constitutional development', 80–3.
48 Huang Tai-lin, 'Pan Blue camp slams Chen's call for a new Constitution', *Taipei Times*, 30 September 2003, 3.

49 President Chen's Inaugural Speech 'Paving the Way for a Sustainable Taiwan', *Taipei Times,* 20 May 2004, 1.
50 Caroline Hong and Huang Tai-lin, 'Chen, Soong sign 10-point consensus', *Taipei Times,* 25 February 2005, 1.
51 For details, see Cabestan, 'A New Constitutional Balance and the Prospect for Constitutional Change in Taiwan', 41–42.
52 Lin, Jih-wen, 'The Politics of Reform in Japan and Taiwan', 118–31.
53 Ko Shu-ling, 'Draft Constitution Moves Ahead', *Taipei Times,* 3 April 2007, 3.
54 Ma made this point in discussions with academics in London, February 2006.
55 Ho, 2015, 'Occupy Congress in Taiwan', 69–70.
56 Chris Wang, 'Sunflower leaders reject Ma's conference plan', *Taipei Times,* 3 April 2014, 1.
57 'Eric Chu presents platform for KMT chairman at event', *Taipei Times,* 30 December 2014, 1.
58 Alison Hsiao, 'Activists assail KMT over failed reform', *Taipei Times,* 18 June 2015, 1.

5 Electoral politics

Milestones, electoral systems and political communication

Democratization transformed Taiwan's electoral politics. Multi-party elections, perhaps more than any other political phenomenon, have widened the gulf between Taiwan and China. Under martial law elections there were candidates from only one political party, almost all political communication was KMT dominated and there was no real policy debate. In contrast, the democratic era brought political advertising, a free media, intense partisan competition, open policy debate and extremely expensive election campaigns. Within less than two decades, Taiwan made the transition from what Pippa Norris calls the 'premodern campaign' to the 'postmodern campaign'.[1] The degree of change to Taiwan's electoral politics can be compared to the switch from black and white to colour television or from vinyl records to digital music downloads. But there is much continuity as well. Taiwanese elections offer a unique blend of the old and new, with practices borrowed from US political marketing blended together with traditional communication that gives elections the atmosphere of a Chinese festival.

For many academics who study Taiwanese politics, elections are the topic that most fascinates us. When I visit Taiwan, I try to make it coincide with an election campaign. For someone who has grown up on a diet of short and dull campaigns in Europe, the noise, colour, passion, policy richness and participatory nature of elections on Taiwan explains my love affair with these democratic festivals. This contrast was driven home to me when I returned to the UK after seven years in Taiwan in the late 1990s. I recall vividly my disappointment at the low-key nature of the first ever direct election for London mayor in 2000. Taiwanese visitors to the UK often comment that they are hardly aware that election campaigns are even taking place here. In Taiwan, no matter how hard you may try, you can never escape from election campaigns. It is for this reason that I can understand why one of my fellow election watchers equates Taiwan's election days with Christmas Day.[2] Each year, the weeks on my Taiwan politics courses where we look at elections are the ones I look forward to the most.

I will first set the scene by outlining the key events in Taiwan's recent electoral history and which parties are perceived as having won those elections. Next, the chapter introduces the island's electoral systems, detailing how they have been reformed and the political consequences of these systems. The focus will then turn to how political communication has developed since the late 1980s. We will look at questions such as whether campaigns focus on issues, personalities or ideology, and whether Taiwanese campaigns are overly negative. Although political scientists often focus on the modern public face of campaigns, we will see how many traditional methods of campaigning remain in vogue in twenty-first century Taiwan. Lastly, the analysis will be tied in with the political communications debate over whether campaigns matter, and if we are seeing an Americanization or modernization of campaigning in new democracies.

Basic history of Taiwanese elections since the mid-1980s

Taiwanese have often told me that they have more elections than any other country. One of Ma Ying-jeou's cabinet ministers publically complained that the frequency of Taiwan's elections was detrimental to good governance.[3] Taiwan holds elections for a wide range of offices from the presidency and national parliament to city mayors, county councillors and, at the lowest grassroots level, ward (*li zhang*) and village heads. After reaching a peak in the number of offices directly elected in the mid-1990s, there has been a slight decline in the number of elections since 2000 as a result of changes in the political system described in the previous chapter. However, we cannot deny that there is a high frequency of elections in Taiwan. In the 30 years since the DPP was formed in 1986, there have been major elections held in 23 of them. The only years without major elections during this period were 1987, 1988, 1990, 1999, 2003, 2007, 2011, 2013 and 2015.[4]

I have summarized Taiwan's major election results in Tables 5.1–5.5. Table 5.1 shows the main parties' vote shares in national parliamentary elections (the Legislative Yuan and National Assembly). Table 5.2 shows parliamentary election seat shares. Table 5.3 shows the presidential election vote shares and Table 5.4 shows local executive vote and seat shares. Lastly, Table 5.5 offers a judgement on which party was viewed in Taiwan as having won each major election between 1989 and 2016. This last table is important as often in Taiwan it is not the seat or vote share that is the key determinant for which party is seen as having emerged victorious.

Before moving on, we need to review some key dates in Taiwan's recent electoral history. The first set of elections that I have included in these tables is the local executive elections of 1985. This year is important in being the last year in which the KMT faced the opposition movement, or de facto party, known as the *Tangwai*. The vote and seat shares that year were quite representative of the way the KMT had dominated electoral

Table 5.1 Vote shares in national parliamentary (Legislative Yuan and National Assembly) elections

	1986	1989	1991	1992	1995	1996	1998	2001	2004	2008	2012	2016
KMT	69.2	60.2	71.2	53	46.1	49.7	46.4	28.6	32.8	51.2	44.5	26.9
DPP	22.2	28.3	23.9	31	33.2	29.9	29.6	33.4	35.7	36.9	34.6	44
NP					13.0	13.7	7.1	2.9	0.1	4	1.5	4.1
PFP								18.6	13.9		5.5	6.5
TSU								8.5	7.8	3.5	9	2.5
GPT											1.7	2.5
NPP												6.1

Source: Election Study Centre, National Chengchi University.

Note 1: The PFP won one seat out of its three official candidates in 2008. The PFP only had one (unsuccessful) district level candidate in 2008, who won 47.04 per cent of the vote in Lienchiang County. This only amounted to 2,064 votes and represents 0.02 per cent of the national vote share. The successful PFP candidate won an aboriginal constituency seat with 11,925 votes; however, votes for the aboriginal constituencies were not included in the Central Election Commission's party vote share figures.

Note 2: The party vote share figures for the 2008, 2012 and 2016 legislative elections are from the party list votes

Note 3: Figures for 1986, 1989 and 1992 from Hsieh (2002: 37).

Note 4: Figures for 1991 from *Lianhebao*, 12 December 1991, 1

KMT: Kuomintang; DPP: Democratic Progressive Party; NP: New Party; PFP: People First Party; TSU: Taiwan Solidarity Union; GPT: Green Party Taiwan; NPP: New Power Party

Table 5.2 Seat shares in national parliamentary (legislative Yuan and national assembly) elections

	1986	1989	1991	1992	1995	1996	1998	2001	2004	2008	2012	2016
KMT	80.8	68.6	78.2	59	51.8	55	54.7	30.2	35.1	71.7	56.6	30
DPP	16.7	20.6	18.6	31.7	32.9	30	31.1	38.7	39.6	24	35.4	60
NP					12.8	14	4.9	0.4	0.4	0	0	0
PFP								20.2	15.1	0.9	2.7	2.7
TSU								5.8	5.3	0	2.7	0
NPP												4.4

Source: Election Study Centre, National Chengchi University.

Note 1: Figures for 1986 from Chao and Myers (1998: 139).

Note 2: The seat share for 1989 is based on my own calculations from *China Times*, 3 December 1989, 1.

Note 3: Figures for seat shares in 1991 and 1996 from Chao and Myers (1998: 237 and 285).

Table 5.3 Vote shares in presidential elections

	1996	2000	2004	2008	2012	2016
KMT	54	23.1	49.9	58.45	51.6	31
DPP	21.1	39.3	50.1	41.55	45.6	56
NP	14.9	0.1				
PFP		36.8			2.7	13

Source: Election Study Centre, National Chengchi University

Note 1: The vote share for the NP in 1996 refers to the Lin Yang-kang ticket, which was supported by the NP but not officially a nominated NP candidate.

Note 2: The PFP vote share in 2000 and 2012 refers to James Soong's independent candidacy.

politics for most of the martial law era. Next, 1986 stands out as the first multi-party election following the formation of the DPP in September that year.

The final supplementary election was in 1989, featuring Legislative Yuan, county- and city-level local executive and Provincial Assembly elections. The election was viewed as a serious setback for the KMT, as the DPP made major breakthroughs, winning a third of the national vote and six local executive posts. Although not listed in these tables, the last indirect presidential election took place in 1990, where Lee Teng-hui was elected by the old National Assembly.

The first full re-elections of the national parliaments took place in 1991 and 1992, replacing the senior parliamentarians from China. Although the KMT won clear majorities in terms of seats and votes, the verdicts were quite different on which party had won these two elections. By gaining almost 80 per cent of National Assembly seats in 1991 the KMT had won the most overwhelming victory of the multi-party era, while the DPP seemed to have lost support. In contrast, the 1992 legislative election is viewed as showing that the DPP had recovered and was on the long road to becoming a potential ruling party. The KMT saw this as a serious setback, as it lost votes and seats, and the campaign featured severe and open inner-party splits.

The local executive elections of 1993 and 1994 saw the DPP continue to grow, but the KMT still retained its position as the dominant party. This was the first time that the local executives for the offshore island districts of Kinmen and Lienchiang (Mazu) were

Table 5.4 Local executive vote and seat shares

	1985	1989	1993	1997	2001	2005	2009	2014
KMT	61.1 (81)	52.7 (66.7)	47.3 (65.2)	42.1 (34.8)	35.2 (39.1)	51 (60.9)	47.9 (70.6)	40.7 (27.2)
DPP	13.5 (19)	30.1 (28.6)	41.2 (26.1)	43.3 (52.2)	45.3 (39.1)	42 (26.1)	45.3 (23.5)	47.5 (59.0)
NP			3.1 (0)	1.4 (0)	9.9 (4.3)	0.2 (4.3)		
PFP					2.4 (8.7)	1.1 (4.3)		
TSU						1.1 (0)		
Seat Numbers	KMT: 17 TW: 4 Total: 21	KMT: 14 DPP: 6 Other 1 Total: 21	KMT: 15 DPP: 6 Other 2 Total: 23	KMT: 8 DPP: 12 Other 3 Total: 23	KMT: 9 DPP: 9 NP:1 PFP:2 Other 2 Total: 23	KMT: 14 DPP: 6 NP:1 PFP:1 Other 1 Total: 23	KMT: 12 DPP: 4 Other 1 Total: 17	KMT: 6 DPP: 13 Other: 3 Total: 22

Source : Election Study Centre, National Chengchi University.

Note 1: The 1985 and 1989 vote share figures are from Cheng and Hsu (1996: 138). It should be noted that I have seen quite variable figures for 1985 and 1989. For instance, Huang Teh-fu (1998: 109) lists the KMT vote share for 1985 as 60.93 per cent and in 1989 as 56.11 per cent. On the day after the 1989 contest the *China Times* gives the KMT 55.7 per cent and the DPP 34.7 per cent (3 December 1989, 1). The seat shares for 1985 and 1989 are based on my own calculations
Note 2: The table shows the main parties' vote and seat shares in local executive elections. The party seat shares are shown in parenthesis.
Note 3: While in 2005, 23 local executives were elected, in 2009 due to administrative district changes, only 17 local executive posts were elected.
Note 4: The DPP had not yet been formed in 1985, so I have used the *Tangwai* (TW) figures for that year.
Note 5: The bottom row lists the total number of seats won by the main parties in these elections.
Note 6: In 2014, the special municipality executive elections were held on the same day as county magistrate/city mayor elections for the first time.

directly elected, thus increasing the total number of seats from 21 to 23. In the 1993 local executive contests, the DPP exceeded 40 per cent of vote share for the first time but was unable to make a breakthrough in seat share and actually lost a seat.[5] In 1994, the three key elections were for Taipei and Kaohsiung mayors and the Provincial Governor. This year was viewed as being a tie as, although the KMT won Kaohsiung city and Taiwan province, it lost the capital to the DPP candidate Chen Shui-bian.

There was a gap of just four months between the December 1995 legislative election and first direct presidential election in March 1996. However, as with 1991–2, the verdicts on these two elections were quite different. The first election was seen as a defeat for the KMT as it only retained a very narrow overall legislative seat majority, while the DPP was disappointed in having made only limited gains. Instead, it was the NP that emerged as the perceived winner, gaining 13 per cent of seats and votes in its first national-level election. In contrast, the KMT was viewed as the winner in 1996 after Lee Teng-hui gained 54 per cent of the vote share in the presidential election to defeat his rivals from the DPP and NP by a wide margin.

Table 5.5 Principal elections and verdict on results, 1989–2016

Year	Elections held	Verdict
1989	Legislative and (supplementary) and Local Executive	DPP won
1991	National Assembly	KMT won
1992	Legislative Yuan	DPP won
1993	Local Executive	KMT won
1994	Special Municipalities and Provincial Governor	Tie
1995	Legislative Yuan	NP won
1996	Presidential and National Assembly	KMT won
1997	Local Executive	DPP won
1998	Legislative Yuan Special Municipalities	KMT won
2000	Presidential	DPP won
2001	Legislative Yuan Local Executive	DPP and PFP won
2002	Special Municipalities	Tie
2004	Presidential	DPP wins (contested)
2004	Legislative Yuan	KMT won
2005	Local Executive	KMT won
2006	Special Municipalities	Tie
2008	Legislative Yuan	KMT won
2008	Presidential	KMT won
2009	Local Executive	DPP won
2010	5 Special Municipalities	Tie
2012	Legislative Yuan and Presidential	KMT won
2014	6 Special Municipalities and Local Executive	DPP won
2016	Legislative Yuan and Presidential	DPP won

Source: Fell (2005c: 14).

Note: The table shows my verdict of how these elections are viewed in Taiwan. This is based on reading of individual campaign coverage, and interviews with politicians and political scientists in Taiwan.

A year and a half after the KMT's presidential triumph, it was to suffer its worst election result to date in the 1997 local executive elections. The DPP not only exceeded the KMT's vote share for the first time, but actually won 12 seats compared to the KMT's 8. However, the KMT looked to have recovered a year later in the Legislative Yuan and special municipality elections. Once again the DPP could not make progress in the parliamentary election, while the KMT won enough seats from the NP to give it an increased majority of seats. Although the KMT and DPP both won one of the two special municipalities' mayoral seats, the fact that the DPP's star Chen Shui-bian lost to the KMT's Ma Ying-jeou in Taipei reinforced the DPP's sense of this being a disappointing year. Narrowly winning the Kaohsiung mayoral seat was the DPP's only real consolation in 1998.

In 2000, Taiwan had its first change of ruling parties under ROC rule, as the DPP's Chen Shui-bian won the presidential election. However, as shown in Table 5.3, it was only because of a KMT split that he was able to win with 39 per cent of the vote. As the DPP had won less than a third of the legislative seats in 1998, Taiwan began its first period of divided government. Things would get even worse for the KMT as it suffered its largest ever parliamentary seat and vote loss in 2001, while the DPP had its best parliamentary seat share to date and became the largest parliamentary party. The year 2001 was also noteworthy for the emergence of the People First Party (PFP), winning more seats than the NP at its peak and challenging the KMT's position as the leading opposition party. From this election the terms Pan Blue and Pan Green became more widely used, with the former referring to the KMT and its splinter parties, the PFP and NP, and the latter referring to the DPP and its ally the Taiwan Solidarity Union (TSU).[6] Despite the KMT's losses, this election left the Pan Blues with a clear majority.

Although the DPP had been behind in the polls for most of the 2004 presidential campaign, it was able to win by a very narrow margin of only 0.2 per cent in March. The assassination attempt on Chen Shui-bian and KMT allegations of vote fraud made this a highly controversial and contested election. On the same day as the presidential election, Taiwan also held its first ever nationwide referendum. In December, the legislative election saw some recovery on the part of the KMT at the expense of the PFP but little real change to the balance of power. The DPP remained the largest party, but the KMT and its ally the PFP retained their parliamentary majority. However, the election is viewed as a DPP setback as it failed to achieve its stated goal of winning a Pan Green parliamentary majority.

The 2005 local executive elections were the DPP's worst ever local executive results, as it fell back to its 1989 level of just six seats, while the KMT and its Pan Blue allies held a similar seat share to the party's late martial law levels. There was no major shift in the balance of power in the special municipal elections of 2002 and 2006, with the KMT and DPP both maintaining control of Taipei and Kaohsiung respectively. The KMT was then able to maintain its momentum from 2005 to win landslide majorities in the 2008 legislative and presidential elections. During the 2008 elections, the KMT gained record high parliamentary seat and presidential vote shares. These victories brought a return to KMT control of the national executive for the first time in eight years and left the party looking more politically dominant than at any point since the lifting of martial law.

Ma Ying-jeou's mid-term election tests came in the local executive contests of 2009 and special municipality elections in late 2010. As a result of administrative district mergers and upgrades, only 17 local executive posts were contested in 2009. On this occasion the KMT won an even better seat share than it did in 2005, with the party gaining 14 out of the 17 seats. However, the election was viewed as a KMT defeat because the DPP improved its overall vote share and won back Yilan County, and most districts saw significant vote share swings towards the DPP. In 2010, elections were being held for the five special municipality mayors. Apart from Taipei and Kaohsiung city (now expanded to include former Kaohsiung county), these include the upgraded Taipei county, now known as New Taipei City, and the new cities of Tainan and Taichung, which combined them with their respective counties. These elections were widely seen as a tie. Although the KMT won three out of five, the DPP's total vote share exceeded the KMT's and the DPP won exactly the same number of city council seats as the KMT (130). Although the DPP had a degree of recovery in the parliamentary and presidential elections in 2012, the KMT was still able to win retain power with comfortable majorities.

The political pendulum swung back in the DPP's direction in 2014. That year, the special municipality elections were combined with the county/city mayoral elections for the first time. Table 5.4 reveals that the DPP enjoyed its best ever local executive results, while the KMT went from controlling three quarters of local executive posts to just 6. In 2016, the DPP then won landslides at the national level, again enjoying record vote and seat shares. These elections gave the DPP unprecedented political power, as for the first time it held a majority of seats in parliament, together with the presidency and the majority of local executive posts.

Electoral systems

Under martial law, Taiwan used two main electoral systems. For executive posts, such as city mayors and county executives, it used a Single Member District (SMD) majoritarian system. These SMD elections did not require a run-off election when the leading candidate failed to reach 50 per cent. In contrast elections for the provincial, city and county assemblies, as well as supplementary national parliamentary elections, used what Rigger referred to as the Single Non-Transferable Voting in Multi-Member Districts (SVMM system).[7] Under this system, the top vote-getters up to the district magnitude are elected. Thus, if the magnitude of a district is six, the top six vote-winners are elected. This system had first been used in Taiwan under the Japanese colonial period, and was used in Japan and Korea until the 1990s. Under martial law, the supplementary national elections for National Assembly and Legislative Yuan also used this SVMM system.

With the advent of full national elections for the Legislative Yuan and National Assembly, Taiwan needed to devise an appropriate electoral system. In the 1992 Legislative Yuan, there were 161 seats available. These were divided as follows: (1) 119 elected under SVMM elections in districts with magnitudes between 1 and 16, with an average district magnitude of 4.41 (2) two three-seat multiple member districts reserved for indigenous peoples, and (3) two sets of proportional representation seats (30 and 6) were distributed to parties based on their district vote share. Although there was a gradual expansion in the number of Legislative Yuan seats (rising to 225 after 1998), this was the system employed for Legislative and National Assembly elections through until 2004.[8]

Operation and consequences of the electoral systems

We can get a clearer picture of how the SVMM system worked by examining two case studies in my adopted hometown of Kaohsiung city. Table 5.6 shows the results for the Kaohsiung North legislative district in 2001, which had a district magnitude of six. All five major parties nominated candidates. There were also two well-known rebel candidates, making this a highly competitive district. The DPP was by far the most successful, with all three of its candidates coming in the top six. Two of the KMT's three candidates won election, and the sole TSU candidate won election by coming in third place. The party that made the biggest strategic error was the PFP. It received 18 per cent of the vote, but these votes were spread too thinly among multiple candidates and thus none of its candidates were elected. If it had nominated two it might have got both elected.

The second case in Table 5.7 shows the results for the Kaohsiung South legislative district in 2001, which had a district magnitude of five. With the smaller magnitude, all five major parties nominating and three strong independents, this was perhaps even more competitive than Kaohsiung North. Once again, the DPP and TSU got all their candidates elected in the top five, but this time the PFP was able to concentrate its votes on a single successful candidate. In contrast, it was the KMT that over-nominated, with all three of its candidates falling outside the top five. With almost 25 per cent, the KMT could have got at least two into the top five, but its over-ambitious nomination resulted in only wasted votes.

The first lesson of those two cases is the importance of getting nomination numbers right and distributing a party's votes among its candidates evenly. In both these Kaohsiung districts, the DPP achieved these requirements perfectly and thus got all its candidates elected. However, if the DPP had had a star politician that attracted too many votes, it

Table 5.6 SVMM at work: Kaohsiung North Legislative Yuan District in 2001

Candidate (incumbent/gender)	Party nominating	Vote share and elected
Lin Chin-hsing (林進興) (i) (M)	DPP 1	14.87 (Yes)
Chen Chi-mai (陳其邁) (i) (M)	DPP 2	14.49 (Yes)
Su Ying-kui (蘇盈貴) (M)	TSU 1	11.38 (Yes)
Lo Shih-hsiung (羅世雄) (M)	KMT 1	8.59 (Yes)
Chiang Yi-wen (江綺雯) (i) (F)	KMT 2	7.97 (Yes)
Chu Hsing-yu (朱星羽) (i) (M)	DPP 3	7.48 (Yes)
Yang Se-yu (楊色玉) (F)	PFP 1	6.89
Lin Shou-shan (林壽山) (M)	PFP 2	6.64
Tseng Chang-fa (曾長發) (M)	KMT 3	6.02
Mei Tsai-hsing (梅再興) (M)	PFP3	4.6
Hsieh Chi-ta (謝啟大) (i) (F)	NP1,	3.89
Ye Yao-peng (葉耀鵬) (M)	DPP rebel	2.45
Wang Tian-ching (王天競) (i) (M)	PFP rebel	2.01

Source: Central Election Commission.

Note: (i) = incumbent legislator, (F) = female, (M) = male

could have undermined the prospects of fellow DPP candidates. In Kaohsiung North, the PFP, and in Kaohsiung South, the KMT, both paid the price for over-nominating and failing to distribute their votes well.

To succeed in SVMM elections requires a well-organized party to correctly estimate vote share, coordinate vote distribution and nominate an appropriate number of candidates. Under martial law, only the KMT had the level of organization to run the kind of coordinated campaigns that are needed to succeed under SVMM. Thus, Hsieh shows how, between 1969 and 1989, the KMT tended to perform best in either small districts with a magnitude of or districts with over 6. In contrast, the *Tangwai* performed best in districts of between 3 and 5 magnitude.[9]

By comparing the party vote and seat shares in Tables 5.1 and 5.2, we can see how the KMT's superior organization enabled it to gain significant seat bonuses. In other words, it received a higher seat share than its vote share. For example, in 1991 the KMT received 71.8 per cent of the vote but gained 78.2 per cent of seats. Moreover, the KMT received a large seat bonus in all SVMM parliamentary elections until it lost power in 2000. In the two post-2000 SVMM parliamentary elections, the KMT still had a seat bonus, but it was much reduced. In contrast, the DPP initially tended to suffer from a seat deficit in its early years. In 1989, it gained 28 per cent of the vote but only won 20 per cent of the seats. As the DPP's organization improved, it was able to achieve vote and seat share parity for most of the 1990s. In the 2001 and 2004 legislative elections, it was even able to gain higher seat bonuses than the KMT.

The parties adopted distinct methods for distributing their votes evenly. The KMT tended to divide districts into responsibility zones, which would be assigned to different candidates and in which other candidates should not campaign. In addition, the KMT had its so-called iron votes (mobilizing military veterans or civil servants) that it could deploy to help prop up weaker candidates at the last minute. Over time, greater political party competition, more independent voters and internal KMT splits have severely undermined the effectiveness of the responsibility zone system, particularly when politicians encroached on each other's zones.

Table 5.7 SVMM at work: Kaohsiung South Legislative Yuan District in 2001

Candidate (incumbent/gender)	Party nominating	Vote share (%) and (elected)
Kuo Wen-cheng (郭玟成) (M)	DPP 1	13.66 (Yes)
Tang Chin-chuan (湯金全) (i) (M)	DPP 2	13.09 (Yes)
Chiu Yi (邱毅) (M)	PFP 1	12.86 (Yes)
Lo Chih-ming (羅志明)	TSU 1	12.38 (Yes)
Liang Mu-yang(梁牧養) (i) (M)	DPP 3	10.07 (Yes)
Yao Kao-chiao (姚高橋) (M)	KMT 1	9.34
Lin Kun-hui (林崑海) (M)	Independent 1	8.46
Lin Hong-tsung (林宏宗) (i) (M)	KMT 2	7.79
Li Fu-hsing (李復興) (M)	KMT 3	7.71
Kao Hsin-wu (高新武) (M)	NP 1	1.55
Tsai Ma-fu (蔡媽福) (M)	PFP rebel	1.4
Chu Kao-cheng (朱高正) (M)	Independent 2	0.83

Source: Central Election Commission, 1–2.

Note: (i) = incumbent legislator, (F) = female, (M) = male

With a smaller vote base and limited financial resources, the opposition parties developed vote allocation programmes that relied on their voters. In the 1990s, both the NP and DPP trialled vote allocation schemes, particularly in metropolitan districts and had a degree of success. For instance, in the two Kaohsiung legislative districts during the 2004 parliamentary elections, the DPP and TSU chose to nominate four candidates, and asked voters born in January–March to vote for Candidate 1, those born in April–June to vote for Candidate 2, and so on.[10] These requests would be widely publicized in party TV and newspaper advertisements prior to voting day. On that occasion, seven out of the eight were successfully elected. This should be seen as being successful as the PFP and KMT both nominated much more conservatively than 2001 in these districts. Nevertheless, we cannot be 100 per cent certain whether we are seeing correlation or causation here, as I struggled to find voters who would admit to having followed their party's vote allocation requests.

Another important variable in succeeding under SVMM was avoiding both rebel and allied party candidates who would disperse your support. One particularly infamous case for the KMT came in 1992 when its rebel candidate Jaw Shaw-kong (趙少康) gained 235,887 votes, almost 17 per cent of the vote share, in 16-seat Taipei County, thus severely undermining the officially nominated KMT candidates. The KMT has suffered more from the problem of allied party candidates under the SVMM system than the DPP. At the district level we can see this in Kaohsiung North (Table 5.6), where the KMT had to compete with four allied party candidates (three PFP and one NP), while the DPP faced just the one allied party candidate. On the national level in 2001, there were 131 candidates from KMT allied parties (42 NP and 89 PFP), while the DPP faced only 58 allied party candidates (55 TSU and three from the Taiwan Independence Party). This partly explains why the KMT's seat bonus declined in 2001 and 2004.

By comparing the elections held under the SVMM (Tables 5.1 and 5.2) and SMD systems (Table 5.4), we can see some clear differences. Tables 5.1 and 5.2 show that though SVMM is not a proportional representation system, it generated quite proportional results until 2004. In other words, there is not a huge gap between the parties' vote and seat share under SVMM. In contrast, the SMD local executive results shown in Table 5.4

generated far more disproportional outcomes, as the seat bonus or deficits tended to be much greater. For instance, in the 2009 local executive elections, the DPP gained only 23.5 per cent of the seats with 45.3 per cent of the vote, while the KMT gained 70.6 per cent of seats from 47.9 per cent of the votes. If we regard each vote as being of equal value to be a democratic standard, then SVMM appears to be a more representative system than SMD.

Under SMD, the dangers of rebel and allied candidates are even greater than under SVMM, as split votes can allow the rival party to benefit. Three cases particularly illustrate this effect. First, in the 1994 Taipei mayoral election the DPP's Chen Shui-bian won with 43.7 per cent of the vote against a divided KMT camp. The KMT's official candidate, Huang Ta-chou (黃大洲) won 25.9 per cent of the vote, and NP candidate Jaw Shaw-kong won 30.2 per cent. The second case was the 1997 local executive elections, where numerous KMT rebel candidates severely split the party's vote, enabling the DPP to win its best ever local executive seat share. The last case was the 2000 presidential election where the KMT rebel James Soong out-polled the official KMT candidate Lien Chan, and thus allowed the DPP's Chen Shui-bian to win with just 39 per cent.

The two electoral systems also have consequences for the party system. Maurice Duverger argued that SMDs promote a two-party system, while proportional representation favours a multi-party system.[11] We can see some support of this proposition in the Taiwan case. Table 5.2 shows that third parties had far greater success in the SVMM (semi-proportional) system than the SMD presidential or local executive elections in Tables 5.3 and 5.4. The NP, TSU and PFP were all able to gain significant numbers of seats under SVMM, while their impact on the SMD local executive elections was negligible. The exception appears to be 2001 and 2005 when both the PFP and NP won local executive posts, but this is a little deceptive as this seat share was largely due to their success in the tiny off-shore island districts of Kinmen and Lienchiang.[12] Under SMD, voters tend to vote strategically to ensure their least preferred candidate does not get elected. This explains why Pan Blue voters tended to concentrate their votes on KMT candidates rather than the splinter parties in SMD elections. The exceptions mentioned earlier occurred in cases such as 2000, when voters were unsure who the strongest Pan Blue candidate was. In short, voters under SVMM were given greater choice, as niche parties had greater potential to win election and thus such a vote was not necessarily a wasted one.

Although SVMM gives voters more choice and is more proportional, it has some drawbacks too. A number of studies in the 1990s highlighted some serious negative political consequences. One such issue is that it tends to encourage inner-party rather than interparty competition. Individual success requires not appealing to floating voters or persuading opposition party supporters, but competing against fellow partisans for their own party supporters. Thus, candidates often spend more effort attacking fellow party candidates than other parties. Such inner-party attacks were especially serious in the KMT during the 1992 legislative campaign. This has potential consequences for democratic consolidation as strong political parties are widely viewed as a prerequisite for long-term democratic stability.[13]

Hsieh argues that the system makes factional politics almost inevitable and notes how 'In the Legislative Yuan today, fights among the numerous "secondary groups" within the KMT often are fiercer than those between the KMT and other parties.'[14] Moreover, Rigger argues that SVMM encourages candidate rather than party- or issue-based voting.[15] If we consider the democratic standards suggested by Grugel or Budge in

Chapter 3, then the candidate-centred nature of campaigning under SVMM could be taken as a similar negative feature of the system.

Another negative argument is that since candidates can win an election with a small proportion of the vote in districts with a large magnitude, this gives scope for radical politicians or parties to get elected. Thus, for instance, more radical politicians from the NP or DPP did get elected under SVMM but had less success under SMD. Hsieh compares how in 1989 DPP candidates ran on much more radical pro-independence platforms in the SVMM legislative election, but how its candidates for the SMD local executive contests steered clear of such issues.[16] Similarly, Lin Jih-wen (林繼文) has compared Chen Shui-bian's more radical positions in SVMM legislative elections with his more moderate stance in the 1994 SMD Taipei mayoral election.[17]

Some scholars have even suggested that SVMM encourages political corruption. The reasoning is that since candidates may just require a small percentage of the vote and voting is candidate centred, they can rely on vote buying, personal connections and even alliances with gangster groups to get elected.[18] Cases that are used to back up this argument include the long-term electoral success of Lo Fu-chu (羅福助) in Taipei County and Yen Ching-piao (顏清標) in Taichung County. Lo was a leading figure in the Celestial Alliance gangster group and a KMT aligned legislator in the 1990s, while Yen has a lengthy criminal record for corruption and firearms offences, but has an impressive electoral record and close KMT links. Therefore, from the late 1990s there were increasing calls for a major reform of Taiwan's electoral system. This seemed all the more urgent as Japan moved away from SVMM in major electoral reforms in 1993–4.

Taiwan's new electoral system

As I mentioned in the previous chapter, constitutional reforms approved in 2005 brought about a radical overhaul of Taiwan's parliamentary electoral system. First, the number of seats was halved from 225 to 113. Second, in place of the old SVMM system arose what was widely called the SMD two-vote system. In this system voters vote for a candidate in one of 73 SMD districts and cast a second vote for their preferred party. The party vote is distributed proportionally for parties receiving more than 5 per cent of the vote to allocate to a further 34 seats. The remaining six seats are for two three-seat districts reserved for aboriginals. The system was largely borrowed from Japan's 1993–4 model. The main differences are that Japan did not choose to halve its parliamentarians, and in Taiwan the SMD candidates could not also be included on the proportional representation party lists. Lastly, the proportion of seats allocated to SMD districts was higher in Taiwan than in Japan.

By comparing the results from 2008's legislative election in Tables 5.1 and 5.2 with elections under the old system, we can see the huge impact of the new system. Taiwan's electoral system has gone from being roughly proportional to highly disproportional. The KMT gained three-quarters of the seats with just 50 per cent of the vote in 2008, while the DPP increased its vote share to almost 37 per cent but saw its seat share fall to 24 per cent. The SMD system seemed to favour the KMT, which won almost all the district seats outside southern Taiwan.[19] The first election under the new system also saw the virtual disappearance of the smaller parties, which failed to win a single seat.[20] Although the smaller parties concentrated their efforts on the proportional representation party list, there was not enough split ticket voting for any of them to cross the 5 per cent threshold to qualify for seats. As voters became accustomed to the new electoral system, we can see how the results became slighty less disproportional in 2012. The DPP was able to reduce its seat deficit and the KMT's seat surplus declined. The election also saw the return of smaller parties, with the TSU and PFP exceeding the 5 per cent threshold. The DPP's landslide victory in the 2016 parliamentary election revealed that although the KMT has a systematic advantage, the 10 per cent vote swing in favour of the DPP allowed it to enjoy its best ever seat bonus. Moreover, smaller parties continued to increase their seats in parliament in 2016.

We can get a further picture of the impact of the new system on the district level in Table 5.8. This shows the two SMD Kaohsiung City Legislative Yuan Districts 4 and 5 in 2008, which are the equivalent of the five-seat Kaohsiung South under the old system we saw in Table 5.7. As we can see, the number of seats has been reduced by more than half. In 2001, the KMT and its ally had won only one seat and the Pan Greens four. But this time, each major party won one of the SMDs each. As we saw at the national level, third parties had effectively disappeared, concentrating competition between the two main parties. Lastly, the proportion of wasted votes is much higher under the SMD. In both districts in 2008, the almost 48 per cent of votes on the losing side were wasted votes. In contrast under, the old system if parties got their nomination strategy right, a voter's vote had a far greater chance of contributing to a winning candidate. Four years later in 2012, the DPP won back Kaohsiung City District 4. However, it went on to lose one of its safest seats, Kaohsiung City 5, because former President Chen's son stood as a rebel candidate, splitting the pro DPP vote and allowing the KMT to win with only 38 per cent.[21] More recently, in 2016 the DPP won a clean sweep of all SMD seats in southern Taiwan.

One major puzzle we face, especially considering the momentus impact of the new system is why did the DPP allow such an unfavourable system to be introduced when it was the ruling party? Naturally, the KMT and DPP both hoped to be rid of troublesome splinter parties; however, both had quite different ideal system preferences. Despite the problem of such a disproportional system, new reforms to Taiwan's electoral system were not on the political agenda until late in the Ma era. Reforming the system requires changing the constitution and, as we discussed in the previous chapter, the high threshold

Table 5.8 Kaohsiung City Legislative Districts 4 and 5 in 2008 (equivalent of Kaohsiung South in Table 5.7)

Kaohsiung City District 4		
Huang Chao-hui (黃昭輝) (i) (M)	DPP	46.6
Lin Ching-yuan (林景元) (M)	Independent	1.1
Liu Hui-wen (劉慧雯) (F)	Taiwan Farmers Party	0.8
Lin Chih-tsong (林志聰) (M)	Civil Party	0.2
Li Fu-hsing (李復興) (i) (M)	KMT	51.3
Kaohsiung City District 5		
Kuo Wen-cheng (郭玟成) (i) (M)	DPP	52
Tsao Wen-wen (曹文玟) (F)	Hakka Party	0.3
Yang Chang-chao (楊掌朝) (M)	(Minor party)	0.4
Chao Lian-chu (趙連出) (M)	(Minor party) KMT rebel	0.8
Yang Mei-lan (楊美蘭) (F)	Civil Party	0.4
Lin Kuo-cheng (林國正) (M)	KMT	46

Source: Central Election Commission.

Note: (i) = incumbent legislator, (F) = female, (M) = male for constitutional reform makes this challenging to achieve. Even at the time of writing, although the DPP had been supportive of limited reform prior to the 2016 elections, it appears no longer to be a party priority.

Election campaigning change and continuity

Elections campaigns are critical in a democracy. Campaigns are a central venue for determining policy and party leadership, distributing power and legitimating democratic government. The winners of an election thus claim to have won a mandate for their political manifesto and will argue that their defeated opponent's policies have been rejected by voters. Similarly, elections are a tool to make politicians accountable for their record in office, thus election outcomes are often taken as rewards or punishments for parties' achievements or failures in government.

Before moving on to examine patterns of change in political communication, it is useful to offer some definitions of the key concepts and introduce some potential frameworks of analysis. Pippa Norris defines political communication as 'an interactive process concerning the transmission of information among politicians, the news media and the public. The process operates downwards from governing institutions towards citizens, horizontally in linkages among political actors and upwards from public opinion towards authorities.'[22] She goes on to define campaigns as 'organized efforts to inform, persuade and mobilize.'[23]

Norris also suggests a typology of three stages in the development of political communication, from premodern to modern to postmodern campaigning.[24] Modernity in campaigning is marked by longer and more expensive campaigning, professionalization and an increased role of new and electronic media. Clearly, this framework is based on the evolution of campaigning in Western democracies, but it will be useful for comparing change in Taiwan's case.

For some scholars, the modern campaign is seen as synonymous with an Americanized campaign. According to Swanson and Mancini, 'campaigning in democracies around the world is becoming more and more Americanized as candidates, political parties and news media takes their cues from their counterparts in the United States'.[25] They claim that 'Many campaign methods and practices that have been adopted by other countries developed first in the United States.'[26] The key features they identify as part of this model are the (1) personalization of politics (candidate centred with the role of the party and ideology diminished), (2) scientificization of politics (professionalization), (3) detachment of parties from citizens (reduced membership), (4) autonomy of structures of communication (the political message is indirect via the media) and (5) shift from citizenship to spectatorship (reduced political participation).

Shelley Rigger suggests that there are two sides to Taiwanese campaigns – a public face and a private face.[27] The former includes practices like speeches, rallies and political advertising and is often called the propaganda battle (*wenxuan zhan*). This public face also includes attendance at traditional settings such as the weddings and funerals of constituents, as well as exploiting more modern practices such as Internet campaigning. The private face, or what Taiwanese often call the organizational battle (*zuzhi zhan*), refers to election mobilization using clientelistic methods. As Rigger explains, 'Clientelism is a political style in which the politicians (the patrons) form lasting relationships with people below them (their clients). These relationships are based on mutually beneficial exchanges. The patron gives the client access to the spoils of power and, in turn, the client supports the patron's political ambitions and activities.'[28] Vote buying is often a key component of the private face of election campaigning, with the vote brokers, or *tiau-a-ka,* purchasing votes and persuading voters on behalf of their political patron.

As we look at change in the Taiwanese campaigns, we should consider how useful these frameworks are for understanding patterns of political communication.

Campaigning in the immediate transition period, 1987–94

As discussed in Chapter 2, open political communication was dominated by the KMT under martial law. The democratic transition brought new opportunities for alternative forms of political communication, but also maintained much continuity.

Following the lifting of martial law, there was a gradual liberalization of Taiwan's political communication environment. Opposition parties took advantage of these changes to hold demonstrations and political rallies to try to get their message across and break the KMT monopoly on political communication. At the time, such political events attracted large numbers, especially as under martial law police had dealt with political rallies in the same kind of harsh manner as Communist authorities in Eastern Europe. Writing in the late 1980s, Tien stated, 'it is not unusual to have over twenty thousand to attend, compared to several hundred that show up at rallies for KMT candidates'.[29] The novelty of street demonstrations at the time was captured in the 1989 Taiwanese rap song titled *Song of Madness (zhuakuang ge)*. This describes the confusion of a country boy on seeing his first ever political rally on a visit to Taipei. The best received speeches were passionate, radical and often in Taiwanese. The atmosphere in KMT candidate rallies tended to be starkly different. There it often was the prospects of free banquet food, scantily dressed performers and red envelopes rather than political speeches that attracted attendees.

Although the ban on new newspapers was lifted in 1988, the overall media structure did not change radically in the transition period. The newspapers and electronic media remained dominated by the KMT. Coverage tended to be overwhelmingly on KMT politicians, and references to the opposition were largely negative. KMT political rituals such as the National Day rally would be broadcast live, while opposition events were subjected to news blackouts. Even after the transition this kind of news bias remained in effect. The main alternative media forms were political magazines and the *Independence Evening News (zili wanbao)*, both of which lacked the distribution networks that KMT publications had. The sense of political bias in the mainstream media is shown in Wan Jen's 1996 film *Super Citizen Ko* (超級國民). In a number of scenes, the protagonist views biased TV news reports of DPP demonstrations and parliamentary violence designed to reinforce the negative image of the DPP.

Despite these structural disadvantages, the DPP and other opposition groups were able to gain greater media attention through their political performances. Although opposition politicians were vastly outnumbered in the old parliaments, they drew attention through the quality of their speeches and performances. For instance, three DPP legislators, Chen Shui-bian, Lin Cheng-chieh (林政杰) and Hsieh Chang-ting (謝長廷), gained the nickname of the 'Three Musketeers' due to their lively speeches. Another key stage was the Central Election Commission's candidate policy forums that were organized during the campaign. These gave opposition politicians the opportunity to shine against their KMT rivals in front of the constituents. As Chu Kao-cheng (朱高正) recalled, 'In the past my main source of votes was the public policy platform meetings, as all the candidates were together. This was the best way for me to get votes.'[30]

Another major means of opposition political communication was what I call 'stunt politics'. At times, this involved a limited use of political violence in parliamentary settings. Two famous cases illustrate this. First was Chu Kao-cheng, the DPP legislator who gained the nickname Taiwan's 'Rambo' for his attacks in the late 1980s on the Legislative Yuan speaker. The second case occurred in 1990 during a banquet at the National Assembly for the last indirect presidential election. In front of President Lee Teng-hui, DPP National Assemblyman Huang Chao-hui (黃昭輝) began overturning table after table, spilling food, soup and wine everywhere.[31] At the time, the unfairness of the political system was the justification of such stunts, and in Huang's case he was protesting the arrest of his fellow DPP National Assemblyman. Such stunts did give opposition politicians cult status, media attention and often helped them win elections. Although the DPP's use of violent antics was mainly a form of political theatre with few real injuries, the KMT did try to paint the DPP as a violent party in its propaganda. As we will see in the next chapter, this was a negative image that the DPP struggled to shake off.

Stunt politics were not limited to parliamentary settings. One especially noteworthy event was when DPP candidate Lu Hsiu-yi (盧修一) promised his rally in November 1989 would feature the head of the World United Formosans for Independence, Guo Peihong (郭倍宏).[32] Since Guo was a blacklisted political exile who had been smuggled into Taiwan and was on the run from the police, the rally attracted a huge crowd.[33] After Guo had made his speech and given a press conference, the police were ready to arrest him. However, in unison Guo and the whole audience put on identical black masks and the lights were turned out, allowing Guo to escape in the confusion.[34] This stunt certainly paid dividends for Lu, who was the highest vote-getter in Taipei County that year. Of course, not all the stunts paid off electorally. A prime example was the Labour Party candidate and striptease artist Hsu Hsiao-tan (許曉丹). Hsu produced one of the most talked about newspaper advertisements of the 1989 campaign, which showed a naked Hsu breaking through a KMT flag and the slogan 'the breast resists the fist' (*naitou duikang quantou*).[35] Moreover, Hsu was able to attract large (mostly male) crowds for her campaign performances and social democratic appeals. Unfortunately for Hsu, breasts were not a critical determinant of voting behaviour, as she failed to win election in 1989, 1992 and 1995.

The emergence of political advertising

In this transition period the two main parties took quite different approaches to campaigning. With its superior organization and resources, the KMT was primarily reliant on the private face of campaigning. For the DPP and other opposition groups, their limited resources dictated an emphasis on the public face or propaganda battle.

One key change in this period was the liberalization of regulations prohibiting campaign advertising. In Table 5.9, I have tried to summarize some key trends in campaign advertising. The first step came in 1989 when for the first time newspaper advertisements were permitted. One scholar estimated that in 1989, NT$165,650,000 was spent by the KMT on newspaper campaign advertisements[36] which tended to be more focused on candidate image building compared to the more ideological and policy focus of DPP advertisements. In a trend that was to reoccur in most subsequent campaigns, KMT candidates were also far less likely to use their party badge or name on their advertisements than other parties.

Table 5.9 Development of newspaper and television election advertising in Taiwan, 1989–2016

Year	Number of newspaper ads	Broadcast time of TV ad (minutes)	Spending on TV ads (in New Taiwan dollars)
1989	Data N/A	No. TV ads	No TV ads Newspaper ads 165,650,000
1991	KMT: 34 DPP: 91 Total: 125	KMT: 149 DPP: 65 SDP: 31 Total: 245	Free on terrestrial channels
1992	KMT: 90 DPP: 83 Total: 173	KMT: 159 DPP: 75 SDP: 27 Total: 261	Free on terrestrial channels
1993	KMT: 27 DPP: 43 NP: 3 Total: 73	No TV ads	No TV ads
1994	KMT: 116 DPP: 88 NP: 18 Total: 222	Data N/A	Total: 23,665,000
1995	KMT: 97 DPP: 72 NP: 43 Total: 212	Data N/A	Total: 55,000,000
1996	KMT: 61 DPP: 47 NP: 19 NP Supported: 14 Total: 141	KMT: 5,490. DPP: 3,381 NP Supported: 2,614 Indep: 8,997★ Total: 20,482	KMT: 54,900,830 DPP: 33,815,333 NP Supported: 26,142,500 Indep: 89,970,000 Total: 204,828,663
1997	KMT: 21 DPP: 44 NP: 13 Total: 78	Data N/A	Data N/A KMT: 232,824,000 DPP: 158,745,000 NP: 37,308,000
1998	KMT: 110 DPP: 88 NP: 31 Total: 229	KMT: 15,580 DPP: 8,027 NP: 2,049 Total: 25,656	KMT: 119,482,000 DPP: 62,734,000 NP: 14,578,000 Total: 196,794,000
2000	KMT: 209 DPP: 94 NP: 16 PFP: 93 Total: 412	KMT: 28,212 DPP: 15,517 NP: 0 Soong: 12,314 Total: 56,043	KMT: 1,694,236,000 DPP: 747,539,000 PFP: 680,235,000 Total: 3,122,010,000
2001	KMT: 56 DPP: 44 NP: 90 PFP: 32 TSU: 16 Total: 238	Data N/A	KMT: 351,123,000 DPP: 153,469,000 NP: 0 PFP: 204,014,000 TSU: 32,933,000 Total: 741,539,000
2002	Data N/A	Data N/A	DPP: 343,973,000 KMT: 225,633,000
2004 Presidential	KMT: 155 DPP: 76 Total: 231	Data N/A	KMT: 184,164,000 DPP: 189,870,000 Total: 374,034,000

Table 5.9 continued

Year	Number of newspaper ads	Broadcast time of TV ad (minutes)	Spending on TV ads (in New Taiwan dollars)
2004 LY	KMT: 49 DPP: 69 PFP: 12 TSU 11 NP: 3 Total: 144	Data N/A	KMT: 4,976,000 DPP: 8,318,000 PFP: 0 TSU: 3,053,000 NP: 767,000 Total: 17,116,000
2005	KMT: 34 DPP: 39 TSU: 3 Total: 76	Data N/A	Data N/A
2008 LY	Data N/A	Data N/A	KMT: 86,166,000 DPP: 54,660,000 Total: 140,826,000
2008 Presidential	Data N/A KMT:138 DPP: 92 Total: 230	Data N/A	KMT: 20,951,000 DPP: 40,351,000 Total: 61,302,000
2012 Combined	KMT:53 DPP:57 PFP:30 TSU: 6 Total: 146		KMT: 201,898,000 DPP: 129,373,000 PFP: 3,584,000 TSU: 922,000 Total: 335,777,000
2016 Combined	KMT: 51 DPP: 28 PFP: 16 TSU: 4 NPP: 1 Total: 100		KMT: 27,078,000 DPP: 24,773,000 PFP: 6,172,000 TSU: 3,003,000 NPP: 0 Total: 61,026,000

Sources: Cheng Tzu-leong (1995); other data supplied by Rainmaker (潤利事業有限公司).

Note 1: 'Number of newspaper ads' refers to the frequency of ads appearing in the three main newspapers over the 31 days prior to each election: *China Times*, *Liberty Times* and *United Daily News*.
Note 2: In 1996, NP supported refers to the presidential candidates Lin Yang-kang and Hao Pei-tsun, who were not official NP candidates but received NP endorsement.
Note 3: The independent team in 1996 were Chen Li-an (陳履安) and Wang Ching-feng (王清峰).

A few advertisement slogans can give us a taste of the moment. KMT candidate Yang Shih-chiu said to voters, 'Don't let the National Father (Sun Yat-sen) weep' (*buyao rang guofu kuqi le*).[37] With the DPP in mind, the KMT's Jaw Shaw-kong appealed, 'They love to fight, so don't vote for them' (*tamen ai daren jiu buyao xuan tamen*).[38] While political advertising expert Cheng Tzu-leong (鄭自隆) questioned the appropriateness of the KMT's Chin Hui-chu's (秦慧珠) advertisement, which showed a group of female stars and the slogan 'Their first time' (*tamen de diyi ci*).[39] Overall, he rated the DPP's advertisements as much more outstanding. Cheng felt that this was partly because many DPP politicians had such rich propaganda experience from their *Tangwai* magazine days. DPP slogans that Cheng particularly noted included Chen Shui-bian's now famous 'Long live Taiwan independence' (*Taiwan duli wan wansui*) and Hsieh Chang-ting's 'Taiwan, community of destiny' (*Taiwan mingyun gongtongti*).[40] Another common DPP theme was what I call

the 'tragic Taiwan' appeal, which seeks sympathy for those that suffered political persecution under the KMT. An example of this was Ye Chu-lan's (葉菊蘭) use of the 'Widow
of Cheng Nan-jung' as a slogan.[41] Cheng Nan-jung (鄭南榕) had long fought for freedom
of speech and in 1989 chose suicide by self-immolation rather than be arrested for printing
a draft Taiwan Constitution.

The next stage in liberalization came with the first legal television election advertisements for the 1991 National Assembly and 1992 Legislative Yuan elections.[42] At this
point, Taiwan chose a model of election advertising closer to the UK Party Political
Broadcasts than the US free market approach. In other words, parties were allocated free
advertising time on the three terrestrial channels according to their number of nominated
candidates. As shown in Table 5.9, in 1991 the KMT received 149 minutes of TV
advertising, the DPP 65 and the Chinese Social Democratic Party (CSDP) 31, while in
1992 the KMT had 159 minutes, the DPP 75 and the SDP 27.[43] Cheng argues that the
quality of the KMT's TV advertisements was higher than those of the DPP in 1991, as
KMT ads were like normal TV ads, with simple messages and easy catchphrases.[44] In
contrast, many of the DPP's advertisements either contained messages too abstract for
ordinary voters to understand or involved long interviews with party leaders. Another
major difference was that the KMT had more advertisements attacking their opponents
while the DPP was more defensive. One KMT slogan gives a picture of the choice they
presented to voters: 'Reform or Revolution, Stability or Chaos, Prosperity or Recession'
(*gexin huo geming, anding huo baoluan, fanrong huo xiaotiao*).[45]

There was a significant improvement in the quality of the DPP's TV and newspaper
ads a year later. This was partly due to the efforts of its new propaganda department
chief, Chen Fang-ming (陳芳明). DPP advertisements were more focused on attacking
the KMT for political corruption and against KMT Premier Hau. Also, many DPP
advertisments employed humour to attack the KMT. However, there was some
continuity, such as the imagery of a tragic Taiwan in its appeals. A series of long DPP
advertisments told some tragic stories of political persecution under martial law. The
KMT continued to highlight the DPP's use of violence and also put stress on the popularity
of President Lee Teng-hui, an approach that became known as 'playing the Lee Teng-
hui card'. At the time, KMT advertisements were criticized as old-fashioned or in the
style of social education broadcasts.[46]

Come 1993, where was Taiwan located on those key frameworks that we set out at
the start of this section? Despite the advent of political advertising in the early 1990s, the
practices associated with what Rigger calls the private face of the campaign were still
dominant in the early 1990s. In a sign that television advertising had not yet revolutionized campaigns, there were no TV advertisements in 1993. Taiwan seemed to come
somewhere between Norris's premodern and modern campaign. Many traditional
Taiwanese style elements of campaigning remained visible. For instance, during campaigns
the streets would be lined with flags bearing candidates' names, reminiscent of Chinese
battle flags. These were often so common that they would block traffic lights and street
signs, causing 'democratic' traffic accidents. Election banquets, to the delight of the poor,
remained in vogue. Candidates would patrol their districts in campaign trucks, behind
which would be thrown firecrackers, again giving the campaign the atmosphere of a
traditional Chinese festival. Although UK door-to-door canvassing has never taken off
in Taiwan, politicians interact with voters by making appearances at weddings, funerals
and the open traditional markets. Chao and Myers report how 'A candidate in the
Sungshan section of Taipei hosted a large dinner party for voters, but when he spoke,

all eyes were riveted on the nude young woman he had asked to sit on the platform.'[47] When we consider how strippers have become a common ingredient in Taiwanese funerals, it is not surprising that some politicians have also incorporated the practice into their election activities.[48] This also adds to the festival nature of the campaign.

Taiwanese campaigns in the age of cable TV

The rapid growth of cable television during the 1990s had a transformative effect on Taiwanese campaigns – namely, cable television played a critical role in raising the importance of the propaganda battle compared to the organizational battle. In 1990, only 16.1 per cent of households subscribed to cable. However, this had risen to 68.1 per cent by 1998 and 84.4 per cent by 2013.[49] The 1993 Cable TV Act facilitated this rapid expansion in cable television. The number of cable channels has risen rapidly since the mid-1990s, bringing with it the establishment of numerous local 24–hour news channels and breaking the old KMT monopoly on the electronic media. This revolutionized election communication in Taiwan, offering politicians a new range of campaigning methods to reach voters directly in their living rooms.

One such method was election advertising. Making good election TV advertisements went from being a minor sideshow to becoming a prerequisite of a successful campaign. Just as in the US, Taiwanese newspapers analyse and compare the quality of the previous day's slots, which often become the subjects of everyday conversation.[50]

Table 5.9 shows three indices of how election advertising has developed since 1989. These are: (1) the number of newspaper election advertisements placed in the main three newspapers in the 31 days prior to each election; (2) the broadcast time for television advertisements in each campaign, and (3) the amount spent on television advertisements in each campaign. This table shows a number of significant trends.

First, the expenditure on newspaper advertisements rose throughout the 1990s, reaching its peak in 2000. Although the amount spent on newspaper advetisements has been overtaken by television spots, the number of newspaper advertisements has remained high in the post-2000 period. In fact, in the 2008 presidential campaign, the KMT spent NT$57,369,000 on newspaper advertisements, almost three times higher than its TV ad expenditure. This is partly because the cable TV market is so fragmented, while now there are only four major national daily newspapers. Therefore, newspaper advertisements often reach a wider audience.

Second, the role played in campaigns by television advertising has shot up since the arrival of cable TV in the mid-1990s. Taiwan shifted to a US-style free market in buying advertising time on cable channels. The degree of change is clear from the comparison of free television campaign ads shown in 1991 with the 56,043 minutes of purchased advertising time in 2000. The amount of election advertisements has meant that it is almost impossible to avoid exposure as such ads were even regularly shown on documentary channels such as National Geographic and kids' cartoon channels.

Third, both the newspaper and television columns show that after an advertising peak in 2000, there has been a decline in both the numbers of and expenditures on election advertisements. For high-level campaigns, TV ads remain the highest spending item, but in interviews with Taiwanese politicians after 2000, there was a consensus that television advertising was most effective in 1998 and 2000, but had become less effective since. In the post-2000 period, where elections are more competitive, parties have tended to spend more heavily, such as 2001, 2004 (presidential) and 2012. However, where polls suggested a clear winner, then parties have spent less, such as in 2008 and 2016. It also appears that combining national parliamentary and presidential elections voting days since 2012 has also led to reduced spending.

Fourth, the table shows how the KMT increasingly tried to win elections by out-spending its rivals in campaign advertising in most campaigns through to 2001. In the early 1990s, the KMT still felt that it could win elections with its combination of the organizational battle, friendly television coverage and traditional campaign methods. However, by the mid-1990s, the party leaders perceived these methods as less effective and so invested more in the propaganda battle. Therefore, in Table 5.9 we can see that from 1994 the KMT had more newspaper ads, TV ads and higher TV ad expenditure than its rivals in almost every election until 2001. The KMT's status as the richest polit-ical party in the world has enabled it to outspend its rivals, even after it became an opposition party. However, after the KMT lost power in 2000, there was parity in the two main parties' advertising spending in most elections. However, when it felt the need, the KMT was still able to outspend its rivals, such as in 2012.

Comparing Table 5.9 with election results in Tables 5.1 to 5.5 reveals that there is not a direct correlation between advertising spending and election results. Although the KMT rapidly increased its propaganda expenditure and vastly outspent its rivals through-out the 1990s, its vote share progressively declined from a high of 71.2 per cent in 1991 to only 23.1 per cent in 2000. In fact, in 2000 the KMT spent more on TV advertisements than the combined total of its two election rivals, but came in a poor third in the race.

Trends in election advertising that cannot be shown in Table 5.9 are the changes in the production quality and format of Taiwan's election slots. In 1991 and 1992, many advertisements resembled the long and serious party political broadcasts of the UK. By the mid-1990s, these had largely been replaced by the 30-second slots common in the US. Moreover, according to advertising scholar Hung Ya-hui (洪雅慧), the quality of Taiwanese election slots eventually overtook those of the US.[51] Although the opposition could not afford to purchase advertising on the scale of the KMT, there is a consensus that the quality of their advertisments has often exceeded those of their rival. As a former KMT party propaganda chief complained, 'The DPP has always been strong at propaganda.'[52]

The DPP was initially slow to recognize the increased significance of television adver-tising. Some in the DPP saw this as a factor in the party's loss of the Taipei mayoral election in 1998. That year, the KMT's Ma Ying-jeou performed well in a series of candidate image advertisements, which showed him jogging, chatting to city residents and making tough anti-corruption speeches. As a DPP campaign manager recalled:

> In 1998 we didn't adjust to media developments. We spent too much money on newspaper ads, but ignored two new trends: the TV ads and 24-hour news channels. We had less TV ads than they did and ours were of poorer quality.[51]

By the 2000 presidential election, the DPP had improved the quality of its television advertising. This election is viewed as being a battle of TV ads, as the DPP's Yu Mei-mei (余莓莓) commented, 'The only year that the TV ads were really effective was in 2000.'[52] The advertiements showed clearly the contrasting acting abilities of the three main candidates. A critical factor was that Lien was clearly uncomfortable about putting on a show. In fact, a KMT advertisement even admitted Lien's lack of showmanship compared with Chen and Soong. The slogan was, 'A person that can talk can't always get things done. A person that can get things done can't always talk.'[55] While Chen and Soong were veteran election campaigners, this was Lien's first campaign, as he had followed a career of unelected government positions, and it showed.[56] Lien clearly suffered from a lack of charisma, and when he did try to use advertisements to show his strength, the message was just too far from his public image to be convincing. For instance, in 2001 the KMT ran a TV ad that was a blatant copy of a Nike football boots ad, with Lien (in place of Ronaldo and Luis Figo) beating an assortment of monsters at football. In contrast, both the opposition candidates James Soong and Chen Shui-bian were far more comfortable at acting in TV ads. For instance, many voters were impressed with Soong's advertisement showing him trying to help flood victims and then contrasting this with Lien's apparent indifference at the disaster zone. Once again, the candidates who gave the best political theatre did the best in this campaign, with the DPP's Chen winning the election with 39 per cent, closely followed by the independent Soong with 36 per cent, while the KMT's Lien gained the party's record low vote share of 23 per cent.

Another major consequence of the rise of cable TV has been the proliferation of political talk shows. While in the UK there are only one or two shows such as *Question Time* per week, at their peak in Taiwan there were at least ten shows each night.[57] In these shows politicians from the major political parties debate the issues of the day, offering them free advertising time. As DPP legislator Lai Chin-lin (賴勁麟) explained, 'They can increase your exposure and make you better known. When you're out electioneering you can only meet a minority of constituents. If you can appear on TV, especially if it's a channel with high viewing rates, many people can see you.'[58] There was particular pressure for urban-based politicians to regularly appear on these shows. For instance, many of the politicians I interviewed in 2000–1 appeared on at least four shows a week. In the initial post-2000 period, I held a very positive view of these shows, arguing that they contributed to the high levels of political knowledge among the Taiwanese electorate. More recently, changes in the nature of the call-in shows have caused me to be more critical of their impact. Since 2004, the number of these shows has declined, suggesting they are less popular, but my main concern is that they no longer offer a diverse range of political opinions. Instead, the guests on the shows sing from the same hymn sheet. Thus, shows now are almost exclusively populated by representatives of either the Green or Blue camp. Moreover, elected or party politicians now are a minority, as the shows are now dominated by more extreme professional political pundits, known in Taiwan as the 'famous mouths' (*mingzui*).[59]

The popularization of cable TV has allowed televised candidate debates to become a regular feature of every campaign. The precedent was set in Taiwan's first live televised candidate debate for the 1994 Taipei mayoral contest. The DPP's Chen Shui-bian was scathing in his criticism of the incumbent KMT mayor, but also attempted to show his own competence in governance. The NP's Jaw Shaw-kong gave by far the most theatrical performance, opening with the statement, 'Taiwan is going to be destroyed! Destroyed in the Nazi Fascist hands of the DPP!'[60] In a later exchange Jaw challenged Chen, 'I shout "Long live the Republic of China." Do you dare to shout "Long live the Republic of China, long live the Republic of China, long live the Republic of China?"' Pundits concluded that the winners of the debate had been the NP's Jaw and DPP's Chen, while all agreed that the KMT's Huang Ta-chou had performed very poorly. This was not surprising considering that Huang had been a government appointed mayor and had never stood for any elected offices before. In contrast, both Chen and Jaw had been star legislators since the late 1980s. The candidates' debate performances were reflected in the actual election results, in which Chen won, while Jaw came second.

The rise in 24-hour cable news has also had an impact on the speeches that political leaders give. While in the past no more than a few soundbites from a speech would be shown on the TV news, since the late 1990s the cable news channels have broadcast rallies live. This has meant that a different speech is needed for each rally and that the speech must be written to appeal to both the rally and TV audiences. Within the DPP, it is felt that initially the DPP's star politician Chen Shui-bian failed to adjust to this new stage, which damaged his 1998 mayoral re-election campaign. As the DPP's Chang Yi-shan (張益贍) explained:

> Before, Chen Shui-bian tended to use mainly Taiwanese in his rally speeches. With much Taiwanese slang, he tried to incite the audience. However, this kind of speech came across very differently to a middle-class audience, and this gave the other side much ammunition to attack Chen Shui-bian.[61]

Therefore, following Chen's 1998 defeat, he began using both Mandarin and Taiwanese, stopped making unscripted speeches and created a professional speech-writing team.

Casting citizens in the role of spectators in campaigns?

The above descriptions of the increasing role that television plays in Taiwanese election campaigns should not be taken as meaning that the electorate has become armchair voters or what Swanson and Mancini refer to as 'casting citizens in the role of spectators'.[62] In fact, since the late 1990s the reverse has happened, as citizen participation in election activities has actually increased.

By the mid-1990s, the old-style outdoor political rally had lost its novelty and voters were no longer so attracted by serious political speeches. Politicians who still persisted with this method, such as Chu Kao-cheng and Lin Cheng-chieh, failed to win election in both 1998 and 2001. Instead, these older-style rallies and speeches have been replaced by a new style of televised mass rally. One of the first political figures to adapt to the new media environment was the DPP's Propaganda Chief from 1995 to 1997, Chen Wen-chien (陳文茜). She tried to liven up the DPP's election rallies to give the party a more modern image that could attract younger voters. Chen designed rallies that would look good on both TV news and also for rally audiences. The most famous of these were the Spice Girls Campaigning Team (*lamei zhuxuan tuan*) rallies of 1997 that combined scantily dressed dancers with pop music, short political speeches and the chance for the audience to directly address questions to party leaders. For this, Chen was criticized by some party elders as trivializing politics. However, the election results, particularly in 1997 when the DPP vote share exceeded that of the KMT for the first time, ensured that even after Chen left the DPP, the party continued its more youth-orientated rallies.

Since the late 1990s. these televised campaign rallies have become a competition in themselves. In the 2000 presidential election, there was a clear contest over which party could hold the largest and most passionate rallies. Although at times the KMT was able to muster larger crowds than the DPP in 2000, on close observation I found that many participants were forced to go by their work units or were being paid to attend. James Soong's rallies in 2000 showed how well he had adapted his election rally performances. Soong is from the Mainlander ethnic community, but he increased his nationwide appeal by learning Taiwanese. Although not a great orator, Soong had the charisma to attract and entertain large crowds. Soong responded to the rise in Taiwanese identity by projecting a more inclusive Taiwanese image in his performances.[63] For instance, in his 2000 rallies Soong appealed to all ethnic communities by mixing his Mandarin speeches with slogans in Hakka, Taiwanese and even aboriginal languages.

Despite the rise in television campaigning, the significance of mass election rallies actually increased after 2000. There was a clear correlation between the increasing emphasis on mass rallies and reduction in spending on television advertisements. The 2004 presidential election was even more a battle of rallies than those witnessed four years earlier. The DPP's keynote political event was the Hand in Hand Rally featuring a human chain linking the far north with the far south of Taiwan that was attended by at least one and a half million people. This event was designed to show Taiwanese unity in the face of the PRC missile threat. In contrast, the KMT held a series of simultaneous anti-Chen rallies on 13 March under the slogan of 'Change the President, Save Taiwan' (*huan zongtong jiu Taiwan*) in which up to three million people participated. Since 2004, although the rally phenomenon has remained central to election campaigns, my impression is that subsequent campaigns have struggled to match the levels of participation seen that year. Nevertheless, despite the rise in TV campaigning, Taiwanese voters have not been relegated to the role of spectators.

The use of Internet campaigning

Since the mid-1990s, one rapidly developing facet of what Pippa Norris calls the post-modern campaign has been Internet campaigning. There has been a huge surge in the number of Internet users in Taiwan, from only 603,000 users in 1996, to 10.46 million in 2008 and 17.64 million in 2014.[64] Taiwan's parties have adapted rapidly to this new means of political communication, and by the late 1990s all political parties had developed websites that are high quality, state-of-the-art and content rich. In addition, the vast majority of legislative and elected local executive politicians also have set up their own websites. Of course, there is a huge variety in the quality of these individual politicians' sites. Politicians from urban-based constituencies tend to have the most extensive sites and employ full-time Web managers, while rural-based politicians interviewed often were unsure whether they even had a website. In fact, in 2001 advertising consultant Fu He-kang (伏和康) was still advising against his clients investing too heavily in campaign websites.[65] My interviews since 2004 suggest that parties are placing far more importance on Internet campaigning and investing more resources on this method, particularly during presidential campaigns. Jonathan Sullivan has shown how recently parties and candidates have enthusiastically adopted Web 2.0 tools for communicating with constituents and voters.[66] In the first edition, I noted: 'the impact of (new media) is not yet as great as TV or newspaper advertising as the largest group of Internet users are under 30, the cohort least likely to vote.' However, the increasing importance of the Internet and social media for political communication has been clearly apparent since 2012. In addition to purchasing TV time, mainstream parties also can share their advertisements on YouTube and social media. In fact, now many advertisements only appear on the Internet and this has served to reduce overall advertising spending. This has benefited smaller parties as they were unable to raise the funds to purchase TV ad time. For example, the NPP and GPT produced a number of TV ads in the 2016 campaign, but these were only distributed via YouTube and social media. The fact that the NPP was able to enter parliament in

2016 despite almost no use of traditional media reveals how new technology is changing political communication. With the continued expansion of Internet and social media usage, its electoral importance will continue to increase. From our perspective of being students of Taiwan politics, the party and candidate websites and social media are a rich research resource, as they allow us to study Taiwanese politics without leaving home.

The rise of political consultants

As predicted in the modern and Americanized models of election campaigning, there has been a professionalization of electioneering in Taiwan. Parties have increasingly sought the help of experts in both polling and advertising. However, these experts have tended to play only an advisory role, with campaigns remaining dominated by party politicians. As in many Western democracies (excluding the US), Taiwan's election consultants have tended to be incorporated within the political parties, rather than operating as independent political consultants.

In addition to making use of commercial and academic survey centres, Taiwan's two leading parties have invested heavily in establishing their own high-tech survey centres. Particularly within the DPP, the head of the survey department has become a powerful party position. The DPP has paid much more attention to public surveys in designing its election campaigns than the KMT. As the advertising expert Fu He-kang explained, 'its [the DPP's] election campaigns have always been based on the results of opinion surveys', while in contrast, the 'KMT doesn't seriously [use surveys] to analyze with which kind of voters and what kind of situation it is the weakest and how to tackle these weaknesses'.[67]

In Taiwan, opinion polls are also viewed as powerful campaign tools. On the eve of voting day, candidates often cite polls in advertisements known as 'Saving Ads' (*qiangjiu guanggao*) to show that they are on the borderline between election and defeat and need your sacred vote to ensure election.[68] In a three-horse race, a common tactic is to cite polls to prove that a rival is already out of the race and that their supporters should switch allegiance. For instance, in the 2000 presidential election, the KMT used polls to convince voters to abandon independent candidate Soong and unite behind the KMT's candidate to defeat the DPP's Chen Shui-bian.[69] However, polls are often misused in Taiwanese campaigns, with doctored polls or polls from unknown polling organizations appearing in newspapers and party propaganda. An example of the way polls can be manipulated was the KMT's practice in 2000 of placing advertisements in leading newspapers that were disguised to look like the newspapers' survey analyses proving that only the KMT candidate could save the island from war.[70] As it is believed that opinion polls are highly influential on voting behaviour, Taiwan's Election and Recall Law prohibits the release of opinion poll results in the last ten days of presidential campaigns.

Since the commencement of legal campaign advertising in the early 1990s, Taiwan's leading parties have sought the help of advertising companies to design their campaign propaganda. However, all major parties have remained suspicious of giving too much power to outsiders, and thus political consultants in Taiwan have never had the same influence on the design of election campaigns as those in the US. Delving further, there are variations in the roles that these experts have in parties within Taiwan itself. This is due in part to the different organizational structures within individual parties. For example, in the DPP the Propaganda Chief has the freedom to design the election campaign in conjunction with selected advertising experts. For instance, in 2000 when

DPP propaganda chief Lo Wen-chia (羅文嘉) teamed up with advertising expert Fan Ke-chin (範可欽), they were able to create one of the best designed and effective election campaigns. In contrast, there is much more political interference from above in the more hierarchical KMT, which affects the quality of the advertising product. As Hung Ya-hui explained regarding the KMT's 2000 campaign, '[it] used a number of ad agencies, and there were many high-level figures to please. When the ad companies were happy with something, the big shots insisted on several revisions. When the KMT was satisfied, the ad companies were not.'[71] The impact of political consultants on Taiwan's elections should not be exaggerated. This was made clear when Fan Ke-chin switched to working on the KMT's 2001 parliamentary campaign. Despite a series of well-designed slots, the electorate responded by giving the KMT its worst ever parliamentary results.

Personalization instead of issues

The Americanized model of election campaigns predicts a dominance of personalities and images at the expense of debate over substantive political issues. During Taiwan's martial law period, elections were already candidate centred. Since Taiwan's liberalization and democratic transition, though candidates remain a critical variable affecting voting behaviour, their importance has declined relative to party identification and issue voting.

I attempted to address the question of the nature of Taiwan's political propaganda in a series of content analysis studies. Table 5.10 shows the results from newspaper ad analysis in the 1990s and post-2000 period. In both eras I found that propaganda was issue rich, with political corruption, democracy and Taiwan independence issues especially salient. Liu Tsung-wei's (劉從葦) study reached a similar conclusion that parties do stress issues in his study of legislative election gazettes.[72] More recently, Jonathan Sullivan conducted a content analysis of both TV and newspaper ads, dividing appeals into issues, ideology and candidate traits. Although he used a different methodology, his conclusion was similar. He found that at least 75 per cent of appeals belonged to issues and ideology, while only 17 per cent of newspaper ads and 25 per cent of TV ad appeals focused on candidate traits.[73] Naturally, the trend in television advertisement from party political broadcasts to 30-second slots has led to greater stress on image rather than on issues. However, the high issue content of newspaper advertisements, the regularity of political talk shows and televised election debates and the intensive media coverage of campaign issues ensure that issues are still central to Taiwanese political communication.

Negativity in Taiwanese political campaigns

Another feature that is often associated with the modern campaign is a high level of negative appeals. A number of scholars have highlighted that Taiwan also suffers from such problems. For instance, Gary Rawnsley talks of the island's 'extraordinary scale of negative campaigning.'[74] A number of accusations and adertisements have been used to support the claim that Taiwanese campaigns are so negative that they undermine its democracy. For instance, there was a series of especially provocative KMT ads in 2004 that tried to associate Chen with Hitler, Osama Bin Laden and Saddam Hussein. However, Sullivan has convincingly challenged these assertions with empirical data showing that Taiwanese campaigns actually have a similar level of negativity with the US, and that there is not a clear linear trend towards greater negativity.[75] One of his most interesting findings is that negative advertisements actually can have a positive side. In other words,

Table 5.10 Issue content of Taiwanese political propaganda

Ranking	1990s newspaper ads (Fell)	2000–4 newspaper ads (Fell)	Election gazettes (1989–98) (Liu's study)
1	Political corruption	Party: positive	Welfare state expansion
2	Party: positive	Taiwan nationalism	Technology and infrastructure
3	Taiwan independence: negative	Candidate: positive	Non-economic demographic groups
4	Candidate: negative	Diluted Taiwan independence	Education expansion
5	Government ability	Economic growth and prosperity	Social justice
6	Party: negative	Taiwan independence: negative	Law and order
7	Democracy	Democracy	Environmental protection
8	Other parties' lack of government competence	Political stability	Political corruption
9	Diluted Taiwan independence	Political corruption	Efficiency of the Legislative Yuan
10	Political stability	Other parties' lack of government competence	Productivity
11	Women	Chinese nationalism	

Source: Fell (2006a: 28; 2005c: 23)

Note: The second and third columns show the top issue mentions in election newspaper advertising in the 1990s and 2000–4 periods. These are based on Fell's content analysis studies. The fourth column shows the top issue mentions in Liu Tsung-wei's content analysis of legislators' policy proposals in election gazettes between 1989 and 1998.

he shows that negative advertisements are far more issue-rich and backed up with evidence. Thus, these negative advertisments can actually serve a greater democratic educational role.

The decline of old campaigning methods?

With the rapid rise of modern campaigning methods, we would expect electioneering practices that originated in the martial law era and democratic transition period to gradually fade away as they lose effectiveness. This section examines the degree that the modern propaganda battle has taken the place of (1) the organizational battle, (2) traditional campaign methods and (3) direct action. Although certain traditional methods have lost their effectiveness, others have been highly resilient and have remained influential in slightly modified forms.

The decline of the organizational battle?

During interviews with KMT politicians in the post-2000 period, there was a consensus that because of the declining effectiveness of its organizational battle, the party had been forced to pay more attention to the propaganda battle. Although it is difficult to prove empirically, most believe the effectiveness of vote buying has declined considerably. As former KMT Secretary General Hsu Shui-teh (許水德) lamented, 'Before, vote buying worked using just scarves or other things. Now offer people hundreds of dollars and they still don't care.'[76] However, it appears that vote buying still is common in rural regions, and new forms of the practice have appeared. For instance, gambling on election results is seen in Taiwan as a novel form of vote buying. This involves a candidate's agent offering favourable odds on the preferred politician winning election, hoping that this will encourage the gambler to campaign hard to win the bet.[77] The large number of vote-buying cases in 2008 and 2009 suggests that despite repeated anti-vote buying crackdowns, the practice remains an invaluable electoral tool for some politicians.

A facet of the organizational battle that the KMT was highly reliant on during the martial law era was mobilizing numerous pro-KMT groups, such as trade unions, civil servants and the military. However, after democratization the KMT found its hold on these groups had declined, as many of these voters became attracted by other parties' issue positions or grew tired of having their votes taken for granted. For instance, on the election eve in March 2000, I met China Steel workers who were pressured to attend the KMT rally in Kaohsiung. However, many just turned up briefly and then either went home or went to the livelier DPP or Soong rallies.

One area of campaigning that has shown the least change has been candidate support organizations and the provision of constituency services. Even today, although a candidate may be initially elected due to having a good reputation, party identification or a special issue focus, when striving for re-election it is essential to create a strong local support organization and to be seen as having given constituents 'service' (*fuwu*). The term 'service' refers to the provision of benefits such as free legal advice or helping constituents in their dealings with officials. The decline of the NP was closely related to its failure to comprehend the importance of organization and service in Taiwan's electoral politics. In 1995, after the NP's fine election performance, its magazine editor Yang Tai-shun warned: 'If the NP is unable to create grassroots organization and an image of party service, it is doubtful that the party will still be able to win votes with the appeal of highly educated candidates and anti-money politics.'[78] In interviews with NP politicians, it was clear that many looked down upon the provision of the services that Taiwanese voters expect from politicians. As a NP party worker explained: 'The NP is not based on service, but ideals. DPP candidates will help constituents when they get in trouble with the police and threaten the police. There is no way that the NP would do this.'[79] Unfortunately for the NP, it failed to heed Yang's advice, and this contributed to its electoral downfall.

Fading away of traditional campaign methods?

In addition to the new campaign methods, it remains essential for candidates at all levels not to neglect traditional electioneering practices. In fact, many of these have become part of the televised campaign. Months prior to voting day, the 24-hour news channels show the candidates on the streets shaking hands or attending religious ceremonies or sporting events. Another feature of traditional campaigning that has transferred well into the modern campaign has been the use of candidate motorcades, behind which firecrackers are set off to attract attention. In fact, in the 2004 election assassination attempt on Chen Shui-bian, it was because of the noise of the firecrackers that Chen's security and TV camera crews were initially unaware of gunshots.

Personal contact also remains highly significant in Taiwan's elections. Therefore, as mentioned briefly above, candidates not only go out and shake countless hands during their campaigning, but they must also spend much time attending weddings and funerals. One PFP politician I interviewed in August 2001 explained how relieved he was that it was Chinese ghost month, as this meant there were no weddings to attend.[80] Such practices are frowned upon by many highly educated politicians, but remain popular among voters. As NP legislator Yu Mu-ming (郁慕明) complained, 'The further south you go, the more they demand. If your family has a funeral, they want you to attend. Like [DPP legislator] Chu Hsing-yu (朱星羽), he'll kneel and crawl in from the door [at a funeral]. Therefore he can get votes and gets elected every time he stands.'[81]

In the 2001 Legislative Yuan election, the NP paid the price for not embracing such traditional campaign methods. In this election the NP's high-profile Chairwoman, Hsieh Chi-ta (謝啟大) stood for election in one southern city in an attempt to expand party seats outside of northern Taiwan. In 2001, I spent a day as an observer accompanying Hsieh on the campaign trail. She was out of her depth in this constituency, unable to speak Taiwanese and unfamiliar with the city. When we visited a temple, Hsieh clearly was unsure how to interact with the worshippers and felt uncomfortable in the midst of Taiwanese speakers. In that campaign, Hsieh spent more on newspaper advertisements than the combined total of the NP's previous six campaigns. However, such modern campaign methods did not pay off, as the NP not only lost in that city, but was wiped out in the whole of Taiwan.[82]

Taiwanese elections remain colourful and festive occasions. Although the candidate election banners have become less common in Taipei, where city government regulations only allow flags at candidate campaign headquarters, as soon as you cross the boundary into Taipei County, you face a sea of flags fighting for voters' attention. In addition, though many intellectuals view election banquets as a form of vote buying, the practice still persists in rural areas. In urban Taiwan these have been replaced by fundraising meals. However, these differ from their counterparts in the US where the main objective is to attract celebrities or the business elite. In Taiwan, these events are more of a competition between candidates to see who can attract the most people. As former DPP legislator Huang Huang-hsiung (黃煌雄) explained about his 1995 campaign, 'He [a fellow DPP candidate] could only manage 480 tables. But I could get 1,000 tables. That is more than 10,000 people.'[83]

Fading away of direct action?

During the late 1980s, many Taiwanese viewed limited political violence as tolerable in the light of the unfair political and media environment. However, by the mid-1990s, the island's democratic transition and media liberalization had basically been completed and all restrictions on freedom of speech removed. As a result, the opposition DPP decided to shift its tactics from street protests to parliamentary opposition. Audience tastes had shifted and violence appeared no longer justifiable. In fact, most opposition politicians had dropped direct action by this point. The price for DPP legislators such as Stella Chen (陳婉真), Huang Chao-hui and Chen San-si (陳三思) who still used direct action, was defeat in the December 1995 Legislative Yuan elections. In the words of the *Far Eastern Economic Review*'s Julian Baum, Stella Chen 'had exhausted the patience of voters with her violent tactics in parliament'.[84]

After the change in ruling parties in May 2000, there appears to have been a resurgence of direct action. In 2004, the KMT ran a series of large-scale marches contesting the fairness of the presidential election, a number of which turned violent.[85] In fact, the aftermath of this election saw the most serious political violence since the late 1980s. PFP legislators led their supporters to attack the Central Election Commission offices and attempted to break down the gates of the Kaohsiung District Court with a campaign truck. Moreover, after a lull in parliamentary violence, such practices have re-emerged since 2004, once again helping increase Taiwan's global YouTube visibility. It will be interesting to see whether voters will punish more violent politicians in future elections, as we saw in the mid-1990s.

Conclusion: do election campaigns really matter?

A final question should now be: can Taiwanese campaigns change electoral outcomes? This may seem like an odd question considering the huge amounts spent in the process. Politicians and pundits often take the impact of campaigning for granted. Finding empirical data to prove campaigns matter has been easier said than done. In my studies I have tried to show the linkage between issue emphasis strategies and political performances with electoral outcomes. I will return to the question of parties' electoral success and failure in the next chapter by examining their issue appeals in more detail. New research techniques such as focus groups and experimental studies are beginning to give us a clearer picture of campaign effects. However, Taiwan's political communication remains an underdeveloped field, at least in English, as some of its leading scholars only publish in Chinese. I am still waiting for a definitive volume on Taiwanese elections.

Before ending this chapter, I urge you to pay Taiwan a visit during election season. You may, like me, come away wishing elections in your own country could learn some lessons from Taiwan.

Discussion questions

1   What are the most important turning points in Taiwan's electoral history?
2   What are the consequences of Taiwan's electoral systems?
3   How should the system be reformed?
4   Assess levels of continuity and change in Taiwanese elections.
5   Compare Taiwanese electioneering with that of other new or mature democracies.
6   How useful are concepts of modernization and Americanization in understanding Taiwanese campaigns?
7   Do Taiwanese elections promote or undermine democracy?
8   Can we prove a relationship between Taiwanese campaigns and election results?
9   Have the Internet and social media transformed political communication in Taiwan?

Further reading

Rich, Timothy and Jonathan Sullivan. 2016. 'Elections and the Electoral System.' In *Handbook of Modern Taiwan Politics and Society*. Abingdon: Routledge. Useful and up-to-date review of electoral politics.

Rigger, Shelley. 1999. *Politics in Taiwan*. London: Routledge. Sections on the electoral system (Chapter 2), martial law electioneering (Chapter 4) and 1989 (Chapter 6) are especially relevant to this chapter.

Sullivan, Jonathan. 2009. 'Campaign Advertising in Taiwanese Presidential Elections'. *Journal of Contemporary China*, 18(61): 675–88. This short article gives a taste of the groundbreaking research Sullivan has started conducting on Taiwan's political communication.

Tien, Hung-mao. 1989. *The Great Transition*. Taipei: SMC Publishing. Chapter 7 on electoral politics is a useful structured account of late martial law elections.

Useful websites

http://esc.nccu.edu.tw/english/ – Election Study Center, National Chengchi University. This offers an unrivalled online database on elections results and key trends in political attitudes in Taiwan since 1992.

http://frozengarlic.wordpress.com/ – This blog, *Frozen Garlic*, written by political scientist Nathan Batto, is the best place to find detailed and academic analysis of developments in Taiwanese electoral politics. I look forward to updates with bated breath.

www.youtube.com – Searching can offer huge numbers of clips of Taiwanese election rallies, talk shows and election advertisements. The only thing missing are clips from the 1990s.

Notes

1 Norris, 'Campaign Communications', 127–46.
2 Nathan Batto's wonderful electoral politics blog, *Frozen Garlic*, available online at: http://frozengarlic.wordpress.com/category/electoral-system/
3 The minister in question was Yaung Chih-liang (楊志良), see 'China Times: Elections hijack Taiwan' on Central News Agency's Focus Taiwan News website, available online at: www.etaiwannews.com/etn/news_content.php (accessed 12 March 2011); to get a taste of how I joined this debate, see Ho Ai Li, 'Taiwan's Polls Poser,' *Straits Times*, 24 March 2010, available online at: www.asianewsnet.net/news.php?sec+3&id+10924 (accessed 12 March 2011).
4 To say that these years did not feature election campaign is not entirely accurate as 1999, 2003, 2007, 2011 and 2015 saw extensive campaigning for the presidential elections held early the next year. The final indirect presidential election was held in March of the 1990s.
5 Although the DPP won the same number of seats (six) as it did in 1989, the total number of seats had increased from 21 to 23 and, having won a by-election in 1992 in Penghu, the DPP had gone into the 1993 election with seven seats.
6 Blue and Green are the colours chosen because they are the principal colours of the KMT and DPP flags respectively.
7 Rigger, *Politics in Taiwan*, 21.
8 In the final election under this electoral system in 2004, there were 225 legislative seats, divided into 168 districts seats and two four-seat Aboriginal districts elected by SVMM and two nationwide proportional representation districts of 41 and 8 seats respectively.
9 Hsieh, 'The SNTV System and its Political Implications', 201.
10 For an example of the DPP's vote allocation appeal, see its newspaper advertisement in *United Daily News*, 10 December 2004, A10.
11 Duverger, *Political Parties*, 217 and 239.
12 The other successful case for the Pan Blue allied parties was Hsu Ching-yuan (徐慶元) winning Taitung for the PFP for one term only in 2001. In 2005, the PFP candidate won the Lienchiang local executive post with just 2,592 votes. In contrast, the winning candidate for Taipei County received almost one million votes.
13 Lipset, 'The Indispensability of Political Parties,' 48–55.
14 Hsieh, 207–8.
15 Rigger, 43–44.
16 Hsieh, 209
17 Cited in Rigger, 44.
18 Hsieh, 209.
19 The only DPP victories outside the south in 2008 were Taipei County 2 and Taipei County 3.

20 This statement is debatable as at least on paper the PFP did win one aboriginal seat in 2008. However, since most PFP politicians actually stood as KMT candidates, the party could arguably be viewed as no more than a faction within the KMT by this time.
21 Due to the merging of Kaohsiung city and county, after 2012 Kaohsiung City District 4 became District 7 and Kaohsiung District 5 became District 9.
22 Norris, 127.
23 Ibid.
24 Ibid., 133–4.
25 Swanson and Mancini, *Politics, Media, and Modern Democracy*, 4.
26 Ibid.
27 Rigger, 41.
28 Ibid.
29 Tien, *The Great Transition*, 183.
30 Interview with author, Kaohsiung, 9 October 2001.
31 This is the same Huang Chao-hui listed as losing the election in 2008 in Kaohsiung City in Table 5.8.
32 For the case of Guo Peihong I have followed Chao and Myers's Romanization.
33 Guo was one among hundreds of Taiwanese on a blacklist that the government banned from returning to Taiwan because of their political activities abroad.
34 Cheng, *Campaign Advertising*, 298.
35 Ibid., 299.
36 Ibid., 293.
37 Ibid., 294.
38 Ibid., 294.
39 Ibid., 295.
40 Ibid., 296.
41 Ibid., 297.
42 Unfortunately, these advertisements are quite hard to view. The only place I managed to see them was at the Wu San-lien Foundation: 10th Floor, 215, Nanking East Road, Section 3, Taipei City.
43 The only other parties qualifying for free time were the Non Partisan Alliance in 1991 and the Truth (*Zhenli*) Party in 1992.
44 Cheng, 303.
45 Ibid., 303
46 Ibid., 314.
47 Chao and Myers, *The First Chinese Democracy*, 235.
48 For more on the colourful world of funeral strippers in Taiwan, see Marc Moskowitz. 2011. *Dancing for the Dead: Funeral Strippers in Taiwan* (DVD).
49 The 1990 figure is from Chiu and Chan-Olmsted. 'The impact of cable television on political campaigns in Taiwan', 491–509; the 1998 and 2013 figures are from Directorate-General of Budget, Accounting and Statistics, available online at: http://eng.stat.gov.tw/ct.asp?xItem= 36500&ctNode=3480&mp=5 (accessed 9 February 2016).
50 For an example of newspaper coverage of election slots, see *China Times,* 6 December 1991, 6. In the elections I have observed, election advertisements were especially popular dinner table topics in 1998 and 2000.
51 Hung Ya-hui, interview by author, Taipei, 18 June 2001.
52 Former KMT Propaganda Chief, interview by author, Taipei, 19 October 2001.
53 Chang Yi-shan, interview by author, Taipei, 23 October 2001.
54 Yu Mei-mei, interview by author, Taipei, 27 September 2001.
55 The advertisement compared Lien's modesty, hard work and numerous achievements while Premier with Chen's big showmanship but alleged lack of policy achievements while Taipei Mayor.
56 Although this was only Soong's second election campaign, he had been a key figure in KMT election planning since 1989 and first appeared on a television campaign slot in 1991.
57 My impression is that these shows reached peak popularity in the immediate post-2000 period.
58 Lai Chin-lin, interview by author, Taipei, 25 September 2001.
59 The term *mingzui,* meaning 'famous mouth', began to be widely used after 2004 to refer to the pundits that appear nightly on the politics talk shows. Generally, these *mingzui* are not

elected politicians but offer viewers highly partisan and often extreme analysis of Taiwan's political scene. For more on politics talk shows, see Chu, 'Political call-in shows in Taiwan: Animating crisis discourse through reported speech'.

60 These quotes are based on my viewing of a recording of the debate viewed at Wu San-lien Foundation.
61 Chang Yi-shan, interview by author, Taipei, 23 October 2001.
62 Swanson and Mancini, *Politics, Media, and Modern Democracy*, 252.
63 Surveys show that respondents self-identifying as Taiwanese rose from 16 per cent 1989 to 41.6 per cent in 2001. For details, see Chapter 8.
64 The 1996 and 2008 figures are from Directorate-General of Budget, Accounting and Statistics, *Taiwan, Republic of China 2009, Statistics*, available online at: http://eng.dgbas.gov.tw/public/data/dgbas03/bs2/yearbook_eng/y131.pdf (accessed 12 March 2011). For the figure for 2014, see Taiwan Network Information Study, available online at: www.twnic.net.tw/download/200307/20140820d.pdf (accessed 3 April 2017).
65 Fu He-kang, interview by author, Taipei, 1 November 2001.
66 Sullivan, 'Legislators' blogs in Taiwan', 471–85.
67 Fu He-kang.
68 For example, see DPP Legislator Tang Chin-chuan's (湯金全) advertisement in *China Times*, 29 November 2001, 19.
69 See *Liberty Times*, 7 March 2000, 1.
70 At first glance I was also taken in by this advertisement. See *Liberty Times*, 4 March 2000, 7.
71 Hung Ya-hui, interview by author, Taipei, 18 June 2001.
72 Liu, 'The Effects of Election Laws on Party Competition in Taiwan', Table 8.1.
73 Sullivan, 'Campaign Advertising in Taiwanese Presidential Elections', 675–88.
74 Rawnsley, 'The 1996 presidential campaign in Taiwan', 47–61.
75 Sullivan, 675–88.
76 Hsu Shui-teh, interview by author, Taipei, 11 October 2001.
77 See *Taipei Times*, Staff Writer, 'Crackdown on election gambling gets under way', *Taipei Times*, 8 March 2000, 1; Jimmy Chuang, 'Justice Chief Says election betters to be indicted soon', *Taipei Times*, 10 March 2004, 4.
78 *China Times*, 3 December 1995, 11.
79 NP campaign worker and party radio station broadcaster, NP Kaohsiung headquarters, 7 September 2001.
80 During the ghost month of the Chinese lunar calendar, people avoid activities such as weddings or moving house.
81 Yu Mu-ming, interview with author, Taipei, 5 October 2001.
82 The party fell from 11 seats in 1998 to only 1 in 2001, and this was from the small offshore island of Kinmen.
83 Huang Huang-hsiung, interview with author, Taipei, 9 November 2001.
84 Baum, 'All Politics is Local', *Far Eastern Economic Review*. 14 December 1995: 14–15.
85 Huang, Tai-lin and Joy Su, 'Rallies Turn Violent: Ma Takes Action', *Taipei Times*, 11 April 2004, 1.

6 Party politics in Taiwan

Only a few months after arriving in Taiwan in 1989, I witnessed my first election campaign. At the time it seemed like a David versus Goliath struggle, as the former ruling party of all of China (KMT) competed against a party only legally registered a few months earlier (DPP). Even before I knew what career path I would take, the two souvenirs from my first year in Taiwan that I particularly treasured were my KMT and DPP party flags. I could never have imagined that I would later devote so much of my career to studying these two political parties. Those two party flags were to make up two-thirds of the cover of my first book, *Party Politics in Taiwan*. Despite the enormous changes to Taiwanese society, after almost three decades of multi-party politics the same two parties dominate Taiwan's political scene today. This chapter is devoted to examining patterns of continuity and change in Taiwan's party politics.

After discussing some of the central concepts in the field of party politics, the first substantive sections of this chapter will examine party change through the following dimensions: (1) ideological and policy positions, (2) party images, (3) leadership and candidate selection methods and (4) inner-party balance of power. Next I will examine how we can best explain these patterns of party change. The chapter will then move on to consider explanations for the success and failure of Taiwan's main parties. This will be followed by a section analysing the smaller challenger parties, a topic that has attracted scant academic attention. The remainder of the chapter will focus on Taiwan's changing party system. This will lay out changes in the main dimensions of the party system, such as party system fragmentation, the openness of the party system to new entrants, interparty party ideological distances and interparty relations. In the concluding section some of the challenges facing party politics in Taiwan will be raised.

Central concepts

As with almost all other central concepts in political science, how to define political parties is a much debated topic. Alan Ware suggests, 'A political party is an institution that (1) seeks influence in a state, often by attempting to occupy positions in government and (2) usually consists of more than a single interest in society and so to some degree attempts to "aggregate interests".'[1] This would be applicable to both parties in authoritarian and democratic political systems. Hague and Harrop offer a similar definition but one that better fits our focus in this chapter on parties in Taiwan during the democratic era. For them, 'political parties are permanent organizations which contest elections, usually because they seek to occupy the decisive positions of authority within the state. Unlike interest groups, which seek merely to influence the government, serious parties aim to secure the levers of power.'[2] The second guiding concept in this chapter is the party system. Ware defines a party system 'as patterns of competition and cooperation between different parties in that system'.[3] Thus, while studies on political parties treat individual parties as the unit of analysis, party system research examines the interactions of all relevant parties within a political system.

In the last two decades, as voters' party loyalties have declined in many older democracies, some writers have questioned the role that parties play in modern democracies.[4] The catchy research question is 'Is the party over?' However, regardless of whether we are studying new or older democracies, parties remain central actors in the political realm. Despite falling party membership numbers, it seems that no democracy can function without parties. They continue to be central in offering policy direction to governments, conducting elite recruitment, acting as agents for interest aggregation and as a point of reference for supporters to simplify the increasingly complicated political world. Half a century ago, Schattschneider argued that 'modern democracy is unthinkable save in terms of political parties'.[5] This remains a valid observation even today.

The final working concept to consider at this stage is party change, which Harmel and Janda define as 'any variation, alteration or moderation in how parties are organized, what human and material resources they can draw upon, what they stand for and what they do'.[6] Thus, party change is a very broad concept. Due to space limitations, I have had to be selective in the aspects of party change covered in this chapter.

Parties in Taiwan and international party families

In March 2017, there were 314 political parties registered with Taiwan's Ministry of Interior.[7] Naturally, the vast majority of these are insignificant, lacking any grassroots membership, political resources or influence. They are mainly just parties on paper. Instead, I will focus my analysis on the dozen or so relevant parties that have contested multiple national elections, won parliamentary seats and affected the party system. Although the DPP and KMT have dominated Taiwan's party politics, at times the challenger parties have left significant imprints on Taiwan's political development.

Studies on Western political parties tend to categorize parties as belonging to one of the following types: (1) Far Right, (2) Conservative, (3) Christian Democrat, (4) Liberal, (5) Social Democratic, (6) Ecological, (7) Regional and Ethnic and (8) Communist.[8] This typology of political parties lends itself to thinking in terms of a left–right ideological spectrum, as all but the Ecological or Regional parties fit easily on the left–right scales. Scholars have employed a variety of methods to locate parties from a range of democracies on this kind of spectrum.[9]

A question for us to consider is whether Taiwanese parties can fit well into these kinds of categories. There are overlapping international organizations for different party families. Taiwan's KMT chose to join the International Democratic Union, the home for parties such as the UK's Conservative Party, the US Republican Party and the German Christian Democrats. In contrast, after much internal debate the DPP opted to join Liberal International rather than Socialist International. Thus, the DPP is part of the group including the UK Liberal Democrats and German Free Democrats. However, as with many 'Third Wave' democracies, trying to analyse Taiwan's party politics through a left–right framework is not very fruitful. In fact, at times the KMT has adopted policies we would usually associate with social democratic parties, while the DPP has taken pro-business and anti-immigration stances that in the UK are the territory of either conservative or even far right parties. The party in Taiwan that has most embraced its international party grouping is the Green Party Taiwan (GPT), a member of Global Greens.

Party change

Ideological and policy positions

One dimension of party politics that has particularly fascinated me has been measuring how Taiwan's parties have changed ideologically.[10] It is very common to hear political observers talk of how parties have moderated or moved to more extreme positions. However, actually proving this kind of change empirically is easier said than done. In my first book, *Party Politics in Taiwan,* I tried to measure ideological change based on four main methods. These were a quantitative content analysis of parties' newspaper election ads, qualitative content analysis of newspaper and television ads, reviews of elite discourse during campaigns (from newspaper reports) and elite interviews with long-term politicians and established political scientists.

I argued that in the initial stage (1986–91), Taiwan's parties moved towards highly polarized positions on many core political issues. For instance, by 1991 the DPP and KMT were poles apart on national identity issues, with the former proposing the establishment of a Republic of Taiwan, and the latter talking about unification under the National Unification Guidelines. There were similar divisions on other political dimensions in the early 1990s, with clear differences between the parties on pensions, constitutional issues, method of presidential election, political corruption and environmental protection. I then contended that the three main parties (KMT, DPP and NP) gradually converged towards the centre ground on core political issues, although they still remained distinct. I termed this pattern 'moderate differentiation'. At least for the two main parties, this convergence reached a peak in the late 1990s, as the DPP and KMT worked together on constitutional reform and at least tacit consensus on national identity and cross-Strait relations. This convergent party movement initially continued in the first years of the post-2000 era, but during the second DPP term the parties became highly polarized.

Before I examine how the parties changed in detail, it is useful to get an idea about what the core issues were that individual parties focused on in the 1990s and post-2000 periods. This is distinct from Table 5.10 in the previous chapter which displayed the combined top issues for all major parties. Table 6.1 shows the main parties' most stressed issues in their newspaper advertisements over nine campaigns in the 1990s. As can be seen from the table, the KMT gave greatest attention to government competence, attacking Taiwan independence, political stability, promoting itself, attacking opposing parties and their candidates, law and order, and political corruption. By far the DPP's most stressed appeals were attacking political corruption and promoting Taiwan independence and nationalism. In addition, it also gave attention to women's issues, democracy, and human rights and social welfare. The NP's appeals were rather different, having some appeals in common with the KMT, such as opposing Taiwan independence, but it also shared the DPP's concern with political corruption. It was also the only major party to consistently promote Chinese nationalism, closer ties with China, peace and education issues in its newspaper advertisements. I generated quite similar results when I calculated the top party appeals based on the frequency these appeals appeared in the parties' annual top tens.[11] Table 6.2 also suggests that the parties had quite distinct issue

Table 6.1 Top issues for the main parties in 1990s newspaper advertisements

Ranking	KMT	DPP	NP
1	Government competence	Political corruption	Party: positive
2	Other parties' lack of government competence	Party: positive	Taiwan independence: negative
3	Taiwan independence: negative	Diluted Taiwan independence	Political corruption
4	Political stability	Non-economic demographic groups (women's issues)	Candidate: negative
5	Party: positive	Democracy	Peace
6	Economic growth and prosperity	Party: negative	Democracy
7	Candidate: negative	Pure Taiwan independence	Chinese nationalism
8	Law and order	Freedom and human rights	Party: negative
9	Political corruption	Taiwan nationalism	Foreign special relationships: positive
10	Party: negative	Social welfare	Education expansion

Source: Fell (2005c, p. 24).

Note: This table shows the top issues stressed by the main political parties in their newspaper advertisements in the 1990s.

appeals during the 1990s. This table is based on the issues that politicians from the main parties I interviewed felt their parties had given the greatest emphasis from 1991 to 2001. The findings are quite similar to the newspaper data, with national identity (which here includes issues of opposing or supporting Taiwan independence and competing national identity appeals), seen as by far the most stressed issue area. The KMT's other core appeals were the economy and stability. The DPP and NP shared concern for corruption and the DPP dominated appeals on social welfare and environmental protection.

The DPP actually started off as a relatively moderate party in 1986, promoting democracy, ethnic justice and Taiwanese self-determination rather than outright independence. However, it gradually became more radical over the next few years. In 1991, the DPP adopted a more extreme position on Taiwan independence and a new constitution while focusing most of its energies on national identity issues. Following that year, it changed tack by moderating its national identity appeals, or what I call repackaging Taiwan independence into more electorally acceptable appeals such as applying for membership into the United Nations. It also reduced its national identity emphasis and instead broadened its issue appeals to include social welfare, environmental protection and, most important of all, political corruption. This process continued into the mid-1990s when it also began to stress women's welfare issues, such as childcare and personal safety. Not all elections followed this moderating and broad appeal formula. For instance, during the 1996 presidential campaign it reverted back to many of the themes it stressed in 1991– namely, that of Taiwan nationalism and independence. However, for its successful 1997 local executive campaign, the DPP was back on track with its broader appeals, particularly

Table 6.2 Elite views on the most stressed election issues, 1991–2001

Ranking	KMT	DPP	NP
1	National identity	National identity	National identity
2	Economy	Money politics	Money politics
3	Stability	Democracy	Economy
4	Prosperity	Social welfare	Social welfare
5	Education	Environmental protection	Democracy

Source: Fell (2005c, p. 27).

Note: These figures are based on my interviews with 61 experienced Taiwanese politicians in 2000–1. The question asked was 'What issues have you and your party stressed most in elections over the last decade (1991–2000)?'

on corruption and crime. In the 2000 presidential campaign, the DPP's appeals could not have been more different from 1996, with anti-corruption and social welfare its dominant issue appeals. At the outset of democratic elections, the DPP had been a radical party focused on Taiwan nationalism. However, by 2000 it had moved towards the centre on identity and offered a broad range of issue appeals.

There was also a degree of continuity and change in the KMT's ideological positions in the 1990s. At the outset of the decade it was a promoter of Chinese nationalism and unification, opposed universal welfare expansion and was prepared to turn a blind eye to many forms of political corruption. By the mid-1990s it moved to the centre on national identity to compete with the DPP. For example, its promotion of Taiwan's international space and the 'New Taiwanese' appeal were interpreted as shifting away from core KMT values. It also tried to steal DPP control over welfare issues in a number of campaigns from 1995 to 2000. However, the KMT was also consistent in arguing that only it could guarantee political stability and economic prosperity, and it attacked the DPP for violence and promoting Taiwan independence in most campaigns.

The NP began its first campaigns on a radical line, promoting Chinese nationalism and opposing Taiwan independence with vigour. We get a taste of their early appeal in quotes from Jaw Shaw-kong in the 1994 Taipei mayoral debate cited in Chapter 5. However, the NP also shifted to a broader issue emphasis in the mid-1990s. For instance, it stressed anti-corruption and handicapped welfare and tried to paint itself as the party of the ordinary urban citizen (*xiao shimin zhengdang*). Having worked seven-day weeks in my first few years in Taiwan, I did appreciate the NP's 1995 slogan of a two-day weekend. This broad approach continued through to 1998, when approximately a third of NP issue mentions were focused on anti-corruption appeals.[12] After the NP's poor showing in 1998, it drifted back to a narrow and extreme position in 2000 and 2001. A sign of this trend was that 75 per cent of NP issue mentions in their newspaper advertisements in 2000 were opposing Taiwan independence and in 2001 it adopted a position similar to China's One Country, Two Systems.

We can get a picture of party change in Table 6.3, which shows the main parties' top issues in newspaper advertisements in the initial post-2000 period. This table is not entirely comparable with Table 6.1 as it only includes data for the 2001 and 2004 parliamentary elections. However, it can show changed issues priorities for the three main parties from the 1990s and also give us a preliminary picture of the new entrants, the TSU and PFP.

The major changes for the KMT were that after 2000 it gave much greater emphasis to economic issues, dropped its attacks on Taiwan independence and employed a mixed identity message, with appeals to both Chinese and Taiwanese identities. Although it had also dropped the stability appeal, it replaced this with calls for social harmony and multiculturalism. The DPP largely dropped references to Taiwan independence, and in their place gave greater emphasis to Taiwan identity appeals. Another major shift was how the DPP was attempting to steal KMT ownership of the stability and economy appeals. The NP, however, was more consistent than the other two parties. Its main change was dropping concern with political corruption and becoming completely focused on a narrow appeal of Chinese identity and opposing Taiwan independence. Based on this data the TSU looks quite similar to the DPP in the early 1990s, with its radical Taiwan independence and Taiwan identity appeals. In contrast, the PFP appears different from any earlier party models. Its propaganda issue emphasis was extremely low, and

Table 6.3 Main parties' top ten issues in parliamentary elections in the post-2000 period

	KMT	DPP	NP	PFP	TSU
1	Party: positive	Party: positive	Taiwan independence: negative	Party: positive	Diluted Taiwan independence
2	Other parties' lack of government competence	Political stability	Party: positive	Candidate: positive	Taiwan nationalism
3	Economic growth and prosperity	Taiwan nationalism	Chinese nationalism	Taiwan nationalism	Pure Taiwan independence
4	Party: negative	Political corruption	Special foreign relationships	Economic growth and prosperity	Party: positive
5	Chinese nationalism	Candidate: positive	Candidate: positive	Party: negative	Candidate: positive
6	Uncategorizable/ others	Economic growth and prosperity	Peace	Education expansion	Democracy
7	Taiwan nationalism	Democracy	Uncategorizable/ others	Government competence	Political stability
8	Social harmony	Social harmony	Social harmony	Peace	Economic growth and prosperity
9	Multiculturalism	Peace	Party: negative	Law and order	Government and administrative efficiency
10	Education expansion	Uncategorizable/ others	Economic growth and prosperity	Taiwan independence: negative	Government competence

Source: Fell (2007b, pp. 23–39).

Note 1: This table shows the top issues stressed by the main political parties in their newspaper advertisements in the parliamentary elections by the DPP, KMT, NP, TSU and PFP in the post-2000 period.
Note 2: The elections included in this analysis for the post-2000 period are 2001 and 2004 legislative elections.

instead it concentrated on party and candidate image creation. In particular it emphasized its prize asset, its chairman James Soong.

Although I have not yet completed the comparable newspaper advertisement content analysis for the 2008 elections, I have used alternative data in a number of publications to assess how the parties have developed ideologically since the first Chen Shui-bian term.[13] In one such study I examined the parties' main appeals in TV election advertisement in legislative campaigns in 2001, 2004 and 2008. Overall, the DPP was quite consistent in attacking the KMT for blocking good legislation and corruption. It also stressed welfare and Taiwan identity appeals. Using other data in other studies, I have tried to argue that the DPP did fluctuate between more radical and extreme national identity positions, but I claim that it was most extreme in the last two years of Chen's second term. I found that the KMT was quite consistent in 2001 and 2004, focusing on attacking DPP governance, economic management failures and Chen Shui-bian and promoting ROC Chinese nationalism. The major shift for the KMT came in 2005 when it began an appeal model that it would continue through to 2008. This involved dropping the ROC Chinese identity appeals and in its place emphasizing heavily on attacking the DPP for political corruption and focusing on the candidate image of Ma Ying-jeou. Other components continued, such as blaming the DPP for Taiwan's economic recession and personal attacks against Chen. The TSU continued to stress Taiwanese identity and opposition to cross-Strait economic integration, but seemed to moderate in 2008, dropping Taiwan independence and offering a broader appeal that tried to attract disadvantaged groups such as students, the unemployed and the disabled. The NP remained basically unchanged in 2008 from four years earlier. It was as focused on Chinese nationalism as ever. I will discuss the more recent election campaigns in more detail in Chapter 13.

My analysis suggests that Taiwan's relevant parties do not fit well into the standard Western party typology. The focus on national identity gives some of the parties characteristics similar to ethnic or regional parties, although this does not apply to the KMT which appeals to all ethnic groups in Taiwan. My analysis suggests that at times the main parties have mixed appeals that in Europe we would associate with social democratic, liberal, conservative or even far right parties. One characteristic of all five parties is that their core issue has tended to be national identity. This is the issue that most Taiwanese analysts view as the most salient among party members. However, this seems to put the parties at odds with most voters, who tend to rank cross-Strait or identity issues lower on issue salience surveys. For instance, a Taiwan Election and Democratization survey in 2016 showed respondents listing economic development and unemployment as by far the most important countries facing the country.[14]

Party image change

Another fruitful method for plotting party change has been through using party image surveys. This kind of research has shown that most voters do have clear images of the main parties and are able to locate them on policy spectrums quite accurately. There have been three main approaches to assessing voters' party images. The first asks voters for their impressions of the leading political parties and the respondent is usually given a number of options on a display card to choose from. The second approach is to ask respondents to place themselves and the main parties on core policy spectrums. The third method asks respondents whether they regard the main parties as meeting certain standards, such as stressing public opinion, being free of corruption or having party unity.

The first approach is displayed in Table 6.4, where I have listed the top five impressions of the main parties in party image surveys conducted in 1995, 2000 and 2004.[15] Although there have been some changes over time, the majority of public images of the KMT are negative. It is viewed as being divided, corrupt and being a party representing the rich or big business. The worst year for the KMT's reputation was 2000, when all five of the public's top KMT impressions were negative. That year, many voters even associated it with organized crime. The KMT's only more positive impressions were its contribution to democracy (1995) and economic development (2004). The most consistent DPP images were that it contributed towards democracy, supports independence, is radical and loves Taiwan. One notable change was that after 2000 it appeared to have lost its image of being violent that arose from its stunt politics of the democratic transition era. The most common impression of the NP was that it represents the Mainlander ethnic group. Its public image deteriorated considerably from 1995 to 2000, with almost all its top impressions negative in the latter survey. The TSU image in 2004 overlaps quite closely with my own newspaper advertisement data, showing a focus on Taiwan independence and identity. Considering the PFP's ambiguous campaign issue positions, it is not entirely surprising to find that the public was confused about what the party stood for. The fact that within four years the party was viewed as going from loving Taiwan (2000) to promoting unification (2004) is a reflection of the party's vague and changeable appeals. More recently, Lin has returned to the study of party images in Taiwan. In a 2014 survey, she found that although respondents still have more negative impressions of the KMT than the DPP, overall negative impressions seem to dominate both party images. The most common images of the KMT were (1) Corrupt and embezzling (9.4 per cent), (2) Invidious (6.8 per cent), (3) No ability to govern (4.7 per cent), (4) Rotten (3.4 per cent), (5) Loveable (3.2 per cent), (6) Conservative (2.9 per cent) and (7) Represents the rich (2.0 per cent). In contrast, the most common impressions of the DPP were (1) Radical (4.6 per cent), (2) Invidious (3.9 per cent), (3) Creates disorder (3.9 per cent), (4) Corrupt and embezzling (3.2 per cent), (5) Violent (2.8 per cent), (6) Fraudulent (2.5 per cent), (7) Have performance (2.2 per cent).[16]

The main party image spectrum surveys aimed to locate the parties and respondents on spectrums regarding reform versus stability, independence versus unification, environmental protection versus economic development and social welfare versus economic growth. I will return to some of these surveys in subsequent chapters in more detail. The overall patterns were that the DPP was viewed as more pro-reform, pro-Taiwan independence and giving priority to environmental protection and social welfare. In contrast, the KMT was perceived as more pro-unification and giving priority to stability and economic growth. Respondents were sensitive to party change too, and these perceptions correspond quite well with my propaganda content analysis findings. For instance, respondents did view the DPP and KMT as moving from polarized positions towards the centre on the independence versus unification spectrum in the 1990s, but then returning to opposite poles in the post-2000 period.

The third approach has been utilized by the TVBS polling centre since the late 1990s. These studies ask respondents whether they view the main parties as being attentive to public opinion, free of corruption, stressing reform, having vigour (*you huoli*), being united and being able to conduct self-examination (*fanxing nengli*). The DPP was viewed as being more attentive to public opinion until 2004, after which the KMT surpassed it during the DPP's second term. There was a similar pattern with regard to corruption, with the DPP having a cleaner reputation though to 2005, when the KMT surpassed it

Table 6.4 Party images, 1995–2004

	KMT	DPP	NP	PEP	TSU
1995	1. Infighting and fragmented 2. Corrupt and embezzling 3. Contribute to democracy 4. Represent the rich 5. Love the ROC	1. Seek Taiwan independence 2. Radical 3. Violent 4. Contribute to democracy 5. Love Taiwan	1. Represent Mainlander interests 2. Check and balance 3. Full of talented leaders 4. Love the ROC 5. Honest and upright		
2000	1. Corrupt and embezzling 2. Associate with business interests 3. Infighting and fragmented 4. Has connections with organized crime 5. Rotten and useless	1. Contribute to democracy 2. Seek Taiwan independence 3. Radical 4. Attentive to public opinion 5. Love Taiwan	1. Represent Mainlander interests 2. Infighting and fragmented 3. Lack of talented leaders 4. High ideals 5. Create disorder	1. Attentive to public opinion 2. With high ideals 3. Represent Mainlander interests 4. Love Taiwan 5. Check and balance	
2004	1. Corrupt and embezzling 2. Full of talented leaders 3. Infighting and fragmented 4. Contribute to economic development 5. Associate with business interests	1. Contribute to democracy 2. Seek Taiwan independence 3. Love Taiwan 4. Radical 5. Lack of talented leaders		1. Represent Mainlander interests 2. With high ideals 3. Attentive to public opinion 4. Seek unification with China 5. Infighting and fragmented	1. Seek Taiwan independence 2. Love Taiwan 3. Rotten and useless 4. Represents Taiwanese interests 5. Lack of talented leaders

Source: Lin Chiung-chu (2006, pp. 34–7).

for the rest of the DPP's second term. This pattern remained consistent throughout the surveys into the KMT period, with the KMT tending to have a more positive party image than the DPP after 2004–5. Although there was a dip in the KMT's party image in the middle of Ma's first term, it was able to recover enough to win re-election in 2012. However, in Ma's second term, there was a clearer reversal of party images. In a June 2015 survey on seven criteria of party image, the DPP earned higher scores than the KMT on all seven.[17] These were: (1) understands public opinion, (2) clean governance, (3) has vitality, (4) puts people' interests above the party's, (5) unity, (6) likeability and (7) satisfaction. In the past, Lin Chiung-chu's (林瓊珠) work suggested that the KMT's shift from positive to negative party images and the DPP's improving images in the 1990–2000 period contributed to the KMT's fall from power.[18] If Lin is right, then these recent surveys can tell us part of the story of why the DPP (2008) and the KMT (2016) fell from power.

Leadership and candidate selection methods

Candidate selection is another area of party change that I have become fascinated with. Schattesshneider reminds us of the importance of candidate selection, stating, 'he who can make nominations is the owner of the party. This is therefore one of the best points at which to observe the distribution of power within the party.'[19] The stability of the party system and remarkable innovation of Taiwanese parties' nomination systems make candidate selection there a subject of interest to comparative party scholars.

The year 1989 was not only a critical year for interparty democracy, but was also noteworthy for inner-party democracy. That year, both the KMT and DPP introduced closed member primaries for selecting their legislative and local executive candidates.[20] With the KMT's long history of authoritarian top-down decision-making and nomination, this was a radical reform. It was equally so for the tiny and young DPP, which at the time only had 15,009 members compared to the KMT's two million. However, when it came to leadership selection, the parties remained poles apart. Lee Teng-hui owed his position as KMT chair to being handpicked by the former dictator Chiang Ching-kuo. The DPP's system was slightly more inclusive, with highly competitive chairman elections decided by a few hundred party delegates from 1988 to 1996.[21]

In Tables 6.5 and 6.6, I have attempted to plot the main parties' nomination practices for the subsequent two decades on a scale of inner-party democracy, in which point 7 equals a nomination decision made solely by a supreme party leader, while at point 1 the electorate includes all eligible voters in a constituency. This scale was based on one devised by Rahat and Hazan (2001) but slightly revised to fit the Taiwan case.[22] The tables show that unlike the progressive trend towards democratic expansion in interparty politics, Taiwan's parties have fluctuated between more authoritarian and democratic nomination methods. Comparatively, the DPP has been more democratic in its candidate and leadership nomination than the KMT. Through to 2008, the DPP maintained some form of primary for most elections, while the KMT used top- down nomination for most of the 1990s. It was only in the post-2000 period that the KMT reverted to primaries. In contrast, the smaller parties have favoured top-down nominations in the vast majority of campaigns.

After the KMT's initial experiment with primaries in 1989, it quickly moved to a more exclusive nomination method. In 1991 and 1992, it employed a mixed primary in which the ordinary member primary vote counted for 50 per cent and cadres vote for the other 50. After 1993, it then totally abandoned primaries for the rest of the decade.

Table 6.5 Categorization of Taiwan's parties' candidate selection procedures, 1989–98

Year	Elections held	KMT	DPP	NP
1989	Legislative and Local Executive	3	3	N/A
1991	National Assembly	4	3	N/A
1992	Legislative	4	3	N/A
1993	Local Executive	5	3	6
1994	Provincial Governor, Taipei and Kaohsiung Mayor	7	4	6
1995	Legislative	5	4	6
1996	Presidential	7	4 & 1	6
1997	Local Executive	5	2	6
1998	Legislative and Taipei and Kaohsiung Mayor	5	2	1

Source: Wang Yeh-li (2003, pp. 166–8, 179–80, 189); Fell (2006b, pp. 172–4).

Note: Explanations of categories:
1   Electorate: including primaries in which all eligible voters may participate or selection by opinion surveys in which survey results account for 100 per cent of the selection weighting.
2   Mixed system of closed member primaries and opinion surveys.
3   Party members: closed member primaries.
4   Mixed system of party cadre primary and closed member primary.
5   Local/centre negotiation: this involves negotiations between three parties: the local party branch, local party factional leaders and the party centre. This normally allows a candidate to be selected by conciliation.
6   Non-Selected Party Agency: a selection committee at the national level makes the nomination decision. This may involve candidates from outside the constituency being parachuted in.
7   Party Leader: the national party leader makes the nomination decision.

Table 6.6 Categorization of Taiwan's parties' candidate selection procedures, 2000–16

Year	Elections held	KMT	DPP	NP	PFP	TSU
2000	Presidential	7	6	7	7	N/A
2001	Legislative and Local Executive	2	2	6	6/7	6/7
2002	Taipei and Kaohsiung Mayor	6	6	N/A	N/A	N/A
2004	Presidential	7	7	N/A	7	N/A
2004	Legislative	2	2	6	6/7	6/7
2005	Local Executive	2	2	N/A	6/7	6/7
2006	Taipei and Kaohsiung Mayor	2	2	N/A	7	6/7
2008	Legislative	2	2	6	6/7	6
2008	Presidential	3	2	N/A	N/A	N/A
2009	Local Executive	2	6	N/A	N/A	N/A
2010	Special Municipality	1 & 6	1 & 6	N/A	N/A	N/A
2012	Presidential and Legislative	1&2	1	7	7	6/7
2016	Presidential and Legislative	1&2	1	7	7	6/7

Source: Wang Yeh-li (2003, pp. 166–8, 179–80, 189); Fell (2006b, pp. 172–4). Figures for 2006–16 are based on the author's calculations.

Instead, it either used a negotiated approach between the local party, central party and local factions or simply let the party leader dominate the process. For instance, in 1996 Lee Teng-hui essentially nominated himself as KMT presidential candidate and four years later he handpicked his successor, Lien Chan. On both occasions Lee rejected internal KMT calls for a return to primaries. In contrast, for legislative and local executive posts, nomination was a three-way struggle between local factions, the local party and the central party, leaving no formal role for grassroots party members or ordinary cadres.

The DPP continued using closed member primaries for nominating its candidates through to 1993. Then, for the mid-1990s it also adopted a mixed primary system, with equal weighting for members and cadres. Perhaps the DPP's most interesting nomination experiment of the 1990s was for its 1996 presidential candidate. After a first round using the mixed primary system, it then used a form of open primary to determine which of the final two candidates would represent the party in that historic election. The two leading candidates were Hsu Hsin-liang, the former *Tangwai* pioneering leader and former DPP chair, against Peng Ming-min, who had been a political prisoner in the 1960s and spent two decades in exile. They took part in 50 candidate policy forums throughout Taiwan, after each of which any eligible voter could cast their vote. Peng eventually triumphed, but the fact that he performed so badly in the presidential election may partly explain why the DPP never repeated this method. In 1997, the DPP began its first trials of a new mixed primary. In place of the cadre vote, the party held public opinion surveys while maintaining a 50:50 weighing for the member primary. Later in 2001, the weighing was shifted to 70 for the survey and 30 for the member vote. This was the standard nomination method for any DPP contested nomination through to 2008, and in 2007 was even used for the DPP's presidential nomination. The DPP also moved to democratize its leadership selection in the late 1990s. Since 1998, it has used closed member primaries to select its party chairperson.

It was only after the KMT's disastrous defeat in 2000 that it reverted to a more democratic nomination and leadership selection process. The KMT attempted to design a close imitation of the DPP's mixed survey/member primary nomination system, maintaining it though to the 2009 local executive elections. Its other radical shift was introducing a closed member primary for selecting its party chairman. Although the first such primary was won by Lien Chan in an uncontested election in 2001, in 2005 there was a highly competitive contest between Legislative Yuan Speaker Wang Jin-pyng and Taipei mayor Ma Ying-jeou. This election was won by Ma and actually served as the party's de facto primary for the 2008 presidential nomination. Therefore, while in the 1990s the two main parties took diametrically opposite nomination approaches, for most of the post-2000 period they were converging on a system of inclusive nomination.

Although the politicians that formed the NP had been highly vocal in calling for inner-party democracy while in the KMT, they employed a top-down nomination committee approach for most of the 1990s. The one exception was its experiment with open primaries in 1998 for legislative and city council nominations, where any ID card-carrying citizen could participate. However, it subsequently returned to an increasingly authoritarian style. Although in theory it reverted to a nomination committee system, it tended to be the party chairperson who had a decisive say on nominations. For instance, in 2000 NP chairman Lee Ching-hua (李慶華) handpicked the party's presidential candidate, and since 2001, chairs Hsieh Chi-ta and Yu Mu-ming have been able to determine the legislative nominations. The situation in the PFP and TSU was also similarly authoritarian. For instance, PFP party chairman James Soong had the dominant say in his party's nomination process. In the case of the TSU, Lee Teng-hui's age meant that he tended to delegate decision-making to his secretary general. Their smaller membership and the fear of the major parties trying to influence their nomination process meant that these smaller parties preferred to keep the nomination power tightly controlled.

After the KMT's return to power in 2008, the two main parties' nomination systems again went through a period of change. For 2009, while the KMT continued the survey/primary system for contested nominations, the DPP dropped primaries for the first time.

Instead, DPP nomination was determined centrally using a nomination committee, with no formal survey or member participation. It was the DPP's most radical change since 1989. After the KMT's disappointing election performance in 2009, it also got cold feet about primaries. The two parties have once again converged on their nomination methods since 2010. At least where nomination is contested (where more than one candidate registers), then both parties tend to use public opinion polls to determine the candidate. Generally, the DPP is more likely to have competitive inner-party elections for its presidential candidates. For example, in 2012 three candidates contested the presidential primary with Tsai Ing-wen (42.5) only wining by a narrow margin over former Premier Su Tseng-chang (41.1). One of the most controversial party primaries was for the KMT's presidential nomination in 2016. In this case, most of the party's major figures did not register and only Deputy Legislative Yuan Speaker Hung Hsiu-chu garnered enough member signatures to be a primary candidate. With only a single candidate, there was no need to go through the party member vote and public opinion primary mechanism. Once opinion surveys showed her support rate exceeded 30 per cent, she was officially nominated in July 2015. However, as the campaign developed, Hung was unable to narrow Tsai's lead and in October she was replaced by party chair Eric Chu.

Inner-party balance of power

It is possible to go into great detail discussing the changing factional balance of power within Taiwan's main parties. Usually, each central standing committee election or party nomination process is examined to analyse which factions have come out on top and who are the losers. In a number of studies, I have tried to simplify this process by understanding it as a struggle between election-oriented and ideology-oriented factions and leaders.[23] Such a perspective also ties in quite nicely with the political science debate over whether parties give priority to votes, seats or policy.

Inner-party balance of power within the KMT

The most common factional terms used to discuss the KMT's inner-party politics during the late 1980s and 1990s are the Mainstream faction (*zhuliu pai*) and non-Mainstream faction (*fei zhuliu pai*). These two groupings emerged during the struggle for party control after the death of Chiang Ching-kuo. Simply put, the Mainstream faction referred to politicians loosely allied with the president Lee Teng-hui, while the non-Mainstream faction tended to oppose Lee. These factions had both ethnic and ideological differences. Thus, which faction came out on top would have a significant impact on political developments in a number of chapters in this book. There was not one dominant leader of the non-Mainstream faction, but one particularly representative figure was the former general, Hau Pei-tsun. The non-Mainstream faction tended to be disproportionally first- and second-generation Mainlanders, although there were also some prominent Taiwanese members who were ideologically opposed to Lee or had fallen out with him. Ideologically, the non-Mainstream tended to vehemently oppose Taiwan independence and support eventual unification and accordingly stressed symbols of ROC Chinese nationalism. They tended to be based in urban areas, were uncomfortable with local KMT factional politicians and often were unable to speak Taiwanese. Prior to democratization, their career track had been within the state or party bureaucracy and thus they had not needed to join elections. However, the younger generation did have an electoral following in

Taiwan's major cities. The two important subfactional divisions of the non-Mainstream were the *Huang Fu-xing* party branch and the New KMT Alliance. The former was the KMT's military veterans' party branch for retired servicemen, which tended to support KMT candidates who were ideologically orthodox. The New KMT Alliance was a subgroup in the late 1980s and early 1990s that opposed Lee and supported orthodox KMT ideology.

In contrast, the politicians of the Mainstream KMT faction tended to be Taiwanese and had experience with local elections. The most important subdivision within the Mainstream faction was known as the Wisdom Club (*jisi hui*). These politicians tended to be loyal to Lee and less attached to KMT Chinese nationalist ideology. The Wisdom Club's more Taiwan-first approach to politics led some to being accused of being closet supporters of the DPP or Taiwan independence.

The struggle between the Mainstream and non-Mainstream KMT was obvious in a number of incidents during the transition period. When Lee first became President, he lacked a strong political base, and many of the party's old guard viewed him as a stop-gap figure. The KMT's divisions were revealed in the 1990 presidential election. Rather than nominate a potential political rival like Premier Lee Huan (李煥) to be his candidate for Vice President, Lee Teng-hui chose the constitutional expert Lee Yuan-tzu (李元簇). He was challenged by Lin Yang-kang and Chiang Wei-kuo (蔣緯國 Chiang Kai-shek's adopted son), although they eventually were persuaded to withdraw. Following Lee's election, he tried to split the non-Mainstream faction by sacking its leading figure, Premier Lee Huan, and replacing him with another non-Mainstream politician, Hau Pei-tsun.

The period of cohabitation between Lee and Hau was probably the height of the struggle between the two factions. This was especially the case in the 1992 legislative campaign when Wisdom Club and New KMT Alliance politicians openly attacked each other. However, Lee emerged victorious after sacking Hau in March 1993 and replacing him with his protégé, Lien Chan, as Premier. Lee was able to further dominate the party after many of the non-Mainstream politicians split off in the summer of 1993 to form the NP. This meant that those non-Mainstream politicians who stayed on were increasingly marginalized within the KMT power structure for the rest of the decade. This was apparent when Hau and Lin joined forces for a rebel KMT challenge that allied with the NP in 1995–6.

In Lee's second term he was more dominant than ever in the KMT. He also moved quickly to try to marginalize a new political grouping around the popular Provincial Governor James Soong. After Soong declared his independent presidential candidacy in 1999, he was also able to attract supporters from both the non-Mainstream KMT and the NP, forming the basis of the PFP.

After the KMT's defeat in 2000, Lee left the power centre and Lien Chan became chairman. There was another major shift in the factional balance of power, as Lien invited many non-Mainstream politicians back to the party centre. Those loyal to Lee became marginalized and some even left to join the TSU. In this post-2000 period, I continued to use the terms 'Mainstream' and 'non-Mainstream' factions, though this usage has become less common in Taiwan itself. Others have talked about a localized KMT faction (*bentupai*) as the equivalent of the Mainstream faction of the 1990s. However, what this actually consists of is something that still requires more research. The figure that is most associated with this localized KMT in this era is Legislative Yuan Speaker Wang Jin-pyng.

The other rising grouping at this point were politicians closely associated with Ma Yingjeou. This became apparent in the build-up to the KMT's 2005 chairman election.

Lien was keen to stay on but did not want to fight Ma in an open primary. When it was clear that Lien would not stand, there was an odd alliance of some non-Mainstream politicians supporting the de facto leader of the localized KMT, Wang Jin-pyng. Although Ma's victory left him in a strong position within the KMT, elements of the localized KMT, non-Mainstream KMT and members close to Lien Chan remained influential in the party.

The KMT's factional power struggle became clear again in Ma's second term. In September 2013, Ma attempted to remove Legislative Speaker Wang by expelling him from the KMT. The remaining strength of the KMT's more conservative wing was apparent in the fact that Hung Hsiu-chu was nominated as presidential candidate in 2015 and, despite being replaced by Eric Chu, she was still able to win the KMT's leadership election in 2016. At the time of writing, another KMT leadership election was held in May 2017, with former Vice President Wu Den-yih, Hung and former Taipei mayor Hau Lung-bin the strongest candidates. Wu emerged victorious and it remains to be seen in what direction he will take the KMT.

Inner-party balance of power within the DPP

The initial early split in the DPP was between the New Tide and Formosa factions. These groups developed from divisions within the *Tangwai* movement in the last years of martial law. The Formosa faction originally referred to politicians involved in the Kaohsiung incident and their relatives. In contrast, the New Tide emerged from younger generation activists involved in opposition magazines in the 1980s. Apart from the generational difference, the Formosa faction tended to be more willing to negotiate with the KMT, took a more moderate national identity stance and preferred to work through existing political institutions, such as the supplementary elections. In contrast, the New Tide took a more radical stance on *de jure* independence and preferred to focus on direct action, such as street protests, even if these at times turned violent. Another distinction according to Cheng and Hsu is while 'the Formosans advocated a liberal democracy, the New Tide tilted towards a social democracy'.[24]

The struggle between the New Tide and Formosa factions was especially intense in the DPP's first five years. However, the two sides reached a compromise in 1991 with Formosa getting the chairmanship and the New Tide being placated with the inclusion of the Taiwan Independence Clause (TIC) in the party charter. For the rest of the decade there was a rough factional balance of power within the DPP. In the mid-1990s, the Formosa faction began to gradually split and weaken, with Hsu Hsin-liang being the last influential Formosa leader. The new factions that emerged in the 1990s included the Justice Alliance and Welfare State, groupings particularly associated with two rising stars of the new generation of DPP leaders, Chen Shui-bian and Hsieh Chang-ting respectively. Moreover, the party leadership was in the hands of election-oriented moderates such as Hsu Hsin-liang and Shih Ming-teh (施明德) for most of the 1990s.

After Hsu Hsin-liang left the DPP in 1999, Formosa ceased to be a recognized faction. Thus, for much of the post-2000, New Tide, Welfare State and Justice Alliance were the dominant groupings within the party. As the DPP was the ruling party, there was now a struggle not only for nomination but also for government positions. In 2006, the DPP decided to officially abolish its factions, as there were concerns they were damaging the parties' reputation and exacerbating internal splits. However, in reality the factions continued to exist, although, apart from the New Tide, they tended to be groupings

allied with Chen Shui-bian and the three or four politicians who ho
These were Hsieh Chang-ting, Su Tseng-chang (蘇貞昌), Yu Shyi-k
a lesser extent, Annette Lu (呂秀蓮).

With the DPP's defeat in 2008 and election of a new party chair, Ts
factional balance of power changed significantly. It took Tsai some time
her position in the party. Nathan Batto suggested in 2010 that there wei
left: Hsieh, Su, Yu, Chen, New Tide and Grandparents (older DPP leaders su
Chai (蔡同榮) and Annette Lu).[25] Even before her landslide election victory
by far the most powerful politician in the DPP. However, other important g
involve alliances with former party chairs Hsieh and Su, as well as key local ex
such as Chen Chu (陳菊 Kaohsiung) and Lai ching-te (賴清德 Tainan).

Inner-party politics in the smaller parties

Despite the size of the NP, it was also riddled with factional divisions in its first decade
The party was formed out of a group of half a dozen leaders of the New KMT Alliance.
In the mid-1990s the party founders took more of a back-seat role, allowing moderates
to have greater influence. Between 1997 and 1998, there was an intense struggle for
leadership between moderates and the party founders. However, from 1998 there was a
significant shift in favour of Chinese nationalist radicals such as Lee Ching-hua. As most
moderates, and even some party founders, left the party for either the PFP or KMT, the
party was left in the hands of a handful of extremists. The trend continued in 2000–1
under the control of Hsieh Chi-ta and since 2002 under Yu Mu-ming's leadership.

Neither the PFP nor TSU have become as factionalized as the older parties. The PFP
was so dominated by Soong that it has often been called a one-man party. Although
Soong liked to talk of the PFP as being a team and stressed the role played by his vice
chair Chang Chao-hsiung (張昭雄), in reality Soong has always been the key decision-
maker. For the TSU, the power centre was whoever Lee designated as party chairman.
In the cases of both the PFP and the TSU, when the party founders lost popularity, their
politicians chose exit to the KMT or DPP rather than to challenge the leader. Currently,
the situation remains the same with Soong and Yu still emperors in their skeleton parties
and Lee's latest designated chairman the dominant personality in a once again legislator-
less TSU.

Explaining party change

In this section I will briefly consider how to explain the ideological and candidate selection
patterns of party change described above.

In the 1990s, Wu Yu-shan and Ming Chu-cheng (明居正) stressed the role of moderate
public opinion in encouraging the main parties to move towards the centre on issues
such as national identity.[26] In contrast, Cheng and Hsu gave prominence to the role of
internal factional politics in explaining why the DPP moved towards more radical
positions on Taiwan independence, in particular focusing on the relationship between
the New Tide and Formosa factions.[27] Another important variable, which I raised in
Chapter 3, is the electoral system, whereby parties take more radical positions in SVMM
and move to the centre in SMD contests.

The way that I have tried to explain party change has been to build upon these earlier
studies by considering both internal and external variables. I applied a framework

who view party change as products of two inner-party
...ange in the internal factional balance of power, and an
...particular a reaction to election results.[28] I argue that
...ed by election-oriented factions and leaders, they tended
...and public opinion by moving the party towards more
...st, when the party was dominated by more ideologically
...erving party unity and policy orthodoxy was most import-
...s the party may adopt electorally unpopular positions, or
...escribed to me as 'election poison'. However, there is always
...secondary faction, which can prevent the dominant faction
...ng party values or going to unacceptably extreme positions.
...w how I have applied this framework.

...DPP's moderation on national identity and broadening of
...1. A key impetus for this change was a widespread though not
...the party had been punished for its radical Taiwan independence
...tion defeat. However, equally important in party change was leader-
...a change. For the rest of the 1990s, the DPP was dominated by more
...ted party leaders such as Hsu and Shih. They appointed new propaganda
...o played a key role in the rebranding of the party. The factional balance within
...P, which shifted away from the more radical New Tide, also facilitated these
...anges. In addition, although not part of the DPP party centre, the rise of new more
election-oriented stars, Chen Shui-bian and Hsieh Chang-ting, also contributed towards
the DPP's new moderate image. Of course, there were limits to how far the election-
oriented politicians could go, and at times Hsu was constrained on changing the DPP's
China policy.

The second case was the KMT's shift away from unification and Chinese identity
appeals after 1993. In this case, there was an election setback in 1992, but what was more
important here was the change in party leadership and factional balance. With Hau ousted
from the premiership, Lee and his Mainstream faction were able to shift the party towards
the centre. We saw this with changed KMT positions on UN membership, constitutional
reform and direct presidential election. However, there were limits to how far Lee could
go. For instance, when Lee tried to persuade the KMT to accept a DPP-style pensions
policy he was blocked by party colleagues.

The third classic case of change was the KMT after its defeat in 2000. This time there
was not only change in its ideology but also candidate selection. In addition to the humiliating defeat, the inner-party balance of power contributed to the KMT's reforms. The
new leadership under Lien and return to the fold of the non-Mainstream politicians
enabled the party to radically change direction. We saw this with the return to primaries
and re-embracing of ROC nationalist appeals that Lee had dropped. In fact, this case is
remarkably similar to that of the DPP after losing in 2008. After defeat, the old Chen
faction was marginalized and many of the Tangwai era leadership were discredited. This
power vacuum allowed Tsai to win the leadership and gradually consolidate power. Under
Tsai's leadership, the party engaged in organizational reforms, reconnected with civil
society, and rebranded the party. Tsai was even able to shift the party slightly closer to
the centre on the DPP's China policy, at least enough to allow the party to win election
in 2016.

A final case of change is that of the NP's move to extreme Chinese nationalism after
1998. There had been election setbacks in 1998 and 2000, but what was especially

important was the departure and marginalization of party moderates. The moderates, such as Yao Li-ming (姚立明) had tried to move the NP towards a more centrist position in 1997, but after this failed reform, the party became entirely dominated by extremists such as Hsieh Chi-ta. The extremists turned a small but relevant party into one able to win only a single legislative seat within a matter of three years.

How to best explain the success and failure of Taiwan's main parties?

This brings us to one of the most interesting questions in party politics: how do we explain success and failure? In my own research, I have tackled this question from three angles: (1) political performance, (2) issue strategies and (3) candidate selection.

The concept of political theatre and performance was touched upon in the previous chapter. My basic argument was that candidates and parties need to adjust their style of political performance or style of putting on a show (*zuoxiu*) according to changing audience tastes.[30] Thus, I tried to show a link between parties' performance skills and electoral results. Of course, you need key actors, and thus some of Taiwan's Oscar winners were Lee (1996), Chen Shui-bian (1994 and 2000), Jaw (1994), Soong (2000) and Ma (1998, 2008 and 2012).[31] Of course, as with stage actors, audience tastes change, and today perhaps all five would now possibly be contenders for the Golden Raspberry awards.

The second angle has been to argue that although issue appeals alone cannot determine election results, parties have benefited from employing the right kind of issue formula. Thus, for instance, when the DPP adopted very narrow national identity and radical Taiwan independence positions, it performed very poorly electorally, such as in 1991 and 1996. In contrast, when it repackaged, moderated and downplayed national identity while also stressing a broad range of salient issues such as attacking corruption, welfare and women's issues, it was able to expand its vote share and win elections such as in its many successes in the 1990s. There was a similar pattern with the NP benefiting from its moderate and broad appeals in the mid-1990s, but going into terminal decline as it became more narrowly focused. I have also argued that the KMT's changed electoral appeals after 2005 contributed to its return to power three years later.[32]

Lastly, I have tried to show a link between candidate selection and election results.[33] What seems to matter is having an institutionalized and rule-based nomination system, rather than a democratic system. Thus, for instance, the DPP's consistent use of primaries was a key factor in its ability to avoid rebel candidates and thus not split the party vote. In contrast, the KMT's top-down and negotiated approach in the 1990s led to party splits and rebel candidates who repeatedly divided the party's vote. There were clear links between nomination failures and the KMT's defeats in 1997 and 2000, as rebels split the KMT vote and allowed the DPP to win the majority of local executive posts and the presidency.

Taiwan's smaller challenger parties

The vast majority of research on Taiwan's party politics naturally focuses on the DPP and KMT. I have always had a soft spot for the island's third parties, perhaps because my first Taiwanese election featured a huge variety of diverse (and unsuccessful) parties, with one party's candidate even stripping during the campaign.[34]

The next three tables can give us a picture of the impact that the main third parties have had on Taiwan's party politics. As we discussed in the last chapter, the challenger parties have almost never been able to win seats in the SMD elections, but at times have been quite successful in SVMM contests.[35] First, Table 6.7 shows the new parties' vote and seat shares in national level elections. Table 6.8 shows their numbers of nominated and elected candidates in the Taipei and Kaohsiung city councils since 1989. Table 6.9 shows numbers of nominated and elected candidates in city and county council elections in the post-2000 period. I should note that I have been selective in the parties included in the analysis, limiting it to ones that have contested more than one election and nominated more than just a handful of candidates. The other grouping that I excluded is the Non Partisan Solidarity Union, as this is just a front for KMT-allied politicians not directly affiliated with any party and without any membership structure or ideological foundation.[36]

These tables suggest four distinct phases for the development of challenger parties. In the initial transition period (1989–92) the majority of the challenger parties were leftist organizations led by politicians that had split away from the DPP. For instance, the founder and only elected politician of the Chinese Social Democratic Party (CSDP), Chu Kao-cheng, had left the DPP in 1989. The founder of the Labour Party (LP) Wang Yi-hsiung (王義雄)was originally elected in 1986 as a DPP legislator, but lost his re-election bid as a Labour Party candidate in 1989. Apart from Chu, the only successful case of a leftist party winning a seat was Zhang Yi-lang (張益郎) for the Labour Party in the 1989 Kaohsiung city council elections. The CSDP does represent the most serious attempt to create a party not based on national identity at its core. In 1991 and 1992 the party ran a coordinated nationwide campaign, nominating 58 and 25 candidates respectively. It also ran TV and newspaper advertisements and gained significant media attention. However, it was unable to make any major breakthroughs and eventually merged with the NP in 1993.

The second phase came in the mid-1990s with the emergence of two splinter parties of politicians dissatisfied with the main parties: the NP and Taiwan Independence Party (TIP).[37] The exception to this pattern was the Green Party (GPT), but it only managed one seat in the National Assembly in 1996. The NP has been far more resilient than the TIP, which only had a minimal impact in 1998. The NP managed to win national legislative seats in the 1990s and was especially successful in Taipei city council elections. Even after the NP's collapse in national elections in 2001, it continued to win seats in the Taipei city council in the post-2000 period.

In the third phase, during the DPP era, two more splinter parties, the TSU and PFP, broke off from the KMT. While the TSU allied with the DPP, it recruited candidates from both major parties. The PFP poached politicians from the NP and the KMT. Like the TIP and NP, the PFP and TSU appealed to voters and politicians dissatisfied with the national identity line of the main parties. However, the PFP and TSU had a far greater impact than either of their counterparts in the 1990s, with the PFP gaining 20 per cent of parliamentary seats at its peak (2001) and the TSU gaining almost 6 per cent. However, after 2004 both parties were on declining trajectories. In Table 6.9 we can see how there was a drastic decline in the PFP's local council candidates and elected candidates in 2005/6. In 2008, with the new voting system in place, more political parties than ever contested the Legislative Yuan election. I have not included the many new entrants in Table 6.7, as for most of them this was their first and last election. New choices presented to voters included the Civil Party, Hakka Party, Third Society Party, Red Party, Taiwan Farmers Party and Home Party. This gave the campaign the appearance of being highly diverse, but most of these new parties only contested the second

Table 6.7 The vote and seat share for new parties in national parliamentary elections

	1989	1991	1992	1995	1996	1998	2001	2004	2008	2012	2016
NP				13 (12.8)	13.7 (14.7)	7.1(4.9)	2.9 (0.4)	0.1 (0.4)	4 (0)	1.5 (0)	4.1 (0)
PFP							20.3 (20.4)	13.9 (15.1)	0 (0.9)	5.5 (2.7)	6.5 (2.7)
TIP						1.5 (0.4)	0.0 (0)	0.0 (0)			
TSU							8.5 (5.8)	7.8 (5.3)	3.5 (0)	9 (2.7)	2.5 (0)
LP	0.92 (0)	0.1 (0)	0.4 (0)					0.0 (0)			
CSDP		2.1 (0)	1.6 (0.6)								
GP					1.1(0.3)		0.0 (0)		0.6 (0)	1.7 (0)	2.5 (0)
NPP											6.1 (4.4)

Sources: Central Election Commission; Fell (2005c); Schaferrer (2003).

Note 1: This table shows the vote share and seat share for new parties in national parliamentary elections.

Note 2: Seat shares are shown in parenthesis.

Note 3: 1989 is for the supplementary Legislative Yuan election; 1991 and 1996 the National Assembly elections; 1992, 1995, 1998, 2001, 2004, 2008, 2012 and 2016 are the Legislative Yuan elections.

Note 4: For 2008, 2012 and 2016 I have used proportional representation vote share.

Note 5: The PFP won one seat out of its three official candidates in 2008. The PFP only had one (unsuccessful) district level candidate in 2008, who won 47.04 per cent of the vote in Lienchiang County. This only amounted to 2,064 votes and represents 0.02 per cent of the national vote share.

Table 6.8 Candidates nominated and elected for new parties in Kaohsiung (KH) and Taipei (TP) city councils

	1989 KH	1989 TP	1994 KH	1994 TP	1998 KH	1998 TP	2002 KH	2002 TP	2006 KH	2006 TP	2010 KH	2010 TP	2014 KH	2014 TP
NP			5 (2)	14 (11)	6 (1)	16 (9)	1 (0)	6 (5)	1 (0)	4 (4)	1 (0)	5 (3)	1 (0)	7 (2)
PFP							8 (7)	17 (8)	8 (4)	8 (2)	2 (1)	7 (2)	3 (1)	7 (2)
TSU							7 (2)	7 (0)	6 (1)	6 (2)	4 (0)	4 (1)	7 (1)	6 (1)
GP					5 (0)	4 (0)		1 (0)		2 (0)		4 (0)	1 (0)	
TIP						4 (0)								
LP	3(1)	1(0)												
Total Seats	43	51	44	52	44	52	52	44	44	52	66	62	66	62

Sources: Central Election Commission; Schaferrer (2003); Lasater (1990).

Note 1: This table shows the number of candidates nominated and elected by new parties in Kaohsiung and Taipei city council elections.
Note 2: The number of candidates elected are shown in parenthesis.
Note 3: The increased number of seats in 2010 are due to administrative mergers and upgrading.
Note 4: Although the GPT did not nominate in Taipei city in 2014, its splinter party, the Tree Party, had five unsuccessful candidates.

Table 6.9 Small party candidates and candidates elected in county and city council elections

	2002	2005/6	2009/10	2014
TSU	53 (9)	58 (14)	15 (5)	41 (9)
PFP	197 (65)	82 (37)	17 (4)	36 (9)
GP	1 (0)	2 (0)	5 (0)	9 (2)
NP	19 (10)	13 (6)	9 (3)	19 (2)
PDF				13 (0)
LP			1 (1)	1 (1)
Tree				10 (1)

Source: Central Election Commission.

vote party list section and none crossed the 5 per cent threshold for winning seats. Then small parties reached a new low in the 2009/10 local elections. These left only 13 local council politicians representing small parties.

Since the publication of the first edition of this book I argue that we are witnessing a new phase in the development of small parties. We saw this first in the return of the splinter parties to the national parliament in 2012 and a continued expansion in seats in local councils in 2014. It was also noteworthy to see that for the first time alternative (prophetic parties) were becoming competitive. For instance, in 2014 two GPT candidates were elected in Hsinchu and Taoyuan. In the aftermath of the Sunflower Movement a number of social movement linked parties were established and there was much talk about a third force in Taiwanese politics. In the 2016 elections, one of the new parties, the NPP, did make a breakthrough. However, the GPT/Social Democratic Party was still well short of the required 5 per cent threshold. The 2016 election also suggested that the splinter parties are running out of steam. Although the PFP managed to retain its three legislators, both the NP and TSU were left without any national seats.

A clear pattern in these three tables is that purifier parties performed far better than prophetic parties, at least prior to 2014.[38] Purifier parties base their appeals on ideology that has been neglected or abandoned by the main parties. Thus, in Taiwan this would include the NP, TIP, PFP and TSU. In contrast, prophetic parties adopt completely new ideological appeals from those of the dominant parties. Thus, the LP, CSDP, GPT and Third Society Party all fall into this less successful category. Moreover, it is the purifiers on the KMT or Pan Blue side that have had far more success than those splitting off from the DPP.

So how do we explain the success and failure of these challenger parties? Thus far, we have only tackled this question via electoral systems and ideological positions. In other words, there is more space in SVMM elections than under their SMD counterparts. In an earlier study I adopted a framework suggested by Paul Lucardie in which third-party success and failure can be explained by three factors: (1) political project, (2) resources and (3) political opportunity structure. I argued that 'new party success depends on the ability to propagate a clear and distinct party appeal that addresses salient political issues; their human, financial, organizational and media resources; and the ability to take advantage of their electoral environment'.[39] I will briefly show how I applied this framework to explain the impact of one prophetic party (SDP), one purifier (PFP) and one hybrid party (NPP).

The CSDP represented the most serious attempt at the creation of a nationwide prophetic party that offered a radical alternative to the main parties. However, despite a strong campaign it only had one candidate elected and it merged with the NP in 1993. We can see elements of its failure through all three dimensions of the framework. First, it did have a comprehensive manifesto that tackled a range of salient issues, something quite rare in Taiwanese elections, but its platform had some fatal weaknesses. The welfare state was a strong appeal due to the inequality of Taiwan's welfare system at the time. However, by the early 1990s both the main parties had taken clear pro-welfare expansion positions, thus limiting its value for the CSDP. Moreover, the CSDP chose a strong anti-Taiwan independence stance and called for unification under a Chinese federation, making it look very similar to the KMT. Lastly, its appeal was delivered in too intellectual a manner. Thus, it struggled to get its message across to ordinary voters. The party also suffered a severe lack of resources compared to the main parties. It did have the well-known Chu Kao-cheng as its party leader, but although the rest of its candidates were highly educated and had clean images, they were electorally inexperienced and lacked the kind of grassroots networks the other parties had developed. The political environment in 1991 and 1992 did leave space for new parties, as these elections used the SVMM electoral system. The problem that Chu admitted to me in an interview was that the KMT party machine was still strong at the time, while the DPP was still growing, limiting the political space for the CSDP.[40] If the CSDP had made a breakthrough in 1991 the story might have been different, but as elections became so expensive in the mid-1990s Chu had little choice but to throw in the towel and join the NP.

The PFP made a far greater impact on party politics than the NP and even challenged the KMT's position as the dominant Pan Blue party for a couple of years. However, it began a long decline after 2004 and now, while the NP remains a marginal party, the PFP has effectively disappeared. The PFP tried to learn from the NP's mistake and thus tried to be ambiguous and moderate on national identity. It did not have a very comprehensive issue appeal and instead focused on candidate Soong and his record for government competence. The difference between the PFP and the NP was that it had a superstar in Soong who could attract financial and human resources from both the KMT and NP. There was also a window of opportunity when the party emerged, as the NP was in decline and the KMT was in disarray after losing the 2000 presidential election. Therefore, the PFP was able to take advantage of SVMM elections to win significant numbers of seats.

So why did the PFP go into seemingly terminal decline after 2004? First, it lacked a clear appeal beyond Soong, so once the KMT looked more orthodox it won votes and politicians back. At the same time the PFP's violent protests made it look more radical after the 2004 election, scaring off the Taiwanese voters it had won in 2000–1. As Soong's own appeal dried up, so did the PFP's support. The party thus lost its key human and financial resources and its legislators began switching back to the KMT from 2005. Lastly, the overall political environment changed, as the KMT under Ma Ying-jeou recovered support and became the clear dominant Pan Blue party by 2005. In the run-up to the first election under the new SMD Legislative Yuan election system, it was clear that the party would struggle to survive, so the PFP reached an agreement with the KMT to allow its politicians to stand as KMT candidates. However, the PFP was able to achieve a limited recovery after 2012. Again, Lucardie's framework can help us understand its survival. First, the party attempted to take a position between the two main parties, but did so by mainly attacking the KMT. Its key human resource remained Soong, as he was able to hold on to a number of loyal politicians and poach some back from the KMT. Lastly, the party was able to survive by using Soong's presidential campaigns in 2012 and 2016 as a means of raising the visibility of its party list candidates.

The newest addition to Taiwan's party scene is the NPP. I see it as a hybrid party as it has used both traditional appeals together with those we normally associate with alternative parties. Its advertising tended to stress the parties' involvement in key social movements such as the Sunflowers, anti-nuclear movement and supporting gay rights. However, it also took a clear stance against economic and political ties with China and worked in alliance with the DPP. Thus, the NPP was appealing to both alternative party supporters but also those inclined to vote TSU or DPP. In addition, the NPP had a major resource advantage over its rival smaller parties in that it had a number of political stars, such as the Sunflower leader Huang Kuo-chang (黃國昌) and musician Freddie Lim (林昶佐).

Party system change

Although it is easy to dismiss party system studies as little more than counting the number of parties, the answers to the core party system questions have critically important implications for the state of any political system. As we see in Singapore or Taiwan under martial law, a one party or one-party dominant system may be democratic on paper, but in reality often operates like an authoritarian system. Similarly, there are dangers for a democracy where the parties become too polarized or the interparty relationship is so antagonistic that politics become a form of war. The consequences of an extremely antagonistic party system were seen in the tragic developments following the 2007 Kenyan presidential election. The four dimensions of party system change discussed in this section are: (1) party system fragmentation, (2) ideological distance between parties and (3) whether the relationship between parties is adversarial or cooperative.[41]

Party system fragmentation

Party system fragmentation looks at the number of relevant parties and their relative size. I have simplified the key patterns of development in Table 6.10. We can divide the party system fragmentation into a number of stages. For the ten-year span of 1989 to 1998 I have categorized Taiwan as having a predominant party system, whereby the KMT won an absolute majority of the seats in parliamentary elections and was the sole large party. However, this period can be subdivided into the early period when the KMT was completely dominant with 70–80 per cent of seats until 1991 and the rest of the decade when, although the KMT remained dominant, the party system became more competitive, with the continuous growth of the DPP and emergence of the NP. Thus, for most of the mid to late 1990s elections, there was one large (KMT), one medium (DPP) and one small (NP) relevant party.

The key turning point was the three-way 2000 presidential election which represents the commencement of the multi-party era. As for the next few elections, there were four or even five relevant parties in legislative, city assembly and even some SMD local executive elections. In the post-2000 period, there was much more fluctuation in the parties' relative size than during the relative stability of the 1990s. In 2001, the DPP was

Table 6.10 Party system fragmentation

	1989	1991	1992	1993	1994	1995	1996	1997	1998	2000	2001	2002	2004	2005	2006	2008	2009	2010	2012	2014	2016
Relevant parties	2	2	2	3	3	3	3/4	2	3	3	4/5	4	4	2	5	2	2	2	4	4	4/5
Party sizes	1L 1M 1C	1L 1M 1C	1L 1M 1C	1L 1M 1S	1L 1M 1S	1L 1M 1S 1C	1L 1M 1S 1C	2L 1C	1L 1M 1S 1C	2L 1M	1L 2M 1S 1C	1L 3M 1C	2L 1M 1S	2L 3C	1L 1M 3S	1L 1M 3C	2L	2L	2L 2S	2L 2S 2C	2L 2S 3C
System type	P	P	P	P	P	P	P	T	P	M	M	M	M	T	M	P	P	T	T	T	T

Source: Based on the author's interpretation of Central Election Commission data.

Note 1: A party needs to gain 5 per cent of seats or votes to be counted as relevant.

Note 2: For the relative party sizes: Large = L: over 35 per cent of seats and votes; Medium sized = M: 15–35 per cent of seats or votes; Small = S: 5–15 per cent of seats or votes, Minor challenger party = C: 1–5 per cent of seats or votes.

Note 3: System types: P = Predominant; T = Two Party; M = Multi-Party.

the large party, against two medium (KMT and PFP) and one small party (TSU), while in 2004 there were two large parties (KMT and DPP), one medium party (PFP) and one small (TSU). After 2005, there was a shift away from multi-party politics towards a two-party system. My categorization of 2006 as having a multi-party system is debatable, as I have taken Taipei and Kaohsiung city councils as my standard. If I had chosen the mayoral elections, then it would also appear that, as in 2005, Taiwan had a two-party system.

The third distinct phase comes after 2008 when we saw a brief return to a KMT dominant system, with the KMT winning absolute majorities of the seats. If we think in terms of seat shares, then the party system in 2008–9 looks remarkably like Taiwan during the immediate transition period (1986–91). In contrast, the vote shares show that the system is still competitive, as the DPP recovered from its 2008 defeat. If I had taken vote share as my main standard, then I could call 2009 a two-party system.

We get a similar picture of party system fragmentation in the party identification trends shown in Table 6.11. Unlike election results, these surveys are conducted more frequently and reflect party preference rather than voting behaviour. We should note some key differences here from the election data: (1) party identification is almost always lower than the vote share, and (2) there is a high number of respondents choosing no party identity. As with the voting figures in the initial period (1992), the degree of KMT domination is striking with 34.4 per cent of respondents preferring the KMT compared to a miniscule 3.3 per cent for the DPP. However, the system gradually became more competitive as DPP support grew in the mid to late 1990s and with the rise of the NP. Once again, 2000 marks the start of a multiparty system, with the DPP as the largest party and the KMT and PFP as medium-sized parties. In terms of identification levels, it is clear how close the PFP came to replacing the KMT as the strongest Pan Blue party in 2000–2. Despite their success in winning seats, surveys could barely pick up voter identification with the TSU and NP.

The next critical turning point in the party system appears to be 2004–5 when the KMT showed a historic increase in identification from 21.2 to 31.2 per cent, and the DPP a significant fall from 24.7 to 21.6 per cent. The challenger parties also suffered consistent declines from then, as Taiwan looked to be moving back towards a KMT-dominated two-party system. One interesting finding from the party identification data is that identification levels were quite stable from 2005 to 2009. In other words, the change in ruling parties in 2008 did not have the same kind of impact on the party system as its earlier equivalent in 2000. This has led me to argue that Taiwan's real critical election year should be seen as 2005 rather than 2008.[42] Thus, an important task for students of political science is to try to unravel what happened in 2005 to create this kind of tectonic shift. I will return to this question in Chapters 11 (political corruption) and 13 (post-2008 Taiwan).

The party identification trends in Table 6.11 suggest that there was a significant shift in party support levels during Ma's second term. The KMT fell from an all-time high in popularity of 39.5 on the eve of the 2012 elections down to 20.8 in 2016. The KMT's decline in support appeared to be especially rapid between 2012 and 2014. Initially, these KMT defectors were switching to selecting no party affiliation and it was only late in the presidential term that the DPP experienced a significant increase in support. Table 6.11 reveals that unlike in the initial post-2000 period, the splinter parties were unable to benefit from the KMT's decline in popularity and it is only in the most recent 2016 survey that we see the NPP appearing in the figures.

Table 6.11 Party identification for Taiwan's main parties, 1992–2016

	1992	1994	1995	1996	1997	1998	1999	2000	2001	2002	2003	2004	2005	2006	2007	2008	2009	2010	2011	2012	2013	2014	2015	2016
KMT	34.4	29	30.8	32.1	24.9	29.2	33.6	21.1	14.8	14.4	24.5	21.2	31.2	35.5	34	35.5	33.9	32.8	39.5	32.7	26.7	22.9	22.1	20.8
DPP	3.3	12.1	12.8	12.8	16.5	21	22	26	25	25.5	21.9	24.7	21.6	18.7	20.1	21.2	19.5	26.2	24.9	25.7	25.7	26.7	31.2	29.9
NP		5.6	8.4	9.8	6.4	4	3.8	2.4	0.9	0.5	0.8	1	0.5	0.6	0.6	1.6	0.9	0.8	1.1	0	0.9	0.8	0.6	0.4
TIP				0.4	0.9	0.6	0.4	0.2	0.2															
PFP								10.9	18.9	15.9	11.6	9.6	4	2	1.1	1.5	1.2	2	3.3	3.4	3.1	2.7	3.7	2.3
TSU									0.6	1.6	2.1	2.4	3.4	2.7	1.2	1.9	1.2	1.1	1.1	2.3	1.8	1.9	1.2	0.2
Indep	62.3	53.3	48	44.9	51.3	45.2	40.2	37.2	42.6	42.1	39.1	41.1	39.3	40.5	42.9	38.3	43.3	37.1						

Source: Election Study Centre, National Chengchi University.

Ideological distance between parties

Previous chapters and the section on individual parties' ideological changes have given us a taste of some of the overall trends in party system ideological shifts on the core issues. Here I will not go into much detail on these core issues, such as national identity, social welfare and political corruption, as I will return to these again in subsequent chapters. However, the broad trends have been as follows. The initial transition phase (1986–91) witnessed a period of gradual polarization as the parties remained wide apart on independence versus unification, national identity, constitutional issues and foreign affairs. There were some areas of convergence such as on health insurance and some democratic reforms, but consensual issues were in the minority. Next, for most of the 1990s there was a general trend towards convergence on the core issues of social welfare, cross-Strait relations and even political corruption. In the late 1990s there was some movement towards the poles by the smaller parties such as the TIP and NP, while the main parties converged towards the centre on many core issues.

The first Chen term featured mixed trends in ideological distance. On welfare, referendums, constitutional reforms and economic policy the parties did manage to reach some important agreements, such as the 2002 Pensions Bill. However, there were also areas of divergence on national identity and nuclear power. To a certain extent, the clash of personalities in the 2004 presidential election has left us with an exaggerated picture of polarization. However, in the second Chen term divergence was the more common trend. What was especially noteworthy was how previously consensual issues became polarized, such as arms procurement from the US. The parties were also diverging on China policy and national identity symbols. This was apparent in the different interpretations of the Pan Blue leaders' visits to China in 2005 and debates over Chiang Kai-shek's legacy in 2007.

Since 2008, there have been significant shifts in the ideological distance between the main parties. The KMT returned to power in 2008 on a moderate platform but gradually moved towards the centre-right and at times even far right of the national identity spectrum. The initial nomination of Hung Hsiu-chu 2015 and her party leadership after 2016 reflect this shift away from the centre. In contrast, the DPP moved gradually closer to the centre in its bid to make itself electable in the run-up to the 2016 elections. A notable feature of the 2016 elections was that there were record numbers of parties appealing to voters at the two poles, but none of their politicians were actually elected.

Cooperative or antagonistic interparty relations

I have attempted to summarize the patterns of interparty relations in Table 6.12. To a certain extent the findings overlap with those on ideological distance, with more cooperation at times of convergence. However, it is worth discussing some of the key trends. The seven dimensions examined are: (1) meetings of party leaders, (2) policy cooperation, (3) interparty conferences, (4) cooperation on speaker elections, (5) negative propaganda, (6) cooperation for election nomination and (7) interparty violence.

There has been considerable variation over time in the state of interparty relations. Of the three periods of multi-party competition, interparty relations were at their most antagonistic between 1986 and 1992. During this period, meetings between the parties' leaders were few and far between. The KMT leaders did not regard the DPP as a suitable partner for negotiation or even a legitimate party. This was clear from KMT Premier

Table 6.12 Adversarial or cooperative strategies

	1986–92	1993–99	2000–10	2011–2016
Meetings of party leaders	Few	DPP–KMT DPP–NP	KMT–PFP KMT–NP DPP–TSU	KMT–NP DPP–TSU/NPP
Policy cooperation	Little	DPP+KMT DPP+NP NP+KMT	KMT+PFP+NP TSU+DPP	DPP+TSU DPP+NPP
Interparty conferences	Yes (1990)	Yes (1996)	Yes (2001)	No
Cooperation on speaker elections	No	DPP+NP	KMT+PFP+NP TSU+DPP	DPP+TSU DPP+NPP
Negative propaganda	KMT vs. DPP DPP vs. KMT	KMT vs. NP KMT vs. DPP DPP vs. NP DPP vs. KMT NP vs. KMT NP vs. DPP	Green vs. Blue Blue vs. Green	Green vs. Blue
Cooperation for election nomination	No	No	KMT+PFP+NP TSU+DPP	KMT+NP DPP+TSU DPP+PFP DPP+NPP
Interparty violence?	DPP vs. KMT	DPP vs. NP KMT vs. DPP	Green vs. Blue	Green vs. Blue

Note: This table compares the adversarial or cooperative interparty relationship over seven dimensions, in four time periods.

Hau Pei-tsun's proposal to legally dissolve the DPP for its advocacy of Taiwan independence in 1991. In this period, the tone of party propaganda was highly antagonistic. While the KMT repeatedly denounced the DPP as an irresponsible, radical and violent party, the DPP was not averse to stirring up ethnic tensions by depicting the KMT's Mainlander premier as a fat pig in election advertisement cartoons.[43] In the parliaments, physical violence reached a peak, as opposition parliamentarians attempted to make up for their lack of members with violent antics. The major exception to the hostile interparty environment of this period was the 1990 National Affairs Conference in which former political prisoners and their persecutors acted like old friends and reached consensuses on the direction of political reform.

We have a mixed picture when comparing the interparty relationships in the Lee Teng-hui period of 1993–2000.[44] The relationship between party leaders showed much improvement. Meetings between the DPP and Lee were commonplace, as the opposition party increasingly viewed Lee as someone with whom they could work. This is apparent from the veteran DPP politician Chang Chun-hong's comment on the 1996 election: 'Instead of saying the DPP did badly that year, we could say the DPP did very well as Lee Teng-hui, the actual DPP chairman, was elected President.'[45] Similarly, in the mid-1990s under the leadership of Shih Ming-teh, the DPP attempted a policy of reconciliation with the NP, with the two parties holding their famous coffee meeting in 1995. Despite the deep ideological gap, they were able to work together on the 1996 Legislative Speaker election and a few pieces of legislation. For instance, in May 1996 the DPP and NP combined to block legislation for the construction of the Fourth Nuclear Power Station.[46] On other issues, such as pensions or national identity, the NP and KMT worked together to oppose the DPP.

Despite the fact that the NP had split from the KMT and shared many ideological similarities with it, the relationship between these parties was often antagonistic. Attacking Lee was a central theme of NP propaganda. It appeared that the NP blamed Lee for all Taiwan's contemporary problems, including the impasse on cross-Strait relations, corruption and ethnic tensions. Similarly, the KMT attempted to smear the NP, accusing it of being a spokesman for the CCP; one 1994 KMT advertisement even likened NP leader Jaw Shaw-kong to Hitler.[47] Unsurprisingly, Lee had little interest in meeting NP leaders. The highpoint for interparty cooperation between the KMT and DPP was the 1996 National Development Conference. Here the two parties were able to negotiate a package of constitutional revisions on a far more equal basis than in 1990.

Although there were clearly numerous signs of cooperative party behaviour in the Lee era, we should not ignore the adversarial components of the party system. The close relations between the DPP and NP in 1995–6 and the KMT and DPP in late 1996 were the exception to the rule. As soon as an election approached, antagonism again ruled. There were high levels of negative propaganda between all three major parties in this era. Finally, although there was a gradual decline in parliamentary violence, political violence between rival supporters reached its peak. There were a number of particularly serious violent incidents between NP and DPP supporters in Kaohsiung and Taipei in 1994–5. In September 1994, there were a large number of injuries when DPP supporters attempted to disrupt the first NP political rally staged in Kaohsiung and DPP activists demanded that the NP 'go back to the Mainland'.[48] In Taipei, there was a series of violent clashes between NP supporters and pro-DPP taxi drivers following the murder of one driver by an allegedly NP-linked gangster.[49]

The party system of the Chen Shui-bian era rightly acquired a reputation for interparty conflict. The major difference from the two earlier periods is that between 2000 and 2008 antagonistic relations were between Pan Green and Pan Blue blocs, while within the blocs cooperative interparty relations were more common. In other words, the KMT, PFP and NP tended to cooperate on nomination, policy and efforts to block DPP government legislation. On the Pan Green side, the TSU tended to support the DPP government.

There was significant change in the relationships between party leaders. Unlike the hostility between the KMT and the NP in the 1990s, after 2000 NP politicians were invited into the KMT chair's (Lien Chan) inner circle of advisers. Similarly, despite the trading of insults between Soong and Lien in the 2000 presidential election, relations between the two became increasingly cordial, culminating in their joint presidential ticket in 2004. There was a similar brotherly relationship between the DPP and their Pan Green allies the TSU, and Chen Shui-bian held frequent meetings with the TSU spiritual leader Lee Teng-hui.

In contrast, the relationship between the Pan Blue and Pan Green parties became increasingly hostile. During his first term as President, Chen Shui-bian only met the KMT and PFP chairs on one occasion each. Two presidential defeats created deep mutual hatred among both KMT leaders and Chen supporters. This was apparent in the serious attempt to recall Chen in 2000–1, the anti-Chen rhetoric of the 2004 presidential campaign and Pan Blue violence following their defeat in 2004.

Negative propaganda was also highly antagonistic between the two camps, rather than within the Blue camp as it was in the 1990s. The principle targets for the Pan Blue attacks were Chen Shui-bian and Lee Teng-hui, while the Greens talked of terminating the 'Lien–Soong system'.[50] This period also saw the worst cases of political violence since the mid-1990s. Particularly serious were the post-election protests in the spring of 2000 and 2004, and violent clashes between rival camps' supporters at Taoyuan Airport in April 2005.

There were few exceptions to the antagonistic relationship between party blocs in the DPP era. Most of these were in Chen's first term. For instance, at the 2001 Economic Development Conference the major parties were able to reach significant consensus on economic policies. Similarly, cross-party cooperation enabled important legislation to be passed on pensions in 2002, enhancement of women's and workers' rights, a Referendum Bill in 2003 and Party Donations Law in 2004.[51]

Originally, I thought that the fading away of Chen, Lien and Soong from the political scene might lead to a more consensual style of politics in the post-2008 period. However, the scars of the Chen era remained unhealed. There was a return to parliamentary violence, as the DPP could no longer block KMT legislative measures with such a small parliamentary party. Ma's parliamentary majority meant that he did not need to negotiate to press through his agenda on expanding relations with China. On one of the very rare occasions when the DPP and KMT chairs did meet in 2014 to discuss the fate of the controversial Fourth Nuclear Power Station, it was clear they were talking past each other.[52]

Conclusions

This chapter has examined the colourful story of party and party system change in Taiwan since the late 1980s. Although the same two parties dominate Taiwanese politics in 2016 as they did in 1986, the parties and party system have witnessed remarkable change. These parties have been the engines of democratic politics, fulfilling the core roles of offering policy direction to government, conducting elite recruitment and acting as both agents for interest aggregation and as a point of reference for supporters to simplify the complicated political world.

Rather than ending on a congratulatory conclusion, I prefer to add a note of caution. Taiwanese parties have become highly unpopular in recent years. The drive to halve the size of the legislature was part of a public mood to punish parties and their representatives. One of the critical challenges ahead for Taiwan's parties is how to reconnect with new voters and lost supporters. The rise in social movements in the Ma era was partly the result of the growing frustration with mainstream party politics. However, as we saw in the post-2008 elections, new parties have struggled to translate alienation from the main parties into parliamentary seats. The limited electoral breakthroughs of the GPT in 2014 and NPP in 2016 show that it is possible for alternative forces to break into the seemingly closed party system.

A final question will be who will be the new opposition to the current ruling DPP. The KMT appears to be deeply divided and at least under the leadership of Hung, it was a party quite distant from the median voter on identity issues. In contrast, the NPP still lacks the human and financial resources to become a true challenger to the DPP, and it is unclear whether the party will retain its loose alliance with the DPP or seek greater autonomy.

Discussion questions

1   What types of parties dominate Taiwanese politics?
2   How have the parties changed (especially ideologically) over time?
3   How has the party system changed since the late 1980s?
4   How can we best explain party success and failure in Taiwan?
5   How can we best explain party or party system change?
6   How and why have Taiwan's parties changed their nomination practices?
7   How can we best explain the impact of third parties in Taiwan?
8   What are the major challenges facing Taiwan's party politics?

Further reading

Fell, Dafydd. 2005. *Party Politics in Taiwan*. London: Routledge. Examination of party change from 1991 to 2001, focusing on parties' election issue emphasis and inner-party balance of power shifts.

Fell, Dafydd. 2006. 'Democratization of Candidate Selection in Taiwanese Political Parties'. *Journal of Electoral Studies*, 13(2): 167–98. I discuss the how and why of candidate selection from 1989 to 2004.

Fell, Dafydd. 2014. 'Measuring and Explaining the Electoral Fortunes of Small Parties in Taiwan's Party Politics'. *Issues and Studies: An International Quarterly on China, Taiwan, and East Asian Affairs*, 50 (1): 153–88. In this piece I plot the impact of the challenger parties and try to explain their successes and failures.

Fell, Dafydd. 2016. 'Parties and Party Systems'. In Schubert, Gunter (ed.), *Routledge Handbook of Contemporary Taiwan*. Abingdon and New York: Routledge, pp. 87–103. In this chapter I analyse Taiwan's changing party system.

Lin, Chiung-chu. 2006. 'The Evolution of Party Images and Party System in Taiwan, 1992–2004'. *East Asia: An International Quarterly*, 23(1): 27–46. This remains the best study on changing party images available in English.

Rigger, Shelley. 2001. *From Opposition to Power: Taiwan's Democratic Progressive Party*. Boulder, CO: Lynne Rienner. Best single party study on the rise of the DPP from its birth to winning power in 2000.

Useful websites

All of Taiwan's main and many challenger parties have websites, although only the KMT and DPP have extensive and well-maintained English language sites.

http://esc.nccu.edu.tw/english/ – The Election Study Center's website is an invaluable source of information in party identification, political attitudes, parties' vote and seats shares.

www.dpp.org.tw/ – (Democratic Progressive Party)

www.greenparty.org.tw/ – This site gives a taste of a challenger party.

www.kmt.org.tw/ – (Kuomintang Party)

Notes

1   Ware, *Political Parties and Party Systems*, 5.
2   Hague and Harrp, *Comparative Government and Politics*, 167.
3   Ware, 7.
4   Dalton and Wattenberg, *Parties without Partisans*.
5   Schattschneider, *Party Government*, 1.
6   Harmel and Janda, 'An Integrated Theory of Party Goals and Party Change', 259–87.

7 See Ministry of Interior: List of Political Parties, 28 March 2017: available online at: www. moi.gov.tw/dca/02people_005–1.aspx?sn=10. In contrast, the figure quoted from 2009 in the first edition was 148 registered parties.

8 Ware, 22.

9 The most important of these are publications based on Manifesto Research Group data and Laver and Hunt's expert surveys. See Budge *et al.*, *Mapping Policy Preferences*; Laver and Hunt, *Policy and Party Government*.

10 I discuss some studies on this question in Fell, 'Measurement of Party Position and Party Competition in Taiwan', 101–35.

11 Fell, *Party Politics in Taiwan*, 25.

12 Ibid., 27.

13 Fell, 'Taiwan's Party System in Transition: More or Less Space for Identity Politics?'; Fell, 'Polarization of Party Competition in the DPP Era'.

14 http://teds.nccu.edu.tw/teds_plan/list.php?g_isn=118&g_tid=1&g_cid=11 (accessed 3 April 2017).

15 Lin, 'The Evolution of Party Images and Party System in Taiwan, 1992–2004', 27–46.

16 National Science Council, 'Party Image: Measurement, Connotation, and Its Application'. National Science Research Project (NSC 102-2410-H-031-046-MY2).

17 TVBS Poll Center, 'Poll on Party List Legislators and Party and Party Images' (*bufenquliwei ji zhengdangxingxiang mindiao*), available online at: http://other.tvbs.com.tw/export/sites/tvbs/file/other/poll-center/0405281-.pdf (accessed 3 April 2017).

18 Lin, 44.

19 Schattschneider, 64.

20 In closed-member primaries only formal registered party members can vote, while in open primaries any citizen can vote.

21 The first two DPP chairmen were chosen by the Central Executive Committee. Initially these elections were held annually, and then after 1989 two-year terms were introduced.

22 Rahat and Hazan, 'Candidate Selection Methods: An Analytical Framework', 297–322, 301.

23 For example, Fell, *Party Politics in Taiwan*.

24 Cheng and Hsu, 'Issue Structure, the DPP's Factionalism, and Party Realignment,' 137–73, 145.

25 Nathan Batto, *Frozen Garlic Blog*, 'DPP Standing Committee Election', (22 July 2010), available online at: http://frozengarlic.wordpress.com (accessed 13 July 2010).

26 Wu, 'Convergence of Mainland Policies: Standard Distribution of Voters' Preferences and Vote Maximizing Strategy,' 5–22; Ming, 'Centrifugal Competition and the Development of the Republic of China's Party Politics,' 142–56.

27 Cheng and Hsu, 'Issue Structure, the DPP's Factionalism, and Party Realignment,' 137–73.

28 Harmel and Janda, 'An Integrated Theory of Party Goals and Party Change', 259–87.

29 I develop these arguments in depth in *Party Politics in Taiwan*. For a more succinct version, see Fell, 'Measuring and Explaining Party Change in Taiwan: 1991–2004',105–34.

30 Fell, 'Putting on a Show and Electoral Fortunes in Taiwan', 133–50.

31 One particularly creative KMT advertisement attacking Soong in the 2000 presidential advertisement carried the slogan 'Money, Lies and Hsingpiao Case: The Oscar Golden Soong Award has been Announced', *Liberty Times,* 3 February 2000, 16.

32 Fell, 'Lessons of Defeat: A Comparison of Taiwanese Ruling Parties' Responses to Electoral Defeat', 660–81.

33 Ibid.

34 Please see Chapter 5.

35 The only exceptions to this pattern were PFP and NP local executive victories in Kinmen (2001 and 2005), Lienchiang (2001 and 2005) and Taitung (2001). The recent exception came in 2016 when the NPP won three SMD legislative seats in 2016 after the DPP did not nominate in these districts.

36 Previously (1995–2001), this alliance operated under the title Nationwide Democratic Non-partisan Union.

37 In addition, a group known as the New Nation Alliance emerged in 1998 with a similar platform to the TIP and won a single seat. However, it did not contest further elections as its sole legislator returned to the DPP in 2001.

38 For a discussion of the concepts of purifiers and prophetic parties, see Lucardie, 'Prophets, Purifiers and Prolocutors', 175–85.

39 Fell, 'Success and Failure of New Parties in Taiwanese Elections', 217.

40 Chu Kao-cheng, interview with author, Kaohsiung, 8 October 2001.

41 In the first edition I had a section on party system openness, but on rereading I felt that question is already covered in the section on smaller parties.

42 Fell, 'Was 2005 A Critical Election in Taiwan?', 927–45.

43 *Liberty Times,* 5 December 1992, 1. The use of a pig in this cartoon is a clear derogatory reference to Mainlanders that became commonly used after the 1940s.

44 I term this the Lee Teng-hui period as it was only after 1993 that Lee was dominant in both the KMT and government.

45 Chang Chun-hong, interview by author, Taipei, 26 September 2001.

46 Lin, 'Paths to Democracy', 443–5.

47 *Liberty Times,* 2 December 1994, 20.

48 Wang Fu-chang, 'Ethnic consciousness, nationalism and party support', 10–11.

49 *Liberty Times,* 22 December 1994, 5.

50 Chang Yun-ping, 'Chen denies termination campaign', 4 August 2004, *Taipei Times,* 3.

51 For more on political developments after 2000, see Fell *et al.* (eds) *What has Changed? Taiwan Before and After the Change in Ruling Parties after 2000.*

52 Available online at: http://englishnews.ftv.com.tw/Read.aspx?sno=2DA6FAF6BACE9C4BB0 48052CE499103C

7 Local and factional politics

Unlike the relatively new national-level elections, local elections have been conducted in Taiwan since the 1930s, over a decade before the arrival of the ROC regime. The patterns of local political competition have often been radically different from those at the national level. A glance at Taiwan's recent grassroots elections will leave the uninitiated observers scratching their heads, wondering whether the data or dates are correct. Even in districts where the DPP runs the county government, over two decades after the lifting of martial law, the KMT is often still the dominant party in grassroots elections.

After reviewing the state of local politics prior to 1987, this chapter moves on to examine change and continuity in local level politics after democratization. A central feature of local politics under martial law was the patron–client alliance between the KMT and local factions. This partly explained the KMT's dominance of the authoritarian era elections. Thus, a key area of discussion will be how this relationship changed after democratization and the inroads the opposition made into the KMT's local dominance. Evidence shows that the KMT has been far more successful at maintaining its control of grassroots elections than national ones. Lastly, the impact of changes of ruling parties, electoral and administrative reform on local politics, will be considered.

Scope of analysis and definitions

This chapter focuses on politics below the national level, which I interpret as the layers of governance below the provincial or special municipality levels (Taipei and Kaohsiung cities after they were upgraded). Since I have already discussed local executive elections in Chapter 5, I will thus look in more detail at elections from the county/city assembly level downwards. These layers are displayed in Table 7.1, which shows the variations in administrative structures and elected positions from the city or county level down to the lowest elected level of the neighbourhood (*li*) or village (*cun*). Thus, most parts of the country have either five or three different types of local elections, from the city mayor/county magistrate down to the neighbourhood chief (*lizhang*).

The most influential player at the grassroots level of local Taiwanese politics has been the local factions. Local factions are subgroups that operate within political organizations, have their members recruited by a leader and are based at the local rather than national level. Landé suggests a definition in which a faction is 'a dyadic non-corporate group' that is based on a patron–client relationship.[1] He goes on to explain that in this patron–client relationship 'two persons of unequal status, power or resources each of whom finds it useful to have as an ally someone superior or inferior to himself'.[2] The attraction of this alliance for the client (local faction) is generally not ideological but economic or

Table 7.1 Grassroots administrative levels and elected posts

Level	County			City
Elected executive	County (county magistrate)			City (city mayor)
Elected representative	County council			City council

Level	Rural township (xiang)	Urban township (zhen)	City (shi)	District (Qu)
Elected executive	Township chief (xiangzhang)	Township chief (zhenzhang)	City mayor (shizhang)	District head (Quzhang) Appointed by city mayor
Elected representative	Township councillor (xiangmindai)	Township councillor (zhenmindai)	City councillor (shimindai)	None

Level	Village (cun)	Neighbourhood (li)	Neighbourhood (li)	Neighbourhood (li)
Elected representative	Village chief (cunzhang)	Neighbourhood chief (lizhang)	Neighbourhood chief (lizhang)	Neighbourhood chief (lizhang)

Level	Community (lin)	Community (lin)	Community (lin)	Community (lin)

symbolic rewards. The patron in turn hopes to profit from the client's ability to supply votes and mobilize supporters on the patron's behalf. In addition to these exchanges, affective social ties are the glue that hold the faction and its followers together. Key components of such ties include networks of relationships (*guanxi*), interactions (*jiaowang*), affections (*ganqing*), face (*mianzi*) and human sentiments (*renqing*).[3] Landé has suggested that some other core features one can observe are an 'uncertain duration, personalistic leadership, lack of formal organization and a greater concern with power and spoils than with ideology or policy'.[4] Bosco notes that Taiwan's factions correspond with these characteristics, 'except that they are more group-like, permanent and sharply defined than factions elsewhere. They have permanent names, a strong sense of identity and a stable leadership.'[5]

In a conference paper, Huang Hsin-ta (黃信達) and Wang Yeh-li (王業立) suggest that Taiwan's local factions have the following unique characteristics:[6]

1 They are geographically bound by administrative districts.
2 They grew out of the competition among local elites for elected political posts, and there tends to be two or more competing factions in each administrative district.
3 Although they do not have a formal structure, factional politicians can be identified using interviews.
4 Factions are actively involved in elections for the public and quasi-public sector with the aim of monopolizing economic resources.
5 Under martial law, factions were closely allied with the KMT. However, since democratization, some factions have also allied with other parties.

Although the term 'local faction' is widely used in political analysis on Taiwan, actually identifying who belongs to factions and to which factions is a challenging task. In fieldwork, the German researcher Stefan Braig was often told 'There are only members of the KMT, and there is no *bentupai* or factions within the KMT.'[7] Part of the problem is that the term has negative connotations, particularly among elite or well-educated urban Taiwanese. Thus, politicians would not openly admit belonging to factions.

Wu Chung-li (吳重禮) suggests two core methods of overcoming this identification problem.[8] The first is to conduct intensive fieldwork in a location, with large numbers of interviews with factional leaders, candidates, party workers, government officials, local politicians and local journalists. A number of foreign scholars such as Bosco, Rigger and Jacobs have employed this kind of method to produce some outstanding studies of how local politics work in Taiwan.[9] Wu calls the second method the 'ruler identifying' approach, which involves relying on internal KMT and DPP documents.[10] The time investment required for comprehensive studies of local politics is one reason for the relative lack of literature compared to some other fields in Taiwanese political science where the researcher does not need to leave home.

There are two main approaches to understanding the emergence and perpetuation of local factions in Taiwanese politics. Huang and Wang term these 'patron–client hierarchism and social network approaches'.[11] The first views local factions as a product of early KMT rule and focuses on the interaction between the two. If either the patron (KMT) or client (factions) is unwilling or unable to supply their side of the bargain, the system will be in danger of breaking up. The second approach involves examining local factions through the lens of social networks. This approach views factions as formed from the bottom-up with the basis of the factions' development being their ability to maintain interpersonal relations and common identity within their core community. However, changes in the social and economic structure within a faction's districts can erode its ability to mobilize its original support networks.

Local factions and the KMT under authoritarian rule

During the 50-year colonial era, the KMT had not developed any significant organization to fight Japanese rule in Taiwan. Thus, when the KMT regime arrived in the late 1940s, it lacked any power base beyond the largest cities. It is debatable whether it introduced local elections to please its American allies or out of its desire to implement Sun Yat Sen's political philosophy. Nevertheless, the adoption of grassroots elections so early in the KMT era meant that it needed local allies; these allies were to be the local factions, many of which emerged in the first decade of KMT rule. In fact, as Kuo shows, some factions even had their roots in the Japanese colonial era.[12] Similarly, Kao Yuang-kuang (高永光) notes how the Xie and Su faction families that have dominated Keelung politics the last four decades were already rich and influential under the Japanese.[13] In both eras, the factions were to play an intermediate role between state and society.

As discussed in Chapter 2, the KMT was able to reward factions with a range of economic and power resources, which the factions would then distribute among their supporters. Chu argues that there were five core components that the local factions sought from their KMT patron:[14]

1   Local monopolistic activities such as banks, credit unions and bus companies.
2   Special loans from provincial banks.
3   Preferential procurement from provincial and local government agencies.

4 Other economic benefits bestowed by government such as favourable land use, zoning laws or public construction schemes for land speculation.

5 Government protection of factions' illegal activities, such as underground dance halls, prostitution or casinos.

The government during the pre-reform era, a period also known as the White Terror, maintained a one-party political system and was diligent in maintaining its control, as we saw with the 1947 2–28 Incident. Thus, it is not surprising that most local political elites chose to affiliate with the KMT in this period. Although local politicians did have the option of remaining independent, the KMT's almost complete control of economic resources and active recruitment of popular independents meant that most succumbed to the KMT's charms.

Wu lists over 100 factions that existed in Taiwan from the 1950s through to the early post-2000 period.[15] In Table 7.2, I have just included those factions that he claims still existed at the time of writing. Factions tended to be county or city level in their network scope, with 16 out of the 23 falling into this category. The six exceptions are Taipei, Nantou, Penghu, Yunlin, Taitung Counties and Tainan City, which instead had multiple township-based factions. The one district viewed as not featuring local factions is Taipei City. Wu argues that this is due to Taipei's levels of modernization and urbanization. Equally important are the deeper social penetration of the KMT in Taipei and the city's exceptional ethnic and sociological structure. The social groups least likely to be involved in local factions are Mainlanders and those working in the public sector (military, civil servants and education sectors, labelled *jungongjiao*), both of which are more concentrated in Taipei than any other location. It is worth reminding readers that trying to understand Taiwanese politics solely through the prism of Taipei is as useful as trying to understand the UK without leaving London or the US being solely based in Manhattan.

Table 7.2 also reveals the diversity in the factional labels. Some take the surnames of their founders, such as in Keelung County or Taichung City. Others use colours as their labels, as we see in Kaohsiung and Taichung Counties. Another variation is ethnic labels for factions, such as in Taoyuan and Hualien Counties, where there are distinct Hakka and Hoklo groupings, the latter being the ethnic group from which most Taiwanese originate. In Kaohsiung City, as a result of significant migration from rural counties, factions have taken the name of their founders' place of origin, such as the Penghu and Chiayi factions.

The local factional politicians enabled the KMT to dominate, at least on paper, martial law era elections at the local level. These included not only grassroots local elections but also elections for the leadership of powerful civic organizations such as the farmer, fishermen and irrigation associations. Control of the local farmers' association was especially prized as it was a key vote mobilization tool and its credit department could become the faction's private treasury.

Bosco gives a case study of a farmers' association election for a village in Pingtung County in the mid-1980s.[16] With parties and issues not salient in such grassroots elections, personal relations and vote buying tend to be more influential. In this case, the contest was between the Lai and Wu factions in a four-seat district. In the end, the Lai Faction won three out of the four seats, with the fourth-placed winner beating the fifth by only two votes (30 and 28 votes, respectively). As with national-level multiple member district elections, how factions distributed their supporters' votes was the key to success and failure. Bosco discovered that a major reason for the Lai faction's success was that it had

Table 7.2 Local factions in Taiwan

District	Faction	Comment
Keelung City	1. Su faction **2. Hsieh faction** 3. Chen (mainstream) faction	Kao lists them as (1) Hsieh, (2) Su-Zhang, (3) Chen-Lin factions
Taoyuan County	**1. Wu faction (Hakka)** 2. Liu faction	Kao lists the following factions for Taoyuan nominations in 2008: (1) Wu, (2) Peng Zhang, (3) Hsu faction, (4) Huang faction
Hsinchu County	1. Su faction **2. Sung faction** 3. Chen faction (Hsinpu) 4. Lin faction 5. Fan faction	
Hsinchu City	1. West Hsu faction 2. East Hsu faction	Kao lists KMT as nominating Hakka faction in 2008
Miaoli County	**1. Old Huang faction** **2. New Huang faction** 3. Hsiao Liu faction 4. Ta Liu faction	Tien lists only (1) Liu faction and (2) Huang faction. Kao lists (1) Old (2) New Huang faction for 2008
Taichung County	**1. Chen (Black) faction** **2. Lin (Red) faction** 3. Yang (Third Force) faction	
Taichung City	**1. Chang faction** 2. Lai faction 3. Ho faction 4. Liao faction	Kao lists (1) Lai, (2) Chang and (3) Ho as all having candidates in 2008
Changhua County	1. Lin faction **2. White faction** 3. Chen faction **4. Red faction**	Tien lists just (1) Lin-White (2) Chen Red factions and Kao in 2008 just lists Red and White factions
Nantou County	1. Li faction 2. Hung Chiao-jung faction 3. Chen faction 4. Tangwai/DPP faction	
Chiayi County	**1. Huang faction** **2. Lin faction**	Note: Lin faction defects to DPP after 2000
Chiayi City	1. Hsiao faction 2. Hsu faction (Not KMT)	Kao also lists Huang faction in 2008
Yunlin County	1. Tangwai faction **2. Lin faction** 3. Anti-Lin faction 4. Hsu faction 5. Liao faction	
Tainan County	1. Sea (Beimen) faction **2. Mountain (Hu) faction** 3. Kao faction 4. Shan Hsin faction	
Tainan City	1. Lin faction	Kao lists Kao faction for 2008

Table 7.2 continued

District	Faction	Comment
Kaohsiung County	1. Red faction 2. White faction 3. Black faction (Yu/DPP)	

Kaohsiung City	**1. Chia Ti (local born)**
	   old faction
	2. Chia Ti (local born)
	   new faction
	3. Tainan faction
	4. Penghu faction
	5. Chiayi faction (DPP)	

Pingtung County	1. Chang faction 2. Lin faction	
Taitung County	1. Wu faction 2. Shao Chung (youth) faction	
Hualien County	1. Fukienese faction 2. Hakka faction	
Yilan County	1. Chen faction 2. Lin (Lo Hsu) faction 3. Chen Huo-tu faction 4. Lu faction	

Sources: Wu (2003: 109–11); Tien Hung-mao (1996, pp. 168–69); Kao (2010).

Note 1: I took Wu Chung-li (2003) as my standard and only included factions he claims exist in the post-2000 period. I have emboldened the factions with nominated candidates in 2008, as a measure for where factions remain strong.

Note 2: Taipei county was excluded as it lacks countywide factions.

bought votes at a far higher price than the Wu faction. Vote buying was a standard method of persuasion of faction vote brokers, the *tiau-a-ka*. We get a taste of this when Shelley Rigger was explaining to some teenagers why she was researching local politics in southern Taiwan. One of the teenagers responded, 'What's to study? They just run around buying votes.'[17]

We can see the mutual dependence of the KMT and its local factions from its nomination statistics for the Provincial Assembly and local executive elections since the 1950s in Tables 7.3 and 7.4. Table 7.3 shows that, with the exception of 1972, factional candidates made up the majority of KMT candidates in Provincial Assembly elections through from 1954 to the body's final election in 1994. The average proportion for this period was 61.89 per cent. The dependence on factional candidates was even higher in the local executive races with an average factional candidate nomination rate of 63.47 per cent. In fact, prior to 1972 factional candidates made up over 80 per cent of KMT candidates. Moreover, factional candidates were far more effective at getting elected than their non-factional KMT counterparts, with factional candidates having a remarkable election rate of 92.63 per cent compared to non-factional candidates' 73.14 per cent success rate in Provincial Assembly elections.

The vote-mobilizing power of the factions was critical to the KMT's success in elections during this period. We can see this by examining the vote and seat shares of the KMT

Table 7.3 KMT factional nomination for provincial assembly elections

Year	Total seats	KMT candidates number	Faction candidates number	Faction candidates as percentage of KMT candidates	KMT non-faction candidate number	Non-faction candidates as percentage of KMT candidates
1954	57	44	33	75	11	25
1957	66	55	33	60	33	40
1960	73	58	37	63.79	21	36.21
1963	74	74	48	64.86	26	35.14
1968	71	60	38	63.33	22	36.67
1972	73	60	30	50	30	50
1977	77	69	42	60.87	27	39.13
1981	77	38	27	71.05	11	28.95
1985	77	60	41	68.33	19	31.67
1989	77	62	36	58.06	26	41.94
1994	79	55	28	50.91	27	49.09
Total	801	635	393	61.89	242	38.11

Source: Wu (2003: 98).

Note: Data for 1965 is missing.

Table 7.4 KMT factional nomination for local executive elections

Year	KMT candidates number	Faction candidates number	Faction candidates as percentage of KMT candidates	Non-faction candidate number	Non-faction candidates as percentage of KMT candidates
1954	21	18	85.71	3	14.29
1957	21	17	80.95	2	19.05
1960	21	19	90.48	2	9.52
1963	21	17	80.95	4	19.05
1968	20	16	80	4	20
1972	20	8	40	12	60
1977	20	3	15	17	85
1981	18	9	50	9	50
1985	18	11	61.11	7	38.89
1989	20	13	65	7	35
1993	19	8	42.11	11	57.89
Total	219	139	63.47	80	36.53

Source: Chen (1998: 179).

Note: Data for 1965 is missing.

in local executive elections shown in Figures 7.1 and 7.2. These show how, at least prior the arrival of the DPP, the KMT was able to gain at least 80 per cent of these prized seats, actually gaining over 90 per cent on four separate occasions. Another sign of the strength of the KMT factional alliance's organizational strength was that it was able to maintain seat domination even when its vote share dipped. Thus, the party regularly had a seat bonus of over 20 per cent prior to democratization. In other words, the KMT local faction alliance paid dividends for the KMT.

The KMT was, of course, aware that the factions were not the ideal alliance partners. Factional politicians had no genuine interest in KMT ideology, and their reputation for political corruption damaged the KMT's party image. Therefore, the KMT had a number of mechanisms to make sure they kept factions in check and subordinate. First, the KMT forbade factions from operating beyond their administrative territory (single city or county) or to establish alliances with factions in other localities. Second, the KMT adopted a divide-and-rule strategy to deal with factions. It tried to prevent any one faction from becoming totally dominant within a district by encouraging two or more competing factions. Where it looked like one faction was too powerful, the KMT would often support the weaker faction. Thus, factions sometimes would alternate the most coveted positions of city mayor/county magistrate and the county/city assembly speaker. For example, in Taichung County there has been quite a stable and regular pattern of power alternation between the Red and Black Factions since the early 1950s.[18] According to Wu, where factions were quite even in strength, 'the KMT nominated non-factional candidates under the guise of pacifying factional strife while, in reality, it was attempting to strengthen its influence in local politics'.[19]

We can get a sense of how the KMT's divide-and-rule tactics with local factions worked in a case study that Tien gives of the factional balance of power in Kaohsiung County in the 1980s. In this case, elected positions were divided between KMT's White and Red factions, non-factional KMT cadres and the *Tangwai* Black faction. Table 7.5 shows their respective control of county council and township chiefs in 1986. Although Taiwan was a one-party state, the way that factional politics developed gave its local elections some elements of multi-party competition.

Although the factions officially ran the local government, the actual powers of local government were in reality quite limited. The KMT control of resource allocation meant that it could cut off the supply of oxygen to overly independent factional politicians.

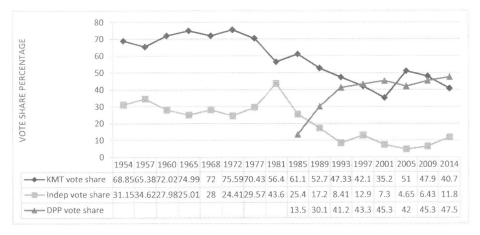

	1954	1957	1960	1965	1968	1972	1977	1981	1985	1989	1993	1997	2001	2005	2009	2014
KMT vote share	68.85	65.38	72.02	74.99	72	75.59	70.43	56.4	61.1	52.7	47.33	42.1	35.2	51	47.9	40.7
Indep vote share	31.15	34.62	27.98	25.01	28	24.41	29.57	43.6	25.4	17.2	8.41	12.9	7.3	4.65	6.43	11.8
DPP vote share									13.5	30.1	41.2	43.3	45.3	42	45.3	47.5

Figure 7.1 Vote share in local executive elections, 1954–2014

Sources: Huang, Teh-fu (1998: 109–10); Cheng, Tun-jen and Hsu Yung-ming (1996: 138); Election Study Center, National Chengchi University.

Note: This figure shows vote shares for the KMT, *Tangwai*/DPP and Independents in local executive elections. I did not include data for other third parties.

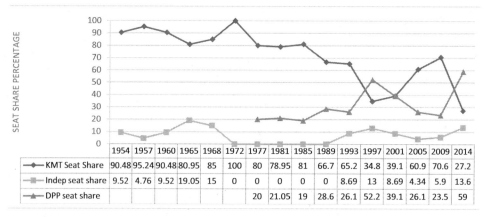

	1954	1957	1960	1965	1968	1972	1977	1981	1985	1989	1993	1997	2001	2005	2009	2014
KMT Seat Share	90.48	95.24	90.48	80.95	85	100	80	78.95	81	66.7	65.2	34.8	39.1	60.9	70.6	27.2
Indep seat share	9.52	4.76	9.52	19.05	15	0	0	0	0	0	8.69	13	8.69	4.34	5.9	13.6
DPP seat share							20	21.05	19	28.6	26.1	52.2	39.1	26.1	23.5	59

Figure 7.2 Seat share in local executive elections, 1954–2014

Sources: Huang, Teh-fu (1998: 109–10); Cheng, Tun-jen and Hsu Yung-ming (1996: 138); Election Study Center, National Chengchi University.

Note: This figure shows seat shares for the KMT, *Tangwai*/DPP and Independents. I did not include data for other third parties.

Table 7.5 Factions in Kaohsiung County, 1986

	White faction	Red faction	Direct KMT control	Black faction	Total
County councillors	21	10	9	13	53
Heads of townships and rural districts	9	11	3	4	27

Source: Tien (1989).

Note: Black faction was a *Tangwai* faction.

The last method that the KMT had to control factions was nomination, or the threat not to nominate factional politicians and instead select someone who was loyal to the party centre and ideologically orthodox. Initially, the KMT did not have the grassroots strength to challenge factions. However, by the early 1970s the KMT, with Chiang Ching-kuo increasingly influential, was prepared to challenge the factions. Thus, in 1972 the KMT chose to nominate 12 party cadres for local executive posts and reduce the factional nomination from 16 to 8 (see Table 7.4). In Table 7.3 we can also see a similar pattern of decreased nomination of factional candidates for that year's Provincial Assembly. The fact that all the non-factional local executive candidates were elected for the KMT in 1972 suggested that it no longer needed to compromise with the factions. Therefore, in 1977 it accelerated this process, with almost all local executive candidates non-factional for the first time. On this occasion, however, as we mentioned in Chapter 2, the anti-factional campaign backfired as the KMT lost four mayoral seats and 22 Provincial Assembly seats. When the KMT failed to nominate factional candidates, the factions sometimes responded by undermining or boycotting the official KMT candidate's campaign. They did this by not mobilizing their supporters and buying votes for the official candidate or even secretly helping the *Tangwai's* candidate.

Table 7.6 KMT factional nominations in supplementary Legislative Yuan elections

Year	KMT candidates number	Faction candidates number	Faction candidates	Non-faction candidate number	Proportion of non-faction candidates
1980	30	11	36.66	19	63.33
1983	45	20	44.44	25	55.56
1986	46	19	41.3	27	58.7
1989	58	29	50	29	50
1992	98	58	59.18	40	40.82
Total	277	137	49.46	140	50.54

Source: Chen (1998: 189).

Nomination statistics for the next few years after the 1977 setback shown in Tables 7.3 and 7.4 reveal how the KMT returned to nominating factional candidates for the next decade. The arrival of the *Tangwai* complicated the electoral picture and the KMT factional relationships. Although the KMT elite distrusted the factional politicians, the heightened *Tangwai* competition meant that they needed the factions more than ever. From the KMT's point of view, the good old days were over, as the saying that KMT nomination guaranteed election was no longer valid. This was to mean that the superior–inferior or patron–client relationship was becoming less clear-cut and the two would gradually move to a more equal relationship.

Although the supplementary elections for the national parliaments began in 1969, the numbers of seats open for direct election really only began expanding significantly in the 1980s. Initially, the KMT preferred to avoid nominating factional candidates for these new national posts, hoping to keep their power limited to the local level. We see this in Table 7.6, which shows the numbers and proportions of factional and non-factional nominated candidates for Legislative Yuan elections between 1980 and 1992. Initially, factional candidates only made up just over a third of KMT candidates for both the Legislative Yuan and National Assembly in 1980. However, there were significant increases in both cases after democratization. This was particularly evident in the proportion of factional candidates nominated in the 1992 Legislative Yuan election, with almost 60 per cent of KMT-nominated candidates falling into this category. Although at first the proportion of KMT factional nominees for the National Assembly in the post-democratization era was not quite so high, the increase in the number of factional candidates moving from local to national politics was quite noteworthy. In 1986, the KMT nominated 15 factional candidates for the supplementary National Assembly, but in 1991 it selected 79, of whom 77 were successfully elected.

Local factions after democratization

The gradual democratization process that began in the late 1980s brought both challenges and new opportunities to the local factions and their alliance with the KMT. Media liberalization meant that the old factional deals faced much greater public scrutiny, and the KMT's ties with corrupt local factions were widely condemned by political commentators. Similarly, the opposition parties found the KMT's factional links and the behaviour of KMT factional-linked politicians fruitful targets in their attacks on the party.

This was a theme both the DPP and NP used quite effectively, particularly in the mid to late 1990s. For instance, a 1995 NP advertisement carried the slogan 'Who brought consortiums, factions and yes men into the Legislative Yuan?'[20] The advertisement went on to list a number of what the NP viewed as dubious KMT nominees, such as leaders from the Taichung Black faction, Sanchong Bang and the Miaoli Liu faction. In other words, the NP was hoping that reminding voters of the KMT's factional nomination would persuade Pan Blue voters that the NP was the only clean Blue party.

Although the KMT stepped back from its anti-factional campaign after setbacks in 1977, the suspicion of factions among party elite remained. Thus, it launched a new move against factions in 1989 with its introduction of party primaries for nomination. A central motivation for this reform was that primaries would force factional members to become KMT members and enable the party to retake control of local politics from the corrupt and potentially unreliable factions. Many factional politicians realized that this was a KMT attempt to replace them. For instance, in Taipei County the KMT centre ensured that its preferred non-factional candidate won the primary for the local executive candidate. However, as Rigger shows, although the local factions did not openly oppose the official KMT candidate, they *held his leg back* (*che ta houtui*) enough to allow a narrow DPP victory.[21] Similar to what was seen in 1977, there was another reappraisal of the anti-factional programme following the KMT's poor electoral performance in 1989. We can see how the KMT once again embraced the local factions in its nominations for 1991 and 1992 (Table 7.6) and also its abandonment of primaries in the early 1990s.

As we discussed in Chapter 6, the KMT was wracked with internal power struggles in the late 1980s and early 1990s between Lee's Mainstream and the non-Mainstream factions. The local factions played a key role in allying with Lee in these struggles and thus also moved into the national political arena. After the full re-election of parliaments, it was now possible for the DPP to replace the KMT as the ruling party through elections. In other third-wave democracies, most former authoritarian parties lost power after the first democratic elections. However, the KMT is an exception to this trend, continuing to win elections over a decade after democratization. Chen Ming-tong has argued that the KMT's alliance with local factions was a critical explanation for its continued success.[22] Of course, Lee had to repay the factions by continued nomination and the economic incentives of the martial law era. In the long term, this would serve to erode KMT popularity.

Clearly, the KMT–local factional relationships became more tightly knit even as the factions moved on to the national level and were no longer restricted by their original geographic territory. Thus, we see factional figures such as Liu Sung-fan (劉松藩) (Taichung Black faction) or Wang Jin-pyng (Kaohsiung White faction), both rising to the influential post of Legislative Speaker. Other factional figures with reputations for organized crime linked to the KMT, such as Lo Fu-chu, Yan Ching-piao and Chang Jung-wei (張榮味), also rose to national political prominence.

In the 1990s the KMT struggled to control factions on a number of dimensions. For instance, Lin shows reduced KMT discipline in the Legislative Yuan in the 1990s on a number of critical Legislative votes.[23] Similarly, the party struggled to reach agreement on unified candidates in local executive elections. This again led to large numbers of rebel or open nominations in both 1993 and 1997, which in the latter case was especially destructive for the KMT, with its worst ever local executive results.[24]

The issue of local factions put the KMT into a severe dilemma that it had not faced in the authoritarian era. The local factions' reputation for political corruption meant that these links were extremely damaging for the KMT, offering the opposition valuable ammunition. However, if the KMT did not have the factional support, it could not win national or local elections. Moreover, these faction politicians had the ability to stand unendorsed as rebel candidates, sometimes to win or at least stop the KMT from winning.

During the 1990s, despite the Mainstream–local faction alliance, there were continued cases of attempts to break the factional alliance or at least deal with the worst aspects of this phenomenon. One of the best illustrations of this was Ma Ying-jeou's struggle against vote buying while Minister of Justice in the mid-1990s. On one sweep in 1994, around a fifth of the island's 858 city/county councillors were indicted for vote buying, the vast majority of whom were KMT local factional politicians.[25] The KMT's distrust of local factions again emerged in the National Development Conference in 1996 when KMT leaders actually backed DPP proposals to end grassroots elections, such as for township chiefs, and make these positions appointed by county magistrates. Wu also argued that part of its motivation for scrapping the provincial assembly and government was to reduce the power of local factions, as 'In past decades, the provincial government and assembly were important vehicles by which resources and largesse were allocated to local factions in exchange for support, delivery of votes and campaign contributions.'[26] The KMT eventually had to give into local factional pressure and change its position on nominating district township heads, as it needed their support for the 1998 legislative and 2000 presidential elections.

In 1998, the KMT's factional nomination levels were high again at almost 60 per cent, suggesting that it had once again abandoned its anti-factional drive. With the scrapping of the Provincial Assembly, the KMT had to find a way out for the large numbers of factional KMT politicians facing the political scrapheap. Thus, the KMT arranged for many of these Provincial Assembly members to be nominated for the 1998 legislative elections. If they had not done so, it is quite likely that many of these factional politicians would have stood as independents and undermined the official KMT candidates' campaigns. Naturally, nominating these factional politicians and sharing stages with them in the presidential campaign gave the NP and DPP ammunition to attack the KMT for corruption. The 2000 presidential election showed the challenge that local factions created for the KMT, as former Provincial Governor Soong had gathered considerable factional support. This meant that the factional vote was divided in 2000 between the official KMT candidate, Lien and the rebel, Soong.

Despite the challenge of the DPP and other parties in the 1990s, to what extent did factions switch their loyalty to other parties? To what extent did the factions and KMT lose control of local grassroots elections? The first place we can look to answer these questions is in the county/city council elections in 1998 displayed in Table 7.7. By comparing these to the electoral tables of the Legislative Yuan, National Assembly or even local executive and special municipalities' city council elections, what is clear is that on paper the KMT remained dominant at the local level. That year, the KMT won almost 60 per cent of all seats and held majorities in most councils. The second largest grouping was independents, the majority of whom were local factional politicians close to the KMT, further reinforcing its dominance. In contrast, the DPP was a minor player with only 14.3 per cent of seats, while the third largest party, the NP, held only 20 seats.

Of course, this raises the question of why did the local politicians not join the DPP or other new parties in the age of multi-party politics? Under martial law, a few factions chose the non-party route; particularly important were the Black faction in Kaohsiung

Table 7.7 County/city council seats, 1998–2014

	1998	2002	2005/6	2009/10	2014
KMT	58 (572)	42.1 (428)	45.1 (450)	46.2 (419)	42.6 (386)
DPP	14.3 (141)	17.4 (177)	22.5 (225)	28.4 (258)	32.1 (291)
NP	2 (20)	0.9 (10)	0.6 (6)	0.3 (3)	0.2 (2)
PFP		6.3 (65)	3.7 (37)	0.5 (5)	0.9(9)
TSU		0.8 (9)	1.4 (14)	0.5 (5)	0.9 (9)
TIP	0.1 (1)				
Labour Party				0.1 (1)	0.1 (1)
GPT					0.2 (2)
Independent	25.5 (252)	32.1 (327)	26.5 (265)	23.7 (215)	22.6 (205)
Total	986	1016	997	906	905

Source: Central Election Commission.

Note: This table shows the proportion of county and city council seats held by the main parties. The number of seats is shown in parenthesis. This includes seats for both city/county councils (including special municipality councils).

County and the Xu faction in Chiayi City. However, after democratization there were no large-scale defections, only a few isolated individuals such as Ho Chia-jung (何嘉榮) in Chiayi County from the Lin Faction who defected to the DPP. In the majority of cases, it was for nomination reasons rather than ideology that caused such party switches. The most common types of party switching for factional politicians were from the KMT to become independent and vice versa. A primary reason was that the KMT still controlled the purse strings at central government, so although less reliable, the economic incentive to stay with the KMT remained in force.

Even where the DPP held the local executive post, they tended to face a KMT or factional-controlled city/county council as well as the KMT central government. Like the KMT non-Mainstream faction, most DPP leaders were well-educated urbanites and thus less comfortable with grassroots politicians. We should recall that the DPP first rose mainly in the major cities such as Taipei and Kaohsiung, and tended to be weakest in geographic areas where the factions were strongest. This elite side to the DPP was reinforced in the 1990s as the student movement generation rose up through the party ranks. Thus, there was a cultural gap between many DPP politicians and the average local factional leader, which we can see in its anti-local factional and political corruption appeals in the 1990s. As the DPP became stronger in local governance, this gap narrowed but was not removed. The picture with the NP, the other main opposition party, was even more severe as they looked upon local factions and their way of doing politics with disdain and suspicion.

The other question that these tables raise is why the DPP and its fellow opposition parties were such abject failures at the grassroots level even in places where they had won in the Legislative Yuan or at the local executive level. A key place to start in explaining this has to be resources. The DPP lacked the financial resources to buy votes on the same scale as the KMT. This is not to say that local DPP politicians have not bought votes; there have been numerous cases. However, they have never been on the same scale as their KMT counterparts. In UK football terminology, the KMT was in the Premier League of vote buying, while the DPP was in League Two. Equally important has been the interparty asymmetry in human resources. For example, the DPP had only

15,000 members in 1989, fighting against a party that had two million members during the same period. Thus, the DPP traditionally struggled to find candidates with electoral strength at the grassroots. A third critical resource factor was the DPP's failure to develop grassroots networks in factional strongholds. County branches tended to be under-resourced, and their national party has always put the priority on national-level elections. Lastly, there is a cultural factor, with DPP politicians not adapting as well as their KMT counterparts to providing the services a local politician is expected to deliver to constituents.

Local and factional politics after the first change of ruling parties

The KMT's defeat in the 2000 presidential election brought new challenges to its domination of local politics and relationship with factions. For the first time, central government resources and the majority of local county/city governments (after 1997) were controlled by the DPP. Moreover, the Mainstream KMT faction that had maintained close relations with local factions under Lee was marginalized after 2000. The non-Mainstream faction, the source of most anti-factional drives, in turn became far more influential. Post-2000 reforms to the KMT's nomination system, such as the revival of primaries and the complete reregistration of party members, were both aimed at rooting out local factions. Under Lien (2000–5) and Ma (2005–7 and 2009–14), the party headquarters was far less welcoming to factions than under Lee.

The electoral patterns in Table 7.7 show a mixed picture in local politics during the DPP era. Initially, the KMT did suffer serious losses in the 2002 city and county council elections, falling from almost 60 per cent to 42 per cent of council seats, resulting in the majority of councils falling from KMT control and becoming hung councils. The DPP's seat share rose to 17 per cent. The PFP gained 6 per cent of council seats in its first local elections, making it the largest third party at both the local and national level. However, the main beneficiary in 2002 was independent councillors, who, as we have mentioned before, are generally pro KMT. In 2005 and 2009/10, the KMT recovered at the expense of the PFP and independents, but was not as dominant as in the 1990s. The KMT did win back control of a number of councils in 2005 and, with the help of sympathetic independents, most councils remained KMT dominated. The DPP continued its steady increase in councillors in 2005 and 2009/10, reaching almost 30 per cent of seats, but it was only competitive with the KMT in a small number of districts such as Yilan, Chiayi Counties and Tainan City. In fact, Chiayi County was the only place where the DPP had, with the help of a few independents, a workable council majority. The large proportion of cases of divided government shows that split-ticket voting is common for voters in local elections. In other words, it is extremely common for voters to choose a DPP local executive at the same time as voting for a KMT or independent county councillor. If we compare these local election results with national party politics, Taiwan remained a one-party dominant system at the county/city council level prior to 2014.

At the lower level of village chiefs/neighbourhood head and township councillor, party politics appear at first glance less important. In the 2010 elections, independents won 73.1 per cent of the former and 61.8 per cent of the latter, followed by the KMT's 25.1 and 30.8 per cent success rate.[27] In contrast, the DPP won only 1.3 per cent of village chiefs and 7 per cent of township councillor elections. If we take independents as generally more pro KMT, then it clearly also remains on paper dominant. Of course, there are dangers for the KMT to overestimate its strength based on these local election results.

Mattlin has conducted some interesting research on party defections at the grassroots level during this period (see Table 7.8).[28] He found that politicians were far more likely to switch parties at the national level than at any of the grassroots levels – namely, Mattlin found the numbers of KMT to DPP defections particularly limited. However, he observed large numbers of cases of local politicians leaving the KMT and becoming independent. These findings offer a number of explanations why local politicians remained loyal to the KMT or at least did not defect to the DPP, even where it ran city/county governments.[29] First, many may have considered that the KMT would return to power in 2004 (and then 2008), so defection was too risky. Second, after 2000 the KMT was far more institutionalized in its nomination practices and thus expelled rebel candidates and blocked their return more than in the past. He also points out that the DPP has tended to be more wary of welcoming opportunistic defectors than other parties. Lastly, the KMT has remained the most generous party financially and thus remains attractive to local factional politicians. The defections of small party politicians to large parties seen at the national level in the run-up to 2008 was also mirrored at the local level. Thus, by 2010 the small parties had almost completely disappeared from city councils.

During the run-up to the 2008 elections, the KMT remained anxious to maintain its alliance with local factions despite Ma's dominant position in the party. During Ma's campaign his long-stay in the country campaign was an attempt to reach out to grassroots and factional KMT politicians, with whom Ma had traditionally maintained some distance. In fact, some still resented his anti-vote-buying campaign of the mid-1990s. Similarly, out of the 73 single member districts in the 2008 Legislative Yuan election, Kao estimates the KMT-nominated factional candidates for almost half these seats.[30] Naturally, the new electoral system will have a long-term impact on factions. Previously, under the multiple member district system, it was easier to divide nomination between factions within a district, but under the single-member district, factions need to work together or face certain defeat by the DPP or being replaced by KMT-imposed candidates.

Table 7.8 Political parties' net gain or loss of candidates in city/county councillor elections in 2002 and 2005

2002	Gain from other parties	Gain from independents	Loss to other parties	Loss to independents	Net gain or loss
KMT		37	(30)	(83)	(76)
DPP	4	19	(3)	(14)	6
NP			(12)	(7)	(19)
PFP	37	18			55
TSU	7	6			13
Other parties			(3)		(3)

2005	Gain from other parties	Gain from independents	Loss to other parties	Loss to independents	Net gain or loss
KMT	6	45	(3)	(29)	19
DPP	1	18		(9)	10
NP			(1)		(1)
PFP	1	3	(5)	(11)	(12)
TSU	3	7		(2)	8
Other parties			(1)		(1)

Source: Mattlin (2006: 77).

In a recent study, Göbel has returned to the topic of local politics to examine the factional operation after electoral reform. He concludes that 'In rural areas (and presumably also in traditional urban neighbourhoods), local factions managed to entrench themselves deeply enough in local society to not be affected by electoral reform.'[31] He argues that where factional strength is fading, this is instead best explained by urbanization and modernization.

After coming to power, Ma Ying-jeou faced the same old dilemma of wanting to eliminate or at least reduce the KMT's ties with local factions, but at the same time still needing their assistance to win local and national elections. In an indirect way, Ma helped partially achieve some of the DPP and KMT non-Mainstream faction's goals for curbing local factions from the 1996 National Development Conference. For example, the administrative mergers of 2010–14 removed elections for township chiefs for Taichung, Taipei, Taoyuan, Tainan and Kaohsiung Counties. Braig argues that these reforms have already had a negative effect on local factions.[32]

On the question of factional nomination, we saw a mixed picture in 2009, where only 8 out of 17 KMT candidates were categorized as factional candidates.[33] Although the KMT did nominate some candidates with clean reputations in other districts, it had to support factional candidates in places such as Hsinchu, Chiayi, Taoyuan Counties and Keelung City. There were also cases where local factions did not fully support the official KMT campaign after their candidates were not nominated, such as in Yunlin. There were also signs in the 2010 by-elections that the KMT was trying to reduce the power of factions or local politicians through direct nomination. Once again, history repeated itself with a number of cases of factional backlash contributing to some quite extraordinary election results, with the DPP winning seats in some of the strongest KMT strongholds such as Taitung and Hsinchu County.[34]

Sunflower earthquake in local politics?

Coming just over half a year after the end of the Sunflower occupation, the November 2014 local elections represented a chance for an earthquake in local politics. There was a clear attempt by a number of alternative parties to make a breakthrough in local politics. Noteworthy examples of this included a well-organized nationwide campaign by the GPT, extensive nominations by the GPT splinter party, the Tree Party, as well as the leftist Democratic Front. In addition, numerous activists stood for election without party labels. When we examine Table 7.7 and Figure 7.2, we see a mixed picture of change. The best case for an earthquake appears to be at the local executive level, where the DPP rode the Sunflower wave to win historic victories. The social movement-based parties had very little success, apart from the GPT's first two seats. Despite increased nomination, even the splinter parties only experienced limited recoveries and were well short of their 2002 peak in local representation. The DPP appears to have enjoyed a continued expansion in local seats, but this has been part of a long-term trend since the early 1990s. The year 2014 represents the KMT's worst ever local council seat total and share, but with 42 per cent of seats, it still has a ten-point lead on the DPP.

Future of local factions and local politics

So what are the prospects for local factions and local politics today? Power alternation at the local and national levels has undermined the old patron client exchange system that was so prevalent in the authoritarian era. Similarly, social and economic changes have eroded the old social networks that were so crucial to factions' vote mobilizing in more urbanized locations such as Taichung City. Almost three decades after the start of full democratic elections, are local politics finally moving in the same direction as national level politics, from the one party dominant system to more competitive multi-party politics? Will political parties displace local factions and take direct control over local politics? Much of the evidence suggests that there are not universal answers to these questions and it may just depend on where we are looking. There are some cases where factions have declined as the district's politics move towards the party political model of Taipei. Table 7.7 suggests this appears to be taking place in much of Taiwan, as the local level seat shares are moving closer to those seen at the national level. In fact, in the special municipalities the space for independent non-party councillors has been increasingly squeezed. There are also cases of factions adapting and transforming to the new political environment. Two successful cases of transformation are in Taichung and Chiayi Counties. In the former county, the Red and Black Factions were able to recover from defeat in 1997 and have dominated elections and KMT nomination since 2000. Huang and Wang go as far as to say they have become 'barons in (an) electoral district'.[35] In Chiayi County, the former KMT Lin faction defected to the DPP in 2001, and over time has actually taken over the DPP machine in the county. A major future challenge for factions will be the new administrative districts following the 2010 mergers. Will the local factions of Kaohsiung and Taichung Counties become absorbed by the more party-oriented politics of the cities or will the factions take over the parties as we saw in Chiayi?

Discussion questions

1   How can we best explain the emergence and development of local factions in Taiwan?
2   How did democratization affect local politics?
3   Why has the KMT struggled to break free of its dependence on local factions?
4   What has been the impact of electoral and administrative reform on local politics?
5   What are the prospects for local factions and politics in the next decade?
6   Why have the opposition parties (or small parties) made less of an impact in attracting votes and politicians at grassroots levels?

Further reading

Braig, Stefan. 2016. 'Local Factions'. In Schubert, Gunter (ed.) *Routledge Handbook of Contemporary Taiwan*. Abingdon and New York: Routledge, pp. 137–52. In this chapter Braig reviews the development of local factions before and after democratization.

Chao, Yung-mao. 1992. 'Local Politics in Taiwan: Continuity and Change'. In Denis Fred Simon and Michael Kau (eds). *Taiwan: Beyond the Economic Miracle*. Armonk, M.E. Sharpe, pp. 43–68. Detailed analysis of local level politics through to the late 1980s by one of the foremost scholars of local politics in Taiwan.

Göbel, Christian. 2012. 'The Impact of Electoral Reform on Taiwan's Local Factions'. *Journal of Current Chinese Affairs*, 41 (3): 69–92. In this piece Göbel tests the conflicting arguments about how factions have coped since electoral reform.

Mattlin, Mikael. 2006. 'Party Opportunism among Local Politicians after Taiwan's Power Transition'. *East Asia*, 23(1): 68–85. Currently the best study in English on local politics in Taiwan in the DPP era, based on extensive fieldwork and accessible use of statistics.

Rigger, Shelley. 1999. *Politics in Taiwan*. London: Routledge. Chapter 4 is especially useful on local level politics under martial law.

Wu, Chung-li. 2003. 'Local Factions and the Kuomintang in Taiwan's Electoral Politics'. *International Politics of the Asia-Pacific*, 3(1): 89–111. Useful discussion of the KMT–faction relationship, with a focus on nomination and elections.

Notes

1 Landé, 'Introduction: The Dyadic Basis of Clientelism', xiii.
2 Ibid.
3 Wu, 'Local Factions and the Kuomintang in Taiwan'Electoral Politics', 89–111, 92.
4 Landé, xxxii.
5 Bosco, 'Taiwan Factions: *Guanxi*, Patronage and the State in Local Politics', 115.
6 Huang and Wang, 'Local Factions after Twin Transitions of Government in Taiwan: Decaying or Transforming?' 4.
7 Braig, 'Local elites and Intra-party dynamics: the KMT *bentupai*', 5.
8 Wu, 93–4.
9 Bosco; Rigger, *Politics in Taiwan*; Jacobs, *Local Politics in Rural Taiwan under Dictatorship*.
10 Wu, 94.
11 Huang and Wang, 6–11.
12 Kuo, 'The Origins of State-Local Relations in Taiwan: A New Institutional Perspective', 29–58.
13 Kao, 'The Future Development of Political Factions in Taiwan: An Analysis from 2009 Local Elections', 3.
14 Chu, 'Authoritarianism and Economic Oligopoly in Taiwan',151–2.
15 Wu, 109–11.
16 Bosco, 116–18.
17 Rigger, *Politics in Taiwan*, 94.
18 Huang and Wang, 26. The only exception to the pattern was when the DPP won the county magistrate post in 1997.
19 Wu, 96.
20 See NP ad, *United Daily News,* 25 November 1995, 41.
21 Rigger, 145–6.
22 Chen, 'Local Factions and Elections in Taiwan's Democratization', 174–92.
23 Lin, 'Paths to Democracy', 442–9.
24 Open nomination refers to cases where the party is unable to settle on a single endorsed candidate and instead permits two party candidates to stand without the threat of punishment. This is overwhelmingly a KMT practice. In safe seats like Kinmen, this may not make a difference, but in 1997 this did contribute to the KMT's damaging setbacks in Tainan City and Taichung Counties.
25 For details on this case, see Baum, 'Spring Cleaning', 18; Baum, 'One Dollar, One Vote'.
26 Wu, 103.
27 Central Election Commission database, available online at: http://db.cec.gov.tw/cechead.asp (accessed 12 March 2011).
28 Mattlin, 'Party Opportunism among Local Politicians after Taiwan's Power Transition', 76–81.
29 Ibid., 81–2.
30 Kao, 8–11.
31 Göbel, 88.
32 Braig, 148.
33 Ibid., 11–14.
34 I will return to discuss these by-elections in Chapter 13.
35 Huang and Wang, 21.

8   Competing national identities

Over the last three decades, national identity has been the most studied topic in Taiwanese political science. Few scholars would contest Hsieh's assertion that in Taiwan, 'Among the political issues, national identity is often regarded as the most significant in distinguishing among the various political parties.'[1] The size of the literature was apparent from the fact that articles on Taiwan's national identity and nationalism made up the whole first volume of *The Politics of Modern Taiwan*. The popularity of identity studies is not without its drawbacks. With so much research in this field, it is not easy for scholars to find new and innovative angles. In response to the glut in publications on national identity, I coined the term 'national identity and cross-Strait fatigue'.[2] Although national identity is a salient issue in Taiwan, there is also a danger of exaggerating its importance. When voters are asked which issues they view as most pressing, identity issues usually get ranked rather lower than many politicians or electoral scholars would like. Nevertheless, identity issues often get entangled with other seemingly unrelated issues, such as social welfare and political corruption. Moreover, politicians tend to view it as the most powerful issue. As the former DPP presidential candidate, Peng Ming-min, explained, 'In election speeches you have to talk about what people want to hear (i.e. national identity).'[3]

Another difficulty we face in studying national identity in Taiwan is that both the general public and politicians' views on the topic cannot always be taken at face value. For instance, some surveys in the 1980s showed that the majority of respondents viewed retaking the mainland as the government's most pressing task. However, this may be more of a reflection on political correctness at the time than a genuine desire to achieve Chinese unification by launching an all-out war against the mainland. We can see similar patterns at the elite level. This was summed up in the words of a senior DPP politician:

> There are some things that you can do, but cannot say. You can be independent, but you cannot say you're independent. And there are some things you can say but you cannot do. The KMT says it wants to retake the mainland. But if you tell the KMT not to say this, it'll lose much of its legitimacy.[4]

We also need to remember that respondents' understanding of key concepts may well have changed over time. For instance, the term 'unification' may have meant the ROC retaking the mainland in the martial law era, but today it is almost universally going to be viewed as the PRC taking over Taiwan.

Core concepts and definitions

Before tackling this fascinating topic in detail, we first need to set out some core working definitions of the key concepts and how they are applied in the Taiwan case. For Gellner, 'Nationalism is primarily a political principle, which holds that the political and national units should be congruent.'[5] A simple way of thinking about nationalism is to view it as two core questions: Who are the people and what are the boundaries of the nation state? In other words, are the people Chinese or Taiwanese, and are the boundaries of the state limited to Taiwan and its surrounding islands, or should the Chinese mainland also be regarded as part of the territory of the state?

Currently, in Taiwan there is fierce competition between two rival forms of nationalism: on one side we have Chinese nationalists promoting a unified China and identifying themselves as Chinese. On the other, Taiwanese nationalists hope for a fully independent Taiwan where its citizens identify themselves as Taiwanese rather than Chinese. A key foundation for both types of nationalists then is the process of nation building, the attempt to mould common identification among citizens with the nation state. This is a process that is promoted both from the top down by the state, but also upwards from the grass-roots level. Thus, in the twentieth century we witnessed three major nation-building projects in Taiwan. First, the Japanese tried to make Taiwanese into Japanese imperial subjects during the colonial era. Then, after 1945 the KMT tried to impose its own form of Chinese nationalism under martial law. Later on, this ROC Chinese nation building was openly challenged after democratization by a rival Taiwanese nation-building project. It is often argued that Lee Teng-hui and Chen Shui-bian attempted to impose their form of Taiwanese nationalism from the mid-1990s. More recently, the Ma government attempted to revive ROC Chinese nationalism. However, equally important in this pro-ject is the societal resistance to state-led nation building and the bottom-up advocacy of Taiwanese nationalists.[6]

Although often overlapping, we can also distinguish between national and ethnic iden-tity. While the former refers to identification with an actual or desired nation state, the latter denotes the often politicized identification with an ethnic group within a state's boundaries. Thus, the term 'ethnic politics' is often used to describe tensions between the four main recognized ethnic groups: (1) Mainlanders (*waisheng ren*), (2) indigenous peoples (*yuanzhu minzu*), and Taiwanese, which are further subdivided between the (3) Minnan (*minnan ren*) or Hoklo (*heluo*) and (4) Hakka (*kejia ren*). Three decades ago it was still quite common to hear writers describe these group distinctions as subethnic identities, although this term appears to have gone out of fashion.[7] Looking ahead, it is likely that the Taiwanese expatriates living in China (*Taishang*) and overseas spouses (*waiji peiou*) will increasingly be treated as new politicized ethnic groups, particularly as their numbers already exceed the indigenous peoples.

Cracks in the KMT's ROC nation-building projects

In Chapter 2, I discussed some of the ways the KMT tried to cultivate its own brand of Chinese nationalism on Taiwan and also use Chinese nationalism as a tool to legitimize its one-party rule. Total control of the education system, media, military and political system were all employed by the KMT to persuade Taiwanese that they should identify themselves as Chinese and desire the ROC to retake the mainland.

Later, domestic and international developments in the 1970s and 1980s began to under-mine at least some of the foundations of the KMT's nation-building project. Taiwan's diplomatic setbacks such as losing its UN seat in 1971, US recognition of the PRC in 1979 and the ROC's dwindling number of diplomatic allies all eroded its claim to be the government of all China. As China returned to the international stage in the decade after the Cultural Revolution, Taiwan's slogan of retaking the mainland sounded more of an anachronism than ever before, even to many KMT politicians. Social, economic and political changes within the island also had an impact. The better educated and wealthier middle class was far less receptive to the KMT's traditional nationalist message. Gradual political liberalization and the rise of an opposition also meant that for the first time there was open debate over identity issues. By the late 1980s, the Mandarin-only official language policy was being challenged by the DPP. Along with democra-tization came the demands of ethnic justice and self-determination.

As we move into the democratic era, it was no longer possible for the KMT to domin-ate the process of nation building single-handedly in a top-down manner. Instead, nation building became a competitive and interactive process between state and society. Under martial law, the alternative forms of nationalism, such as Taiwanese nationalism, could only exist in exile abroad or underground on the island. However, since the 1990s there have been four competing types of nationalisms fighting for the loyalty of Taiwanese voters and elites. I term these (1) ethnic Taiwanese nationalism, (2) civic Taiwanese nationalism, (3) ROC Chinese nationalism and (4) PRC or Greater Chinese nationalism. This is also often described as the unification versus independence debate, or *Tongdu* question.

It is quite common for Taiwanese political analysts to discuss issues of national identity in Taiwan as a spectrum with a left, right and centre. At the far left, I take the key com-ponents of ethnic Taiwanese nationalism as being the call for an immediate declaration of independence or *de jure* independence (I have also used the term 'pure Taiwan independence') and exclusive ethnic Taiwanese identity appeals that discriminate against Mainlanders and non-Taiwanese (*Taiyu* or *Minnanyu*) speakers. At the centre-left is civic Taiwanese nationalism, which encompasses opposition to unification, but rather than outright independence it views Taiwan as already independent, so there is no need to declare independence (I have also termed this diluted Taiwan independence, but it is more commonly labelled de facto independence). The identity appeals are Taiwan centred but treat all citizens, regardless of their ethnicity, as equally Taiwanese. It was best encap-sulated in Lee Teng-hui's 1998 New Taiwanese appeal, arguing that all inhabitants of the island are Taiwanese so long as they identify and work hard for Taiwan. An alternative but similar term that has emerged recently is natural independence (天然獨). In a post-election seminar, sociologist Michael Hsiao (蕭新煌) defined this as the 'mindset of Taiwanese youth in which a separate national and political identity from that of China's is just the natural order of things'.[8] It is hard to actually call the middle of this spectrum as representing a coherent form of nationalism, although of course a large proportion of the population would fit into this category of 'wait and see' and holding dual Chinese and Taiwanese identities. At the centre-right we see opposition to independence but no mention of unification. The key symbolic appeal is the ROC and ROC Chinese nationalist images such as Chiang Ching-kuo. Like the centre-left, it can be viewed as a form of civic nationalism, but the citizens are expected to be loyal to the ROC rather than Taiwan. At the far right is what I call PRC or Greater Chinese nationalism. This focuses on the primacy of rapid unification, positive references to the PRC and includes Chinese identity symbols such as Chiang Kai-shek.

Below in Table 8.1 I have listed some of the political appeals that can be used to identify these competing models of nationalism on the *Tongdu* spectrum. We can examine the state of play of these competing identity projects on three main levels: (1) government, (2) political parties and (3) mass public opinion.

Competing identities: government and party level

1985–92: polarized identities

For the sake of simplicity and space, I will first discuss developments of the competing nationalisms at the government and party level together following democratization. In the first 15 years of multi-party politics (if we take the *Tangwai* as representing a de facto party by the mid-1980s) the two central actors were the KMT/national government and the DPP/*Tangwai*. We can use a number of methods to plot change such as elite interviews, government and party documents, public opinion surveys and campaign propaganda.

In the initial five years of this period, the main parties were wide apart on the identity spectrum. The KMT government continued the slogan of unification under the Three Principles of the People and its rigid One China policy in which it maintained that the ROC was the sole legitimate government of China. There were still severe limits on freedom to challenge the KMT's national identity orthodoxy. For instance, the 1987

Table 8.1 A spectrum of Taiwanese versus Chinese nationalism

Far left: Ethnic Taiwanese nationalism	*Centre-left: Civic Taiwanese nationalism*	*Centre*	*Centre-right: ROC Chinese nationalism*	*Far right: PRC or Greater Chinese nationalism*
Republic of Taiwan	Anti-unification	Status Quo	Anti-Taiwan independence	Positive references to unification
Taiwan independence	Anti-one country, two (three) systems	Dual identity	Pro ROC	National Unification Guidelines
New Taiwan constitution	UN application		Protect the ROC ROC flag	One country, two systems
Anti-Mainlander appeals	Anti One China Pragmatic diplomacy		ROC national anthem	Anti-Secession Law
Tragedy of being Taiwanese	Self-determination		Chiang Ching-kuo	Anti-pragmatic diplomacy
February 28 Incident	Oppose Anti-Secession Law		1992 Consensus (One China Different Interpretations)	Mainlander appeals
Accusations of betraying Taiwan	Taiwan First Love Taiwan New Taiwanese Map of Taiwan Natural independence			Chiang Kai-shek Anti-Japanese war Pro CCP Pro PRC Confucianism One China Principle

Source: Fell (2005c: 87–8).

Note: This table combines some of the main sub-issues on the independence versus unification and Taiwanese versus Chinese identification spectrums.

National Security Law forbade advocating communism or division of the national territory (i.e. Taiwan independence). Similarly, Article 100 of the Criminal Code had been repeatedly used to imprison political dissidents for merely advocating Taiwan independence. For instance, Huang Hua (黃華) was arrested three times under this article in his almost 24 years behind bars, with his final arrest in December 1990.[9] Similarly, in 1989 the dissident Cheng Nan-jung chose martyrdom by self-immolation rather than be arrested for publishing a draft Taiwan constitution. The martial law era cultural policies aimed at promoting ROC Chinese nationalism were also maintained after the outset of democratization. For instance, the education curriculum remained Sino-centric and Mandarin the dominant and sole official language in the electronic media and public spaces. On the symbolic level, the KMT still employed Chinese nationalist symbols, such as continuing to erect statues of Chiang Kai-shek and Sun Yat Sen. In short, initially democratization did not serve to localize the KMT regime and thus it remained to the far right of the identity spectrum in Table 8.1.

At the time the DPP was established in 1986, it was actually located at the centre-left, what I label here as civic nationalism, rather than exclusive Taiwanese nationalism. For instance, it did not incorporate Taiwan into its party name and included leaders from both the Hakka and Mainlander community and even advocates of eventual unification. On the *Tongdu* question, it adopted the position of supporting Taiwan's self-determination. In other words, unification or independence were both options. However, what mattered was that the ultimate decision would be made democratically by Taiwan's population rather than by secret negotiations between the KMT and CCP.

Nevertheless, the DPP soon began moving away from the centre-left. For example, in 1989 some DPP candidates chose to openly advocate Taiwan independence in the legislative election campaign. This radicalization led to the departure of some politicians that preferred at least to keep an open mind about the possibility of an eventual unified China. For instance, this was a factor in Lin Cheng-chieh and Chu Kao-cheng's departures from the party. It also increasingly gave the image of being an ethnic Taiwanese party, leading many of its Mainlander leaders and supporters to defect. Lin explained the atmosphere in the party's early years like this:

> In fact the DPP never had many Mainlanders. A minority of people made statements that made me feel uncomfortable, but it was never directed against me personally. In the DPP Fei Hsi-ping (費希平), Fu Cheng (傅正) and I were all well respected. They may have hated Mainlanders, but they didn't hate us.[10]

By the outset of full democratic national elections in 1991, the parties were highly polarized on national identity. The gulf between parties was especially visible in the 1991 National Assembly election campaign.[11] The KMT had staked its position a year earlier with the establishment of the National Unification Council (NUC) and National Unification Guidelines (NUG). The NUG envisaged a three-stage process leading to unification of a free and democratic China. During the campaign, the KMT bitterly attacked Taiwan independence and warned that it would bring war, destruction and economic recession to Taiwan. Premier Hau even proposed dissolving the DPP for its advocacy of Taiwan independence and rejected the call to decriminalize peaceful advocacy of independence. The KMT also continued its use of Chinese nationalist symbols such as Chiang Kai-shek, who appeared prominently in the party's advertising.[12] In contrast, the DPP adopted its most radical identity position to date. The culmination of this gradual radicalization of the DPP was its adoption of the Taiwan Independence Clause (TIC) that year. This controversial (and still existent) clause in the DPP Charter calls for the establishment of a Republic of Taiwan (ROT) after approval by a plebiscite and a new Taiwan constitution. In the campaign, the majority of DPP candidates made this appeal central to their propaganda. For instance, the drafter of the TIC, Lin Cho-shui (林濁水), called himself the 'Engineer of the Taiwan Nation'.[13] Other candidates included their version of an ROT flag in their advertising. My own content analysis found that almost 80 per cent of DPP candidates included references to the more extreme form of nationalism that I have termed 'pure Taiwan independence'. The DPP also used significant symbolic appeals that fall into the category of exclusive ethnic Taiwanese nationalism. In both 1991 and 1992, the DPP employed anti-Mainlander appeals. For instance, in 1991 a candidate boasted of his involvement in the attempted assassination of Chiang Ching-kuo in the US.[14] A year later, the DPP attempted to profit anti-Mainlander sentiments in a series of advertisements that attacked KMT Premier Hau Pei-tsun.[15] The last major identity appeal the DPP used heavily at this time is what I call the tragic appeal. These focus on the many tragic cases of political persecution the Taiwanese suffered, such as the 2–28 Incident and White Terror. These were used quite extensively in the early 1990s. For instance, in 1992 three lengthy DPP TV advertisements told the distressing stories of how the families of political dissidents suffered under martial law. On first viewing they reduced me, a stony-hearted political scientist, to trying to hold back tears. In short, in the early 1990s the two main parties were poles apart at the right and left of my national identity spectrum in Table 8.1.

Stuttering moves towards the centre: 1992–2002

For the subsequent decade there was a gradual process of elite convergence on the national identity spectrum, as the leading actors moved towards the moderate centre. Naturally, there were some exceptions as the parties occasionally swung away from moderation to appeal to their core supporters. However, the predominant elite trend between 1992 and 2002 was convergent. The parties, however, did not become indistinguishable; instead, the pattern on this issue corresponded to my argument in Chapter 3 that party competition could be categorized as featuring moderate differentiation.

Instead of actually abandoning the TIC, the DPP chose to de-emphasize Taiwan independence and to repackage it into a more moderate and voter-friendly product. As I mentioned in Chapter 5, it broadened its issue appeal by giving much greater emphasis from 1992 to 1993 to other issues such as social welfare, political corruption, women's issues, environmental protection and crime. The term 'repackaging Taiwan independence' means that it stopped openly advocating a ROT and rarely even mentioned the term 'Taiwan independence'. In its place it stressed more popular dimensions of Taiwan independence, such as opposing unification and calling for admittance into the United Nations (UN). When the DPP first launched its appeal for Taiwan to apply to rejoin the UN in 1991, it was denounced by the KMT who argued that it would serve to undermine Taiwan's security. However, less than two years later, the KMT had been persuaded, and the government officially launched its first petition to rejoin the UN in 1993.

The KMT followed a similar pattern to the DPP's treatment of TIC regarding its core guidelines of the One China policy and NUG. As the decade progressed, these were seemingly swept under the carpet, given less and less government attention. It continued to attack the DPP for Taiwan independence, but its positive references to unification became few and far between. Instead, the KMT put greater emphasis on promoting pragmatic diplomacy or Taiwan's international space. Although it may seem odd to classify this as a shift towards the centre-left of *Tongdu,* the PRC certainly did view it as part of a bid for independence. This is why the PRC reacted so furiously to Lee Teng-hui's visit to the US in June 1995. In essence, pragmatic diplomacy was a bid to secure Taiwan's de facto independence and thus I locate it at the centre-left.

The degree that parties were moving towards the centre by the mid-1990s was visible in the election campaigns of 1995–6. In those years, the KMT stressed its pragmatic diplomacy successes, constantly showing in their TV advertisements images of Lee visiting the US and meeting world leaders. In addition, it stressed how the government was standing up to the military threats from China, giving the image that the KMT and DPP were united in opposing unification. Although the DPP's 1996 presidential campaign did have some of the hallmarks of the pure Taiwan independence appeals of 1991, it was the exception to the rule and did not receive wholehearted support from many within the party. Instead, DPP Chairman Shih Ming-teh's remark in 1995 reflected the bid to move the party towards the centre-left and make it more electable. Shih argued that 'If the DPP becomes the ruling party, we will not need to, nor will we, declare independence . . . because Taiwan has already been independent for half a century.'[16]

On the Taiwanese versus Chinese identity dimension of the national identity spectrum, there was also a degree of convergence in this period. The DPP continued to appeal to voters with Taiwanese identity themed messages, but generally moved away from its anti-Mainlander and tragic Taiwanese appeals.[17] Two major figures in this changed campaign style were Chen Shui-bian and Chen Wen-chien. The first key instance of the new youth-oriented campaigns was Chen Shui-bian's 1994 Taipei mayoral campaign under the slogan 'Happiness, Hope, Chen Shui-bian'. At the national party level, Chen Wen-chien also tried this most successfully with the 1997 local executive campaign's TV advertisements and Spice Girls campaigning troupe. As the decade progressed, the KMT moved away from its use of Chinese nationalist symbols such as Chiang Kai-shek and Sun Yat-Sen and instead tried to steal the DPP's ownership of the Love Taiwan appeal. Thus, maps of Taiwan increasingly took centre stage in KMT advertisements, and its candidates often avoided using the full title of the party in their propaganda. In other words, if they did use the party title, it tended to be KMT rather than Chinese KMT.

Hughes argues that 'Lee's masterstroke was to effectively appropriate the civic conception of national identity that was central to DPP thinking'.[18] Key examples he cites are Lee's description of Taiwan as a *Gemeinschaft* (community of shared lives) and his slogan 'manage great Taiwan, establish a new Central Plains'. Hughes argues that this was an attempt to advocate 'a new sino-centralism with Taiwan as the focus'.[19] The KMT appeal that best represented its choice of a centre-left position on this dimension was Lee Teng-hui's promotion of the inclusive 'New Taiwanese' concept. Lee first used this in a campaign speech for Ma Ying-jeou in late 1998. Lee defined New Taiwanese in these terms: 'No matter if you came 400 or 500 years ago, or 40 or 50 years ago from the mainland, or if you are aboriginal, we are all Taiwanese, so long as we work hard for Taiwan and the ROC, then we are New Taiwanese.'[20] Polls at the time tended to show that the concept was popular among all major ethnic groups.[21]

There was even change in cultural policies for the first time. Nowhere was this more apparent than in textbook reforms and the introduction of a set of junior high school textbooks known as *Getting to Know Taiwan.* These were to be used for geography, society and history courses, and were designed to rectify the severe lack of coverage of Taiwan in the school curriculum. On this occasion, the KMT and DPP stood side by side in supporting these localizing reforms, while it was politicians from the NP that bitterly fought their introduction. Under martial law, school curriculums had been a central tool for ROC nationalist nation building, but now for the first time the KMT government was openly accused of promoting Taiwanese nationalism.[22]

Following Lee's re-election in 1996, the DPP and KMT convergence actually accelerated on *Tongdu* matters. The two worked together to implement constitutional reforms that effectively scrapped the provincial level of the ROC political system. Although this was justified as an efficiency measure, removing an unnecessary overlapping layer of government, from the perspective of both Chinese and Taiwanese nationalists the provincial government did have deep symbolic meaning. Both viewed this reform as a step in the direction of Taiwan independence, as a provincial government implied that Taiwan remained a province of China. Once again, it was the NP that was the main opponent of this reform.

It was only the parties on the political margins that failed to embrace this consensus on the centre or centre-left of the spectrum. One factor in the formation of both the Taiwan Independence Party and the NP was their parent parties' movement away from nationalist orthodoxy. The NP did start off on the far right of the spectrum. However, in the mid-1990s, like the DPP, it downplayed the issue and broadened its appeal. In fact, in 1997 some reformers in the party even proposed moving towards the centre with the idea of 'one China two countries' (*yizhong liangguo*).[23] However, the reformers lost the power struggle and after 1998 the party moved even further to the right than when it was first formed.

In late 1999, on the eve of the 2000 presidential election, the main parties were closer than ever. Earlier that year, the DPP had passed its Resolution Regarding Taiwan's Future which formalized Shih Ming-teh's verbal statement of 1995 stating that there was no need to declare independence as Taiwan was already independent under the title ROC. Similarly, Lee argued that relations between Taiwan and China should be categorized as a state-to-state or special state-to-state relationship. These comments are also sometimes referred to as Lee's 'Two State Theory'. This was perceived by many within Taiwan, and especially in China, as tantamount to independence and reflected the narrowing of party differences.

Mixed identity messages and then polarization: 2002–8

On coming to power, the DPP's moderate approach was made clear by Chen's inaugural 'Five Noes' pledges that promised he would not declare independence, change the national title, put the state-to-state theory into the constitution, hold a referendum on independence or abolish the NUG/NUC. In fact, in Chen's first two years in office his government made a number of gestures aimed at reaffirming its moderate nature on identity. Thus, in the initial period after the 2000 change of ruling parties, we could still talk of moderate differentiation on national identity. Another scholar who came to this conclusion was Gunter Schubert, who offers a detailed examination of the political party divisions on national identity in the aftermath of the change in ruling parties.[24] He found that despite the common image of confrontational politics, the parties had reached an overarching consensus on a civic Taiwanese nation.

One way we can test the patterns of party/government convergence and divergence is in how the parties are perceived by the public on the unification versus independence spectrum. Table 8.2 shows the results from party image surveys that ask voters to place themselves and the main parties on a spectrum where 0 equals immediate independence, 5 equals the status quo and 10 equals immediate unification. This reveals that respondents tended to view the parties as moving towards the centre in the 1990s. In other words, the voters perceived the KMT as moving from the right towards the middle under Lee Teng-hui. Their perception of change is more limited for the DPP, which is seen as being at the far left for most of the 1990s, with only Chen's 2000 campaign seemingly receiving some acceptance of moderation. Voters then view the parties as diverging again in the post-2000 period. The KMT is seen as reverting back to the centre-right under Lien and Ma's leadership. Similarly, respondents perceive the DPP moving back to the far left as the DPP term progressed. Voters generally viewed the three other relevant parties, the NP, TSU and PFP, as occupying radical positions. The most recent figures from 2016 show that the public perceive the KMT as remaining at the edge between the centre and far right. However, the public do see the DPP as becoming more moderate under Tsai and that the PFP has moved from the centre-right towards the centre.

In Chen's first term, this perceived divergence was partly a result of the increasingly confrontational state of party politics. When we actually examine party positions and appeals, they remained quite close to the centre for much of the period. The DPP largely adhered to its Five Noes pledge and reaffirmed them in Chen's second inaugural speech in 2004. In order to reach out to other ethnic groups, the DPP promoted its own version of Lee's New Taiwanese appeal, as it claimed to be trying to turn Taiwan into a multi-cultural society. Cabestan described these efforts as having the 'avowed aim of diluting the Chinese cultural legacy into a melting-pot where Japanese, American and European contributions are given equal importance to the Chinese inheritance'.[25] DPP cultural policies radically expanded support of Hakka and aboriginal cultures – for instance, in broadcasting, mother-tongue language education and cultural centres. The commonly stated exception to this moderation was Chen's 2002 controversial statements arguing that there is 'one country on either side' of the Taiwan Strait and Taiwan should 'go its own way'.[26] However, based on my method of classification, such statements are closer to the centre-left than far left of the spectrum. Nevertheless, the general DPP trend was

Table 8.2 Party image survey on the Taiwan independence versus Chinese unification spectrum

	1992	1994	1996	1998	2000	2001	2002	2004	2008	2012	2016
Public	7.0	5.9	5.1	5.0	5.3	5.1	4.7	4.7	4.6	4.5	4.3
KMT	8.0	6.8	6.1	6.5	6.4	7.2	7.2	7.4	7.3	7.0	7.3
DPP	2.0	3.0	2.0	2.3	3.2	2.6	2.4	2.2	1.9	2.6	3.1
NP		6.5	6.5	7.2	7.2	7.6	7.5				
PFP					7.0	7.2	7.5	7.3	7.2		5.8
TSU						2.6	2.0	1.8	2.6		2.5
NPP											3.0

Source: Figures for 1992–2001: Fell (2005c: 94); figures for 2002–4 supplied by Professor Wu Chung-li; figures for 2008–16 from *Taiwan Election and Democratization Study*.

Note 1: This table shows where respondents place themselves and the main political parties on an issue spectrum in which the fastest independence equals 0, maintaining the status quo is 5, and immediate unification is 10.
Note 2: The 2002 survey only covered Taipei and Kaohsiung city, so these figures represent the average placement for these two cities.

moderation, exemplified by its decision in 2001 to elevate the Resolution Regarding Taiwan's Future to the same level as the TIC in the party charter.[27] Referendums are often viewed as being an integral component of the Taiwan independence project in Taiwan. Thus, the 2003 Referendum Bill could also be seen as indicative of changing party positions. However, in this case it was actually something that the DPP and KMT both supported and was mostly drawn up by the KMT.

In this period, though, there were signs of the KMT shifting back away from the centre-left. For instance, the KMT under Lien dropped references to the 'special state to state' formula and floated a proposal for a confederacy model for cross-Strait unification in 2001.[28] Similarly, it began reverting to more Chinese identity appeals after 2000, such as using images of Chiang Ching-kuo and Sun Yat Sen, and versions of the ROC national anthem in its election advertising. The sense of polarization was enhanced by the three smaller parties – the TSU, NP and PFP – all of whom were appealing to radical audiences.

The 2004 presidential election is often viewed as being the most polarized due to the abundance of negative campaigning. This was exemplified by the KMT advertisements likening Chen to Hitler, Bin Laden and Saddam Hussein.[29] However, the parties' actual positions and identity messages appeared once again converging on the centre-left. As mentioned earlier, there was cross-party support for the referendum legislation in late 2003. Moreover, as in the late 1990s, the two competed over who best loved Taiwan. We can see this in the two parties' most important campaign events. On the anniversary of the 2–28 Incident, the DPP organized a human chain from the far south to the far north of the island. This was known as the 'Hand in Hand Rally' and was designed to bring all Taiwanese together in protest against the PRC's missile threat. The KMT gave its prime rally the title of 'Change the President, Save Taiwan'. A key feature of the event was the image of its presidential candidates Lien and Soong kissing the ground to show their love for Taiwan.[30]

One of the most common Pan Blue criticisms of both Lee Teng-hui and Chen Shui-bian was that they were attempting to desinify Taiwan. In other words, they were trying to cultivate their own Taiwanese nation-building project to reverse the work of the two Chiangs. A central piece of supporting evidence for this accusation was their cultural policies, particularly education reforms. Under Chen, the focus of these accusations was the controversial education minister, Tu Cheng-sheng (杜正勝). Under Tu, principles previously employed in the 'Getting to Know Taiwan' textbooks were extended to the Senior High School history curriculum. The new Taiwan-centric approach involved separating Taiwanese history from Chinese history in a course titled 'Domestic History' and placing the study of China post 1500 (including the ROC until 1949) in the course on 'Modern World History'.[31] Similar complaints were made of attempts to expand the scope of mother-tongue education. On the matter of language education, the case is not convincing, as Klöter shows that Mandarin remains the dominant language and to a large extent local language education has been a disorganized failure.[32]

In many ways, the DPP appeared to be taking a leaf out of the KMT's book in its cultural policies. We get a sense of this in Phil Deans's analysis of the role that postage stamps have played in Taiwanese regime legitimation before and after democratization. Deans shows how, under the KMT rule, stamps emphasized Chiang's virtuous leadership, the ROC's international status and the island's economic achievements. However, after democratization the stamp design remained highly politicized. Deans notes that under the DPP, stamps 'have been predominantly related to promoting a Taiwanese culture and identity distinct from that of China'.[33]

When Lien visited China in 2005, he explained the Blue Camp's perception of DPP desinification, arguing that things had become so bad that parents now had to take their own initiative to 'allow young people to receive Chinese culture'.[34] However, such KMT accusations need more scrutiny. Was there really a genuine attempt to desinify the education system and, if so, how thorough was it? Or should we regard it just as an attempt to continue rebalancing the overly sinocentric curriculum left over from martial law?[35] This area of cultural politics still requires much more research and I would argue that these remain unanswered questions.

While we can safely say that the pattern of party/government movement was inconsistent and fluctuating in the first five years of the DPP era, there was a more consistent pattern of polarization for the final years in Chen's second term. In 2005, Lien and Soong individually visited China and reached agreements with the CCP on a number of issues, including working together to fight Taiwan independence. After Ma Ying-jeou replaced Lien Chan as KMT Chairman in the summer of 2005, the party continued its rightwards direction, as Ma made increasingly pro-unification statements. In a December 2005 interview with *Newsweek* magazine, Ma argued that 'For our party, the eventual goal is unification.'[36] During Ma's UK tour in 2006, he called for a return to the '1992 Consensus' of 'One China different interpretations'.

The DPP followed a similar divergent direction from 2006. First, Chen announced in early 2006 that the NUG would cease to apply and NUC cease to function.[37] This created a political storm, as such a move meant breaking one of Chen's Five Noes pledges. Then, in spring of 2007, Chen made his most comprehensive repudiation of the Five Noes when he declared that 'Taiwan wants independence, wants name rectification, wants a new Constitution and development'.[38] In short, by the summer of 2007, the leaders of both main parties had dragged their parties to their most polarized positions on the *Tongdu* spectrum since the early 1990s.

In the second term, the DPP also first showed signs of moving away from its moderate position on symbolic identity issues in election campaigns when it began calling for name rectification in December 2004. In Chen's first term the only significant step in this area was the inclusion of Taiwan on the front cover of ROC passports from 2003.[39] However, it was not until 2007 that the DPP actually began implementing name changes of government-owned enterprises. In February 2007, Chen's administration succeeded in changing the company names of Chunghwa Post and Chinese Petroleum Corporation to Taiwan Post and Taiwan CPC Corporation respectively.[40] In a highly symbolic move, the first postage stamp in which the ROC was replaced with Taiwan (in English and Chinese) showed the 2–28 Incident Memorial Museum.[41]

The DPP's more exclusive Taiwan identity message was accelerated in 2006–7 with the campaign against the cult of Chiang Kai-shek. Although the DPP framed such moves as part of democratization and transitional justice, in some circles it was perceived as an attack on the Mainlander community. In the first step, Chiang Kai-shek International Airport was renamed Taiwan Taoyuan International Airport in September 2006.[42] The anti-Chiang campaign continued into 2007 with the removal of the huge Chiang statue from the Kaohsiung Culture Centre and the Ministry of Defence pledged to remove all Chiang statues from its bases. In Taipei, the central government also renamed Chiang Kai-shek Memorial Hall into Taiwan Democracy Memorial Hall.[43]

The KMT also took a sharply different approach to the greater Chinese nationalist symbols. As in Chen's first term, Sun Yat Sen was employed in KMT election communication. On the day after the Pan Blues retained their legislative majority in December

2004, the KMT ran a full page advertisement with a portrait of Sun and the slogan 'Thank you for allowing me to continue to be the Nation's Father'.[44] However, the change in KMT party values was more apparent in its treatment of the Chiang Kai-shek statue debate. The KMT took its most pro-Chiang Kai-shek stance since the early 1990s. The KMT-run Taipei City government attempted to block the name change of the Chiang Kai-shek Memorial Hall. On 31 March 2007, the KMT even organized a rally to protest against the anti-Chiang campaign, in which demonstrators shouted, 'Long live Chiang Kai-shek!'[45] KMT leaders repeatedly condemned the anti-Chiang campaign as similar to the Chinese Cultural Revolution and as inciting ethnic tensions. Increasingly, KMT politicians emphasized Chiang Kai-shek's contribution to Taiwan rather than his role in the White Terror era.[46]

In short, on both core dimensions of the identity spectrum, the parties had gone from a tacit consensus at the centre-left in the late 1990s to their most polarized state since 1991. Schubert talks of the DPP shifting from a civic to ethnic nationalist message in the post-2000 period and argues that it paid the price electorally for pushing this agenda too hard.[47] Cabestan also comes to a similar conclusion in his study of the limits of Taiwanese nationalism, claiming that the DPP's new fundamentalism contributed to its electoral defeat, the loss of domestic consensus on core identity questions and increased levels of polarization on Taiwan.[48] Nevertheless, as I hope this section has shown, both major parties played a role in the identity polarization and loss of national identity consensus in this period. We will come back to the question of competing nation-building projects in the Ma era in Chapter 13.

Measuring national identities at the mass level

Perhaps no country in the world conducts more frequent political opinion polls than Taiwan. The most commonly asked identity-related questions revolve around whether respondents prefer Taiwan independence or unification with China, and whether voters see themselves as primarily Taiwanese or Chinese. Examining this data can give us some idea of the legacies of the nation-building projects and the impact of post-democratization developments.

A bewildering array of polling companies, newspapers and political parties conduct frequent polls on national identity in Taiwan. However, finding easily accessible and reliable time series figures are not as straightforward as you might expect. The media frequently conduct and cite surveys, but their data is rarely, if ever displayed in a time series format. The four sources that maintain online accessible time series data are TVBS Polling Center, Global View Monthly (GVM) Polling Center, Taiwan Indicator Survey Research (TISR) and National Chengchi University's Election Study Center (ESC). Other issues that we also need to keep in mind when citing Taiwanese survey sources are whether the methodology used is professional and whether there is any partisan bias involved. Thus, if a media-cited survey is from an unknown survey company or if there is a clear partisan bias of the newspaper, then this data must be taken at least with caution. It is quite common for parties to try to manipulate surveys for their own benefit. For instance, surveys are often used as a component in party advertising and there are even cases where advertisements focused on polls are portrayed as real news stories. Another problem, at least with TVBS, TISR and GVM surveys, is that they are relatively new, so tend to start their data in the post-2000 period.

In Figure 8.1, I track changing public positions on the unification versus independence question based on ESC data.[49] One issue with the ESC data is that it gives voters many options. For simplicity, I chose to combine some categories to create just four options: (1) independence (includes independence as soon as possible and status quo move towards independence); (2) unification (unification as soon as possible and status quo move towards unification); (3) status quo (maintain status quo indefinitely and maintain status quo, decide at a later date); and (4) don't know/no response. We can see a number of clear trends. First, the proportion of voters supporting immediate or eventual unification declined drastically from over 50 per cent in 1989 to only 20 per cent in 1994. It then showed a more gradual decline in the DPP era, falling to only 9.5 per cent by 2016. Second, support for Taiwan independence options rose quite fast from almost nothing in the late 1980s to 17.2 per cent in 1997. It then was quite stable through to 2002. Since then, it has gradually crept up to 23.4 per cent in the most recent survey in 2016. For most of the early surveys, around half of respondents expressed a preference for maintaining the status quo of neither unification nor independence. However, the proportion preferring this in-between option has risen to approximately 60 per cent in more recent surveys. Lastly, the proportion of respondents who did not know has dwindled significantly. This figure reveals that the vast majority of Taiwanese voters are moderates. This is further reinforced when looking at the unmerged statistics which show that the combined scores of the most radical options of immediate independence and unification as soon as possible never gets more than 10 per cent after 1994.

This movement of voters from the centre-right towards the centre or centre-left on the *Tongdu* spectrum corresponds with the party image surveys on Table 8.2. When asked to locate themselves on the unification versus independence spectrum, the median voter has shifted from the centre-right to the centre and then centre-left. This does suggest that the parties are out of step with the public on the *Tongdu* issue, as voters perceive a widening gap between themselves and all major parties on the issue. Lin found some

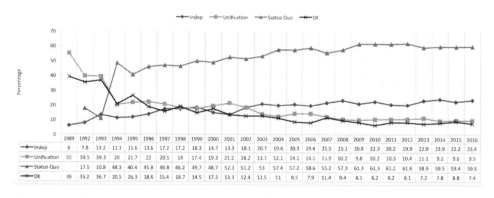

	1989	1992	1993	1994	1995	1996	1997	1998	1999	2000	2001	2002	2003	2004	2005	2006	2007	2008	2009	2010	2011	2012	2013	2014	2015	2016
Indep	6	7.8	13.2	11.1	11.6	13.6	17.2	17.2	18.3	14.7	13.3	18.1	20.7	19.6	20.3	19.4	21.5	23.1	20.8	22.3	20.2	19.9	22.9	23.9	22.2	23.4
Unification	55	39.5	39.3	20	21.7	22	20.5	18	17.4	19.3	21.2	18.2	13.7	12.1	14.1	14.1	11.9	10.2	9.8	10.2	10.3	10.4	11.1	9.2	9.6	9.5
Status Quo		17.5	10.8	48.3	40.4	45.8	46.8	46.2	49.7	48.7	52.3	51.2	53	57.4	57.2	58.6	55.2	57.3	61.3	61.3	61.2	61.6	58.9	59.5	59.4	59.6
DK	39	35.2	36.7	20.5	26.3	18.6	15.4	18.7	14.5	17.3	13.3	12.4	12.5	11	8.5	7.9	11.4	9.4	8.1	6.2	8.2	8.1	7.2	7.8	8.8	7.4

Figure 8.1 Public opinion on unification versus independence

Sources: Lin, Chia-long (1998: 508); Election Study Centre, National Chengchi University.

Note 1: This shows the proportion of respondents supporting Taiwan independence, unification with China or the status quo. In order to simplify the table I merged some categories. Thus, independence includes those opting for independence as soon as possible and maintain the status quo, move towards independence. Status quo includes maintain status quo indefinitely and maintain status quo, decide later. Unification includes unification as soon as possible and maintain status quo, move towards unification. DK stands for don't know/no response.
Note 2: The range of options was more limited in the earlier surveys cited by Lin Chia-long.

similar results when comparing elite and mass responses to the same survey questions, finding, for instance, a much higher preference for Taiwan independence among elites than ordinary voters.[50]

One facet that has frustrated researchers is that most respondents chose the in-between category of the status quo; moreover, there is uncertainty as to what voters really mean by their answers. It is likely that the way that voters actually view terms such as independence, unification or the status quo have changed over time. In the late 1980s, many voters might still have associated the term unification with unification under the ROC, but by 2016 this would be unlikely. Similarly, we need to remember that a respondent giving a preference for Taiwan independence in a 1980s survey was quite courageous or foolhardy. We have to consider the pervasiveness of the Taiwanese intelligence services in martial law society and that independence advocacy had been punished by firing squads at the height of the White Terror period and could land you in prison as late as 1992.

One way researchers have tried to unravel respondents' true preferences has been to add conditionality to the questions. Voters are asked if they would agree to Taiwan independence if Taiwan could still maintain peaceful relations with China. The reverse question asks if Taiwan and China should reunite if China catches up economically, socially and politically. These studies tend to show that around half of respondents could accept either unification or independence if the conditions are right. Scholars such as Marsh use these conditional answers to divide voters into four categories: (1) Pragmatists, who can accept either outcome if the conditions are right; (2) Taiwan nationalists, who only accept Taiwanese independence and reject unification regardless of Chinese progress; (3) Chinese nationalists, who reject Taiwanese independence regardless of conditions and support unification after China further develops; and (4) Conservatives, who reject both outcomes and prefer indefinitely maintaining the status quo.[51] In Table 8.3, I have tried to show opinion change using this approach. The table shows how flexible or pragmatic most voters are. In other words, they can generally accept either unification or independence if the conditions are right. However, once again, preferences are changing over time. Regardless of favourable conditions, support for unification halved over a ten-year period, while there has been a gradual rise in support for independence.

Table 8.3 National identity in Taiwan using the conditional questions

	1992	1993	1994	1996	2001
Pragmatist	25	25.4	24.1	39	22.7
Taiwan nationalist	9.3	10.3	9.4	21.2	20.3
Chinese nationalist	38	27.6	24.7	16.9	18
Conservative	11	7.4	5.9	2.4	11.2

Sources: Marsh (2002: 123–43); Niou (2005: 91–104).

Note 1: This table shows the percentage of survey respondents classified as Pragmatists, Taiwan nationalists, Chinese nationalists or Conservatives on the unification versus independence spectrum. This is created by asking respondents if they would agree to Taiwan independence if Taiwan could still maintain peaceful relations with China. The reverse question asks if Taiwan and China should reunite if China catches up economically, socially and politically. Note 2: Pragmatists are those who can accept either outcome if the conditions are right; Taiwan nationalists only accept Taiwanese independence and reject unification regardless of Chinese progress; Chinese nationalists reject Taiwanese independence regardless of conditions and support unification after China further develops; Conservatives reject both outcomes and prefer indefinitely maintaining the status quo. I have excluded the others category.

Of course, a stumbling point is which of the two ideal scenarios is more likely. Marsh argues that he sees the probability of the PRC catching up as more likely than for it to peacefully accept Taiwan's *de jure* independence.[52]

Niou has critiqued the three standard methods of measuring one's identification with their state and instead proposed bringing further elements of conditionality by using four conditional questions.[53] This may well help unravel the true meaning of respondents' answers, but may also serve to cloud the simple picture of change we get from the standard methods.

Some more recent survey data suggests that even if the conditions are right, support for unification continues to decline. Global Views Monthly (GVM) surveys asked voters whether, if the PRC caught up economically, politically and socially, unification would be facilitated or remain unnecessary?[54] What is interesting is that in the first GVM survey in 2002, the results were similar, with 35.9 per cent agreeing to unification if the conditions were right and 38.2 per cent opposing unification regardless. However, in the subsequent six years the gap has widened, as support for unification, even if the PRC catches up, has plummeted to only 12.1 per cent. In contrast, in 2010, 66.1 per cent of respondents felt that unification would be unnecessary in the unlikely event that the PRC democratizes. More recently, a TEDS 2013 survey found that 35.7 agreed to unification if China catches up economically, socially and politically, while 52.9 disagreed. Such figures suggest China's Taiwan policy has failed.

Self-identification as Chinese, Taiwanese or dual identities

Perhaps the second most asked identity-related survey question is whether respondents view themselves as Chinese, Taiwanese, or both. This is a key measure we have to actually assess impact on or at least correlation with the major nation-building projects of the authoritarian and post-authoritarian eras. I have tried to sum up the major shifts in the self-identification dimension as Chinese, Taiwanese, or both in Figure 8.2. There are some similarities but also marked differences to the patterns we saw in Figure 8.1 on *Tongdu* public opinion. The drop in pure Chinese identity is quite similar in scale to falling support for unification. Also, the most common response, at least until the middle of the DPP era, was dual identity just as most voters expressed a preference for maintaining the status quo. The major difference is that while support for independence stalled or at least grew very slowly after the late 1990s, self-identification as Taiwanese has grown consistently throughout the democratic era. Interestingly, Taiwanese self-identification has continued to grow and exceeded dual identity in 2008 after the return of the KMT to power, hitting a peak of over 60 per cent in the Sunflower Movement year of 2014. Figure 8.2 suggests that significant numbers of respondents have moved from Chinese identity to dual and Taiwanese identification over a period of less than two decades.

Naturally, there is much variation in responses for different demographic backgrounds. Liu and Ho's study found that in 2000 the groups most likely to have stronger Taiwanese identity were: people of Hoklo (they use the term *Fulao*) origin, people aged between 50 and 59, those with only an elementary school education, females and DPP supporters.[55] In contrast, the only group with a significant likelihood to maintain a Chinese identity was Mainlanders. However, they do find that regardless of background, the consistent trend of identity change during the 1990s was one of declining Chinese and rising Taiwanese identity. Even for the Mainlanders there was significant change, with the proportion identifying themselves as Chinese falling from 55.6 per cent in 1994 to only

29.9 per cent in 2000, with most presumably switching to dual identity. These figures naturally also reveal why even the KMT needs to appeal to Taiwanese identity to win elections, as the market for the old exclusive Chinese identity has almost disappeared.

One of the foremost Western scholars working on the identity patterns of Taiwan's Mainlander ethnic group has been Stéphane Corcuff. Corcuff (2002) conducted a unique 178-question survey of members of this group's identity attitudes in the mid-1990s. He found that most Mainlanders do have a degree of Taiwanese identification in their daily lives, but that when these issues become politicized at election times, their Taiwan identity vanishes. Lastly, Corcuff calls for abandoning the term 'Mainlander' and replacing it with the more neutral 'New Taiwanese' or 'New Inhabitants'. I was delighted to see that in the post-2000 period he has followed up with a new set of surveys that examine trends in Mainlander identity at the end of the Chen era (surveys were conducted in 2007).[56] In the later survey, he finds that increasingly this group is no longer comfortable with the term Mainlander. He also finds that close to 70 per cent could accept independence if the conditions were right. In contrast, though, he finds a strong backlash against what his respondents perceived as desinification policies under Chen. This led him to conclude that we are seeing a shift from political to cultural Chinese identity among this group.

Based on the above public opinion survey data, can we actually say that any of the rival nation-building projects has succeeded? Writing in the late 1990s, Hughes argued that Taiwan should be categorized as being in an intermediate post-nationalist state, as neither the integrationist nor separatist forces had 'proved strong enough to move Taiwan decisively in either direction'.[57] Lin actually comes to similar conclusions to Hughes. He employs a combination of mass and elite surveys to show how an inclusive civic national identity developed in the 1990s, in which 'a significant portion of the population actually have multiple identities, claiming to be politically Taiwanese and culturally Chinese'.[58] Although there has been elite radicalization in the decade since Lin and Hughes reached these conclusions, the most recent survey data suggests that voters remain moderate and pragmatic on the core identity questions. At the mass level, Taiwanese still appear to embrace a civic rather than ethnic nationalism. Writing in mid

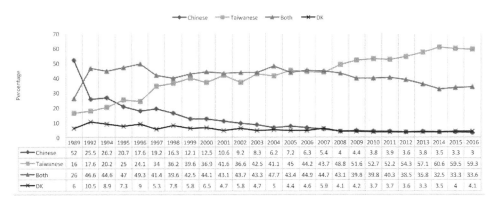

	1989	1992	1994	1995	1996	1997	1998	1999	2000	2001	2002	2003	2004	2005	2006	2007	2008	2009	2010	2011	2012	2013	2014	2015	2016
Chinese	52	25.5	26.2	20.7	17.6	19.2	16.3	12.1	12.5	10.6	9.2	8.3	6.2	7.2	6.3	5.4	4	4.4	3.8	3.9	3.6	3.8	3.5	3.3	3
Taiwanese	16	17.6	20.2	25	24.1	34	36.2	39.6	36.9	41.6	36.6	42.5	41.1	45	44.2	43.7	48.8	51.6	52.7	52.2	54.3	57.1	60.6	59.5	59.3
Both	26	46.6	44.6	47	49.3	41.4	39.6	42.5	44.1	43.1	43.7	43.3	47.7	43.4	44.9	44.7	43.1	39.8	39.8	40.3	38.5	35.8	32.5	33.3	33.6
DK	6	10.5	8.9	7.3	9	5.3	7.8	5.8	6.5	4.7	5.8	4.7	5	4.4	4.6	5.9	4.1	4.2	3.7	3.7	3.6	3.3	3.5	4	4.1

Figure 8.2 Public opinion on self-identification as Taiwanese, Chinese or both

Sources: Lin, Chia-long (1998: 508); Election Study Centre, National Chengchi University.

Note: This shows the proportion of respondents self-identifying as Taiwanese, Chinese or both. DK stands for don't know/no response.

2017, survey trends still show most voters adopt moderate positions with civic Taiwanese self-identification and support for de facto independence as core shared values. Naturally, this means that national identity survey results are very frustrating from the perspective of PRC Taiwan analysts.

Explaining elite and mass patterns of identity change

Having traced major trends in elite and mass positions on national identity, a major question we need to ask is how we explain these trends, especially in the post-democratic era. To what extent can elite-led nation-building projects really mould voters' identification? It is quite common to hear KMT or PRC figures blame DPP leaders for the creation of Taiwanese nationalism. Or is it a matter of parties following public opinion on national identity issues? With the huge abundance of survey data and the intensive scrutiny of politicians' identity positions during elections, politicians need to avoid being rejected for being too extreme on identity.

In my own work, I have tended to focus on explaining party positions on identity with reference to inner-party balances of power and election results. In other words, when more electorally oriented factions and leaders dominate a party, it tends to move towards positions closer to the median voter, while if the party is dominated by more ideological or radical factions and leaders, it tends to try to persuade voters of the validity of its more radical positions. Party positional change tends to come in response to electoral setbacks and changes in the inner-party balance of power. For instance, the DPP's shift towards the centre after 1992 was driven by both a reaction to its disastrous defeat in 1991 (on the back of its ROT campaign) and a shift in favour of more moderate party leaders. The NP's shift to extreme nationalist positions after the late 1990s was also a reaction to the widespread departure of party moderates and subsequent domination by extremists. In the case of the NP, it appears that defeats no longer have any effect; instead, it operates consistently. This kind of framework also works for explaining the stronger Chinese identification and pro-unification message the KMT employed after falling from power in 2000. Again, there was soul searching after its disastrous defeat and also a radical shift in the internal balance of power. Thus, my analysis views politicians as being torn between their own party ideology, which is often out of step with the ordinary voters, and the desire to respond to public opinion and win elections.

One weakness in my approach is undoubtedly that it neglects the importance of external variables. Here, the key actors we need to consider are, of course, China and the US. Given Taiwan's reliance on the US for security, it needs to consider US concerns that if Taiwan adopts more radical positions on the *Tongdu* issue, it might jeopardize US–China relations. If it was felt that Taiwan had needlessly provoked China by declaring independence, it is unlikely that the US would come to Taiwan's aid. Taiwanese politicians thus must consider the possibility that its policies or statements will provoke China. The missile crisis of 1995–6 did serve to reinforce the elite view that the Chinese military threat was credible and that the US security guarantee was not unconditional. This can, of course, work both ways as politicians are also aware that voters do not wish to see their leaders openly kowtowing to China. Therefore, to a certain extent we have seen politicians trying to reap the benefits of provoking China and being seen to stand up to them. One way we can see the effect of external forces on government positions is in the drafting of presidential inaugural speeches, as the writers need to consider the way the speech will be received in both Beijing and Washington. In short, as Hughes shows, the international context, public opinion and electoral pressures encouraged a moderate domestic consensus among politicians on formerly divisive identity issues.[59]

We face similar difficulties in explaining the trends in mass identities. Clearly, we can be certain from the sea of changes over the last two decades that identity in Taiwan is not immutable. But which of the various processes had the decisive impact? Is it a matter of generational replacement? Lin contends that political democratization and China's military threats were the key driving forces in the development of the new civic nationalism.[60] The intense electoral debates over matters of *Tongdu* and Chinese versus Taiwanese identity must also be a contributing factor in the competing identities. We can be sure that top-down nation building has only limited effects in modern Taiwan. If top-down nation building was decisive, then we would expect a rise in support for independence under Chen and a revival in Chinese identity under Ma. In fact, Figures 8.1 and 8.2 show the opposite, as there was little change in support for independence under Chen and under Ma Taiwanese rather than Chinese self-identification hit record levels. Nevertheless, although we can plot correlation for a range of political, social and economic processes and changing identities, proving causation will remain a challenge for the future.

Future prospects for contending identities

As we look to the future, what are the prospects for the competing national identities in Taiwan? Lynch found a widespread anxiety among Taiwanese nationalists over the dangers of the increasing economic integration with China and their belief in the importance of cultural desinification for their nation-building objectives.[61] The limited growth in support for Taiwan independence and declining electoral performance of the DPP after 2004 and its fall from office have been used to suggest a failure of the Taiwanese nationalist project. As early as 2006, Robert Ross wrote that 'Political developments in Taiwan over the past year (2005) have effectively ended the independence movement there.'[62] However, the picture is clearly far more complex, as after the DPP fell from power we actually saw a continued rise in Taiwanese identity and support for independence. The Sunflower Movement and subsequent decline in the KMT's support levels have led to a similar argument on the failure of Ma's resinification efforts.

We should not, however, just take for granted that the key trends we have witnessed since the 1980s will continue. The growing economic integration between Taiwan and China means that there is a rapidly growing Taiwanese population working and studying in China. Estimates on this population vary from 1 to 2 million, and these people are largely absent from the surveys we see coming out of the main polling centres. Will they be influenced by growing Chinese nationalism or will the direct daily contact with Chinese citizens actually promote their sense of distinct Taiwanese identities? In addition, increasing numbers of Taiwanese have contact with Chinese tourists, businesspeople and even students coming to Taiwan. Will these interactions have any impact? Another variable will be the huge numbers of migrant spouses coming to Taiwan from both China and South East Asia. Will they become Taiwanized by their host families or, as some Taiwanese nationalists fear, will those spouses from China spread Chinese nationalism? Looking further ahead, what kind of national identities will the children of these interracial marriages adopt? In short, there are still many unanswered questions and new avenues for research in the study of identities in Taiwan.

Discussion questions

1 What are the competing national identities in Taiwan?
2 How and why has public opinion changed on the central identity questions?
3 How and why did the government adjust its nation identity positions?
4 How reliably is public opinion on identity measured?
5 Assess the claims that Taiwan was desinified under Lee and Chen and then resinified under Ma.
6 What has been the impact of China's rise or the economic integration with China on national identity in Taiwan?
7 How and why have the parties changed their positions on identity questions?
8 Does the divisive identity dispute prevent Taiwan from becoming a consolidated democracy?
9 How will migration trends to and from Taiwan affect future identity patterns?

Further reading

Corcuff, Stéphane (ed.). 2002. *Memories of the Future: National Identity Issues and the Search for a New Taiwan*. Armonk, NY: M.E. Sharpe. Unrivalled collection of essays on identity in the late 1990s and early post-2000.

Fell, Dafydd. 2011. 'The Polarization of Taiwan's Party Competition in the DPP Era'. In Robert Ash, Penny Prime and John Garver (eds). *Taiwan's Democracy and Future: Economic and Political Challenges*. London: Routledge. In this chapter I try to update my analysis of party change on identity in the post-2000 period.

Fell, Dafydd. 2005. *Party Politics in Taiwan*. London: Routledge. Chapter 6 examines party change on national identity issues in detail for the 1990s.

Fell, Dafydd (ed.). 2008. *Politics of Modern Taiwan*. London: Routledge. Vol. 1 includes fifteen key articles on national identities in Taiwan, including three from Corcuff's *Memories of the Future*.

Hughes, Christopher. 2011. 'Negotiating national identity in Taiwan: Between nativization and de-sinification'. In Robert Ash, John Garver and Penny Prime (eds). *Taiwan's Democracy and Future: Economic and Political Challenges*. London: Routledge, pp.51–74. Great discussion of the debates surrounding nativization and desinification.

Schubert, Gunter and Jens Dam (eds). 2011. *Taiwanese Identity in the 21st Century*. London: Routledge. This collection includes up-to-date research on identity in Taiwan in the post-2000 period from some of the leading scholars of the subject.

Useful websites

http://esc.nccu.edu.tw/english/modules/tinyd2/index.php?id=6 – Election Study Centre, National Chengchi University. This is the best set of time series data on the unification versus independence and Chinese versus Taiwanese identity surveys.

www.tvbs.com.tw/news/poll_center/index.htm – TVBS Polling Center has perhaps the widest selection of online available polls on a huge variety of topics, including identity.

www.gvm.com.tw/gvsrc/eng/index.asp – Global Views Monthly Research Center has a growing user-friendly collection of surveys that complement the ESC data. Also, the site has both Chinese and English reports.

Notes

1 Hsieh, 'Continuity and Change in Taiwan's Electoral Politics', 32–49, 38.
2 Fell, 'A Welcome Antidote to National Identity and Cross-Strait Fatigue', 256–63.

3 Peng Ming-min, interview by author, Taipei, 31 October 2001.

4 Chang Chun-hung, interview by author. Taipei, 26 September 2001.

5 Gellner, *Nations and Nationalism*, 1.

6 Rigger, *Taiwan's Rising Rationalism*.

7 Lamley, 'Subethnic Rivalry in the Ch'ing Period', 282–318.

8 Albert Tseng, 'A Time to Realign Policy', *Ketegelan Media*, 3 February 2016: available online at: www.ketagalanmedia.com/2016/02/03/a-time-to-realign-policy/

9 Chao and Myers, *The First Chinese Democracy*, 226.

10 Lin Cheng-chieh, interview with author, Hsinchu, 21 September 2001.

11 For details, see Fell, *Party Politics in Taiwan*, 98–100 and 110–11.

12 *Liberty Times*, 25 November 1991, 1.

13 Fell, *Party Politics in Taiwan*, 99.

14 Ibid., 111.

15 Ibid.

16 Cited in Fell, *Party Politics in Taiwan*, 102–3.

17 Of course, there were notable exceptions to this pattern, such as the anti-Mainlander appeals that accused Ma of being part of a 'Betray Taiwan Consortium' in the 1998 Taipei campaign. See Wang Chao-chun, 'Ye Chu-lan: Ma is a Pawn in a Betray Taiwan Consortium', *China Times*, 19 October 1998, 18.

18 Hughes, 'National Identity', 158.

19 Hughes, 'National Identity', 158.

20 *United Daily News*, 3 December 1998, 5.

21 Hsu Hsiao-tzu, 'Gallup Poll: Almost Fifty Per Cent of People Identify themselves as New Taiwanese', *China Times*, 13 December 1998, 4.

22 Corcuff, 2005.

23 Fell, 106.

24 Schubert, 'Taiwan's Parties and National Identity', 534–54.

25 Cabestan, 'Specificities and Limits of Taiwanese Nationalism', 32–43, 33.

26 Lin Chieh-yu, 'Chen Raises Pitch of Anti-China Rhetoric', *Taipei Times*, 4 August 2002, 1.

27 Joyce Huang, 'DPP makes minor revisions to stance on independence', *Taipei Times*, 21 October 2001, 3.

28 See Staff Writer, 'KMT urges serious consideration of Confederation', *Taipei Times*, 16 July 2001, 3.

29 For the infamous KMT Hitler advertisement, see *China Times*, 12 March 2004, A7.

30 See KMT advertisement, *China Times*, 15, March 2004, A5.

31 See Chang, 'Constructing the Motherland: Culture and State Since the 1990s', 187–206, 200.

32 Klöter, 'Mandarin Remains More Equal: Changes and Continuities in Taiwan's Language Policy', 207–24.

33 Deans, 'Isolation, Identity and Taiwanese Stamps as Vehicles for Regime Legitimation', 8–30, 8.

34 *United Daily News*, 'Lien Chan's Question and Answer session at Beijing University', 29 April 2005.

35 For a discussion of this issue, see Hughes, 2011.

36 Newsweek International Edition, 'Conditions aren't right', available online at: www.msnbc.msn. com/id/10511672/site/newsweek/ (accessed 7 April 2007).

37 Taipei Representative Office in the UK Press Release, 'President Chen announces National Unification Council and Guidelines to Cease'. Available online at: www.roc-taiwan.org/uk/TaiwanUpdate/nsl010306a.htm (accessed 6 April 2007).

38 China Post Online edition, 'Chen declares Four Wants and One Without', *China Post*. Available online at: www.chinapost.com.tw/backnews/archives/front/200735/103826.htm (accessed 7 April 2007).

39 Monique Chu, 'ROC Passports will get makeover,' *Taipei Times*, 13 June 2003, 3.

40 Shih Hsiu-chuan, 'Chen pushes corporate name-change', *Taipei Times*, 9 February 2007, 3.

41 See Taiwan Post website. Available online at: www.post.gov.tw/post/internet/w_stamphouse/stamphouse_eng.htm (accessed 7 April 2007).

42 Jimmy Chuang, 'Chiang Kai-shek Airport enters dustbin of history', *Taipei Times*, 7 September 2006, 1.

43 Flora Wang, Rich Chang and Shih Hsiu-chuan, 'CKS statues' removal nears completion', *Taipei Times,* 6 February 2007, 1. The choice of Taiwan Democracy Memorial Hall is an odd one, seeming to imply that democracy is something Taiwan has already lost.
44 KMT advertisement, *China Times,* 13 December 2004, A11.
45 Mo Yan-chih, 'Thousands Protest anti-Chiang campaign', *Taipei Times,* 1 April 2007, 3.
46 See KMT website. Available online at: www.kmt.org.tw/category_3/category3_1_n.asp?sn=502 (accessed 8 April 2007).
47 Schubert, 'Taiwan's Evolving National Identity since the DPP Takeover: From Civic to Ethnic', 85–115.
48 Cabestan, 'Specificities and Limits of Taiwanese Nationalism', 32–43.
49 The data for 1989, 1992 and 1993 is from Lin, 'Paths to Democracy: Taiwan in Comparative Perspective', 508.
50 Ibid.
51 Marsh, 'National Identity and Ethnicity in Taiwan: Some trends in the 1990s', 144–59.
52 Ibid., 157–8.
53 Niou, 'A new measure of preferences on the independence-unification issue in Taiwan', 91–104.
54 Global Views Monthly Research Center, 'Survey on Signed Cross-Strait Economic Cooperation Agreement, People's Views on Unification-Independence Issue and President Ma Ying-jeou's Approval Rating,' 28 July 2010. Available online at: www.gvm.com.tw/gvsrc/20100714S01AP00PR2R.pdf (accessed 10 October 2010).
55 Ho and I-chou, 'The Taiwanese/Chinese identity of the Taiwan people in the 1990s', 149–83.
56 Corcuff, 'Taiwan's Mainlanders under President Chen Shui-bian', 113–132.
57 Hughes, 63–81.
58 Lin, 'The Political Formation of Taiwanese Nationalism'' 144–59.
59 Hughes, 63–81.
60 Lin, 144–59.
61 Lynch, 'Taiwan's Self Conscious Nation-Building Projects', 513–33.
62 Ross, 'Taiwan's Fading Independence Movement'.

9 Taiwan's external relations

Balancing international space and cross-Strait relations

Taiwan represents a puzzle for students of international relations. It is sometimes categorized as a contested or unrecognized state, but it is in reality quite distinct from others in those categories such as Ngorno Karabakh or Somaliland. It has all the key ingredients of a state set out in the 1933 Montevideo Convention. First, it has a permanent population of over 23 million, which is larger than most countries in the United Nations.[1] Second, it has a defined territory that has not changed since the 1950s and is of almost the same size as the Netherlands.[2] Third, it does have a functioning, well-educated, meritocratic and multi-layered government. And fourth, it has a range of government (including its Ministry of Foreign Affairs) and non-government agencies with the capacity to enter into relations with other states. Yet Taiwan has been excluded from the United Nations since 1971 and is only officially recognized by a dwindling number of minor players on the world stage. Since the loss of South African and South Korean recognition in the 1990s, Taiwan's most prized remaining diplomatic allies are the Vatican and Paraguay.[3] That failed states such as Somalia and Afghanistan or rogue states such as North Korea and Zimbabwe are part of the formal system of international relations centred on the United Nations, while Taiwan is shut out, is perplexing to outside observers and a source of great frustration for most Taiwanese.

If Taiwan's external relations were just limited to the international minnows that it currently maintains formal ties with, it is likely it would have been annexed by China long ago. It has, however, developed unofficial but substantive relations with most UN members. Under a range of titles, its overseas offices are virtually indistinguishable from regular embassies in their operations. Even after losing official diplomatic relations with the US in 1979, Taiwan has maintained de facto diplomatic ties with the US. Relations with the US are particularly critical as it alone provides Taiwan with advanced defensive arms sales and an ambiguous security guarantee. In addition, Taiwan has been a major player in the international trading system since the 1960s and in 2015 was the seventeenth largest exporting nation in the world.[4] This involvement in international trade has not only contributed to Taiwan's economic success, but also to its ability to maintain its international relations and independence. One country alone stands in the way of Taiwan's entrance into the UN system – that, of course, is the PRC. Over the last few decades, the PRC has attempted to squeeze Taiwan's international space at every possible opportunity. Taiwan's external relations have always been complex. Over the last four hundred years, the island has changed hands five times. On each occasion the control of Taiwan has been determined externally, depending on the balance of power between Chinese and international actors in the region.

We generally refer to the external relations between China and Taiwan as cross-Strait relations. Should we regard these ties as international relations? Some in Taiwan view these as state-to-state relations. In contrast, from the PRC perspective cross-Strait relations are purely a domestic matter. For them, Taiwan is just another province or at most a special administrative region belonging to the PRC, on par with Hong Kong or Macau. Other than occasional battles over the remaining ROC-controlled islands off the Chinese coast, there were almost no contacts across the Taiwan Strait for most of the martial law era. From the early 1990s until 2008, cross-Strait relations featured a paradoxical development of ever closer economic integration but political divergence. Even after the improved cross-Strait relations following the KMT's return to power in 2008, the PRC continued to increase its 1,000-plus missiles targeted at Taiwan and refused to rule out the use of force against the island. After the DPP returned to power in 2016, there appears to be a return to the political divergence in cross-Strait relations.

In this chapter, after first reviewing Taiwan's external ties under martial law, the focus will be on developments after political liberalization. Preserving cross-Strait peace has been a delicate balance as a result of the often conflicting values and objectives of the three main actors: Taiwan, the US and China. More often than not when Taiwan appears in international news, it is on account of cross-Strait tensions or disputes between the US and China centred on Taiwan. As Rigger noted in the late 1990s, cross-Strait relations remain a challenge for Taiwan's democracy, as it faces the ever-present Damocles' sword of Chinese invasion and Chinese attempts to undermine Taiwan's democratic political system.[5] The state of Taiwan's external relations has implications beyond the immediate region. Along with the Korean peninsula, Taiwan represents the only other potential flashpoint that could trigger a major conflict between the US and China.

For over five decades the status quo of neither independence nor unification has survived. This is not the ideal scenario for either China or many in Taiwan, but is preferable to their nightmare scenarios. China's ideal outcome is unification under the One Country, Two Systems model. In Taiwan, there is a broad consensus against unification, but opinion appears divided over whether the ideal solution is continuing de facto independence or eventually moving towards de jure independence. The position of Washington is also ambiguous. Although it is often accused of opposing unification and even covertly supporting independence, the US has repeatedly reiterated that it can accept any outcome so long as war is avoided and it has the consent of the Taiwanese side. Reading the tea leaves suggests that the US is most satisfied with an indefinite status quo.

Given the sheer importance of the issue for all three parties' security, economic and political considerations, it is not surprising that external relations have been one of the most popular topics in the field of Taiwan politics. The literature in English is particularly large. This is partly due to the fact that scholars can work on this topic without the kind of language skills or extensive fieldwork that is required in areas such as local politics. The field attracts both theoretically informed but also much policy-centred research. If a London- or Washington-based think tank is planning a Taiwan conference, nine times out of ten the central topic will be external relations, particularly cross-Strait relations.

Frameworks of analysis

Taiwan's external relations are a huge topic that deserves much greater space. Therefore, I have had to restrict my coverage in this chapter to a few core areas. The examination of cross-Strait relations will focus on political rather than economic ties. Also, although

China's and the USA's changing policies towards Taiwan will be touched upon, the analysis will mainly be Taiwan centred. The four major dimensions of Taiwan's international relations that we will consider will be its formal diplomatic relations, attempts to join international organizations, its substantive but unofficial international relations, as well as its public diplomacy efforts. Rawnsley defines public diplomacy as 'Conscious act of communicating with foreign publics, and therefore is an important facilitator of soft power.'[6]

One of the most productive writers on Taiwan's external relations has been Dennis Hickey. He has suggested distinctive time periods for examining Taiwan's external relations. For foreign policy he suggests: (1) a golden era from 1950 to 1971, (2) diplomatic isolation from 1971 to 1988 and then (3) pragmatic diplomacy from 1988 to the present day.[7] For cross-Strait relations the periodization is slightly different with: (1) Cold War 1949 to 1987, (2) warming ties 1987 to 1994, (3) economic convergence vs. political divergence 1995 to 2008, and then (4) a new start under Ma. Given my focus on the democratic era, I will first examine the Cold War or pre-democracy era in one section that incorporates both Hickey's golden and isolation periods. Next, I will discuss the transition period from 1987 to 1994 when Taiwan tried to have its cake and eat it too. In other words, it tried to achieve an equal balance between international space and closer cross-Strait ties. During the next period, which I date from 1995 through to 2008, the KMT and DPP governments appeared to give priority to international space and faced the paradox of economic convergence vs. political divergence through until 2008. The classification of a new era after 2008 is a debatable one, as we should also recognize considerable continuity from the DPP era. However, the question of whether Ma brought a revolution in Taiwan's external relations is a useful topic for us to consider. Lastly, I will discuss the impact and prospects for Taiwan's external relations after the latest change in ruling parties in 2016.

The key time periods for China's Taiwan policy should be slightly different. Hickey suggests that we can think of the following four: (1) armed liberation (1949–79), (2) One Country, Two Systems (1979–87), (3) reconciliation and conflict (1987–2005) and (4) post-2005 carrots and sticks.[8]

The next question to consider is how to explain Taiwan's changing international status and policies. Hickey has proposed a set of potential explanatory frameworks for the Taiwan case. For foreign policy, he considers four.[9] The first is system level analysis. This approach views external factors as decisive in shaping Taiwan's fate and foreign policy. Thus, Taiwan is like a shrimp between whales, the whales being China and the US. The second is state-level analysis, which focuses on the role of government institutions in shaping policy. Thus, key players would be the Ministry of Foreign Affairs, the parliament, Executive Yuan or presidency. The third framework stresses the role of societal influences, such as parties, think tanks, interest groups or public opinion. Lastly, he considers the role of the individual, particularly the influence of Taiwan's five presidents. A couple of years later in a paper on cross-Strait relations, Hickey suggested that in addition to individual level analysis (or what he calls the 'President the Great'), the other frameworks he considers are 'paradigm shift' and 'bureaucratic politics'.[10] By paradigm shift he means policy adjustments can be traced back to radical change in the basic assumptions due to generational change or changes in international context. In contrast, the bureaucratic politics approach tries to explain policy according to the organizational culture or standard operating procedures of different branches of government. Thus, to a certain extent we can take this as equivalent to state-level analysis. As the subsequent analysis will show, in each period there is much variation in how best to explain Taiwan's changing international status and external policies.

External relations prior to democratization

The former Chairman of Mainland Affairs Council, Su Chi (蘇起) commented that prior to the mid 1980s; contacts were 'so few and far between that even the term cross-Strait relations did not exist'.[11] This is not entirely accurate for the 1950s, as from mid 1948 through to the end of 1950, up to two million people fled to Taiwan with the remnants of the ROC government. This was the largest ever wave of cross-Strait migration in Taiwan's history. Moreover, there was also a series of military clashes over the off-shore islands during that decade. However, after the end of 1950, Taiwan was cut off from China to an even greater degree than during the Japanese era and remained so until the 1980s. There was almost no direct or indirect trade and it was close to impossible and illegal for citizens of either side to physically set foot in the rival's territory. One of the few exceptions to this pattern of isolation were occasional incidents of air force pilots defecting to the other side for handsome rewards.

By early June 1950, Taiwan was gripped with pessimism over the KMT's ability to withstand what seemed an imminent Chinese invasion. In April, the ROC had lost control of Hainan Island and the PLA was assembling a large force in Fujian to finish the job of liberating Taiwan and thus ending the Chinese Civil War. After repeated defeats on the mainland, morale was at an all-time low in the ROC military. By this time the US had essentially given up Chiang's regime as a lost cause and ceased military aid. Chiang was so desperate that he was willing to appeal to former Japanese war criminals to save his regime.

The outbreak of the Korean War in June 1950 completely changed the equation, as in response Truman ordered the US Navy's Seventh Fleet into the Taiwan Strait to prevent a Chinese attack on Taiwan. This security guarantee was formalized in the 1954 US–ROC Mutual Defence Treaty, which would last until 1979.[12] Chiang had hoped that this military alliance with the US would be the foundation for his plan to reconquer the mainland. The slogan of retaking the mainland (*fangong dalu*) was ever present in the government's rhetoric under martial law. Chiang lobbied the US for support in this sacred mission. However, the US saw the alliance differently. It was more concerned with containing communist expansion than the prospect of engaging in a land war in China. To get the Mutual Defence Treaty, Chiang had to agree in writing not to attack the mainland without US consent. Chiang and the US also differed over the offshore islands of Kinmen and Mazu that were still held by the ROC. These had not been included in the treaty and the US doubted their viability to survive sustained PRC attacks. Chiang, on the other hand, saw them as critically important for retaking the mainland and Taiwan's defence. The alliance was put to test in the 1954 and 1958 cross-Strait crises, when the ROC forces on Kinmen came under heavy artillery attacks from the PLA. By the 1958 crisis the US had come round to Chiang's position on Kinmen and actually offered critical support. Despite Chiang's rhetoric of retaking the mainland, Tsang notes that 'he simply did not have the military capabilities to put into effect his avowed object of retaking the mainland'.[13] By 1958, even Chiang publicly conceded that 'the implementation of Dr Sun Yat-sen's Three Principles of the People . . . and not the use of force' was the main way to achieve its mission to recover the mainland.[14]

Even in the world of literature readers were reminded of the need to retake the mainland. Lucy Chen's comments give us a taste of the atmosphere in the 1950s:

Almost all the creative writing by refugee mainland writers of this time concerned itself with the anti-Communist struggle. The setting was always the mainland. A typical plot would portray a great love; the lovers would be inhumanly separated by the arrival of the Communists, and the last chapter would provide the moral that the only hope for reunion was a fighting return to the mainland. Nostalgia was the ruling emotion: the heart of the writer remained in a Peking restaurant or drifted along the Yangtse River. Spy novels were popular. The most overworked theme was that of a handsome anti-Communist secret agent with whom one or more female Communists would fall in love and sacrifice their lives so that he could carry out his mission and return safely to Formosa. So many of these novels were published and sold that they tended to create an impression that the one thing which stood in the way of a triumphal return to the mainland was the shortage of handsome spies to prepare the way.[15]

Direct military clashes dried up after 1958, and the Chinese Civil War was put on hold with an undeclared ceasefire. Both sides adopted competing One China policies, as each presented itself as the sole legitimate government of all China and their rivals as rebels controlling renegade provinces. Both Chinas employed similar slogans. While the ROC's official policy was to retake mainland militarily, the PRC talked of liberating Taiwan militarily. Within Taiwan, the continuation of the Chinese Civil War was used to justify both martial law and the suspension of many constitutional rights. The slogan of reunification remained for the rest of Chiang Kai-shek and Chiang Ching-kuo's presidencies, but there was a gradual acceptance that retaking the mainland would rely mainly on political rather than military campaigns. The priority shifted to making Taiwan into a model Chinese province to showcase what the ROC could achieve on the mainland in the future.

The ROC was able to benefit from the international system of the Cold War era as a key US ally. Taiwan played an important support role for the US during the Vietnam War in the 1960s and early 1970s. US support went beyond just military and economic aid. It enabled the ROC to retain its seat in the UN and even as a permanent member of the Security Council. The US backing also meant that Taiwan had the advantage over China in most other international governmental organizations. With a few exceptions, such as the UK, countries on the Western side in the Cold War tended to follow the US lead in recognizing the ROC rather than the PRC as the legitimate government of China. As large numbers of former colonies achieved independence in the 1950s and 1960s, the two Chinas fought hard for their recognition. However, neither was prepared to accept dual recognition. Thus, if one country recognized the PRC, the ROC would immediately cut ties with them, or if the PRC gained membership to an international organization, the ROC would immediately withdraw in protest. One of the major methods Taiwan adopted to maintain its ties with these newly independent states was by sending technical development teams. While the US was Taiwan's core backer, the Soviet Union and other communist states, particularly Albania, called for the PRC to take China's seat in the UN. An annual vote was held over which side should hold the UN China seat. To give the ROC breathing space, the US successfully sponsored a resolution proscribing that this should be considered an 'important question' which would require a two-thirds vote to pass. It looked like Taiwan was losing its battle by 1970 when the votes supporting the PRC's membership exceeded the ROC's for the first time.

Although there were some notable diplomatic defections to the PRC prior to 1971, such as France in 1964, Taiwan still had the edge over the PRC in terms of formal diplomatic ties. At its peak in 1971, the ROC had 68 diplomatic allies to the PRC's 53. However, by the late 1960s, the US was seeking rapprochement with China, with a view to withdraw from Vietnam while taking advantage of the Sino–Soviet split. The US had hoped to find a compromise that would allow the PRC to take the China seat at the UN, but also allow the ROC to remain in the UN as an ordinary member. We can never be sure whether this proposal could have been approved, and it is quite likely that the PRC would not have been willing to join under these circumstances. However, the ROC rejected it outright and, with the US dropping its lobbying for the ROC, it was expelled and replaced by the PRC in October 1971.

The ROC went from its diplomatic peak or golden year in the summer of 1971 to endure diplomatic setback after setback for the rest of the decade after its UN debacle. Derecognitions were particularly numerous in the 1970s, with 49 countries switching sides. The process continued into the 1980s, and the only countries that newly recognized the ROC tended to be small nation states like Tuvalu and Nauru. The loss of the UN seat also meant that Taiwan became excluded from the various UN affiliated International Government Organizations (IGOs). In fact, by 1981 the ROC remained a member of only nine IGOs.

Nevertheless, throughout most of the 1970s the ROC's critical international relationship remained that with the US, as the Mutual Defence Treaty remained in force, and the US embassy in Taipei. However, by 1972 it was clear that the US was moving towards recognizing the PRC. The process was set in motion by Nixon's 1972 China visit, although Taiwan remained a stumbling block in US–China relations. Naturally, there was a fear that the US was going to sell out Taiwan to China, which was reflected in anti-US protests in Taiwan in 1972 and 1978–9. The inevitable finally occurred in January 1979, with US recognition of the PRC and abrogation of the defence treaty. However, pro-Taiwan politicians in the US were able to pass the Taiwan Relations Act in April 1979, which codified how the US should conduct its relations with Taiwan. Particularly important were the pledge to provide Taiwan with defensive arms, its expectation that the future of Taiwan be determined by peaceful means and that it would treat Taiwan as an independent state.

At the same time that Taiwan was losing the diplomatic battle to China, it also faced changes within the PRC itself. As China emerged from the Cultural Revolution (1966–76), it returned to the international stage, more actively joining international organizations and seeking overseas investment. At this point, China tried to appeal to Taiwan with concrete peace proposals that it hoped would lead to unification. In 1979, the National People's Congress issued its 'Message to Compatriots on Taiwan', which called on the two sides to begin unification talks and to establish the three links (trade, transportation and mail). Then in 1981, PLA Marshal Ye Jianying (葉劍英) made a nine-point unification proposal, which promised to give Taiwan considerable autonomy and even allow it to retain its own armed forces. Soon afterwards, it was made clear that the concept of 'One Country, Two Systems' adopted for Hong Kong and Macau was also designed for Taiwan. Chiang Ching-kuo responded to these overtures with the 'three noes' policy of no contacts, no negotiations and no compromise with the CCP. The view that the KMT had been tricked by the CCP in its earlier United Front cooperation with the communists was reiterated. As Chiang explained, 'To talk with the Chinese Communists is to invite death.'[16]

At the same time as we saw the first signs of what we today call a 'rising China' in the 1980s, US–Taiwan ties were often strained. Relations were severely damaged when ROC security agencies arranged a gangster assassination of the Chinese American author Henry Liu (江南) in California in 1984. Since Liu had written a critical biography of Chiang Ching-kuo, Chiang was indirectly implicated. Roy notes that this incident 'was a disastrous setback to the KMT's image in the United States',[17] which was another sore point, for the US was Taiwan's trade surplus, with the US particularly critical over intellectual property issues. The US was increasingly vocal in calling for political reforms and improvement of Taiwan's human rights record in this period. On Taiwan's side there were also concerns over whether the US would betray Taiwan to China. Originally, the defeat of Jimmy Carter by the anti-communist Ronald Reagan in the 1980 presidential election raised hopes for warmer US–ROC relations. However, in the August 1982 China–US communiqué there was a pledge to gradually reduce arms sales to Taiwan, and in 1984 Reagan also visited China as relations bloomed. In reality, though, arms sales to Taiwan continued, as did the de facto diplomatic relations. Over time, the US post-derecognition security commitment to Taiwan became known as 'strategic ambiguity'. This meant that the US kept both Taiwan and the PRC guessing over whether it would intervene in the event of a Chinese attack on Taiwan. The outset of dem-ocratization in the late 1980s was extremely well received in the US, particularly when it coincided with the PRC's crackdown on student protestors in 1989.

Despite Chiang's seemingly inflexible three noes response, there were some signs of ROC pragmatism in the final years of his presidency. In 1984, a compromise was reached, enabling Taiwan to remain in the Olympics for the Los Angeles games under the name Chinese Taipei. Similarly, it was able to stay in the Asian Development Bank under the title Taipei, China, after the PRC was admitted. In the past, the ROC would have withdrawn as soon as the PRC gained admission to an international organization, but by the mid-1980s the ROC was willing to take a flexible position on its membership title to avoid total isolation. The 1980s also saw a rapid expansion in indirect cross-Strait trade, mainly via Hong Kong. As is the case today, Taiwan benefited more than China, as it enjoyed a trade surplus with the mainland.

A major breakthrough in relations came in 1986, following the hijacking of a China Airlines flight to China. The pilot wished to defect to China, while the crew wanted to return to Taiwan. Reluctantly, Chiang agreed to allow negotiations in Hong Kong which ensured the return of the crew and aircraft.[18] A year later, this was followed by an even more significant opening, legalizing Taiwanese with relatives in China to visit the mainland via Hong Kong or Tokyo. This allowed the first wave of cross-Strait visits for decades, and even thousands without relatives in China found loopholes in the system to finally visit China. However, it should be pointed out at this point that visits were only one way, as it still remained impossible for PRC citizens to come to Taiwan.

Nevertheless, despite these breakthroughs at the end of Chiang's life, cross-Strait relations as we know them today were in their infancy. At least formally, Taiwan was isolated internationally and the PRC was actively attempting to further squeeze Taiwan's remaining international space. This applied both to international organizations but also to Taiwan's few remaining diplomatic allies, which the PRC pressured to switch ties. By 1988, the year Chiang died, Taiwan was down to only 22 formal diplomatic allies.

So how should we best explain Taiwan's international status and external relations during the martial law era? It is clear that societal, bureaucratic and state level analyses have little explanatory value for the period. Under martial law, foreign policy-making, like other policy areas, was insulated from public opinion, and the various political institutions such as the Executive Yuan and Legislative Yuan were essentially rubber-stamp bodies. Instead, individual level analysis is most useful, as power lay in the hands of the two Chiangs. Nevertheless, Hickey's analogy of Taiwan being a shrimp between whales is also relevant, as Taiwan's international standing and de facto independence depended on US support as well as the PRC's international isolation. Normalization of Sino–US relations and China's return to the international stage contributed to the subsequent narrowing of Taiwan's international space.

External relations under democracy: trying to have the best of both worlds?

Although we tend to associate pragmatic diplomacy with Lee Teng-hui, as we have seen some of the roots of this policy lay in the flexibility of the final years of Chiang Ching-kuo. The same was true of closer cross-Strait ties, as Chiang had taken the first measures in breaking his own three noes in 1986 and 1987. In the first six years of Lee's presidency, there was an attempt to have the best of both worlds, as Taiwan tried not only to improve cross-Strait relations, but it also sought to expand its international status. This was a delicate balance to keep and by the middle of 1995 it had collapsed.

Pragmatic diplomacy under Lee: achievement and limitations

As Rubinstein notes, 'When Lee Teng-hui took command of his party in July 1988, he made it clear that a vigorous, effective and innovative foreign policy, "pragmatic diplomacy," would be central to his new administration.'[19] The case of Grenada revealed the new Taiwanese flexibility, as when in 1989 it established full diplomatic ties with the ROC, Taiwan did not insist it cut ties with the PRC. For a month it held dual recognition with the two Chinas, until the PRC cut ties. From Table 9.1, which shows the numbers of official diplomatic allies, we can see how Taiwan's allies shot up from only 22 in 1988 to 29 by 1991. Taiwan was accused of employing dollar diplomacy or cheque book diplomacy in winning these new allies. It is true that recognition switches tended to be part of generous assistance packages. The new allies tended to be concentrated in Latin America, the Pacific Ocean and Africa, and partially compensated for losing recognition of some long-standing key allies such as Saudi Arabia (1989) and South Korea (1992).

Under Lee, Taiwan was also highly proactive in attempting to expand the island's unofficial or quasi-official international relations. For instance, following the collapse of communism in Eastern Europe, Lee's administration moved quickly to establish de facto embassies in the form of trade offices in places such as Latvia, Hungary and the Czech Republic. It also tried to use its economic muscle to strengthen its international relations. For instance, it had major contracts for overseas companies to bid for its new Taipei metro system, nuclear power stations and later its high-speed rail system. Another tool was arms purchases. Particularly important was the 1992 US sale of 150 F-16 jet fighters and, even more remarkable, the French sale of 6 Lafayette frigates and 60 Mirage fighters. Additionally, since the early 1990s, visits by foreign governments' trade ministers have become increasingly common.

By the late 1980s, it was clear that its old public diplomacy themes of being the real government of all China and the preserver of Chinese culture were no longer working.

Table 9.1 Taiwan's diplomatic allies

Period	Number of formal diplomatic allies in the first and last year	Major losses	Major gains
1971–79	68–22	Austria, Mexico, Turkey, Iran, Japan, United States, Australia, Brazil, Malaysia, Vietnam, Philippines, Thailand, Portugal	South Africa, Tonga
1979–88	22–22	Columbia, Uruguay, Bolivia,	Nauru, St Lucia
1988–96	22–30	Saudi Arabia, South Korea	Grenada, Liberia
1996–2000	30–29	South Africa	Macedonia
2000–8	29–23	Chad, Costa Rica, Senegal, Macedonia	
2008–2017	23–20	Gambia, São Tomé and Príncipe, Panama	

Sources: Tien (1989: 223); Hickey (2006: 77).

Similarly, while Taiwan remained a one-party state, its claim to be Free China was not convincing to foreign audiences. Particularly in the decade after the 1989 *Tiananmen* Incident, Taiwan also used its democratization as a key tool in its public diplomacy. In speeches abroad and in government publicity material, Taiwan's democratic achievements were highlighted. However, the numbers of diplomatic allies did not show much improvement following democratization. Nevertheless, these reforms have improved Taiwan's international image and made US security guarantees steadier. If Taiwan had remained a soft authoritarian state on a similar model to Singapore, it is doubtful that the US would feel obliged to protect it.

In order to break through the PRC's diplomatic stranglehold, the ROC needed to find loopholes. One of these was to disguise visits in the form of what became known as 'vacation' and at times even 'golf' diplomacy. During the early to mid 1990s, Premiers Hau and Lien and President Lee were able to visit non-diplomatic allies such as Singapore under the pretext of vacationing in these countries. During these visits, private meetings with politicians or golf games with state leaders would take place. Another tool was to use plane transfers on the way to allies in Latin America as a means to visit the US. In one particularly infamous case in 1994, Lee Teng-hui requested that he be allowed to stay overnight in Hawaii to rest and refuel his plane on his way to Central America. The State Department turned down his request, only allowing him to rest in an airport lounge. In both Taiwan and the US, this was widely condemned as insulting treatment to the leader of a democracy.

One region that Taiwan worked particularly hard at developing quasi-diplomatic relations in was South East Asia. These efforts were known as the Go South Policy. It aimed to encourage Taiwanese business to invest in South East Asia in order to both reduce economic dependence on China and also strengthen Taiwan's links with these countries. During the early to mid 1990s, Taiwan's leaders were able to make a number of high-profile but unofficial visits to these countries. One country in which Taiwan made particular progress in developing ties where nothing had existed since the 1970s was Vietnam. An aspect of international relations that blossomed as a result of Taiwanese investments in this region was interracial marriages, as the region became a source of brides for Taiwanese men. This was the subject of the Public Television series *Don't Call Me an Overseas Bride Anymore* (*biezai jiaowo waiji xinniang*), which tells the stories of four Vietnamese women who marry Taiwanese husbands and struggle to settle in their new home country.

Taiwan also doubled its efforts to rejoin international organizations. The keystone in this process was its attempts to rejoin the UN after 1993.[20] This was followed by an annual bid supported by its diplomatic allies to rejoin the organization. Taiwan argued that its UN membership would not contravene the One China principle and that this kind of divided China or one country two equal political entities formula could be a first step towards eventual unification. Its appeals stressed how Taiwan's 23 million people were effectively excluded from the UN and its democratic political system. Although these failed bids generated sympathy for Taiwan overseas, they did not make any progress and infuriated the PRC. Beijing ensured that the issue never even made it on to the agenda for the UN General Assembly. Fear of Beijing's wrath means that few nations are prepared to back Taiwan's bid to join the UN and not even all its diplomatic allies were enthusiastic about the campaign. The UN bid idea had been extremely popular in Taiwan and its repeated failure caused much frustration and anti PRC sentiment.

Taiwan faced similar setbacks in other international organizations[21] – for instance, PRC pressure ensured that it was only able to join General Agreement on Tariffs and Trade as an observer in 1992 under the title of 'Taiwan, Penghu, Kinmen and Mazu Customs Territory'. Taiwan was repeatedly disappointed that Lee was not invited as its representative to attend the annual Asia Pacific Economic Cooperation meetings. Taiwan has also promoted membership of International NGOs as a form of pragmatic diplomacy, with well over 900 memberships by the mid 1990s. Even in this NGO sector, Taiwan has often faced resistance to full participation from the PRC.

The importance that Taiwan placed on international space was apparent in the 1995–6 election campaigns. The KMT's propaganda was saturated with images of Lee on the world stage, meeting world leaders and his historic US trip of 1995. At the time, Lee's private visit to the US and his speech at Cornell University was seen as a triumph of pragmatic diplomacy and the source of much pride within Taiwan. For many, it symbolized that Taiwan was breaking out of its lengthy international isolation. Although the US had promised China that Lee would not get a visa, the Senate and House of Representatives passed resolutions asking the US government to allow Lee to visit the US. Lee's speech at Cornell University received extensive domestic and international media attention. It was well received in Taiwan but furiously condemned in China. When PRC military intimidation reached its height on the eve of the March 1996 presidential election, the US finally felt compelled to step in to reaffirm its support for Taiwan by sending two aircraft carrier battle groups, the *Independence* and *Nimitz* into the area. Lee's Cornell trip marked the end of Taiwan's bid to have the best of both worlds; it suggested that Taiwan placed priority on international space above cross–Strait relations.

Cross–Strait breakthroughs and setbacks

In the early Lee Teng-hui years, there were no immediate breakthroughs in cross-Strait relations. However, at the non-government level, cross-Strait relations flourished. The value of indirect trade rose from US$0.95 billion in 1986 to US$20.99 billion by 1995.[22]

There were similar trends in the area of cross-Strait investment, as by 1995 50 per cent of Taiwan's overseas investment went to China.[23] Many Taiwanese firms chose to relocate production to China to take advantage of lower labour costs and laxer environmental regulations. The expansion of economic ties with China was not affected by the PRC's crackdown on the student protestors in 1989. Despite the ROC government condemnation of the *Tiananmen* Incident, and much sympathy for its victims, Taiwan did not follow many Western countries' decision to apply trade sanctions on China.

During the early 1990s, the ROC moved to institutionalize cross-Strait relations. In 1991, Lee finally abolished the Temporary Provisions Effective during the Period of Mobilization for the Suppression of the Communist Rebellion, in effect formally ending the Chinese civil war. In 1990, the National Unification Council (NUC) was established to draw up the National Unification Guidelines (NUG) and debate unification-related issues. The NUG called for a three-stage process leading to eventual unification. These were as follows:

1 Reciprocal exchanges (indirect links, reduce hostility).
2 Mutual trust and cooperation (establish official communication links, the three links, high-level visits, joint participation in International Government Organizations).
3 Negotiating unification (establish joint bodies to design a Chinese constitution based on democracy, economic freedom and social justice).

As Julian Kuo (郭正亮) notes, the NUG set up a number of challenging preconditions for the PRC before the two sides could move to the second stage: 'The PRC does not deny the Republic of China (ROC) as a political entity, the PRC renounces the use of force against the ROC, and the PRC respects the right of the ROC to join the international community.'[24]

Another important body created at the time was the Mainland Affairs Council (MAC). This Executive Yuan body was given the task of researching and setting guidelines for mainland policy. The MAC's counterpart in China was the Taiwan Affairs Office. However, the MAC could not engage in direct talks with the PRC in the first stage of the National Unification Guidelines, so a non-government body called the Straits Exchange Foundation (SEF) was created for unofficial talks. The PRC followed suit by creating its own semi-official body called the Association for Relations Across the Taiwan Strait (ARATS). A series of secret envoy meetings were held between December 1990 and November 1991 before the two sides were ready to begin formal SEF–ARATS talks.[25] From the outset a key sticking point was the question of how to define one China, as both sides had very different interpretations. Here we come to a controversial question: Did the two sides reach an agreement in late 1992 that both accept there is one China but accept they have different interpretations of one China? According to Su Chi, they agreed on what he called One China Respective Interpretations (OCRI) or, as it is now more commonly known, the 1992 consensus.[26] For Su, this was critical in the subsequent progress in the SEF–ARATS talks. This is how Su describes developments: 'The OCRI consensus was the first political compromise reached between Taiwan and mainland China in over 40 years, and it focused on the most central, and thorniest cross-Strait issue: sovereignty.'[27]

The high point in these talks was the April 1993 Koo–Wang talks held between the heads of SEF and ARATS in Singapore. Considering the years of mutual hostility and divergent political values, it is not entirely surprising that despite the numerous meetings between 1992 and 1995, little was actually achieved in terms of formal agreements. Agreements were reached on registered mail and document authentication, and there was much discussion about dealing with cross-Strait crime. Much time was spent on meeting preparations and meeting etiquette. The PRC was more enthusiastic to move on to political discussions, while Taiwan insisted on sticking to practical substantive economic issues.

By 1993–4, when the semi-official talks were at their high point, conflicting tensions began to undermine cross-Strait trust. By this time, Taiwan was enthusiastically promoting pragmatic diplomacy, such as its UN bid, and its leaders toured other countries on their vacation diplomacy. In March 1994, 24 Taiwanese tourists were murdered at Qiandao Lake in China. The PRC's poor handling of the incident led to a temporary Taiwanese tourist boycott of China and aroused anti-Chinese sentiments. A month later, Lee gave his infamous interview to the Japanese writer Shima Ryotaro, which infuriated China. As Rigger explained: 'The president compared himself to Moses leading Taiwan to freedom, and he bemoaned the fate of the Taiwanese, who he said had fallen under the power of one foreign regime after another, including the Nationalists (KMT).'[28] These comments were taken by Chinese nationalists on both sides of the Taiwan Strait as evidence that Lee was a supporter of Taiwan independence.

However, as we saw earlier, 1995 was the watershed year. In January 1995, CCP Secretary General Jiang Zemin (江澤民) made his Eight Point Proposal to Taiwan. Jiang argued that so long as both sides accepted the One China principle, they could begin negotiations on ending the state of cross-Strait hostility and move towards unification on a step-by-step basis. He also stressed that negotiations should be on an equal basis rather than between a central and local government. Beijing was to be disappointed when Lee responded in April 1995 with his Six Points. According to Kuo, Lee reiterated:

> the PRC's acceptance of Taiwan's separate jurisdiction as a political pre-condition for discussing the implication of One China, and refusing to deal with One China as a principle. At best, Lee would only accept that 'the definition of one China is subject to respective interpretations by each side,' and hoped to shelve the sovereignty dispute for the time being.[29]

Nevertheless, as late as May 1995, preparatory talks were held for the second Koo–Wang talks to be held in Beijing in August. However, these talks were postponed indefinitely following Lee's US visit.

The PRC tried to intimidate Taiwan with threatening military exercises close to the island. In July 1995, it test-fired missiles off the Taiwan coast, and in both August and November large-scale naval exercises were carried out with Taiwan as the clear target. Then, on the eve of the first presidential election in March 1996, missile tests were carried out close to Taiwan's main ports of Kaohsiung (my home at the time) and Keelung. These military threats were used in conjunction with extremely vitriolic propaganda attacks against Lee designed to turn Taiwan's public opinion against him. Lee was called 'a traitor and sinner who sought to split the mainland'.[30] They called on Chinese to sweep Lee into the dustbin of history. Within Taiwan, the NP joined the PRC in condemning Lee for taking Taiwan to the edge of war, while the KMT and DPP looked united in taking a firm stand against China.[31] The Chinese threats in 1995–6 backfired. Not only did they help Lee to win re-election, but they also were damaging for Chinese identity and support for eventual unification. However, they did make Taiwan's public and elite believe that PRC military threats were genuine and thus undermined support for declaring independence.

Economic convergence vs. political divergence

Part 1: Lee's second term, 1996–2000

After Lee's US trip in June 1995, it was clear that Taiwan was prioritizing international space over cross-Strait relations. This was to remain Taiwan's position through to 2008 under the rest of Lee and Chen's presidencies. At the same time as the lengthy political standoff, Taiwan and China's economic ties continued to expand rapidly. Therefore, I have called this period one of economic convergence versus political divergence.

Compared to Lee's first term, the ROC's progress on both foreign and cross-Strait relations in his second term was, in a word, disappointing. By 2000, cross-Strait talks were stalled again and tensions almost as high as 1995–6. Moreover, no real improvement had been made in its numbers of diplomatic allies or joining IGOs. More worrying for Taiwan was that by 2000, US support for Taiwan looked to be waning, with some in the US viewing Lee as a troublemaker. Therefore, Kuo claims that Lee was 'buying time without strategy'.[32]

After winning re-election, Lee tried to respond to the PRC's military threats and his fear of economic dependency on China by calling on businesses to limit investment in China. This was called the 'Go Slow, Be Patient' policy and shared a similar motivation with the Go South policy. Once codified, this stipulated that single Taiwanese investment projects in China should not exceed US$50 million, Taiwanese should not invest in Chinese infrastructure projects and investment in the high-tech sector in China should be more strictly regulated.[33] However, by the late 1990s, financial liberalization meant that the Taiwanese state could no longer regulate capital flows in the same way it had under martial law. Thus, businesses were able to find ways to continue their Chinese investments.

Mutual suspicion ensured that it was not until October 1998 that the second Koo–Wang talks were convened in Shanghai. However, despite the handshakes and smiles, these talks revealed how wide the gulf between the two sides had grown. The two sides were once again clashing over the meaning of One China, issues of meeting etiquette and democracy. Of course, by this time Taiwan was avoiding positive references to One China and unification. In contrast, Su argues that 'Chinese policy toward Taiwan had gone from preventing the Taiwan independence to striving for reunification'.[34] As Jiang commented in March 1999, 'our desire to realize the complete unification of the motherland is urgent'.[35] By the end of 1999, Jiang had overseen the return of both Hong Kong and Macau to Chinese sovereignty and was looking to cement his legacy by also achieving a breakthrough with Taiwan.

After the elation of Lee's 1995 US tour, progress on international space in the second term fell far short of expectations. No progress was made on the UN campaign. Lee only made one overseas trip to Central American allies in 1997, although his vice president and premiers were able to visit both diplomatic and non-diplomatic allies. Although there was only a net loss of one diplomatic ally, losing South African recognition was a symbolic blow, one not really compensated by gaining ties with Palau or the Marshall Islands. After 1995, the PRC intensified its efforts to isolate Taiwan. In 1997, news broke of the PRC's Three Empties policy (*sanguang zhengce*) that aimed to remove Taiwan's remaining diplomatic allies and formal international presence by 2000.[36] However, Taiwan's biggest diplomatic setback came during Clinton's 1998 China visit. Clinton made his so-called 'Three Noes' comments, stating that the US did not support Taiwan independence, Two Chinas or One Taiwan, One China, or Taiwan's membership of IGOs requiring statehood. Although this was painted by the US as not marking any real change in its Taiwan policy, this was the first time the US had been so explicit in supporting the PRC's position on Taiwan.

In 1999, as Taiwan and China were preparing for another round of Koo–Wang talks, the process was once again derailed by Lee Teng-hui. In a German radio interview in July, Lee stated that since 1991 the ROC had 'redefined its relationship with Mainland China as being state-to-state relations (*guojia yu guojia guanxi*) or at least special state-to-state relations (*teshu guo yu guo guanxi*)'.[37] This became termed by Lee's critics as the 'Two State Theory'. Lee's comments were generally welcomed in Taiwan but harshly attacked in the PRC, and even Washington expressed disapproval.[38] Tensions reached their highest level since 1995–6, but this time the US and the PRC appeared to be jointly constraining Taiwan. External pressure did pay off as Lee eventually backed down from including special state-to-state relations in the next round of constitutional revisions.

As the Lee Teng-hui era reached a conclusion, it is clear that the explanatory frameworks used after democratization are more diverse than under the martial law system. Competitive multi-party politics meant that leaders had to pay attention to public opinion in devising foreign and cross-Strait policy. Policies such as UN membership and pragmatic diplomacy were designed to attract votes. In contrast, support for the PRC's proposal for unification under One Country, Two Systems was so low that no serious politician would dare speak in defence of the idea.[39] In addition, the government had to face a new powerful constituency from the business community, lobbying for liberalizing cross-Strait economic policy. In short, societal pressures played a major role for the first time in shaping foreign policy since the early 1990s. There are also signs of continuity, too. Even after democratization, Lee left a significant personal imprint on Taiwan's external policies. As Su shows, he was often prepared to ignore or override his more cautious advisers and government colleagues. Lastly, the Lee Teng-hui era shows how system level factors remained influential. In particular, pressures from the US and China placed limits on Taiwanese politician's room to devise external policy and expand the island's international space.

Part 2: External relations under the DPP, 2000–8

Following the 2000 presidential election, the DPP came to power for the first time. This was a shock and challenge for Beijing as the DPP was unambiguous that its ultimate objective was a fully independent Taiwan. During the 2000 campaign, cross-Strait issues were highly salient again. However, the main parties' handling of external policy issues was quite distinct from four years earlier. Since 1996, the DPP had become far more pragmatic on China policies. For instance, in 1998 it held its China policy conference, showcasing a more moderate stance and willingness to engage with China. It had passed the Resolution Regarding Taiwan's Future, arguing that there was no need to declare independence and accepting the ROC as the national title. In the campaign, Chen was actually condemned as reckless by Lien for calling for the establishment of the three links. The KMT and Soong heavily emphasized the dangers of Chen winning, warning voters that this would lead to cross-Strait war breaking out. Thus, the KMT message was in stark contrast with 1996, as it largely dropped references to pragmatic diplomacy or standing up to China. In 2000, the PRC did not employ military exercises to intimidate Taiwan's voters, but it did issue advice on how to vote. Three days before the election, Premier Zhu Rongji (朱鎔基) warned, pointing his finger, that Taiwanese should not choose the 'wrong candidate'. He stated: 'Let me advise all these people in Taiwan: do not act on impulse at this juncture, which will decide the future course that China and Taiwan will follow. Otherwise I am afraid you won't get another opportunity to regret.'[40] This made it look like the KMT and PRC were on the same side.

The PRC reacted cautiously to Taiwanese voters' choice of 'the wrong candidate'. A Taiwan Affairs Office statement noted that it would 'listen to what Taiwan's new leader says and observe what he does in regard to the direction he takes in cross-Strait relations'.[41] Naturally, Chen's election created much concern of cross-Strait instability. To reassure Beijing, Washington and Taiwanese, Chen made his inaugural Five Noes pledge. These promised that he would not:

1   declare Taiwan's independence;
2   change the name of the nation;
3   push for the inclusion of former President Lee Teng-hui's 'special state-to-state relationship' in the constitution;
4   hold a referendum to change the status quo on the question of independence or unification;
5   move to abolish either the National Unification Guidelines or the National Unification Council.

In Chen's first two years he made a number of gestures meant to show his moderation and willingness to engage in constructive relations with China. He expressed willingness to talk to China so long as the One China principle was not a precondition and was prepared to discuss a future One China. On occasion, he spoke positively about OCRI and the spirit of 92 (rather than the 1992 Consensus). The DPP Chairman, Hsieh Chang-ting, mentioned 'returning to the constitutional One China framework'.[42] In another positive sign at the 2001 Economic Development Advisory Conference, it was officially agreed to drop the 'Go Slow, Be Patient' policy. Although the DPP did not establish the three links, it did open what were known as the mini three links. These were direct shipping between the offshore islands Kinmen and Mazu with the Chinese province of Fujian. However, the PRC ignored these conciliatory gestures, and SEF–ARATS negotiations were not renewed. Developments in the second half of Chen's first term convinced the PRC that Chen was not trustworthy. In August 2002, he stated: 'Taiwan can never be another Hong Kong or Macau, because Taiwan has always been a sovereign state. In short, Taiwan and China stand on opposite sides of the Strait, there is one country on each side.'[43] Both within Taiwan and China, this was taken as going further than Lee's special state-to-state interpretation of cross-Strait relations. The holding of referendums on the same day as the 2004 presidential election was also taken by the PRC as a step towards independence. In short, despite the conciliatory measures taken by Chen's government initially, by 2004 the PRC had lost patience with Chen and there were no prospects for even talks about talks.

Initially, the election of US President George W. Bush in 2000 suggested improved US–Taiwan relations, particularly at a time of US–Chinese tensions following the detention of a US spy plane crew in Hainan in April 2001. Shortly afterwards, Bush made his pledge that the US would do whatever it took to defend Taiwan if it were attacked by China.[44] This suggested that the US was abandoning its long-held position of strategic ambiguity on China–Taiwan security issues. The US also offered Taiwan a major arms sales package, which featured 'an unprecedented array of major new weapons systems for Taiwan, including weapons that had been denied many times by previous administrations'.[45] The US was also initially pleased with improved communication with the Chen administration compared with under Lee. Michael Swaine also noted another less reported but significant change in US–Taiwan policy in early 2002.

For the first time, the US government stated that neither Beijing nor Taipei should set any preconditions for the resumption of a cross-Strait dialogue. US officials such as Richard Bush (at the time director of AIT) particularly emphasized that Beijing should not insist that Taipei accept its 'One China' principle as a precondition for such talks. In making such a statement, Washington seemed to move away from its past neutral stance on the issue of a cross-Strait dialogue, towards Taiwan's position of rejecting Beijing's One China principle.[46]

After this high point in 2002, relations between the US and Taiwan deteriorated. This was partly due to the US needing to avoid conflict with China in the post-9/11 and Iraq War world order. Additionally, domestic factors within Taiwan served to damage relations. The US became increasingly irritated by what it regarded as actions provoking China, such as the 2002 One Country on each side of the Strait comments, the 2004 referendums and scrapping the NUG and NUC in 2006. On each occasion the US was highly critical of Taiwan's actions. Once again, it looked like the PRC and the US were jointly managing the Taiwan question. US dissatisfaction with Taiwan was not restricted to the DPP. The US was also annoyed by the KMT's blocking of legislation for the US arms package in Chen's second term. The comments of US Secretary of State Colin Powell in October 2004 reflect the more hostile US stance, arguing, 'there is only one China. Taiwan is not independent. It does not enjoy sovereignty as a nation and that remains our policy, our firm policy.'[47] Hickey portrays the changed view of Chen in the White House, noting that he 'began to be described as President Bush's least favourite democratically elected leader'[48] and he is alleged to have 'described Chen as a son of a bitch'.[49]

Taiwan's difficulties with its external relations were not limited to those with the US, and the island's international space continued to be squeezed under the DPP. This can be seen in the PRC's increasing success at pushing countries to openly support its positions on opposing Taiwan independence, supporting the One China principle and even One Country, Two Systems.

Under the DPP, Taiwan's one major success was joining the World Trade Organization in 2001. However, Taiwan continued to make no progress in its annual UN bid. Although it attracted broad international support to join the World Health Assembly as an observer, Chinese opposition continued to prevent accession. Table 9.1 shows how Taiwan suffered a steady erosion of its formal diplomatic allies, falling to only 23 during Chen's two terms, just one more than its record low.

Another way to observe Taiwan's international space is its leader's ability to visit non-diplomatic allies, something quite common under Lee. Under Chen, visits to formal allies were extremely frequent, but the only cases of visiting non-diplomatic allies came when Vice President Annette Lu visited Hungary and Indonesia in 2002. The latter case revealed how Taiwan's diplomatic clout had declined compared to the 1990s. Lu had a visa to take a vacation in Bali, but then chartered a flight to Jakarta to try to join National Day celebrations. However, she was denied permission to leave the airport, and her aides' claims that Lu had met the Indonesian president at the airport were denied.[50] The model of vacation diplomacy of the 1990s no longer seemed to work. The controversial case of Taiwan's attempt to secure diplomatic relations with Papua New Guinea also suggested that its old practices of dollar diplomacy were no longer effective. In 2006, Taiwan's Ministry of Foreign Affairs transferred almost US$30 million to a Singapore based go-between to help secure diplomatic ties with Papua New Guinea.[51]

As under Lee Teng-hui, the DPP placed heavy emphasis on Taiwan's democracy in its public diplomacy. However, the DPP government placed more stress on the process being a bottom-up struggle, rather than the KMT's discourse that focused on the role of Lee and Chiang Ching-kuo. One example of the new approach was the creation in 2003 of the Taiwan Foundation for Democracy. There was also much greater stress on Taiwanese rather than Chinese culture. For example, towards the end of the DPP administration, it sponsored the dark metal band ChthoniC's UNlimited Tour in 2007, a band known for its support for Taiwanese nationalism. The government hoped that the tour would help boost international support for its bid to rejoin the United Nations.

Hickey views 2005 as the start of a new era for the PRC's Taiwan policy – what he calls 'Carrots and Sticks'.[52] In other words, the hard gets harder and the soft gets softer. Despite Chen's reaffirmation of the Five Noes on re-election in 2004, the PRC had no interest in negotiating with him, preferring to wait for the KMT to return to power in 2008. A range of developments show how the PRC's hard was getting harder. First, in March 2005, the PRC passed its Anti-Secession Law. This legislated that the PRC should use military means to resolve the Taiwan question if Taiwan declared independence or if all possibility of peaceful unification had been exhausted. The PRC has also continued to increase the numbers of missiles targeted at Taiwan, with almost 1,000 in place by the end of the Chen era. In addition to beating Taiwan at dollar diplomacy, such as buying back Senegal's recognition in 2005, the PRC sought to belittle Taiwan on the international stage at every possible occasion. Hickey lists a large number of often petty but humiliating cases for Taiwan.[53] For instance, 'During the 40th International Children's Games (ICG) in Bangkok, members of the PRC team thrice wrest away the ROC flag draped over Taiwan's gold medal winners.'[54]

The key instance of the soft getting softer was the establishment of KMT–CCP dialogue. This was one of the products of the historic Pan Blue leaders' visits to China in April–May 2005. These visits coming only a month after the PRC passage of the Anti-Secession Law were controversial. At a time when the law was being condemned in Taiwan and abroad, the KMT leader Lien Chan chose to ally with the CCP against Taiwan independence.

As with the Lee Teng-hui era, there was a mix of variables affecting Taiwan's international status and external policies. External constraints of the US and PRC played key roles in restraining the DPP from adopting more radical policy measures. Taiwan was more of a shrimp between whales than ever. The same could also be true of societal restraints, as public opinion remained moderate. We can see this from the polls, but also from the fact that the DPP failed to win the kind of majorities it needed to govern alone. The influence of business on more liberal cross-Strait policies was also clearly greater than in the past under Lee. For the first time, the state-level framework was also important as the Legislative Yuan had a major restraining role on the DPP government. Unlike in the past, the individual level is far less useful. As no matter what Chen would have liked to do on external relations, the Pan Blue majority ensured that without their agreement he was limited only to largely symbolic gestures.

In the 2008 presidential election, unification versus independence was not on the issue agenda. However, for the first time there was significant debate over cross-Strait economic integration. The Green parties warned of the dangers of a One China Common Market, while the KMT was more positive on the benefits of closer economic ties. The DPP tried to warn of the dangers of factory closures and also importing mainland labour and accused the KMT of planning to sell out Taiwan.[55]

Taiwan's international space did receive some attention in the campaign. There was an odd charade where both the KMT and DPP were promoting referendums on Taiwan's UN application. A Government Information Office press release laid out the two proposals: (1) The DPP proposed 'National Referendum Proposal No. 5 calls on the government to apply for new membership in the United Nations under the name "Taiwan."'[56] (2) While the KMT proposed 'National Referendum Proposal No. 6 calls on the government to apply for restoration of the nation's UN membership, and for entry into other international organizations, under the name "Republic of China" or other appropriate name.' Perhaps due to the years of failed bids, the appeals were not able to generate much enthusiasm, and clearly both parties were using these as instrumental goals to help mobilize support. The case of the KMT's UN referendum was especially cynical as in the end it chose to ask its voters to boycott both its own and the DPP referendums. This meant that neither referendum reached the required turnout levels and that both domestically and internationally the Taiwan UN drive was harmed.

Therefore, in the 2008 presidential election voters were presented with a clear choice on external relations. The DPP proposed continuity in giving foreign relations priority over cross-Strait relations, but had no new ideas about breaking through the cross-Strait stalemate or Taiwan's international isolation. In contrast, the KMT vision included international space, but it was secondary to cross-Strait relations. The KMT argued that it would be able to better handle relations with China and that economic integration with the mainland would be the answer to Taiwan's economic problems. Ma's 58 per cent electoral victory suggested that he had won the argument.

Was there a revolution in Taiwan's external relations under Ma?

Just as we saw when Chen came to power in 2000, there were serious domestic concerns about the potential consequences of the change in ruling parties in 2008. Ma immediately sought to reassure domestic and external concerns that he would not be too radical. Thus, in his inaugural speech he offered his Three Noes pledge of no unification, no independence and no use force.[57] In short, he pledged to maintain the status quo. He did make clear that he would accept the 1992 Consensus and try to resume cross-Strait dialogue. The way that Ma's government defined the 1992 Consensus was that there is only One China but the two sides have different interpretations of One China. Of course, it should be noted that the PRC's understanding of the 1992 Consensus does not include different interpretations. The KMT hoped that closer cross-Strait ties would also allow Taiwan to expand its international space.

While Ma was highly conservative on domestic political reforms, he moved to rapidly transform Taiwan's external relations policy. Ma's impact on cross-Strait relations is likely to be cited by historians as his greatest long-term legacy. With Ma's acceptance of the 1992 Consensus, he was able to resume the SEF–ARATS talks and alongside a continuation of the CCP–KMT forum. This first bore fruits in November 2008 when Taipei and Beijing inked four agreements, agreeing to drastically expand flights and allow direct shipping links across the Taiwan Strait. Another product of the new regime was the major expansion of Chinese tourists visiting Taiwan, so that by 2010 China became the largest source of overseas visitors to Taiwan. Readers can get an insight into these tour groups in Wan Jen's cross-Strait comedy *It Takes Two to Tango* (車拼) and this has also become an exciting new topic in the cross-Strait relations literature.[58] In 2010, legislation was passed to allow Chinese students to enter Taiwan's universities.[59] This became an increasingly important source of income for some of Taiwan's private universities. Some of these developments were quite popular and consensual, such as direct flights. However, even in his first term there were concerns that Ma was moving too fast towards economic integration and that he would sacrifice Taiwan's sovereignty. This was reflected in a number of large-scale demonstrations, some of which the police handled in a manner reminiscent of the martial law era.

The most important achievement for the first Ma administration was the signing of the Economic Cooperation Framework Agreement (ECFA) in 2010. The agreement allowed for even greater liberalization of cross-Strait trade. The KMT argued that this would benefit Taiwan's exports and also help it to establish similar trade deals with other countries. In fact, Taiwan was able to sign free trade agreements with New Zealand and Singapore. In contrast, the DPP focused on the dangers of Taiwan being flooded by cheap Chinese imports, undermining local industries and the dangers of Chinese labour entering the Taiwan market. An important moment in the run-up to ECFA was a televised debate between Ma and Tsai, which most observers felt Ma won. The TSU made repeated efforts to request a national referendum on ECFA, but the KMT used its control of the Referendum Review Committee to block these attempts. A key feature of the Ma era was that the two sides of Taiwanese politics did not make serious attempts to reach any internal consensus on China policy in the way achieved under Lee.

Taiwan's public diplomacy showed a significant shift after 2008. Rawnsley argues that while the Ma government downplayed the democratic achievements narrative seen under the DPP, it instead gave greater emphasis on the preservation of traditional Chinese culture.[60] This was highlighted in a KMT election advertisement in 2012 that boasted of the government's promotion of Confucian education in mainland China. Rawnsley has questioned both the effectiveness of the message and changes in Taiwan's public diplomacy institutions. For example, he was critical of the decision to close Taiwan's Government Information Office.

Despite Ma's talk of expanding Taiwan's international space, it became clear that he would give greater priority to cross-Strait relations over foreign ones. Rather than applying for UN membership, the emphasis shifted to asking for Taiwan to join specialized UN agencies. A major initiative of Ma's foreign policy was known as the diplomatic truce. In other words, Taiwan wished to cease the old struggle over diplomatic allies, whereby they try to outspend each other to win allies. Ma clearly had distaste for the old accusations of dollar diplomacy. Under Ma, Taiwan only lost a single formal ally, Gambia. However, this was more to do with internal Gambian politics than PRC poaching. As with previous administrations, the Ma government worked hard at substantive diplomacy with non-diplomatic allies. One key success was the agreement on visa-free entry for ROC passport holders to 35 European countries starting in January 2011.[61] The Ma regime was particularly proud that from 2009 Taiwan was able to join the World Health Assembly as an observer. This had been a long-standing Taiwanese aspiration and one that had the support of the US and other non-diplomatic allies. Even this should not be exaggerated as it was on a yearly invitational basis and to a large extent would be based on PRC goodwill. After the cross-Strait tensions and unpredictability of the Lee and Chen era, Taiwan–US ties improved after 2008. The US welcomed closer cross-Strait ties. In a sign of improved relations, the US approved selling a major arms package to Taiwan in 2009. What was interesting was that the PRC was strongly critical of the US and cut off military dialogue, but that it did not directly criticize Taiwan.

External relations in the 2012 elections and Ma's second term

The debates over external relations in the 2012 elections were quite different from four years earlier. The DPP stopped opposing ECFA, warning of the dangers of Chinese labour migration and no longer mentioned its UN campaign. Tsai proposed what she termed the Taiwan Consensus instead of the 1992 Consensus. For Tsai, this meant that Taiwan needed to achieve a domestic consensus through democratic means over how to manage relations with China. Thus, Tsai was proposing a model of policy-making similar to the consensus-seeking conferences of the Lee Teng-hui era. While the DPP tried to downplay external relations, the KMT campaign focused on its cross-Strait economic record. It stressed how various sectors had enjoyed economic benefits of the ECFA and warned of how this could all be lost if the DPP returned to power. The KMT was quite vague on its vision for cross-Strait relations in its second term. The one major policy proposal was for a cross-Strait peace accord. However, when public opinion reacted negatively to the idea, Ma explained that such an agreement would need to be approved by a referendum and quietly dropped this from his campaign. Overall, it appeared that the cross-Strait issue favoured the KMT in 2012. This was reflected in the front page headline in the *United Daily News* the day after the election: 'Ma Ying-jeou has won; the 1992 Consensus has won' (馬英九贏了 92 共識贏了).[62]

Both Ma and the PRC attempted to accelerate economic and politics integration in Ma's second term. This was clear in February 2012 when in a meeting with Chinese President Hu Jintao, the KMT's Wu Po-hsiung (吳伯雄) argued that cross-Strait relations should be handled under the framework of One Country, Two Areas.[63] Initially, it seemed that Ma would be able to continue progress on integration as he had a strong majority in parliament and the DPP took time to recover from the 2012 defeat. A key achievement was the signing of the Cross-Strait Services Trade Agreement (CSSTA) in June 2013. This was followed by the inaugural visit by Taiwan's Mainland Affairs Council Minister to China in February 2014 and the reciprocal visit by China's Taiwan Affairs Office Minister to Taiwan in June. This created the conditions for an historic first meeting between President Ma and Chinese President Xi Jinping in Singapore in November 2015.

Although improved cross-Strait relations represent Ma's main achievement and helped him to win re-election in 2012, they would also contribute to the KMT's loss of power in 2016. For the first time, elements of integration process were stalled in Ma's second term. However, this time the key actor was not the DPP but civil society resistance. In 2013, the Anti-Media Monopoly Movement played a crucial role in the blocking of the pro-CCP Want Want group's attempt to take over the Next Media Group. Then in the spring of 2014 came the Sunflower Movement, the result of which was a pledge that before the Cross-Strait Services Trade Agreement would be ratified, a Cross-Strait Agreement Supervisory Act would be passed to deal with all future agreements. Despite the KMT's parliamentary majority, it was not able to make any progress in the remainder of Ma's second term on these items or other integration projects such as establishing mutual representative offices.

In the 2016 election campaign, domestic issues dominated the agenda. It was clear that external relations no longer favoured the KMT. This was partly due to public opinion becoming more cautious on further economic and political integration. However, both major parties played their part in the changed environment. The DPP attempted to project a more moderate stance on external relations. Tsai took the status quo as her guiding position and ceased attacking the 1992 Consensus. In contrast, the original KMT candidate Hung Hsiu-chu's call for accelerating integration with her One Country, Same Interpretation left the party looking out of step with public opinion. The KMT did try to attack the DPP on its inability to handle China ties without the basis of the 1992 Consensus, but these attacks no longer seemed effective.

A new start under the DPP?

The DPP's presidential and parliamentary victories in 2016 represent the worst possible scenario for the PRC and a major setback in its Taiwan policy. Although Tsai has recognized the historical fact of the China–Taiwan negotiations in 1992, she has not endorsed the 1992 Consensus. China has attempted to punish Tsai in a number of ways. First, there has been a reduction in the numbers of Chinese tour groups and students visiting Taiwan. In addition, the negotiations have been postponed again and there is a renewed push to squeeze Taiwan's international space. For example, Taiwan lost further allies as São Tomé and Príncipe and Panama switched diplomatic recognition to the PRC during Tsai's first 14 months in office. Nevertheless, much of the foundation of economic integration left by both Chen and Ma presidencies remains intact.

Although the DPP has not initiated a renewed UN campaign, it is clear that the new government places greater emphasis on foreign relations. A key element of this is known as the New Southbound policy that targets not only ASEAN countries, but also South Asia and the Pacific region. For instance, visa liberalization has been offered for ASEAN and South Asian countries to fill the gaps left by declining numbers of Chinese tourists. However, maintaining strong ties with the US remains the priority in Taiwan's external relations. Therefore, the phone call between the incoming US President Trump and Tsai Ing-wen in December 2016 was seen as a small breakthrough. However, Trump quickly mended relations with China and reaffirmed the US One China policy.

The international context remains quite similar to the past, limiting Taiwan's room for manoeuvre. However, the domestic explanatory variables since 2008 have been slightly different from those witnessed under Chen. With the KMT controlling both the Legislative Yuan and Presidency under Ma, the Legislative Yuan did not play an important constraining role until 2013. Ma was able to push his agenda of economic and political integration. However, societal factors, especially changing public opinion and social movements were to be far more effective in constraining Ma than the opposition party.

Future prospects and challenges in Taiwan's external relations

Almost 70 years since the relocation of the ROC from mainland China to Taiwan, the island's political system has been transformed into a model democracy and economy, and the international system is almost unrecognizable from that of the Cold War era. Despite these remarkable changes, Taiwan's de facto independence, the half-way house between independence and unification that we often call the status quo, remains intact.

Almost thirty years ago, one of the first books I ever read on Taiwan was Simon Long's *Taiwan: China's Last Frontier*. In the final chapter, Long evaluated which of the following six possible scenarios was most likely to occur by 2000. These were: (1) status quo; (2) peaceful reunification under one country, two systems; (3) reunification under the three principles of the people; (4) independence of Taiwan as a separate nation; (5) reunification by military means, or (6) peaceful reunification on a compromise formula, which preserved Taiwan's de facto independence. Long argued that by the end of the century the status quo would have collapsed and saw the sixth option of compromise as the most likely outcome.

Three decades later, the status quo remains intact. Will this be the case in another twenty years? Long's second scenario remains highly unlikely as surveys show that One Country, Two System is as unpopular as ever in Taiwan.[64] The third option is unlikely even if the CCP collapsed, so at least for now can be discounted. Independence is the most preferred eventual outcome for people in Taiwan and would be acceptable to the global community, if China agreed, but it does seem that China would respond with a military attack. We cannot rule out a military reunification, especially as China grows militarily and if the US takes a more withdrawn position in East Asia. It is also possible that the PRC will grow impatient even with the more conciliatory KMT or DPP cross-Strait policies adopted since 2008. However, all three main parties will try to avoid this scenario as much as possible.

Lastly, we come to Long's final scenario. For much of the Ma administration it appeared that some kind of compromise might be on the cards in the medium term. The PRC hoped that the ever closer cross-Strait economic integration would spill over into the political arena. Of course, in the 2012 election the KMT did raise the idea of an interim peace agreement with the PRC. However, anti-unification public opinion, the Sunflower Movement and the 2016 election defeat of the KMT means that at least in the short term, Long's sixth option is not viable. Reaching an acceptable cross-Strait compromise will depend on political skill on both sides. Taiwan and China will both need to show flexibility in dealing with competing pressures. Getting the balance between societal pressures for international space and self-determination, and the PRC pressure for unification remains a challenge for Taiwan, as does maintaining a degree of US security. One great challenge for Taiwan is to revive a greater sense of internal consensus on external relations, something achieved by Lee but lost since. This will strengthen Taiwan's hand in external relations. Those in China supporting a compromise solution also need to appease the military hawks and angry Chinese nationalists baying for rapid unification. Although it seems unlikely, it is even possible that some kind of half-way house between independence and unification will still exist in 2030.

Discussion questions

1   How has democratization changed policy-making on Taiwan's external relations?
2   Compare the influence of external and domestic variables on Taiwan's foreign and cross-Strait policies.
3   Have changes in Taiwan's ruling parties transformed the island's external relations?
4   How and why has public opinion in Taiwan changed on external relations?

5 Should Taiwan continue to seek diplomatic recognition/membership in international bodies like the UN?
6 How has Taiwan coped with the 'Rise of China'?
7 Is Taiwan's search for international space incompatible with stable cross-Strait relations?
8 How and why has China's Taiwan policy altered since the late 1980s?

Further reading

Bush, Richard. 2005. *Untying the Knot: Making Peace in the Taiwan Strait*. Washington, DC: Brookings. Best single volume on the development of cross-Strait relations available in English, written by someone with first-hand experience as the head of the US de facto embassy, the American Institute in Taiwan.
Goldstein, Steven and Julian Chang (eds). 2008. *Presidential Politics in Taiwan: The Administration of Chen Shui-bian*. Norwalk, CT: Eastbridge. Chapters 7–10 offer the best available discussions of external relations under the DPP.
Hickey, Dennis. 2007. *Foreign Policy Making in Taiwan: From Principle to Pragmatism*. London: Routledge. Best available single volume on Taiwan's international relations. The author makes good use of his own extensive interviews with key policymakers.
Schubert, Gunter (ed.). 2016. *Routledge Handbook of Contemporary Taiwan*. London: Routledge. Chapters 25–34 offer detailed and up to date discussions of Taiwan's China policies, foreign policy and public diplomacy.
Su, Chi. 2009. *Taiwan's Relations with Mainland China: A Tail Wagging Two Dogs*. London: Routledge. Examination of cross-Strait relations since the late 1980s written by the former MAC Chairman and influential Figure in the post-2000 KMT. Sections on the Lee Teng-hui era are especially useful. Partisan bias does seep into the discussion of the post-2000 period.

Useful websites

The survey sites listed in Chapter 8 also offer rich data on public views on Taiwan's external relations.
www.mac.gov.tw/mp.asp?mp=3 – Mainland Affairs Council website offers extremely rich data on government policies, speeches, statistics and public opinion related to cross-Strait relations.
www.mofa.gov.tw/en/default.html – Ministry of Foreign Affairs website is not quite as user friendly as the MAC one, but also provides useful policy and news release data on Taiwan's diplomatic activities.

Notes

1 It ranks as the country with the 51st largest population, coming between Mozambique and Syria.
2 It has the 136th largest land area, being slightly smaller than the Netherlands.
3 As I was completing the second edition, Panama switched sides.
4 *Republic of China Yearbook 2016*. Available online at: https://english.ey.gov.tw/cp.aspx?n=A98E E53BDE2EF371 (accessed 20 April 2017).
5 Rigger, *Politics in Taiwan*, 190–3.
6 Rawnsley, 'Approaches to Soft Power and Public Diplomacy in China and Taiwan', 123.
7 Hickey, *Foreign Policy Making in Taiwan*, 8–13. This is quite similar to the scheme proposed by Chao Chien-min of (1) period of expansion (1950–71), (2) period of retreat (1971–9), (3) recuperation (1980–8), (4) readjustment of diplomatic strategies (1988–present). See Chao, 'The Republic of China's Foreign Relations under Lee Teng-hui: A Balance Sheet', 179–84.

8 Hickey, 'Beijing's Evolving Policy toward Taipei: Engagement or Entrapment', 31–70.
9 Hickey, *Foreign Policy making in Taiwan*, 1–7.
10 Hickey, 'Beijing's Evolving Policy toward Taipei: Engagement or Entrapment', 56–63.
11 Su, *Taiwan's Relations with Mainland China*, 276.
12 For a detailed discussion of the US–Taiwan relationship and Chiang's plan to retake the Chinese mainland, see Tsang, 'Chiang Kai-shek and the Policy to Reconquer the Mainland', 48–72.
13 Ibid., 64.
14 Ibid., 48.
15 Chen, 'Literary Taiwan', 78.
16 Cited in Roy, *Taiwan: A Political History*, 148.
17 Ibid., 145.
18 Long, *Taiwan: China's Last Frontier,* 205–6. The pilot, Wang Hsi-chuen, was allowed to stay in China.
19 Rubinstein, *Taiwan: A New History* (2007 edn), 462.
20 For a discussion of Taiwan's UN campaign, see Wang, 'Taiwan's Bid for UN Membership', 174–92.
21 For a discussion of Taiwan's participation in international organizations, see Wang, 'Taiwan's Participation in International Organizations', 149–73.
22 Zhao, 'Economic Interdependence and Political Divergence', 24.
23 Ibid., 24.
24 Kuo, 'Cross-Strait Relations', 205–6.
25 For details on these secret envoy meetings, see Su, *Taiwan's Relations with Mainland China,* 8–9.
26 Ibid., 15.
27 Ibid., 15–16.
28 Rigger, *Politics in Taiwan*, 169.
29 Kuo, 'Cross-Strait Relations', 208.
30 Roy, 197.
31 For instance, one NP advertisement carried the slogan, 'Don't let our Children become the Cannon Fodder for Taiwan independence. If you don't want War, then Vote NP.' See *United Daily News*, 8 March 1996, 9.
32 Kuo, 204.
33 Ibid., 213.
34 Su, 46.
35 Ibid., 47.
36 Chao, 'The Republic of China's Foreign Relations under Lee Teng-hui: A Balance Sheet,' 191.
37 Cited in Roy, 221.
38 The MAC showed in a series of surveys there was strong Taiwanese support for the concept. See Mainland Affairs Council, 'Public Support for "Special State-to-State Relationship"', issued September 1999. Available online at: www.mac.gov.tw/ct.asp?xItem=54854&CtNode=5954&mp=3 (accessed 12 March 2011).
39 Ibid. In the above survey, support for the One Country, Two Systems formula stood at under 10 per cent and opposition at almost 80 per cent.
40 *Taipei Times,* 16 March 2000.
41 Cited in Su, 87.
42 Ibid., 131.
43 Chen Shui-bian, 'President Chen's Opening Address of the 29th Annual Meeting of the World Federation of Taiwanese Associations'. Available online at: www.gio.gov.tw/taiwan-website/4oa/20020803/2002080301.html (accessed 12 March 2011).
44 Charles Snyder, 'US will defend Taiwan', *Taipei Times,* 25 April 2001, 1.
45 Swaine, 'Managing Relations with the United States', 180.
46 Ibid., 182–3.
47 Hickey, 'Change and Continuity: US Policy and Taiwan', 113.
48 Ibid., 112.
49 Ibid.
50 Su, 183–4.

51 Jenny Hsu *et al.*, 'Huang apologizes for PNG scandal', *Taipei Times,* 3 May 2008, 1; Staff Writer, 'Singapore court orders return of embezzled funds', *Taipei Times*, 20 October 2010, 1.

52 Hickey, 'Beijing's Evolving Policy Toward Taipei', 37.

53 Ibid., 50–1.

54 Ibid., 50.

55 Fell, 'The China Impact on Taiwan's Elections'.

56 Government Information Office, 'March 22, 2008 Presidential Election and Referendums – PRESS KIT Fact Sheet No. 6', available online at: www.gio.gov.tw/elect2008/kit_06.htm (accessed 19 March 2011).

57 Ma's Inaugural Speech (2008). Available online at: www.president.gov.tw/Portals/4/Features Section/Other-feature-articles/20080520_PRESIDENT_INAUGURAL/e_speech.html (accessed 25 March 2011).

58 Rowen, 'Touring in Heterotopia', 20–34.

59 Shih Hsiu-chuan, 'MOE takes on Chinese diplomas', *Taipei Times,* 16 October 2010, 1.

60 Rawnsley, 'Taiwan's Soft Power and Public Diplomacy'.

61 Shih Hsiu-chuan, 'EU approves plan to grant visa free entry to Taiwanese', *Taipei Times*, 26 November 2010, 1.

62 *United Daily News*, 15 January 2012, A1.

63 *Taipei Times*, 23 March 2012, 1.

64 The MAC surveys between 2000 and 2008 asked the question:'Is the One Country, Two Systems formula suitable for solving the problem across the straits?' Those supporting the proposition ranged from 7.4 to 17.6 per cent, while those opposing ranged between 67.8 and 83.7. See MAC, 'Public Opinion on Cross-Strait Relations in the Republic of China (statistic charts) (2008/03)'. Available online at: www.mac.gov.tw/ct.asp?xItem=54556&ctNode= 5948&mp=3 (accessed 30 March 2011).

10 From Leninist corporatist state to vibrant civil society

The emergence and role of social movements

When thinking about Taiwan's political miracles, it is easy to concentrate on electoral change and the emergence of competitive party politics. Another domestic sphere where we can see an equally remarkable transformation is in Taiwan's associational life. Under martial law, the KMT's Leninist control and penetration of society was so extensive that there was almost no space for any kind of independent interest groups, to say nothing of a civil society. The only interest groups able to operate under martial law, such as the farmers' associations, trade unions and the ROC Women's Association, were so dominated by the KMT that they were in effect front organizations manipulated by the KMT branches. Even when Taiwan moved into the period of soft authoritarianism, the KMT continued to repress attempts at creating independent social movements.

Immediately before and after the lifting of martial law, a large number of new social movements emerged to challenge the KMT regime on a range of political and social issues. These movements contributed to Taiwan's democratic transition by not only calling for political and social reforms, but also by eroding the KMT's dominant position in the country's associational life. Since the democratic transition, social movements have continued to grow and diversify. They play a critical intermediary role between the state and society. Often they are able to lobby for legislative action where the mainstream political parties struggle to represent constituents' interests. Their importance was reinforced in 2014, when an alliance of social movements was able to block core KMT government policy in the areas of cross-Strait relations and nuclear power. Other key functions they perform include political recruitment, scrutinizing government and promoting social capital. In short, they enrich Taiwan's democracy. From having almost no independent interest groups in the late martial law era, Taiwan now has one of the most vibrant civil societies of any state in Asia.

After reviewing some of the definitions of central concepts for the study of civil society and social movements, I will then discuss how the KMT tried to control associational life in the hard authoritarian era. Two groups that did challenge the KMT during martial law were the overseas Taiwan independence movement and the Presbyterian Church. Next, I will introduce the remarkable blossoming of new social movements in the period immediately before and after the lifting of martial law. The core part of the chapter will focus on the activities and impact of the following four influential movements: women's rights, labour, environmental protection and students.

Core concepts

The term 'civil society' has grown in popularity over the last two decades. The popularity of the concept actually contributes to its fuzzy meaning. It means different things to different people and is promoted by academics and practitioners with contrasting political objectives, as neo-conservatives, liberals and radicals alike see it as a critical variable in economic and political reform.

There is no consensus in the literature on a single definition for civil society. One of the most often cited is Hegel's from the *Philosophy of Right,* which claims that 'civil society comprises the realm of organizations that lie between the family at one extreme and the state at the other'.[1] But this is just too broad to be of much use for our analysis. Another often cited definition from the London School of Economics (LSE) Centre for Civil Society is more specific:

> Civil society refers to the arena of uncoerced collective action around shared interests, purposes and values. In theory, its institutional forms are distinct from those of the state, family and market, though in practice, the boundaries between state, civil society, family and market are often complex, blurred and negotiated. Civil society commonly embraces a diversity of spaces, actors and institutional forms, varying in their degree of formality, autonomy and power. Civil societies are often populated by organisations such as registered charities, development non-governmental organisations, community groups, women's organisations, faith-based organisations, professional associations, trade unions, self-help groups, social movements, business associations, coalitions and advocacy groups.[2]

Michael Edwards calls this understanding 'civil society as associational life'.[3]

As the LSE definition suggested, boundaries between civil society groups and the state can often be blurred. Although civil society groups often do have political goals, they are usually not aiming to control government and do not contest elections; instead, they mainly seek to influence policy. However, social movements can make the transition to political parties; obvious cases include the ecological movement in Germany or the *Tangwai* in Taiwan. Moreover, many Non-Government Organizations (NGOs) are fronts for political parties. For instance, many think tanks in both the UK and Taiwan are funded directly by political parties and operate as de facto party spokespersons or branches.

Michael Edwards suggests that another major school of thought views 'civil society as the good society'.[4] But should actors in civil society always be civil? In other words, should we regard it as a realm of service rather than self-interest and a breeding ground for attitudes and values like cooperation, trust, tolerance and non-violence? If a group must be civil to qualify, then Al Qaeda would naturally be excluded. However, the picture is not so clear-cut in cases such as Sinn Féin, the African National Congress or the *Tangwai,* all of whom have been accused of being terrorists at certain points in their history, but are regarded as leading social movements in their countries. Other writers stress the role of civil society as a public sphere.[5] In other words, civil society should be seen as an arena for public deliberation, rational dialogue and the exercise of active citizenship for the common good.

In this chapter, the area of civil society that I am particularly interested in examining is social movements. According to the *Oxford Dictionary of Politics,*

> [they] may encompass political parties and campaigning organizations, but also include individuals who are not part of any formal organizational structure. They are organized around ideas which give individuals who adhere to the movement new forms of social and political identity.[6]

Thus, social movements feature elements of the associational life and public sphere under-standing of civil society actors.

As we discussed in Chapter 3, civil society plays a vital role in both democratic transition and post-transition democratic politics. For instance, Grugel argues that a core feature of a consolidated democracy is a strong participatory and critical civil society.[7] Diamond stresses the democratic role that civil society plays in limiting state power, scrutinizing government, developing democratic values and lowering the burdens and demands on the state.[8] Grugel distinguishes between Diamond's liberal view on civil society as an aid to the state and a radical perspective that expects civil society to challenge and transform the state. 'Civil society thus becomes an instrument to correct the imbalances of the capitalist state, and the struggle between civil society and the state is a means to achieve democracy.'[9]

Two terms that are frequently used to discuss the KMT's control of Taiwanese society under martial law are 'Leninist' and 'corporatist'. The former is defined by Selznick as the concentration of 'total social power in the hands of a ruling party'.[10] Ho Ming-sho (何明修) goes on to explain that from a Leninist perspective, the party's task was to remake what is a malleable society.[11] Thus, this overlaps with the standards for a total-itarian state raised in Chapter 2. While Leninism is almost always associated with non-democratic regimes, corporatism features in a variety of regime types, such as democracies in Scandinavia or authoritarian Latin America and Taiwan. For Philippe Schmitter, corporatism is

> a system of interest representation in which the constituent units are organized into a limited number of singular, compulsory, non-competitive, hierarchically ordered and functionally differentiated categories, recognized or licensed (if not created) by the state and granted a deliberate representative monopoly within their respective categories in exchange for observing certain controls on their selection of leaders and articulation of demands and supports.[12]

He later notes that this kind of system helps ruling elites to 'repress and exclude autono-mous articulation of subordinate class demands'.[13]

Interest groups under martial law

Under martial law there was a substantial expansion in the number of registered interest groups and members, growing from 2,560 groups and 1.3 million members in 1952 to 11,306 groups and 8.3 million members by 1987.[14] What on the surface suggested a pluralistic society, masked a high degree of KMT penetration and control of associational life, at least until the last decade of authoritarianism. We can observe how KMT cor-poratism dominated this sector by examining some cases of the most influential interest groups under martial law. These groups included peasants, workers and students, whose lack of support was perceived by the KMT as contributing to their loss of the mainland to the CCP. KMT leaders thus devoted much effort to controlling these sectors of society through its puppet interest groups.

The KMT did not outlaw trade unions. Instead, it encouraged them to be established in state-owned enterprises and large private companies. By 1987, about a quarter of Tai-wan's 8 million workers were unionized. However, unions operated as vehicles of KMT control rather than for protecting workers' rights. As Ho Ming-sho explains:

state corporatism was characterized by two layers of control. At the workplace, individual labor unions were closely monitored and manipulated by Kuomintang (KMT) party branches. The latter made sure that only KMT loyalists were elected as union officers so that the state and management could effectively control the unions. At the national level, the KMT pre-emptively recognized one federation of trade unions as the only legitimate representative of Taiwan's labor. The Chinese Federation of Labor (CFL, *quanguo zonggonghui*) was patronized, financed and staffed by the KMT, and as a result, labor unions became mere extensions of state rule. They did not represent the rank and file.[15]

Moreover, workers were deprived of the right to strike and to form independent unions.

Unions represented one of a host of ways the KMT tried to control labour in large state-run enterprises. Union officer positions were lucrative and thus were a key way for the party to reward loyalist workers. Moreover, the unions tended to control the distribution of workers' welfare benefits, which gave them another tool to control employees. From the 1950s, the KMT was also highly active in recruiting worker members and 'establishing a party branch in every nationalized factory and a party cell in every workshop'.[16] Ho explains another KMT control method in China Petroleum Corporation's Kaohsiung Refinery. 'The new section, later notoriously known as the Personnel II, was in charge of monitoring employees by establishing an invisible network of informants throughout the factory. The Personnel II kept secret files of its supervised populace.'[17] Party membership and open loyalty to the party were also critical for gaining promotion in state-owned enterprises, as much as in the civil service. Promotion from a worker to a white-collar staff member involved both examinations and a superior's evaluation, so pro-KMT enthusiasm was a crucial ingredient to upward mobility.[18]

The levels of KMT control and penetration went even further in the education system. All campuses had a KMT branch office and the party's youth organization, the China Youth Corps (*jiuguo tuan*). There was no space for campus democracy; instead, the student government chair selection was dominated by the university authorities and KMT affiliated groups. University students were a key recruiting target for the KMT. Membership brought a range of benefits, while failure to join could be costly. Membership could help admission to graduate school, tolerance of poor academic performance, more desirable military service allocations and career advancement in the civil service. It was basically essential for university administrators at middle or higher ranks to be party members. Even the curriculum was heavily political, with students still forced to take compulsory courses in ROC Constitution, Sun Yat Sen Thought and military training. Universities, particularly in the state sector, were party universities.

In every campus, each student was assigned a military instructing officer (*junshi jiaoguan*) who kept an eye on their behaviour and views. The military instructing officers were invariably KMT members. In addition, these officers were assisted by student informers in every class, who often had joined the party even before college. Teresa Wright notes that 'These unidentified class spies were responsible for scouting prospective recruits and keeping an ear to the ground for anti-party opinions and activities.'[19] Students who failed to meet the standards expected by the KMT military instructing offices and school administration faced expulsion or damaged career prospects if they accumulated sufficient penalty demerits. She goes on to explain that 'KMT-affiliated student groups also maintained control over student activities' allowances and grant nominations'.[20] Even posters or campus publications required the stamp of approval from KMT-dominated committees.

In rural Taiwan, the interest groups most useful for the KMT project to penetrate and control society were the farmers' and fishermen's associations. These associations were built on the foundations of the extensive system of farmers' associations that had been established under Japanese colonial rule. As we discussed in Chapter 7, the farmers' associations were a prized asset for election mobilization and as a source for funds from their credit department. Thus, they tended to be a key component in the KMT local faction patron–client relationship. Like local elections, farmers' association elections were also highly competitive. Statistics suggest that the KMT's representation at all levels of the farmers' association was actually increasing through the martial law years. At the provincial farmers' association level, almost all elected assembly representatives were already KMT members by 1969.[21] Even at the local farmers' association level, almost 100 per cent of chairmen of the board and chiefs of the board of supervisors were members by 1975.[22] In addition, the KMT also had much credit in the countryside from its success at land reform. Although the KMT operated in coordination with its local factional affiliates in controlling these farmers' associations, they provided powerful vote machines for the party well into the democratic era. Nevertheless, since the KMT operated through its proxies, the farmers' associations were less valuable as a tool for ideological indoctrination than labour unions, campuses or the military. Just as we saw with labour unions, the farmers' associations were not run with the primary purpose of promoting the interests and rights of their members. Instead, their overriding function was to draw millions into KMT-controlled networks.

Under martial law, the KMT was much more willing to grant freedom of religion than its rival on the mainland. Rather than becoming a more secular society with rapid economic modernization, organized religion has grown in Taiwan. Robert Weller notes that 'The number of temples per capita has been increasing since the 1970s and has probably never been as high as it is now.'[23] At the local level, many temples did become part of local factional networks, but the KMT generally took a negative view on the excesses of popular religion. According to Shih Fang-long, 'From the KMT government's point of view, people wasted their time, money and commodities at religious festivals and such behaviour was conceived as an obstacle to economic take-off.'[24] Thus, it produced a series of guidelines to encourage temples to economize their religious festival activities. Despite their potential for mobilization, the vast majority of religious groups chose to take an apolitical stance prior to democratization.

Challenge from the Presbyterian Church in Taiwan

The one major exception to this apolitical pattern was the Presbyterian Church in Taiwan (PCT). The PCT had become established in Taiwan in the final decades of Qing rule in the late nineteenth century. In addition to the church's missionary work, they developed important educational and medical centres. Many of these centres continue operating to this day and were even able to continue operations for much of the Japanese colonial period. In an era of severe discrimination against Taiwanese in the tertiary education sector, the Presbyterian-run schools played a key role in educating local elites. The PCT stressed using local dialects as the main language of preaching and instruction in their establishments, and employed a system of Romanized Bibles and hymn books in Hokkien and other Taiwanese languages.

The February 28 Incident was to be a crucial moment in the PCT's history. As Rubinstein notes, 'The open and very public role that the leaders of the Presbyterian

Church played during the 2–28 Incident and the degree of suffering that they and other church members experienced during the event and its aftermath, led to defining moments of consciousness for Presbyterians.'[25] The chaotic return to Chinese rule after 1945 and KMT policies under martial law were to make the PCT increasingly anti-KMT. Naturally, the PCT could not openly oppose the KMT in the first two decades of martial law; instead, Rubinstein describes it as 'lying low and defending turf' during this period.[26] However, one early point of conflict lay with the KMT's policy of Mandarinization and its attempt to suppress the use of local dialects. Government directives banning local dialects in schools and for preaching were a challenge to the PCT.

It was not until 1971 that the PCT actually came out to openly challenge the KMT. *The Public Statement of Our National Faith* was the first of a series of bold documents the PCT issued under martial law.[27] This called for Taiwan's fate to be decided by Taiwanese rather than outsiders and for full democratization. These were radical demands when Taiwan was still under hard authoritarian rule. Similar statements had landed political dissidents such as Lei Chen and Peng Ming-min in jail with lengthy sentences. In the mid-1970s the two sides continued to clash over local language promotion, with the KMT confiscating thousands of Romanized Hokkien Bibles in 1975. Another important public statement was issued in 1977 and was addressed to US President Jimmy Carter. This was titled *A Declaration of Human Rights by the PCT*. What was particularly groundbreaking was that it openly called for 'our government to face reality and to take effective measures whereby Taiwan may become a new and independent country'.[28] Such a challenge to KMT nationalist orthodoxy led to confiscation of the *Taiwan Presbyterian Church News,* but not mass arrests of Church leaders. To a certain extent, the PCT's links with overseas Presbyterian churches gave it a degree of protection that other dissidents lacked.

During the late 1970s and 1980s, the PCT became increasingly an ally of the *Tangwai* movement. Following the Kaohsiung Incident, *Tangwai* leader Shih Ming-teh was hidden by the General Secretary of the PCT Kao Chun-ming (高俊明). Both were soon arrested. Thus, Church leaders joined the *Tangwai* in the military trials of 1980s and also received long jail sentences. During the 1980s, the KMT continued to suppress the PCT – for instance, using legal measures to try to close down the PCT's Tainan Theological College.[29] We can get a taste of the oppositional role of the PCT in the film *Formosa Betrayed,* as the central demonstration scene occurs at a Presbyterian church and US investigators discover that the assassinated professor had been remitting money to a Taiwanese church.

The lifting of martial law and inauguration of a Presbyterian Taiwanese President, Lee Teng-hui, marked the end of government suppression of the Church. Many of its demands on a range of issues such as language policy, democratic reforms and national identity became mainstream government policies during the transition period. The Church was thus able to return to its main focus on education, medical provision and religious work. Despite the relatively small size of the PCT, it played a key role in challenging the KMT directly at a time when no other organized group dared to do so.

Overseas Taiwan Independence Movement

During the height of the White Terror, one of the only instances of a genuinely independent social movement was the exiled Taiwan Independence Movement (TIM). This movement initially emerged after the 2–28 Incident with a group of Taiwanese exiles in Hong Kong. In 1948, the League for the Reliberation of Formosa sent a petition to the UN requesting that Taiwan be placed under UN trusteeship before eventual independence.[30] In the 1950s and early 1960s, the main base for the TIM was Japan. The early centre of the movement was the Thomas Liao-led Provisional Government of the Republic of Formosa, founded in 1956. In 1960, a rival student-led Taiwan Youth Association was established, publishing Japanese and English language journals. In addition to lobbying foreign governments, the early TIM attempted to offer an alternative and critical portrayal of the political situation in Taiwan. These TIM publications were designed to inform not only foreign governments and media but also the growing overseas Taiwanese communities. Thus, the TIM abroad represented a severe challenge to the Free China image that the KMT was striving to promote abroad.

As increasing numbers of Taiwanese migrated to the US for work or higher education, the centre of gravity of the TIM shifted to North America in the 1960s and 1970s. Thus, once Peng Ming-min escaped from Taiwan in 1969, after a brief stay in Sweden he chose to be based in the US. A major landmark in the movement's history came with the establishment of the World United Formosans for Independence in 1970. This was designed to bring together anti-KMT groups in Japan, North America and Europe under one umbrella organization.

The activities of the overseas TIM were predominantly peaceful, focusing on lobbying the US government and trying to influence the foreign media and overseas Taiwanese community. Use of violence was extremely rare. One exception was the attempt to assassinate Chiang Ching-kuo during his visit to the US in May 1970.

Even though the TIM operated abroad, participation entailed great risk. The KMT strove to undermine these exiled organizations and encourage overseas governments to outlaw their operations. Those suspected of involvement in the TIM were put on a KMT blacklist, which barred thousands from returning to Taiwan. The KMT also employed spies within the overseas Taiwanese community and on overseas campuses to report on the behaviour of compatriots. Association with TIM activists could result in harassment of family members back in Taiwan and also rule out many career avenues after returning to the island. At its most extreme, the KMT was prepared to make use of its Chinese mafia links, such as the Bamboo Union, to punish overseas dissidents. In the film *Formosa Betrayed,* the US-based Professor Henry Wen is assassinated for his political activities against the KMT regime and advocacy for an independent Taiwan. This fictional character is meant to be modelled on aspects of actual cases such as Chen Wen-chen and Henry Liu.

What kinds of people were willing to make the risky decision to join this social movement? Shu Wei-de's (許維德) study of the life histories of a number of these US-based TIM activists reveals some common characteristics.[31] The majority were male, Taiwanese and from southern Taiwan. They also tended to be born in the 1930s or 1940s and thus had experienced the high period of KMT White Terror in their youth. Shu also finds that activists tended to be from well-educated and professional occupational backgrounds. In almost all his cases, the activists joined the movement after coming to the US for graduate study.

Although the KMT devoted considerable resources to attacking the TIM abroad, its actual impact on Taiwan was quite limited. Opposition dissidents within Taiwan were at pains not to be associated with these groups, as it was just too dangerous. Moreover, under martial law Taiwan suffered from a serious brain drain. In other words, the vast majority going abroad to study or work preferred not return to Taiwan. Thus, Taiwanese exposed to TIM ideas abroad did not bring these back to Taiwan. With the media so controlled by the KMT, the TIM also had no legitimate channels to challenge KMT nationalist discourse within Taiwan.

After the lifting of martial law, many activists returned to Taiwan and joined the DPP. However, this alliance was not as productive as these activists hoped for. Former exiled independence activists have tended to be on the margins of the DPP and many became disillusioned with the party's moderation and limited progress towards full independence under DPP rule. However, the TIM still exists both abroad in groups such as the World United Formosans for Independence and the Formosan Association for Public Affairs, and within Taiwan there are also a range of pro-independence civic groups promoting their cause.

The birth of Taiwanese social movements before and after the lifting of martial law

The lifting of martial law opened the floodgates to the emergence of a large number of independent social movements. For the first time in Taiwan's history, protest demonstrations became an acceptable form of political activism. Statistics show how the number of protests skyrocketed in the late 1980s. In 1983, there were 143 social protests in Taiwan, but in 1987 there were 676.[32] Chu Yun-han (朱雲漢) found that the most frequent categories of protests in 1987 were economic in nature, followed by political, environmental and labour protests.[33] According to Michael Hsiao (蕭新煌), 'By the end of 1989, at least eighteen social movements had emerged to make claims on the state.'[34] These were: (1) consumers' movement; (2) local anti-pollution protest movements; (3) conservationists' movement; (4) women's movement; (5) aborigine human rights movement; (6) student movement; (7) New Testament Church protests; (8) labour movement; (9) farmers' movement; (10) teachers' rights movement; (11) handicapped and disadvantaged welfare group protests; (12) veterans' welfare protests; (13) human rights movement; (14) Mainlanders' home-visiting movement; (15) Taiwanese home-visiting movement;[35] (16) anti-nuclear power movement; (17) Hakka rights movement; and (18) non-homeowners' shell-less snail movement.[36]

Fan Yun's (范雲) research on social movement activists in the 1990s had some similar findings to Shu's study of the overseas TIM. For example, she found that social movement activists also tended to be from privileged backgrounds, well educated and from the middle or upper classes. In contrast, workers and farmers were not well represented in Fan's sample of activists. The major difference in the two studies is that social movement activists in the 1990s tended to be much younger than those in the overseas TIM, with over 60 per cent born between 1953 and 1964.[37]

Since 1987, some of these movements have ceased their oppositional role, often after achieving their central objectives. For instance, after a long and bitter struggle the New Testament Church won the right to return to its spiritual home of Mount Zion in Kaohsiung County in the late 1980s. Thereafter, its followers reverted to their reclusive religious lifestyle and stopped anti-KMT activism. Subsequently, large numbers of new movements and interest groups have arisen that further enrich Taiwan's associational life. During the final decade of martial law, the number of national and local registered associations was already rising gradually. But the lifting of martial law was followed by a rapid acceleration in the proliferation of new civic groups. In 1980, 3,960 civic groups were registered with the local or national government, with the number rising to almost

6,000 by 1987. However, the figure had risen to 18,465 by 2001 and 50,093 by 2016.[38] Rather than try to be comprehensive, I will next discuss the development of four of the most influential social movements: women, labour, environmental protection and student movements. In particular, I consider their methods, objectives, relationship with the state and political parties, and their impact.

The women's movement: a successful but rootless movement?

Under authoritarianism, Taiwanese politics were completely dominated by men. Although the ROC constitution promised equality of the sexes, women were both politically and socially second-class citizens. The KMT promoted a highly patriarchal political culture that stood in stark contrast to the CCP's egalitarian ideology of women holding up half the sky. Prior to the 1980s, women were completely excluded from the key decision-making institutions of the Executive Yuan cabinet or KMT Central Standing Committee. The major women's association was the ROC Women's Association which, with Madame Chiang serving as its president, operated like a KMT branch.

It was not until the 1970s that an embryonic women's movement emerged. The key player was Annette Lu who had risen from a small merchant family background to graduate from National Taiwan University's law school and then went on to postgraduate study in the US.[39] On returning to Taiwan she initially worked as a civil servant in the Executive Yuan. Lu initially began campaigning against gender injustice in the education and legal system through newspaper articles and public lectures. Her initial attempts to create an effective women's organization were frustrated, and it was not until 1976–7 that she had more success. She was able to establish a Women's Information Centre in Kaohsiung and Taiwan's first women's telephone helpline. Another central dimension was publishing feminist works through establishing a Pioneer Press. Lu had to find loopholes in the martial law system to develop her campaigns. However, she faced a great deal of resistance and harassment, including much hate mail. Some of her books were banned and her initial attempt to register a Modern Women's Association was blocked as it would have been overlapping with the puppet KMT Women's Association. The intelligence agencies also were able to infiltrate Lu's various organizations to both spy on and sabotage their operations. By the late 1970s, Lu shifted her focus towards democratization and became an integral part of the *Tangwai*. Like the PCT leadership, the women's movement paid a high price for this alliance, as Lu joined the other Kaohsiung Incident defendants in the dock, and the remnants of her organizations were closed down in 1979–80.

It was not until 1982 and the establishment of the *Awakening Magazine (funu xinzhi zazhi)* that the movement's second stage began. The crackdown in 1979 forced Lu's former collaborators to devise a new set of approaches to promote women's rights. First, it focused on elitist rather than grassroots mass activism. Thus, it lobbied for gender equality legislation and ran small-scale academic seminars and publications. Second, it took a clearly non-partisan approach, trying to keep its distance from both the *Tangwai* and KMT. This low-key non-partisan method enabled the women's movement to develop in the final five years of martial law with far less KMT suppression than other new movements were facing. In 1984, the Awakening even had its first success in lobbying in support of the Eugenics Protection Law, which legalized abortion.[40]

The lifting of martial law in 1987 allowed Awakening to become the Awakening Foundation and for a large number of new women's civic groups to be created. However, the basic mode of activism remained quite consistent from that set by Lee Yuan-chen

(李元貞) in the early 1980s. In other words, they engaged in what Fan Yun calls 'politics without parties', and a continued focus on lobbying rather than confrontational street demonstrations.[41] Fan shows that this is not entirely surprising given the elite nature of women's movement activists compared to both environmental and labour movements.[42]

In Table 10.1, I have listed a series of important pieces of legislation that the women's movement lobbied for both during the KMT and DPP eras. These addressed a range of areas where severe inequality had existed under martial law. One piece of legislation that the movement is particularly proud of is the 2001 Equal Employment Law. This was first drafted in 1987 by the Awakening Foundation but faced strong resistance from the business sector. Only after 14 years' hard struggle was the bill finally passed. Legislation has established measures against child prostitution, domestic violence, sexual harassment and rape within marriage. Taiwan's patriarchal education curriculums were also a target for feminists; thus, the 2004 Gender Equity Education Act was another important achievement. Fan and Wu argue that the classrooms have become 'the front line of promoting gender equality'.[43] In addition, there is now more of a legal level playing-field on matters such as child custody and property rights after divorce. In terms of legislative achievements, the women's movement must rank as Taiwan's most successful movement. The women's movement has also managed to change many patriarchal norms such as wider acceptance of the same pay for men and women. In addition, women's groups have gained access to increasingly large budgets, as many have been commissioned by local or central government to run social welfare programmes. Thus, women's groups have greater financial resources than the other leading movements.

As multi-party politics developed, it became harder to remain as apolitical as they once were, particularly as parties began to employ women's issues in election campaigns in the 1990s. In the 1990s, both DPP and KMT Taipei governments appointed women's movement leaders as policy advisers and cabinet ministers. After 2000, Chen Shui-bian

Table 10.1 Legislation promoted by Taiwan's women's movement in the KMT and DPP eras

KMT Era	*DPP Era*
1. Eugenic Protection Law (1984)	1. Equal Employment Law (2001)
2. The Tenth Amendment of the Constitution (1994)	2. Conjugal Property Law (2002)
3. Prevention of Child and Youth Prostitution Law (1995)	3. Gender Equality Education Bill (2004)
4. Sexual Assault Protection Law (1997)	4. Sexual Harassment Prevention Law (2005)
5. Women's quota in legislative party list seats (2005).	
5. Revision of the Family Section of the Civil Code (1998)	
6. Domestic Violence Prevention Law (1998)	
7. Revision of the Criminal Law on Rape (1999)	
8. Creation of Executive Yuan Women's Rights Promotion Committee (1997)	

Sources: Weng and Fell (2006: 152); Fan and Wei-ting (2016).

Note 1: The 1994 Constitution Amendments stipulated that the state should preserve women's dignity, protect women's safety, eliminate sexual discrimination and promote equality between the sexes.
Note 2: The revisions of the Family Section of the Civil Code revised articles that had favoured the male party in child custody, conjugal property and conjugal residence, making these comply with the principles of gender equality.

even brought some into the national government cabinet, such as the Director of the Peng Wan-ju Foundation Lin Fang-mei (林芳玫). Parties were also recruiting women's leaders as election candidates. This shift towards 'politics with parties' has helped improve the gender balance in Taiwan's politics. The trend was accelerated by the 2005 reforms to the electoral system that required half the party list seats be given to women. Currently, 38 per cent of Taiwan's legislators are female, and since 2000 women have often held a number of important cabinet posts. And, of course, between 2000 and 2008 the founder of the women's movement, Annette Lu, was Vice President. One other major policy implication of closer ties to parties was that under the DPP, for the first time the women's movement had much greater access to government ministers. The fact that Taiwan elected its first female president in 2016 also has received international attention. Although the Executive Yuan Women's Rights Promotion Committee was established under the KMT in 1997, it began to have a greater effect after the DPP came to power in 2000. From inside government, women's leaders were able to promote the idea of gender main-streaming. As Huang Chang-ling explained, 'The gender commission model was expanded into local government in almost every city and county after 2002, and by 2008, when the conservative party returned to power, a commission-like working group was also established in every ministry.'[44] Nevertheless, the politicization of women's groups served to erode their human resources and often split the movement.

One key issue that has divided the women's movement since the mid-1990s has been sexual politics. The younger generation of women's activists tended to be more sym-pathetic to the sexual liberation discourse espoused by Josephine Ho (何春蕤). Thus, the founder generation and those joining after martial law often took distinct positions on issues such as pornography. However, the issue that was most divisive were licensed prostitutes in Taipei. The DPP's Taipei mayor, Chen Shui-bian, took the advice of the women's advisory council (dominated by senior women's movement leaders) in scrapping the system of licensed prostitutes in 1997. However, many younger generation activists chose solidarity and protecting the human rights of these sex workers. The issue became further politicized as the KMT candidate Ma Ying-jeou came out in support of their human rights during the 1998 Taipei mayoral election. Thus, women's activists lined up supporting different party camps in the election. After winning, Ma delivered on his promise to give the licensed prostitutes a two-year reprieve. Although the intensity of this dispute has decreased, the scars have not fully healed. Even today there are still divisions within women's groups over whether to legalize prostitution. The licensed prostitutes issue developed from a movement that initially was narrowly focused on protecting the rights of a relatively small number of licensed prostitutes to a broader approach today. Chang Mau-kuei (張茂桂) lists a range of the sex workers' rights movement's demands from a 2006 conference. These included calls for legalizing the sex trade, protecting the work rights of local and immigrant sex workers, freedom to migrate and ending the suppression of prostitutes and immigrants.[45]

The women's movement now also faces other weaknesses and challenges. By becom-ing so financially reliant on social welfare programme provisions from the state, it has become part of the state and thus lost its ability to be independent and criticize govern-ment for fear of losing its financial lifeline. Also, its elitist methods have meant that it often struggles to get its message across at the grassroots level. Although legislation has changed, many patriarchal norms remain intact. An example of this has been the huge rise in Taiwan-style mail-order brides, whereby through agents, Taiwanese males effectively buy wives from South East Asia and China.[46] The women's movement's elitist approach has also meant that it has failed to create a mass following, thus making it unable to mobilize large demonstrations to promote its causes. This led Weng and Fell to describe the women's movement as a 'rootless movement'.[47] Lin Fang-mei has a similar conclusion, suggesting that the civil society and state partnership resulted in civil society as a whole seeming to disappear.[48] One problem the movement faces is that the issue is one the parties will embrace for party political purposes but are willing to sacrifice, as it remains of low priority compared to economic or identity matters. As a veteran women's leader stated before the DPP fell from power:

> In the past the KMT wouldn't have responded to the women's groups' demands if the DPP hadn't goaded them . . . But now that the DPP's in power, it is not any better because this government is so obsessed with political ideology.[49]

Given the progress that feminist activists made during the Chen Shui-bian administration, there was concern among some activists on the return to power of the KMT in 2008. Huang has referred to the relationship between the movement and KMT government from 2008 to 2016 as an 'uneasy alliance'.[50] There was some continuity. For instance, in 2012 the newly created cabinet level Department of Gender Equality was tasked with continuing the drive towards gender mainstreaming and implementing a Gender Equality Policy Framework. However, there was a shift in the balance of members of the gender commission in favour of more conservative groups such as the National Women's League (婦聯會) and conservative groups began more open challenges to gender equality education programmes.[51] A key battle ground became the issue of LGBT rights, a topic I will return to in Chapter 11.

Despite these reservations about the state of Taiwan's women's movement, overall it is a remarkable success story. The efforts of this movement have transformed gender-related legislation and social values, contributing to making Taiwan arguably one of the most gender-equal societies in Asia if not the world. In fact, according to Taiwan's government in 2014, the island ranked as the world's fifth best performing state on the Gender Inequality Index, only being surpassed by the Netherlands, Denmark, Switzerland and Sweden.[52] When I was asked on the BBC radio show *Women's Hour* why Taiwan has been more successful at promoting gender equality than its East Asian neighbours such as Japan or Korea, my immediate answer was to credit its women's movement.

Labour movement

The KMT's extreme fear of communism partly explains why socialist or labour movements developed later than the religious or women's movement. However, late in the martial law era, both political and economic changes created a window of opportunity for a labour movement to emerge. Ho has shown how the rise of private industry from the 1960s created abundant opportunities for state-owned enterprise workers to moonlight. This served to make these workers far less reliant on the clientelistic controls of the KMT and no longer a source of KMT iron votes.[53] Similarly, the shift to soft authoritarianism did create some space for labour activism.

After decades of successfully controlling the labour sector, the late 1980s saw a sudden rise in labour activism. This is clear from the comments of the Council of Labour Affairs Director in 1989. 'We never heard such expressions as "the rise of labor consciousness" or "strike" until two years ago.'[54] This new rising movement employed a number of core methods in its initial period. Ho terms one of these the 'unionizing strategy'.[55] In other words, activists tried to create new unions in the private sector where KMT unions had not been established or to take over existing pro-KMT unions. Although there was limited scope for labour unionizing in family-run small and medium-sized enterprises, there were opportunities in larger private enterprises that had kept KMT-run unions out in the past. We can see how this strategy was bearing fruit from the increase in industrial unions from 1,160 in 1987 to a peak of 1,354 by 1990.[56] Ho shows how. in the late 1980s, anti-KMT workers took control of the Taiwan Petroleum Workers' Union in the China Petroleum Corporation's Kaohsiung refinery by beating KMT loyalists in union elections.[57] Through into the early 1990s, the KMT party branch and refinery management attempted to defeat independent unionism in internal elections. However, by the late 1990s, the KMT branches and affiliated offices had either been removed or become powerless. Ho reports how in the 1999 Taiwan Petroleum Workers' Union elections the independent union activist won all 33 seats, while the KMT no longer even nominated a slate of candidates.[58] In addition, unions attempted to create cross-union alliances to increase effectiveness. For instance, in May 1988 the National Federation of Independent Trade Unions was established and accepted as a member of the World Federation of Labour. However, it was not until 12 years and after the fall of the KMT in 2000 that an independent union federation gained legal recognition under the title Taiwan Confederation of Trade Unions (TCTU).[59]

Another dimension of the movement was to contest elections through its own political parties. Although some individual DPP politicians have worked with labour activists, the party as a whole was trying to be a catch-all party and in order to attract corporate donations it wanted to avoid an anti-business image. Thus, the DPP's ambiguous stance on labour activism encouraged activists to establish the Labour Party (*gongdang*) in 1987 and the Workers' Party (*laodongdang*) in 1989. For example, the Labour Party founder Wang I-hsiung had originally been elected as a DPP legislator. However, both socialist parties were electoral flops, and after the early 1990s they ceased nominating election candidates. At a time when the KMT party machine was still strong and the DPP was still expanding rapidly, these labour parties failed to make headway.

In the transition period, the KMT and big business attempted a series of initiatives to challenge the rising labour movement. During the early 1990s, greater numbers of businesses began relocating production to lower labour cost locations such as South East Asia and mainland China, leading to large-scale redundancies of unionized workers. Also, there was increased resistance to unionization within the private sector – for instance, in the electronics sector. The KMT also encouraged the police to suppress worker protests harshly. One such case was police suppression of a strike at the Far Eastern Chemical Fibre Company in 1989.[60] Moreover, at a time when Taiwan was politically liberalizing, labour activists received very severe prison sentences.[61] Therefore, economic and political changes have contributed to the decline in the numbers of industrial unions and union members since the early 1990s. In 1990, there were 1,354 unions, with almost 700,000 members. By 2000, this had fallen to 1,128 unions and 588,832 members, and in 2008 to only 959 unions and 523,289 members.[62]

The KMT also began initiating a series of legislative measures to control organized labour and protect its business allies. For instance, one way of undermining labour was to legalize the importation of overseas contract labour from 1992.[63] These workers were not unionized and could easily be fired and thus eroded labour's trump card of a labour shortage. In the early 1990s, Ho notes how the KMT planned to 'further restrict legal protection of labor rights by revising the Labor Union Law, the Labor Dispute Law and Labor Standard Law in a way designed to favour management'.[64] In the early to mid-1990s, the labour movement had to adjust its tactics to try to defend labour rights against these KMT pro-business policies. It worked together with the DPP to block these new proposed bills. However, the labour movement did not make any significant legal gains in the 1990s, leading Ho to describe it as its 'lost decade'.[65]

The KMT continued to try to use the Chinese Federation of Labour as a key mobilizing tool and thus blocked the legal recognition of a rival national union body. However, labour activists worked together with local executives to establish independent local union federations at the city or county level. By 2000, eight such local federations had been created, six of which were in DPP-run administrative districts. The KMT continued to resist recognizing a national independent rival to the Chinese Federation of Labour, but by 2000 the tide had turned as the Chinese Federation of Labour was facing financial difficulties and unions were withdrawing from it. The changed political climate was apparent in the 2000 presidential election, with the DPP and James Soong supporting legalization of an independent union federation and even the KMT's Lien not opposing the idea.[66]

The election of the DPP's Chen Shui-bian seemed to mark the start of a new era for independent unionism and a final nail in the coffin of KMT corporatism in the industrial sector. Back in 1988, Chen already had close links with labour activists, offering them legal advice.[67] In Chen's first term, the labour movement had a number of important achievements. In May 2000, Chen attended the official founding ceremony of the TCTU and it received legal recognition four months later. It had also worked together with women's groups in lobby for the Equal Employment Law. Other important legislative successes included the Protective Act for Mass Redundancy of Employees, the Protection for Workers Incurring Occupational Accidents Act and the Employment Insurance Act.[68] The latter two laws improved existing legislation by ensuring much wider coverage of unemployment insurance benefits and work injury compensation.

Another major change after 2000 was that for the first time, independent labour activists were given access to government decision-making processes. In the past, this privilege had been limited to the KMT's puppet unions. Ho cites the case of the veteran union activist Pai Cheng-hsien (白正憲), who was invited to join a series of government advisory bodies related to labour disputes, social welfare, the Council of Labour Affairs and pensions. The TCTU participation was also able to make sure that labour demands were heard at the 2001 Economic Development Advisory Conference, where, according to Ho, 'labour not only stymied most of the attempts by business to deregulate the current labour regime, but also placed its demands in the joint conclusion'.[69]

As we saw in the case of the women's movement, the post-2000 political environment also brought serious challenges for the labour movement. During the mid-1990s, the KMT had begun a process of privatizing certain state-owned enterprises, such as banks. In the 2000 presidential election, Chen Shui-bian had pledged to reconsider privatization policies. However, on coming to power, the DPP actually accelerated the process, privatizing the financial sector, Chunghwa Telecom, China Shipbuilding Corporation, Taiwan Machinery Company and Taiwan Motor Transport Corporation. Such measures were opposed by unions as their members tended to be laid off or suffer cuts in wages and work benefits. Although the DPP claimed that this policy was motivated by economic considerations, it had long viewed the state-owned sector as a hotbed of KMT networks, and thus hoped to undermine its rival's mobilization tool.

The KMT also hoped to revive its strength in the labour sector by appeals that were in stark contrast to its time in office. It began criticizing the DPP's privatization policies and the import of overseas labour, even though these had been KMT projects. In addition, it joined labour in fighting against the DPP administration in calling for lowering the working week to 42 hours.[70] In 2001, the KMT tried to appeal to workers by organizing a nationwide demonstration against high unemployment, health insurance fees and tuition. Lastly, it tried to revive the Chinese Federation of Labour union networks as a mobilization tool.

Ho argues that in the post-2000 era Taiwanese labour had political representation without a mass base. We can see this in the fall in the numbers of industrial unions and their members by 2008. Ho's fieldwork found other worrying signs for the state of independent unionism.[71] For instance, the TCTU became viewed by some as a puppet of the DPP, just like the Chinese Federation of Labour had been of the KMT. Similarly, as labour unions shifted their focus to national-level legislation, many workers felt they had become detached from the grassroots bread-and-butter concerns of workers. The TCTU suffered from financial problems due to member unions refusing to pay fees and some chose to leave the TCTU structure. In fact, like the Chinese Federation of Labour, the TCTU has become dependent on state subsidies. Thus, like the women's groups, this dependence undermines its ability to critique the state. Lastly, the TCTU suffered from increasingly intense internal factional power struggles between pro- and anti-DPP groupings. In a sign that the TCTU was striving to detach itself from the DPP, it chose not to back either presidential ticket in 2004 or 2008.

According to Chiu, the return to KMT rule represented a fresh challenge for the labour movement because 'Ma's economic and financial policies strongly favoured the capitalist class, in particular the large corporations and the business groups who invested in China'.[72] However, one important legal change for the labour movement came with the 2011 Trade Union Law. One of the causes of low union membership had been the restrictions on industrial unions, which had been company or factory based and required a minimum of 30 initiating members. The new law allowed for the creation of industrial unions that cut across workplaces. Chiu argues that since 2012 we have seen a resurgence of labour militancy in three core areas. First, new industrial unions have been established as a result of the new legislation with the aim of protecting previously non-unionized workers. For instance, the Taiwan Higher Education Union was established in 2012. A second trend has been increasing use of strike action. For instance, in 2015 and 2016 there were a number of high-profile and successful strikes involving staff at China Airlines. The third trend identified by Chiu was a return to electoral politics. One example of this was the alliance between a number of independent unions and the GPT/SDP in the 2016 election campaign and their nomination of a number of union leaders as candidates.

Environmental protection movements

Taiwan's economic record under martial law was remarkable, with rapid growth and growth with equity. One of the prices it paid for this economic miracle was serious environmental damage. We can get a taste of this in Linda Arrigo's article titled 'The Environmental Nightmare of the Economic Miracle'.[73] Arrigo describes how, on leaving an elegant coffee shop, she was assaulted by a whirl of grit and trash in the humid eddies of air, the noxious fumes of motorcycles, and the growl and honk of nearby traffic. The mounting nausea you feel when you cannot avoid eyeing slop spilled from restaurant pails left for pickup by pig farms, mounds of used Styrofoam bowls and drink cartons, mangy dogs rooting in the garbage heaps awaiting early morning collection, and scraps of rotting and rusting metal from long-abandoned carts. The unease you feel when you seek escape from the congested city center and find debris from construction sites egregiously scattered in supposedly scenic spots, and industrial and household waste piled up on every otherwise open piece of land, whether vacant lot or graveyard knoll. The choke and dry cough that becomes habitual after too many hours in stop-and-go city traffic, evenings of endless banquets with chain smokers, and nights in which the smoke of chemical emissions from faraway factories – venting illegally but with impunity under cover of darkness – seeps into your apartment, where you thought you were safe with your cool tiled floors and humming air conditioners.[74]

Arrigo's description corresponds with my own first impressions of Taiwan in the late 1980s and was the point when I first became aware of the importance of environmental protection.

Large numbers of environmental protests first occurred in the early 1980s. These early anti-pollution protests shared many similarities with cases in contemporary China and authoritarian-era South Korea. They tended to be localized in nature and focused on a specific case of environmental damage. Generally, the target of protests was a single factory or local government rather than the national government. Usually, protestors would first use petitioning, but even under martial law there were cases of direct action against polluters in the 1980s. These protests thus fit the commonly used term 'NIMBY' or 'not in my back yard' and could often be resolved through payment of compensation to be distributed by local politicians. The KMT government, with its economic growth-at-all-costs philosophy, tended to take the side of business in these disputes.

There was not yet any linkage between these early isolated protests and intellectuals who began raising environmental issues in the media. A key figure in this regard was Edgar Lin (林俊毅), widely known as the 'Father of the anti-nuclear movement'.[75] He began writing articles that were critical of Taipower's nuclear policy as early as 1979 and, like Annette Lu, Lin developed close ties with the *Tangwai* movement. Lin recalled how,

> During the 1970s, when the political consciousness began to emerge in Taiwan, we knew that we couldn't talk about practical politics, so the environment was a good cause. The environmental movement is a political movement. It was safe to use. A supposedly innocuous topic, but it could form the momentum for a political coalition. But at that time any critical articles about anything would cause a lot of tension.[76]

Even this kind of environmental advocacy in the media carried risks, and by the mid-1980s Lin was pressured to leave the country to avoid arrest and then put on the blacklist from returning to Taiwan. Nevertheless, environmental issues were beginning to gain more attention in the parliaments by the mid-1980s, particularly from Taiwan-elected politicians. For instance, in April 1985, 61 KMT and *Tangwai* legislators signed a petition against the proposed construction of the Fourth Nuclear Power Station.[77]

Emergence of a grassroots environmental movement

The final four years of the 1980s saw the emergence of a grassroots environmental move-ment. A key moment in this process was known as the Lukang Rebellion of 1986–7.[78] A series of well-organized protests were held at the Changhua County historical town of Lukang against a proposed Du Pont titanium dioxide plant. If it had gone ahead, it would have been Taiwan's largest single foreign investment project, and so had very strong central government backing. The protests received support from politicians from the newly established DPP in the late 1986 elections. In fact, the alliance between the environmental movement and the DPP would become the closest of all the social move-ments. For the first time, an environmental protest received extensive media attention. There had been concerns that the central government would suppress the protests, but finally Du Pont decided to withdraw the proposal.

Following the Lukang victory, the numbers of environmental protests skyrocketed, and the movement's DPP ties became closer. For instance, Kaohsiung DPP city coun-cillor Chu Hsing-yu staged a hunger strike as part of protests against Taiwan Cement's emissions. The first national environmental organization, the Taiwan Environmental Protection Union (TEPU), was established in 1987. It rapidly expanded into a nationwide body, with local chapters throughout the island and a large grassroots membership. The TEPU has since played a critical role in organizing protests, lobbying the Environmen-tal Protection Administration and conducting environmental research investigations. The relationship between the DPP and TEPU has been intimate since its establishment. The dependence was more than just financial. As Ho notes, 'some DPP politicians were also TEPU members and not a few local branches were managed directly by them. In some places, the DPP politicians' offices and local TEPU branches shared the same floor and even were staffed by the same workers.'[79]

One of the most vigorous grassroots arms of the environmental movement has been the anti-nuclear campaign. This also made a transition from an elitist movement to one with an active grassroots base and political party ties in this period. Taipei-based academics and student activists worked together with the local town of Gongliao in Taipei County, where Taipower planned to locate its Fourth Nuclear Power station. They created the Yenliao Anti-Nuclear Self-defence Association in March 1988. The moving story of this grassroots movement is told in the documentary *How are You, GongLiao? (gongliao nihaoma?)*. Anti-nuclear campaigning has been a mainstay of the TEPU, with it launching in 1988 the first of what has become an annual anti-nuclear demonstration in Taipei. This was resoundingly backed by the DPP, with an anti-nuclear stance in its party charter and its legislators leading the way in attacking the Fourth Nuclear Power Station budget in the Legislative Yuan in the 1990s. In the mid to late 1990s, DPP local executives in Taipei City, Yilan and Taipei Counties conducted referendums on the Fourth Nuclear Power Station, in which clear majorities opposed the scheme. In Taipei County, the DPP local executive You Ching (尤清) tried administrative means to block the project, such as refusing a construction licence.

The KMT responded in a number of ways to this challenge of a DPP-allied environ-mental movement. First, it established the Environmental Protection Administration in 1987 along with a system for routinizing environmental impact assessments. There were increased local government efforts at raising recycling levels, although as Arrigo notes, some of these were designed as political patronage for pro-KMT local factions and reported quantities of recycled waste were often faked.[80] The close DPP–environmental movement links also served to politicize the issue and thus fewer KMT politicians were prepared to openly oppose nuclear power in the Legislative Yuan from the early 1990s. After 1990, the new Premier Hau Pei-tsun attempted to crack down on environmental as well as labour activists, or what he called 'hooligans' (*liumang*).

The new atmosphere was apparent from the manner Hau tried to revive the stalled Fourth Nuclear Power Plant project in 1991. The Yenliao Anti-Nuclear Self-Defence Association responded by barricading the construction site. However, the police took more forceful actions to dismantle the barricade, leading to a violent clash with protestors. In the confusion of the clashes, one policeman was accidently killed by Lin Shun-yuan (林順源), the young driver of a protest truck. The judiciary and police responded in a manner reminiscent of martial law terror. Large numbers of protestors were rounded up and 17 found guilty by courts, including a life sentence for Lin.

In the mid to late 1990s, some cracks appeared in the environmental movement's alliance with the DPP. In May 1996, the DPP joined forces with the NP and some rebel KMT politicians to pass a bill to terminate all nuclear plants under construction. However, when the government asked the Legislative Yuan to reconsider the bill four months later, the anti-nuclear alliance in the Legislative Yuan had weakened. Although the DPP claimed to be still opposing the Fourth Nuclear Power Station, it secretly 'traded the nuclear bill for other concessions from the KMT'.[81] When anti-nuclear protestors outside parliament discovered they had been betrayed, they angrily blamed the DPP legislators.

Similar divisions were also visible in 1997–8 when the DPP magistrate for Taichung County joined environmental activists in opposing a proposed Bayer US$1.7 billion chemical plant. Liao Yung-lai (廖永來), proposed a local referendum on the project and eventually Bayer chose to locate the factory in Texas. The DPP central party leadership actually came out against Liao, hoping to avoid the anti-business image. In a sign of growing dissatisfaction with the DPP's environmental credentials, the Green Party was formed in 1996 by anti-nuclear veteran Kao Cheng-yan (高成炎). Since then, the Green Party has consistently nominated candidates for local and national elections. However, like the labour-oriented parties, the Green Party has had little success and also failed to persuade other stars of the anti-nuclear movement, such as Chang Kuo-long (張國龍) and Edgar Lin, to join.

The 2000 presidential election raised hopes of many environmental activists. During the campaign, Chen had taken clear stands against both the Fourth Nuclear Power Station and the Meinong dam. During the DPP administration it appointed key environmental activists as Environmental Protection Administration Directors, including Edgar Lin (2000–1) and Chang Kuo-long (2005–7). There was also much greater access for environmental activists to government officials and the policy-making process than in the past. Both the Meinong dam and the Bin-nan industrial zone were put on hold. Chen regularly stressed sustainable development and the profile of the National Council for Sustainable Development was increased. Another eye-catching measure was the ban on free plastic bags being supplied by retailers, something not achieved in the UK until 2015. The residents of Gongliao were also delighted to hear Premier Chang Chun-hsiung (張俊雄) announce the halting of construction of the Fourth Nuclear Power Station in October 2000. Another environmental success DPP supporters like to cite is the clean-up of Kaohsiung's Love River, which when I first visited Kaohsiung was black and stank of pollution. Today, fish can be seen, and it is now lined with open-air coffee shops and tourist boats.

Nevertheless, the period was one of continued disappointment and frustration for the environmental movement. First, the DPP government was forced to backtrack on the

Fourth Nuclear Power Station and ordered construction to continue. The KMT had been joined by the other splinter Blue parties in opposing halting construction, threatening to impeach the president. We should recall that in the 1990s the NP had taken an anti-nuclear position, but changed party politics had further politicized the issue. Arrigo and Puleston suggest that another factor was that Chen exchanged the Fourth Nuclear Power Station for support from Lee Teng-hui's new TSU.[82] Although some continued to oppose nuclear power in the DPP, they became increasingly isolated. For instance, former DPP Chairman Lin I-hsiung organized a series of events for the Association for Promoting a Public Vote on Fourth Nuclear Power Station in the post-2000 period. However, the DPP did not try to make the issue the subject of a national referendum, as once again it revealed that environmental issues were not its top priority.

Another environmental setback came in 2003 when Chen's bid to create the Makao National Park was also defeated in the Legislative Yuan. The DPP showed its lack of environmental commitment in the Economic Development Conference of 2001. The DPP promised to respond to business complaints about speeding up the Environmental Impact Assessment procedure. In fact, Chen called Environmental Impact Assessments a road-block to economic development and offered to 'kneel down to the Environmental Impact Assessment reviewers on behalf of business'.[83] Similarly, in 2007 the Vice Premier Tsai Ing-wen (蔡英文) intervened on behalf of Formosa Plastic Group's steel plant proposal which was being challenged by the Environmental Impact Assessment Review Committee. This pro-business shift was apparent in how the DPP administration dismissed a number of active environmentalists from the Environmental Impact Assessment Review Committee in 2007, sparking off new protests.[84] That year, Chang Kuo-long also resigned as Environment Protection Administration Director. His wife explained the decision to the press:

> President Chen [Shui-bian (陳水扁)] has already said that concern for the environment cannot become a hurdle for economic development. This made it impossible for my husband to continue to serve in his present capacity . . . Chang is a man of action and does not covet high office. He will not sacrifice his beliefs for the sake of economic development.[85]

So how can we explain the limited impact of the environmental movement while its ally the DPP was in power through to 2008? First, there were limits to what the DPP could achieve as it never won a legislative majority. Thus, in the antagonistic political climate, environmental issues also became politicized, and many DPP pro-environment measures were defeated. Second, although the DPP is generally more concerned about environmental issues than the KMT, green issues, like gender equality matters, are always secondary – something that can be sacrificed if necessary. The DPP is also reliant on business donations and needed to avoid an anti-business image. On the nuclear power issue, the DPP also faced pressure from the US, as major contracts for US firms were at risk if the Fourth Nuclear Power Station really had been abandoned.[86] Increasingly, the environmental movement, like its labour counterparts, also faced a business counter-movement. We saw this in the business attempts at the Economic Development Conference to water down Environmental Impact Assessments, but also there were other business protests against banning disposable bags and food utensils, and attempts to reduce river water pollution in southern Taiwan met severe resistance from pig farmers and illegal scrap-metal refineries. Ho also suggests a convincing structural explanation for the

DPP's failures in environmental protection, as reduced state capacity limited both its ability to deliver pro-environmental policies and resist business counter-mobilization.[87] This is a useful framework that we can consider for other social movements, such as the women's and labour movements. Lastly, like other social movements, the environmental movement also lacked a strong mass base and suffered from loss of its human resources, as many leaders and activists were recruited into government.

The return to power of the KMT in 2008 represented numerous challenges for the environmental movement. Its earlier long-term alliance with the DPP meant that under Ma environmentalists were no longer welcome in governing circles. Ma also adopted an even more aggressive economic growth philosophy and openly supported the completion and operation of the controversial Fourth Nuclear Power Station. Politically, the environmental movement had also been weakened as not only had its ally (DPP) lost power, but also the relationship with the DPP had broken down in the latter part of the Chen era. The politicization of environmental issues under the DPP contributed to the more conservative KMT stance. According to Ho, critics of the new government's environmental policy were intimidated, and he reported how he was phoned by the Environmental Protection Administration to express concerns over one of his newspaper articles.[88]

Despite the obvious challenges to the environmental movement since 2008, there have been significant achievements. As discussed in Chapter 6, the GPT grew to become a potential relevant party for the first time. A sign of its potential was that two of its former leaders were recruited as legislators by the DPP in 2016. Environmental groups make up a significant component of the resurgence of social movements in the post-2008 period. The most noteworthy environmental success of Ma's first term was the government's decision to drop the planned Kuokuang petrochemical project in Changhua in 2011.[89] In this case, there had originally been strong local and national government support and even the DPP was not part of the original opposition campaign. However, opponents were able to develop a very broad coalition of environmental and local groups that successfully pressured the government to back down.

The other major success for environmentalism came in Ma's second term. This was the mothballing of the Fourth Nuclear Power Station in 2014.[90] Even before Ma came to power in 2008, it appeared inevitable that the power station would be completed and start operation. The Fukushima nuclear disaster in Japan did have an effect on public opinion, but it did not lead to an immediate government change of heart. In the 2012 election, while the DPP called for a nuclear-free homeland, the KMT pledged it would complete the Fourth Nuclear Power Station and gradually phase out the older plants. Although the issue did not derail Ma's re-election, it was clear that by early 2013 the public and political mood had changed. For much of that year there was intense debate about the proposal to hold a national referendum to decide the fate of the power station. The final moment that the plant was mothballed, though, came in April 2014 in the immediate aftermath of the Sunflower occupation. By this time the KMT itself was deeply divided over the issue and in the light of a new series of anti-nuclear protests and Lin Yi-hsiung's hunger strike, the government announced its decision on 27 April 2014.

Now the DPP has returned to power it will be interesting to see whether it will be more successful at developing sustainable developmental policies than the previous DPP government. One such test case will be whether it can resolve the controversial problem of removing the nuclear waste site on the indigenous Lanyu Island.

Despite the disappointments of the environmental movement under democracy, there has been enormous progress. When I read Arrigo's description of the Taiwanese environmental nightmare to my (then) teenage son, it did not really tally with his experience of living in Taiwan in the post-2000 period. Nowhere is this more apparent than in the major cities, which are much more liveable as a result of metro systems, factory relocation away from Taiwan to China and changed waste-treatment policies. Four decades of environmental activism have transformed the environmental conscious-ness on Taiwan. This has meant that politicians from all parties try to look green, even those from the KMT camp. While Ma was Taipei mayor, he tried to cultivate a green image, with the continued development of the metro system and bicycle trails throughout the city and implementing the mandatory recycling programme. When I tell the story of Taiwan's movement to British anti-nuclear audiences, they are often impressed and envious of its success. In contrast, Taiwanese environmentalists are often surprised to hear how little public reaction there was to the UK Government's decision to promote a new generation of nuclear power stations.

Student movements

At a time when the *Tangwai* was beginning to openly challenge the KMT in the late 1970s and early 1980s, KMT control of the university campuses remained as strong as ever. From the early 1980s, however, an embryonic student movement began to emerge from this constrained environment. Initially, a small group of NTU students began to challenge KMT domination through existing campus associations and publications. Their central demand was popular election of student government. One of their riskiest projects was producing and distributing flyers about the 2–28 Incident on campuses in early 1983 and hanging a banner outside the house of the KMT general responsible for the killings in Kaohsiung, stating, 'The blood of February 28 is on Peng Meng-chi's hands.'[91] Such campaigns had to be conducted with the utmost secrecy. As one activist recalled:

> At the very start, we only dared to sneak into classrooms in the very early morning and write "popular elections" (*pu xuan*) on the blackboard; [also,] in the middle of the night, [we would] distribute pamphlets on campus advocating a popular election.[92]

The KMT, via university authorities, worked to curtail this movement and its demands. Student activists received demerits as punishment and reformist publications were closed down. In May 1985, a famous student activist at NTU, Lee Wen-chung (李文忠), was refused permission to register for classes and then summarily called up for immediate military service.[93] Lee's supporters were warned that any further protests would result in their expulsion. In 1986, when NTU closed *University News* for a year and punished its leaders, the publication prepared to hold a protest meeting. The school wrote to students' parents warning that 'if your child speaks they will definitely be punished'.[94] However, NTU students became increasingly defiant, holding marches, distributing pamphlets and even submitting a petition to the Legislative Yuan. Despite resistance from authorities, the students finally achieved popular election in May 1987, with the reformist candidate Lo Wen-chia winning election.

Following the lead of NTU, student activism spread through campuses throughout Taiwan, and by mid 1988 most had adopted popular election. In addition, inter-univer-sity student alliances began to develop, focusing both on reform of university law and also on establishing links with other social and political movements. In September 1989, Taipei held the largest student demonstration to date, with over 2,000 participants calling for campus liberalization. However, in a sign that the KMT was still sensitive to student dissidence, many participants were interrogated by university officials on returning to their campuses and some were punished.[95]

The next year, in the run-up to the last indirect presidential election of 21 March, the most famous episode of the student movement took place. This became known as the Month of March or Wild Lily Movement. First, on 14 March, a group of NTU students unfurled banners with four demands near the KMT party headquarters: (1) to re-elect the National Assembly, (2) to abolish the old constitution, (3) to present a schedule for political reform and (4) to convene a National Affairs Conference to discuss such reform.[96] Student protestors began their sit-in at Chiang Kai-shek Memorial on 16 March and over the next few days their numbers grew and also received much support from Taipei residents, their professors and DPP politicians. This time, President Lee chose to talk to the students rather than crack down on them and held a long exchange of views with them at his office, promising to hold a National Affairs Conference to discuss political reform. In this way, the student movement contributed towards the conference that set the blueprint for political reform for the next five years.

Having achieved its central goal, the students thus withdrew from the square, but this was not the end of the student movement. Its activists returned to campuses to be leading figures in student government, working to accelerate the undermining of KMT campus domination. Many of these activists were later to continue activism in other social movements or even to join political parties and stand as candidates. For instance, Lo Wen-chia worked for years as a campaign manager for Chen Shui-bian and later both Lo and Lee Wen-chung became DPP legislators.

From the Wild Strawberries to the Sunflowers

By the Chen Shui-bian presidency, campuses had gained the image of being increasingly apolitical. Some of the first-generation student activists I spoke to talked of a generation gap between themselves and the new student cohort. This began to change in the second Chen administration. Some student and academic groups echoed the calls for Chen Shui-bian's resignation for political corruption in 2006 and were also involved in the protests to protect the historic Losheng sanatorium.

The scale of the student movement saw a significant rise following the next change of ruling parties in 2008. The first notable case was the protest movement known as the Wild Strawberry Movement. This emerged as a result of harsh police treatment of demonstrations protesting against the PRC ARATS envoy Chen Yunlin (陳雲林) in November 2008. The Wild Strawberries had the following core demands: (1) Apologies from the President and Premier, (2) resignation of police chiefs responsible for police violence and (3) liberalization of the Parade and Assembly Law.[97] Their tactics included sit-ins at Chiang Kai-shek Memorial Hall and live webcasts of their protests. Readers can gain a sense of the rise and fall of this movement in Jiang Wei-hua's (江偉華) remarkable documentary *The Right Thing* (廣場). At the time, the movement was seen as having failed as Ma's government did not respond to any of the core demands and in December the occupation ended. However, it would have long-term consequences. Many of the original activists went on to join the subsequent social movements of the period. Subsequent movements built on the Wild Strawberry experience of using the Internet and social media as effective mobilization and communication tools.[98] Third, most of the subsequent movements followed the model of keeping autonomy from the mainstream political parties. Lastly, the way the government responded to protests by dismissing or ignoring demands and employing tough police treatment would be a common feature of the Ma era.

For the rest of the Ma era, students would play a leading role in a wide range of influential social movements. Increasingly, student groups worked in alliances with new and existing civil society groups. An important subsequent case was the 2012–13 Anti-Media Monopoly Movement.[99] In this case, we see an alliance of students, journalists and academics working against the attempt by the Want Want China Times Group to monopolize Taiwan's media scene, but also to promote a legal framework that would create a more diverse and democratic Taiwanese media. As with the Wild Strawberries there was both a China factor and democratic crisis element to this movement. The owner of the Want Want group has brought a pro CCP and pro-unification discourse into Taiwan's media scene and thus could be seen as a part of the PRC's United Front programme to unify Taiwan. In addition to protests in Taiwan, the Anti-Media Monopoly Movement was able to mobilize large numbers of protesters abroad. Eventually, Want Want's acquisition bids failed. However, despite positive pledges, the ruling KMT did not allow passage of the draft anti-media monopoly legislation. The movement also contributed to the rise of key student leaders such as Lin Fei-fan (林飛帆) and Chen Wei-ting (陳為廷).

When I try to persuade students at my university to study Taiwanese politics, one of my methods is to cite the example of the 2014 Sunflower Movement.[100] The fact that students could occupy Taiwan's parliamentary debating chamber for over three weeks and push government to make a major policy shift often impresses students in London. The movement is a perfect place to start when discussing the role of civil society after democratic transition. Students have made the case for the Sunflowers as promoting Taiwan's democratic consolidation, while others have argued that it undermined a democratically elected government. One thing we should highlight here is that the Sunflower Movement was not just a student movement, but a very broad alliance of student groups and civil society actors.[101] Hsu's study reveals the diversity of the movement's member organizations and the different motivating factors that kept the movement together.

The Sunflower Movement emerged in response to the attempt by the Ma administration to force through ratification of the Cross-Strait Services Trade Agreement. Although it began as a protest involving just a few hundred people, it would grow into one of the largest ever protests in Taiwan's history. It includes both the occupation of the Legislative Yuan but also the surrounding streets, as well as protests throughout Taiwan. The movement's core demands were to reject the Cross-Strait Services Trade Agreement and for new legislation that would supervise future Cross-Strait agreements. In terms of substantive effects, the movement had a mixed record. Eventually, occupation ended after the Legislative Yuan speaker announced that the Cross-Strait Services Trade Agreement would not be reviewed until the supervision legislation had been passed. However, at the time of writing, this legislation has yet to be passed, even after the DPP returned to power in 2016. The level of support shown in the large support demonstrations as well as public opinion surveys should also be viewed as a mark of success, especially when we consider that the movement's use of occupations of government buildings was something new and radical.

Nevertheless, the Sunflower Movement did have an enormous effect of Taiwan's politics. A social movement rather than the opposition party had been able to halt the process of integration with China. The movement served to boost the fortunes of a wide range of progressive issues such as the anti-nuclear movement, LGBT rights and the cause of constitutional reform. Politically, the movement seriously undermined the support base of the KMT as it suffered disastrous electoral defeats in 2014 and 2016. It also had a major effect on the DPP as it embraced many social movement issues in 2016 and nominated numerous social movement activists as its candidates. As we discussed earlier, the movement also served to boost the fortunes of a third force in Taiwanese politics, with the best example the success of the NPP in 2016.

A number of factors can help us understand the success of the Sunflowers. In the first place, the very broad alliance of actors involved was critical in making such a long occupation possible. Unlike the Wild Strawberry case, the Sunflower Movement had a more effective decision-making system and it created star leaders. The movement's communication methods in both traditional and new media were also highly effective in maintaining domestic support, but also in gaining international media attention. The movement leaders were also able to frame their actions in a way that allowed it to appeal to different audiences. The focus on protecting democracy and Taiwan's way of life was important in this appeal. Although there was a China factor in the movement, the appeals generally were not framed as being anti-Chinese. Instead, the potential threat of the PRC to Taiwan's democracy was highlighted. Contextual factors also helped. For instance, by 2014 Ma's government had lost popularity and public opinion had become more conservative on further economic or political integration with China. The protestors were also able to take advantage of the changing media environment, as the rise of social media played a critical role in the movement's communication and mobilization. Lastly, divisions within the ruling KMT were critical in the movement's ultimate success. It was able to take advantage of the KMT's power struggle between Ma and legislative speaker Wang Jin-pyng. Thus, Wang was able to prevent a forceful police eviction of the protestors from parliament and it was Wang who made the announcement on not reviewing CSSTA until supervision legislation was in place.

Conclusions

Since the late 1970s, Taiwan has gone from being a KMT-dominated society with almost no space for independent associational life, to one of the most diverse civil societies in Asia. That Taiwan hosts the largest annual gay pride parade in Asia is the perfect reflection of this diversity. Of course, civil society still faces significant challenges. We saw this in the KMT's resistance to liberalizing the Parade and Assembly Laws and also how Taiwan's NGOs face harassment from the PRC on the world stage. Taiwan's social movements are central actors in this new civil society. They have an intimate relationship with the island's democracy. Social movements contributed to democratic transition, but also were given the space to develop as a result of democratization, which meant that political parties and civil societies developed a complex relationship of mutual dependence after transition. However, social movements have continued to play a key role of supervising political parties, sometimes supporting them and sometimes challenging them when they abandon their ideals. Social movements have also enriched Taiwan's democracy by ameliorating the failures of Taiwan's national identity and election-crazed parties. If the third force in Taiwan's party system does become more influential, it is likely to be a product of civil society rather than another mainstream party splinter. Critically important has been their ability to lobby government, parties and business to conduct progressive reforms, such as on gender equality or environmental protection. Lastly, we should not underestimate their educational role in transforming social norms. Social values have been transformed on human rights, gender equality, environmental protection and worker's rights. In short, social movement activists have contributed to what I think we should regard as a series of social miracles.

Discussion questions

1   How did the KMT use civic groups to control Taiwanese society?
2   Compare the impact and methods of Taiwan's main social movements.
3   How did social movements undermine KMT rule in the 1980s and 1990s?
4   How did the changes in ruling parties in 2000 or 2008 present challenges and opportunities to social movements?
5   Analyse the relationship between democracy and Taiwanese social movements.
6   Are we seeing a new type of social movement in the post-2008 period?
7   How can we measure social movement success?
8   What frameworks can explain social movement success or failure?
9   What are the future prospects for Taiwan's social movements?

Further reading

Fell, Dafydd (ed.). 2017. *Taiwan's Social Movements under Ma Ying-jeou From the Wild Strawberries to the Sunflowers*. Abingdon and New York: Routledge. This volume includes a diverse set of social movement case studies from the Ma Ying-jeou era.
Grano, Simona. 2016. *Environmental Governance in Taiwan*. London: Routledge. In this wonderful new book Grano examines the environmental movement by looking at four controversial cases studies from the Ma era.
Schubert, Gunter (ed.). 2016. *Routledge Handbook of Contemporary Taiwan*. London: Routledge. Chapters 16–20 offer broad historical overviews of key social movements.
Tsui, Shu-hsin (崔愫欣). 2004. *How are you: GongLiao?* This moving documentary on the community protest movement against the Fourth Nuclear Power Station brings to life the reality of what constitutes a social movement far better than any academic essay.

Notes

1   Ottaway, 'Civil Society', 122.
2   Centre for Civil Society, 'What is Civil Society?'. Available online at: www.lse.ac.uk/collections/CCS/what_is_civil_society.htm (accessed 18 March 2009).
3   Edwards, Michael (2005). Civil Society, the *Encyclopaedia of Informal Education*. Available online at: www. infed.org/association/civil_society.htm (accessed 8 November 2010).
4   Ibid.
5   Ibid.
6   McLean, *Oxford Concise Dictionary of Politics*, 458–9.
7   Grugel, *Democratization*, 36.
8   Diamond, 'Rethinking Civil Society: Towards Democratic Consolidation', 4–17.
9   Grugel, 95.
10   Selznick, *The Organizational Weapon*, 5.
11   Ho, 'The Rise and Fall of Leninist Control in Taiwan's industry', 162.
12   Schmitter, 'Still the Century of Corporatism?', 93–94.
13   Ibid., 25.
14   Tien, *The Great Transition*, 43. In correspondence with the author Ho Ming-sho pointed out that 'the official statistics on membership numbers was never reliable. Because the government did not keep updating the change annually, but simply added up the data from the time these organizations were established'.

15 Ho, 'Challenging State Corporatism', 107.
16 Ho, 'The Rise and Fall of Leninist Control in Taiwan's industry', 169.
17 Ibid., 170.
18 Ibid., 173.
19 Wright, 'Student Mobilization in Taiwan', 988.
20 Ibid.
21 Tien, *The Great Transition*, 63.
22 Ibid., 63.
23 Weller, 'Identity and Social Change in Taiwanese Religion', 350.
24 Shih, 'From Regulation and Rationalisation, to Production: Government Policy on Religion in Taiwan', 272.
25 Rubinstein, 'The Presbyterian Church in the Formation of Taiwan's Democratic Society, 1945– 2001', 160.
26 Ibid.
27 The text of these statements can be found at Presbyterian Church in Taiwan: Public Statements. Available at: http://english.pct.org.tw/enArticle_public_main.htm (accessed 28 November 2010).
28 Presbyterian Church in Taiwan, 'A Declaration of Human Rights by the Presbyterian Church in Taiwan', (16 August 1977). Available at: http://english.pct.org.tw/Article/enArticle_public_19770816.html (accessed 28 November 2010).
29 Rubinstein, 170.
30 Ong, 'A Formosan's View of the Formosan Independence Movement', 110.
31 Shu, 'Who Joined the Clandestine Political Organization?' 47–72.
32 Fan, 'Taiwan: No Civil Society, No Democracy', 167.
33 Ibid.
34 Hsiao, 'The Rise of Social Movements and Civil Protests', 59.
35 This movement fought for the right of return for Taiwanese that had been stranded in China after 1950.
36 The phrase 'shell-less snail' became a common way to refer to people unable to buy their own houses from the late 1980s.
37 Fan, 168.
38 Ibid., 176–7; *Ministry of Interior, Statistical Yearbook: Social Affairs*. Available online at: http://sowf.moi.gov.tw/stat/year/elist.htm (accessed 10 May 2017).
39 For a review of Lu's life story through to the late 1970s, see Rubinstein, 'Lu Hsiu-lien and the Origins of Taiwanese Feminism, 1944–1977', 244–76.
40 This initiative was not an unqualified success as many of the articles still reflected patriarchal values. For instance, abortion required permission from the women's father or husband.
41 Fan, 'The Women's Movement During Political Transformation', 156.
42 Ibid., 133–94, 150.
43 Fan and Wu, 'The long feminist march in Taiwan', 318.
44 Huang, 'Uneasy Alliance', 261.
45 Chang and Chang, '"Rosy Periwinkle": The Politics of the Licensed Prostitutes Movement in Taiwan'.
46 This popular practice is portrayed in the Public Television Service soap opera, *Don't Call Me Overseas Spouse Anymore* (*bie zai jiao wo waiji xinniang*).
47 Weng and Fell, 'The Rootless Movement: Taiwan's Women's Movement in the KMT and DPP Eras', 147–63.
48 Lin Fang-mei, 'Women's Movement and the Development of Civil Society in Taiwan', paper given at the Fifth European Association of Taiwan Studies Conference, March 2008, Prague.
49 Shih Chi-ching, quoted in Weng and Fell, 161.
50 Huang, 'Uneasy Alliance'.
51 Ibid.
52 This measure takes account of five indicators: maternal mortality ratio, adolescent fertility rate, the share of parliamentary seats, educational attainment (secondary level and above) for age 25 and over, and labour force participation rate. See www.gender-indicators.org.tw/zh-tw/equal/index (accessed 10 May 2017).
53 Ho, 175–6.

54 Quoted in Ho, 'Challenging State Corporatism', 113.
55 Ibid.
56 Ibid., 115.
57 Ho, 'Rise and Fall of Leninist Control in Taiwan's Industry', 176–8.
58 Ibid.
59 Ho, 'Challenging State Corporatism', 114.
60 Ibid.
61 Ibid.
62 Ibid., 115.
63 In fact, business had been using overseas labour since the late 1980s, but this legislation institutionalized the practice.
64 Ibid., 114–15.
65 Ho, 'Neo-Centrist Labour Policy in Practice', 131.
66 Ho, 'Challenging State Corporatism', 119.
67 Ho, 'Neo-Centrist Labour Policy in Practice', 129.
68 Ibid., 134–5.
69 Ibid., 136.
70 For a discussion of the working hours dispute, see Ho, 137–9.
71 Ho, 'Challenging State Corporatism', 123–6.
72 Chiu, 'Rising from the Ashes', 215.
73 Arrigo, 'The Environmental Nightmare of the Economic Miracle', 21–44.
74 Ibid.
75 Ho, 'The Politics of Anti-Nuclear Protest in Taiwan', 690.
76 Edgar Lin interview by author, London, 9 November 2005.
77 Ho, 692.
78 This case is discussed in detail in Reardon-Anderson, *Pollution, Politics and Foreign Investment in Taiwan.*
79 Ho, 695.
80 Arrigo and Puleston, 'The Environmental Movement in Taiwan after 2000', 167.
81 Ho, 702.
82 Arrigo and Puleston, 179.
83 Ho, 'Weakened State and Social Movement', 350.
84 Sandy Ku, 'Environmentalists Protest in front of the Environmental Protection Administration's Taipei Office', *China Post,* 20 July 2007.
85 Shelley Shan, 'Newsmaker: EPA Chief Goes out Fighting', *Taipei Times,* 22 May 2007, 2.
86 Arrigo and Puleston, 178.
87 Ho, 'Weakened State and Social Movement', 339–352
88 Ho, 'Understanding the Trajectory of Social Movements in Taiwan (1980–2010)', 17.
89 Grano, *Environmental Governance in Taiwan*, 92–117.
90 Grano, *Environmental Governance in Taiwan*, 60–91.
91 Wright, 'Student Mobilization in Taiwan: Civil Society and its Discontents', 993.
92 Ibid., 993.
93 Ibid., 995–6.
94 Ibid., 998.
95 Ibid., 1004.
96 Ibid., 1005.
97 For more details about the Wild Strawberries, see http://taiwanstudentmovement2008.blogspot.com/ (accessed 10 May 2017).
98 Hsiao, 'Virtual ecologies, mobilization and democratic groups without leaders'.
99 Ebsworth, 'Not Waning Wang: The Anti-Media Monopoly Movement in Taiwan'.
100 For analysis of the Sunflower Movement, see Cole, *Black Island*; Beckershoff 'The Sunflower Movement'; Hsu, 'The China factor and Taiwan's civil society organizations in the Sunflower Movement'; Rowen, 'Inside the Sunflower Movement'; and my favourite documentary on the movement is *Sunflower Occupation* by the Taipei Documentary Film Union.
101 Hsu, 'The China factor and Taiwan's civil society organizations in the Sunflower Movement'.

11 Is democracy working in Taiwan?

Social welfare, political corruption and LGBT rights

In the aftermath of Taiwan's disputed 2004 presidential election, it became common to see the slogan 'Democracy is Dead in Taiwan' at Pan Blue rallies. After the KMT's 2008 return to power, many DPP supporters in turn complained of a return to authoritarian government practices. Even many outside observers who had been full of praise for Taiwan's democratization in the 1990s began to question the state of the island's democracy in the post-2000 period. Taiwan is not alone in this respect. After the optimism of the height of the Third Wave of democratization, there was stagnation in the number of new democratic transitions and concern about democratic reversals. The focus of democracy research became less on how to engineer transition and more towards how and why countries were unable to consolidate their democracies. A common complaint in new democracies is that though they offer reasonably fair and regular elections, they have failed to bring tangible improvement to the everyday lives of citizens. In many newly democratic countries there are signs of nostalgia for authoritarianism among older generations.

As discussed in Chapter 3, ideally in a democracy we would expect parties to take into account public opinion in designing policies or risk being rejected by voters in elections. Thus, one of the best ways to assess the quality of a country's democracy is its ability to resolve central issues that the public are concerned about. In this chapter I focus on how democracy has performed in dealing with three of Taiwan's most salient political issues: (1) social welfare, (2) political corruption and (3) LGBT rights. During the 1990s and post-2000 period, the first two issues received much attention from political parties during election campaigns. LGBT rights only became politically controversial recently in Taiwan, but this represents an important test for how democracy can deal with newly salient issues. Democracy represents one of the main differences between Taiwan and China and a core element in Taiwanese national identity. If Taiwan's democracy is unable to deal with the most salient political issues facing the country, then it is likely to undermine trust in its political system.

Why social welfare?

The *Oxford Dictionary of Politics* defines a welfare state as 'a system in which the government undertakes the main responsibility for providing for the social and economic security of the state's population.'[1] This therefore incorporates a wide range of welfare provisions, including pensions, social care, social housing, social security benefits and subsidized healthcare and insurance.

Social welfare is one of the most salient political issues, both in authoritarian and democratic states. Under Mao, the Chinese Communists employed extensive work unit welfare provisions as a tool to legitimize its rule in urban China. Similarly, in both authoritarian Taiwan and South Korea, the state used social welfare to reward pro-ruling party occupational groups. The influence of welfare systems is perhaps even greater in democracies. According to Richard Rose, 'most politicians believe that their continued electoral success depends on their ability to maintain or increase an already high level of state provision of welfare'.[2] Opinion polls in democracies consistently find welfare-related issues to be ranked by the public as the most or one of the most pressing issues facing the country. In the UK's Ipsos MORI polls over the last three decades, the National Health System has been one of the most salient issues, almost never out of the top five ranked issues by the public.[3] The quality of a country's welfare system has significant ramifications for its levels of social equality. For instance, there is a link between the extensive welfare state of Scandinavian countries and high levels of gender equality. Similarly, with today's growing income disparities, social welfare can potentially play a critical redistributive role in reducing social inequality. Once again, Scandinavian countries appear to offer the best levels of correlation between these variables, with their generous welfare state and small poverty gap.

Changing patterns in global politics have served to raise the salience of social welfare issues since the end of the Cold War. While other dimensions of the traditional left–right political cleavage, such as relations with the Soviet Union or nationalization, have faded away, the welfare state has become the core remaining left–right issue. This was reinforced by neoliberal efforts to promote welfare state retrenchment, such as those espoused under Reagan in the US and Thatcher in the UK. The issue's divisive potential has been revealed in the bitter disputes surrounding attempts to establish quite modest universal health insurance programmes in the US under the Clinton and Obama presidencies.

The heavy emphasis placed on social welfare by parties in electoral campaigns is closely related to the symbolic power of such issues on voters. This was exemplified in the much discussed UK Labour Party's party political broadcast from the 1992 General Election known as 'Jennifer's Ear'.[4] The spot shows the contrasting fates of two young girls requiring ear operations. While the one wealthy enough to afford private healthcare received immediate treatment, the one on the National Health Service had to endure the pain during months stuck on the long waiting list. We see similar emotional appeals in Taiwanese welfare advertisements. For instance, a 1998 KMT TV ad shows a baby undergoing a heart operation. Then the doctor explains how before Universal National Health Insurance (UNHI), many parents were unable to afford such operations and thus lost their children. Finally, we see a couple consoling each other, supposedly after suffering a pre-UNHI loss.

Taiwan's welfare system under martial law

Under martial law, the KMT government began implementing welfare programmes from the 1950s. Ku and Hsueh argue that this was the first of three golden decades of welfare development as the first social insurance programmes were established.[5] However, instead of universal coverage, these schemes were targeted at pro-KMT occupational groups. The two key beneficiaries of martial law welfare were the *jungongjiao* or military, civil service and education sector workers, and unionized workers from large state-owned enterprises. For the KMT, welfare provisions were a means to reward these occupational groups for political loyalty. Since Mainlanders made up a disproportionate number of workers in the *jungongjiao,* the martial law era welfare imbalance also contributed to a sense of ethnic injustice among many Taiwanese. In contrast to these privileged groups, the rest of the population was left to fend for themselves and their families when it came to medical treatment or old age and childcare. For Ku and Hsueh, the second golden decade was the 1970s, as this saw the first national policy guideline for welfare and an expansion of personal social services.[6] In the later years of martial law, there was a gradual expansion of the existing programmes. Thus, for instance, in the late 1970s Labour Insurance was opened up to workers in smaller firms of more than five employees, resulting in a doubling of those covered from 2.3 million in 1979 to 4.15 million in 1985.[7] These incremental expansions ensured that by 1994, 60 per cent of the population was covered by health insurance.

Nevertheless, there were still huge gaps and disparities in coverage and insurance premium levels between those under the *jungonjiao* schemes and those with standard Labour Insurance. Those under *jungongjiao* schemes had the best welfare provisions, with post-retirement pensions, lower premiums and even health insurance for dependents. Those on the Labour Insurance scheme could get a retirement lump sum payment, but this was half that received by government employees and meant losing their healthcare insurance. This meant that workers on the Labour Insurance programme were far less likely to take up the old age benefits than those on *jungongjiao* schemes. Thus, even among KMT-controlled groups there were large disparities. For the rest of society, children, unemployed and retired workers, those groups most likely to require medical care, were excluded from health insurance schemes. The imbalance of the system is clear from the fact that as late as 1991, 74 per cent of central government welfare expenditure went to the *jungongjiao.*[8]

Taiwan's martial law era welfare system had some core characteristics of what Gosta Esping-Anderson terms conservative welfare capitalism.[9] In other words, as in West Germany, social security schemes were occupationally based rather than universal, thus limiting their redistributive impact and tending to emphasize traditional family values. In fact, Taiwan's authoritarian welfare system also shared many similarities with other Asian cases, such as South Korea. Holliday has termed these cases as *productivist welfare capitalism,* which feature, 'a growth-oriented state and subordination of all aspects of state policy, including social policy, to economic/industrial objectives'.[10] Some writers even talk of the concept of an *Asian* or even *Confucian welfare state.*[11] The elites in these states tended to adopt a highly conservative ideology on welfare systems, viewing Western welfare states as economically wasteful and culturally inappropriate for Asian states. One Japanese writer talked of the dangers of succumbing to the 'British disease' of over-dependence on the welfare state.[12] Among both mass and elite, the idea of welfare as an entitlement was not widely accepted. Asian welfare states tended to feature low spending compared to Western states, with highly selective and contributory schemes rather than universal programs. Lastly, the Asian model featured a central welfare role for the family, while the state was principally a regulator rather than the main provider of services.

The standard framework for explaining welfare state system developments in Europe views welfare states as a consequence of changing balances of class power.[13] Cross-national studies show that the strength of independent labour unions and social democratic parties was especially important for welfare system expansion. In the Taiwan case, as in most Asian states, there has not been a strong leftist party or union movement. At least under martial law, societal or democratic explanations for welfare development are not very useful, as policy-making was largely insulated from societal pressures. In fact, even after the *Tangwai* began contesting elections in the late 1970s and early 1980s, it did not give welfare much attention. Thus, instead a state-centred approach is more fruitful for this period. This approach assumes that the state is the key agent of change in welfare policy. In short, under martial law the KMT state was able to dictate the content of welfare policy and mould this welfare system for its own political interests.

One useful way of thinking about social welfare in Taiwan is to picture it as a spectrum as listed below:

- Far right: government priority is economic growth, the main welfare provider is the family and the martial law welfare system that favours pro-KMT groups is sufficient.
- Centre-right: also prioritizes economics and the family first, although it supports limited expansion into broader contributory welfare schemes.
- Centre-left: calls for a broader or universal and equitable welfare state but not so generous as to require tax increases.
- Far left: Scandinavian-style welfare state: high taxes and a very comprehensive and generous welfare system.

For most of the martial law era we can safely place the KMT at the far right of this spectrum.

Social welfare under multi-party politics

During the transition period, welfare issues began to get more partisan attention. First, the *Tangwai* and then DPP began calling for pensions and universal health insurance from the mid-1980s. Initially, however, it was not a top-priority issue. For instance, in 1991 welfare did not feature in the DPP's top-ten issues in its newspaper advertising for the National Assembly elections.[14] Nevertheless, the KMT was beginning to feel pressured by this early welfare emphasis along with the rise of a labour movement and democratic challenge. Thus the KMT chose to try to steal or co-opt the DPP's appeal of UNHI. In 1986. Premier Yu Kuo-hua (俞國華) announced that UNHI would be introduced by 2000; two years later the start date was brought forward to 1995. The design and passage of the UNHI Bill revealed the KMT's continued political dominance. Essentially, the KMT and government bureaucrats at the Department of Health (DOH) dominated the design of the legislation as the process was largely insulated from interest groups or public opinion. Similarly, when the bill went to the Legislative Yuan in 1993–4, the KMT majority was large enough to ensure its smooth passage, with only limited amendments.

After its introduction in 1995, the UNHI was in many ways extremely successful and popular. Within three years, it reached 96.8 per cent coverage of the population and enjoyed a 70 per cent public satisfaction rate.[15] Each insured citizen carries a *jianbaoka* (UNHI card), which can be used in almost all public and private hospitals, private clinics and dentists. Even most Chinese medical establishments welcomed UNHI patients, allowing me to recover from frequent football injuries in time for the next match. Patients generally only need to pay nominal registration and medicine fees. The system works highly efficiently compared to the UK National Health Service, as almost all practitioners are part of the system. Thus, in Taiwan the waiting lists that plague our National Health Service are unheard of. Generally, there is no need to make an appointment to see a general practitioner, dentist or even a specialist. On one occasion, I saw a specialist without an appointment and then had the required operation within the week. I, not the hospital, chose the time and date I would go under the knife.

Under the UNHI, the former bewildering array of health insurance programmes was united under one single-pipe mechanism that is managed by the Bureau of National Health Insurance (BNHI). The BNHI is responsible for collecting insurance premiums and payments to the medical care providers.[16] Joseph Wong argues that the scheme was highly successful at promoting social economic equality, as the lower and middle-level income groups increased their medical care visits to a much greater extent than the most wealthy.[17] One study concluded that under the new UNHI, 'the poor pay less but get more, (and) the rich pay more but get less'.[18] This redistributive element was especially important at this moment in Taiwan's history, as after reaching quite impressive levels of income equality by the early 1980s, during the 1990s and post-2000 period the gap between rich and poor widened considerably. The standard way of measuring income inequality is the GINI index, for which in 1980 Taiwan's GINI index was 0.278, rising to 0.312 in 1990, 0.326 in 2000 and 0.345 in 2009.[19] The KMT's adoption of a universal UNHI reveals why it is hard to apply traditional Western left–right dimensions to Taiwan's party politics. As DPP legislator Chen Chi-mai (陳其邁) noted, 'The KMT is a rightist party, closer to your (British) Conservative Party, but it passed the UNHI, closer to your Labour Party.'[20]

Developments in the 1990s

As I showed in Chapters 5 and 6, social welfare became one of the most salient political issues of the 1990s. This was partly because the DPP was searching for a new set of issues to broaden its support base, but Liu's examination of election gazettes found that KMT candidates were as enthusiastic as their DPP counterparts in making welfare appeals.[21] Although both parties stressed welfare, the welfare sub-issues they focused on were slightly different.

The year in which welfare issues first received significant election attention was 1992. The DPP began using the slogan 'welfare state', listing this as one of the party's three major objectives for the future. But that year the KMT was actually more likely to stress welfare issues than the DPP, with six TV ads trumpeting its plans for an UNHI. Some KMT legislators even joined the DPP in talking about a welfare state.[22] The KMT would make its NHI programme one of its central election themes for the rest of the decade. The other welfare issue that was placed on the electoral agenda at this point was pensions or old age allowances. In Tainan County, DPP legislative candidate Su Huan-chih (蘇煥智) made this proposal. However, this did not have much impact beyond his constituency, and his call was not echoed by the DPP party centre.

If we consider the welfare spectrum outlined earlier, the DPP could be considered at the centre-left, based on its strong use of the welfare state slogan. Nevertheless, the party had not yet made it a core issue compared with democratization, national identity or even political corruption. The KMT was actually giving the issue more attention, and it moved from the far right to the centre-right during the transition period. This shift was best exemplified by its acceptance of UNHI. Ku and Hsueh reach similar conclusions on the relative positions of the main parties. They do this by reference to a comparison of the DPP's 1993 white paper on social welfare and the KMT government's 1994 Social Welfare Policy Guidelines. They conclude that the KMT's vision fits well the productivist welfare regime, while the DPP proposes a social democratic style welfare state.[23]

A key moment in the electoral politics of welfare issues came in the pensions debates of 1993–4. These would be critical in the development of distinct party images on welfare and for promoting old age care policies. This time, the DPP party centre and its candidates for local executive posts pledged that they would pay old age allowances if elected. DPP propaganda claimed that raising taxes would not be needed as pensions could be funded by cracking down upon KMT corruption.[24] Other advertisements justified DPP welfare expansion proposals by citing the unfair martial era welfare system and its ethnic bias. For instance, one DPP ad claimed that 'Actually Taiwan has the best welfare in the world, but only veterans enjoy it, while the Taiwanese are seen as slaves to provide for these people.'[25]

The KMT's response to the DPP playing the pensions card was largely negative. KMT candidates and the party centre alike condemned the DPP policy proposal. For instance, the Minister of Interior, Wu Po-hsiung, took the traditional position that 'The government advocates that the elderly people live with or near their sons and daughters, so that care will be close by and the elderly will enjoy the natural bonds and ethical relationships between members of their family.'[26] President Lee spoke the language of the person on the street saying, 'Making pension pledges but asking others to wipe their arse; this is not reasonable.'[27] Others, such as Lien Chan and James Soong, condemned pensions as a form of vote buying or argued that pensions would bankrupt the treasury. Once the elected DPP local executives took office in late 1993, their pensions pledges quickly hit difficulties, as the KMT-run central government refused to finance the campaign cheque. This meant that DPP local governments soon ran out of funds and had to stop or reduce old age payments within a matter of months. When the DPP again called for pensions in the 1994 campaign, the KMT responded with the slogan, 'DPP: Let me cheat you one more time.'[28] Overall, the NP tended to take a similar conservative attitude to welfare expansion, noting the party was opposed to 'vote buying style or free-spending social welfare'.[29] However, one new niche welfare dimension it did place on the agenda was greater care for disabled people.

As we move into the mid 1990s, the DPP broadened its welfare appeals to also incorporate women's welfare and childcare issues. For instance, one of its 1995 TV ads ended with the slogan, 'Women's Welfare State. Give Taiwan's Women the Chance of Happiness.'[30]

By the mid-1990s, cracks began to appear in the KMT's conservative position on old age allowances, as it was aware of the popularity of DPP-style pensions. In 1995, Welfare Allowance for Old Farmers was introduced, on a model similar to the DPP proposal of 1993–4. Like UNHI, this came just in time for the 1996 presidential election. The Executive Yuan also began researching the feasibility of a contributory national pension scheme. In October 1997, Lee Teng-hui even tried to steal the appeal of DPP-style pensions. At an election rally he pledged that if the KMT candidate in Taipei County was elected, everyone over 65 would receive an old age allowance of NT$5,000, even if they already received payments under other retirement schemes (such as *jungongjiao* or Labour Insurance).[31] The DPP tried to take advantage of this KMT U-turn by proposing a pensions bill in the legislature.

Nevertheless, Lee faced stiff resistance from welfare conservatives in the subsequent KMT party Central Standing Committee meeting. For instance, James Soong argued that a greater priority was to universalize running water, while Lien Chan preferred the contributory scheme under review in the Executive Yuan. The NP condemned Lee for breaking his earlier promise on pensions and instead proposed a filial subsidy to encourage three generations to live together. Lee was unable to overcome this internal resistance, and finally KMT and NP legislators combined to defeat the DPP pensions bill.

Only two years after the introduction of the UNHI, the KMT was beginning to get cold feet. The popularity of the scheme, such as rapid increases in outpatient visits, was leading to a depletion of the health insurance fund. In response, the DOH commissioned a study which recommended a new privatized and competitive multi-carrier system. Under the new scheme, all enrolled would receive the same basic healthcare services, but competing carriers could also offer additional health services for higher premiums. Thus, the new system threatened to erode the redistributive nature of the original scheme. The DOH scheme was introduced at the Legislative Yuan in early 1998. However, opposition from both DPP and KMT legislators ensured that it did not get beyond its first reading. Why would the KMT fail to pass its own bill despite having a legislative majority? Joseph Wong argues that the key factor was the remarkable coalition that emerged to oppose welfare retrenchment. This coalition included over 200 civic groups, incorporating medical professionals, labour unions and a range of social movements. This coalition was able to exert sufficient pressure on legislators to persuade them that it was in their own interests to kill the reform bill.[32]

The incident revealed the impact of democratization on policy-making, for it was no longer possible, as in the original introduction of UNHI, for the KMT to just impose its own policies on society. Now public opinion and interest groups needed to be consulted and engaged with. The state's policy-making could no longer be insulated from societal pressures. Democratic politics meant that welfare retrenchment was just too costly for the ruling party. DPP legislator Shen Fu-hsiung (沈富雄) explained the KMT's predicament, 'The government's biggest mistake was to make its first attempt at universal healthcare such a generous programme. It is impossible in a democracy to now convince people that what is best for them is to be less generous.'[33]

In the final two campaigns of the KMT era, the two main parties were back to their early 1990s' positions at the centre-left and centre-right of the welfare spectrum. The KMT was again mocking the DPP's failure to deliver on old age allowances, the financial irresponsibility of DPP-style pensions and promising to eventually introduce the contributory pensions scheme. In one of the 2000 presidential debates, Lien once again called DPP pensions 'policy vote buying'.[34] In 1998, this issue also featured heavily in its TV advertisements. One ad contrasted the KMT's success at implementing UNHI with the failure of the Clinton welfare programme. The KMT actually gave record emphasis to welfare issues in 2000, but the core focus was to trumpet its UNHI. For instance, one advertisement claimed: 'Even if you curse Lien Chan every day, you still carry Lien Chan's transcripts, the *jianbaoka* (UNHI) card.'[35] In contrast, the DPP's Chen Shui-bian offered voters one of the most extensive welfare packages in Taiwan's election history. First was the '333 Welfare Plan' of NT$3,000 pensions per month, free healthcare for the under-threes and 3 per cent first-time buyer mortgages. The second was the '555 Childcare Plan' that included provisions for more childcare workers and reducing women's childcare burden and domestic violence.

Electoral competition after the lifting of martial law contributed to a rapid expansion of welfare provisions in Taiwan. Particularly on healthcare, Taiwan had gone from a biased and narrow system of coverage, to a universal and redistributive scheme. During democratization, we can see this by the acceleration in the proportion of government spending on social welfare in this period shown in Table 11.1. From the democratic breakthrough year of 1986, when only 6.6 per cent of government spending went to social welfare, the figure had almost trebled by 2001. Thus, Lin and Chou note the 1990s gained the reputation as the 'golden decade of social welfare development'.[36]

Although both parties gave the issue quite heavy emphasis over the decade, it was the DPP that emerged with the reputation as the more pro-welfare state party. Party image surveys, which asked respondents to locate parties on a spectrum with one pole prioritizing economic growth and the other social welfare, placed the KMT on the side of the former and the DPP on the latter.[37] Similarly, surveys asking which party was best able to design a fair and reasonable welfare system showed far greater trust in the DPP than the NP or KMT.[38]

Social welfare after the first change of ruling parties

The DPP's welfare emphasis over the 1990s and its pro-welfare party image suggested that the election of Chen Shui-bian as president in 2000 would facilitate a more extensive welfare state. On coming to office, Chen did move to fulfil his welfare election pledges. Free healthcare for the under-threes began in 2001. In 2002, the Elderly Welfare Allowance Temporary Law was passed, offering those over 65 not covered by existing schemes NT$3,000 per month. This non-contributory scheme naturally placed a severe financial burden on the state. It was hoped that this would later be replaced by the national pensions scheme. To meet the problem of growing unemployment levels, the Employment Insurance Act was passed in 2002, giving six months' unemployment benefits and free UNHI premiums.

Nevertheless, many welfare scholars and social welfare activists became disappointed in the DPP government's welfare performance. Within his first year in office, Chen had stated that he placed priority on the economy over social welfare and that he planned to postpone many of his planned welfare programmes.[39] As with environmental issues, welfare is not a core ideological issue for the party and thus could be sacrificed. On coming to office, the DPP faced both severe difficulties being a minority party in the parliament and also with the financial challenges of the economic downturn. In fact, the DPP did often try to blame the KMT for its brutal slashing of welfare schemes in repeated TV elections advertisments during the DPP era. Table 11.1 shows the percentage of government expenditure on welfare and how welfare spending actually was quite stable between 1996 and 2011 and only rose again significantly in the second Ma term.

Compared to the 1990s, much of the post-2000 period featured reduced salience of welfare issues on the electoral agenda and a degree of partisan convergence on welfare. Content analysis of election TV and newspaper advertising shows that both parties were less interested in using welfare appeals than in the past.[40] Undoubtedly, this was related to the economic climate and that many core and costly welfare schemes were already in place. Another factor was the parties' increasing polarization on identity issues, which often served to narrow the issue agenda and drown out other concerns. But there was

Table 11.1 Proportion of government spending on social welfare

Year	1981	1986	1996	2001	2004	2008	2012	2015
%	3.9	6.6	15.7	17.5	15.4	15.7	20.2	20.1

Source: 'Net Expenditure on Social Welfare,' in 2016 Statistical Yearbook of the Republic of China (Taiwan). http://ebook.dgbas.gov.tw/public/Data/610281138403HCL2D3O.pdf (accessed 10 May 2017).

also welfare convergence. In fact, without a degree of consensus, the DPP government's welfare legislation, such as 2002 old age allowances, could not have been passed. This shift in attitudes was brought home to me on seeing a Pan Blue campaign poster at Keelung train station during the 2004 presidential election. In the poster, Lien and Soong pledged that if elected they would raise the old age allowance to NT$5,000, thus trying to outbid the DPP government's NT$3,000. We should recall that these two politicians had been the most vocal in opposing universal old age allowances in the 1990s. Thus, this case shows how democratic competition has promoted welfare value change even at the elite level and a more equal welfare system.

State of social welfare developments after 2008

During the final years of the Lee Teng-hui era, the DPP had been highly critical of the KMT's failure to deliver on its promise to establish a National Pensions Scheme. However, it was not until the final year of the DPP administration that the National Pension Insurance Act was passed, and the scheme came into operation on October 2008 after the KMT was back in power. The scheme is neither mandatory nor universal and is designed to cover those not included in Labour Insurance or various *jungongjiao* retirement programmes. In other words, something like 3.5 million people could be covered. In contrast to the 2002 old age allowance scheme, this National Pensions Insurance is a contributory programme. In addition to a government contribution, those enrolled aged over 25 have to pay premiums for between 10 and 40 years. Since it is non–mandatory and only those most disadvantaged in society are included in the scheme, it is questionable how effective and redistributive it will be. The other major old age welfare shift was a revision to the Labour Insurance Act, so that from August 2008 those enrolled would receive a monthly pension rather than a lump sum on retirement.[41]

Another area of welfare in flux is the UNHI, which has been suffering from an increasing fund deficit. In late 2010, the DOH proposed a 'Second Generation UNHI' scheme that its promoters believed would fill the gap in the fund's finances and also make the premium payment closer to actual household income. A particularly controversial feature was that the premiums set for the unemployed or housewives would assume they had an income of NT$17,280. However, as in 1997, the DOH reform was blocked by a cross-party coalition. Many legislators from the KMT refused to back their own government policy, fearing a voter backlash. Eventually, on 4 January 2011 a compromise amendment to the National Insurance Act was passed, which left the original system largely intact. Premiums remained based on salaries and were actually reduced from 5.17 to 4.91 per cent. To fill the revenue gap, a new supplementary premium was introduced for income from investments, rents or bonuses.[42]

It would appear that social welfare has returned to salience in the last few years. Perhaps as Taiwan has a rapidly ageing population, issues related to elderly welfare have been prominent on the political agenda again. Ku and Hsueh note how, 'After four years of debating, the Act (Long-Term Care Service Act) was finally adopted by the Legislative Yuan in May 2015.'[43] This issue also received significant attention during the 2016 election campaign, with Tsai proposing a tax-based, long-term care system. Ku and Hsueh suggest that this has the potential to be as important in Taiwan's welfare system as UNHI and the National Pension Insurance.[44]

Even more controversial, though, has been the question of Taiwan's pension system. Under Ma, a pension reform task force was set up and numerous public forums were held. However, the reforms stalled in the KMT-controlled parliament in 2014. During Tsai's presidential campaign and in her inaugural speech she stressed the importance of pension reform. Key challenges facing the system include the unequal pensions available across Taiwanese society and problems of financial sustainability. Tsai's government set up a pension reform committee, ran numerous public forums and a national pension reform conference. Groups that feel threatened by reform, such as the military and civil servants, have engaged in angry and at times violent protests against the draft reform bills. Creating a fairer but also sustainable pension system will be a major test for Tsai's government. If she fails to deliver, her pledge to promote social and generational justice will be severely undermined.

Democracy has transformed Taiwan's welfare system, shifting it from a limited and unfair system to one of the most extensive and efficient systems in Asia. Through democratic debate, the main parties have converged on most welfare issues. In the first edition of this book, I argued that there was less interest in welfare issues than in the past and suggested it was unlikely that we would see major new welfare programmes proposed. The picture in 2017 looks quite different as welfare issues have returned to the agenda and have again featured partisan divergence. Although there are still problems in the social welfare provision, the fact that Taiwan could develop a significant and broad social security network at a time of global welfare retrenchment is a real achievement. Thus, in answer to my core question, I would give it a cautious 'yes', as on welfare policy, democracy has had an overall positive effect.

Politics of political corruption

Since the end of the Cold War, political corruption has developed into one of the most influential political issues in global politics. Prior to the 1990s, corruption had been a marginal issue in most Western democracies, one that was more associated with authoritarian states. Since the Cold War, however, almost no Western democracy has been immune from the impact of the issue. In the 1990s, corruption allegations contributed to the downfall of long incumbent parties in Italy, the UK and Spain. This salience was maintained in the post-2000 period. The reputation of the whole UK parliamentary system was damaged by the expenses scandal of 2009–10. There were similar trends in new democracies. Corruption allegations led to the overthrow of Joseph Estrada in the Philippines in 2001 and the justifications for the coup in Thailand against Thaksin Shinawatra were allegations of widespread corruption and nepotism in 2006.

Political corruption has been equally, if not more, prominent in Taiwan than in most other democracies. If we take issue emphasis as our standard, then we can regard political corruption as the most salient issue since democratization. It repeatedly receives more electoral emphasis than national identity and played a central role in both the downfall of the KMT in 2000 and the DPP after 2005. However, because it is a valence (no politician will openly support corruption) rather than positional issue, political scientists in Taiwan often underplay its importance, and so the question we need to ask is whether democracy actually helped tackle or promote corruption in post-transition Taiwan.

A number of factors have contributed to the rising global prominence of the corruption issue. We cannot be certain whether actual levels of corruption have declined globally, but the liberalized, scandal-seeking media and investigative journalism have given the issue much coverage and made it harder for politicians to get away with corrupt practices. Both elite and mass norms on corruption have also shown significant change, with trends shifting towards lower toleration of corruption. Politicians have successfully exploited this new issue as a very powerful tool for political exposure and electoral mobilization. Moreover, the fading of the left–right divide has opened up space on the political agenda for the issue and therefore it is an issue that politicians of both traditional left and right parties readily use.

Apart from the undoubted salience of the corruption issue, there are other reasons for us to study this topic. According to the World Bank, 'corruption is the greatest obstacle to economic and social development. It undermines development by distorting the rule of law and weakening the institutional foundation on which economic growth depends.'[45] Democracy is unfortunately not always a panacea for tackling corruption. Some studies have found that medium-level democratic countries have higher levels of political corruption than authoritarian states. Paul Heywood points out that political corruption is more undermining of democracies than authoritarian states as, 'By attacking some of the basic principles on which democracy rests – notably, the equality of citizens before institutions, corruption contributes to the delegitimation of the political and institutional systems in which it takes root.'[46] Nevertheless, in my own work on Taiwan I have generally been supportive of Michael Johnston's argument that 'high quality, well institutionalised political competition can help reduce levels of corruption'.[47]

Definitions and frameworks of analysis

There is much debate within political studies over how to best define political corruption. Arnold Heidenheimer notes that 'recent political scientists have fairly consistently defined corruption in terms of transactions between the private and public sectors such that collective goods are illegitimately converted into private-regarding payoffs'.[48] A problem here is that there is often a blurred distinction between the public and private sectors in authoritarian states and new democracies. Moreover, employing legal standards for political corruption carries the risk that a dominant party can use its control of the state to institutionalize corruption. An alternative approach is to take public opinion as the standard for defining what constitutes political corruption. Even this method can be challenged as what is perceived as corruption varies over time, cross-nationally and even within single states. Heidenheimer has proposed a public opinion based framework that distinguishes between black, grey and white corruption. Black corruption occurs when a 'majority consensus of both elite and mass opinion would condemn and would want to see punished'.[49] For grey corruption, 'some elements, usually elites, may want to see the actions punished, others not, and the majority may well be ambiguous'.[50] White corruption is where 'the majority of elite and mass opinion probably would not vigorously support an attempt to punish a form of corruption that they regard as tolerable'.[51]

One of the most widely cited methods for measuring levels of political corruption also relies on public opinion. This is the Corruption Perception Index (CPI) managed by the NGO Transparency International.[52] This uses expert surveys of business people and analysts to rank states on a scale of corruption that ranges between 100 (highly clean) and 0 (highly corrupt). Respondents are asked for their perception of the degree of corruption among public officials and politicians. The CPI gives both a corruption score and also a global ranking. These surveys have been conducted for a gradually larger number of countries since 1995, rising from an initial 40 to 178 in 2010. We can thus use the CPI to measure time-series change in Taiwan's perceived corruption since 1995 and also how Taiwan's perceived corruption compares with other states with similar and different political systems.

Political corruption under martial law

Although corruption only began to feature prominently on the political agenda after democratic transition, Taiwan already suffered from pervasive corruption under martial law. As we discussed in Chapters 2 and 7, the patron–client relationship between the KMT and KMT local factions institutionalized a range of corrupt practices such as vote buying, economic monopolies, profiting from control of land planning and zoning, and the right to run illegal businesses. There is a common perception that under authoritarianism corruption was restricted to the local level, while at the national level the ROC state was squeaky clean. However, the KMT took advantage of its political dominance to create a huge business and property empire, making it arguably the richest political party in the world. The party's political dominance meant that it could also ensure that its cronies and own companies won lucrative government contracts or enjoyed economic monopolies. Since the KMT controlled the judicial system, both local and national level corruption by the party and its members were free from direct legal challenge. Even at the level of public opinion, KMT corruption was not openly challenged for most of the martial law period. Thus, the case corresponds quite well with Heidenheimer's concept of white corruption, as these practices were regarded as normal by most elites and ordinary people.

Nevertheless, Taiwan's level of political corruption was lower than many other authoritarian states, such as South Korea. Kong argues that a key reason for this was the regime type.[53] He terms Taiwan as having a quasi-monolithic regime, in contrast to the bureaucratic authoritarian South Korean case. In other words, while there was a mutual hostage relationship between big business and the military rulers in Korea, in Taiwan the KMT was not challenged by business and was itself a dominant player in the economic sector through its party enterprises and its control of the state-owned enterprises.

Political corruption issue in the Lee Teng-hui era

During the democratic transition period, political corruption did receive some attention from the *Tangwai* and then early DPP. However, as with social welfare, it was not yet a core opposition issue, as democratic reforms, human rights and national identity appeals dominated dissident propaganda. As Chu and Lin noted, 'concerns about money politics, if any, had little effect on party preferences in the 1980s'.[54] In fact, in the first full democratic election for the National Assembly in 1991, corruption received little attention from any of the major parties.[55] However, at this point the local factional and big business-linked politicians were moving from the local level to the national political arena. Democratization created new opportunities for the politicians to gain national-level elected office and thus offer further protection for their economic interests. Moreover, these politicians were critically important for the KMT as it faced the challenge from the DPP and as a tool to win the power struggle against the non-Mainstream faction within the KMT. Therefore, some writers, such as Ramon Myers, blame Lee Teng-hui for allowing political corruption to move up from the local to national level during this period.[56] Lee indeed must take a degree of responsibility as KMT factional nomination and even nomination of gangster-linked politicians was an undeniable feature of the 1990s. However, as described earlier, the roots of KMT corruption were already present under the two Chiang presidencies. Kong stressed the role of simultaneous economic and political liberalization in the perceived rise in corruption:

Dual transition opened up enormous scope for the private appropriation of public assets not only by big business, but also by other forces, notably local factions and organised crime. The ruling party also emerged as a major business force. It is this multiplicity of actors and alliances between them (and especially those involving gangsters) that gave Taiwan's dual transition its chaotic image.[57]

Political corruption emerged as a central election issue in 1992 and remained firmly on the electoral agenda for every major election for the rest of the 1990s.[58] The 1992 legislative election in particular set the stage for how the issue would be treated. The DPP gave the issue heavy emphasis for the first time, including 'Anti-money Politics' in its campaign slogan and a large section of its manifesto-style TV advertisement called 'Because of Us' (*yinwei you women*). Much DPP propaganda focused on exposing cases of KMT corruption and vote buying. In contrast, the KMT and its candidates, knowing the issue to be unfavourable, tried to steer clear of the matter and move the campaign focus on to its preferred issues such as stability and the economy.

In the next few elections, the DPP continued to own the anti-corruption issue, with 70, 37 and 36 per cent of its official newspaper ad issue mentions focusing on this question in 1993, 1994 and 1995 respectively.[59] The breadth of its corruption attacks gradually widened to include also attacks on KMT local executive corruption, corruption involving central government officials and KMT party assets. For instance, many DPP advertisements alleged KMT involvement in corruption cases linked to the Taipei metro construction project. In 1995, the DPP began its first concerted campaign of protests against KMT party assets, calling for them to be investigated and returned to the state. From 1995, the DPP was also joined in the anti-corruption appeals by the NP. Many of the NP's attacks on KMT corruption corresponded with those adopted by the DPP, but it also often tried to direct the blame for corruption on to its hate figure, Lee Teng-hui. One such NP advertisement called for authorities to 'Catch Taiwan's Rho Tae-woo'.[60] The KMT occasionally tried to defend itself or accuse DPP local executive candidates of being equally corrupt. For instance, in 1995 it defended the legal status of its party assets and in 1994 ran a campaign alleging the DPP's provincial governor candidate Chen Ting-nan (陳定南) to be an 'expert at cultivating corruption.'[61] However, these were the exceptions to the rule, as the KMT preferred to avoid the issue where possible.

There was a brief lull in the political corruption debates during the 1996 presidential election as the campaign was almost completely dominated by cross-Strait and national identity issues. However, political corruption was to return to its place as the most stressed issue for the final three elections of the Lee Teng-hui era. The newspaper ad statistics for 1997 suggest that there was quite a different pattern of issue emphasis, as the KMT gave the most emphasis to anti-corruption appeals (9.8 per cent of issue mentions), while the DPP ignored the issue in its official newspaper ads that year.[62] As in 1993, the KMT tried to accuse a number of DPP local executives of involvement in corruption cases, particularly focusing on Taipei and Kaohsiung Counties where the DPP had held office for at least two terms. For instance, one anonymous anti-DPP ad likened the DPP Kaohsiung County local executive's wife to the most infamous criminals of the day, asking 'Where can Red Envelope Lien escape?'[63] However, the DPP did give much attention to the issue in its campaign speeches and TV ads in 1997. For instance, in its 'Spokesman Ad', the animated KMT spokesman tries to explain away KMT corruption cases. As more cases are reported, his nose becomes longer and on hearing that the KMT's

Pingtung County Council Speaker has been given a life sentence for murder, the spokesman collapses and is carried away on a stretcher.[64]

A year later in 1998, all three parties gave corruption much coverage in their election appeals. With Ma Ying-jeou as the KMT's Taipei mayoral candidate, the party had more confidence on the corruption issue. It even issued a TV ad focusing on how Ma had cracked down on vote buying while Minister of Justice, and a member of the public was quoted as saying 'All the gangsters that ought to be caught have been caught or have fled.'[65] DPP attacks on KMT 'black gold' (a common Taiwanese euphemism for political corruption) were also widespread in both its TV and newspaper advertisements that year. However, the NP gave the most emphasis to anti-corruption appeals, with almost a third of its newspaper issue mentions on this question.[66]

Unlike the 1996 presidential election, in 2000 corruption was the most stressed election issue. Even the KMT gave the issue its second highest proportion of issue emphasis for any campaign over the whole of the 1990s. However, most KMT anti-corruption ads were focused on smearing its rebel candidate James Soong rather than the DPP's Chen Shui-bian. These accusations were known as the *Hsing Piao* case and centred on how Soong had allegedly embezzled KMT funds while he was the party's Secretary General and Provincial Governor. One particularly infamous advertisement claimed that Soong's changing press conference explanations for the funds deserved an acting award. The ad carried the slogan '*Money, Lies, Hsing Piao* Case. The Oscar Golden Soong Award has been announced. Congratulations!'[67] The readers were then told that Soong has won the best actor award and best film went to *Money, Lies, Hsing Piao Case,* which we were told was an X-rated film. As many NP politicians were more sympathetic to Soong than to either their own candidate or the KMT's Lien, they gave less emphasis to anti-corruption than in previous years.

The DPP once again gave this issue more attention than ever, as the appeal could enable the party to attack both the KMT and the KMT rebel Soong. Chen's words from the first presidential debate reflect an anti-corruption message the party had made since 1992:

> According to surveys about 70 per cent of the people think that under KMT rule the black gold question is getting worse. From grassroots financial institutions to big public construction projects, from insider trading on the stock exchange to corruption in military procurement cases, the KMT has relied on a system of corruption that reaches all levels of our country. Since the end of martial law the KMT has relied on gangsters and money politics to maintain its power. So hoping for the KMT to tackle black gold is like dying charcoal white, it is impossible. Only if A-bian [Chen Shui-bian's nickname] is elected can the danger of black gold be dealt with.[68]

DPP newspaper and TV advertisements also focused on this issue. One such ad showed a picture of Lien with Wu Tse-yuan (伍澤元) (former KMT Pingtung Local Executive who had been removed from office due to corruption cases) and Lo Fu-chu (gangster-linked independent legislator) and Soong with Yan Ching-piao (Taichung County Council speaker with a black gold reputation). These were contrasted with pictures of Chen and Nobel Prize winner Lee Yuan-che (李遠哲), who had come out in support of Chen. Voters were then asked, 'Who are you going to trust Taiwan's future with?'[69]

By the end of the 1990s, the corruption issue was clearly benefiting the DPP. Party image surveys showed that the proportion of voters viewing the KMT as clean fell from 37 per cent in 1992 to 21 per cent in 1997, and the proportion seeing the KMT as corrupt rose from 28 per cent to 50 per cent. In contrast, the proportion of voters seeing the DPP as clean rose from 26 per cent in 1992 to 47 per cent in 1997.[70] When voters were asked why they disliked the KMT, the most frequent answers tended to be related to its black gold image.[71] Other surveys that asked voters for their first impression of the KMT also increasingly tended to cite corruption-related images by the end of the decade.[72]

The DPP and NP's control of the anti-corruption issue contributed to their impressive electoral rise in the 1990s. KMT politicians I interviewed often cited their party's corruption image as contributing to their setbacks, particularly in 1997 and 2000. For instance, KMT party officials in Pingtung complained to me of how the DPP's stress on the gangster–KMT linkage in its 1997 TV advertisements (such as the Spokesman ad) had undermined the KMT's campaign that year. Of course, the corruption appeal did not always pay dividends. For instance, although the NP gave record emphasis to this issue in 1998, many of its supporters returned to the KMT as Ma Ying-jeou's candidacy suggested that the KMT was cleaning up its act. Nevertheless, in the aftermath of the KMT's presidential defeat in 2000, black gold was viewed as one of its key reasons for its loss of ruling power.

The consistent election emphasis also resulted in tougher anti-corruption policy. In 1993, the DPP cooperated with the non-mainstream KMT to pass the Mandatory Disclosure and Mandatory Trust clauses to the Financial Disclosure Law of Government Officials. This forced senior government officials to disclose their assets and place them in trusts. The KMT was also under increased pressure to crack down on vote buying. For instance, when Ma Ying-jeou was Minister of Justice he launched a sweeping campaign against vote buying in county council elections that mainly caught KMT local politicians. By 2000, the KMT even expressed a willingness to end involvement in profit-making businesses, thus resolving the party assets question.

Therefore, if we consider the Heidenheimer corruption framework, we can see how after democratization most corruption sub-issues made a transition from being white to grey, with some even transitioning to black corruption. By the late 1990s, many political activities that had been at least tacitly accepted under martial law were now viewed as unacceptable by both elites and ordinary voters. For instance, at least in major cities, open vote buying became far less common and visible by the end of the decade.

I argue that the key factors explaining the changing norms over political corruption after the late 1980s were democratization and media liberalization.[73] Democracy enabled politicians to place political corruption on the electoral agenda, forcing the ruling party to respond with anti-corruption measures. However, the impact of the anti-corruption messages would have been muted without the media liberalization seen in the 1990s. The emergence of a liberalized print and electronic media meant that opposition politicians and investigative journalists had a platform for exposing ruling party corruption. The under-the-table patron client deals between the KMT and local factions were repeatedly exposed in the media by both the DPP and NP. One of the key arenas for corruption allegations was the cable TV political talk shows that became so popular from the late 1990s.

There were limits to how far the KMT could respond to the anti-corruption appeals. It was financially too reliant on party assets for campaigns and needed the alliance with corrupt local factions to win grassroots elections. Thus, removing its black gold reputation, even though it wanted to, would have severely undermined its electoral prospects.

In short, by the end of the Lee Teng-hui era the political corruption issue had contributed to the rising support for the DPP and NP, the loss of KMT ruling power at the local and then national level, and to a broader awareness of corruption issues and consensus on the need for tougher anti-corruption measures. Therefore, in the first period of multi-party politics, democracy did have a positive impact on dealing with political corruption.

Political corruption in the first DPP term, 2000–4

When the DPP came to power on the back of its anti-corruption platform, there were high hopes for a new era of clean government. It was in the DPP's interests to deal with the black gold issue not only because of the public's anti-corruption sentiment but also because the old system of institutionalized corruption created an uneven electoral playing-field that favoured the KMT.

The new Minister of Justice, Chen Ting-nan, set out on an ambitious anti-corruption campaign. For instance, there were much more vigorous anti-vote buying efforts. Christian Göbel noted that 'The Legislative Yuan elections in December 2001 were accompanied by massive campaigns aimed to dissuade the Taiwanese populace from accepting money for their votes and by even more massive crackdowns on vote captains and the legislators who had hired them.'[74] The DPP government also proposed a wide range of administrative changes and legislation to tackle political corruption. These included proposals to create an anti-corruption task force, Political Party Law (to deal with KMT party assets), Lobby Law, Party Donations Law, Money Laundering Law and other sunshine bills (anti-corruption bills are called 'sunshine' bills in Taiwan). However, by the end of the first DPP term, only the Party Donations Law had been passed, as the DPP had failed to gain sufficient cross-party support. Despite an extensive Control Yuan investigation into the KMT's party assets in 2001 that proposed nationalizing the assets on a model similar to East Germany, little progress was actually made on the issue. The DPP initially began a major programme of mergers and takeovers of local grassroots financial institutions that had long been the major source of finance for corrupt KMT politicians. Here again, the results were mixed, as when farmers began protesting against these financial reforms on the eve of elections in 2002, the DPP government halted them.[75]

Although the KMT largely blocked many of the DPP's sunshine bills, it did endeavour to deal with its own black gold image. It revised its nomination regulations to try to avoid nominating candidates with a corrupt record or reputation, leading to some of its incumbents failing to gain nomination in 2001. Also, the fact that it no longer held national office and had lost control of most local government posts meant that it was harder to accuse it of corruption.

In the first post-2000 election in 2001, the DPP continued to make political corruption its most stressed issue that year.[76] However, the overall pattern in the first five years of the DPP era was that corruption declined in salience. It fell from being the most stressed issue in newspaper ads from 1991 to 2000 to only the ninth most stressed issue between 2001 and 2004. Even for the DPP it fell from its most stressed issue in the Lee Teng-hui era to its sixth most stressed issue.[77] The NP completely seemed to lose interest in its 1990s core appeal, as it became totally obsessed with Chinese nationalism and cross-Strait integration. In the 2004 presidential election, the DPP candidate Chen Shui-bian came under attack for corruption from an economic fugitive, Chen Yu-hao (陳由豪), in the final week of the campaign. However, it appears that the impact was not significant as Chen was still able to win by a very narrow margin. In the December 2004 legislative elections, none of the major parties gave the issue much attention in their propaganda, suggesting a declined salience of the issue.[78] Table 11.2 shows the proportion of voters viewing the two main parties as free of corruption from TVBS surveys. This reveals that the DPP's early anti-corruption efforts after 2000 had earned it an improved party image, but that there had been a gradual decline in its clean governance image by mid-2004. Although the KMT had gradually improved its image after losing power, the political corruption issue still favoured the DPP as late as May 2005.

The picture concerning political corruption by the end of the first Chen administration was thus a mixed one. Göbel writes that,

> the influence of 'black gold' on Taiwan's polity was significantly reduced simply because the new administration did not or could not take the KMT's former position as a hub in the informal network. The large conglomerates' influence on politics was weakened as economic liberalisation subjected them to competition with the new conglomerates, which had emerged without political protection.[79]

Comparing the KMT and DPP administrations' anti-corruption efforts he concluded that,

> the major difference between the two administrations' anti- 'black gold' policies was that the DPP had nothing to lose, but much to gain from revamping the administrative, legal and financial apparatus and indiscriminately persecuting vote buyers, organised criminals and corrupt politicians alike. On the contrary, failure to do so might catapult it back into the opposition. Even so, institutional and organisational change proved difficult to achieve. Accordingly, the DPP too had to rely more on symptom-oriented than on cause-oriented policies to prove its resolve, but here it achieved more than the KMT ever had. Top-level crime figures were arrested, others have fled the country, and vote buying has decreased significantly. The bureaucracy has become more assertive towards the Legislative Yuan, and the KMT's big business cronies' political influence has been weakened.[80]

When we examine the Corruption Perception Index (CPI) data for Taiwan, we can see that there was a gradual perception of decreased corruption from the mid-1990s (50) through to until after the first change of ruling parties in 2000 (55). However, between 2001 and 2010, the perception of corruption was quite stable, fluctuating between 59 and 56 on the CPI score. Compared to other Asian countries, Taiwan's perceived level of corruption is higher than Japan and Singapore but better than South Korea and Malaysia. Taiwan was ranked 31st out of 176 countries with a score of 61 in 2016. In contrast, China was ranked 79 globally and had a CPI score of 40.[81]

Table 11.2 Party image of clean government

	Nov 1999	March 2001	March 2002	Aug 2004	May 2005	Sept 2005	Nov 2005	July 2006	Oct 2007	Jan 2008	Sept 2009	Jan 2010	Oct 2012	June 2015
KMT	21	22	27	31	30	34	29	40	29	38	31	26	20	17
DPP	47	41	48	38	34	31	17	14	21	23	21	31	30	38

Source: TVBS Poll Center, 'Poll Party List Legislators and Party Image', 1 June 2015. Available online at: http://other.tvbs.com.tw/export/sites/tvbs/file/other/poll-center/0405281-.pdf (accessed 18 May 2017).

Political corruption in the second Chen administration

From 2005, political corruption reverted to its position as one of the most salient issues in Taiwanese politics. That year saw the first of what seemed an endless string of DPP-linked corruption scandals that emerged first in late 2005 and dominated the political agenda throughout the final months of the campaign. The allegations that were particularly damaging for the DPP were related to corruption in the Kaohsiung Mass Rapid Transit (MRT) construction project and also high-level DPP involvement in stock market insider trading.[82] The former Deputy Secretary General of the Presidential Office, Chen Che-nan (陳哲男), was the focus of the Kaohsiung MRT scandal and so this also indirectly implicated President Chen. Pictures of Chen Che-nan and the former head of Kaohsiung Rapid Transit Corporation in a casino in South Korea were used by the KMT as ammunition against the DPP.[83] Although Chen Che-nan was expelled from the DPP, the scandal seriously tarnished the image of the party. The importance the KMT placed on anti-corruption can be seen from how it stressed the issue in its advertising and campaign rallies. For instance, its main pre-election rally was titled the 'Oppose Corruption Save Taiwan, All People Rally'.[84] This was in stark contrast to many previous elections, where the KMT had tried to steer clear of the corruption issue. Following what was the KMT's first post-2000 landslide election victory, one of Taiwan's leading political scientists, Wu Yu-shan, commented that in 2005, 'Corruption brought down the Green Camp's Domain'.[85] This was the DPP's worst local executive election defeat. As had been the case for the KMT in 1997, the image of political corruption was critical for this DPP electoral setback. If we look back at Table 6.11, we can see that in 2005 there was one of the KMT's largest year-on-year rises in party identification and major fall for the DPP. We will look in more detail at evidence of the importance of the corruption issue for the downfall of the DPP in Chapter 12.

In addition to the DPP's corruption scandals, some of the KMT's institutional reforms were beginning to pay off by the second Chen term. For instance, its nomination primaries and anti-corruption nomination regulations helped avoid the nomination of the kind of politicians that had been so damaging for the party in the 1990s. Equally important for the KMT's improved image was the election of Ma Ying-jeou as party chairman in July 2005. Ma was one of the few KMT politicians who were seen as corruption free, a reputation that he initially cultivated, cracking down on KMT vote buying when he was Minister of Justice in the early to mid 1990s. In 2005, as in 1998, when Ma was the most prominent KMT candidate, accusations of KMT corruption were less effective.

The corruption allegation scandals against the DPP, and particularly Chen Shui-bian, continued for the remainder of his second term. The pro-Blue TV politics talk show pundits (*Mingzui,* literally 'famous mouths') claimed to have a limitless supply of corruption scandals to reveal on a nightly basis to their loyal viewers. First, in May 2006 Chen's son-in-law was taken into custody over stock market insider trading allegations. Then in November 2006, Chen's wife, Wu Shu-chen (吳淑珍), was indicted for corruption involving the special presidential funds. These accusations seriously eroded the legitimacy and popularity of the DPP and its government.

In 2006, a group of scholars, some of whom had been sympathetic to the DPP in the past, organized a petition urging Chen to resign to take responsibility for the corruption allegations.[86] Then in the autumn of 2006, the DPP faced one of the largest ever social movement protests known as the Red Shirt movement.[87] This anti-corruption movement was led by former DPP chairman Shih Ming-teh, and strongly backed by both Pan Blue politicians and also by many former DPP supporters. There was a series of huge demonstrations in Taipei, with protestors calling for Chen to step down from the presidency. The KMT also tried to take advantage of this wave of opinion by organizing a series of impeachment votes in the Legislative Yuan against Chen. On each occasion these failed as they were unable to gather the required two-thirds majority. In the post-2005 election campaigns, the KMT also gave heavy emphasis to the corruption issue. For example, in the 2008 legislative election political corruption was the KMT's second most stressed issue in its TV advertisements.[88] In a series of ads featuring what were meant to look like ordinary voters, housewives and taxi drivers complained bitterly about the DPP's economic failures and reputation for corruption.

The KMT also faced corruption allegations during this period. In fact, both Chen and Ma faced quite similar accusations of having made improper use of their special funds, and Ma was also indicted for corruption during the presidential campaign. However, by this time contrasting party images meant the issue was highly unfavourable for the DPP. Although the DPP's presidential candidate Hsieh Chang-ting tried to keep some distance from Chen during the campaign, many voters were taking the election as an opportunity to punish Chen and the DPP. Perhaps more so than for the KMT in 2000, political corruption was a critical factor in the DPP's landslide defeats and loss of national office in 2008.

Political corruption after the second party turnover

After leaving office, Chen lost his presidential immunity against prosecution and soon faced a number of serious corruption case indictments. Chen was taken into custody and remained there throughout the trial process. In September 2009, Chen received a life sentence for money laundering and embezzlement, although this was later reduced to 19 years in a subsequent trial. On 3 December 2010, Chen formally began his prison sentence as prisoner number 1020.[89]

There are two competing political interpretations of the handling of political corruption after 2008. From the KMT government's perspective, it was attempting to clean up corruption by prosecuting cases of corruption from the DPP era. The alternative understanding is that the KMT was conducting a witch hunt against Chen and former DPP government officials. It does appear that there was serious political interference and judicial bias in the prosecution process in a number of these cases. Such incidents undermined the legitimacy of the prosecution process. The KMT government was under heavy pressure from both its hardline politicians and supporters to take revenge on Chen, thus making his case a priority. However, judicial malpractices in some of these cases led to much criticism from overseas scholars and contributed to accusations of a return to KMT authoritarian practices. I will return to these issues in Chapter 13.

One important development after 2008 was that a number of KMT legislators had their election victories cancelled as a result of vote buying cases. In the past, it was only the grassroots vote brokers who were caught, while the high-level candidates avoided prosecution. On each occasion a by-election was held to fill the vacant legislative seat and non-KMT candidates won all related seats. Once again, we can see evidence of voters punishing parties for perceived corruption.

Much of the analysis on why the KMT fell from power in 2016 focuses on the Sunflower effect. Nevertheless, political corruption was one of the factors in the fall in the KMT and Ma's popularity. Ma had relied heavily on attacking the DPP for political corruption in his bid to bring the KMT back to power in 2008, thus when corruption scandals emerged involving politicians close to him they were very damaging. From Table 11.2 we can see that the KMT retained a better reputation for clean governance for most of Ma's first term. However, it suffered a major fall in its reputation between surveys in April and October 2012 from 32 per cent seeing it as free of corruption to only 20 per cent.[90] During the same period, presidential satisfaction also collapsed from 40 per cent to 15 per cent in July. A key event shaping this change was the emergence of a serious corruption scandal involving Lin Yi-shih (林益世), Ma's Executive Yuan Secretary General.[91] This was further reinforced by corruption cases such as the one surrounding Taipei City Councillor Lai Su-ju (賴素如) in 2013.[92] Lai had been closely associated with Ma for many years, serving as the director of his 2012 campaign office, KMT party spokesperson and director of the KMT's propaganda department. We can see from Table 11.2 that as KMT scandals emerged in Ma's second term and the DPP's reputation improved under Tsai, the DPP developed a much better image for clean governance than the KMT as Taiwan approached the 2016 elections.

The struggle over LGBT rights

When I wrote the first edition of this book, LGBT rights were only touched upon briefly. However, today an examination of the issue can help us assess how well democracy is working in Taiwan. If we accept the more demanding definition of democracy, then there should be a close link between public opinion and government policies. Given the increasingly tolerant views towards homosexuality in Taiwan, we should expect to see adjustments in relevant policies. Democracies often struggle to deal with new issues that do not neatly follow existing partisan divides. Thus, the emergence of LGBT issues on to the political agenda in recent years offers another test of the vitality of Taiwan's democracy.

Since the early 1990s, Taiwan has developed the reputation of being more tolerant of homosexuality than its Asian neighbours. Taiwan has held the largest gay pride rally in East Asia since 2003. Cinematic representations of homosexuality have been common in Taiwanese film for over three decades. Gay themed films such as *Wedding Banquet, Vive L'amour, Blue Gate Crossing, Formula 17* and *Girlfriend, Boyfriend* have not just received critical acclaim as well as commercial success, but they have also been championed by the Taiwanese state.

While LGBT issues were developing into an important cultural theme in the 1990s, they were just not yet politically salient. Such issues had received slightly more attention in the more socially liberal Taipei. While Ma Ying-jeou was Taipei mayor, he made some overtures to the gay community. Simon notes how Ma appeared on the front page of the *G&L* magazine and that his city govenment issued a *Getting to Know Comrades* handbook in which Ma apologized for past human rights violations against gays.[93] An initial low-key attempt at legalizing gay and lesbian marriage came from Chen's Executive Yuan in 2003. However, like most of Chen's proposed reforms, this did not make progress through the Pan Blue controlled parliament and was not a major priority for the DPP at the time.

A number of factors have caused the rising salience in LGBT rights in recent years. Public opinion has clearly grown more tolerant. Cheng, Wu and Adamczyk show how, while Taiwanese and Koreans held similar levels of acceptance of homosexuality in the mid 1990s, by 2012 Taiwanese showed much faster growth in acceptance.[94] This study, as well as TVBS surveys, suggest that younger, better educated and non-Christians are more likely to be supportive of homosexuality. Most surveys suggest that well over 50 per cent are supportive of LGBT marriage and while less than a third are opposed, the remaining 20 per cent tend to be apathetic.[95] The Cheng *et al.* study found that acceptance of homosexuality was higher in Japan than Taiwan. Thus, despite lower public acceptance, legalizing same-sex marriage has received greater political support in Taiwan than in Japan. Therefore, we also need to look for political explanations of change.

Both civil society and political pressure contributed to the new environment. An important moment was the establishment of the Taiwan Alliance to Promote Civil Partnership Rights (TAPCPR) in 2009. The first political party to take an openly pro-LGBT rights stance was the Green Party Taiwan (GPT). It started nominating openly gay candidates in 2010 and made this a central campaign theme in both 2014 and 2016. There has also been strong support for LGBT rights from Taiwan's leading feminist groups such as the Awakening Foundation.[96] In October 2013, a group of DPP legislators submitted a bill (based on TAPCPR proposals) to revise the Civil Code to legalize same-sex marriage, which passed its first reading. There was an immediate response from conservatives with the establishment of the Alliance for Protecting Families, who went on to organize a number of large and controversial counter protests aimed at preventing the legalization drive making further progress through parliament. Cole has looked in great detail at how this counter movement has developed in cooperation with evangelical groups in the United States and Taiwanese politicians.[97] Despite the fact that Christians make up a small minority in Taiwan, he argues that the 'alliance tends to punch well above its weight'.[98] At this stage, the Alliance for Protecting Families was able to successfully lobby enough politicians from both the DPP and KMT to see the bill dropped in early 2014. The counter movement was even able to lobby the Ministry of Education to include two of its figures in the Commission on Gender Equality.

The mood, though, changed quite radically during the 2016 presidential campaign. The GPT/SDP Alliance nominated a record number of openly LGBT candidates and highlighted the issue in their advertising. They also nominated the co-founder and CEO of the TAPCPR, Victoria Hsu (許秀雯), on their party list. Unsurprisingly, the NPP also came out supportive of marriage equality. Adding to the salience of the issue in 2016 was the creation of a new political party, the Faith and Hope Alliance in early 2015, with the sole aim of contesting the progress of same-sex marriage legislation. The alliance was able to spend heavily in the campaign as a result of support from evangelical churches as well as business leaders such as Cher Wang (王雪紅), the co-founder of HTC. However, what made this election especially interesting was the mainstream parties' treatment of the issue. Even the KMT's original candidate, Hung Hsiu-chu, stated she maintains an 'open and optimistic' attitude towards the LGBT community. Unlike its relatively vague stance in 2012, the DPP took an unambiguously pro-LGBT stance in its 2016 campaign communications. In the DPP's best known *Walk with the Children* TV advertisement, we see the gay pride flag and a man holding a flag stating 'legalize same-sex marriage'.[99] On the day of the 2015 Gay Pride parade, Tsai issued a short clip on her Facebook in which she states, 'I'm Tsai Ing-wen, I support marriage equality'.[100] Another DPP advertisement titled *Born Equal* (生而平權) that was also issued on the eve of the Gay Pride parade shows two loving couples (one gay and one lesbian) happily sharing breakfast.[101] Tsai's victory and the strong showing by gay candidates revealed that Taiwanese voters could accept a presidential candidate taking an openly pro LGBT rights position and openly gay candidates.

Once Tsai had been elected, there was an expectation she would move to fulfil her clear campaign promise. Not only did she have a clear mandate with her presidential victory, but she also had a DPP majority in parliament and record numbers of parliamentarians with clear pro-LGBT rights positions. There has been a degree of impatience among activists about the pace of reform under Tsai. The issue came to a head in late 2016 when draft bills were discussed in parliament. The overall pattern was that the DPP and NPP were supportive, while the KMT and PFP have led opposition to legalization. However, one new KMT legislator has taken an openly pro-marriage equality stance, while among their DPP the party list legislators have tended to be much more supportive than those elected from districts. During the latter half of 2016, there were large pro- and anti-legalization demonstrations. Writing in late February 2017, Cole suggests that in the face of stiff resistance, Tsai was stalling on marriage equality.[102] At the time of writing, it appears that the issue has been now resolved. In May 2017, the Constitutional Court issued its ruling that laws preventing members of the same sex from marrying violated their right to equality and were unconstitutional. Moreover, it set a two-year time limit for the Legislative Yuan to make the required legal adjustments.[103] Despite the current stalemate over same-sex marriage, growing support from civil society, political parties, as well as public opinion suggests that Taiwan will be the first Asian country to legalize same-sex marriage. Such a move would be a major boost for Taiwan's soft power.

Conclusions

Back in the immediate post-2000 period, I reached positive conclusions on the relationship between democracy and both social welfare and political corruption.[104] I began to reassess such positive evaluations in the light of the corruption scandals after 2005 and the financial difficulties facing the UNHI system. Nevertheless, I would argue that both cases still support my original conclusion that democracy is working in Taiwan. In the field of social welfare, the UNHI remains popular, efficient and universal, while there has also been a continued broadening of other welfare schemes, particularly regarding old age pensions and, more recently, long-term care. Democracy continues to encourage welfare state development and to prevent welfare system retrenchment. On political corruption, the process of widening norms on what constitutes corruption has continued, as more of what was considered white or grey corruption under martial law has become black corruption. Public toleration of political corruption has thus declined drastically. We can see this in the anti-corruption protests in 2006 and the way that voters have punished parties and politicians for perceived corruption in numerous elections before and after 2008. The LGBT rights issue has also shown how Taiwan's democracy has dealt with a new issue area. Although the outcome of the same-sex marriage debate was still ongoing at the time of writing, we can see how government policies are being forced to respond to societal pressures on the issue. Of course, whether or not we regard democracy as still being healthy in Taiwan will depend on the policy issue we are examining. We have also seen positive trends in Chapter 10 with regard to improvements on environmental protection and gender equality. Of course, in some areas, such as income disparities, the picture may be less promising. Nevertheless, we have seen how on a variety of policy dimensions Taiwan's democracy is still working.

Discussion questions

1 What has been the relationship between democracy and welfare system development in Taiwan?
2 What was the impact of the change in ruling parties for welfare system development and political corruption?
3 How can we categorize the current welfare system in comparison with global welfare practices?
4 Has democracy undermined or promoted political corruption?
5 How can we explain the changing patterns of issue saliency of political corruption, welfare or LGBT rights since 2000?
6 How well has democracy in Taiwan dealt with debates over LGBT rights?

Further reading

Cheng, Yen-hsin Alice, Fen-chieh Felice Wu and Amy Adamczyk. 2016. 'Changing attitudes towards homosexuality in Taiwan, 1995–2012'. *Chinese Sociological Review* 48(4): 317–45. A systematic study of changing public opinion on the LGBT issue.

Chin, Ko-lin. 2003. *Heijin: Organized Crime, Business and Politics in Taiwan.* Armonk, NY: M.E. Sharpe. Best single volume on the links between gangster groups and politics in contemporary Taiwan.

Fell, Dafydd. 2005. 'Political and Media Liberalization and Political Corruption in Taiwan'. *China Quarterly*, 184: 875–93. I examine the role that democratization and media liberalization played in reducing political corruption.

Fell, Dafydd. 2005. *Party Politics in Taiwan.* London: Routledge. Chapters 4 and 5 examine in detail the electoral politics of social welfare and political corruption from the late 1980s through to 2002.

Göbel, Christian. 2016. 'Taiwan's Fight Against Corruption'. *Journal of Democracy*, 27 (1): 124–38. Göbel returns to discuss more recent developments regarding political corruption.

Wong, Joseph. 2004. *Healthy Democracies: Welfare Politics in Taiwan and South Korea.* Ithaca, NY: Cornell University Press. Based on extensive fieldwork and engagement with democratic and welfare theories, this is a wonderful comparative study of welfare politics in these two East Asian democracies.

Notes

1 McLean and McMillan (eds), *Oxford Concise Dictionary of Politics*, 561.
2 Rose, 'Common Goals but Different Roles: The State's Contribution to the Welfare Mix', 15.
3 IPSOS MORI, 'The Most Important Issues Facing Britain Today'. Available online at: www.ipsosmori.com/researchpublications/researcharchive/poll.aspx?oItemId=56&view=wide (accessed 28 November 2010).
4 Labour Party Political Broadcast March 1992. Available online at: www.youtube.com/watch?v=4PAIZGPSoEI (accessed 31 March 2011).
5 Ku and Hsueh, 'Social Welfare', 345.
6 Ku and Hsueh, 'Social Welfare', 345.
7 Aspalter, *Democratization and Welfare State Development in Taiwan*, 53.
8 Kwon, 'A Comparison of East Asian Welfare Systems', 47–8.
9 Esping-Anderson, *Three Worlds of Welfare Capitalism*, 21–23.
10 Holliday, 'Productivist Welfare Capitalism', 709.
11 White and Goodman, 'Welfare Orientalism and the Search for an East Asian Welfare Mode', 3–24, 11.
12 Ibid., 12.

13 For example, see Esping-Anderson, *Three Worlds of Welfare Capitalism.*
14 Fell, *Party Politics in Taiwan*, 33.
15 Ibid., 39.
16 For an organization chart of the UNHI, see Wong, *Healthy Democracies*, 64.
17 Ibid., 113.
18 Ibid.
19 Directorate General of Budget, Accounting and Statistics. Available online at: http://win. dgbas.gov.tw/fies/a11.asp?year+98 (accessed 28 November 2010).
20 Chen Chi-mai, interview by author, Kaohsiung, 20 August 2001.
21 Liu Tsung-wei, 'The Effects of Electoral Laws on Party Competition in Taiwan: 1989–1998', Table 8.9.
22 *Liberty Times,* 9 December 1992, 21.
23 Ku and Hsueh, 'Social Welfare', 347–8.
24 *China Times,* 29 November 1994, 40.
25 *Liberty Times,* 17 November 1994, 17.
26 Government Information Office, ROC Yearbook, 1994.
27 Cited in Fell, 42.
28 *China Times,* 25 November 1994, 1.
29 *China Times,* 5 November 1993, 2.
30 Cited in Fell, 37.
31 For details on the 1997 pensions debate, see Aspalter, *Democratization and Welfare State Development in Taiwan*, 95–110.
32 For details on this episode, see Wong, Chapter 6.
33 Cited in Wong, 130.
34 *China Times,* 5 March 2000, 2.
35 *China Times,* 4 March 2000, 5.
36 Lin and Chou, 'Globalization, Regime Transformation and Social Policy Development in Taiwan', 101–24, 111. Similarly, Ku and Hsueh see it as the third golden decade for welfare policy.
37 Fell, 34.
38 Ibid., 35.
39 Lin and Chou.
40 For example, see Fell, 'Change and Continuity in Taiwanese Party Politics since 2000', 30–5.
41 National Policy Foundation, 'Establishment of the Pension System in Taiwan'. Available online at: www.npf.org.tw/printfriendly/5577 (accessed 3 December 2010).
42 Flora Wang and Vincent Chao, 'KMT caucus passes amendment to NHI', *Taipei Times,* 5 January 2011, 1.
43 Ku and Hsueh, 'Social Welfare', 350.
44 Ibid., 353.
45 World Bank, 'Overview of Anti-Corruption'. Available online at: http://web.worldbank.org/ WBSITE/EXTERNAL/TOPICS/EXTPUBLICSECTORANDGOVERNANCE/EXTAN TICORRUPTION/0,,contentMDK:21540659~menuPK:384461~pagePK:148956~piPK:216 618~theSi tePK:384455,00.html (accessed 28 November 2010).
46 Heywood, 'Political Corruption: Problems and Perspectives', 1–19, 5.
47 Johnston, 'Party Systems, Competition and Political Checks against Corruption', 777–96, 777–8.
48 Heidenheimer, 'Introduction to Part 1', 3–14, 6.
49 Heidenheimer, 'Perspectives on the Perception of Corruption', 149–63, 161.
50 Ibid.
51 Ibid.
52 For details, see *Transparency International* at: www.transparency.org/ (accessed 10 May 2017).
53 Kong, 'Corruption and the Effect of Regime Type', 346.
54 Chu and Lin, 'Elections and Elite Convergence: The Path to Political Consolidation in Taiwan', 21.
55 Fell, *Party Politics in Taiwan*, 60.
56 Myers, Chao and Kuo, 'Consolidating Democracy in the Republic of China on Taiwan', 80–3.
57 Kong, 347.

58 For details on the electoral politics of corruption in the 1990s, see Fell, Chapter 5.
59 Ibid., 60.
60 *China Times,* 29 November 1995, 5. The former Korean president Roh was convicted of corruption and treason charges in 1996 and given a life sentence.
61 *Liberty Times,* 29 November 1994, 18.
62 Fell, 60.
63 *China Times,* 27 November 1997, 5.
64 Fell, 71.
65 Ibid.
66 Ibid., 60.
67 Ibid., 67.
68 Ibid., 72.
69 *Liberty Times,* 15 March 2000, 16.
70 Fell, 61.
71 Ibid.
72 Lin, 'The Evolution of Party Images and Party System in Taiwan: 1992–2004', 40.
73 Fell, 'Political and Media Liberalization and Political Corruption in Taiwan', 875–93.
74 Göbel, 'Beheading the Hydra: Combating Political Corruption and Organised Crime in the KMT and DPP Eras', 61–82, 73.
75 Leou, 'Financial Reform under the KMT and the DPP (1996–2004)', 107–28.
76 Fell, 'Change and Continuity in Taiwanese Party Politics Since 2000', 21–40, 35.
77 Ibid.
78 Ibid.
79 Göbel, 'Beheading the Hydra', 77.
80 Ibid., 78.
81 See *Transparency International,* 'Corruption Perception Index 2016'. Available online at: www.transparency.org/news/feature/corruption_perceptions_index_2016#table (accessed 1 May 2017).
82 Ko Shu-ling, 'KMT crushes DPP in landslide victory', *Taipei Times,* 4 December 2005, 1.
83 See KMT newspaper election advertisement, *China Times,* 10 November 2005, A8.
84 KMT advertisement, *United Daily News,* 26 November 2005, A1.
85 Wu Yu-shan, 'Corruption Brought Down the Green Camp Domain' (*Tanfu Yakua le Lüying Bantu*), (*China Times*), 4 December 2005, A15.
86 Mo Yan-chih, 'Pan Green Academics turn on Chen', *Taipei Times,* 16 July 2006, 1.
87 For more on this movement and its implications, see Shih, 'The "Red" Tide Anti-Corruption Protest: What Does it Mean for Democracy in Taiwan?' 87–98.
88 Fell, 2011b, 'Taiwan's Party System in Transition', 99.
89 Staff Reporter, 'Chen Shui-bian now Prisoner 1020', *Taipei Times,* 4 December 2010, 1.
90 TVBS Poll Center, 'Poll on Party List Legislators and Party Image', 1 June 2015. Available online at: http://other.tvbs.com.tw/export/sites/tvbs/file/other/poll-center/0405281-.pdf (accessed 18 May 2017).
91 Jason Pan, 'Lin Yi-shih sentenced to more than 13 years in jail', *Taipei Times,* 27 February 2016, 1.
92 Jason Pan, 'Lai Su-ju guilty verdict upheld by High Court', *Taipei Times,* 1 September 2016, 1.
93 Simon, 'From Hidden Kingdom to Rainbow Community', 83–4.
94 Cheng, Wu and Amy Adamczyk. 2016. 'Changing Attitudes towards Homosexuality in Taiwan'.
95 TVBS Poll Centre. Poll on Attitudes Towards Homosexuality, 16 April 2012. Available online at: http://other.tvbs.com.tw/export/sites/tvbs/file/other/poll-center/5lge5lexqf.pdf (accessed 18 May 2017).
96 Huang, 'Uneasy Alliance', 268–9.
97 Cole, *Black Island,* 189–247.
98 Cole, *Black Island,* 218.
99 Available online at: www.youtube.com/watch?v=jeIFbqHmpGs (accessed 18 May 2017).
100 Available online at: www.facebook.com/tsaiingwen/videos/10152991551061065/ (accessed 18 May 2017).

101 Available online at: www.youtube.com/watch?v=xLv3wL73RnM (accessed 18 May 2017).
102 Michael Cole, 'Yes, Tsai is stalling on marriage equality,' *Taiwan Sentinel*, 21 February 2017: https://sentinel.tw/tsai-stalling-marriage-equality/ (accessed May 18, 2017).
103 'Taiwan's top court rules in favour of same-sex marriage'. Available online at: www.bbc.co.uk/news/world-asia-40012047 (accessed 29 May 2017).
104 See Fell, *Party Politics in Taiwan*.

12 Taiwan under divided government, 2000–8

The Chen Shui-bian era

On 18 March 2000, the DPP's candidate, Chen Shui-bian, won Taiwan's second direct presidential election. The election was a historic milestone on a range of accounts. It brought an end to a period of uninterrupted KMT rule over Taiwan since 1945. If we include the KMT's period of rule over mainland China, then its defeat in 2000 ended over seven decades of ruling party status. The DPP's victory represents the first election-driven change of ruling parties not only in Taiwan but for any Chinese majority political system. For Taiwanese nationalists, the election marked the end of the KMT party state that had imposed decades of harsh authoritarian rule and a Chinese nation-building project. Many then hoped for progress in their own alternative Taiwanese nation-building programme while Chinese nationalists feared this would bring the start of an era of cultural desinification. For optimists in the KMT, the smooth handover of power in May 2000 reflected the maturity of Taiwan's democracy and also created a golden opportunity for their party to reform itself and put it once more on the road to recovering government office. PRC threats prior to the election, memories of the 1996 missile crisis and KMT election advertisements all contributed to fears that a Chinese invasion was possible if the wrong team won the election. Lastly, after 2000 Taiwan had its first experience of divided government, as though the DPP now held the presidency, it controlled only about a third of seats in the Legislative Yuan.

The year 2000 marked the beginning of a fascinating, controversial but turbulent period in Taiwan's political history. The period saw two electoral changes of ruling parties in 2000 and 2008, in addition to a close call in 2004 when the DPP won by a very narrow margin. These momentous election results brought genuine political and social change to Taiwan, although far less than the winners promised or the losers had predicted. Despite the emotional campaigning, both changes of ruling parties were followed by significant political continuity on a range of dimensions. As discussed in earlier chapters, this period featured hostile interparty relations and an increasingly polarized party system. These trends seem to have affected academic analysis of the Chen Shui-bian era. We saw in Chapter 3 how in this period many scholars began more critical assessments of the state of Taiwan's democracy. The KMT has tried to frame the Chen Shui-bian era as a wasted eight years, but we should not forget the important reforms of the period as well as the political legacy it has had on the subsequent administrations.

This chapter focuses on four closely related questions on the Chen Shui-bian period: (1) How can we best explain the results of the three presidential elections? (2) How can we assess the impact of the change of ruling parties in 2000? (3) Were any of these elections genuine turning points in Taiwan's political history or what political scientists call 'critical elections?' (4) To what extent did the losing sides in these elections learn the lessons of defeat from these setbacks?

Definitions and frameworks

Between 2000 and 2008, there were two changes of ruling parties, first in 2000 when the DPP won the presidency and then in 2008 when the KMT returned to power on the back of landslide presidential and legislative victories. At first glance, these both look like watersheds in Taiwan's political history and thus potential critical elections. Critical elections are defined by Evans and Norris as 'Those exceptional contests which produce abrupt, significant and durable realignments in the electorate with major consequences for the long-term party order.'[1] In the UK case, both the Conservative general election victory in 1979 and New Labour's triumph in 1997 can be taken as examples of critical elections, as they were followed by long periods of political domination. At this stage, we can only talk about potential critical elections in the post-2000 period in Taiwan, as we still need to consider subsequent election results to determine whether we are witnessing a durable partisan realignment.

'Critical' elections are naturally extremely rare political phenomena; 'maintaining' or 'deviating' elections are more common. Maintaining elections are those that feature a continuation of the partisan status quo, while in deviating elections there is a temporary shift in party seat or vote shares, followed by a return to normality in the subsequent election. The other two commonly used concepts regarding party realignment relate to long-term patterns of change. 'Secular dealignment' describes a process of long-term loosening of partisan attachments among voters while 'secular realignment' refers to gradual shifts in party allegiances due to generational change or the impact of new issue cleavages. Looking back at party identification trends (see Table 6.11), we could argue that Taiwan experienced secular realignment, as from the early 1990s there was a steady long-term period of growth in the DPP's support level. The introduction of new political issues contributed to the DPP's party identification rise from 3.3 per cent in 1992 to 26 per cent by the end of the decade.

A number of the chapters in this book have addressed the question of whether or not changes in ruling parties make a difference. This question is highly relevant when we think about the definition of democracy, which requires parties to put into practice what they promised during the campaign once they come to power. Analysing the impact of changes in ruling parties is a mammoth task, and so in this chapter I will only attempt to summarize some key trends from the Chen era. I will return to this question for the Ma and Tsai eras in Chapter 13.

How to explain electoral results and learn the lessons of defeat (and victory) are popular topics for politicians, political scientists and political pundits alike. The day after each election in Taiwan, round tables are organized by think tanks and newspapers in order to analyse the campaign and figure out how to explain the results and expected consequences. In the week after the election, the main political parties hold similar but often closed-door meetings to try to reach conclusions on what went wrong (or right) in their campaigns. However, comparative studies show that parties often do not learn the true lessons of defeat and may well misread the election tea leaves.[2] For instance, both the UK Labour and Conservative Parties reacted to defeats in 1979 and 1997 respectively by appealing to their own core voters rather than the decisive swing voters in the subsequent general election. Similarly, Taiwan's New Party reacted to its setback in 1998 not by reaching out to the middle-class voters who had enabled it to become Taiwan's first significant third party, but by appealing to the dwindling band of hard-core Chinese nationalists. In all these cases, misreading the lessons of election defeat contributed to further setbacks. Internal power struggles rather than scientific data tend to determine whose interpretation of election results is decisive within parties.

Explaining the first change of ruling party in 2000

Fifteen months before losing power in March 2000, the KMT had won a landslide legislative victory in December 1998. It won 54.7 per cent of seats, increasing its overall majority largely at the expense of the NP. Having also survived the Asian Financial Crisis of 1997–8 relatively unscathed, the KMT looked to be in a strong position to retain control of the presidency. The KMT had the advantage of incumbency and its party assets meant it could vastly outspend its rivals. So how could the KMT go from winning a comfortable victory in 1996 with 54 per cent of the vote to coming third place with only 23.1 per cent in 2000?

A range of short- and long-term variables, as well as internal and external ones, contributed to this historical setback for the KMT. The first place to look in explaining the result is the KMT's nomination system. Although the KMT lost in 2000, the Pan Blue vote share reached almost 60 per cent, with the rebel candidate James Soong coming second with 36.8 per cent. Thus, the KMT's inability to field a single presidential candidate split the Pan Blue vote sufficiently enough to enable the DPP to win with only 39.3 per cent. The KMT had multiple warning signs of the dangers of rebel candidates in splitting the vote. In 1996, there had been two sets of rebel KMT presidential candidates, and in 1997 rebel KMT candidates had cost the party dearly in its local executive campaign. However, the difference between 1996 and 2000 was that in 1996 it was always clear that the official candidate Lee Teng-hui was the leading candidate, while the rebels had no real chance of winning.

Table 12.1 shows the support levels for the main candidates from May 1999 to ten days prior to voting day in March 2000. This shows that for most of the campaign the KMT rebel, Soong, was leading the field. However, after December all three candidates were evenly matched. During the final weeks of the campaign, both the KMT's Lien and Soong each tried to convince voters that they were the strongest Pan Blue candidate and that voters should either abandon Soong to save Lien or abandon Lien to save Soong. KMT voters were unsure who the stronger Pan Blue candidate was and thus a divided Pan Blue camp lost to a united DPP. A key question that arises from Table 12.1 is why Soong's support level declined after December 1999. The key factor was the KMT's

Table 12.1 Polls on support for the 2000 presidential candidates

	May 1999	August 1999	Sept 1999	Dec 1999	5 Jan 2000	23 Jan 2000	29 Feb 2000	6 March 2000
Lien	17.2	21	19	21	23	22	24	25
Chen	22.6	22	25	23	24	29	24	26
Soong	36.7	31	33	34	25	27	27	24
DK	22.2	24	22	20	27	21	23	23

Source: TVBS Poll Center: 'Ten Days Before the Election', 6 March 2000. Available at: www.tvbs.com.tw/code/tvbsnews/poll/200003/0305.asp (accessed 20 March 2011).

Note 1: The candidates are Lien Chan for the KMT, Chen Shui-bian for the DPP and James Soong, the rebel KMT candidate.
Note 2: DK stands for undecided voters.

accusations that Soong had embezzled large amounts of money while a senior KMT official in the 1990s. In other words, the *Hsing Piao* case that was discussed in Chapter 11 seriously eroded Soong's support levels. However, placing this issue at the centre of the election agenda was actually detrimental to the KMT itself, as by 2000 it also had a party image for political corruption, thus indirectly benefiting the DPP. This represents another major difference from 1996, where political corruption was not an influential issue in a national identity and cross-Strait dominated campaign.

When we compare the election results of 1996 and 2000, we need to explain three puzzles that contributed to the DPP's success in 2000: (1) Why was Lien so unpopular? (2) Why was the KMT rebel more successful in 2000? (3) Why was Chen more popular than Peng in 1996?

Although Lien's campaign was able to vastly outspend Soong and Chen, in 2000 he struggled to generate momentum to his campaign. First, Lien did not have the kind of charisma of Lee Teng-hui, thus he was unable to enthuse his supporters in the same way as his rivals. Also, Lien had far less election experience than both Chen and Soong and this was clearly apparent in the televised debates. It is sometimes argued that Lee undermined Lien's campaign to allow Chen to win the election. In the final weeks of the campaign, some of Lee's close associates such as the President of Chimei Corporation, Hsu Wen-long (許文龍), did come out in support of Chen. However, I am not convinced by this conspiracy argument, as Lee campaigned extremely hard for Lien throughout the campaign. Nevertheless, Lee was not able to transfer his charisma to Lien and by 2000 Lee had anyway lost much of the popularity that had won him the 1996 election.

Second, voters still recalled Lien's record while Premier for the first two years of Lee's second term. During this period Taiwan suffered an unprecedented crime wave and large anti-crime protests.[3] Dissatisfaction with Lien's record had contributed to the KMT's poor election results in 1997 and his eventual dismissal as Premier in August 1997.

Third, though Lien ran a very expensive campaign, most analysts were critical of its effectiveness. Since Lien's campaign delegated its advertising to multiple companies and maintained multiple campaign headquarters, voters were often confused about the party's message. Since the KMT was fighting to both undermine Soong and the DPP, it also made some strategic errors in its issue emphasis. As mentioned earlier, the anti-corruption attacks against Soong benefited the DPP far more than Lien. Similarly, the advertisements warning that Chen's victory would bring war with China seemed to have a counterproductive effect. In other words, those who wanted Taiwan to stand up to China were more likely to vote for Chen, while those who feared war switched to the candidate seen as most friendly to China, Soong. Lien's appeals on China therefore alienated voters who had supported Lee in 1996 for standing up to China. Lastly, in the final weeks of the campaign, Lien attempted to reach out to Soong's supporters by using Chinese nationalist appeals. For instance, Madame Chiang Kai-shek's (宋美玲) open letter in support of Lien became a KMT newspaper advertisement.[4] Again, this may not have helped win supporters back, but would have alienated KMT voters with strong Taiwanese identification that had voted for Lee in 1996.

In contrast, Soong had many of the attributes that Lien lacked. He was charismatic and a fine rally performer. Of the rallies I attended in 2000, I found similar levels of supporter enthusiasm at Soong's and Chen's events. Soong had also won much popularity while serving as Provincial Governor from 1994 to 1999 and thus gained support from many grassroots politicians. While in 1996 Lin Yang-kang and Hau Pei-tsun's rebel candidacy was more reliant on the support of dark Blue, Mainlander and pro-NP voters,

Soong was able to create a cross-ethnic support base. If there had been an open KMT primary, it is likely that Soong would have been the KMT candidate. One of the most effective TV advertisements during the campaign was set in a post-earthquake disaster zone, and contrasted an uncomfortable and aloof Lien with Soong talking sympathetically with victims. The only thing that Soong lacked was Lee's support, since he had fallen out with Lee over scrapping the provincial government.

In 2000, Chen gained a far greater vote share than Peng's 21.1 per cent in 1996, but only slightly more than the 38.7 per cent the DPP's provincial governor candidate, Chen Ting-nan, had won in 1994. Having contested elections since the mid 1980s, Chen had rich election experience, enabling him to excel at the campaign rallies and TV debates. Second, Chen's advertising is viewed as having been especially effective. This campaign was centralized around his young assistant, Lo Wen-chia, and the advertising specialist, Fan Ke-Chin. The advertisement that was viewed as especially influential showed Chen's relatives and childhood acquaintances in his hometown of Kuantien in Tainan County. The ad was designed to contrast Chen's humble background and Taiwanese credentials with the rich KMT candidates, who had many family members holding US passports. The DPP also benefited from the fact that both welfare and political corruption were high on the electoral agenda, as these were both issues that favoured the DPP over the KMT.

In the final weeks of a campaign, Taiwanese parties like to use the endorsement of influential figures to appeal to undecided voters. In the run-up to the 2000 election, a number of respected academics, business people and artists openly endorsed Chen. These included the Nobel Prize winner Lee Yuan-che, the Founder of the Cloud Gate Ballet Troup, Lin Hwai-min (林懷民) and the Hsu Wen-long.[5] The DPP had never before received the open support of so many high-profile and respected figures.

Unlike in 1996, the cross-Strait issue benefited the DPP rather than the KMT. In 1996, Peng's strong Taiwan independence position meant that his appeal was limited to Taiwanese nationalists. In contrast, the DPP's 1999 adoption of the Resolution on Taiwan's Future gave it a much more moderate image, enabling it to reach out to voters who preferred the status quo. In 2000, the PRC did not employ military exercises and missile tests off the Taiwan coast. However, as discussed in Chapter 9, Chinese Premier Zhu Rongji did sternly warn Taiwan's voters about voting the wrong way. This time it was the DPP that was seen as the only party willing to stand up to China, while the KMT's warnings of the dangers of Taiwan independence made it look soft on China.

What changed? The impact of eight years of DPP rule

When the DPP came to power in 2000, there were contrasting expectations among voters on the losing and winning side. The DPP had raised completely unrealistic expectations of change among its supporters, while some KMT supporters feared imminent cross-Strait conflict. However, the DPP began on a moderate note, with its Five Noes pledge and appointed a KMT member as Premier. Initially, Chen actually had an approval rate as high as 77 per cent.[6] However, within a year serious domestic problems had begun to emerge. The KMT's threat to impeach Chen over his decision to halt construction on the Fourth Nuclear Power Station project in late 2000 marked the start of highly antagonistic interparty relations that would plague the rest of the DPP era.[7] Moreover, the DPP had to face the consequences of the dotcom recession, as Taiwan suffered negative growth in 2001 and record levels of unemployment. Although the DPP economic policies were not dissimilar from those of the previous KMT government, the KMT routinely blamed the DPP for economic mismanagement.[8] External and domestic appraisals of the state of Taiwan's democracy grew increasingly negative after 2001.

We need to be careful to avoid taking sides when attempting to tackle this complex question. DPP rule did not, as KMT election advertisements predicted, bring immediate outbreak of war with China. Although some important reforms were passed during the DPP era, even many of the party's supporters were largely dissatisfied by the results of eight years in power. One of the most important variables constraining the DPP from transforming Taiwan was that it never managed to gain a parliamentary majority. This meant that other than for symbolic moves, it needed KMT support to promote its reform programme. Externally, the DPP government was also limited in its ability to adjust Taiwan's international status both by the threat of Chinese military action and US preference for maintaining the ambiguous status quo of neither independence nor unification. Lastly, the degree of policy continuity suggests that on a range of policy areas Taiwan's main parties are actually far less polarized than appears the case in politicians' electoral rhetoric or as explicated by the politics talk show *mingzui*.

Although Taiwan was under divided government for the DPP era, some important domestic reforms were achieved during this period. We have discussed many of these in earlier chapters. For instance, there was a continued expansion of social welfare schemes, particularly in the field of pensions. Major progress was made in the area of gender equality legislation and a more balanced pattern of female political representation. The DPP did attempt to follow up on its pledges to tackle political corruption. We have also seen the impact of constitutional reform of the electoral system on party politics. Policy-making also became more inclusive, as for the first time civil society actors gained greater policy influence and access to government ministers. We saw in Chapter 10 how this partnership with civil society allowed for gender mainstreaming to be brought into the policy-making process. In other areas, such as labour politics and environmental protection, the relationship between civil society and the DPP government became increasingly hostile over time. However, most of the more progressive legislation came in the first DPP term, as the DPP struggled to get its legislation through parliament in the more hostile partisan atmosphere witnessed after 2004. The party's compromises with big business and its growing reputation for corruption after 2005 were also the source of great disappointment to many of the DPP's supporters.

As the DPP was constantly frustrated in its domestic reform agenda, it often fell back on employing Taiwan identity appeals. Even in this policy realm, the DPP impact was limited. Klöter's study on language policy details how, despite the introduction of native language education after 2000, Mandarin remained the dominant language in Taiwan.[9] Similarly, attempts to establish a commonly accepted system for writing Taiwanese and promoting a new Mandarin Romanization system known as *Tongyong Pinyin* were both abject failures.

Externally, the DPP's impact looks even less impressive. The cross-Strait stalemate that began in the final years of the Lee presidency continued, as the PRC refused to reopen the semi-official talks with Taiwan. While Taiwan and China converged economically, they continued to diverge politically. Internationally, Taiwan did retain its de facto alliance with the US, but the US was often frustrated by Chen's handling of external relations and by 2008 appeared to prefer a KMT victory in the presidential election. Under the DPP, the PRC continued to squeeze Taiwan's international space as its number of formal diplomatic relations declined and no progress was made in its UN bid. Nevertheless, the

DPP could argue that it institutionalized Taiwan's de facto independence and, as we saw in Chapter 8, support for independence and numbers of people identifying themselves as Taiwanese both rose, while support for unification and numbers of people identifying themselves as Chinese continued to decline. Moreover, eight years of DPP rule persuaded the PRC that it would need to take a slightly more flexible approach towards Taiwan than in the 1990s once the KMT returned to power.

Lessons of defeat?

Losing the 2000 presidential election was a traumatic experience for the KMT. As had been the case after losing power in China in 1949, the KMT tried to learn the lessons of defeat by introducing a series of party reforms to put it back on the road to recovery.[10] The KMT's new approaches fell into four broad categories: (1) organizational change, (2) party leadership change, (3) policy position and issue emphasis change and (4) change in interparty relations. Trends in election results and party identification suggest that at least up to December 2004 the KMT had learnt some but not all the key lessons of the 2000 setback.

The KMT rightly saw organizational failures as a key factor in its fall from power and moved to institutionalize and democratize the nomination process. As we discussed in Chapter 6, the KMT introduced the mixed survey and primary system (modelled on the DPP's system) for candidate nomination and also a party member primary for selecting the party chair. It was hoped that this would give the chairperson greater legitimacy and also help avoid the rebel candidates that had plagued the party since the late 1980s. The party also tried to remove its reputation for political corruption by changing nomination regulations to prevent candidates with criminal records from being nominated. As in the early 1950s, the KMT ran a complete membership reregistration process, with the aim of rooting out unreliable or dormant party members.

The KMT also tried to make a fresh start in its leadership from the Lee era. Many politicians blamed Lee rather than Lien for the defeat and thus Lee was pressured to resign the KMT chairmanship early. Lien then became the acting chair until the first direct chair election in 2001, while Lee and his close supporters were increasingly marginalized in the party. Thus, the charismatic Lee was replaced by the wooden Lien. Lien's advisers did try to liven up his image. The prime example of this was the TV advertisement described in Chapter 5 that showed Lien in superhero attire defeating an assortment of monsters at football. Lien also brought a very different set of party leaders and advisers into his inner circle compared with Lee, many of whom came from the non-Mainstream KMT.

The KMT also tried to adopt a radically different policy approach from that seen in Lee's second term: it disowned Lee's special state-to-state concept and 'no haste, be patient' guidelines for cross-Strait relations. Instead, Lien proposed a confederacy model for unification in 2001, and the KMT once again talked about One China.[11] In the 2001 election it attacked the DPP for economic mismanagement and also stressed Chinese nationalist symbols that Lee had dropped, such as Sun Yat Sen and Chiang Ching-kuo. Such appeals on the centre-right of the national identity spectrum may appear irrational considering the overall public opinion trends at the time. However, they were designed to try to win back Pan Blue voters that had shifted to the PFP or NP. The last important lesson that the KMT learnt from 2000 was the need for Pan Blue unity and cooperation against the DPP. Serious efforts were made to promote cooperation between the PFP,

NP and KMT and to heal some of the scars from the vicious attacks between Lien and Soong in the 2000 campaign. The three Pan Blue parties cooperated successfully in the Legislative Yuan in the first Chen term – for instance, they were able to exert sufficient pressure to force the DPP government to resume construction on the Fourth Nuclear Power Station. This improved interparty relationship eventually did bear fruit in the joint Pan Blue presidential ticket of Lien and Soong in 2004.

We can judge the KMT's success in learning the lessons of the 2000 defeat by examining its subsequent election results and presidential campaign. As Table 5.2 shows, the KMT suffered its worst ever legislative results in 2001, and was even threatened to be replaced by the PFP as the largest Pan Blue party. In fact, in 2001 and 2002 the PFP enjoyed higher party identification than the KMT. Despite the improved Pan Blue legislative cooperation, in the 2001 legislative election the Pan Blue rivalries were as damaging as in 2000. The DPP once again benefited from a divided Pan Blue camp. However, by early 2003 the KMT's prospects were looking vastly improved, its party identification had bounced back and its candidate (Lien) was the presidential rather than vice-presidential candidate on the Pan Blue ticket.

2004 election

When the PFP and KMT leaders agreed on a joint ticket for the 2004 presidential campaign in March 2003, it looked like the end for the DPP era. In 2000, the Pan Blues had gained almost 60 per cent of the vote and had retained a majority in the Legislative Yuan after 2001. Table 12.2 shows how they had a huge poll lead for most of the 2004 campaign of over 20 per cent. However, the gap narrowed rapidly from the autumn of 2003, with the Pan Blue lead fluctuating between 10 and 3 per cent for the remainder of the campaign. Finally, on 20 March 2004, the DPP's Chen Shui-bian won re-election by the narrowest of margins against the joint Pan Blue ticket. Chen gained 6,471,970 (50.11 per cent), compared to the Pan Blues' 6,442,452 (49.89 per cent). As occurred in 2000, the campaign mattered. In other words, the DPP was able to persuade enough voters to change their voting intensions to allow it to win.

The KMT and their allies refused to accept the legitimacy of the result, accusing the DPP of electoral fraud on a number of counts. The KMT suspected the DPP of having faked the 19 March assassination attempt (known as the 3–19 shooting) on Chen and Lu and blamed this for the election result. It also accused the government of abusing the

Table 12.2 Polls on support for the 2004 presidential candidates

	14 April 2003	16 Sept 2003	30 Oct 2003	25 Nov 2003	26 Dec 2003	30 Jan 2004	27 Feb 2004	8 Mar 2004	17 Mar 2004	19 Mar 2004
Lien	53	54	41	46	45	47	41	40	46	39
Chen	32	31	35	33	34	35	38	36	37	38
DK	16	15	25	21	21	18	21	24	17	24
Lien lead	21	23	6	13	11	12	3	4	9	1

Source: TUBS Poll Center: 'Survey one day before the election after the shooting of Chen Shui-bian', 19 March 2004. Available online at: www.tvbs.com.tw/fiLE_DB/files/osaka/200404/osaka-20040427193847.pdf (accessed 1 April 2011).

Note 1: The candidates are Lien Chan for the KMT/PFP and Chen Shui-bian for the DPP.
Note 2: DK stands for undecided voters.

National Security Mechanism after the assassination attempt to cancel leave for military and security personnel, thus preventing thousands of traditionally Pan Blue voters from returning home to vote.[12] Instead of a mild acceptance of defeat speech, Lien called on the Central Election Commission to declare the election invalid and demanded a full recount.[13] In response, the KMT instigated a series of large and sometimes violent protests and legal cases demanding the result be declared invalid. A recount was held but it only produced a slight adjustment in Chen's majority, and the lawsuits challenging the election's legitimacy were ultimately unsuccessful.

Table 12.2 does suggest that the assassination attempt may well have swung some undecided voters behind the Chen ticket on the final day. However, proving causation is not straightforward and, as the table shows, the KMT's poll lead had already been narrowed by October 2003. Moreover, a common pattern in many Taiwanese surveys is that DPP voters are often under reported. The problem for the KMT was that it became obsessed with the shooting incident and failed to fully examine why it lost its commanding lead in the campaign.

The campaign suggests that the KMT had not fully learnt the lessons of 2000. First, although it had a single unified presidential ticket, the party once more decided nomination behind closed doors and thus it was party hierarchy rather than popularity that determined the final selection. Therefore, Chen faced the uncharismatic Lien once more. Soong was only the vice-presidential candidate this time as his own personal popularity had declined after 2002. If the party had nominated its most popular politician at the time, Taipei Mayor Ma Ying-jeou, the KMT would probably have returned to power. With public satisfaction rates of almost 80 per cent in 2003, Ma would have represented a formidable challenge for the incumbent Chen.[14]

Another KMT failure was that it once again ran a poor campaign compared to that of the DPP. The DPP was able to dominate the election agenda, particularly stressing the island's first referendums and held the Hand in Hand Rally featuring a human chain from the far south to the far north of the island on 28 February 2004. The rally was meant to show Taiwanese solidarity against the PRC missiles targeting Taiwan. The DPP's promotion of Taiwan's first-ever referendums and the KMT's call on voters to boycott the referendums allowed the DPP to accuse the KMT of being anti-democratic. Overall, the DPP ran quite a positive campaign combining Taiwanese identity appeals (such as the Hand in Hand Rally) with an emphasis on the many reforms it had made in the first term (such as on gender equality and welfare). The KMT campaign did not use the anti-Taiwan independence rhetoric of 2000, but instead ran a highly negative campaign, particularly against Chen's personality. KMT advertisements likened Chen to Hitler, Saddam Hussein and Bin Laden.[15] It also boycotted the Hand in Hand Rally and encouraged its supporters to boycott the two referendums. Like Lee Teng-hui in the past, the KMT tried to steal the DPP Taiwan identity appeal. As mentioned in Chapter 8, in one of the largest pre-election Pan Blue rallies, its candidates kissed the ground to show their love of Taiwan. However, unlike Lee, Lien and Soong were not viewed as convincing on the Taiwan identity appeal. By placing this issue at the centre of the political agenda, therefore, they were helping the DPP. In the final weeks of the campaign, the economic fugitive Chen Yu-hao made a number of corruption allegations against Chen Shui-bian. However, this may not have actually damaged Chen Shui-bian, as it looked like an economic criminal was supporting the KMT, and in 2004 the political corruption issue still favoured the DPP. In contrast to the DPP advertisements listing its various successes, the KMT attempted to frame the first four years as one of government failure.

One such KMT advertisement visualizes this through the lens of an office setting. One office worker throws a piece of crumpled paper into the cigarette bin, which then catches light and sets off a series chaotic scenes. The ad ends with the slogan, 'If you vote the wrong way, we will not have a good life' (投錯了, 不會有好日子). In other words, the message was that voting DPP would only lead to a disaster.

The KMT's obsession with the 3–19 shooting meant that to a certain extent it wasted a year – a year that could have been used reforming and learning lessons from 2004. Although the KMT did show signs of recovery in the December 2004 parliamentary elections and viewed them as a KMT victory, this interpretation is not entirely accurate. One reason why this was seen as a DPP setback was that Chen set an unrealistic target of a Pan Green majority and thus the DPP over-nominated. The KMT's seat share gain was entirely at the expense of the PFP, with the DPP remaining the largest party and increasing its vote and seat share. KMT cooperation with the PFP ensured that the PFP remained a relevant party that continued to split the Pan Blue vote. The election results were almost exactly the same as in 2001, suggesting real limitations to the KMT and an overall Pan Blue recovery under Lien's leadership.

The bitterness felt on both sides from the 2004 presidential election contributed to the highly polarized and antagonistic party politics of the second Chen term. We saw this in the trend of polarization on the national identity issue discussed in Chapters 6 and 8. In addition, numerous formerly consensual issues became polarized and partisan. There had been a cross-party agreement that Taiwan needed to bolster its defences against China by buying advanced weapons. However, the inclusion of a referendum on purchasing anti-missile systems on the same day as the 2004 presidential election turned this into a contested issue and the Pan Blue controlled legislature repeatedly blocked the government's attempts to gain approval for the US arms package. There was a similar pattern in Pan Blue obstruction of the government budget in 2006 and endorsement of Chen's Control Yuan nominations. These were unprecedented developments on formerly relatively consensual issues.

Was 2005 a potential critical election or critical year?

When we try to apply party realignment concepts to Taiwan's recent political history, a number of elections appear to be turning points. For instance, 1992 marks the start of a long period of consistent growth in DPP party identification that continued through until late 2004, corresponding with the concept of secular realignment. Another important year is 1994, which saw the emergence of the NP as Taiwan's first 'third party'. We can see this in election results (see Tables 5.1 and 5.2) and party identification surveys (see Table 6.11). However, the party soon faded away in the late 1990s, suggesting that we can view those mid-1990s contests as deviating elections, before a return to two-party competition. Both 2000 and 2008 also appear strong candidates as potential critical elections. The year 2000 marks the start of a period of multi-party competition with four or even five relevant parties that lasted through until December 2004. Table 6.11 shows the huge shift in party identification, as between 1999 and 2001 KMT support fell from 33 per cent to only 14 per cent. The weakness of the 2000 argument is that this multi-party system collapsed between 2005 and 2008, as Taiwan became a pure two-party system. We may also be able to consider 2000–4 a deviating period, before a return to the normality of two-party competition. The key bases to the 2008 claim to be a potential critical election are the landslide KMT presidential and parliamentary victories that year. They gave the KMT the kind of control of Taiwanese politics not seen since the late authoritarian era.

In a study published in 2010, I argued that rather than 2008 we should regard 2005 as the potential critical election.[16] The December 2005, local executive elections set a pattern for a two-party competition and KMT domination in seat shares that would be repeated in 2008 and 2009. 2005 also saw record shifts in party identification; with KMT support rising from 21.9 to 33.2 per cent and DPP support falling from 26.3 to 20.6 per cent (see Table 6.11). This was then followed by four years of quite stable party identification, which did not seem to be affected by momentous events such as the 2006 Red Shirt Movement or 2008 change in ruling parties. If we also consider the seat shares of the 2009 local executive and 2010 special municipality executive elections, we could argue that the period of KMT domination set in 2005 was maintained through to 2010. On the other hand, the 2010 party identification figures (see Table 6.11) and the even share of city council seats in 2010 suggest a more competitive two-party system.

There are other reasons for considering 2005 a watershed moment in Taiwan's political history. The Pan Blue leaders' visits to China and resulting CCP–KMT dialogue set the pattern for cross-Strait relations that would be implemented at the government level once the KMT returned to power after 2008. Also highly influential was the reform of the election system in 2005, which contributed to the highly disproportional election results in favour of the KMT in 2008. This, of course, raises the question of what caused the historic shifts in public opinion in 2005.

The most obvious answer would appear to be the Pan Blue visits to China in April 2005, the first such party-to-party talks since the 1940s. Although these visits were quite controversial, they were more popular than some had expected. In Table 12.3 I have laid out the party identification figures from TVBS polls between April 2004 and December 2005. These show that although KMT support did rise slightly after the trips, DPP support also rose at that moment. But what is clear is that the most dramatic rise for the KMT (32 to 47 per cent) and fall for the DPP (21 to 12 per cent) occurred between August and December 2005. I argue that the two most important explanations for these shifts in public opinion were the DPP's loss of its reputations for clean government and Ma's election as KMT party chairman in the summer of 2005.[17]

The shifting party images on clean governance in Table 11.2 do suggest a potential relationship with the respective parties' popularity and 2005 election results. The KMT's image for clean governance shows a significant improvement after Ma became party chairman in June 2005. But what is especially striking is how, following the emergence

Table 12.3 TVBS party identification surveys, 2004–5

	April 2004	*July 2004*	*2 Feb 2005*	*30 March 2005*	*28 April 2005*	*23 May 2005*	*24 Aug 2005*	*15 Dec 2005*
DPP	23	23	26	24	18	23	21	12
KMT	21	16	23	23	24	31	32	47
PFP	10	10	7	8	5	5	4	3
TSU	2	5	4	4	4	4	4	3
Indep	40	41	36	37	45	33	37	31

Source: TVBS Poll Center, 'Survey on the reputation of the nine major politicians after the three in one election', 15 December 2005. Available online at: www.tvbs.com.tw/fiLE_DB/DL_DB/yijung/200512/yijung-20051216 190351. pdf (accessed 1 April 2011).

of the Kaohsiung MRT corruption scandal in late 2005, we see a simultaneous deterioration in the DPP image on the corruption issue and its party identification levels. For the rest of the DPP era and through into the Ma era, the corruption issue remained favourable to the KMT. The heavy media coverage of the Chen family trials after 2008 ensured that the issue cast a long shadow over the DPP's post-2008 election recovery. It was not until 2010 that party images returned to the pre-2005 pattern of the KMT having a worse reputation for political corruption.

Ma's victory in the 2005 KMT party chair primary ensured KMT nomination for the presidential election, and thus by 2005 the nomination issue was resolved. Moreover, as we mentioned earlier, Ma's nomination was important for the party to offer a clean governance image as Ma is one of the few leading KMT politicians seemingly immune to corruption attacks, gaining nicknames of 'non-stick pan' or 'Teflon man'.[18]

Lessons of defeat: Part 2

In first January and then March 2008 the KMT won landslide election victories in both the parliamentary and presidential elections (see Tables 5.2 and 5.3). Explaining these results requires examining a range of long- and short-term variables. By comparing the 2008 campaign to previous contests, it is clear that the KMT benefited from learning the lessons of its earlier defeats.

As with so many Taiwanese elections, the first place to look for explanations of election results is nomination. For the presidential election in 2008, the KMT had a clear advantage over the DPP on this dimension. Its competitive party chair primary in 2005 meant that the KMT presidential candidate would be Ma, as he had beaten his challenger Wang Jin-pyng so convincingly throughout Taiwan. This meant that there was no need for a KMT presidential primary, as no one was strong enough to challenge Ma's nomination after 2005. Thus, Ma had two and a half years to prepare his campaign for 2008. Unlike in 2000 and 2004, where party hierarchy had determined KMT nomination, in 2008 it was popularity.

In contrast, the DPP had four contestants for its presidential primary election in May 2007. The process generated much animosity between supporters of the main camps. The timing left the winner, Hsieh Chang-ting, less than a year to reunite the DPP and revive the party's morale. Hsieh did try to reach out to his opponents by nominating for vice-president the primary runner up, Su Chen-chang. However, as we can see in Table 12.4, the Hsieh camp had a mountain to climb trying to narrow Ma's 20-point poll lead. The table also shows that unlike in 2000 and 2004, the DPP failed to make inroads into the Pan Blue poll lead. In fact, the stability of polls in the eight months prior to voting day is remarkably different from the previous campaigns. This suggests that the campaign did not have any major effect on voters.

The KMT also had an advantage when it came to legislative nomination. Although both parties used similar primary methods that combined party member votes and public surveys, the DPP's primary process was especially acrimonious and divisive compared to the KMT's primaries and the DPP's earlier ones. For the KMT, nomination and primaries played a unifying and conflict resolution role. First, many PFP politicians chose to abandon their party and return to the KMT to contest its primaries. For those remaining PFP legislators, the KMT either found them legislative districts (as KMT candidates) or nominated them on the KMT's proportional representation list. This meant that the PFP was effectively merged into the KMT and thus, for the first time since 1992, there was

Table 12.4 Presidential candidate support levels, 2007–8

	15 Aug 2007	19 Sept 2007	15 Jan 2008	31 Jan 2008	15 Feb 2008	29 Feb 2008	9 Mar 2008	13 Mar 2008	17 Mar 2008	19 Mar 2008	21 Mar 2008
Ma	51	53	56	56	53	54	50	47	54	52	51
Hsieh	30	30	26	30	29	30	31	32	28	30	29
DK	19	17	18	14	19	16	19	21	18	18	20
Ma lead	21	23	30	26	24	24	19	15	26	22	22

Source: TVBS Poll Center, 'Poll one day before the 2008 presidential election', 21 March 2008. Available online at: www.tvbs.com.tw/fiLE_DB/DL_DB/even/200803/even-20080328162638.pdf (accessed 1 April 2011).

Note 1: The candidates are Ma Ying-jeou for the KMT and Hsieh Chang-ting for the DPP.
Note 2: DK stands for undecided voters.

only one relevant Pan Blue party in district-level elections.[19] Where there was competition for KMT district nomination, generally competitive primaries were held and this did contribute to the low level of KMT rebel candidates.

Two developments made the DPP's legislative nomination especially divisive. First, the party introduced a new element to the survey dimension of its primary known as the 'remove the blues survey'. This meant that if respondents stated they were supporting the KMT or other Pan Blue parties, they would not be included in the survey, thus effectively removing swing voters from the selection process. However, it was because this reform was introduced so late and was seen as being designed to favour more radical elements of the party that it created such divisions. This system might have worked under the old multiple-member district system, but with single-member districts, parties now needed to appeal more to the swing voters in the middle. A second problem for the DPP's primaries was the allegations of party candidates using fraudulent methods to manipulate the survey portion of primaries. These allegations involved candidates buying vast numbers of telephone lines so that they could channel survey calls to their own supporters. In short, nomination contributed to a united Pan Blue camp facing a divided DPP in 2008.

The new electoral system for the legislative election also played a role in the KMT's landslide victory. Tables 5.1 and 5.2 show that although the DPP increased its vote share from 35.7 per cent (2004) to 36.9 per cent (2008), its seat share fell from 39.6 to a mere 24 per cent. In contrast, the Pan Blues did benefit from an effective 11-seat head start, as its strongholds of the offshore islands (3 seats), east coast (2 seats) and aboriginal districts (6 seats) were largely unaffected by the reforms. For instance, tiny Kinmen and Mazu both retained their seats, while Kaohsiung City went from 11 seats to only 5. Under the new system, the KMT swept the board, winning almost all district seats north of Chiayi County, while the DPP was only competitive in the south and in the proportional representation vote. The new single-member district system meant that, unlike in the past, there were large numbers of wasted votes. In Yilan in 2004, for example, the three winning candidates shared 82 per cent of the vote, but in 2008 the winning candidate gained 53 per cent and the remaining 47 per cent of the votes were wasted.

An obvious question is why the DPP would, and particularly Chen, have been so foolish to support this new unfavourable system? There had been voices within the DPP, such as Lin Cho-shui, warning of the potential damaging consequences of electoral reform. The DPP's ability to gain over 50 per cent of the vote share for the first time in the

2004 presidential election had convinced Chen that the DPP could win a majority under a single-member district system. We also need to consider that the DPP's calculations were probably based on the prospect that there would still be a divided Pan Blue camp consisting of the KMT, PFP and maybe even the NP. If these three had remained divided, as in 2001 and 2004, then the 2008 election result would have looked much more favourable for the Greens.

Major swings in public opinion also contributed to the KMT's return to power. In 2005, the KMT once again became the most popular party and was led by Taiwan's most popular politician, Ma Ying-jeou. In contrast, the DPP's support rates and Chen's presidential satisfaction rates plummeted and remained low for the years up to 2008. As we can see in Table 12.4, the KMT maintained its lead throughout the campaign regardless of DPP efforts. So here we need to ask three questions:

1   Why was the KMT so far ahead at the outset?
2   How did it maintain its lead?
3   What did the KMT and DPP do differently from earlier campaigns?

We have already touched upon some of the factors leading to the contrasting party support levels one or two years prior to the election. In 2005, the KMT gained a major advantage on the political corruption issue as corruption scandals first emerged in late 2005 and continued to dominate the political agenda until well after the KMT won power. The DPP also became less attractive to floating voters, as it became more extreme on national identity in the final two years of Chen's second term. As a result of KMT obstruction in parliament, the DPP also had little of note to list in terms of policy achievements in the second term. Thus, it could not campaign hard on its government performance. Even though the economy was recovering by 2007, there was a widespread perception that Taiwan was in economic decline, especially compared with rivals such as South Korea. The picture was also similar on cross-Strait relations. While relations were blooming economically, there was a widespread impatience with the long-term political stalemate and resulting tensions. In contrast, the KMT was led by a politician with a clean image and charisma, and was viewed as more reliable on cross-Strait relations, clean government and the economy.

A number of elements of the KMT campaigns were quite distinct from earlier elections, and some of these did contribute to the party's improved performance. First, the Ma campaign was much more effective at employing the Taiwan identity theme than Lien had been in 2000 or 2004. Ma published a book titled *Taiwan Spirit* in which he discussed Taiwanese historical events and figures. He also used his campaign activities to express his attachment to Taiwan. For instance, in 2007 he led his team on a cycle tour from the far south of Taiwan to the far north, the account of which was later also published in book form.[20] He also employed what became known as his 'Long Stay' programme, whereby Ma would reside with rural people away from Taipei and spend time working with farmers or workers. Images of Ma toiling in a paddy field or on a fruit farm were all part of Ma's skilled political theatre, something that was absent in the Lien campaigns.

Ma also tried to give the KMT a more moderate policy image than under Lien. For instance, Ma did not follow Lien in visiting China to conduct party-to-party talks. His campaign slogan of 'no unification, no independence and no use of force' was designed to place the KMT near the centre on national identity.[21] However, Ma did offer voters a different vision regarding cross-Strait relations, proposing that by accepting the 1992 consensus, cross-Strait relations could help fix Taiwan's economic crisis. Ma also offered voters hope of an improved Taiwan. For instance, he stated that 'We expect to achieve a target economic growth of at least 6 per cent a year from 2008, a per capita income of US$20,000 by 2011 and creation of 100,000 job opportunities as well as an un-employment rate of below 3 per cent.'[22] While Lien had focused on attacking Chen, Ma's official campaign was overwhelmingly positive. Two of his spokesman Lo Chih-chiang's (羅智強) comments reflect his distinct approach compared to Lien:

> He (Ma) deliberately tried to appear civil. He doesn't like extreme emotions in his campaign style and wanted to avoid making personal attacks . . . Our campaign style was what we call a parallel campaign. In other words, 'We run our campaign, you run yours. We do not take any notice of your campaign and it's best if you do not take any notice of ours.'[23]

On a similar note, Ma had tried to keep some distance from the often violent Pan Blue protests, first against the 2004 election and then the Red Shirts protests of 2006. Since Ma was Taipei mayor at the time, he controlled the policing of these demonstrations and thus he was able to remain aloof from these more radical projects.

In his election advertising Ma talked of how Taiwan had wasted too much time under the DPP and how he represented a government in waiting that would set Taiwan back on course. This was encapsulated in an advertisement that showed galloping horses (representing Ma, whose surname means 'horse') and then various KMT local executives talking of change, hope and the message that they were ready for the new Taiwan. Ma finally appeared at the end encouraging voters to cast their vote to change Taiwan's future.[24]

To say that the KMT was completely free of negative campaigning is, of course, not accurate. However, Ma tried to delegate the more negative messages to the KMT legislative camp. Some key KMT attacks focused on Chen's personality, DPP corruption, economic recession and government failure. KMT man-in-the-street advertisements were reminiscent of those used by the DPP in 2000 and showed ordinary voters complaining about DPP corruption and how they struggled to make a living due to economic mismanagement. As mentioned earlier, the economy was on the mend by 2007, but after seven years of relatively poor economic performance there was a perception of economic failure and thus the KMT economic appeal finally seemed to be paying off. Although Chen was not standing for re-election, the KMT's attacks against Chen enabled them to frame the election as a referendum on eight years of Chen rule. Since Chen was so unpopular by this stage, again this favoured Ma and the KMT.

Ma's popularity was such that he was able to withstand corruption accusations from the DPP. In fact, in early 2007 he was indicted on similar charges to Chen for misuse of his special mayoral allowance. However, this failed to undermine his poll standings. Unlike Lien in 2001 or 2004, Ma was a key image appeal for legislative candidates. KMT candidates were desperate for Ma to join their campaign rallies and most used Ma's picture in their campaign literature. There was a clear coat-tail effect for KMT legislative candidates trying to benefit from Ma's popularity. All in all, the KMT's campaign was rather similar to that of Lee Tenghui's in 1996, basically running a positive campaign and ignoring the rivals.

In some respects, the DPP campaign was quite similar to previous ones. However, it failed to have the desired impact of bringing back voters. As in 2004, the DPP was able to hold referendums on the same day as the national elections. These included referendums on recovering KMT assets, together with the January legislative election and one supporting Taiwan's UN campaign with the presidential campaign. Although both are important issues, they were unable to generate much voter enthusiasm compared with 2004, and the KMT boycott of these referendums meant that both failed to reach their required 50 per cent participation rate. The DPP did try to boost the chances of the assets referendum in some novel ways. One advertisement showed the Government Information Office Minister rapping and dancing with youngsters in praise of the assets referendum and singing of how resolving the issue would benefit tuition fees and welfare.[25] In the Noodle Shop TV advertisement, the shop owner explains to her gloomy customers how recovering KMT assets will pay for business start-up loans and other welfare schemes. In contrast, the DPP was far less supporting of its UN referendum bid, seeing it as a lost cause by March.

Another key DPP theme was to blame the KMT for blocking good legislation in parliament. Advertisements on this theme looked to be almost carbon copies of similar ones used in 2001 and 2004 that attacked the KMT for brutal blocking of welfare, and child welfare schemes in particular. There were once again anti-corruption advertisements, particularly focused on Ma. But it would appear that these had limited impact. The lack of innovation in DPP advertising was apparent in that one advertisement used not only the same music but also many of the same images as one in 2000.

A final major DPP theme was to accuse the KMT of disloyalty to Taiwan in its dealings with China and warned of the dangers of economic dependence on China. For instance, one TV advertisement showed images of Lien and Hu Jintao shaking hands and then showed Chinese missiles. Following the break-out of PRC violence against Tibetan monks in March 2008, a DPP advertisement warned of the dangers of agreements with the CCP. It reminded them of the 1951 China–Tibet agreement and the dangers of Taiwan becoming a second Tibet. The DPP also warned of the dangers of what they called the 'One China market', referring to KMT vice-presidential candidate Vincent Siew's proposal for a cross-Strait common market. Such attacks focused on the possibility of free movement of Chinese labour to Taiwan and how it would cause widespread unemployment. Lastly, the DPP questioned Ma's lack of loyalty to Taiwan by accusing him of still retaining his American green card. Even Ma's former spokesman, Lo Chih-chiang, admitted that the DPP campaign style meant that it tended to control the electoral agenda.[26] However, unlike in previous campaigns, it still did not seem to affect public support levels.

Conclusions

This chapter has examined Taiwan's political developments in the eight-year Chen Shui-bian presidency. A recent edited volume notes that 'The Chen Shui-bian era left a complicated legacy for Taiwan.'[27] While the editors see some positives in the area of democratic consolidation, the overall evaluation is more critical, particularly in economic performance, political corruption scandals, media and political polarization, as well as in tense relations with China. It was an era of significant change and continuity. It featured Taiwan's first taste of divided government, first change of ruling parties through elections, lawsuits over the legitimacy of election results and unprecedented polarization and political violence. Both domestic and foreign evaluations of the state of Taiwan's democracy became more critical than they were in the 1990s. However, Taiwan's democracy coped surprisingly well with many of these new challenges. I have argued that 2005 represents the best candidate for being a potential critical election or watershed year. Taiwan's parties showed themselves to be highly adaptable to the more complicated political environment after 2000. The best case of this was the way that the KMT learnt from its electoral setbacks to allow it to return to power in 2008. The impact of the second (2008) and third (2016) changes of ruling parties will be discussed in the next chapter.

Discussion questions

1   How can we best explain the results of the three presidential elections of the Chen era?
2   What was the impact of the DPP's eight years in power?
3   Were any of these elections genuine turning points in Taiwan's political history or what political scientists call 'critical elections?'
4   To what extent did the KMT learn the lessons of defeat?
5   Assess the competing evaluations of the Chen Shui-bian presidency.
6   What have been the main political legacies of this period?

Further reading

Ash, Robert, John Garver and Penelope Prime (eds). 2011. *Taiwan's Democracy: Economic and Political Challenges*. London: Routledge. A collection of essays that examine how Taiwan has coped with its political and economic challenges since 2000.

Chu Yun-han, Larry Diamond and Kharis Templeman (eds). 2016. *Taiwan's Democracy Challenged: The Chen Shui-bian Years*. Boulder, CO: Lynne Rienner. This new volume assesses the period through a range of angles. An advantage this has is that it was written eight years after Chen left office thus has more complete data than the other three volumes which were largely written during Chen's second term.

Fell, Dafydd. 2009. 'Lessons of Defeat: A Comparison of Taiwanese Ruling Parties' Responses to Electoral Defeat.' *Asian Politics and Policy,* 1(4): 660–81. In this article I examine how the KMT and DPP tried to learn the lessons of its electoral defeats. In the case of the KMT, I show how this learning contributed to its return to power in 2008.

Fell, Dafydd. 2010. 'Was 2005 A Critical Election in Taiwan? Locating the Start of a New Political Era'. *Asian Survey,* 50(5): 927–45. This paper applies the concept of critical elections to Taiwan's post-2000 politics.

Fell, Dafydd, Henning Klöter and Chang Bi-yu (eds). 2006. *What has Changed: Taiwan Before and After the Change in Ruling Parties*. Wiesbaden: Harrassowitz. The chapters in this edited volume compare Taiwan before and after the change in ruling parties in 2000.

Goldstein, Steven and Julian Chang (eds). 2008. *Presidential Politics in Taiwan: The Administration of Chen Shui-bian*. Norwalk, CT: Eastbridge. Another outstanding collection of articles focused on developments during Chen's first and second terms.

Notes

1   Evans and Norris (eds), *Critical Elections: British Parties and Voters in Long-Term Perspective,* xxxi.
2   Norris and Lovenduski, 'Why Parties Fail to Learn: Electoral Defeat, Selective Perception and British Party Politics', 85–104.
3   For example, see Chen Hsi-lin, 'Protesting student sit in and 12 hour hunger strike: Weekend Rally's clear message: President admit error and replace the Cabinet', *United Daily News,* 2 May 1997, 5.
4   *China Times,* 15 March 2000, 1.
5   See DPP advertisement, *China Times,* 16 March 2000, 7.

6 TVBS Poll Center, 'Poll on the Popularity of the Main Politicians in the Country', 28 August 2007. Available online at: www.tvbs.com.tw/news/poll_center (accessed 7 February 2011).
7 For a discussion of both the Fourth Nuclear Power Station controversy and environmental politics in the first Chen term, see Arrigo and Puleston, 'The Environmental Movement in Taiwan after 2000: Advances and Dilemmas', 165–84.
8 For a discussion of the DPP's economic policies, see Ash, Lin and Wu, 'The Economic Legacy of the KMT and its Implications for Economic Policy Formulation under the DPP', 83–106.
9 Klöter, 'Mandarin Remains More Equal: Changes and Continuities in Taiwan's Language Policy', 207–24.
10 For an examination of how the KMT tried to recover after losing the Chinese Civil War, see Dickson, 'The Lessons of Defeat: The Reorganization of the Kuomintang on Taiwan, 1950–52', 56–84.
11 Staff Writer, 'Lien Touts Confederation', *Taipei Times*, 5 January 2001, 3.
12 For details on the KMT's suspicions over the election, see *'Bulletgate' Questions on the Legitimacy of the Presidency* (Taipei, National Policy Foundation, 2004).
13 Huang Tai-lin, 'Lien Calls Election Unfair, Demands a Recount', *Taipei Times*, 21 March 2004, 17.
14 For comparative poll ratings of Taiwan's leading politicians at this time, see TVBS Poll Center, 'Poll on the Popularity of the Main Politicians in the Country After the 326 March', 30 March 2005. Available online at: www.tvbs.com.tw/news/poll_center (accessed 7 February 2011).
15 *China Times*, 12 March 2004, A7.
16 Fell, 'Was 2005 A Critical Election in Taiwan? Locating the Start of a New Political Era', 927–45.
17 Ibid.
18 Liberty Times Editorial, 'Beware Ma's KMT Chairmanship', *Taipei Times*, 2 August 2009, 8.
19 The only genuine Pan Blue challenge facing the KMT in the 2008 parliamentary elections came in the proportional representation voting, where the NP attempted to cross the 5 per cent threshold required for seats.
20 Ma and Lo, *Youthful Bicycle Goes Forward: Ma Ying-jeou's Taiwan Bicycle Diary*.
21 Instead of 'no use of force' some translations opt for 'no war'.
22 'KMT nominates ex-chairman as candidate, who pledges economic lift if he wins poll', AsiaNews.it. Available online at: www.asianews.it/news-en/KMT-nominates-ex-chairman-as-candidate,-whopledges-economic-lift-if-he-wins-poll-9653.html (accessed 7 February 2011).
23 Lo Chih-chiang, interview by author, London, 10 June 2008.
24 This advertisement is available on YouTube at: www.youtube.com/watch?v=OT8sxeulXLQ (accessed 1 April 2011).
25 This classically fun advertisement is available on YouTube at: www.youtube.com/watch?v= j5LmTfwia2o (accessed 1 April 2011). The live rally version is at: www.youtube.com/watch?v= U0a17Isll7 U&feature=related (accessed 1 April 2011).
26 Lo Chih-chiang, interview by author, London, 10 June 2008.
27 Chu, Diamond and Templeman (eds), *Taiwan's Democracy Challenged*, 9–11.

13   Taiwan under Ma Ying-jeou and Tsai Ing-wen

In both 2008 and 2016, Taiwan saw two more changes of ruling parties through elections. In both cases the victors came to power on the back of historic landslide victories that left the losing party in disarray. As had been the case in 2000, there were both unrealistically high expectations but also deep-set fears of the consequences of these changes of ruling parties. In this chapter I will discuss how we best evaluate the political consequences of these two changes of ruling parties. To what extent have we seen continuity or change? Will historians view these as successful or failed administrations? I will also look at a number of election campaigns from the post-2008 period and how we can explain the outcome of these contests.

A new era in Taiwanese politics?

Looking back at the Obama-style rhetoric of change coming out of the KMT camp in the 2008 campaigns, it is not surprising that many voters were once again disappointed in the impact of the second change in ruling parties. Nevertheless, the impact of the new administration was greatest in the field of Taiwan's external relations. As we discussed in Chapter 9, the key change was the resumption of cross-Strait talks. Here, the progress of these talks was far greater than the limited agreements of the early 1990s. Substantive agreements were reached on Chinese tourists, direct flights and Chinese investment. These culminated in the signing of the Economic Cooperation Framework Agreement (ECFA). In international relations, there was both continuity and change. The KMT took a more low-key approach, dropping the bid for full UN membership and calling for a diplomatic truce. The KMT government viewed its Observer status at the World Health Assembly, improved US–Taiwan relations, the expansion in countries offering ROC passports visa free entry and that it only lost one further diplomatic ally as proof that its approach was bearing fruit.[1]

What was surprising is that the Ma government was so cautious and conservative domestically. The huge KMT parliamentary majority gave it the power to implement radical reforms to transform the island, something that Chen could only dream of. The Chen era had shown there were serious problems in the design of Taiwan's political system. But there was little of note in the area of domestic reforms. Perhaps the most notable reform was the administrative redistricting whereby Kaohsiung City and County, Tainan City and County, Taichung City and County were merged and then upgraded (Taipei County was upgraded and renamed New Taipei City, and Taoyuan City was also later upgraded) to special municipal status. A major question for future research will be whether this contributes to better government efficiency and accountability. It is also possible these will exacerbate financial difficulties and create a more obvious two-tier system of inequality between the remaining county/cities and special municipalities. The limits of the KMT's domestic impact are apparent in its failure to introduce a genuine second-generation National Health Insurance in late 2010. Instead, it opted for a model that left the original system largely intact. Time and again the pressure for important reforms such on issues of the Parade and Assembly Law, media monopolies, LGBT rights went unanswered.

The KMT clearly did move to try to clear up numerous corruption cases from the DPP era. Perhaps the most obvious case was Chen Shui-bian and his wife, but a number of other former DPP officials were also indicted. This led to accusations of a KMT witch-hunt against DPP politicians.

Under the DPP, both the KMT and some foreign observers became increasingly critical of the state of Taiwan's democracy, particularly in Chen's second term. It was common to see the slogan 'Democracy is Dead' in Taiwan at KMT rallies.[2] The main criticisms of outside observers centred on poor government performance under divided government, party polarization and conflict often leading to legislative gridlock and a return of legislative political violence.[3] The return of a unified government under the KMT did serve to revive Pan Blue confidence in the state of Taiwan's democracy and benefited the image of Taiwan's democracy in China. It is not surprising that Pan Green politicians first warned that a return to KMT rule would bring authoritarian martial law-style rule that would mean an end to Taiwan's liberal democracy. During Ma's first term, a series of open letters signed by respected foreign scholars, and also critical reports by influential NGOs such as Freedom House and Reporters without Borders, highlighted areas of genuine concern regarding the state of Taiwan's democracy under the KMT.

The following areas of concern focused on four core areas:

1   Judicial malpractice in cases related to former DPP officials.
2   Government interference with the media.
3   Government handling of protests.
4   The new government's pro-China policies.

The focus of concerns on the trend towards judicial bias surrounded Chen and other former DPP officials' treatment after leaving office. It would appear that there was pressure exerted on the judiciary from KMT hardliners and dark Blue supporters to punish Chen severely. Even though most accept that the weight of evidence against Chen was convincing that he was guilty on a number of corruption counts, the malpractices in the judicial procedure undermined the legitimacy of the process and even generated renewed sympathy for Chen. For instance, one of the open letters complained about a 'widespread pattern of leaks to the media regarding ongoing cases — leaks which because of their content and nature can only have come from the prosecutors' offices'.[4] In his commentary in the *South China Morning Post* on 8 January 2009, Professor Jerome Cohen presented details of such political interference in the judicial system with regard to the Chen case. Another incident highlighted was a skit performed by prosecutors who were handling the Chen case that mocked Chen Shui-bian at a Ministry of Justice party. This incident was recorded and posted on YouTube and condemned as a sign of both judicial bias and lack of professionalism.[5] It was alleged that there was also KMT pressure to keep Chen in custody throughout the entire trial process and interference in matters such as the selection of presiding judges.

There were also worrying signs of attempts by the KMT to interfere with and even control the media, with similarities to its behaviour under martial law. After the KMT came to power, Freedom House and Reporters without Borders both downgraded Taiwan's ranking for press freedom, with the latter ranking Taiwan below semi-democratic Hong Kong.[6] An area of particular concern was allegations of KMT inter-ference in the state media sector. There were reports that after 2008 there was pressure on Radio Taiwan International to stop reports critical of the PRC. Similarly, the appointment of Ma's former campaign spokesman Lo Chih-chiang as deputy director of Central News Agency was viewed as another attempt by the KMT to control the media. Equally worrying were attempts by the KMT to control the Public Television Service, Taiwan's version of the BBC, which had long been one of the few islands of quality programming and objective news and current affairs. Another long-term, but seemingly growing feature of media politics was government purchasing of news space in the print and electronic media.[7] The problem is that this kind of government or even partisan propaganda is often disguised as regular news reports. In addition, Chinese state organizations also joined in the practice of embedded advertising in the Taiwanese media.

The problems of harsh police handling of protestors and of the antiquated Parade and Assembly Law was raised in Chapter 10. The violent police handling of demonstrators protesting against the PRC's envoy Chen Yunlin visit sparked the emergence of the Wild Strawberry protest movement. Images of police confiscating protestors' ROC flags were put online on to YouTube. Such police actions received attention in both the open letters and Freedom House reports.[8] Similarly, Reporters without Borders raised concerns about the number of journalists injured or arrested during these clashes.

The final area of concern in Ma's first term was the accusation of an overly pro-China policy and its consequences for Taiwan's sovereignty and democracy.[9] Some of these accusations need to be taken with a pinch of salt, as we should recall that the KMT did include pledges for closer economic ties with China in its 2008 campaign literature. It could arguably claim a mandate for the resumption of cross-Strait talks and even ECFA. However, from a democratic perspective the KMT government was less successful at subjecting the new agreements to democratic accountability. This was rather odd when we consider that the KMT held such an overwhelming legislative majority. For instance, neither the various SEF–ARATS agreements nor ECFA were given full legislative reviews. Similarly, the party employed its dominant position on the Executive Yuan Referendum Review Committee to block attempts at holding a referendum on ECFA proposed by the DPP and TSU.[10] Despite these bids gaining the required number of signatures, they were turned down on technicalities. Lastly, after the KMT returned to power, it was not always been clear who or which institution was determining cross-Strait policy and whether there was proper democratic oversight to this process. In addition to the SEF–ARATS talks, the CCP–KMT forum continued to operate. Neither process could claim direct democratic accountability. The issue of democratic supervision of cross-Strait relations would return to haunt Ma in his second term in the form of the Sunflower Movement.

Ma's mid-term malaise

When Ma assumed office in May 2008, there were high hopes that he would bring a new era for Taiwanese politics. His campaign had stressed that Taiwan needed change and that he and his team were ready to deliver. They argued that better cross-Strait relations would be the basis of a new economic prosperity. As discussed earlier, he did bring quite radical change in cross-Strait relations. However, when we examine the patterns seen in his presidential satisfaction and dissatisfaction rates in Table 13.1, it is clear that he enjoyed fluctuating support levels during his first term. This led Rigger to argue that in 2010 Ma was suffering from 'mid-term malaise'.[11]

Although some critics explain this dissatisfaction through the lens of his China policy, domestic and economic issues were more important. Ma had raised unrealistic expectations of change that soon led to disappointment, especially his 633 pledge of 6 per cent economic growth rate, unemployment rate below 3 per cent and average income of US$30,000. As was the case with the DPP in 2000–2, the incoming KMT administration was hit by global economic crisis. Therefore, Ma's support was hit by an economic growth rate of 0.73 per cent in 2008 and minus 1.91 per cent in 2009.[12] The unemployment rate for 2009 was 5.85 per cent, which was also worse than the highest figures under the DPP (5.17 in 2002).[13] Although there was economic improvement in 2010 and 2011, there was still a widespread perception of economic recession. Similarly, many voters perceived the continued development of an M-shaped society, with a wide gap between the rich and poor and a squeezed middle class. Economic issues did contribute to the DPP's downfall in 2008 and in turn also eroded the KMT's popularity after coming back to power.

Ma and his KMT government also were partly to blame for their decreased popularity. Ma's choice of Premier, Liu Chao-shiuan (劉兆玄), a technocrat from the Lee Teng-hui era, struggled to defend government policies and performance in Ma's first year in office. Low points in his popularity seen in Table 13.1 coincided with a food safety scandal in October 2008 and poor handling of the flooding following the Morakot typhoon in August 2009. The government was heavily criticized for slow reactions and poor crisis management during the typhoon. This contributed to Ma's lowest public satisfaction rates in his first term (16 per cent in August 2009) and the resignation of the unpopular Premier Liu and his cabinet in September 2009. The KMT has also suffered from serious internal divisions and open disagreement over nominations in local elections such as in Hualien in 2009. Nevertheless, we can see both in this table and in the party identification figures in Chapter 6 that Ma and his party were able to recover support in time for the 2012 national elections.

Lessons of defeat: Part 3

We have seen how the KMT tried but did not always correctly learn the lessons of its defeats in 2000 and 2004. Its return to power in 2008 came through learning hard lessons but also good fortune from the mistakes of its rival, the DPP. The next question is how well did the DPP recover by learning the lessons of its defeat in 2008? Was the party

Table 13.1 Presidential satisfaction and dissatisfaction rates for Ma Ying-jeou

	June 2008	Oct 2008	May 2009	Aug 2009	May 2010	May 2011	Dec 2011	May 2012	June 2013	Mar 2014	May 2015	May 2016
Satisfaction	41	23	41	16	33	36	40	20	13	14	16	23
Dissatisfaction	37	59	49	65	47	49	45	64	73	72	67	58

Source: TVBS Poll Center (2016): 'Poll on President Ma's satisfaction rates over eight years'. Available online at: http://other.tvbs.com.tw/export/sites/tvbs/file/other/poll-center/0505041.pdf

able to reform itself after defeat as well as it did after 1991 and 1996? If we date the DPP's downfall back to 2005, then we can say that initially it was highly resistant to learning lessons of defeat. For example, party leaders rejected attempts to reform proposed by younger figures such as Lo Wen-chia and Tuan Yi-kang (段宜康), who called for a New DPP Movement in 2005.[14] The party was also unable to deal with its image as a corrupt party, as corruption scandals continued to emerge and DPP politicians that were critical of Chen over this issue were vilified. Lastly, with the presidential election approaching, the party broke two other key rules of going into a presidential election, with a more radical national identity stance and being openly disunited.

In the aftermath of the 2008 elections, the DPP had the key ingredients required for party change. The external variable was that it had suffered a traumatic electoral defeat, one that could only be matched by combining its 1991 National Assembly and 1996 presidential defeats. Internally, there was a transformation of the party's balance of power. In May 2008, Tsai Ing-wen won the DPP chairperson election against a former presidential adviser, Ku Kuan-min (辜寬敏). With Chen Shui-bian leaving office and embroiled in corruption cases, perhaps the most influential figure in the DPP for the previous decade was now marginalized. Although the DPP's other heavenly kings remained influential, they all were tainted to greater or lesser extents with their involvement in the Chen administration.[15] Thus, the factional balance of power was significantly different from that of the Chen era, with no dominant force. It was initially not clear whether Tsai would be able to sail the party on the road to recovery or would just be a stop-gap figure prior to one of the heavenly kings returning to the fore.

On a number of levels, the DPP under Tsai tried to make a clean break from the Chen Shui-bian era and learn the lessons of defeat. Perhaps the most radical reform Tsai made was to the DPP's nomination system. In response to the inner party divisions over nomination in 2008, under Tsai the old mixed primary system was abandoned. First, in 2009 a highly centralized nomination system was used for nominating DPP local executive candidates. Then in 2010 in the two competitive races, the party relied on a primary based solely on opinion surveys. In the past, primaries played a major role in avoiding DPP rebel candidates and resolving nomination disputes.

Tsai also gave the DPP a new party image. Although she had been a minister under Chen, she was far less tainted by association with Chen than the other heavenly kings. Being relatively new to the DPP, a former academic, Western educated, female and younger than the *Tangwai* era generation of DPP leaders distinguished Tsai from all her predecessors and rivals. Tsai even adjusted the party badge used in party propaganda, as now the party flag is surrounded by a circle consisting of a number of colours, suggesting the party's more diverse appeals.

Under Tsai, the DPP's party image gradually improved. This was partly because the Chen corruption cases had gradually fallen off the agenda after he began serving his sentence. While Tsai was quite decisive on party organizational reforms, on policy matters it was less clear how the DPP had changed. She did not tackle the controversial issue of China policy and national identity until the 2012 campaign was under way. Tsai did try to project a more moderate and pragmatic stance on these dimensions, but the long-awaited DPP China policy conference did not take place prior to 2012. Taking a vague position on China and identity is possible for local level elections, but it would prove to be one of the DPP's major challenges for 2012.

If we examine the election results and survey data of 2009 and 2010, it does suggest that Tsai was relatively successful at reviving the DPP. Although the KMT appeared to have been the winner in the 2009 local executive elections, gaining 12 out of 17 seats, the election was viewed in Taiwan as a sign of DPP revival. This was because the DPP's vote share almost matched the KMT's and the DPP regained the hotly contested seat of Yilan. In 2010, the DPP held both Kaohsiung and Tainan special municipalities, exceeded the KMT's total vote share and also won an equal share of the council seats with the KMT. Some of the most remarkable election results came in legislative by-elections in 2009–11, where the DPP won in some of the safest Pan Blue districts with some exceptional swings. The most eye-catching cases occurred in Hsinchu and Taitung Counties, where in 2008 the DPP had not even nominated candidates, but in 2010 it was able to come out on top. The party identification figures (see Table 6.11) show that there was not an immediate recovery after Tsai became DPP chair, but by 2010 DPP support levels had returned to the peak levels of 26 per cent last seen in 2000. Also, as we discussed in Chapter 6, by 2010 the DPP's overall party image on a range of dimensions, including political corruption, was better than the KMT's. In short, in early 2011 it looked possible that there could be a further change in ruling parties in 2012.

The 2012 combined national elections

As we saw in Chapter 5, the KMT won re-election in both parliamentary and presidential elections in January 2012. So how was the party able to recover from the economic setbacks and periods of high presidential dissatisfaction in Ma's first term to win reduced but working majorities?

We can start to answer this question by looking at some public opinion trends. In Table 6.11 we saw how the KMT's party identification dropped slightly after 2008 but recovered on the eve of the election in 2011 to a historic high of 39.5. In contrast, the DPP's peak in popularity in Ma's first term came in 2010, then dropped off slightly as the election approached. There was a similar trend with Ma's satisfaction rate (Table 13.1) recovering and dissatisfaction rate falling in 2010, and both rates showed a gradual improvement up to December 2011 (the eve of the election). Table 13.2 shows the trend in support rates for the three presidential candidates in the 2012 election. This shows both similarities and differences from earlier contests. The election was clearly more competitive than 2008, but in the vast majority of surveys Ma retained a clear lead over Tsai. For the first time since 2000 there was a significant third candidate, James Soong, who polled in the mid teens for much of the campaign. We can also see how by the eve of the election Ma had a clear lead over Tsai and that Soong's support was collapsing. The final polls showed that Ma still had an advantage in support level even when figures were broken down by gender, age, education levels and even in most

Table 13.2 Pre-election presidential polls for 2012

	7/21	8/15	8/30	9/14	10/6	10/26	11/23	12/10	12/29	Jan 13
Ma	38	39	40	42	40	42	39	41	44	43
Tsai	36	35	32	34	33	33	39	37	38	35
Soong	13	16	17	15	14	13	9	8	6	6
DK	12	9	12	11	13	12	12	14	12	16

Source: TVBS Poll Center, 'Polls for the 2012 Presidential Election held in the Restricted Period January 3–13' (13 January 2012). Available online at: www1.tvbs.com.tw/tvbs2011/pch/tvbs_poll_center.aspx

geographical regions (except the south). Tsai was more popular than Hsieh four years earlier, but there were clearly limits to the DPP's recovery. Therefore, considering these trends in public opinion in the run-up to 2012, the KMT's victories are not surprising.

What, then, explains these trends that allowed the KMT to retain power? To answer this we can consider developments in the build-up to the election and, of course, the actual campaign itself. A first step was replacing the unpopular Premier Liu with the experienced legislator and former Kaohsiung mayor, Wu Den-yih. This not only improved the government's relations with the KMT parliamentary group, it also helped overall government communication with the public and media. By the end of 2010, there was a sense that the momentum had shifted back in favour of the KMT. ECFA had been signed, Ma had won the ECFA debate against Tsai and the KMT won three of the five special municipality mayoral elections in 2010. Both the KMT and Ma tried to take the credit for Taiwan's economic growth rate of over 10 per cent in 2010.

This was the first time where the presidential and parliamentary elections were held on the same day. Although this was justified as a means to save resources, both sides hoped that it would benefit their electoral fortunes. For the DPP, there was the hope that a strong presidential campaign could help their relatively unknown parliamentary candidates, while the KMT hoped that mobilization of its incumbent legislators could help a relatively unpopular president. We can be sure that the timing helped the KMT. The subsequent decline in Ma's popularity suggests that if the election had been held a few months later, the outcome would have been quite different. Naturally, the KMT had a number of advantages in 2012. As had been the case in 2008, the parliamentary electoral system favoured the KMT. Similarly, we saw in Table 5.9 that the KMT spent very heavily on election advertising, with the amount the KMT spent on TV advertising almost double that of the DPP in 2012.

The campaign appeals the two main parties adopted saw both continuity and change from 2008. While the 2008 KMT campaign had been quite Taiwan centred in its appeals, one of its core themes in 2012 was dual Republic of China and Taiwan identity. The ROC flag was prominent in KMT advertisements. For instance, the National Flag Ad (國旗篇) shows people from different generations waving and wearing ROC flags with an upbeat version of the national flag anthem as background music. The KMT once again used the Happy Gathering song 歡聚歌) in its TV advertising campaign to project an image of ethnic harmony. Its 2012 version ended with the slogan 'Our Taiwan, our homeland, our ROC, our country' (咱的台灣，咱的家園，咱的中華民國，咱的國家) Generally, the KMT used more negative advertisements than in 2008. For instance, it often tried to remind voters of the corruption scandals of the Chen era and to insinuate that Tsai was surrounded by Chen's allies. More damaging were accusations that Tsai herself had personally profited from a biotech company investment she had approved while Vice Premier under Chen.

Given that its specific 633 pledge had backfired in 2008, forcing Ma to apologize to voters, in 2012 the KMT took a different, vaguer approach. It promised that if it was re-elected voters could enjoy *Ten Golden Years*. Since Ma was the presidential candidate, he naturally featured heavily in KMT advertising. However, there were differences. Many candidates, especially in the South, no longer featured Ma in their campaign literature. Perhaps due to the fact that Tsai appealed to voters with the call to make her Taiwan's first female president, the KMT advertising frequently featured Ma's wife Chou Mei-ching (周美青). In fact, though not as wide as in 2008, Ma still retained a clear advantage in support among female voters in 2012.[16]

There was a higher degree of change in the DPP's campaign communication compared with 2008. Much of the emphasis was on Tsai herself, making clear how different she was from earlier generations of DPP leaders. For instance, her early advertisements showed Tsai in Berlin and London. In the latter location she talks of her experiences as a student at the London School of Economics. Her central slogan was 'Taiwan Next' and there was much talk of change. For instance, one advertisement asked voters to 'Give Tsai Ing-wen a chance to change Taiwan'. Tsai's central theme in 2016 was social justice. While Ma tried to trumpet the previous four years as a time of unprecedented economic success, Tsai's advertisements stressed the widening gaps between rich and poor. Nevertheless, unlike earlier DPP campaigns, Tsai did not offer voters the kind of welfare pledges that could potentially address questions of inequality.

The China issue featured prominently in the campaign. Again, the DPP's approach was very different from four years or even two years earlier. It no longer accused the KMT of selling out Taiwan and ceased its focus on opposing or warning of the dangers of economic agreements with China. Tsai attempted to appear more moderate than her predecessors on China relations. However, she was not prepared to accept the 1992 Consensus that Ma claimed was the basis of cross-Strait relations since 2008. Instead, Tsai proposed an alternative Taiwan Consensus on China relations. This basically meant that various parties within Taiwan should first reach a domestic consensus on how to handle relations with China and that this consensus should be reached democratically. Schubert argued that essentially Tsai was trying to bring the DPP's position back to the 1999 Resolution on Taiwan's Future,[17] thus moving from the far left back to the centre-left of the identity spectrum.

The KMT viewed cross-Strait relations as the key to its success in 2012 and Tsai's weakness. While Tsai attempted to avoid the issue, the KMT repeatedly tried to bring relations with China back on to the agenda. Many KMT advertisements focused on how various sectors, especially agriculture, tourism and the Taishang, had benefited from economic integration. KMT advertisements also attempted to compare its successful economic policies with those of the previous DPP administration. Both in the presidential debate and in numerous newspaper advertisements sponsored by Taishang groups, voters were warned of the dangers of a return to DPP rule without the 1992 Consensus.[18] Key business leaders, including some who had previously also supported Chen such as Evergreen's Chang Yung-fa (張榮發) and Chimei's Hsu Wen-long (許文龍) showed their preference by declaring their support of the 1992 Consensus.[19] Although the DPP's Taiwan Consensus was vague, actually the KMT was also quite vague on its vision for future relations with China. It preferred to campaign on its record and promise continuity. The one occasion that it did propose something new was when Ma raised the idea of a peace agreement with China in October 2011. However, when public opinion reacted badly, he quickly backtracked on the idea and reassured voters that such an agreement would need to be approved by a referendum.[20] Overall, it would appear that Ma once again had won the debate over China policies. Immediately after the election, the *United Daily News* carried the headline, 'Ma Ying-jeou has won, the 1992 Consensus has won'.[21] A post-election TVBS survey found by far the most common reason voters cited for voting for Ma was his cross-Strait policies.[22]

Ma's disastrous second term

Following Ma's re-election in January 2012, it appeared highly likely that politics would follow a similar pattern to that seen in his first term. In other words, there would be a continuation of his policies of increased economic integration with China, while domestic reforms would be minimal. Ma had a clear working majority in parliament and it also looked like he had little to fear from the opposition. Tsai Ing-wen had been defeated and resigned as party chair. Former Premier Su Tseng-chang replaced Tsai as party leader after winning the leadership election. In fact, for the first two years it did not appear that the DPP would be able to challenge the KMT government. New agreements continued to be signed with China, such as the controversial Cross-Strait Services Trade Agreement in 2013. Another significant development was the inaugural visit by Taiwan's Mainland Affairs Council Minister to China in February 2014 and the reciprocal visit by China's Taiwan Affairs Office Minister to Taiwan in June. Increasingly, cross-Strait communications were being conducted directly on a government-to-government basis. This created the conditions for an historic first meeting between President Ma and Chinese President Xi Jinping in Singapore in November 2015.

Despite Ma's meeting with the Chinese president, his second term is universally viewed as a failure. We already have a range of data to show this in earlier chapters. The KMT suffered historic defeats at the local level in 2014 and national level in 2016. In Table 13.1 we can see how the Ma's presidential satisfaction rates plummet after winning re-election, but unlike in his first term, they stayed low throughout his second term. We also saw in Table 6.11 how the KMT's party identification collapsed from a high of almost 40 per cent in 2011 to 20 per cent in 2016. By as early as 2013 the Fourth Nuclear Power Station issue showed how the KMT was struggling to implement its policies and the Sunflower Movement's blocking of the Cross-Strait Services Trade Agreement in 2014 could be taken as the date when the Ma government became a lame duck administration.

The 2016 national elections

We can consider a range of long- and short-term factors to understand the demise of the KMT. First, as we saw in Chapter 11, the KMT's party image suffered badly as a result of a series of corruption scandals involving politicians closely associated with both Ma Ying-jeou and the party's 2016 presidential candidate Eric Chu. Ma's administration suffered a further reverse in July 2013, when public outrage over the death of a young conscript in the military led to large demonstrations and the resignation of the Minister of National Defence. From being a highly united party, the KMT's inner party power struggles severely eroded its power and reputation. In September 2013, Ma attempted to remove his long-term inner party rival, Wang Jin-pyng who had been implicated in an influence-peddling scandal. The affair provoked turmoil within the KMT, as Wang resisted the party's attempt to revoke his KMT membership, which would disqualify him from serving as a KMT legislator and as legislative speaker. In the event, Wang won his legal case against the KMT's attempt to expel him, forcing Ma to reach a temporary truce with his inner party rival. Therefore, for most of the second term Ma was unable to rely on the support of his party in parliament. This would also be significant in the face of the Sunflower Occupation as Wang used this as an opportunity to further undermine Ma.

For much of Ma's second term, he faced a resurgent civil society. We have discussed some of these in Chapter 10. What is important, though, is that these social movements not only represented a nuisance to the KMT government, but they were able to block key government policies such as on trade agreements, push for better food safety and mothball the Fourth Nuclear Power Station. Although generally not successful, they were able to promote more progressive draft legislation on media monopolies, marriage equality and even constitutional reform. We could also argue that social movements were able to promote changes in public attitudes on a range of issues. We can talk broadly of a Sunflower effect contributing to the fall of the KMT.

In the aftermath of the 2014 local elections, the momentum had clearly shifted in favour of the DPP. Under Tsai, it had won its best ever local election results. Ma had been forced to resign as KMT chair to take responsibility for defeat. Even the politician seen as most likely to be the KMT's presidential candidate, Eric Chu, had only narrowly held on to his position as New Taipei City Mayor against a weak DPP candidate. As was the case in 2000 and 2008, nomination would play a major role in the presidential outcome. When it came to register for the KMT's presidential primary, none of the party's heavyweights, apart from senior legislator Hung Hsiu-chu, registered in April 2015. While she was KMT candidate, Hung ran a disastrous campaign. She took a hard-line Chinese identity approach and clearly wanted to accelerate cross-Strait integration. Instead of the 1992 Consensus of One China, Different Interpretations, she called for One China, Same Interpretation. She also revived Ma's call for a cross-Strait peace agreement. Thus, Hung was seen as making the KMT more like the NP. In other words, she was moving the KMT further away from the median voter and failing to learn the lessons of the Sunflower Movement and 2014 local election defeat. Unsurprisingly, her campaign failed to take off and throughout her time as candidate there were constant rumours of her being replaced. It even seemed possible that Hung could be beaten into third place by James Soong. Eventually, in mid October 2015, Hung was replaced as KMT presidential candidate by Eric Chu. However, as we can see in Table 13.3, Chu was not able to narrow Tsai's lead.

Lastly, we need to examine the actual election campaign to understand why the DPP came to power in 2016. Given the divisions leading up to his nomination, Chu faced an almost impossible mission to recover the KMT's support. One key task was to project a more moderate image that brought the KMT closer to its 2008 and 2012 appeals. Chu took 'One Taiwan' as his core campaign slogan and used the tried and tested appeal of ethnic harmony, seen in so many KMT campaigns. Such advertisements tend to be used by the KMT as a means to directly or indirectly accuse the DPP of inciting ethnic tensions. In one such Chu advertisement we see Taiwanese from different ethnic groups, occupations and ages talking about a time when there were no divisions in Taiwan, a time when Taiwan opened up to the world and achieved its (economic) miracle. This was Chu's version of the Happy Gathering Song.[23]

Table 13.3 Pre-election polls for 2016

	May	21 June	7/6	8/11	10/05	10/07	10/19	11/18	12/13	Jan 14
Hung/Chu	17	38	26	17	21	29	29	28	22	24
Tsai	46	41	36	38	46	48	46	46	45	43
Soong/Shih	6	2	21	20	12	10	10	10	10	16
DK	31	20	17	24	22	13	15	16	23	18

Source: TVBS Poll Center, 'Polls Two Days Before the 2016 Presidential Election' (19 January 2016). Available online at: http://other.tvbs.com.tw/export/sites/tvbs/file/other/poll-center/0501131.pdf

Note: Figures on the Soong/Shih row are for Shih Ming-teh in the May and June polls and then for James Soong as Shih left the race.

Like Ma, he challenged Tsai on her ability to handle cross-Strait relations without the 1992 Consensus. However, perhaps sensing the shift towards more conservative public opinion on integration, Chu used this issue far less than Ma. Like Ma in 2012, Chu used ROC identity appeals. Nevertheless, the style was quite different. Ma's ROC appeals exuded a sense of confidence, while Chu was returning to begging voters to 'Save the ROC'. Chu needed to persuade Hung to at least publically support him, partly because the NP was trying to nominate her. However, Hung's campaigning and advertisements undermined Chu's attempt to reach out to more moderate voters. Lastly, in both 2014 and 2016 the KMT attempted to discredit the social movement wave. One such advertisement is known as 'I am the Fifth generation' ad (我是五年級生). In this advertisement a middle-aged manager complains about a 'them', who we can call both the Sunflower Movement and DPP. There are clear references to the opposition to trade liberalization, social justice and denial of the ROC. Tumin's article in *New Bloom* suggests that the KMT was trying to stir up intergenerational conflict with this kind of advertisment.[24] Once again, the ad accuses the other side of stirring up hatred. It ends with the manager saying that he will 'vote for the values and country he resolutely believes in', and the final image is of the ROC flag.

Tsai's DPP did make some clear adjustments and we can see some evidence of learning from defeat, as well as adjusting to the changed political environment. Like Chen in the run-up to the 2000 election, Tsai made a bid to show a moderate position on China. In 2016, Tsai pledged to maintain the status quo and to 'push for the peaceful and stable development of cross-Strait relations in accordance with the will of the Taiwanese people and the existing ROC constitutional order'.[25] While Tsai did not accept the 1992 Consensus, she was no longer denying it. It was also clear in the campaign that when attacked on China policy, Tsai was much more confident. Wu argues that what he calls Tsai's moderation offensive contributed to both her winning the support of voters in the middle but also US approval of her candidacy.[26] He views Tsai's positioning in 2016 as similar to that taken by Chen in 2000.

The one most noticeable feature of Tsai's advertising campaign in 2016 was how the DPP was appealing to its civil society allies. In other words, it was taking the exact opposite approach to the KMT. Brian Hioe compared the way that the KMT and DPP attempted to appeal to younger voters in the campaign, arguing that the DPP was much more successful. He singles out the DPP's 'Walking with the Children ad'. He notes how

> The ad, which consists of different vignettes of Taiwan in freeze frame or slow motion, suggests that progress in Taiwan has halted—hence the slow motion images of Taiwan. The call of the ad would be for the resumption of progress. But what is noteworthy is the incredible density of 'Walking with Children' ad in referencing the different issues which were of concern to Taiwanese civil society in the last year, including abandoned animals, forced housing evictions in Dapu, Miaoli, the campaign to remove Chiang Kai-Shek statues from high school and college campuses, 'new immigrants' from Southeast Asia and marriage equality. The ad also seems to visually cite the film *Kano* several times with shots of baseball, in regards to the ad's call for overcoming political and ethnic divisions to work together for the sake of bettering Taiwan. Tsai herself only appears in the ad near the very end, with a brief shot of her playing together with children.[27]

This was without doubt the most talked about advertisement in the 2016 campaign, perhaps the closest we have to the 'Guantian' ad of 2000.[28] Tsai also made her appeal to civil society by her nomination of record numbers of social activists on her legislative party list and also by allying with the activist based NPP. In fact, in the final week of the campaign, the DPP chose to highlight its nomination of civil society figures in its TV and newspaper advertising.[29]

Much of the media coverage and post-election analysis focused on the so-called Chou Tzu-yu (周子瑜) incident. In this case a Taiwanese singer based in China launched an online campaign accusing Chou (a teenage Taiwanese member of a K-Pop band) of being a supporter of Taiwan independence because she had appeared on a TV show waving a ROC flag. Chou was forced by her Korean production company to issue a televised apology in which she stated ,'there is only one China, the two sides of the Strait are one, and I have always been proud to be Chinese'.[30] Since this was released the day before the voting day, it did dominate the news and political talk shows. Many took this as a humiliation to Taiwan and undermined the KMT's claim that everything would be fine under the protection of the 1992 Consensus. This kind of incident undoubtedly was damaging for the KMT and Wu views this as an example of the China factor playing a role in the election.[31] Of course, Tsai's lead over Chu was so wide that this incident would not have a significant effect, but it is likely to have had an impact on the parliamentary election. For example, it is likely that it would have caused some KMT legislators in marginal seats to lose their elections. My own interviews found that GPT/SDP politicians felt they suffered as the incident shifted the issue agenda on to China and thus favoured parties with a clearer national identity image such as the DPP and NPP.

Taiwan under Tsai Ing-wen: a new era in Taiwanese politics?

Tsai's inauguration ceremony was held on 20 May 2016. With numerous references to Taiwan's social movements and democracy in Tsai's speech, the tone of the event was in stark contrast to Ma's inaugurations.[32] In many ways, Tsai built on themes she had campaigned on. So there was much greater emphasis on domestic than external issues. There was a clear targeting of younger voters and those in the social movement sector. For instance, the musician Lin Sheng-hsiang (林生祥), who had been a prominent supporter in a range of environmental campaigns, was invited to perform at the ceremony. Equally symbolic was Fire-Ex's 滅火器 performance of *Island Sunrise*, a song that had become an anthem for the Sunflower Movement. There were five main themes in her speech: (1) Transforming Economic Structures, (2) Strengthening the Social Safety Net, (3) Social Fairness and Justice, (4) Regional Peace and Stability and Cross-Strait Relations, (5) Diplomatic and Global Issues.[33] Inevitably, Tsai was vague on specifics but there were a number of objectives that will be assessed when Tsai runs for re-election in 2020. For instance, she talked about a New Model of Economic Development that would incorporate sustainable development. She also proposed a New Southbound Policy to reduce economic dependence on a single market (China). In terms of social welfare, Tsai pledged to establish a Pensions Reform Committee, to hold a national pension's conference and to offer a pensions reform programme within a year of coming into office. Tsai also promised to address the issue of transitional justice and reconciliation, including aspects related to Taiwan's indigenous peoples.

The part of her speech most closely scrutinized was how she would address relations with China. Like Chen in 2000, Tsai offered a moderate message. Although she did not endorse the 1992 Consensus, she promised to maintain the existing mechanisms for dialogue and communication across the Taiwan Strait. For Tsai, the basis of her new model of cross-Strait relations would be 'The first element is the fact of the 1992 talks between the two institutions representing each side across the Strait (SEF & ARATS)', when there was joint acknowledgement of setting aside differences to seek common ground. This is a historical fact. The second element is the existing Republic of China constitutional order. The third element pertains to the outcomes of over twenty years of negotiations and interactions across the Strait. And the fourth relates to the democratic principle and prevalent will of the people of Taiwan.[34] Thus, we can see that Tsai was attempting to edge closer to the KMT/PRC position without alienating the median voters or her own party's core values.

I am writing this chapter just over a year after the DPP came into office. To what extent have we seen a revolution in Taiwanese politics? Has Tsai disappointed her supporters and proved her 2016 campaign opponents right? We already have some of the answers in many chapters in this book, but let me summarize some initial developments.

First, when it comes to Taiwan's party system, we are in uncharted waters. The DPP is the dominant party in parliament and in party identification for the first time. The KMT, and in fact the Pan Blue camp, is at a historically weak point. Instead of learning the lessons of 2016, the party elected the unelectable Hung Hsiu-chu as its new chair. Hung's time as party chair was no better than her disastrous presidential campaign. This meant that the KMT retained its far-right image and took an oppositional position on almost all the DPP's proposed reforms, leaving the party system highly antagonistic. It was not until the summer of 2017 that Hung was replaced as party chair by former vice president Wu Den-yih following a competitive leadership election. Under Wu, the KMT is unlikely to split or collapse, but will not pose a serious threat to the DPP in the short term. Also important has been the rise of the NPP. It is poised to make a further breakthrough in the next round of local elections in 2018 and to become the most significant third party since the PFP in the early 2000s.

Despite Tsai's moderation and olive branches towards China, China has not been satisfied with Tsai's refusal to accept the 1992 Consensus. It has attempted to punish her by breaking off negotiations, reducing the number of Chinese tour groups and making renewed efforts to squeeze Taiwan's international space. Following Panama's switching diplomatic recognition from Taipei to Beijing in June 2017, Taiwan was left with just 20 formal diplomatic allies. There was talk of a domino effect. Taiwan was also not able to attend the 2017 World Health Assembly and was prevented from participating in meetings of other world bodies such as Interpol, the International Civil Aviation Organization and the United Nations Framework Convention on Climate Change. Despite Chinese pressure, though, Taiwan has been able actually to increase its tourist and student numbers by liberalizing visa rules for visitors from South East Asia. It has also sought to strengthen its de facto diplomatic relations – for instance, there has been significant progress in its relations with Japan.

Considering the challenging international environment that Taiwan faces, it is not surprising that Tsai has given greater attention to domestic reforms since coming to office. Her new government immediately revoked controversial textbook curriculum guidelines that had been proposed by the Ma administration. Despite strong opposition from certain groups, Tsai has attempted to push ahead with pensions reforms. At times, protests have been quite violent by Taiwanese standards. She has held a series of consultative conferences and overall public opinion is supportive of these reforms. At the time of writing, legislation was being reviewed by parliament. We have seen a similar style of inclusive procedures in preparing for a National Congress on Judicial Reform, something that will also be a priority in Tsai's first term.

Another area that Tsai has attempted to tackle has been transitional justice. Legislation has been passed to deal with the KMT's controversial party assets for the first time. However, the KMT has attempted to resist these measures and tried to frame this as a bid to undermine party competition in Taiwan. Tsai also has attempted to address the question of historical injustice of Taiwan's indigenous peoples. In August 2016, Tsai became the first president to offer a public apology for the historical treatment of Taiwan's indigenous peoples. The Presidential Office Indigenous Historical Justice and Transitional Justice Committee held its first meeting on 20 March 2017 and will move forward on a range of issues, including traditional territories. However, some of the most visible protests against Tsai's government have been related to indigenous land justice, often involving activists who had formerly supported Tsai. There have been long-term occupations on Ketegalan Boulevard protesting about a Council of Indigenous Peoples proposal for the return of traditional indigenous land.

Apart from pension reform and indigenous land rights protests, the other major set of protests have been over the question of LGBT rights, a topic discussed in Chapter 11. Given that Tsai was so openly supportive of marriage equality in the 2016 campaign, there has been a sense of impatience with progress on legislation and at times it appeared that Tsai's government was wavering in the face of loud conservative protests. Although there have been celebrations following the constitutional court ruling in May 2017, Tsai's government has frustrated civil society activists by its apparent lack of enthusiasm and urgency in achieving marriage equality.

Conclusions

As I write this new chapter, we are now well into Tsai's first term. In this chapter, I examined political developments following Taiwan's second and third changes in ruling parties. Although there has been much continuity in the aftermath of these changes in ruling parties, this chapter has shown that elections in Taiwan do matter. In both cases we have seen how new governments led to radical shifts both in Taiwan's external relations but also domestic policies. Although Ma's second term ended in failure and disastrous defeat for his party, this stands in stark contrast to the series of breakthroughs in cross-Strait relations in his first term. Once again, we have seen how Taiwan's voters have punished governments for their performance on a range of issues, leading to the fall of the KMT between 2014 and 2016. It is likely that the DPP will face a similar punishment protest wave if it is unable to deliver on its campaign promises. This is, however, something I will have to leave for the third edition of this book.

Discussion questions

1   Assess the degree of political change following changes of ruling parties in either 2008 or 2016.
2   Are there any similarities between the DPP's fall in 2008 with the KMT's in 2016?
3   Compare the re-election of ruling parties in 2004 (DPP) and in 2012 (KMT).
4   Has Taiwan's democracy deepened or been eroded in the post-2008 period?
5   To what extent did the DPP (2008) and KMT (2014–2016) learn the lessons of defeat?

6 What was the Sunflower effect on Taiwan's politics?
7 Why did the KMT lose landslides in 2014 and 2016?
8 Compare the vision for change proposed by Ma in 2008 with that offered by Tsai in 2016.

Further reading

Cabestan, Jean-Pierre and deLisle, Jacques (eds) 2014. *Political Changes in Taiwan under Ma Ying-jeou.* London: Routledge. This excellent edited volume takes the reader through until half-way through Ma's second term.
Schubert, Gunter (ed.). 2016. *Routledge Handbook of Contemporary Taiwan.* London and New York: Routledge. The majority of chapters in this comprehensive handbook deal extensively with the Ma Ying-jeou administration.

Notes

1 Gambia broke diplomatic ties with Taiwan in 2013 but this was more to do with internal politics in Gambia, and China did not actually re-establish its ties with Gambia until 2016.
2 See Huang Tai-lin and Joy Su, 'Chen replies to Pan Blue rally request', *Taipei Times*, 28 March 2004, 1.
3 For instance, see Rigger, 'Unfinished Business of Taiwan's Democratization', 16–43; Fell 'Democracy on the Rocks: Taiwan's Troubled Political System Since 2000', 21–5; Fell, 'Partisan Issue Competition in Contemporary Taiwan: Is Taiwan's Democracy Dead?' 23–39.
4 Erosion of Justice: Open Letter to President Ma Ying-jeou, 17 January 2009. Available online at: www.taiwandc.org/statement%2017%20Jan%202009.htm (accessed 1 April 2011).
5 See www.youtube.com/watch?v=bvj1B1xU8Q8 (accessed 1 April 2011).
6 See Reporters without Frontiers, 'Press Freedom Index 2010'. Available online at: http://en.rsf.org/pressfreedom-index-2010,1034.html (accessed 1 April 2011).
7 For a report of this development, see Dennis Engbarth, 'Media Fights Propaganda Masked as News, Inter Press Service News Agency'. Available online at: http://ipsnews.net/news.asp?idnews=54291 (accessed 1 April 2011).
8 Freedom House, 'Freedom House Calls for Inquiry into Taiwan Clashes', 20 November 2008. Available online at: www.freedomhouse.org/template.cfm?page=70&release=725 (accessed 2 April 2011).
9 For an example of this type of critique, see Richard Kagan, 'GIO Response Misses the Point', *Taipei Times*, 25 December 2009, 8.
10 Loa Iok-sin, 'Committee Once Again says No to Referendum Bid', *Taipei Times*, 6 January 2011, 1.
11 Rigger, 'Ma's Puzzling Midterm Malaise'. Available online at: www.brookings.edu/opinions/mas-puzzling-midterm-malaise/
12 *DGBAS Statistical Yearbook 2010: Key Indicators of National Income*, 153. Available online at: http://eng.dgbas.gov.tw/public/data/dgbas03/bs2/yearbook_eng/Y093.pdf (accessed 1 April 2011).
13 *DGBAS Statistical Yearbook 2010: Important Indicators of Labor Force Status*, 44. Available online at: http://eng.dgbas.gov.tw/public/data/dgbas03/bs2/yearbook_eng/y022.pdf (accessed 1 April 2011).
14 Jewel Huang, 'New DPP movement dies an early death', *Taipei Times*, 18 October 2005, 3.
15 The term 'heavenly king' (*tianwang*) is often used to refer to the political stars within the DPP.
16 TVBS Poll Center, 'Polls Two Days Before the 2016 Presidential Election' (19 January 19 2016). Available online at: http://other.tvbs.com.tw/export/sites/tvbs/file/other/poll-center/0501131.pdf
17 Schubert, 'No Winds of Change', 147.
18 *China Times*, 22 December 2011, A1.
19 *Taipei Times*, 4 January 2012, 3.
20 Schubert, 'No Winds of Change', 148.

21 *United Daily News*, 15 January 2012, A1.
22 TVBS Poll Center, 17 January 2012, 'Poll Two Days After the Presidential Election'. Available online at: http://other.tvbs.com.tw/export/sites/tvbs/file/other/poll-center/dfbrol1dv8.pdf
23 Available online at: www.facebook.com/llchu/videos/10156462060460128/?theater
24 Tumin, 'The KMT attempting to stir up intergenerational conflict?' *New Bloom*, January 2017. Available at: https://newbloommag.net/2016/01/06/kmt-intergenerational-conflict-ad/
25 Cited in Wu Yu-shan, 'Heading Towards Troubled Waters?', 70.
26 Ibid.
27 Brian Hioe, 2016, 'Aesthetics and Politics in 2016 Presidential Campaign Ads', *New Bloom*. Available online at: https://newbloommag.net/2016/01/05/aesthetic-politics-campaign-ads-2016/
28 To view the advertisement, see: www.youtube.com/watch?v=jeIFbqHmpGs
29 For example, see DPP advertisement, 8 January 2016, *Liberty Times*, A1.
30 Wu, 'Games without Frontiers, War without Tears?', 35–6.
31 Ibid.
32 Brian Hioe, 'Time to Celebrate after the Tsai Inauguration? Or time to rain on the Tsai Parade? *New Bloom*. Available online at: http://newbloommag.net/2016/05/20/tsai-inauguration/
33 For the full text, see 'Full text of President Tsai's Inaugural Address'. Available at: http://focus taiwan.tw/news/aipl/201605200008.aspx
34 Ibid.

14 A multitude of political miracles and future challenges

Having come this far, I hope I have convinced you that Taiwan's politics are worth studying. The innovation and diversity in Taiwanese politics and sheer pace of political change on the island never cease to amaze me. Every morning, the first thing I look forward to is checking for the most recent political developments. In addition to the online newspapers and political blogs, now social media brings an even more diverse range of angles to our subject. Another important means to witness Taiwanese politics that has emerged has been live streaming. Live streaming allowed millions of people outside of Taiwan to have the sense of being in the Legislative Yuan during the Sunflower occupation. Where possible, I attempt to combine family holidays with fieldwork in Taiwan. Listening to Taiwanese taxi drivers' lectures on politics, interviewing politicians, watching the highly partisan talk shows and TV ads, and attending election rallies are just a few of the highlights of any fieldwork trip to Taiwan. I can guarantee that you will not be disappointed if you visit Taiwan during a major election campaign.

Taiwan is not just worth studying for the vibrancy of its democracy, but also because it represents a useful case for applying political science theories and frameworks. For instance, we have considered a variety of approaches for explaining Taiwan's democratic transition and the development of its welfare system. Similarly, Taiwan's status as a new democracy presents a huge range of possibilities for comparison with new and mature democracies. Although the most commonly employed comparative cases are South Korea and Japan, there is also much potential for comparing Taiwan with cases in Eastern Europe and Latin America. Recently, a number of my students have compared Taiwan and Hong Kong, especially their social movements.

When social scientists first began talking of a Taiwan miracle in the 1970s and 1980s, they were referring primarily to its extraordinary economic record. Later, however, it also gained a reputation of having undergone a political miracle due to its smooth and peaceful democratic transition and consolidation from the late 1980s through to the late 1990s.

As I have tried to suggest in this book, Taiwan's political transformation goes far beyond its democratic transition and introduction to regular competitive national level elections. Before considering Taiwan's remaining democratic challenges, it is worth recapping just a few of these political miracles.

In Chapters 2 to 4, we saw how Taiwan was able to make a transition from a hard authoritarian system to what was widely viewed as a model liberal democracy. What was remarkable about this transformation was that it was achieved not through a revolutionary upheaval, but by reforming the original existing Republic of China political institutions. Within Taiwan, there remains much disagreement about whether the national title should still be the Republic of China or Taiwan. Observers in the PRC and also some in Taiwan argue that the Republic of China ceased to exist after the establishment of the PRC or the ROC's expulsion from the United Nations in 1971. However, if we take Taiwan's political institutions as the guideline, then we can say that the ROC is alive and kicking.[1] The political system of the 1947 ROC Constitution that was designed to govern all of China was largely forgotten in its founding capital of Nanjing, but is basically intact and functioning in Taiwan today. What has changed is that while these institutions operated in an authoritarian manner for the first four decades, they have since been democratized and Taiwanized.

Since this democratic transition, Taiwan has instituted national elections that have enjoyed their own remarkable and eye-catching features. Unlike many other new democracies, Taiwan has experienced three changes of ruling parties through elections, going well beyond Huntington's two-turnover test of democratic consolidation. The passion, noise and diversity of Taiwan's political communication also represent a great transformation from the short, controlled campaigns of the martial law era. The quality and content of this political communication contributes to the high levels of political interest, participation and knowledge among the electorate. This is important when we consider how voter apathy has become so common in many contemporary democracies. Taiwanese electioneering proves that campaigns can be both information rich and also fun. Compared to the slow pace of change in political advertising in most European countries, Taiwanese parties have rapidly mastered new campaign technologies to appeal to voters. If we take the US as the birthplace of the modern campaign, then on dimensions such as campaign rallies, TV advertising and Internet/social media campaigning, Taiwan has become a world leader.

Another important feature in the transformation of Taiwan's politics has been the high level of innovation and adaptability. In Chapter 6 we saw how Taiwan's parties invented a range of nomination practices quite unique to the island. Although there was a long history of parliamentary violence in older democracies such as France, the US and the UK, the literally riotous political theatre of the Taiwanese legislature is state of the art. Taiwanese election rallies are also highly innovative and stand in stark contrast to the stage-managed affairs seen in many democracies. Election rallies in Taiwan tend to incorporate music and dance, as well as policy and ideologically rich political speeches. These rallies are effective not only for the armchair TV audience, but also for those physically attending. The audience rally experience is indeed quite special, as you get the chance to join in the chanting and singing, and witness an atmosphere that shares the elements of a Chinese festival and a football match. Try to picture the noise of fire-crackers and the rally's events, smoke from vendors selling Taiwanese-style sausages and other delicacies, and the visual intensity of huge crowds chanting and wearing their club (party) colours.

Taiwan's party politics has seen both huge transformation and also stability. Compared to most new democracies, Taiwan has institutionalized parties and a stable party system. The same two parties that contested the first multi-party election in 1986 remain dominant over three decades later. These two parties have made elections meaningful by stressing political issues and offering diverse policy platforms during the campaigns. After election, they have attempted to implement their manifestos and have been held accountable when they have failed to deliver on their promises. While most former authoritarian parties struggled to adapt to a multi-party democratic environment, Taiwan's KMT was a model of adaptability. It continued to win elections after the transition and then was able to recover from its two disastrous defeats to return to power in 2008. A key ingredient of the adaptability of Taiwan's political parties has been their ability to respond to signals from the public through opinion surveys and election results. Despite how polarized the parties were at the outset of democratic elections, they have been able to move towards the centre ground by responding to moderate public opinion.[2]

On a range of salient political issues we can see how democracy has made a tangible difference in making Taiwan a better place. Electoral debate, along with the free media and pressure from civil society, has forced the government to respond on these core issues. In Chapter 11 we discussed how, after democratization, Taiwan moved from a limited and highly biased welfare system under martial law to a welfare state that is extensive, efficient and has universal coverage. Taiwan's national health insurance system has been so successful that it faces the challenge of medical tourism. In Chapter 11 we also saw how democracy contributed to reduced public toleration of political corruption and tougher anti-corruption legislation and institutions. Taiwan's voters have shown themselves prepared to punish parties or candidates that abused their power, as we saw in the presidential elections of 2000 and 2008.

There is also a similar positive relationship between democracy and gender equality. Here, the women's movement has worked together with political parties to promote legislation that improves women's rights and status in Taiwanese society. In terms of female political representation, Taiwan performs far better than its democratic counterparts in Asia. As was the case regarding changed norms over political corruption, political debate on gender issues has contributed to a sea change in public values. Nowhere is this more apparent than the development of more tolerant views regarding homosexuality. More recently, we have seen how this has led to Taiwan being on the verge of becoming the first Asian country to legalize same-sex marriage.

Even in the controversial field of national identity and external relations, democracy has had a positive impact. The moderate nature of public opinion has forced the nationalists in both party camps to reach tacit consensuses on protecting Taiwan's sovereignty and Taiwanese identity in addition to promoting Taiwan's international space. Democracy has served to marginalize those promoting more radical nationalist solutions, such as the NP, TIP and Chinese Unification Promotion Party (CUPP).

A distinctive feature of authoritarian rule in Taiwan was that policy-making was almost completely insulated from societal pressures. However, as Taiwan's democracy has matured, policy-making has become increasingly transparent and open to social influence. A key player in promoting the inclusion of progressive values into the policy-making process has been Taiwan's vibrant civil society. In Chapter 11 we saw how diverse social coalitions were able to prevent market reforms to the health insurance system that would have reduced its redistributive functions. The women's, labour and environmental movements have all played an increasingly engaged role in trying to guide government policy. Naturally, democratization has exposed the state to greater pressure from big business, whose interests are often starkly opposed to those of liberal civil society groups. For instance, big business initially opposed the call for gender equality legislation. However, after a decade of struggle, the women's movement achieved the critical measure of the Equal Employment Bill in 2001. The importance of civil society was especially evident in the Ma era, as social movements were often more effective at actually constraining government than the main opposition party. From having no independent civil society, Taiwan can now claim to have one of the strongest civil societies in Asia.

In the final decade of martial law, when Taiwan had lost almost all its formal diplomatic allies and the PRC had begun making proposals for peaceful unification, the odds on Taiwan retaining its independence were not good. We saw that in the scenarios that Simon Long considered in his 1991 book *Taiwan: China's Last Frontier.* He predicted that the status quo would not survive until the end of the decade. Although democracy has not helped Taiwan to join the main International Government Organizations such as the UN or enabled it to gain widespread formal diplomatic recognition, it has served to strengthen the island's de facto independence and international space. Taiwan's democracy is a key factor in why it retains its (albeit ambiguous) security guarantee from the US. Moreover, its status as a vibrant democratic state has earned it huge international sympathy and a generally positive image. The success of Taiwan's Sunflower, anti-nuclear and LGBT rights movements have all contributed to Taiwan's soft power. By creating organizations such as Taiwan Foundation of Democracy, Taiwan is now also a player in promoting democratization in the region. At a time when China is widely associated with human rights abuses and persecution of minority groups, Taiwan's free and democratic international image is probably more valuable for protecting its security than any of its advanced weapon systems.

Remaining challenges to Taiwan's democracy

At the end of Shelley Rigger's influential 1999 book *Politics in Taiwan,* she suggested that some key remaining challenges for Taiwan's democracy were (1) transforming political attitudes and behaviour, (2) balancing presidential and legislative power, (3) streamlining Taiwan's administration, (4) reducing clientelism and corruption, (5) strengthening political parties and (6) the challenge of cross-Strait relations.[3]

Almost two decades later, while some of these issues have been largely resolved, others continue to threaten or undermine Taiwan's democratic quality and prospects. In addition, some fundamentally new challenges have emerged. How Taiwan confronts these challenges will determine whether it is able to maintain its reputation as a model Asian liberal democracy. Failure to deal with these challenges could lead to an erosion of domestic confidence and international support for its democracy. The consequences of such a failure could be stalled democratic consolidation, reversion to a Singapore-style electoral authoritarian political system or even Long's worst case scenario of Taiwan becoming another Chinese province following a PLA invasion.

Looking back at the challenges raised by Rigger, Taiwan appears to have made progress on almost all of these dimensions. Since 2000, the legislature has played a much more influential role in policy-making and constraining presidential power than at any time in the ROC's history. There have also been quite radical administrative streamlining reforms, with the abolition of the Provincial Government and National Assembly along with recent county/city mergers. In Chapters 7 and 11 we discussed the impressive progress that Taiwan has made in reducing political corruption and weakening the clientelist local factions. Although there is much widespread dissatisfaction with the performance of its political parties, the KMT and DPP continue to dominate the political scene and represent one of the most institutionalized democratic party systems in Asia. In the first edition of this book I argued that 'Even on the controversial question of cross-Strait relations, the prospects of military conflict look lower today than at any point in the last two decades.' From my vantage point in mid 2017, it appears we have returned to economic convergence and political divergence.

Nevertheless, despite the many areas of democratic deepening since 2000, there have been domestic and international concerns about the state of Taiwan's democracy. Below, I will discuss a few of the areas I view as particularly important facing Taiwan's democracy. These are based on my own impression of Taiwan's current political scene, and my students often propose alternative sets of challenges or even solutions to these problems.

Constitutional reforms to the political and electoral system

Decisions made in the process of constitutional reform have contributed to some of the major crises the island's democracy has faced since 2000. The lack of the requirement for a run-off presidential election when the leading candidate fails to gain over 50 per cent of the vote resulted in Taiwan electing a president in 2000 who had gained only 39 per cent of the national vote. This contributed to the limited domestic legitimacy of the first Chen presidency. We cannot be certain who would have come out on top if there had been a second round between Chen and Soong, but whoever came out on top would have had a stronger mandate to govern. Similarly, the removal of the legislative approval vote for the Premier meant that the DPP President could appoint the Premier without parliamentary backing. This also contributed to the frequent parliamentary stalemate and confrontations and low public satisfaction with politics in the DPP era.

Another serious constitutional problem is the disproportionality of the current parliamentary election system following the 2005 reforms. Despite the numerous drawbacks of the old SVMM system, it was at least quite proportional. Under the new system in 2008, the KMT was able to win three-quarters of the seats with only 50 per cent of the vote, while the DPP seat share fell to less than a quarter on an increased vote share of almost 40 per cent. Although the 2012 and 2016 elections saw some improvement, there remains a problem of serious disproportionality. There are also serious disparities in district sizes, which not only favour the Pan Blues but also mean that votes in certain smaller districts (such as Mazu) are far more influential than other more populous ones. In addition, the new system reduced the space for the smaller third parties that emerged under the old system. Those parties did offer voters greater choice and stressed issues and issue positions that were neglected by the mainstream parties. The current electoral system contributes to the sense that the political system is unfair and unrepresentative, eroding its legitimacy. Thus, we have a strange situation whereby voters are highly dissatisfied with the mainstream political parties, but there are severe limitations for alternative parties to challenge them.

In many democracies, referendums can play an important role in resolving controversial issues. However, in Taiwan the design of the Referendum Law and the way the main parties attempted to manipulate referendums for partisan gain have prevented direct democracy from taking root. In the advent of the Sunflower Movement, electoral and constitutional reform did return to the political agenda. In particular, problems with the Referendum Law, space for small parties and the voting age have been discussed. The Referendum Law has been described as a birdcage Referendum Law due to the obstacles to both holding a referendum and the very high turnout requirements.

Therefore I suggest the following constitutional reforms:

1   Adding a presidential run-off election if the leading candidate fails to gain at least 50 per cent of the vote share.
2   Reviving the legislative approval vote for the premier.

3   Reforming the parliamentary election system to one closer to the German system, whereby there is rough parity between the number of district and proportional representation seats and also equality in district sizes. This would involve an increase in the total number of legislators. In addition, the minimum threshold for parties to win proportional seats should be reduced, thus opening up more space for smaller parties.
4   The voting age should be reduced to 18, which is the norm in most democracies.
5   Liberalization of the Referendum Law to allow greater scope for direct democracy.

Despite the KMT's large majority under Ma, it showed no interest in addressing defects in Taiwan's political system. Although the DPP is seen as more supportive of reform, since Tsai came to power in 2016, it does not seem to be priority for the current administration. It is unlikely that either camp will have the kind of majorities to carry out constitutional reform on their own, and so future reform will require cross-party consensus. However, implementing such reforms would contribute to increased domestic legitimacy in the democratic system and also the efficiency of governance.

Strengthened and diversified political society

A second but closely related challenge to Taiwan's democracy lies in how to diversify its political society. Both Taiwan's leading parties are highly institutionalized and programmatic parties. However, there is much dissatisfaction with the performance and responsiveness of the two main parties. There appears to be a growing pattern of de-alignment among younger voters and also many in the new middle classes. At the root of the problem is the KMT and DPP's obsession with national identity and neglect of other issues. As Rigger noted,

> young Taiwanese have little interest in the issue cleavages that provide the underlying logic for Taiwan's party system. This means that any party which can come up with ideas and strategies that mobilize young people has a chance to gain their support.[4]

To a certain extent, the emergence of the Sunflower and other social movements since 2006 can be partly attributed to dissatisfaction with mainstream parties.

Therefore, Taiwan needs more choice rather than just a freezing of the current two-party system. As discussed above, the first step in the emergence of alternative political parties is reform to the electoral system to make it more proportional. However, as we saw in Chapter 6, for new parties to become relevant they need to offer distinctive political platforms that can attract and mobilize new supporters, but also hold on to their loyalties. Equally important is acquiring rich human and financial resources, as in modern democracies parties seem to need stars, or, in Taiwan's case, heavenly kings.

I am more optimistic on this point than when I wrote the first edition of this book. The emergence of relevant parties with roots in civil society was a notable feature in the 2016 elections. In addition, the DPP has attempted to work much more closely with social movements both in the campaigns and in policy-making since 2014. Thus, civil society looks likely to be an increasingly important actor guiding public policy and keeping government accountable.

Removing authoritarian era legacies

Because Taiwan adopted a pacted transition, many aspects from the old authoritarian era have persisted into the democratic era. While these have contributed to Taiwan's political stability, some of these hold-overs have damaged the fairness and legitimacy of the political system.

One core feature of the martial law era was the KMT party state. This party state was defined by its blurring of the divide between the functions, assets and authority of KMT and the ROC government. The hardest of these issues to resolve has been the KMT party assets, which enabled the party to outspend its rivals after democratic elections began. Although the KMT has talked about resolving the party assets issue since the late 1990s, so far it has not gone beyond selling off some of these to allies in the private sector. Here again, we can see progress since 2016 as legislation has been passed to allow the state to deal with these controversial assets. If successful, this would be an important step in the direction of a more level electoral playing-field and transitional justice.

Another area where the blurred distinction between party and state continued into the democratic era is in the judicial system. In the 1990s, the KMT Secretary General, Hsu Shui-the, claimed that 'the courts belong to the KMT'.[5] Many in the Green camp still believed this to be the case. There were widespread concerns that the KMT continued to use its influence within the judicial system to persecute its political enemies. Now that the DPP is back in power, the party needs to promote genuine judicial reform to make sure that accusations of judicial bias are no longer justified.

Authoritarian legacies also persist on many symbolic dimensions. For instance, the KMT party flag is part of the national flag and the national anthem is a KMT party song. Currently, changing the national flag seems off the agenda, but perhaps a feasible gesture might be for the KMT to adopt a new party flag and badge. An obvious symbolic gesture towards authoritarian rule after the KMT returned to power in 2008 was its renewed respect paid to the former dictator, Chiang Kai-shek. In recent years, there have been growing attacks on Chiang Kai-shek statues, while Chinese nationalist groups have conducted similar protests against symbols of Japanese colonialism.

Removing harmful legacies of the authoritarian era will require difficult and sometimes painful reforms. These will not be easy for the KMT, which has long benefited from its financial and symbolic advantages over its political rivals. However, dismantling the remaining vestiges of the KMT party state will be a major step towards transitional justice and reviving trust in the political system. Many of the DPP's own efforts at promoting transitional justice failed in the highly polarized atmosphere of Chen's second term. It is clear that the post-2016 DPP government is serious about making genuine progress in the area of transitional justice. It will be interesting to see whether it is better able to find some consensus on these important issues than Chen's DPP. If it is, it could prove fruitful for healing the wounds of the martial law era.

Reviving political consensus

One of the major successes of the Lee Teng-hui era was the ability to achieve radical and progressive political reforms, but to do so in a gradual and consensual manner. Key instances of this were the constitutional conventions of 1990 and 1996, which set the tone for the constitutional reforms that made Taiwan's political institutions democratic. Even on external relations and national identity there was at least a tacit consensus among the two main parties by the end of the 1990s. The ability to create cross-party consensus was largely lost in the era of polarization under the DPP and was not revived under Ma. Under Ma, the KMT's overwhelming parliamentary majority allowed it to ignore the opposition and public opinion. This was particularly apparent in its handling of Taiwan's controversial relations with China and contributed to the sense of political alienation in the opposition camp. Again, this refusal to seek domestic consensus was another cause of the Sunflower, as well as other social movements.

The image of the CCP and KMT cooperating against the DPP stands in stark contrast to the unified position that Taiwan's main parties took towards China in the mid 1990s. The KMT's majorities (2008–16) allowed it to ignore dissenting views, but this only served to alienate the opposition further. A first step would be to establish a cross-party consensus seeking convention to examine cross-Strait and international relations. Although we tend to think of confidence-building measures (CBM) in relation to military relations, some such measures could be useful in dealing with the domestic anxiety about cross-Strait negotiations. Potential CBMs could include scrapping the KMT–CCP dialogue, including opposition representatives in cross-Strait negotiating teams and even offering the opposition some kind of veto power over controversial agreements. The Lee Teng-hui era showed that a consensual approach to politics can help deepen Taiwan's democracy and strengthen its domestic and international legitimacy. Internal consensus on external relations will place Taiwan in a stronger position for cross-Strait negotiations and expanding international relations.

Ideally, such consensus-seeking conventions could be adopted to deal with pressing domestic issues as well. A starting point would be for constitutional reform of the electoral and political systems discussed above. Such reforms require the support of three-quarters of legislators and so are unlikely to succeed without a consensual approach to politics.

Dealing with new political and social issues

This book has shown that Taiwan's democracy performed quite well at dealing with a range of salient issues during the first two decades of multi-party politics. Improvements in environmental protection, gender equality and welfare systems along with the enactment of anti-corruption measures are all testaments to this positive impact of democracy. However, it is still not clear whether Taiwan's democracy will be able to cope with the challenge of important newly emerging issues. One such issue is the growing concerns over rising income inequality, a trend that appears to be exacerbated by closer economic integration with China.[6] The widening gap between rich and poor, known as an M-shaped society, is one that faces almost all governments around the world. However, perhaps because Taiwan has had such a proud record of achieving growth with equity in the past, the issue is viewed as a pressing problem at elite and mass levels. Neither the Chen nor Ma governments offered concrete proposals to deal with this growing problem. Given that Tsai put so much emphasis on social justice in her 2012 and 2016 campaigns, she will be expected to make greater efforts on this issue.

Another new challenge that Taiwan faces is how to build a multicultural society. Over the last two decades, there has been a growing trend in female marriage migration from South East Asia and China to Taiwan. As more of these migrants obtain Taiwanese citizenship and their children reach voting age, they are becoming a major political constituency. Initially, the Taiwanese state treated these new citizens, especially those from

China, with suspicion, making their integration into Taiwanese society problematic. There is still much the state can do to protect the human and work rights of this new ethnic group. Failure to integrate them could result in a large constituency that is alienated from the political system. Again, there have been some positive signs such as more inclusive messages to new citizens in campaign communication, more inclusive legislation and the first new citizen legislator elected in 2016. Some of my students have argued that the way that society treats its LGBT citizens should also be factored into our assessment of Taiwan's multiculturalism. This could be taken as another item showing how Taiwan's democracy has engaged with newly emerging social issues.

Tackling political corruption

There was great optimism that the election of Ma Ying-jeou in 2008 on the back of an anti-corruption campaign would be a turning point in how the Taiwanese state dealt with corruption. For many KMT supporters, the trials and sentencing of Chen Shui-bian on corruption charges also symbolized a triumph for Taiwan's democracy and anti-corruption efforts in particular.

Nevertheless, the challenge of political corruption that Rigger raised in the late 1990s continues to trouble Taiwan's democracy. Although Ma himself was not embroiled in corruption cases, his KMT colleagues have featured in a number of high-profile corruption scandals. The seriousness of the problem is clear from the series of KMT legislators that had their 2008 election disqualified due to vote-buying cases. Furthermore, KMT politicians and supporters again dominated the vote-buying cases under investigation for the 2009 and 2010 local elections.[7] Similarly, corruption cases involving politicians close to Ma contributed to his slump in popularity after 2012. Overall, though, the Taiwan case has shown that high-quality democratic competition plus a free media can lead to a gradual and significant reduction in political corruption.

Getting the right balance between cross-Strait and international relations

The final challenge to Taiwan's democracy was also part of Rigger's list. Can we call Taiwan's democracy secure when it has the constant threat of Chinese military intervention? How to find the right balance between cross-Strait relations and Taiwan's international space remains one of the greatest challenges for any Taiwanese government. Taiwanese voters expect their government to strive for international space and dignity. However, if international relations are pushed too far, China will perceive it as a move towards independence and so cross-Strait relations will deteriorate. This is what happened in 1995–6 when China used missile tests off the Taiwan coast to punish Lee Teng-hui for his US visit. On the other hand, if cross-Strait relations are prioritized, it is possible that Taiwan's sovereignty and national security will be damaged. The PRC does not disguise its objective of unification under One Country, Two Systems, hoping to turn Taiwan into another special administrative region like Hong Kong. The accusation that Ma's opponents consistently made was that Taiwan's compromises with China did not actually bring any tangible international benefits and set Taiwan on a course towards unification with China. Although this may be an exaggeration, Ma's regime downgraded the importance of international relations compared to cross-Strait relations. This was apparent in a survey that found that only 1 per cent of voters could actually name the

Minister of Foreign Affairs, while his Mainland Affairs Council Minister was one of the best known cabinet members.[8]

Taiwan's main parties have distinct visions on how best to get this balance right. In a recent blog essay, one of my students noted how in the 2010 ECFA debate Tsai made the following distinction: 'The DPP walks towards the world and walks towards China with the world, while the KMT walks towards China and walks towards the world with China.'[9] Thornton interprets the implications of this distinction on how to develop international space as follows: 'Ma's "cross-Strait policy first, foreign policy second" hard power approach versus Tsai's "foreign policy first, cross-Strait policy second" soft power approach.'[10]

I ended this section in the first edition quite optimistically, noting that 'the recent improved cross-Strait relations have brought about a welcome reduction in tensions'. However, China now poses a greater threat to Taiwan's democracy than ever. In addition to the military threats, it has developed a comprehensive set of strategies for undermining Taiwan's democracy. Key prongs in this strategy include purchasing of Taiwanese media, cooperation with political parties, support for anti-DPP social movements, use of the China market to influence Taiwan and, of course, cooperation with Taishang. Under Tsai, Taiwan is adopting a new model of handling external relations. It remains to be seen whether it will be more successful than the models adopted by her predecessors. Looking ahead, regardless of which party is in power, for Taiwan's democracy to survive in the long term it needs both cordial cross-Strait relations and continued international support.

Conclusion

In this volume we have seen how Taiwan achieved a remarkable series of political miracles. On a range of dimensions, Taiwan's democracy remains healthy compared to most new third- wave democracies. Certain political developments since 2000 did erode domestic and internal confidence in the island's democracy, leading to more pessimistic academic appraisals. However, if we consider the democratic challenges that Rigger proposed in 1999, Taiwan has actually performed admirably on almost all these tests. Comparing the first and second editions of this book, I find myself much more positive about the state of Taiwan's democracy than seven years ago. In this chapter, I have suggested some of the remaining challenges that Taiwan's democracy faces today and some potential ways of addressing them. How Taiwan's voters and political elite deal with these key political challenges will determine whether the country retains its model liberal democracy status.

Discussion questions

1   What are the main challenges facing Taiwan's democratic political system?
2   How can Taiwan deal with these challenges?
3   What are the long-term prospects for Taiwan's democracy?
4   What are the prospects for cross-Strait relations and Taiwan's international space?

Notes

1 Hickey makes a similar point – see Dennis Hickey, 'ROC is alive and well', *Taipei Times*, 21 March 2011, 8.

2 Naturally, there are periods when the main parties moved away from the median voter positions, but they have later moved back after electoral setbacks.
3 Rigger, *Politics in Taiwan*, 178–93.
4 Rigger, *Taiwan's Rising Rationalism: Generations, Politics and Taiwanese Nationalism*, 26.
5 Cited in Taiwan News Editorial, 'KMT stakes claim on Taiwan's courts', *Taiwan News*, 26 December 2008. Available online at: www.taiwannews.com.tw/etn/news_content.php?id=822263
6 Su Yung-yao, 'ECFA benefitting wealthy: Report', *Taipei Times*, 27 March 2011, 1.
7 Shelley Huang, 'Figures show 22 KMT, 6 DPP candidates detained', *Taipei Times*, 26 November 2009, 3.
8 'Survey on Public Awareness of Ma Government Cabinet Members: Forty Percent are One Percent Ministers' (*Ma Zhengfu shouzhang zhimingdu mindiao: Yipa buzhang da sicheng*), *China Times*, 29 December 2009.
9 Mariah Thornton, 17 June 2017, 'Defining and Developing "International Space": Comparing Two Different Approaches and Understandings of "International Space" from Ma Ying-jeou to Tsai Ing-wen'. Available online at: http://mariahtthorntonchina.blogspot.co.uk/2017/06/defining-and-developinginternational.html
10 Ibid.

References

Arrigo, Linda. 1994. 'The Environmental Nightmare of the Economic Miracle'. *Bulletin of Concerned Asian Scholars*, 26(1–2): 21–44.

Arrigo, Linda and Gaia Puleston. 2006. 'The Environmental Movement in Taiwan after 2000: Advances and Dilemmas'. In Dafydd Fell, Henning Klöter and Chang Bi-yu (eds). *What has Changed: Taiwan Before and After the Change in Ruling Parties*. Wiesbaden: Harrassowitz, pp. 165–84.

Ash, Robert, John Garver and Penelope Prime (eds). 2011. *Taiwan's Democracy: Economic and Political Challenges*. London: Routledge.

Ash, Robert, Joseph Lin and C. J. Wu. 2006. 'The Economic Legacy of the KMT and its Implications for Economic Policy Formulation under the DPP'. In Dafydd Fell, Henning Klöter and Chang Bi-yu (eds). *What has Changed: Taiwan Before and After the Change in Ruling Parties*. Wiesbaden: Harrassowitz, pp. 83–106.

Aspalter, Christian. 2002. *Democratization and Welfare State Development in Taiwan*. Aldershot: Ashgate.

Baum, Julian. 1994a. 'One Dollar, One Vote'. *Far Eastern Economic Review*, 24 March, pp. 27–8.

Baum, Julian. 1994b. 'Spring Cleaning'. *Far Eastern Economic Review*, 28 April, p. 18.

Baum, Julian. 1995. 'All Politics is Local', *Far Eastern Economic Review*, 14 December, pp. 14–15.

Beckershoff, André. 2017. 'The Sunflower Movement: Origins, structures and strategies of Taiwan's response against the Black Box'. In Dafydd Fell (ed.). *Taiwan's Social Movements under Ma Ying-jeou: From the Wild Strawberries to the Sunflowers*. London, pp.113–33.

Bosco, Joseph. 1994. 'Taiwan Factions: *Guanxi*, Patronage and the State in Local Politics'. In Murray Rubinstein (ed.). *The Other Taiwan: 1945 to the Present*. Armonk, NY: M.E. Sharpe, pp. 114–44.

Braig, Stefan. 2008. 'Local elites and Intra-party dynamics: The KMT *bentupai*.' Paper presented at the 2008 European Association of Taiwan Studies Conference, Charles University, Prague, April.

Braig, Stefan. 2016. 'Local Factions'. In Schubert, Gunter (ed.). *Routledge Handbook of Contemporary Taiwan*. Abingdon and New York: Routledge, pp. 137–52.

Budge, Ian and Judith Bara. 2001. 'Introduction: Content Analysis and Political Texts'. In Ian Budge, Hans-Dieter Klingemann, Andrea Volkens, Judith Bara and Eric Tanenbaum (eds). *Mapping Policy Preferences: Estimates for Parties, Electors and Governments: 1945–1998*. Oxford: Oxford University Press, pp. 1–18.

Budge, Ian, Hans-Dieter Klingemann, Andrea Volkens, Judith Bara and Eric Tanenbaum (eds). 2001. *Mapping Policy Preferences: Estimates for Parties Electors, and Governments: 1945–1998*. Oxford: Oxford University Press.

Bush, Richard. 2005. *Untying the Knot: Making Peace in the Taiwan Strait*. Washington, DC: Brookings.

Cabestan, Jean-Pierre. 1999. 'The Constitutional Reform: Is Taiwan Moving Towards a French-style Semi-presidential System?' *China Perspectives*, 14: 40–4.

Cabestan, Jean-Pierre. 2005. 'Specificities and Limits of Taiwanese Nationalism'. *China Perspectives*, 62: 32–43.

Cabestan, Jean-Pierre. 2008. 'A New Constitutional Balance and the Prospect for Constitutional Change in Taiwan'. In Steven Goldstein and Julian Chang (eds). *Presidential Politics in Taiwan: The Administration of Chen Shui-bian*. Norwalk, CT: Eastbridge, pp. 29–48.

Cabestan, Jean-Pierre and deLisle, Jacques (eds.) 2014. *Political Changes in Taiwan under Ma Ying-jeou*. London: Routledge.

Carothers, Thomas. 2002. 'The End of the Transition Paradigm'. *Journal of Democracy*, 13(1): 5–21.

Chang, Bi-yu. 2006. 'Constructing the Motherland: Culture and State Since the 1990s'. In Dafydd Fell, Henning Klöter and Chang Bi-yu (eds). *What has Changed: Taiwan Before and After the Change in Ruling Parties*. Wiesbaden: Harrassowitz, pp. 187–206.

Chang, Bi-yu. 2015. *Place, Identity and National Imagination in Postwar Taiwan*. London: Routledge.

Chang, Mau-kuei and Chang Yu-fen. 2010. '"Rosy Periwinkle": The Politics of the Licensed Prostitutes Movement in Taiwan'. In J. Broadbent and V. Brockman (eds). *East Asian Social Movements: Power, Protest and Change in a Dynamic Region*. New York: Springer, pp. 255–86.

Chang, Yu-tzung, Chu Yun-han and Park Chong-min. 2007. 'Authoritarian Nostalgia in Asia'. *Journal of Democracy*, 18(3): 66–80.

Chao, Chien-min. 2002. 'The Republic of China's Foreign Relations under Lee Teng-hui: A Balance Sheet'. In Bruce Dickson and Chao Chien-min (eds). *Assessing the Lee Teng-hui Legacy: Democratic Consolidation and External Relations*. Armonk, NY: M.E. Sharpe, pp. 177–203.

Chao, Linda and Ramon Myers. 1998. *The First Chinese Democracy: Political Life in the Republic of China on Taiwan*. Baltimore, MD: The Johns Hopkins University Press.

Chao, Linda and Ramon Myers. 2000. 'How Elections Promoted Democracy in Taiwan under Martial Law'. *China Quarterly*, 162: 387–409.

Chao, Yung-mao. 1992. 'Local Politics in Taiwan: Continuity and Change'. In Denis Fred Simon and Michael Kau (eds). *Taiwan: Beyond the Economic Miracle*. Armonk, NY: M.E. Sharpe, pp. 43–68.

Chen, Don-yun. 1999. 'A Popularly-Elected Presidency as a Focus of Constitutional Choice: Explaining the Taiwanese Case, 1986–96'. *Issues and Studies*, 35(5): 1–42.

Chen, Edward I-te. 1972. 'Formosan Political Movements under Japanese Colonial Rule, 1914–1937'. *Journal of Asian Studies*, 31(3): 477–97.

Chen, Kuan-hsing. 2005. 'A Borrowed Life in *Banana Paradise*: De-Cold War/Decolonization, or Modernity and Its Tears'. In Chris Berry and Lu Feii (eds). *Island on the Edge: Taiwan New Cinema and After*. Hong Kong: Hong Kong University Press, pp. 39–54.

Chen, Lucy. 1963. 'Literary Taiwan'. *China Quarterly*, 15: 75–85.

Chen, Ming-tong. 1998. 'Local Factions and elections in Taiwan's Democratization'. In Tien Hung-mao (ed.). *Taiwan's Electoral Politics and Democratic Transition*. Armonk, NY: M.E. Sharpe, pp. 174–92.

Cheng, Tun-jen. 1989. 'Democratizing the Quasi-Leninist Regime in Taiwan'. *World Politics*, 41(4): 471–99.

Cheng, Tun-jen and Hsu Yung-ming. 1996. 'Issue Structure, the DPP's Factionalism, and Party Realignment'. In Tien Hung-mao (ed.). *Taiwan's Electoral Politics and Democratic Transition*. Armonk, NY: M.E. Sharpe, pp. 137–73.

Cheng, Tzu-leong. 1995. *Campaign Advertising: Theory, Policy and Strategy: Research Case Studies*. Taipei: Zhongzheng (Chinese).

Cheng, Tzu-leong. 2004. *Election Campaign Communication in Taiwan*. Taipei: Yangzhi (Chinese).

Cheng, Yen-hsin Alice, Fen-chieh Felice Wu and Amy Adamczyk. 2016. 'Changing attitudes towards homosexuality in Taiwan, 1995–2012'. *Chinese Sociological Review*, 48(4): 317–45.

Chin, Ko-lin. 2003. *Heijin: Organized Crime, Business and Politics in Taiwan*. Armonk, NY: M.E. Sharpe.

Chiu, P. and S.M. Chan-Olmsted. 1999. 'The impact of cable television on political campaigns in Taiwan'. *Gazette: The International Journal for Communication Studies*, 61(6): 491–509.

Chiu, Yu-bin. 2017. 'Rising from the Ashes? The Trade Union movement under Ma Ying-jeou's regime'. In Dafydd Fell (ed.), *Taiwan's Social Movements under Ma Ying-jeou: From the Wild Strawberries to the Sunflowers*. London: Routledge, pp. 199–218.

Chou, Wan-yao. 2016. 'Taiwan under Japanese Rule (1895–1945)'. In Gunter Schubert (ed.). *Routledge Handbook of Contemporary Taiwan*. London: Routledge, pp. 22–35.

Chu, A. 2003. 'Political call-in shows in Taiwan: Animating crisis discourse through reported speech'. Ph.D. thesis. Austin, TX: University of Texas.

Chu, Yun-han. 1989. 'Authoritarianism and economic oligopoly in Taiwan'. In Wu Chung-chi (ed.). *Monopoly and Exploitation: The Political Economy of Authoritarianism*. Taipei: Taiwan Research Fund (Chinese).

Chu, Yun-han. 2006. 'Book Review of *Party Politics in Taiwan*'. *China Quarterly*, 185: 189–90.

Chu Yun-han, Larry Diamond and Kharis Templeman (eds). 2016. *Taiwan's Democracy Challenged: The Chen Shui-bian Years*. Boulder, CO: Lynne Rienner.

Chu, Yun-han and Lin Jih-wen. 2001. 'Political Development in 20th Century Taiwan: State Building, Regime Transformation and the Construction of National Identity'. *China Quarterly*, 165: 102–29.

Chu, Yun-han and Lin Tse-min. 1998. 'Elections and Elite Convergence: The Path to Political Consolidation in Taiwan'. Paper presented at the Taiwanese Political Science Association Conference, Taipei, Taiwan, December.

Cole, Michael. 2015. *Black Island: Two Years of Activism in Taiwan*. CreateSpace Independent Publishing Platform Constitution of the Republic of China. Available online at: www.gio.gov.tw/info/news/constitution.htm

Corcuff, Stéphane. 2002. 'Introduction: Taiwan, a Laboratory of Identities'. In Stéphane Corcuff (ed.). *Memories of the Future: National Identity Issues and the Search for a New Taiwan*. Armonk, NY: M.E. Sharpe, pp. xi–xxiii.

Corcuff, Stéphane (ed.). 2002. *Memories of the Future: National Identity Issues and the Search for a New Taiwan*. Armonk, NY: M.E. Sharpe.

Corcuff, Stéphane. 2005. 'History Textbooks, Identity Politics and Ethnic Introspection in Taiwan'. In Edward Vickers and Elisa Jones (eds). *History Education and National Identity in East Asia*. New York: Routledge, pp. 133–69.

Corcuff, Stéphane. 2011. 'Taiwan's mainlanders under President Chen Shui-bian: A shift from the political to the cultural?' In Gunter Schubert and Jens Damm (eds). *Taiwanese Identity in the 21st Century: Domestic, Regional and Global Perspectives*. London: Routledge, pp. 113–32.

Dahl, Robert. 1989. *Democracy and its Critics*. London: Yale University Press.

Dalton, Russell and Martin Wattenberg (eds). 2000. *Parties without Partisans: Political Change in Advanced Industrial Democracies*. Oxford: Oxford University Press.

Deans, Phil. 2005. 'Isolation, Identity and Taiwanese Stamps as Vehicles for Regime Legitimation'. *East Asia: An International Quarterly*, 22(2): 8–30.

Diamond, Larry. 1994. 'Rethinking Civil Society: Towards Democratic Consolidation'. *Journal of Democracy*, 5(3): 4–17.

Diamond, Larry and Marc Plattner (eds). 2001. *Global Divergence of Democracies*. Baltimore, MD: The Johns Hopkins University Press.

Dickson, Bruce. 1993. 'Lessons of Defeat: The Reorganization of the Kuomintang on Taiwan, 1950–52'. *China Quarterly*, 133: 56–84.

Dickson, Bruce. 1996. 'The Kuomintang before Democratization: Organizational Change and the Role of Elections'. In Tien Hung-mao (ed.). *Taiwan's Electoral Politics and Democratic Transition: Riding the Third Wave*. Armonk, NY: M.E. Sharpe, pp. 42–78.

Dickson, Bruce. 1998. *Democratization in China and Taiwan: The Adaptability of Leninist Parties*. Oxford: Oxford University Press.

Dickson, Bruce and Chao Chien-min (eds). 2002. *Assessing the Lee Teng-hui Legacy: Democratic Consolidation and External Relations*. Armonk, NY: M.E. Sharpe.

Duverger, Maurice. 1959. *Political Parties: Their Organization and Activities in the Modern State*. London: Methuen.

Ebsworth, Rowena. 2017. 'Not wanting Wang: the Anti-Media Monopoly Movement in Taiwan'. In Dafydd Fell (ed.) *Taiwan's Social Movements under Ma Ying-jeou: From the Wild Strawberries to the Sunflowers*. London: Routledge, pp. 71–91.

Edmondson, Robert. 2002. 'The February 28 Incident and National Identity'. In Stéphane Corcuff (ed.). *Memories of the Future: National Identity Issues and the Search for a New Taiwan*. Armonk, NY: M.E. Sharpe, pp. 25–46.

Esping-Anderson, Gosta. 1990. *Three Worlds of Welfare Capitalism*. Cambridge: Polity Press.

Evans, Geoffrey and Pippa Norris (eds). 1998. *Critical Elections: British Parties and Voters in Long-Term Perspective*. London: Sage.

Fan, Yun. 2003. 'The Women's Movement During Political Transformation'. *Taiwanese Sociology*, 5: 133–94 (Chinese).

Fan, Yun. 2004. 'Taiwan: No Civil Society, No Democracy'. In Muthiah Alagappa (ed.). *Civil Society and Political Change in Asia*. Stanford, CA: Stanford University Press, pp. 164–90.

Fan, Yun and Wu Wei-ting. 2016. 'The long feminist march in Taiwan'. In Gunter Schubert (ed.). *Routledge Handbook of Contemporary Taiwan*. London: Routledge, pp. 313–25.

Fell, Dafydd. 2002. 'Party Platform Change in Taiwan's 1990s Elections'. *Issues and Studies*, 38(2): 31–60.

Fell, Dafydd. 2004. 'Measurement of Party Position and Party Competition in Taiwan'. *Issues and Studies*, 40(3–4): 101–35.

Fell, Dafydd. 2005a. 'A Welcome Antidote to National Identity and Cross-Strait Fatigue'. *Issues and Studies*, 41(4): 256–63.

Fell, Dafydd. 2005b. 'Measuring and Explaining Party Change in Taiwan: 1991–2004'. *Journal of East Asian Studies*, 5(1): 105–33.

Fell, Dafydd. 2005c. *Party Politics in Taiwan*. London: Routledge.

Fell, Dafydd. 2005d. 'Political and Media Liberalization and Political Corruption in Taiwan'. *China Quarterly*, 184: 875–93.

Fell, Dafydd. 2005e. 'Success and Failure of New Parties in Taiwanese Elections'. *China: An International Journal*, 3(2): 212–39.

Fell, Dafydd. 2006a. 'Change and Continuity in Taiwanese Party Politics Since 2000'. In Dafydd Fell, Henning Klöter and Chang Bi-yu (eds). *What has Changed: Taiwan Before and After the Change in Ruling Parties*. Wiesbaden: Harrassowitz, pp. 21–40.

Fell Dafydd. 2006b. 'Democratization of candidate selection in Taiwanese Political Parties'. *Journal of Electoral Studies*, 13(2): 167–98.

Fell, Dafydd. 2007a. 'Democracy on the Rocks: Taiwan's Troubled Political System Since 2000'. *Harvard Asia Pacific Review*, 9(1): 21–5.

Fell, Dafydd. 2007b. 'Partisan Issue Competition in Contemporary Taiwan: Is Democracy Dead in Taiwan?' *Chinese History and Society*, 32: 23–39.

Fell, Dafydd. 2007c. 'Putting on a Show and Electoral Fortunes in Taiwan'. In Julia Strauss and Donal Cruise O'Brien (eds). *Staging Politics: Power and Performance in Asia and Africa*. London: I.B. Taurus, pp. 133–50.

Fell, Dafydd. 2008a. 'Inter-Party Competition in Taiwan: Towards a new Party System?' In Steven Goldstein and Julian Chang (eds). *Presidential Politics in Taiwan: The Administration of Chen Shui-bian*. Norwalk, CT: Eastbridge, pp. 49–84.

Fell, Dafydd (ed.). 2008b. *The Politics of Modern Taiwan: Critical Issues in Modern Politics*. London: Routledge.

Fell, Dafydd. 2009. 'Lessons of Defeat: A Comparison of Taiwanese Ruling Parties' Responses to Electoral Defeat'. *Asian Politics and Policy*, 1(4): 660–81.

Fell, Dafydd. 2010a. 'Taiwan's Democracy: Towards a Liberal Democracy or Authoritarianism?' *Journal of Current Chinese Affairs*, 39(2): 187–201.

Fell, Dafydd. 2010b. 'Taiwan's electoral and party politics: Towards a one party or multi-party system?' *Stiftung Wissenschaft und Politik (SWP)*. Available online at: www.swpberlin.org/en/common/get_document.php?asset_id=7327

Fell, Dafydd. 2010c. 'Was 2005 A Critical Election in Taiwan? Locating the Start of a New Political Era'. *Asian Survey*, 50(5): 927–45.

Fell, Dafydd. 2011a. 'Polarization of Party Competition in the DPP Era'. In Robert Ash, John Garver and Penny Prime (eds). *Taiwan's Democracy and Future: Economic and Political Challenges*. London: Routledge, pp. 75–98.

Fell, Dafydd. 2011b. 'Taiwan's Party System in Transition: More or Less Space for Identity Politics?' In Gunter Schubert and Jens Damm (eds). *Taiwanese Identity in the 21st Century: Domestic, Regional and Global Perspectives*. Abingdon: Routledge, pp. 95–112.

Fell, Dafydd. 2013. 'Impact of Candidate Selection Systems on Election Results: Evidence from Taiwan Before and After the Change in Electoral Systems'. *The China Quarterly*, 213: 152–71.

Fell, Dafydd. 2014. 'Measuring and Explaining the Electoral Fortunes of Small Parties in Taiwan's Party Politics'. *Issues and Studies: An International Quarterly on China, Taiwan, and East Asian Affairs*, 50(1): 153–188.

Fell, Dafydd. 2015. 'The China Impact on Taiwan's Elections: Cross-Strait Economic Integration through the Lens of Election Advertising'. In Schubert, Gunter (ed.) *Taiwan and the 'China Impact' Challenges and Opportunities*. Abingdon: Routledge, pp. 53–69.

Fell, Dafydd. (ed.). 2017. *Taiwan's Social Movements under Ma Ying-jeou: From the Wild Strawberries to the Sunflowers*. London and New York: Routledge.

Fell, Dafydd and Charles Chen. 2014. 'Lessons of Defeat and Success: Taiwan's 2012 Elections in Comparative Perspective;. *Journal of Current Chinese Affairs*, 43(3): 13–43.

Fell, Dafydd, Henning Klöter and Chang Bi-yu (eds). 2006. *What has Changed: Taiwan Before and After the Change in Ruling Parties*. Wiesbaden: Harrassowitz.

Friedman, Edward (ed.). 2006. *China's Rise, Taiwan's Dilemmas and International Peace*. London: Routledge.

Gates, Hill. 1996. 'Ethnicity and Social Class'. In Emily Martin Ahern and Hill Gates (eds). *The Anthropology of Taiwanese Society*. Taipei: SMC Publishing, pp. 241–81.

Gellner, Ernest. 1983. *Nations and Nationalism*. Oxford: Blackwell.

Göbel, Christian. 2006. 'Beheading the Hydra: Combating Political Corruption and Organised Crime in the KMT and DPP Eras'. In Dafydd Fell, Henning Klöter and Chang Bi-yu (eds). *What has Changed: Taiwan Before and After the Change in Ruling Parties*. Wiesbaden: Harrassowitz, pp. 61–82.

Göbel, Christian. 2012. 'The Impact of Electoral Reform on Taiwan's Local Factions'. *Journal of Current Chinese Affairs*, 41(3): 69–92.

Göbel, Christian. 2016. 'Taiwan's Fight Against Corruption'. *Journal of Democracy*, 27 (1): 124–38.

Gold, Thomas. 1996. 'Taiwan society at the fin de siècle'. *China Quarterly*, 148: 1091–114.

Gold, Thomas. 2016. 'Retrocession and Authoritarian KMT Rule (1945–1986)'. In Gunter Schubert (ed.). *Routledge Handbook of Contemporary Taiwan*. London: Routledge, pp. 36–50.

Goldstein, Steven and Julian Chang (eds). 2008. *Presidential Politics in Taiwan: The Administration of Chen Shui-bian*. Norwalk, CT: Eastbridge.

Government Information Office (Taiwan). 1994. *Republic of China Yearbook 1994*. Taipei: Government Information Office.

Government Information Office (Taiwan). 2009. *Republic of China Yearbook 2009*. Taipei: Government Information Office.

Grano, Simona. 2016. *Environmental Governance in Taiwan*. London: Routledge.

Grugel, Jean. 2002. *Democratization: A Critical Introduction*. London: Sage.

Guy, Nancy. 2005. *Peking Opera and Politics in Taiwan*. Chicago: University of Illinois Press.

Haddon, Rosemary. 2005. 'Hou Hsiao-hsien's *City of Sadness*: History and the Diologic Female Voice'. In Chris Berry and Lu Feii (eds). *Island on the Edge: Taiwan New Cinema and After*. Hong Kong: Hong Kong University Press, pp. 55–66.

Hague, Rod and Martin Harrop. 2001. *Comparative Government and Politics: An Introduction*. Basingstoke: Palgrave.

Hao, Paul. 1996. 'The Transformation of the KMT's Ideology'. *Issues and Studies*, 32 (2): 1–31.

Harmel, Robert and Kenneth Janda. 1994. 'An Integrated Theory of Party Goals and Party Change', *Journal of Theoretical Politics*, 6(3): 259–87.

Heidenheimer, Arnold. 1989. 'Perspectives on the Perception of Corruption'. In Arnold Heidenheimer, Michael Johnston and V.T. Le Vine (eds). *Political Corruption: A Handbook*. New Brunswick, NJ: Transaction Press, pp. 149–63.

Heidenheimer, Arnold. 2002. 'Introduction to Part 1'. In Arnold Heidenheimer and Michael Johnston (eds). *Political Corruption: Concepts and Contexts*. New Brunswick, NJ: Transaction Press, pp. 3–14.

Heywood, Paul. 1997. 'Political Corruption: Problems and Perspectives'. In Paul Heywood (ed.). *Political Corruption*. Malden, MA: Blackwell, pp. 1–19.

Hickey, Dennis. 2006. 'The High Cost of Excluding Taiwan from the WHO'. In Edward Friedman (ed.). *China's Rise, Taiwan's Dilemmas and International Peace*. London: Routledge, pp. 149–73.

Hickey, Dennis. 2007a. 'Change and Continuity: US Policy and Taiwan'. *Journal of Chinese Political Science*, 12(2):105–24.

Hickey, Dennis. 2007b. *Foreign Policy Making in Taiwan: From Principle to Pragmatism*. London: Routledge.

Hickey, Dennis. 2009. 'Beijing's Evolving Policy toward Taipei: Engagement or Entrapment'. *Issues and Studies*, 45(1): 31–70.

Hickey, Dennis. 2011. 'Rapprochement between Taiwan and the Chinese Mainland: Implications for American foreign policy'. *Journal of Contemporary China*, 20(69): 231–47.

Higley, John, Huang Tung-yi and Lin Tse-min. 1998. 'Elite Settlements in Taiwan'. *Journal of Democracy*, 9(2): 148–63.

Ho, Ming-sho. 2003. 'The Politics of the Anti-Nuclear Movement in Taiwan: Case of Party Dependent Movement (1988–2000)'. *Modern Asian Studies*, 37(3): 683–708.

Ho, Ming-sho. 2005. 'Weakened State and Social Movement: The Paradox of the Taiwanese Environmental Movement after the Power Transfer'. *Journal of Contemporary China*, 14(43): 339–52.

Ho, Ming-sho. 2006a. 'Challenging State Corporatism: The Politics of Taiwan's Labor Federation Movement'. *The China Journal*, 56: 107–27.

Ho, Ming-sho. 2006b. 'Neo-centrist Labour Policy in Practice: The DPP and Taiwanese Working Class'. In Dafydd Fell, Henning Klöter and Chang Bi-yu (eds). *What has Changed: Taiwan Before and After the Change in Ruling Parties*. Wiesbaden: Harrassowitz, pp. 129–46.

Ho, Ming-sho. 2007. 'The Rise and Fall of Leninist Control in Taiwan's industry'. *China Quarterly*, 189: 162–79.

Ho, Ming-sho. 2010. 'Understanding the Trajectory of Social Movements in Taiwan: 1980–2010'. *Journal of Current Chinese Affairs*, 39(3): 3–22.

Ho, Ming-sho. 2015. 'Occupy Congress in Taiwan: Political Opportunity, Threat and the Sunflower Movement', *Journal of East Asian Studies*, 15: 69–97.

Ho, Szu-yin and Liu I-chou. 2002. 'The Taiwanese/Chinese identity of the Taiwan people in the 1990s'. In Lee Wei-chin and T. Y. Wang (eds). *Sayonara to the Lee Teng-hui era: Politics in Taiwan, 1988–2000*. Lanham, MD: University Press of America, pp. 149–83.

Holliday, Ian. 2000. 'Productivist Welfare Capitalism: Social Policy in East Asia'. *Political Studies*, 48(4): 706–23.

Hsiao, Michael Hsin-huang. 1992. 'The Rise of Social Movements and Civil Protests'. In Cheng Tun-jen and Stephan Haggard (eds). *Political Change in Taiwan*. Boulder, CO: Lynne Rienner, pp. 57–74.

Hsiao, Yuan. 2017. 'Virtual ecologies, mobilization and democratic groups without leaders: Impacts of Internet media on the Wild Strawberries'. In Dafydd Fell (ed.), *Taiwan's Social Movements under Ma Ying-jeou: From the Wild Strawberries to the Sunflowers*. London: Routledge, pp. 34–53.

Hsieh, John. 1996. 'The SNTV System and its Political Implications'. In Tien Hung-mao (ed.). *Taiwan's Electoral Politics and Democratic Transition*. Armonk, NY: M.E. Sharpe, pp. 193–212.

Hsieh, John. 2001. 'The 2000 Presidential Election and its Implications for Taiwan's Domestic Politics'. *Issues and Studies*, 37(1): 1–19.

Hsieh, John. 2002. 'Continuity and Change in Taiwan's Electoral Politics'. In John Hsieh and David Newman (eds). *How Asia Votes*. New York: Chatham House Publishing, pp. 32–49.

Hsu, Szu-chien. 2017. 'The China factor and Taiwan's civil society organizations in the Sunflower Movement'. In Dafydd Fell (ed.), *Taiwan's Social Movements under Ma Ying-jeou: From the Wild Strawberries to the Sunflowers*. London and New York: Routledge, pp. 134–53.

Hu, Fu. 1990. 'Our System is a Responsible Cabinet System'. *Zhongguo luntan* (China Tribute), 29(12): 34–40.

Huang, Chang-ling. 2017. 'Uneasy Alliance: State feminism and the conservative government in Taiwan'. In Dafydd Fell (ed.) *Taiwan's Social Movements under Ma Ying-jeou From the Wild Strawberries to the Sunflowers*. London and New York: Routledge, pp. 258–72.

Huang, Hsin-ta and Wang Yeh-lih. 2010. 'Local Factions after Twin Transitions of Government in Taiwan: Decaying or Transforming?' Paper delivered at American Political Science Association Conference, 2–5 September 2010, Washington, DC.

Huang, Teh-fu. 1998. 'Elections and the Evolution of the Kuomintang'. In Tien Hung-mao (ed.). *Taiwan's Electoral Politics and Democratic Transition*. Armonk, NY: M.E. Sharpe, pp. 105–36.

Hughes, Christopher. 2001. 'Post-nationalist Taiwan'. In Michael Leifer (ed.). *Asian Nationalism*. London: Routledge, pp. 63–81.

Hughes, Christopher. 2011. 'Negotiating national identity in Taiwan: Between nativization and de-sinification'. In Robert Ash, John Garver and Penny Prime (eds). *Taiwan's Democracy and Future: Economic and Political Challenges*. London: Routledge, pp. 51–74.

Hughes, Christopher. 2014. 'Revisiting Identity Politics Under Ma Ying-jeou'. In Jean-Pierre Cabestan and Jacques deLisle (ed.). *Political Changes in Taiwan Under Ma Ying-jeou: Partisan Conflict, Policy Choices, External Constraints and Security Challenges*. London: Routledge, pp. 120–36.

Hughes, Christopher. 2016. 'National Identity'. In Gunter Schubert (ed.). *Routledge Handbook of Contemporary Taiwan*. London: Routledge, pp. 153–68.

Huntington, Samuel. 1991. *The Third Wave, Democratization in the late Twentieth Century*. Norman, OK: University of Oklahoma Press.

Jacobs, Bruce. 'Taiwan During and After the Democratic Transition (1988–2016)'. In Gunter Schubert (ed.). *Routledge Handbook of Contemporary Taiwan*. London: Routledge, pp. 51–67.

Jacobs, Bruce. 2008. *Local Politics in Rural Taiwan under Dictatorship and Democracy*. Norwalk, CT: Eastbridge.

Johnston, Michael. 2002. 'Party Systems, Competition and Political Checks against Corruption'. In Arnold Heidenheimer and Michael Johnston (eds). *Political Corruption: Concepts and Contexts*. New Brunswick, NJ: Transaction Press, pp. 777–96.

Kao, Yuang-kuang. 2010. 'The Future Development of Political Factions in Taiwan: An Analysis from 2009 Local Elections'. Paper presented at the European Association of Taiwan Studies Conference, Tübingen, Germany, April 2010.

Kastner, Scott L. and Chad Rector. 2008. 'National Unification and Mistrust: Bargaining Power and the Prospects for a PRC/Taiwan Agreement'. *Security Studies*, 17(1): pp. 39–71.

Kerr, George. 2005. *Formosa Betrayed*. Taipei: Taiwan Publishing Co. Available online at: www.pinyin.info/books/formosabetrayed/index.html

Klöter, Henning, 2006. 'Mandarin Remains more Equal: Changes and Continuities in Taiwan's Language Policy'. In Dafydd Fell, Henning Klöter and Chang Bi-yu (eds). *What has Changed: Taiwan Before and After the Change in Ruling Parties*. Wiesbaden: Harrassowitz, pp. 207–24.

KMT. 2004. *'Bulletgate' Questions on the Legitimacy of the Presidency*. Taipei: National Policy Foundation.

Kong, Tat Yan. 2004. 'Corruption and the Effect of Regime Type: The Case of Taiwan'. *New Political Economy*, 9(3): 341–64.

Ku, Yuen-wen and Hsueh Cherng-tay. 2016. 'Social Welfare'. In Gunter Schubert (ed.). *Routledge Handbook of Contemporary Taiwan*. London: Routledge, pp. 342–58.

Kuo, Cheng-tian. 1999. 'The Origins of State-Local Relations in Taiwan: A New Institutional Perspective'. *Issues and Studies*, 35(6): 29–58.

Kuo, Cheng-tian. 2000. 'Taiwan's Distorted Democracy in Comparative Perspective'. *Journal of Asian and African Studies*, 35(1): 85–111.

Kuo, Julian. 2002. 'Cross-Strait Relations: Buying Time without Strategy'. In Bruce Dickson and Chao Chien-min (eds). *Assessing the Lee Teng-hui Legacy: Democratic Consolidation and External Relations*. Armonk, NY: M.E. Sharpe, pp. 204–17.

Kuo, Tai-chun and Ramon Myers. 2012. *Taiwan's Economic Transformation*. London: Routledge.

Kushner, Barak. 2007. 'Nationality and Nostalgia: The Manipulation of Memory in Japan, Taiwan and China since 1990'. *The International History Review*, 29(4): 793–820.

Kwon, Huck-ju. 1998. 'A Comparison of East Asian Welfare Systems'. In Roger Goodman, Gordon White and Kwon Huck-ju (eds). *The East Asian Welfare Model: Welfare Orientalism and the State*. London: Routledge, pp. 27–75.

Lamley, Harry. 1981. 'Subethnic Rivalry in the Ch'ing Period'. In Emily Ahern and Hill Gates (eds). *The Anthropology of Taiwanese Society*. Taipei: SMC Publishing, pp. 282–318.

Lamley, Harry. 1999. 'Taiwan under Japanese Rule 1895–1945: The Vicissitudes of Colonialism'. In Murray Rubinstein (ed.). *Taiwan: A New History*. Armonk, NY: M.E. Sharpe, pp. 201–60.

Lamounier, Bolivar. 1989. 'Authoritarian Brazil Revisited: The Impact of Elections on Abertura'. In Alfred Stepan (ed.). *Democratizing Brazil: Problems of Transition and Consolidation*. New York: Oxford University Press, pp. 43–79.

Landé, C.H. 1977. 'Introduction: The dyadic basis of clientelism'. In S.W. Schmidt, J.C. Scott, C.H. Landé and L. Guasti (eds). *Friends, Followers and Factions*. Berkeley and Los Angeles, CA: University of California, pp. xiii–xxxvii.

Lasater, Martin. 1990. *A Step Towards Democracy*. Washington, DC: American Enterprise Institute for Public Policy Research.

Laver, Michael and Ben Hunt. 1992. *Policy and Party Government*. London: Routledge.

Leng, Shao-chuan (ed.). 1993. *Chiang Ching-kuo's Leadership in the Development of the Republic of China on Taiwan*. Lanham, MD: University Press of America.

Leou, Chia-feng. 2006. 'Financial Reform under the KMT and the DPP (1996–2004): Has the DPP done a better job?' In Dafydd Fell, Henning Klöter and Chang Bi-yu (eds). *What has Changed: Taiwan Before and After the Change in Ruling Parties*. Wiesbaden: Harrassowitz, pp. 107–28.

Liao, Da-chi. 2007. 'An examination of the leadership elite's role in Taiwan's constitutional development'. In Wu Chung-li and Wu Yu-shan (eds). *Constitutional Reform: Background, Operation and Influences*. Taipei: Wunan, pp. 63–93.

Liao, Da-chi and Herlin Chien. 2005. 'Why no co-habitation in Taiwan? An analysis of the Republic of China's Constitution and its Application'. *China Perspectives*, 58, pp. 55–9.

Lin, Chia-long. 1998. 'Paths to Democracy: Taiwan in Comparative Perspective'. Ph.D. dissertation. New Haven, CT: Yale University.

Lin, Chia-long. 2002. 'The Political Formation of Taiwanese Nationalism'. In Stéphane Corcuff (ed.). *Memories of the Future: National Identity Issues and the Search for a New Taiwan*. Armonk, NY: M.E. Sharpe, pp. 144–59.

Lin, Chiung-chu. 2006. 'The Evolution of Party Images and Party System in Taiwan, 1992–2004'. *East Asia: An International Quarterly*, 23(1): 27–46.

Lin, Jih-wen. 2003. 'Transition Through Transaction: Taiwan's Constitutional Reform in the Lee Teng-hui Era'. In Lee Wei-chin and T.Y. Wang (eds). *Sayonara to the Lee Teng-hui Era: Politics in Taiwan, 1988–2000*. Lanham, MD: University Press of America, pp. 63–90.

Lin, Jih-wen. 2006. 'The Politics of Reform in Japan and Taiwan,' *Journal of Democracy*, 17(2): 118–131, April.

Lin, Wan-I and Grace Chou. 2010. 'Globalization, Regime Transformation and Social Policy Development in Taiwan'. In James Lee and Kam-Wah Chan (eds). *The Crisis of Welfare in East Asia*. Lanham, MD: Lexington, pp. 101–24.

Lipset, Martin Seymour. 1959. 'Some Social Requisites of Democracy: Economic Development and Political Legitimacy'. *American Political Science Review*, 53(1): 69–105.

Lipset, Martin Seymour. 2000. 'The Indispensability of Political Parties'. *Journal of Democracy*, 11(1): 48–55.

Liu, Tsung-wei. 2000. 'The Effects of Electoral Laws on Party Competition in Taiwan: 1989–1998'. Ph.D. dissertation. Colchester: University of Essex.

Long, Simon. 1990. *Taiwan: China's Last Frontier*. London: Macmillan.

Lu, Ya-li. 2002. 'Lee Teng-hui's Role in Taiwan's Democratization: A Preliminary Assessment'. In Bruce Dickson and Chao Chien-min (eds). *Assessing the Lee Teng-hui Legacy in Taiwan's Politics*. Armonk, NY: M.E. Sharpe, pp. 53–72.

Lucardie, Paul. 2000. 'Prophets, Purifiers and Prolocutors: Towards a Theory on the Emergence of New Parties'. *Party Politics*, 6(2): 175–85.

Lynch, Daniel. 2004. 'Taiwan's Self Conscious Nation-Building Projects'. *Asian Survey*, 44(4): 513–33.

Ma, Ying-jeou and Lo Chih-chiang. 2007. *Youthful Bicycle Goes Forward: Ma Ying-jeou's Taiwan Bicycle Diary*. Taipei: 2 Fishes (Chinese).

McLean, Iain (ed.). 1996. *Oxford Concise Dictionary of Politics*. Oxford: Oxford University Press.

McLean, Iain and Alistair McMillan (eds). 2009. *Oxford Concise Dictionary of Politics*. Oxford: Oxford University Press.

Mancall, Mark. 1964. 'Taiwan, Island of Resignation and Despair'. In Mark Mancall (ed.). *Formosa Today*. New York: Praeger, pp. 1–42.

Marsh, Robert. 2002. 'National Identity and Ethnicity in Taiwan: Some trends in the 1990s'. In Stéphane Corcuff (ed.). *Memories of the Future: National Identity Issues and the Search for a New Taiwan*. Armonk, NY: M.E. Sharpe, pp. 144–59.

Mattlin, Mikael. 2006. 'Party Opportunism among Local Politicians after Taiwan's Power Transition'. *East Asia: An International Quarterly*, 23(1): 68–85.

Ming, Chu-cheng. 1998. 'Centrifugal Competition and the Development of the Republic of China's Party Politics'. *Theory and Policy*, 12(2): 142–56 (Chinese).

Moore, Barrington. 1966. *Social Origins of Democracy and Dictatorship*. Boston, MA: Beacon Press.

Myers, Ramon, Linda Chao and Kuo Tai-chun. 2002. 'Consolidating Democracy in the Republic of China on Taiwan'. In Bruce Dickson and Chao Chien-min (eds). *Assessing the Lee Teng-hui Legacy: Democratic Consolidation and External Relations*. Armonk, NY: M.E. Sharpe, pp. 73–90.

National Science Council. 2003. 'Party Image: Measurement, Connotation, and Its Application'. National Science Research Project (NSC 102-2410-H-031–046-MY2). Taipei: National Science Council.

Niou, Emerson. 2005. 'A new measure of preferences on the independence-unification issue in Taiwan'. *Journal of Asian and African Studies*, 40(1/2): 91–104.

Norris, Pippa. 2002. 'Campaign Communications'. In Lawrence LeDuc, Richard Niemi and Pippa Norris (eds). *Comparing Democracies 2: New Challenges in the Study of Elections and Voting*. London: Sage, pp. 127–46.

Norris, Pippa and Joni Lovenduski. 2004. 'Why Parties Fail to Learn: Electoral Defeat, Selective Perception and British Party Politics'. *Party Politics*, 10(1): 85–104.

Ong, Joktik. 1963. 'A Formosan's View of the Formosan Independence Movement'. *China Quarterly*, 15: 107–14.

Ottaway, Marina. 2005. 'Civil Society'. In Peter Burnell and Vicky Randall (eds). *Politics in the Developing World*. Oxford: Oxford University Press, pp. 120–38.

Peng, Ming-min. 2005. *A Taste of Freedom: Memoirs of a Formosan Independence Leader*. Taipei: Taiwan Publishing Co. Available online at: www.pinyin.info/books/peng/index.html

Phillips, Steven. 1999. 'Between Assimilation and Independence: Taiwanese Political Aspirations Under Nationalist Chinese Rule, 1945–1949'. In Murray Rubinstein (ed.). *Taiwan: A New History*. Armonk, NY: M.E. Sharpe, pp. 275–319.

Przeworski, Adam. 1991. *Democracy and the Market: Political and Economic Reforms in Eastern Europe and Latin America*. Cambridge: Cambridge University Press.

Puddington, Arch. 2011. 'Freedom in the World 2010: Erosion of Freedom Intensifies'. (Overview Essay for Freedom in the World 2010). Freedom House. Available online at: www.freedomhouse. org/uploads/fiw10/fiW_2010_Overview_Essay.pdf

Rahat, Gideon and Reuven Hazan. 2001. 'Candidate Selection Methods: An Analytical Framework'. *Party Politics*, 7(3): 297–322.

Rawnsley, Gary. 1997. 'The 1996 Presidential Campaign in Taiwan: Packaging Politics in a Democratizing State'. *The Harvard International Journal of Press/Politics*, 2(2): 47–61.

Rawnsley, Gary. 2012. 'Approaches to Soft Power and Public Diplomacy in China and Taiwan'. *Journal of International Communication*, 18(2): 121–35.

Rawnsley, Gary. 2014. 'Taiwan's Soft Power and Public Diplomacy'. *Journal of Current Chinese Affairs*, 43(3): 161–74.

Reardon-Anderson, James. 1992. *Pollution, Politics and Foreign Investment in Taiwan: The Lukang Rebellion*. Armonk, NY: M.E. Sharpe.

Rigger, Shelley. 1999. *Politics in Taiwan: Voting for Democracy*. London: Routledge.

Rigger, Shelley. 2001. *From Opposition to Power: Taiwan's Democratic Progressive Party*. Boulder, CO: Lynne Rienner.

Rigger, Shelley. 2002. 'Political Science and Taiwan's Domestic Politics: The State of the Field Politics'. *Issues and Studies*, 38(4): 49–92.

Rigger, Shelley. 2005. 'The Unfinished Business of Taiwan's Democratization'. In Nancy Berkopf Tucker (ed.). *Dangerous Strait: The US–Taiwan–China Crisis*. New York: University of Columbia Press, pp. 16–43.

Rigger, Shelley. 2006. *Taiwan's Rising Rationalism: Generations, Politics and Taiwanese Nationalism*. Washington, DC: East West Centre.

Rose, Richard. 1986. 'Common Goals but Different Roles: The State's Contribution to the Welfare Mix'. In Richard Rose and Rei Shiratori (eds). *The Welfare State East and West*. Oxford: Oxford University Press, pp. 13–39.

Ross, Robert. 2006. 'Taiwan's Fading Independence Movement'. *Foreign Affairs*, 85(1): 141–48.

Rowen, Ian. 2017. 'Touring in Heterotopia: Travel, Sovereignty and Exceptional Spaces in Taiwan and China'. *Asian Anthropology*, 16(1): 20–34.

Rowen, Ian. 2015. 'Inside Taiwan's Sunflower Movement: Twenty-Four Days in a Student-Occupied Parliament, and the Future of the Region'. *Journal of Asian Studies*, 74(1): 5–21.

Roy, Denny. 2003. *Taiwan: A Political History*. Cornell, NY: Cornell University Press.

Rubinstein, Murray. 2004. 'Lu Hsiu-lien and the Origins of Taiwanese Feminism, 1944–1977'. In Catherine Farris, Lee Anru and Murray Rubinstein (eds). *Women in the New Taiwan: Gender Roles and Gender Consciousness in a Changing Society*. Armonk, NY: M.E. Sharpe, pp. 244–76.

Rubinstein, Murray. 2006a. 'Party Politics in Taiwan: Party Change and the Democratic Evolution of Taiwan, 1991–2004'. *Pacific Affairs*, 79(1): 9–28.

Rubinstein, Murray. 2006b. 'The Presbyterian Church in the Formation of Taiwan's Democratic Society'. In Cheng Tun-jen and Deborah Brown (eds). *Religious Organizations and Democratization: Case Studies From Contemporary Asia*. Armonk, NY: M.E. Sharpe, pp. 109–35.

Rubinstein, Murray (ed.). 1999. *Taiwan: A New History*. Armonk, NY: M.E. Sharpe.

Rubinstein, Murray (ed.). 2007. *Taiwan: A New History* (Expanded Edition). Armonk, NY: M.E. Sharpe.

Rustow, Dankwart. 1970. 'Transition to Democracy: Toward a Dynamic Model'. *Comparative Politics*, 2(3): 337–63.

Schaferrer, Christian. 2003. *The Power of the Ballot Box*. London: Lexington.

Schattschneider, Elmer. 1942. *Party Government*. New York: Holt, Rinehart & Winston.

Schedler, Andreas. 1998. 'What is Democratic Consolidation'. *Journal of Democracy*, 9(2): 91–107.

Schmitter, Philippe. 1979. 'Still the Century of Corporatism?' In Philippe Schmitter and Garhard Lehmbruch (eds). *Trends Toward Corporatist Intermediation*. London: Sage, pp. 43–94.

Schubert, Gunter. 2004. 'Taiwan's Parties and National Identity'. *Asian Survey*, 44(4): 534–54.

Schubert, Gunter. 2008. 'Taiwan's Evolving National Identity since the DPP Takeover: From Civic to Ethnic?' In Steven Goldstein and Julian Chang (eds). *Presidential Politics in Taiwan*. Norwalk, CT: Eastbridge, pp. 85–115.

Schubert, Gunter. 2012. 'No Winds of Change: Taiwan's 2012 National Elections and Post-Election Fallout'. *Journal of Current Chinese Affairs*, 41(3): 143–161.

Schubert, Gunter (ed.). 2016. *Routledge Handbook of Contemporary Taiwan*. London: Routledge.

Schubert, Gunter and Jens Damm (eds). 2011. *Taiwanese Identity in the 21st Century*. London: Routledge.

Schumpeter, Joseph. 1976. *Capitalism, Socialism and Democracy*. London: George Allen & Unwin.

Schweig, Meredith. 2014. 'Hoklo Hip-Hop: Resignifying Rap as Local Narrative Tradition in Taiwan'. *Journal of Chinese Oral and Performance Literature*, 33(1): 37–59.

Selznick, Philip. 1979. *The Organizational Weapon*. New York: Arno.

Shih, Chih-yu. 2003. 'The Global Constitution of "Taiwan Democracy"'. *East Asia: An International Quarterly*, 20(3): 16–38.

Shih, Chih-yu. 2008. *Democracy (Made in Taiwan): The 'Success' State as Political Theory*. Lanham, MD: Lexington Books.

Shih, Fang-long. 2006. 'From Regulation and Rationalisation, to Production: Government Policy on Religion in Taiwan'. In Dafydd Fell, Henning Klöter and Chang Bi-yu (eds). *What has Changed: Taiwan Before and After the Change in Ruling Parties*. Wiesbaden: Harrassowitz, pp. 265–83.

Shih, Fang-long. 2007. 'The "Red" Tide Anti-Corruption Protest: What Does it Mean for Democracy in Taiwan?' *Taiwan in Comparative Perspective*, 3: 87–98.

Shu, Wei-der. 2002. 'Who Joined the Clandestine Political Organization? Some Preliminary Evidence from the Overseas Taiwan Independence Movement'. In Stéphane Corcuff (ed.). *Memories of the Future: National Identity Issues and the Search for a New Taiwan*. Armonk, NY: M.E. Sharpe, pp. 47–72.

Shugart, Mathew and John Carey. 1992. *Presidents and Assemblies: Constitutional Design and Electoral Dynamics*. Cambridge: Cambridge University Press.

Simon, Scott. 2004. 'From Hidden Kingdom to Rainbow Community: The Making of Gay and Lesbian Identity in Taiwan'. In Davi Jordan, Andrew Morris, Marc Moskowitz *et al.*, (eds) *The Minor Arts of Daily Life: Popular Culture in Taiwan*. Honolulu: University of Hawai'i Press.

Slater, Dan and Joseph Wong. 2013. 'The Strength to Concede: Ruling Parties and Democratization in Developmental Asia'. *Perspectives on Politics*, 11(3): 717–33.

Snow, Edgar. 1972. *Red Star Over China*. London: Penguin.

Stavis, Benedict. 1974. *Rural Local Governance and Agricultural Development*. New York: Cornell University Center for International Studies.

Su, Chi. 2009. *Taiwan's Relations with Mainland China: A Tail Wagging Two Dogs*. London: Routledge.

Sullivan, Jonathan. 2009. 'Campaign Advertising in Taiwanese Presidential Elections'. *Journal of Contemporary China*, 18(61): 675–88.

Sullivan, Jonathan. 2010. 'Legislators' blogs in Taiwan'. *Parliamentary Affairs*, 63(3): 471–85.

Swaine, Michael. 2008. 'Managing Relations with the United States'. In Steven Goldstein and Julian Chang (eds). *Presidential Politics in Taiwan: The Administration of Chen Shui-bian*. Norwalk, CT: East Bridge, pp. 171–202.

Swanson, David and Paulo Mancini (eds). 1996. *Politics, Media, and Modern Democracy: An International Study Of Innovations In Electoral Campaigning and Their Consequences*. Westport, CT: Praeger.

Tien, Hung-mao. 1989. *The Great Transition: Politics and Social Change in the Republic of China*. Taipei: SMC Publishing.

Tien, Hung-mao (ed.). 1996. *Taiwan's Electoral Politics and Democratic Transition: Riding the Third Wave*. Armonk, NY: M.E. Sharpe.

Tsang, Steve. 1993. 'Chiang Kai-shek and the Kuomintang's Policy to Reconquer the Chinese Mainland, 1949–1958'. In Steve Tsang (ed.). *In the Shadow of China: Political Developments in Taiwan since 1949*. Honolulu: University of Hawaii Press, pp. 48–72.

Wang, Fu-Chang. 1998. 'Ethnic Consciousness, Nationalism, and Party Support'. *Taiwanese Sociological Review*, 2: 1–45, July (Chinese).

Wang, Fu-chang. 2001. 'National Imagination, Ethnic Consciousness, and History: Content and Context Analysis of the "Getting to Know Taiwan" Textbook Disputes'. *Taiwan Historical Research*, 8(2): 145–208 (Chinese).

Wang, Peter. 1999. 'A Bastion Created, a Regime Reformed, an Economy Reengineered, 1949–1970'.In Murray Rubinstein (ed.). *Taiwan: A New History*. Armonk, NY: M.E. Sharpe, pp. 320–38.

Wang, T.Y. 2006. 'Taiwan's Bid for UN Membership'. In *China's Rise, Taiwan's Dilemmas and International Peace*. Edward Friedman (ed.). London: Routledge, pp. 174–92.

Wang, T.Y., Lee Wei-Chin and Yu Ching-Hsin. 2011. 'Taiwan's Expansion of International Space: Opportunities and Challenges'. *Journal of Contemporary China*, 20(69): 249–67.

Wang, Vincent. 2006. 'Taiwan's Participation in International Organizations'. In Edward Friedman (ed.). *China's Rise, Taiwan's Dilemmas and International Peace*. London: Routledge, pp. 149–73.

Wang, Yeh-Li. 2003. *Comparative Electoral Systems*. Taipei: Wu-Nan Books.

Ware, Alan. 2001. *Political Parties and Party Systems*. Oxford: Oxford University Press.

Weller, Robert. 1999. 'Identity and Social Change in Taiwanese Religion'. In Murray Rubinstein (ed.). *Taiwan: A New History*. Armonk, NY: M.E. Sharpe, pp. 339–65.

Weng, Hui-chen and Dafydd Fell. 2006. 'The Rootless Movement: Taiwan's Women's Movement in the KMT and DPP Eras'. In Dafydd Fell, Henning Klöter and Chang Bi-yu (eds). *What has Changed: Taiwan Before and After the Change in Ruling Parties*. Wiesbaden: Harrassowitz, pp. 147–63.

White, Gordon and Roger Goodman. 1998. 'Welfare Orientalism and the Search for an East Asian Welfare Model'. In Roger Goodman, Gordon White and Kwon Huck-ju (eds). *East Asian Welfare Model: Welfare Orientalism and the State*. London: Routledge, pp. 3–24.

Winkler, Edwin. 1984. 'Institutionalization and Participation on Taiwan: From Hard to Soft Authoritarianism?' *China Quarterly*, 99: 481–99.

Winkler, Edwin. 1994. 'Cultural Policy in Post-War Taiwan'. In Steven Harrell and Huang Chun-chieh (eds). *Cultural Change in Post-War Taiwan*. Boulder, CO: Westview Press, pp. 22–46.

Wong, Joseph. 2003. 'Deepening Democracy in Taiwan'. *Pacific Affairs*, 76(2): 57–90.

Wong, Joseph. 2004. *Healthy Democracies: Welfare Politics in Taiwan and South Korea*. Ithaca, NY: Cornell University Press.

Wright, Teresa. 1999. 'Student Mobilization in Taiwan: Civil Society and its Discontents'. *Asian Survey*, 39(6): pp. 986–1008.

Wright, Teresa. 2001. *Perils of Protest: State Repression and Student Activism in China and Taiwan*. Honolulu: Hawaii University Press.

Wu, Chung-li. 2003. 'Local Factions and the Kuomintang in Taiwan's electoral politics'. *International Politics of the Asia-Pacific*, 3(1): 89–111.

Wu, Chung-li. 2016. 'Games without Frontiers, War without Tears? The Process of Campaigning in the 2016 Taiwanese General Elections'. *American Journal of Chinese Studies*, 23(1): 25–40.

Wu, Nai-teh. 2005. 'Transition without Justice, or Justice without History: Transitional Justice in Taiwan'. *Taiwan Journal of Democracy*, 1(1): 77–102.

Wu, Yu-shan. 1998. 'Convergence of Mainland Policies: Standard Distribution of Voters' Preferences and Vote Maximizing Strategy'. *Theory and Policy*, 12(3): 5–22 (Chinese).

Wu, Yu-shan. 2000. 'The ROC's Semi-Presidentialism at Work: Unstable Compromise, Not Cohabitation'. *Issues and Studies*, 36(5): 1–40.

Wu, Yu-shan. 2007a. 'Legitimacy of Political Power and the Format of Constitutional Reforms: Comparing Taiwan with Post Communist New democracies in Europe'. In Wu Chung-li and

Wu Yu-shan (eds). *Constitutional Reform: Background, Operation and Influences*. Taipei: Wunan, pp. 29–62 (Chinese).

Wu, Yu-shan. 2007b. 'Semi-presidentialism–easy to choose, difficult to operate: The case of Taiwan'. In Robert Elgie and Sophia Moestrup (eds). *Semi-Presidentialism Outside Europe: A Comparative Study*. London: Routledge, pp. 201–18.

Wu Yu-shan. 2016. 'Heading Towards Troubled Waters? The Impact of Taiwan's 2016 Elections on Cross-Strait Relations'. *American Journal of Chinese Studies*, 23(1): 59–76.

Yu, Ching-hsin. 2005. 'The Evolving Party System in Taiwan: 1991–2004'. *Journal of Asian and African Studies*, 40(1/2): 105–23.

Zhao, Suisheng. 1999. 'Economic Interdependence and Political Divergence'. In Zhao Suisheng (ed.). *Across the Taiwan Strait: Mainland China, Taiwan and the 1995–1996 Crisis*. London: Routledge, pp. 21–40.

Zhao, Suisheng (ed.). 1999. *Across the Taiwan Strait: Mainland China, Taiwan and the 1995–1996 Crisis*. London: Routledge.

Index